THE BLOODLESS REVOLUTION

*A Cultural History of Vegetarianism
from 1600 to Modern Times*

TRISTRAM STUART

W. W. NORTON & COMPANY

New York London

Manufacturing by Courier Westford
Production manager: Anna Oler

Library-of-Congress Cataloging-in-Publication Data

Stuart, Tristram.
The bloodless revolution : a cultural history of vegetarianism from
1600 to modern times / Tristram Stuart.
p. cm.
Includes bibliographical references and index.
ISBN-13: 978-0-393-05220-6
ISBN-10: 0-393-05220-6
1. Vegetarianism—Europe—History. 2. Vegetarianism—Religious aspects—
Hinduism—History. 3. Europeans—India—History—17th century.
4. Europeans—India—History—18th century. I. Title.

TX392.S86 2007
613.2'6209—dc22   2006051018

ISBN 978-0-393-33064-9 pbk.

W. W. Norton & Company, Inc.
500 Fifth Avenue, New York, N.Y. 10110
www.wwnorton.com

W. W. Norton & Company Ltd.
Castle House, 75/76 Wells Street, London W1T 3QT

1 2 3 4 5 6 7 8 9 0

To my father
SIMON STUART
(1930–2002)

CONTENTS

viii · THE BLOODLESS REVOLUTION

LIST OF ILLUSTRATIONS

PLATES

John Evelyn's 'pietre dure' cabinet showing Orpheus charming the beasts by Domenico Bennotti & Francesco Ffanelli, 1644–50. *V&A Images/Victoria and Albert Museum, London (ref: CT64605)*

School of Jan Brueghel the Elder, 'Orpheus charming the animals', Flemish, *c*.1600–10. Galleria Borghese, Rome. *Alinari Archives/Corbis*

SECTION TWO

Joseph Highmore, 'The Harlowe Family' from the illustrations of Samuel Richardson's *Clarissa*, 1747–8. *Yale Center for British Art, Paul Mellon Collection, USA/The Bridgeman Art Library, London (ref: YBA 156350)*

Jean Baptiste Greuze, 'Girl weeping over her Dead Canary', *c*.1765. *National Gallery of Scotland/The Bridgeman Art Library, London (ref: NGS 230482)*

Elizabeth Vigée Le Brun, 'Self Portrait in a Straw Hat', 1782. *The National Gallery, London*

Jean-Baptiste Greuze, 'The Milkmaid', before 1784. *Louvre, Paris/The Bridgeman Art Library, London (ref: XIR 90016)*

Frontispiece of Jean-Jacques Rousseau's 'Discours sur l'Origine et les Fondemens de l'Inegalité', Marc Michel, Amsterdam, 1755. *The British Library, London*

Jean Baptiste Greuze, 'The White Hat', by *c*.1780. *Museum of Fine Arts, Boston/ The Bridgeman Art Library, London (ref: BST 216007)*

Attributed to Marie Victoire Lemoine, 'Young Woman with a Dog', *c*.1796 *Bucharest National Museum of Arts/AKG Images, London*

Jean Laurent Mosnier, 'The Young Mother', *c*.1770–80. *Musée Municipal, Macon, France/The Bridgeman Art Library, London (ref: XIR 180450)*

Eugene Delacroix, 'Liberty Leading the People', 1830. *Louvre, Paris/The Bridgeman Art Library, London (ref: XIR 3692)*

C.J. Grant, 'Singular effects of the universal pills on a green grocer!' From 'Grant's Oddities', London, 1841, plate 8. *The Wellcome Trust Medical Photographic Library (ref: V0011125)*

'The Mansion of Bliss. A New Game for the Amusement of Youth', William Darton, London, 1822. *V&A Images/Victoria and Albert Museum, London (ref: CT26924)*

The Old Fort, Playhouse and Holwell's Monument, Calcutta, from Thomas Daniell, 'Views of Calcutta', 1786. *The British Library, London (ref: P88, 88)*

Attributed to Johann Zoffany, 'Portrait of John Zephaniah Holwell', 1765. *Hood Museum of Art, Dartmouth College, New Hampshire (ref: P.961.244)*

Marquis de Valady (1766–1793) and his wife, daughter of the Comte de Vaudreuil. *Courtesy of Christian de Chefdebien*

INTEGRATED

ACKNOWLEDGEMENTS

I would like to thank my agent, David Godwin, for his infectious enthusiasm; and my superlatively patient editors, Arabella Pike and Kate Hyde at HarperCollins, and Bob Weil and Tom Mayer at Norton, and also Annabel Wright and Morag Lyall. Penetrating advice on the manuscript came from a number of selfless readers to whom I am deeply indebted: Alice Albinia, Dr John Lennard, Dr Joan-Pau Rubiés, Dr Hannah Dawson, Corin Stuart, Dr Jim Watt, Steve Haskell and Daniel Wilson. Hannah Dawson, Daniel Wilson and John Lennard have been, over the years, great sources of intellectual inspiration and companionship, and Joan-Pau Rubiés kindly gave me his time and attention at the final stages. For invaluable encouragement and guidance I am also extremely grateful to Professor Nigel Leask, Dr Richard Grove, Dr Lizzie Collingham, Dr Aparna Vaidik and Dr Charlotte Grant. I have also received generous assistance from Patrick French, Dr Kate Teltscher, Dr Raj Sekhar Basu, Dr David Allan, Dr Biddan Bharan Mukerjee, Dr Dilwyn Knox and Dr Deepak Kumar. In the course of my research, the path has been illuminated by the work of Keith Thomas, Dr Timothy Morton, and Dr Anita Guerrini. A special thanks to Martin Rowlands of Milford Haven for his lifelong investigation into the history of John Zephaniah Holwell's mansion, Castle Hall; and to Messrs Christian and Hugues de Chefdebien, relatives of the Marquis de Valady, who provided me with fascinating material including the portraits of the Marquis and his wife.

Most of the research was done in the British Library, London. Many thanks to the librarians, particularly Giles Mandelbrote and Shashi Sen; and to the wonderful staff in the Rare Books Reading Room and the Oriental and India Office Collection, who brightened my daily life; warmest thanks to Paget Anthony, Kwame Ababio, Sita Gunasingham and Cyril Ashley; and to fellow-readers. Thanks to the librarians, curators and staff at Cambridge University Library; the Bibliothèque Nationale, Paris; the Library of the Asiatic Society , Kolkata; the National Library of India, Kolkata; the archives of the Royal Society of Physicians, Edinburgh; the National Library of Scotland; the Victoria and Albert Museum, particularly Rosemary Crill and Amin Jaffer; the Bodleian Library,

Oxford; the Nehru Memorial Library, New Delhi; the Wren Library, Trinity College Cambridge; King's College Library, Cambridge; the London Library; Essex Record Office; and to the compilers and editors of digital libraries, particularly Early English Books Online, Eighteenth-Century Collections Online, Literature Online and latterly, Google Books; they are facilitating a revolution in scholarship.

I have been blessed with idyllic cottages and homes in which to write: by the Goulder family at Ty Hen, by Charity Garnett at The Stone House and by Dr Rosemary Summers at No 9. Love and profound gratitude to my families, the Stuarts and the Mathers, who have helped me and put up with me; in the case of my brothers, Thomas and Corin, this has been a not inconsiderable feat. Nothing could have been done without the love of my life, my principal adviser and collaborator, the aforementioned Alice, whom the reader should thank, in any case, for making this book readable. The friendship of Charlie Layfield, James Parsons and Sangam Macduff helped to keep things in perspective. It would be incomplete if I did not also mention the natural world, and the humans within it, that drove my curiosity to understand them. Finally, to my father, who taught me how to read; I dedicate this book to him.

Introduction

Stranded in the countryside and confronted with a live chicken which he has to roast, Withnail is paralysed. 'I think you should strangle it instantly,' says his anxious friend Peter, 'in case it starts trying to make friends with us.' 'I can't,' he adds, 'those dreadful, beady eyes' (Bruce Robinson, *Withnail & I* (1987)). In 1714 the philosophical wit, Bernard Mandeville, mused on a very similar predicament: 'I question whether ever any body so much as killed a Chicken without Reluctancy the first time,' he commented wryly, 'yet all of them feed heartily and without Remorse on Beef, Mutton and Fowls when they are bought in the Market.'[1] Western society has fostered a culture of caring for animals; and it has maintained humanity's right to kill and eat them. Today, negotiating compassion with the desire to eat is customary, and there are clearly defined lifestyles available for each person's particular taste. But it was only after the word 'vegetarian' was coined in the 1840s, followed by the formation of the Vegetarian Society in 1847, that 'vegetarianism' was applied to a distinct movement that could easily be pigeon-holed, and ignored. Before that, meat-eating was an open question that concerned everyone and it affected not just people's choice of diet but their fundamental ideas about man's status on earth.*

In the era preceding the Industrial Revolution the question of meat-eating was one of the fiercest battle-fronts in the struggle to define humanity's proper relationship with nature. The vital question: 'should humans be eating animals?' was a serious challenge to Western society's belief that the world and everything in it had been made exclusively for mankind. Vegetarians called for a wholesale reappraisal of the human relationship with nature. Man was lord of the creation: but what kind of a lord, vegetarians asked, ate his own subjects?

It started with the Bible – with the very first chapter of Genesis. The

---

* Seventeenth- and eighteenth-century writers generally used 'Man' to denote 'mankind' comprising both genders, usually with a patriarchal bias. It would be a distortion to avoid using their term.

first words God said to Adam and Eve after creating the world were: 'Be fruitful, and multiply, and replenish the earth, and subdue it: and have dominion over the fish of the sea, and over the fowl of the air, and over every living thing that moveth upon the earth' (Genesis 1:28). In the remote world of fourth-century BC Athens, this view was echoed with remarkable consonance by Aristotle, probably the most revered authority in Western culture after the Scriptures: 'plants are created for the sake of animals, and the animals for the sake of men'.[2] These two pillars of cultural authority provided a religious and philosophical sanction for humanity's predatory instincts (a characteristic of hominid behaviour which arose more than a million years ago). Anything that wasn't recognisably *Homo sapiens* stood little chance of being valued beyond its basic utility. But there were always counter-currents and cracks in the edifice, and it was into these fractures that vegetarians thrust their cultural crowbars.

Man was lord of the earth; but in what, exactly, did his dominion consist? In the beginning at least, according to the Bible, man's dominion over the animals apparently did *not* include killing them – for the very next thing God had said to Adam and Eve was: 'Behold, I have given you every herb bearing seed . . . and every tree, in the which is the fruit of a tree yielding seed; to you it shall be for meat' (Genesis 1:29). From this primeval culinary instruction most seventeenth- and eighteenth-century theologians deduced that Adam and Eve were restricted to eating fruit and plants, and all creatures lived together in herbivorous peace. It was only much later (1,600 years by standard chronology), when the earth had been destroyed and renewed again in Noah's Flood, that God altered the charter to mankind.[3] When Noah came down from the Ark, God told him, 'the fear of you and the dread of you shall be upon every beast of the earth, and upon every fowl of the air, upon all that moveth upon the earth, and upon all the fishes of the sea; into your hand are they delivered. Every moving thing that liveth shall be meat for you; even as the green herb have I given you all things' (Genesis 9:2–3). As the scholar John Edwards explained with relish in 1699, this was as much as to say, 'you have as free liberty now, since the Flood, to eat the Flesh of every living Creature, as you had before the Flood to feed on every sort of Herbs and Fruits, tho you were stinted as to Flesh. This is the clear sense and import of the words; and consequently proves, that eating Flesh before the Flood was unlawful.'

The friction between God's permission to prey upon animals and the ideal of mankind in harmony with creation produced a fault line which vegetarians sought to magnify. Even as the biblical strictures faded in society, equivalent values remained prevalent, and their legacy can still be traced in modern society, particularly in the deep-rooted beliefs on either side of the environmental debate.

Meat-eating came under fire from a spectacular array of viewpoints in the seventeenth and eighteenth centuries. Revolutionaries attacked the bloodthirsty luxury of mainstream culture; demographers accused the meat industry of wasting resources which could otherwise be used to feed people; anatomists claimed that human intestines were not equipped to digest meat, and travellers to the East presented India as a peaceful alternative to the rapacity of the West. Radicals and eccentrics contested their society's values head on; but many of the era's foremost thinkers also wrangled over the issues, leading to a reassessment of human nature. The luxury of *choosing* to abstain from meat may have been restricted to small sectors of European society, but these often drew their inspiration from the underfed poor who seemed to live, and labour, without needing vast quantities of meat. The cultural elites in turn influenced agronomic, medical and economic policies which determined the diets of populations as a whole.

The arguments that raged in the formative period between 1600 and 1830 helped to shape the values of modern society. Understanding the history of our ideas sets modern culture in a striking new light and can overturn our most entrenched assumptions. The early history of vegetarianism reveals how ancient ethics of abstinence, early medical science and Indian philosophy have influenced Western culture in profound and unexpected ways.

Returning to a state of harmony free from carnage became a fervent wish for many in the seventeenth century; it remained an idyllic dream even for those who recognised its impossibility. It was part of what can be called *prelapsarianism*: the desire to return to the perfection enjoyed by mankind before Adam and Eve's 'lapse' in Paradise. Prelapsarians often wished to reinstate the harmonious relationship with the animals enjoyed in Eden. Their 'dominion' would be benevolent and kind, not a savage tyranny: an ideal which seventeenth-century radicals used in their attack on oppression and violence in human society.

In 1642 civil war broke out between Royalists and Parliamentarians, plunging England into years of bloodshed. Men and women of all political stripes searched for an alternative to the anarchy around them by trying to recreate a society based on paradisal peace and harmony. The Royalist Thomas Bushell followed his master Francis Bacon's advice by testing whether the primeval diet was the key to long life and spiritual perfection. On the radical wing of the Parliamentary faction, puritanical fighters for democracy used vegetarianism to articulate their dissent from the luxurious mainstream, and called for a bloodless revolution to institute a slaughter-free society of equality. Religious extremists chimed in with the announcement that God dwelt within the creatures and mankind should therefore treat them all with love and kindness.

One other *external* force joined the fray, exerting a surprising influence on Western culture. European travellers to India 'discovered' the ancient Indian religions and the fascinating doctrine of *ahimsa*, or non-violence to all living things. They interrogated Hindus and Jains on its philosophical ramifications; with astonishment, they observed animal hospitals, widespread vegetarianism and extraordinary kindness even to the most lowly creatures. News of Indian vegetarianism proved a radical challenge to Christian ideas of human dominance, and it contributed to a crisis in the European conscience. To many it seemed that the idealists' dreams had become a reality. Vegetarians got down on their knees, calling on the ancient Indian philosophers to lead humanity away from its state of corruption and bloodshed.

Europe's encounter with Indian vegetarianism had a massive impact well beyond the radical fringe. A thriving trade in travel literature inflamed the eager inquiries of serious philosophers and fuelled the curiosity of a wide popular audience. The travellers themselves tended to ridicule Indian vegetarianism as absurd soft-heartedness, but many readers saw in the Indian system a powerful and appealing moral code. Members of the philosophical establishment – John Evelyn, Sir Thomas Browne and Sir William Temple – recognised that the Indian vegetarians proved that people could live happily on the original fruit and vegetable diet. Sir Isaac Newton's reading about Eastern sages helped to convince him that 'Mercy to Beasts' was one of God's first and most fundamental laws from which Europeans had long since apostatized. Sceptics at the end of the seventeenth century used Indian vegetarianism to plant a powerful blow on European religious and social orthodoxies, arguing that Indians upheld the original law of nature: to do unto others (including animals) as you would be done by.

The impact of Indian vegetarianism vitally influenced a shift away from the Bible's mandate of unlimited dominion. It encouraged people to imagine that broadening the sphere of ethical responsibility was beneficial for humans as well as for nature itself. Indian philosophy – and principally the doctrine of *ahimsa* – triggered a debate that has evolved over time into the modern ecological crisis.

The seventeenth and eighteenth centuries were a time of immense scientific development. New discoveries and systematising theories emerged from all over Western Europe and filtered out into the widely educated population. Microscopes plunged the observing eye into thitherto invisible worlds; surgical explorations opened up concealed areas of the human body; ever-growing tables of astronomical observations from bigger and better observatories drove human knowledge deeper into space; accumulated navigational skills extended the known world almost to its limits, bringing new peoples and new species under the scrutiny of Enlightenment science – or 'Natural Philosophy' as the discipline was then known. If the vegetarian argument was to prosper it would have to keep up with the times and adapt its logic to modern systems of thought. Vegetarians developed elaborate scientific ways of defending their philosophy, and plugged their views into the main channels of Enlightenment thought.

Intrepid investigations with the scalpel confirmed that the human body was almost identical to that of apes and very similar to other animals, which put the study of anatomy and physiology centre-stage in philosophical debate. Man was partly an animal: but scientists wanted to know exactly what sort of animal, herbivore or carnivore? A substantial sector of the intellectual world concluded that the human body, in its original form, was designed to be herbivorous – thus substantiating the scriptural evidence that the primeval diet was fruit and herbs.

Science flourished in the eighteenth century, but it was founded on the schism with received modes of thought engineered by the philosophers René Descartes (1596–1650) and his vitally important rival, Pierre Gassendi (1592–1655). Within their new frameworks, Descartes and Gassendi set to work on the most pressing questions: the nature of the soul, of man, and man's place between God and nature. Contrary to all expectations, both Gassendi and Descartes agreed that vegetarianism could be the most suitable diet for humans.

Amazingly, three of Europe's most important early seventeenth-century philosophers – Descartes, Gassendi and Francis Bacon – *all* advocated vegetarianism. At no time before or since has vegetarianism been endorsed by such a formidable array of intellectuals, and by the 1700s their pioneering work had blossomed into a powerful movement of scientific vegetarianism.

Anatomists noticed that human teeth and intestines were more akin to those of herbivores than those of carnivores. Dieticians argued that meat did not break down in the digestive system, clogging blood circulation, whereas tender vegetables easily dissolved into an enriching fluid. Neural scientists discovered that animals have nerves capable of exquisite suffering, just as humans do, and this was discomfiting for people who based their entire moral philosophy on the principle of sympathy. At the same time, the study of Indian populations indicated that abstinence from meat could be conducive to health and long life. This helped to transform the image of vegetarianism from a radical political statement into a sound medical system. The idea that the vegetarian diet could be the most natural was so astonishingly prevalent in university medical faculties across Europe that it appears to have been close to a scientific orthodoxy.

Numerous vegetarian doctors emerged all over Europe, transforming these scientific arguments into practical dietary prescriptions for patients believed to be ailing from over-consumption of flesh. These diet-doctors became conspicuous figures in society, much like the celebrity dieticians of today, but they were also primary movers in pioneering medical research. Meat was almost universally believed to be the most nourishing food, and in England especially, beef was an icon of national identity. It was still common to suspect that vegetables were unnecessary gastronomic supplements and that they were prone to upset the digestive system in perilous ways. The vegetarians helped to alter such suppositions, by presenting evidence that vegetables were an essential nutritional requirement, and that meat was superfluous and could even be extremely unhealthy. The vegetarians thus played a key role in forming modern ideas about balanced diets and put a spotlight on the dangers of eating meat, especially to excess.

Believing that the vegetable diet was healthier and meat was positively harmful invariably led people to the conclusion that the human body was designed to be herbivorous, not carnivorous, and that killing animals was unnatural. Examining natural laws was supposed to provide insights into God's creational design, independent from scriptural revelation. The new scientific observations were seen to endorse the old theological claims for the origins of the vegetable diet, and it gave added force to the view that human society's savage treatment of lesser animals was a perversion of the natural order.

These deductions were backed up by changing perceptions of sympathy which became one of the fundamental principles of moral philosophy in the late seventeenth century, and has remained an abiding force in Western culture. The idea of 'sympathy' in its modern sense as a synonym for 'compassion' was formulated as a mechanical explanation of the archaic idea of *sympatheia*, the principle – spectacularly adapted to vegetarianism by Thomas Tryon – according to which elements in the human body had an occult 'correspondence', like a magnetic attraction, to similar entities in the universe. Descartes' followers explained that if you saw another person's limb being injured, 'animal spirits' automatically rushed to your corresponding limb and actually caused you to participate in the sense of pain. Although the Cartesians thought that sympathy for animals should be ignored, later commentators argued that the instinctive feeling of sympathy for animals indicated that killing them was contrary to human nature. Vegetarians seized upon the unity of the 'scientific', 'moral' and 'religious' rationales and tried to force people to recognise that eating meat was at odds with their own ethics. Although most people preferred not to think about it, the vegetarians insisted that filling the European belly funded the torture of animals in unpleasant agricultural systems, and ultimately the rape and pillage of the entire world.

All these claims were fiercely repudiated and a distinct counter-vegetarian movement quickly rallied in defence of meat-eating. The intensity as well as the wide proliferation of the debate testifies to just how familiar the vegetarian cause became, and just how challenging most people felt it to be. It threatened to oust man from his long-held position as unlimited lord of the universe – and worse still, to deprive people of their Sunday feasts of roast meat. Leading figures in the medical world accepted some of the vegetarians' reforms – that people should eat less meat and more vegetables – but urgently asserted that man's anatomy was omnivorous or carnivorous *not* herbivorous, and that vegetables alone were unsuitable for human nourishment. Several philosophers, novelists and poets likewise insisted that sympathy for animals was all very well, but should not be taken to the extreme of vegetarianism.

Nevertheless, prominent members of the cultural elite espoused at least some of the views of the vegetarians and inspired a considerable back-to-nature movement in which diet played an important role. The novelist Samuel Richardson allowed the vegetarian ideals of his doctor, George Cheyne, to infiltrate his best-selling novels, *Clarissa* and *Pamela*. Jean-Jacques Rousseau, concurring with the anatomical case, argued that the innate propensity to sympathy was a philosophical basis of animal rights, thus spawning a generation of Rousseauists who advocated vegetarianism. The economist Adam Smith took on board the doctors' discovery that meat was a superfluous luxury and this provided an important cog in the taxation system of his seminal treatise on the free market. By the end of the eighteenth century vegetarianism was advocated by medical lecturers, moral philosophers, sentimental writers and political activists. Vegetarianism had sustained its role as a counter-cultural critique, backed up by evidence that many in the mainstream of society could accept.

The history of vegetarianism adumbrates recent revisionary criticism which questions traditional oppositions between the so-called irrationalism of religious enthusiasts and the 'Enlightenment' rationalism of natural philosophers. In the seventeenth and eighteenth centuries, the vegetable diet was munched raw at the communal board of the political and religious extremists – but it was also served with silver cutlery at the high table of the Enlightenment to the learned elite.

In the late eighteenth and early nineteenth centuries, Europe was dominated by a culture of radical innovation – diverse movements bundled together under the name Romanticism. Hinduism became the object of veneration as a new wave of Orientalists travelled to India, learned Indian languages and translated Sanskrit texts to the delight of Western audiences. Some East India Company servants were so overcome by the benevolence of Indian culture that they relinquished the religion of their fathers and employers to embrace Hinduism as a more humane alternative. This played into the hands of radical critics of Christianity, such as Voltaire, who used the antiquity of Hinduism to land a devastating blow to the Bible's claims, and acknowledged that the Hindus' treatment of animals represented a shaming alternative to the viciousness of European imperialists. Even those more dedicated to keeping their Christian identity, such as the great scholar Sir William Jones, found themselves swayed by the doctrine of *ahimsa*, seeing it as the embodiment of everything the eighteenth-century doctors and philosophers had scientifically demonstrated.

As the ferment of political ideas brewed into revolutionary fervour in the 1780s, the vegetarian ideas from former centuries were incorporated once again into a radical agenda. Hinduism was held up as a philosophy of universal sympathy and equality which accorded with the fundamental tenet of democratic politics and animal rights. The rebel John Oswald returned from India inflamed with outrage at the violent injustice of human society and immersed himself in the most bloodthirsty episodes of the French Revolution. Others developed Rousseau's back-to-nature movement and lost their heads on the guillotine defending their vegetarian beliefs. The poet Percy Bysshe Shelley joined an eccentric network of nudist vegetarians who were agitating for social revolution and immortalised their ideas in a series of vegetarian poems and essays. As atheism waxed, the anthropocentric bias of European Christianity was eroded, and humans were forced to acknowledge that they were more closely related to animals than was entirely comfortable. Utopian reformers still had the model of primeval harmony seared into their imaginations even though many of them regarded Eden as no more than a myth, so they learned to treat Judaeo-Christianity as an anthropological curiosity and paved the way for modern ideas about humanity and the environment.

As environmental degradation and population growth became serious problems in Europe, economists turned to the pressing question of limited natural resources. Many realised that producing meat was a hugely inefficient process in which nine-tenths of the resources pumped into the animal were wastefully transformed into faeces.

Utilitarians argued that since the vegetable diet could sustain far more people per acre than meat, it was much better equipped to achieve the greatest happiness for the greatest number. Once again the enormous populations of vegetarian Indians and Chinese were held up as enlightened exemplars of efficient agronomics. Such calculations eventually led to Thomas Malthus' warnings that human populations inexorably grew beyond the capacity of food production, and that famine was likely to ensue.

By the early nineteenth century most of the philosophical, medical and economic arguments for vegetarianism were in place, and exerting continual pressure on mainstream European culture. In the course of the nineteenth and twentieth centuries the ideas inevitably transformed, but continuities can be traced to the present day. Figures as diverse as Adolf Hitler, Mahatma Gandhi and Leo Tolstoy developed the political ramifications of vegetarianism in their own ways, and continued to respond to India's moral example.

When studying ideas that people formulated hundreds of years ago, it is important to understand them on their own terms, irrespective of whether they are 'right' or 'wrong' according to present-day understanding, because to do so allows them to provide insight into assumptions that still prevail in modern society – of which, in their nature, we are commonly unaware. The remarkable and long under-appreciated lives of early vegetarians are inroads into uncharted areas of history; they simultaneously shed light on why you think about nature the way you do, why you are told to eat fresh vegetables and avoid too much meat, and how Indian philosophy has crucially shaped those thoughts over the past 400 years.

PART ONE

Grass Roots

ONE

Bushell's Bushel, Bacon's Bacon and The Great Instauration

Driving out of London over Highgate Hill on a cold March day in 1626, Sir Francis Bacon noticed spring snow still lying on the ground and seized the opportunity to test whether 'flesh might not be preserved in snow, as in salt'. Bacon descended from his carriage in a flourish of compulsive inquisitiveness, purchased a hen from a poor woman, made her gut it, and then stuffed it with snow himself. Before he could publish the results of this, his last experiment, the snow chilled Bacon's own flesh, and he was struck by a coughing fit so severe he could not return home. As he lay in the damp bed in the nearby house of his friend the Earl of Arundel, his condition worsened, and within days Bacon, one of England's greatest philosophers, was dead.[1]

Born in 1561, Bacon had struggled to the very top of the political ladder; he had been a member of Queen Elizabeth's council and Lord Chancellor to King James VI and I. Despite his relatively modest background as the grandson of a sheep-reeve, he had been knighted and ennobled with the titles of Baron Verulam and Viscount St Albans. Above all, he was respected throughout Europe for philosophical works in which he envisaged an intellectual project of limit-defying scale. By gaining comprehensive knowledge of the natural world, Bacon believed that people could improve their control over the environment until eventually they would reinstate the felicity that Adam enjoyed in Eden. In the title of his unfinished work, *The Great Instauration* (from the Latin *Instauratio* – restoration, inauguration), he signified that his vision was the beginning of the restitution of mankind's lost power. His audacious optimism fired the imagination of the keenest minds of the ensuing centuries, and his name became the touchstone of the Enlightenment. When King James first read Bacon's writings he proclaimed that 'yt is like the peace of God, that passeth all understanding'.[2]

Bacon's escapade with the frozen chicken was not an isolated whim. He had been studying the properties of food for years and in 1623 published in Latin *The Great Instauration*'s third part: *The History Naturall and Experimentall, Of Life and Death. Or the Prolongation of Life.* The quest to discover the secret to long life had been an obsession since ancient times, and Bacon himself considered it the 'most noble' part of medicine.[3] For Bacon, no less than people today, diet took centre-stage. Though ironically his investigations into the 'preservation of flesh' actually caused his own flesh to perish, Bacon hoped that discovering the ideal food would help lead men back to their original perfection.

Bacon noticed that it was healthy to eat plenty of fruit and vegetables on a daily basis. But if it was longevity you were after, he advised his readers to ignore the usual chatter about the Golden Mean and go for either of the extremes. Strengthen your constitution by undergoing a 'strict *Emaciating Dyet*' of biscuit and guaiacum tree resin: this would weaken you in the short term, but set you up for a long life. Going to the other extreme, Bacon agreed with Celsus, the first-century AD medical encyclopaedist, that gastronomic excess could also be good for you. This amusing mandate for indulgence – which eighteenth-century medics rallied around when their appetites came under fire from the vegetarian doctors – no doubt informed the approving tone of the contemporaneous biographer, John Aubrey, when he wrote that Bacon's one-time assistant, the philosopher Thomas Hobbes, periodically over-indulged, getting himself blind drunk at least once a year. Dying at the age of ninety-two, Hobbes was later wilfully enrolled by eighteenth-century vegetarians as a fine example of the benefits of temperance.[4]

'*Man*, and *Creatures* feeding upon Flesh, are scarcely nourished with Plants alone,' wrote Bacon in 1623. 'Perhaps, *Fruits*, or *Graines*, baked, or boyled, may, with long use, nourish them;' he added. 'But *Leaves*, of *Plants*, or *Herbs*, will not doe it.' Surviving exclusively on leaves and greens ('herbs' meant herbaceous plants including things like cabbage) had already been attempted with catastrophic effects by the Foliatanes, a convent of ascetic nuns who fed on nothing but foliage. But Bacon did allow that humans and carnivores could survive on vegetables if the ingredients were well chosen, and his Latin original shows him to have been even more open to the vegetarian diet than his disconcerted posthumous translators made it sound.[5] Bacon noticed that there was substantial statistical evidence that vegetarianism was one of the extremes that could aid longevity: Pythagoras, the sixth-century BC Greek philosopher renowned for his theorem on right-angled triangles, also taught his disciples to abstain from meat, and Pythagoreans such as Apollonius of Tyana 'exceeded an hundred yeares; His Face bewraying no such Age'. Indeed, Bacon catalogued numerous vegetarians recorded in history who had lived unusually long lives: the desert-dwelling Jewish sect of vegetarian Essenes, the Spartans, the Indians and plenty of Christian ascetics. 'A *Pythagoricall*, or *Monasticall Diet*, according to strict rules,' concluded Bacon, 'seemeth to be very effectual for long life.'

So while Hobbes swallowed whole Bacon's aphorisms about indulgence, another flamboyant young male acolyte, Thomas Bushell (1594–1674), was ruminating over his master's approbation of the vegetarian way. John Aubrey described both Hobbes and Bushell scurrying along behind Bacon transcribing his thoughts during strolls in his garden – each preparing to carry Bacon's legacy forward in their own divergent ways.

In 1621 Bacon's glittering political career came to an abrupt end. He was made the scapegoat in a political tussle about monopolies and the victim of a personal attack by his rival Edward Coke. Left to the mercy of Parliament by the King, Bacon was accused of taking bribes; he was fined £40,000, briefly imprisoned in the Tower of London and banished from court in disgrace. In the wake of this scandal there followed more severe allegations: that Bacon was a sodomite and paid his young male servants, Bushell among them, for sex. Satirical verses circulated, laughing at the matching of their names: Bacon was 'A pig, a hog, a boar, a bacon/ Whom God hath left, and the devil hath taken', while his servant pecked at his bushel of grain, but 'Bushell wants by half a peck the measure of such tears/ Because his lord's posteriors makes the buttons that he wears'. (The buttons refer to the garish fashion of embellishing suits with buttons, leading to the *double-entendre* nickname 'buttoned Bushell'.)[6]

Taking his fate stoically, Bacon devoted himself to philosophical enquiries, but Bushell – who had joined Bacon's household at the age of fifteen, risen to be his seal-bearer and was entirely dependent on his patron – faced despair. Following Bacon's fall from grace and subsequent death, Bushell was plunged into dejected remorse. Lurching from a life of wanton profligacy, in which his greatest achievement had been running up enormous debts and attracting the attention of

'Thomas Bushell, the Superlative Prodigal' from Thomas Bushell,
The First Part of Youths Errors (1628)

James I for the gorgeousness of his attire, he left behind him London's gaming houses, bawdy Shakespearean plays and buxom whores of Eastcheap, and dramatically refashioned himself as the 'Superlative Prodigall'.

The young man took his penitence to anchoritic extremes. In his later writings, Bushell described how he first retired to the Isle of Wight disguised as a fisherman, and afterwards to the Calf of Man (an islet just off the Isle of Man) where he took up residence on the desolate summit of a cliff 470 feet above the Irish Sea. There, he said, 'in obedience to my dead Lord [Bacon's] philosophical advice, I resolved to make a perfect experiment upon myself, for the obtaining of a long and healthy life.' He shunned meat and alcohol, living instead on a 'parsimonious diet of herbs, oil, mustard and honey, with water sufficient, most like to that [of] our long liv'd fathers before the flood, as was conceiv'd by that lord, which I most strictly observed, as if obliged by a religious vow'.

The austerity of Bushell's diet was clearly rooted in the Christian (and pre-Christian) tradition of abstinence from meat and monastic penitence. By imposing strictures on the body, it was believed, the soul would be regenerated and cleansed of sin. And it was meat and alcohol, above all, that were identified as the principal items of luxury. The problem for Bushell was that in Protestant England ascetic fasting was seen as a superstitious vestige of Catholicism. By giving up meat and living like a monk he risked being accused of having secret Catholic sympathies. In his confessions, *The First Part of Youths Errors* (1628), Bushell vigorously defended himself: if all the saints – Anthony, Augustine, Jerome, Paul the hermit and the Apostles themselves – had been ascetics, he demanded, then why shouldn't he, a terrible sinner, be one as well?[7]

Bacon too was aware of how suspicious his predilection for vegetables could seem. Regardless of being called a Catholic, Bacon was afraid he would be accused of sympathising with the medieval vegetarian heretics, the Manicheans and Cathars, whom the Inquisition had genocidally suppressed with fire and sword. Anxious to avoid such a fate, Bacon issued repeated disclaimers: 'Neither would we be thought to favour the *Manichees*, or their diet, though wee commend the frequent use of all kindes of seedes, and kernels, and roots . . . neither let any Man reckon us amongst those *Hereticks*, which were called *Cathari*.' Bacon was trying to shift discussions of diet away from its old heretical connotations into the new idiom of enlightened philosophy. His opinions, he insisted, were based on empirical facts and not on religious dietary taboos.[8]

Happily, Bacon's healthy vegetable diet appears to have done Bushell a world of good. By the time he was buried in the cloisters of Westminster Abbey in 1674 at the fine old age of eighty, Bushell had become a legendary figure, and is still remembered today as the Calf of Man's most famous inhabitant. For a while, he was also rich. Having come down from his cliff, he pursued Bacon's practical tip on reclaiming silver and lead mines in Wales and established his own mint in Aberystwyth. God was so pleased with his vegetarian penitence, he claimed, that He gave Bushell power to subdue the 'Subteranean Spirits' which usually hindered mining projects. With the profits that flowed from the earth, he proclaimed his intention to realise Bacon's plans for a 'Solomon's House' – the utopian establishment depicted in Bacon's unfinished work, *New Atlantis*. Bacon had imagined an ideal colony where scientific endeavour (including a primitive form of genetic engineering) was enhanced by the inhabitants' rigorous lifestyle, some of them purifying their bodies by living in three-mile-deep caves below the mountains. Bushell's institution was not quite what Bacon had imagined. It was more like a philanthropic dining facility for his miners, where instead of being fed the complete meal Bacon had devised – a fermented-meat drink – they were fed on Bushell's own meagre diet of penitential bread and water.

Bushell himself retreated, meanwhile, to his estate at Road Enstone, near Woodstock in Oxfordshire, where he created a 'kind of paradise' in a grotto garden around a cave which became famous for a natural spring generating a series of spectacular hydraulic contraptions. He was no doubt inspired by Bacon's cave-dwelling multi-centenarian wise men and by the 'paradise' garden at Bacon's mansion in Gorhambury where the pair used to spend hours in meditation. In his new abode Bushell kept up his old dietary resolve, writing that he still 'observ'd my Lords prescription, to satisifie nature with a Diet of Oyle, Honey, Mustard, Herbs and Bisket'. King Charles I and Queen Henrietta visited Bushell in his grotto in 1636, and for their pleasure he organised the performance of a masque about a vegetarian prodigal hermit. The Queen expressed her appreciation by installing an extremely rare Egyptian mummy in Bushell's damp grotto home (where it slowly went mouldy and was lost to posterity).

When civil war broke out in 1642, Bushell roused himself from his tranquil retreat. As political affiliations polarised those who questioned and those who believed subjects had no right to question, Bushell remained fervently loyal to King Charles. Bacon had foreseen the political turmoil and spent his career defending the royal prerogative; faithful to Bacon as always, Bushell became a mainstay of the Cavaliers' military campaign against the Roundheads. He turned his miners into the King's lifeguard, bankrolled the Royalist army with silver and a hundred tons of lead-shot from his mines, put down a mutiny in Shropshire, and defended (yet another island) Lundy in the Bristol Channel. Eventually surrendering to the onslaught of the Parliamentary army, he was arrested and seriously wounded in the head, but then attained the protection of Lord Fairfax. With many of his loans unsettled other than by a quaint but otherwise worthless thank-you letter from King Charles, Bushell went back to his garden, as Horace to his Sabine Farm and the poet Andrew Marvell to Nun Appleton, rejecting the anarchy of Cromwell's interregnum in preference for his own private Eden.[9]

Bushell's dietary strictures followed an ancient Christian tradition which conceived of vegetarianism as a back door to regaining paradisal perfection. Like several Church fathers, the ascetic St Jerome (AD *c.*347– 420) – revered for plucking a painful thorn from a lion's paw and composing the Latin Bible in his penitential cave – associated the gluttony of flesh-eating with Adam's intemperate eating of the forbidden fruit. If people wanted to undo the curse of the Fall, they would have to start by abstaining from flesh: 'by fasting we can return to paradise, whence, through fullness, we have been expelled.' 'At the beginning of the human race we neither ate flesh, nor gave bills of divorce, nor suffered circumcision,' said Jerome. These were concessions granted after the Flood, 'But once Christ has come in the end of time,' he said, 'we are no longer allowed divorce, nor are we circumcised, nor do we eat flesh'.[10] This provided a theological rationale for relinquishing meat which lasted for centuries. As Sir John Pettus suggested in 1674, we 'multiply *Adams* transgression by our continued eating of other creatures, which were not then allowed to us'.[11]

This tradition had come under fire ever since the Protestants had split from the Roman Church. John Calvin (1509–64), co-founder of the Reformation, had tried to untangle such literal-minded dietary loopholes. He cast doubt over the vegetarianism of the early patriarchs by pointing out that God gave Adam and Eve animal skins to wear when he ejected them from Eden's balmy realm, and that ever since the time of Cain and Abel people had sacrificed animals. But even if they didn't eat the animals they sacrificed, he stressed, the important point was that God did eventually give 'to man the free use of flesh, so that we might not eat it with a doubtful and trembling conscience'. Anyone who thought mankind should be vegetarian was being blasphemously ungrateful for God's generosity. He had one message for such hyper-scrupulous quibblers: shut up and eat up.[12] But this was not enough to stem the longing for perfection, even in Protestant countries, and Bushell was one of many who still hoped to reclaim his lost innocence by abstaining from flesh.

In the masque he laid on for the King and Queen, Bushell depicted (and perhaps played) the part of the vegetarian hermit – clearly

The Golden Age, from Ovid's *Metamorphoses*

modelled on himself – who claims to have lived in the same Oxfordshire cave and subsisted on the same vegetable diet ever since the time of Noah. The hermit tells his audience he lives in a reconstructed Golden Age, 'In which no injuries are meant or done'. The masque ended with the hermit inviting the King to join his world (and forget for a while the looming political crisis) by sharing in the feast of home-grown fruit.[13]

Bushell was indulging in the common feeling that the biblical story of original harmony was analogous to the classical Greek and Roman myth of the Golden Age, when justice reigned, iron was yet to be invented and no animals were slaughtered. In 1632, just before Bushell's masque, the travelling poet George Sandys had published his extremely influential translation and commentary on Ovid's *Metamorphoses*. Sandys portrayed the Golden Age menu of wild blackberries, strawberries, acorns and 'all sorts of fruit' in a much more appetising light than translators hitherto, and added enthusiastically that 'this happy estate abounding with all felicities, assuredly represented that which man injoyed in his innocency: under the raigne of Saturne, more truly of Adam.'[14] Eating meat, he added, was 'a priviledge granted after to Noah; because ['hearbes and fruits'] then had lost much of their nourishing vertue'. Meat-eating, according to this reasoning, was an unfortunate consequence of the Flood. In the climactic finale of

Metamorphoses, Pythagoras comes forward and delivers a lengthy diatribe against eating animals – 'How horrible a Sin, / That entrailes bleeding entrailes should intomb! / That greedie flesh, by flesh should fat become!' Sandys noted that Pythagoras' vegetarianism was an attempt to reinstate the peacefulness of the Golden Age because killing animals proceeded 'from injustice, cruelty, and corruption of manners; not knowne in that innocent age'.[15] Pythagoras' example was an inspiration to early vegetarians like Bushell.

Giving up meat altogether may have been rather quirky in early seventeenth-century England, and Bushell was well aware that his notions could be mistaken for 'the Chymera of a phanatick brain'.[16] He further risked his reputation by successfully lobbying the government to release from prison several members of religious groups who were also trying to reinstate the conditions and even the diet of Eden, such as the Rosicrucians, the Family of Love and the Adamites (who took the Adamic lifestyle to its extreme by shedding their clothes and living in the naked purity of Eden before the figleaves).[17]

It may seem as if Bushell had by this time descended into a religious dream world, but his extreme diet was endorsed by scientific rigour. Bushell's immersion into vegetarianism was an act of religious fervour, but it was simultaneously the realisation of a Baconian project: he presented himself as a human guinea-pig in Bacon's 'perfect experiment' for lengthening human life on a vegetarian diet. As Bushell said, his dietary attempt to gain a long and healthy life was based on that of 'our long liv'd fathers before the flood'. It was statistically evident that the average age of the 'antediluvian' patriarchs was in excess of 900 years, topped by Adam's descendant, Methuselah, who lived to 969 (Genesis 5). What – everyone wanted to know – was the secret of their longevity?[18] Once permission to eat meat was granted after the Flood, human life expectancy plummeted from 900 to the current average of around 70. It seemed at least plausible to the enquiring mind that it was eating meat that had curtailed human life so dramatically;[19] perhaps by relinquishing it one could regain some of those lost years. This may sound like it competes in crankiness with today's diet-doctors, but few then dared doubt the basic facts set out in the Bible. Even the philosopher René Descartes seems to have believed it. It may seem surprising that religious extremes and experimental philosophy coincided in such a spectacular way, but it was a trend that would continue for at least two centuries. Bacon and Bushell raised many of the questions about vegetarianism that dominated the ensuing debate.

Far from being the exclusive territory of extremists, undoing certain effects of the Fall was also the basis of Bacon's intellectual endeavour. Bacon's idea of the reclamation of Adamic knowledge became the manifesto for the seventeenth-century advancement of learning. The utopian reformers of the Civil War period Jan Amos Comenius and Samuel Hartlib hoped that their new system for universal education, or pansophism, would restore 'Light, Peace, Health . . . and that golden age which has ever been longed for'. Their contemporary, the radical doctor Nicholas Culpeper, promised that his brand of the regulated temperate diet could mitigate malign celestial influences and make life on earth 'a terrestiall Paradise to him that useth it'.[20] The kabbalists Knorr von Rosenroth and Franciscus Mercurius van Helmont believed that reclaiming knowledge would reinstate the harmony 'which so many thousands of Christians have wished and groaned for, for such a long time'.[21] Even members of the Royal Society – the pinnacle of British scientific exploration chartered by Charles II in 1662 – thought that they were gradually working mankind back to the universal knowledge enjoyed in Paradise.[22]

Bushell's idealistic vegetarianism fitted hand in glove with the intellectual project inaugurated by his master Francis Bacon. Bacon's experimental philosophy would restore mankind to the universal knowledge lost in Adam's Fall and discover the secret to longevity. Vegetarians would join forces by testing the dietary hypotheses and simultaneously restoring mankind to lost innocence and perfection. The dietary means to returning to antediluvian health was also a route to spiritual restoration. In Bushell's 'perfect experiment', the spiritual and the 'scientific' marched side by side.

Bacon did not challenge the universally accepted doctrine that man had rightful dominion over nature; indeed, he held this as his philosophical paradigm. But Bacon did argue that man's power over creation carried an important caveat: 'There is implanted in man by nature,' he wrote in *The Advancement and Proficience of Learning* (1605), 'a noble and excellent Affection of *Piety* [pity] *and compassion*, which extends it selfe even to bruit creatures'. God had given man dominion, but He had also encoded him with a sentiment of compassion which moderated his behaviour to animals. Only 'contracted & degenerate minds', said Bacon, failed to heed the edict encapsulated in the biblical book of Proverbs, 'A Just man is mercifull to the life of his Beast' (Proverbs 12:10).

Bacon's translation of this Proverb took the compassionate treatment of animals further than most Christians were comfortable with. The 1611 King James version rendered it ambiguously, 'A righteous man *regardeth* the life of his beast', and the Latin Vulgate simply says *novit* ('recognises'), while in the original Hebrew the righteous man's concern for his domestic animals may well be purely self-interested. Bacon was partaking in the pervasive, though often frowned-upon, tradition of seeking in the Bible laws that endorsed kindness to animals.

His motive for doing so was partly fuelled by the desire to find an equivalent in Judaeo-Christianity of the laws of humanity that he identified in other cultures. In doing this, he pushed forward one final major philosophical development which was to transform thinking in the seventeenth and eighteenth centuries: that Western and Eastern cultures shared close moral affinities regardless of their religious differences. This had roots in the medieval and Renaissance idea of the 'virtuous gentile', but it took on greater prominence and complexity as travellers had increasing opportunities to observe foreign cultures first hand. Bacon dubiously claimed that the Mosaic law against eating blood, found in Genesis, Leviticus and Deuteronomy, was Moses' counterpart of laws found all over the world that enforced mercy to animals: 'even in the sect of the *Esseans* and *Pythagoreans*, they altogither abstain'd from *eating Flesh*; which to this day is observed by an inviolate superstition, by many of the Easterne people under the Mogol.' The law of pity, Bacon concluded, was not just a Jewish law, it was embedded in human nature, so it was little surprise to find that diverse religions enforced it. When other cultures could provide such useful comparisons that helped to prove his views on the properties of human nature, no wonder Bacon regarded the voyages of discovery as an important aspect of restoring man's universal understanding. The Indians and the Pythagoreans took their opinions to superstitious extremes, but their vegetarianism, Bacon said, was the realisation of a true and noble principle. Misguided as they perhaps were, they nevertheless exemplified natural human mercy more than the 'contracted & degenerate minds' of his own society. This was a daring valorisation of a foreign ethical code, and Bacon later moderated it by comparing their superstitions with the Muslim taboos on pork and bacon.[23] This idea of instinctive sympathy added still more force to the scientific dietary reasons for becoming vegetarian. Richard Baxter (1615–91), one of the chief Puritan ministers in the Civil War, clearly exemplified how the medical and the moral motives propelled each other. When he was told to give up meat to save his ailing health, he consoled himself by reflecting that God had 'put into all good men that tender compassion to the bruites as will keep them from a senseless royoting in their blood'; 'all my daies', he wrote, eating meat 'hath gone, as against my nature, with some regret; which hath made me the more contented that God hath made me long renounce it'.[24]

Bacon's cultural analysis found a common cause in Christian and Indian teaching; as usual Bushell went a step further and cultivated the comparison in himself. In 1664 – more than forty years after Bushell first adopted the vegetable diet – the like-minded advocate of Indian vegetarianism and fellow Royalist John Evelyn called on Bushell in his cave. He was mightily impressed by the hermit's way of life as well as the Edenic garden layout: 'It is an extraordinary solitude,' Evelyn wrote. 'There he had two mummies; [and] a grott where he lay in a hammock like an Indian.' Although he was probably thinking of American Indians not East Indians, in Evelyn's eyes Bushell had taken on the identity of another culture, removed from the turbulent society around him.

Bacon and his assistant Bushell glimpsed many of the philosophical and spiritual developments of the ensuing two centuries – with regard to vegetarianism as much as any other field. Their combination of religion, science and morality forecast the religious debates of the seventeenth century, the medical enquiries of the Enlightenment, and even the Eastern philosophy that forced itself on the conscience of Europe. Bacon and Bushell's 'perfect experiment' would be recast, re-tested and reformed time and time again.

TWO

John Robins: The Shakers' God

In the middle 1600s Adam – father of mankind – rose from the dead, brushed away over 5,000 years of subterranean dust, and came to deliver his descendants from the sin he had brought into the world. Quickly acquiring himself a new Eve – whom he also called 'Virgin Mary' – and impregnating her with a child called Abel who was also Jesus reincarnated, Adam set about accumulating disciples. He entranced all who happened to hear him by raising the dead and speaking in the original language of mankind, and convinced witnesses that they had seen visions of him miraculously riding on the wind like a flame, flanked by dragons and heavenly beasts. Before long, Adam's biblical coterie accompanied him everywhere he went. His faithful associates included Judas the betrayer, the prophet Jeremiah, and the ill-fated Cain. To all these, Adam promised that he would reinstate Paradise on earth as it was before the Fall. Records show that a sizeable number of Londoners believed him.[1]

Adam – otherwise known as John Robins, the radical seventeenth-century prophet – was a classic product of the English Civil War. Were it not for the political, religious and social mayhem the Civil War brought in its wake, Robins would never have gained such a following nor such fame. Seven years of bloodshed had shaken even the strongest nerves. From 1642 to 1649, the nation had turned on itself with such violence that hardly a family escaped unscathed, and in that unsettling environment Robins' fervent preaching appealed to many confused and disillusioned minds.

The worst of war had ended with the execution of Charles I and the establishment of Oliver Cromwell's republic, but in the early days of Cromwell's rule lack of religious state control and the first ever free press combined to foment a plethora of extreme religious and political movements. Royalists all over Europe looked on aghast as God's deputy on earth was overcome by a furious rabble. Parliamentarians, on the other hand, saw the world opening into a new era of justice and purity. But radicals soon became frustrated by the comparative moderation of Cromwell's parliamentary settlement. They had been fighting for liberty against what they saw as monarchical and episcopal tyranny, and had pinned their hopes on a new era of equality in which justice would no longer be stifled and corrupted by a callous and indiscriminate elite. They had staked their lives, belongings and loved ones against a system in which the blood and sweat of the poor paid for the excesses of a frivolous court life – against the right of one man to treat millions as the objects of whim and fancy. To their horror, Cromwell's republic began to look like the same tyranny all over again.

Disillusioned radicals turned for solace to the Bible. The Church had always promised that the Messiah would come again to establish a new heavenly kingdom after a period of violence and turmoil. Millenarian groups began to predict that Jesus' second coming was nigh. Even most ministers of the established Church instructed their parishioners to prepare for Judgement Day.[2]

The time was ripe for Robins' religious debut. When he came forward and declared himself the saviour they had been waiting for, dozens of disciples rallied to his cause. Twenty-three people were eventually charged in court for worshipping Robins, and there were clearly many more. They were mockingly dubbed the Shakers for their quaking fits of divine inspiration, and startled onlookers lumped them together into a larger heterogeneous movement known as the Ranters – those revolutionary fanatics noted for wild preaching, radical politics and stripping naked in public. Some of Robins' contemporaries believed he was also responsible for founding movements that would prove as long-lasting as the Quakers and as important as the Levellers, whose activism in the army had been partly responsible for bringing down the monarchy.[3]

Like Jesus (to whom he compared himself), Robins wrote nothing down, but we do have the records of the state and of his former followers, one of whom said in a memoir that the Shakers 'pray'd unto him, and they fell flat on their Faces and Worshipped him, calling him their Lord and their God'.[4] Buoyed up by his disciples' support, Robins' vanity appears to have reached dizzying heights. He publicly declared that 'the Lord Jesus was a weak and Imperfect Saviour, and afraid of

Death.' Robins himself, by contrast, 'had no fear of Death in him at all'.[5] Even Robins' enemies did not deny his powers; rather, they accused him of witchcraft and even of being the devil himself.[6]

Like other radical sects, the Shakers pooled their worldly goods and lived in a primitive communism with their leader.[7] Upending conventional morality, Robins encouraged his followers to swap spouses and set an example by taking the wife of his head disciple.[8] Characteristically of the seventeenth-century radical sects which often gave women equal status with men, about half of the Shakers were women. It was also rumoured that they liked to gather together naked – the same was said of the Quakers and the Adamites – because covering the body was a sign of the Fall, and anyone who wanted to return to innocence had to start by stripping down to Adam and Eve's state of shameless undress. Understandably, allegations of free-love practices abounded in the popular press.[9]

Decades later, Lodowicke Muggleton, who went on to lead a sect of his own, remembered wistfully that it really had seemed at the time as if Robins were Adam come again. 'For who upon Earth did know, at that time,' Muggleton pondered, 'whether he was False or True: I say none, not one.'[10]

Having established his identity, Robins, like all cult leaders, pledged to guide his followers to a promised land, the Mount of Olives in the Holy Land of Jerusalem where he would feed them on manna from heaven.[11] He elected a stand-in Moses to lead the way, and started gathering people in London to prepare for their escape. Robins vowed that once he had collected a crowd of 144,000 (the number of saints in the tribe of Israel, as prophesied by Revelation), he would part the waters of the English Channel and march them over dry land, away from the uproar of England, to safety and bliss.[12] Robins was the King of Israel; following him to Jerusalem, his supporters thought, would pave the way for Christ's return.[13]

A notorious wild prophet by the name of Thomas Tany (or 'Theauraujohn'), joined forces with Robins by erecting tents for each of the so-called tribes of Israel and declaring that his people would follow Robins to Jerusalem. Some of Robins' followers, and Tany himself, took their enthusiasm for Judaism so seriously that they claimed to have learned Hebrew and even to have circumcised themselves.[14] Tany kept up the mission – even after Robins had been clapped in jail. He claimed on his own behalf that he was the rightful King of France,

Ranters and Shakers from *The Declaration of John Robins* (1651)

A naked rout of Ranters from
Strange Newes from Newgate
(1650/1)

Naked Adamites from
The Adamites Sermon (1641)

England and the Jews, and was arrested for violently wielding a sword at Parliament a week after Oliver Cromwell had been offered the title of King, and for symbolically burning pistols, a sword, a horse's saddle and the Bible. Tany perished many years later in an attempt to effect Robins' journey to Jerusalem. The boat he built to carry him there sprang a leak during the crossing to Holland, and he and his crew were all drowned.

The claims Robins and Tany made of biblical descent probably did not seem strange to their contemporaries. Many Puritans had long envisaged the English as a lost tribe of Israel awaiting deliverance from their own Egyptian-style bondage.[15] Thinkers like Jan Amos Comenius aimed to restore man's lost perfection by converting all the Jews. Iron-ically, these hopes fuelled the philo-Semitism of the seventeenth cen-tury and Robins' followers were instrumental in a successful campaign to force Parliament to allow Jews to live freely in England.[16] More than a century later William Blake (who dabbled in the Muggletonian cult established by Robins' ex-followers) was still living in hope: 'Till we have built Jerusalem,/ In England's green and pleasant land'.[17]

The first Adam had lost Paradise. The second Adam, Christ, had promised to restore everything to its former perfection. John Robins confirmed that he was none other than 'the third *Adam*, that must gain that which the first lost'.[18] His followers obediently declared that '*John Robins* is the same *Adam* that was in the Garden.'[19] As John King, another disciple, put it, John Robins 'is now come to reduce the world to its former condition, as it was before the fall of the first *Adam*'.[20]

The original Adam lived on the pure fruits of Eden, so it was logical for Robins to insist that his followers should adhere to Paradise's strict vegetable diet.[21] Thomas Bushell had taken up the vegetable diet to be *like* Adam before the Fall; John Robins claimed that he *was* Adam, and vegetable cuisine seems to have been an essential adjunct to his cult. There were other millenarian prophets at the same time proclaiming that the return to the pre-fallen state would require a revival of the original vegetarian diet, like the philo-Semite George Foster who prophesied in 1650 that animals would be involved in the universal freedom which was coming to humans.[22] Like many vegetarians to come, Robins also condemned the use of alcohol: 'it was not of Gods making: it is the drink of the Beast (*said he*) a poysonous liquor, and wo be unto all them that drinks it.'[23] Non-radical contemporaries found Robins' dietary antics shocking – it was hardly believable that life could be sustained on vegetable food without flesh – but they knew what he was getting at. 'Their food is onely bread and water, although they have plenty of monies to buy other provisions,' explained one bemused contemporary, emphasising the Shakers' asceticism.[24]

In a neater and more detailed combination of scatology and eschatology, Robins' ex-follower and later arch-rival John Reeve condemned his dietary laws to his face: 'thou didst deceave many People,' he bellowed, 'and then gavest them leave to abstain by degrees from all kind of Food, that should have preserved and strengthed their Natures: But thou didst feed them with windy things, as Aples, and other Fruit that was windy; and they drank nothing but Water.'[25] In the guts of his followers, said Reeve, Robins' high-blown vegetarian doctrines turned into nothing but malodorous hot air. Most contemporaries agreed: vegetables may have been all right for Adam in Paradise, but they were hardly appropriate for the average earthly being. This common prejudice seemed to be empirically demonstrated by Robins' experiments. Reeve narrated a woeful tale which, if true, leaves Robins guilty of irresponsibility in the extreme:

> he commanded his Disciples to abstain from Meats and Drinks, promising them that they should in a short time be fed with Manna from Heaven, until many a poor Soul was almost starved under his Diet, yea and some were absolutely starved to Death, whose Bodies could not bear his Diet.[26]

Reeve squarely identified Robins as a devilish false prophet of the type St Paul had warned would come and deceive the people by 'Commanding to abstain from meats' (1 Timothy 4:1–5).[27] Robins wasn't God, or Adam: he was Satan and he had led many people astray, to their and his own perdition.[28]

Unperturbed, Joshuah Garment, Robins' representative Moses, proudly called their group 'the people that live by water and bread'. They emphasised that their bloodless diet contrasted to the bloodiness of their oppressors, and combined their vegetarianism with vehement anti-war sentiments and pacifism. Garment denounced his persecutors as 'bloudy Prelates' whose 'Law is Sword', and predicted that their 'thirstings after the bloud' will be punished, for God took no pleasure in 'those that delight in bloud'. Robins, by contrast, was 'the peaceable man' and his followers 'the peaceable multitude that shall never bear arms offensive or defensive'.[29]

These stirring words, with their imagery of blood, bloodthirstiness and bleeding, were a reaction against the violence of the Civil War. Garment, who enlisted as a soldier, witnessed murder and had probably been obliged to kill. His conversion was sudden. One day, after three years of fighting against the King, God personally commanded him to leave the army and effect instead a bloodless revolution 'by the sword of the spirit, not by the sword of man'. God's voice ordered him to wait 'in love and peace, till peace and love is established in the Earth'.[30] Garment became convinced that violence could never achieve his idealistic aims, and his aversion to killing humans and drawing their blood appears to have spread into a repulsion towards bloodletting of all kinds. Universal peace was a prerequisite of Christ's millennial kingdom as Isaiah had prophesied in the Bible,[31] and this fusion of pacifism and vegetarianism would become a prevalent motif among blood-sated radicals.

The Shakers' strong repulsion from blood may have been reinforced by their reversion to Jewish law which forbade the eating of blood. To King James I's amusement, groups of 'Christian Jews' earlier in the century had resurrected the Mosaic law, holding that it was 'absolutely unlawful to eat any swines flesh or blacke puddings' (i.e. pork or blood). Contemporaries likened the waywardness of the Ranters to the absurdity of the Judaist leader, John Traske, who had been brutally punished in 1618 and starved on a diet of bread and water until he agreed to break his resolve by eating pork. His wife, who was found still languishing in prison in 1639, twenty-one years after her first arrest, obstinately stuck to her scruples. 'She has not eaten any flesh these seven years, neither drunk anything but water,' reported an appalled commissioner; but there she remained until at least 1645 when a fellow prisoner at last persuaded her to change her diet.[32]

Ridicule from the press and mocking crowds did nothing to sway the Shakers from their course. The strong arm of the law, however, eventually did. By 1650 Parliament had reached the end of its tether with the religious radicals, and in August passed the landmark Blasphemy Act, specifically tailored to suppress John Robins and the Ranters.[33] There was a swift crackdown, and one by one the Ranters were picked off and put behind bars. Several of Robins' followers were arrested and held in the Gatehouse Prison at Westminster, where they were pumped for information about 'where *John Robins, alias Roberts* dwelleth'. Eventually, after almost a year of covert information-gathering, in spring 1651 the authorities caught up with Robins at one of his clandestine meetings in Long Alley in Moorfields and he and his supporters were interrogated and sent to the New Prison at Clerkenwell.[34]

During the trials it was alleged by the prosecution that Robins had encouraged his followers to believe that he was God, for which the Blasphemy Act prescribed a six-month imprisonment on the first offence (with probable whipping and hard labour, the inconvenience of unpalatable lodgings and disease, and the inevitable accumulation of debt from prison charges). In order to encourage the Shakers to recant, it was clearly stated that a second offence would bring banishment, a sentence that, if flouted, would be punished by death 'without benefit of Clergy'.[35] Government sources claimed that in court Robins' followers fell down at Robins' feet, chanting, clapping, screaming, and calling on him for deliverance.[36]

Though Robins and some of his followers strenuously argued that he had never claimed to be more than a prophet, Robins was sentenced.[37] The arrests and trials broke the communalism of the Shakers. Their detractors jeered that their leader couldn't even part the waters of the Thames to save them from jail – let alone whisk them off to Paradise. Eventually most of them got off with a plea bargain by signing a document forswearing their faith in Robins and agreeing that they had been led astray by the devil. Only one recalcitrant follower, Thomas Kearby, remained loyal. He 'cursed and reviled the Justices in open Court', refused to recant, and was condemned to six months in the Westminster House of Correction with corporal punishment and hard labour.[38]

During his initial weeks of imprisonment, Robins continued to preach from the open window of his prison cell. In February of the following year he was either still in jail, or had been re-sentenced. But one ex-disciple claimed that, soon afterwards, Robins wrote Cromwell an apology which secured his release. Thanks to the profits he had made from his followers, he was able to repurchase his old estate and retired to the country.[39] Whether or not this is true, Robins disappeared from view. But his blend of political radicalism, divine inspiration and vegetarianism lasted for decades.

Robins was condemned for flouting the Blasphemy Act's criminalisation of anyone maintaining 'him or her self, or any other meer Creature, to be very God . . . or that the true God, or the Eternal Majesty dwells in the Creature [i.e. the created universe] and no where else'.[40] Robins was not the only one preaching such blasphemies. The Act was designed to suppress a rash of dissidents, such as the Leicester shoe-maker-turned-soldier-preacher, Jacob Bauthumley, who were proclaiming that 'God is in all Creatures, Man and Beast, Fish and Fowle, and every green thing'.[41] This idea that God was in animals as well as in man was deeply subversive, particularly because it blurred the vital distinction between the natural and divine worlds and smacked of the idolatrous practices condemned in the first commandment. It also had dangerous implications for man's treatment of the brutes, and the State did what it could to lance the festering gangrene of heresy.

The leader of the communist Diggers, Gerrard Winstanley, was among the most notorious advocates of such beliefs. In April 1649, Winstanley led a band of comrades to the edge of Windsor Forest to occupy the land. For too long landowning elites had exerted a monopoly over the earth and its produce; food prices had reached record highs and the poor were being deprived of the barest necessities. It was time to reclaim nature's heritage. The Diggers illegally started to dig the soil, manure it, and plant it with crops for their own sustenance: 'everyone that is born in the land may be fed by the earth his mother that brought him forth,' declared Winstanley, 'all looking upon each other as equals in the creation.' Calling on the disaffected masses to join them, the Diggers advertised the virtues of their home-grown corn, parsnips, carrots and beans: 'we have peace in our hearts and quiet rejoicing in our work, and filled with sweet content, though we have but a dish of roots and bread for our food.'[42] Digging the land to grow crops, they promised, would free the poor from enforced labour and from the unreliable and inherently oppressive market economy of food.

Much as Winstanley seized the land to return it to the people, so also he grabbed hold of God and pulled Him down to earth. The Church had always kept God closeted up in heaven where only the established priesthood could access Him. But like many radicals of his time, Winstanley insisted that God was all around us, in every thing on earth. In contrast to traditional theologians who tended to regard matter as dirty and potentially evil, Winstanley stressed that all creatures were inhabited by divinity and should therefore be treated with love and reverence, 'as well beasts as man-kinde'.[43] This egalitarian spirituality upturned the traditional hierarchies between people, and it challenged mankind's disregard for animals. Strictly speaking, Winstanley did not break the Blasphemy Act because he did not claim that God dwells in the created universe *'and no where else'*, and he did not go to the extreme of the pantheists who literally identified the world with God. But his doctrines were nevertheless radical and extremely threatening.

Winstanley did not doubt that man was supposed to be lord of the creation, just as God was lord over man. But he took the radical step of arguing that Christ's most important commandment – to do as you would be done by – applied not just to fellow humans, but also to animals. In order to undo the corruption of the Fall, man had to start by 'looking upon himselfe as a fellow creature (though he be Lord of all creatures) to all other creatures of all kinds; and so doing to them, as he would have them doe to him'.[44]

It might seem logical that with such beliefs Winstanley would have to be a vegetarian. But he did not explicitly state that everyone had to stop killing or eating animals. Most contemporaries with similar beliefs were not vegetarian. If one argued that it was wrong to kill an animal because God dwelt in all living things, it could also be argued that it was wrong to kill cabbages. Indeed, if man, nature and divinity were parts of a unified whole, there would be no reason why animals should not give up their lives for humans who were just another part of that same unity.[45] Jacob Bauthumley, whose theology in this respect was very similar to Winstanley's, explained how one could believe that animals were inhabited by God, and still happily slaughter them. He pointed out that an animal death was no death at all: men and beasts were just different parts of 'one intire Being', so when animals died their flesh returned to dust and their life was reabsorbed into God.[46] It is unsurprising, therefore, to find that in 1652, after the Diggers had been violently disbanded by the Government, Winstanley provocatively incited the poor to ransack butchers' shops and steal from the common flocks for their food.[47]

However, some individuals did argue that it was wrong to take away life which came from God. This line appears to have been taken, for example, by certain English members of the Family of Love. These clandestine confederates were disciples of the sixteenth-century Dutch mystic, Hendrik Niclaes, who taught that God suffused the universe and that it was wrong to do violence of any sort because God 'created all things, that they should have their being'.[48] He told his followers to recreate on earth a new Eden, where people 'kill not. for they have no Nature to Destroying. But all their Desyre is, that it mought all live, whatsoever is of the Lyfe'.[49] In the 1640s, a bricklayer-preacher from Hackney called Marshall who was a soldier-turned-pacifist associated with the Family of Love, echoed Hendrik Niclaes by announcing to many people 'that it is unlawfull to kill any creature that hath life, because it came from God'.[50] The heretic-hunting Presbyterian minister Thomas Edwards added Marshall's vegetarian doctrine to his blacklist of blasphemies, *Gangraena* (1645–6), where he warned that unauthorised preachers like Marshall were teaching that ''Tis unlawfull to fight at all, or to kill any man, yea to kill any of the creatures for our use, as a chicken, or on any other occasion'.[51]

Believing that God dwelt in nature provided a radical theological basis for reforming man's relationship with animals. It was added to the growing arsenal of vegetarian arguments. It led many to egalitarian politics, to pacifism, and in some cases to believing that it was wrong to kill anything at all. Later in the century, Thomas Tryon revived beliefs like Winstanley's and argued that God's presence in the creatures made meat-eating a direct violence against the deity. With Robins, Winstanley and the Family of Love all preaching doctrines related to vegetarianism, a cross-party radical agenda was emerging which included dissent from mainstream society's bloodthirsty eating habits.

THREE

Roger Crab: Levelling the Food Chain

In the same year that Robins retreated from London, another war veteran stepped into the breach as the arch-enemy of meat-eaters. Roger Crab had been fomenting trouble for years, and now he deployed vegetarianism as an attack on political and economic injustice. Like Robins, Crab was hardened to the severity of political censure. His first recorded run-in with the State was back in 1646 when Cromwell's New Model Army had defeated the Royalists and King Charles I surrendered to the Scots. There would be no more fighting until 1648, after Charles escaped from Hampton Court to the Isle of Wight, precipitating the country's second civil war. During the lull between the two wars, arguments raged in Parliament between those who wished to compromise with the King and those, such as Generals Cromwell and Fairfax, who realised that the New Model Army had shed its blood for the cause and was not to be fobbed off. On the radical wing of the debate, the Levellers were stirring up mutiny, demanding the abolition of the monarchy and a massive extension of the franchise.

Even before 1647, when Leveller agitation started in earnest, the young Roger Crab was preaching a religious message of regeneration combined with the most virulent radical politics. Baptising crowds of people who had assembled to hear him speak, he incited them to join the ranks against the king.[1] Having a monarch as God's deputy, he told them, was idolatry. Although by 1649 Parliament would come to agree with Crab, for the moment he had gone too far, and in 1646 the authorities caught up with him while he was haranguing a crowd in Southwark and slung him in jail. It was just as well, said Thomas Edwards (the heretic-basher who hated vegetarians and radicals): Crab was a despicable 'Dipper and a Preacher', leading people astray with 'strange doctrines against the Immortality of the soul', and telling them 'that it was better to have a golden Calfe or an Asse set up . . . then to have a King over them'.[2]

In 1647 Fairfax got wind of Crab's sorry plight and was so incensed that he took the case straight to Parliament where, speaking uncompromisingly to newly empowered statesmen, he raised Crab to the status of a *cause célèbre*. At Crab's trial, Fairfax complained, Justice Bacon had locked the jury up without food and water until they agreed to return a guilty verdict. Crab had been sent in chains to the White Lyon where he was to remain until he found a way of paying the inordinate sum of 100 marks.[3] In being imprisoned for preaching against tyranny, Crab had proved just how tyrannous the system was. As Crab himself later added, he had nearly lost his life on the battlefield when his head was 'cloven to the braine'; imprisoning him now was the depths of ingratitude. The case created a ripple of excitement: Fairfax's complaint was copied down and published, and eight years later the newspapers still remembered Crab as a leading Levelling 'Agitator in the Army'.[4]

Writing in his will at the end of his life, Crab still looked back on this time as the catalyst to his future self; he had nearly 'departed this humane Life' but God saw fit to let him be born again 'upon which account the Lord himselfe took my Soule into his custody'.[5] Disgruntled and disillusioned by parliamentary policies, Crab left the army to set up a hat shop at Chesham in Buckinghamshire. But like Gerrard Winstanley, he soon came to see commerce as con-artistry; it was the grease that oiled the system of decadent consumerism.[6] He started stirring up trouble; as one satirical publication declared 'we have amongst us a Crabbed cavelling fellow, being both a Barber, Hors-Dr. and a Hat-maker, that disturbs and jeers at Ministers that come to preach with us'.[7] In 1652 he sold his hat shop, gave his estate away to the poor and rented an isolated spot in Ickenham near Uxbridge where he built a little hermitage and started digging the land.[8] Thrusting himself metaphorically into the wilderness, Crab cast himself as a John the Baptist figure and proceeded to hurl abuse at the system that exploited the poor to satisfy the material pleasure of the few: 'if *John the Baptist*, should come forth againe,' he exclaimed, 'and call himself *Leveller*, and take such food as the wildernesse yeelded, and such cloathing, and Preach up his former Doctrine, *He that had two coats should give away one of them, and he that hath food should do likewise*; How scornfully would our proud Gentlemen and Gallants look of him'.[9]

Reviling the carnal pleasures of the corrupt 'Sodomite generation', Crab stopped eating meat and took up the bleakest of vegetable diets. Meat was a sign of wealth; renouncing it was an act of solidarity with the oppressed.[10] Home-grown vegetables were the answer to social inequality, and the key to spiritual regeneration:

> instead of strong drinks and wines, I give the old man ["(meaning my body)"] a cup of water; and instead of rost Mutton, and Rabbets, and other dainty dishes, I gave him broth thickned with bran, and pudding made with bran, & Turnep leaves chop't together, and grass.

Crab rejected butter and cheese, and like John Robins despised alcohol as much as flesh. The production of beer used up grain which would otherwise be good as food, pushing up prices and oppressing the poorest of the poor. Luxury, Crab noticed, was not just a sign of inequality, it was a cause of it – an economic argument still being used at the end of the century by Thomas Tryon, and again a century later by radicals including Percy Bysshe Shelley.[11]

Despite his puritanical asceticism, Crab insisted that the vegetable diet was perfectly suited to sustain the body. Standing in a long tradition of vegetarian doctors, Crab opened a folk medical practice, claiming to have up to 120 patients on his books at any one time. The evidence he accumulated from his patients suggested to him that meat was the cause of human ills and abstinence was their cure. 'If my Patients were any of them wounded or feaverish, I sayd, eating flesh, or drinking strong beere would inflame their blood, venom their wounds, and encrease their disease, eating of flesh is an absolute enemy to pure nature.' As one newspaper added in more purple prose, Crab claimed that meat made 'the body a *Dunghill*, filling it with gross Humors and *snakie Diseases*, engenderers of *Lust*, *Sloth* and *Melancholy*, that so corrupt the senses & bodies of men and Women, that take aside a little reason, there is no difference between them and bruit beasts.'[12]

Keeping his body in tune with nature's vegetarian laws, Crab soon achieved spiritual illumination and began consulting the radicals' favourite astrologer William Lilly, about his revelations.[13] Then in 1655 Crab journeyed to London and published the first of his radical vegetarian pamphlets, *The English Hermite, or, Wonder of this Age*. He cut a striking figure – an ex-soldier turned bearded hermit – and his

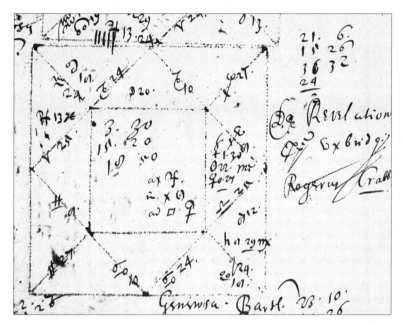

Roger Crab's horoscope consultation with William Lilly, *'de Revelatione'*

unwonted dietary habits created a sensation in the city. His publisher registered the astonishment with which ordinary folk greeted Crab 'who counteth it a sin against his body and soule to eate any sort of Flesh, Fish, or living Creature'; 'his dyet is onely such poore homely foode as his own Rood of ground beareth, as Corne, Bread, and bran, Hearbs, Roots, Dock-leaves, Mallowes, and grasse, his drink is water.'[14]

The press had a field day: Crab 'observes the stricktest life of a Hermet that we have heard of', announced one popular paper.[15] Even though Crab rarely spoke about animals, contemporaries were anxious that he was eroding the distinction between man and beast, as had his fellow Leveller Richard Overton,[16] so the papers satirically suggested that his reluctance to kill animals stemmed from the fact that he had love affairs with them. Comparing him to a Judaist who wouldn't eat pigs, the twice-weekly *Mercurius Fumigosus* claimed that '*Roger Crab* had formerly some such *beast* to his *Valentine*; that makes him now to turn *Hermit*, live in a solitary Cave neer *Uxbridge*, and feed on nothing but *Roots*'.[17] Even his publisher liked to poke fun at him. One of his pamphlets is accompanied by a woodcut apparently showing Crab naked,

Roger Crab, that feeds on Hearbs and Roots, is here,
But I believe Diogenes had better Cheer.   Rara avis in terris.

Herbes and Roots

Roger Crab, *The English Hermite* (1655)

in a compromising position with an unidentified herbivore: Crab, they thought, was taking animal husbandry too far.

Crab swiftly forged a link with the Robins sect by converting the leading Leveller, Captain Robert Norwood, who collaborated with Thomas Tany and was impeached with him for blasphemy in 1651. But the alliance was to be short-lived, for Norwood could not sustain the austerities of his diet-master. Crab's publisher reported that 'Cap. *Norwood* was acquainted with *Roger Crab*, and being enclining to his

Illuminated letter S from Roger Crab,
The English Hermite (1655)

opinion, began to follow the same poore diet till it cost him his life.'

The story that the vegetarian diet starved Norwood to death would scarcely seem credible if we did not know that Norwood did indeed perish in 1654, two years after Crab retreated to his hermitage.[18] This was not a good advertisement for the novel diet and it played into the hands of detractors who preferred their beefsteaks to the grass and turnip leaves proffered by Crab. Norwood's death confirmed John Reeve's accusations against John Robins, and one later commentator made the unfounded claim that Crab 'destroyed himself by eating bran, grass, dockleaves, and such other trash' – even though he actually lived to the impressive age of nearly seventy.[19]

This connection with Norwood suggests that there was a loose association of vegetarian radicals. Crab may also have been connected with the Diggers whose membership was largely composed of disaffected Levellers. Both Crab and Winstanley had been Baptists,[20] they both said that private property was a curse,[21] that the upper classes would wither if peasants lived off their own produce instead of labouring for landowners,[22] and Crab wielded the digging metaphor, for example in his sequel pamphlet, *The English Hermites Spade at the Ground and root of Idolatry* (1657).[23] Like Winstanley also, Crab was said to have extended to animals the commandment to 'do unto others as you would be done by'.[24]

Like the other vegetarian radicals, as well as some of the Quakers,[25] Crab accompanied his retreat into vegetarianism with a conversion to pacifism.[26] He pitted his harmless herbivorous lifestyle against his opponents who 'prepare themselves by thirsting after flesh and blood'.[27] Crab even suggested that flesh-eating had triggered the violent passions that led to the war in the first place: 'that humour that lusteth after flesh and blood,' he said, 'is made strong in us by feeding of it.' Killing animals and eating their flesh was widely believed to inure men to cruelty.[28] Crab saw in this the workings of God's Providence: all aggressive meat-eaters would succumb to their ferocious instincts until they ended up killing each other, thus wiping the carnivorous sinners off the earth.[29] Conflating the two meanings of 'flesh', Crab hoped that just as he gave up 'flesh', so England would give up the 'fleshly' cares that motivated violent conflict. This in turn he saw as an allegory of giving up Moses' old 'fleshly' law for the new spiritual laws of Christ.[30]

According to Crab's observations, nature unambiguously revealed that meat was bad for the body and the soul. Now Crab had to balance that with evidence from the Book of God. In doing so, Crab inaugurated the English school of vegetarian Bible exegesis, and he managed to manipulate just about any passage in the Scriptures to suit his purposes. Engaging in doctrinal disputes with theologians up and down the country, and apparently deriving some arguments from St Jerome, Crab developed a rigorous scriptural defence of vegetarianism.[31]

For Crab, as for others, vegetarianism started in the beginning, with Adam and Eve. Crab even implied that the Fall itself was caused by Adam lapsing from his God-given diet into meat-eating: 'if naturall *Adam* had kept to his single naturall fruits of Gods appointment, namely fruits and hearbs,' he lamented, 'we had not been corrupted.' God permitted mankind to eat the animals after Noah's Flood, he insisted, only because all the water had temporarily killed off the world's vegetation.[32] God intended mankind to return to the vegetable diet as soon as the earth recovered from the Flood. But having once tasted flesh, Crab complained, men were inflamed by a desire for more, and rejected natural vegetables as 'trash in comparison of a Beast, or beastly flesh'. From that point on, man was bound on an inexorable decline into corruption and violence. Like other vegetarians on both sides of the political spectrum, Crab imagined his vegetarian hermitage was a route to 'the Paradise of God from whence my Father *Adam* was cast forth'.[33]

Crab viewed the whole of biblical history as one long saga in God's attempt to return men to their natural diet. Moses led the Israelites into the desert, Crab claimed, to bring them away from their carnivorous Egyptian masters (perhaps this was even latent in Robins and Garment's ideas of themselves as Moses figures). When the recalcitrant Israelites 'murmured, and rebelled against the Lord, lusting after the flesh pots of Egypt', God punished them: the flock of quails God sent was poisoned and they died with the flesh in their teeth.[34] The prophets Ezekiel and Isaiah, and Christ's apostles, had continued the message by either living on vegetable food or practising harsh asceticism for our emulation.[35] The prophet Daniel had confined himself to lentils and water, a diet on which he had achieved divine epiphanies.[36] Just as the saints were assisted by animals, so Crab was brought bread in prison by a spaniel, and he claimed that birds came to him from God to inform him of future events.[37] Even Christ himself, Crab wilfully suggested, was in favour of vegetarianism: we hear of Christ eating various comestibles, he said, 'but we never finde that ever he was drunke, or eate a bit of flesh'.[38] In a rare example of Crab's concern for animal welfare, he defended Christ's feeding of fishes to the five thousand on the grounds that the meal was 'innocent' because it was made 'without hurting any creature that breathed on earth' (excluding aquatic animals from the category of flesh was a standard division of Catholic fasting laws).[39] Even the Passover feast, where Christ decidedly partook of the lamb, was an irregularity which he was obliged to undertake only to fulfil the Jewish prophecies.

Crab's presentation of the Bible as a monolithic vegetarian manifesto became more problematic when his adversaries threw back at him passages in the New Testament that were clearly designed to abolish old Jewish food taboos. Each of the New Testament passages that Crab and his contemporaries referenced in their disputes about vegetarianism had already been used by St Augustine and St Aquinas against vegetarians such as the heretic Manicheans. The doctrinal dispute was new in England, but it had a history that reached back more than a millennium, and the English clergy were happy to rely on such authoritative texts to prove the unorthodoxy of their adversary.[40] But Crab – a Houdini of biblical exegetes – found an answer to all his detractors.

Christ had taught that all food should be accepted with thanksgiving and none of it should be rejected as unclean. Crab retorted that this was manifestly absurd since some things were poisonous, and even if meat wasn't unlawful it was still undesirable. Deftly perverting the sense of St Paul's famous edict, 'if meat make my brother to offend, I will eat no flesh while the world standeth,' and his allusion to one 'who is weak, eateth herbs', Crab appealed for people to 'forbear Flesh for my conscience sake, as *Paul* did declare he would do concerning his weak Brother'.[41] Crab even challenged the passage that John Reeve had used against John Robins' vegetarianism which warned against devilish prophets 'commanding to abstain from meats'.[42] Crab insisted that he *commanded* no one: he just wanted everyone to be enlightened enough to give up of their own accord.[43] By attacking him, he objected, the ignorant English priests were breaking Paul's commandment aimed specifically at the vegetarian dispute: 'Let not him that eateth despise him that eateth not.'[44] Despite his efforts at scriptural justification, Crab was defamed by the local priests as a devil and the Puritan minister of St Margaret's in Uxbridge, Thomas Godboult, told everyone Crab was a witch.[45] Crab retorted that he was willing to meet any of the clergy for a wrangle, and claimed they had lost the argument so many times they were scared to meet him in public. He had in any case absolutely no respect for the incumbent priesthood or the government that supported it: priests compelled the people to pay tithes, which in Crab's eyes made the Church a whore-house and the priests its pimps and the whole idea of forcing people to go to church on Sunday turned religion into idolatry. Despite the puritanical fervour of Cromwell's England, church-goers still saw Sunday as an excuse to dress up in fancy clothes and blow their week's savings on a feast of roast meat. To Crab, therefore, it was the most sacrilegious day and he made a point of flouting Sabbath laws.[46]

Crab's seditious ravings were no less threatening to the authorities than they had been back in 1646 when he was put in prison. The priests whom he attacked could criticise his vegetarianism, but there was little they could do about it. His refusal to abide by the Sabbath laws, however, and his overt encouragement to the people to skive off church provided the authorities with the opportunity they needed. By 1657 Crab had been hauled in front of the magistrates at least four times for Sabbath-breaking. He had been set in the stocks in front of Ickenham church, and locked in Clerkenwell Prison on more than one occasion. Crab even claimed that Cromwell had once sentenced him to death. In January 1655 he was locked up and tried before magistrates but managed to get off the charge of calling the government a tyranny.[47] It was always his vegetarianism that attracted controversy at these times, bringing people in flocks to gaze at him behind bars.[48]

In 1657 Crab stood unrepentantly in court listening to the judges demand that he abide by the laws of the 'Higher Powers'. In his daring and brilliant retort we get a glimpse of Crab at his strongest: not a wizened hermit eccentrically whiling his life away on a patch of ground in the country as many represented him, but a hardened radical taking on the authorities.[49] His reply split open the paradox of revolutionary government: he had fought alongside them when they were Cromwellian rebels, he pointed out, 'with my sword in my hand against the Highest Powers in England, namely, the King and the Bishops, upon which account ye sit here.' How could they tell him now that rebellion was forbidden when their authority was founded on the biggest rebellion in memory? Crab made them address their own hypocrisy in trying and sentencing a rebel whom they had once championed as one of their own.

Unpopular with the authorities, but blessed with eloquence and charisma, Crab soon attracted a band of vegetarian followers. By 1659, a year before the Restoration of the monarchy, he had converted enough people to earn his group a name – the 'Rationals' or 'Rationalists'. Vegetarianism was their key policy, and it was lauded in a ballad by a publisher, one 'J.B.', who counted himself as one of their disciples:

> Illustrious souls more brighter than the morn,
> Oh! how dark mortals greet you still with scorn,
> Admiring at your homely sack-cloth dresse,
> Hearbs, Roots, and every vegetable mess
> On which you live; and are more healthy far
> Than Canibals, that feed on lushious fare;[50]

By this time Crab had become convinced that God was speaking through him, and wrote his pamphlets as if in the voice of God Himself. His competing claims for divine inspiration embroiled him in controversy with the Quakers. In January 1659 the Quaker Thomas Curtis wrote to George Fox with his concerns about a 'very great and precious' meeting in Buckinghamshire attended by 'fish of all sorts', 'many of the world, some baptized, and some of Crab's company'. Crab incited attacks from the well-known Quaker controversialists John Rance and George Salter (who would one day be arrested at a meeting with John Robins' old rival, John Reeve). Salter derisively attacked the Rationals, calling Crab 'a corrupt bulk of Fog, who art like a quagmire that sucks up those that comes upon thee'.[51]

Crab was later said to have joined forces with the leader of one of the most prominent and long-lasting international mystic organisations of the period, the Philadelphian Society – named after the Greek for 'brotherly love'.[52] Crab might have known the spiritual leader of the Philadelphians, Dr John Pordage, since Pordage was a doctor in Cromwell's army.[53] As a deeply subversive clergyman in the parish of Bradfield, Pordage had been ousted from his post for encouraging polygamy, refusing tithes and hosting crazed spiritual revelries with their friends from the Family of Love and the Ranters. Pordage was said to have made an alliance with Thomas Tany, and used fasting as a method of achieving 'visible and sensible Communion with Angels'.[54] Pordage himself claimed that he was hastening Christ's second coming by uniting the dispersed tribes of Israel,[55] and establishing an ideal primitive community practising 'Universal Peace and Love towards All'.[56] Like Crab, Pordage thought one could access God by studying nature, for he said the universe was 'as ye Cloathing of God'.[57]

There is little evidence to suggest that the Philadelphian Society took up vegetarianism as a whole,[58] but they were renowned for their extreme fasting and were mocked for not being able to 'eat and drink their common Dyet'.[59] One of their later members, Richard Roach, recalled that they modelled themselves on the ascetic Jewish sect of Essenes, believing that austerity made them 'more conversant wth ye Mysteries of Religion'.[60] Some Philadelphians believed that animals had souls and would achieve spiritual liberation on Judgement Day, and objected to the abuse of birds, beasts and fishes to satisfy people's luxury and gluttony.[61] And above all, Crab and Pordage shared a fascination for the mystical vision of the German shoemaker Jacob Böhme (1575–1624),[62] whose emphasis on personal enlightenment and the pantheistic search for God in nature inspired generations of thinkers. It is difficult to exaggerate Böhme's influence on European culture: mystics during the seventeenth century revered him; scientists in the Enlightenment clung to his revelations; and the Romantics revived him again for his intense spiritual communication with nature. In the 1650s interest had reached fever pitch with the translation into English of his most important writings. Böhme may not have been vegetarian himself, but judging from the number of vegetarians who shared an interest in Böhme, there was something about his teaching that encouraged it. Perhaps it was his reverence for nature, perhaps his passionate call for all to embrace love in the world and shun the fierce wrath that lay hidden in everything (even God). His specific comments about eating meat are in the vein of traditional Christian asceticism; he complained that the soul is defiled and clad with stinking flesh when 'the body *feedeth upon the flesh of beasts*': 'Dost thou know why God did forbid the *Jews* to eat of *some sort of flesh?*' he asked, 'consider the smell of it . . . and thou *shalt discern it.*'[63]

Böhme aspired to the spiritual purity of Adam before the Fall. He wasn't explicit about any dietary regulations for achieving that goal (which might have been difficult since he believed that before the Fall Adam didn't even have a material body and so ate no food at all). But vegetarians might have been encouraged by Böhme's comment that God 'created so many kindes and sorts of beasts for his *Food* and *Rayment*' only because he had foreknowledge of man's Fall. If man was to 'come againe into his first estate', as Böhme fervently wished, it could follow that he would have to give up eating animals.[64] Crab also shared Böhme's theory that 'Seven Grand Properties', corresponding to the seven planets, governed the seven spirits of the human body. Crab, whose seven properties were actually more akin to conventional astrology, held that it was the Martian spirit that stirred up flesh-eating and murder.[65]

Most of the radicals of the mid-century period died in anonymity. After the Restoration in 1660 their politics became unpopular and dangerous to espouse. Roger Crab, exceptionally, sustained his local fame until he died in 1680. Secondary sources report a large concourse of people attending his funeral on 14 September at St Dunstan's Church in the parish of Stepney. In the churchyard a large monument was erected in his memory with a versified tribute to his vegetarianism:

> Tread gently, Reader, near the Dust,
> Cometh to this Tomb-stone's Trust.
> For while 'twas Flesh, it held a Guest,
> With universal Love possest.
> A soul that stemm'd Opinion's Tyde,
> Did over Sects in Triumph ride.
> Yet separate from the giddy Crowd,
> And Paths Tradition had allow'd.
> Through good and ill Reports he past;

> Oft censur'd, yet approv'd at last.
> Wouldest thou his Religion know?
> In brief 'twas this: To all to do
> Just as he would be done unto.
> So in kind Nature's Law he stood,
> A Temple undefil'd with Blood:
> A Friend to ev'ry Thing that's good.
> The rest, Angels alone fitly can tell:
> Haste, then, to Them and Him; and so farewel.[66]

The lines – written by a more proficient poet than Crab himself – represent vegetarianism as perfectly compatible with orthodox Christianity. To a large degree this agenda seems to have been achieved: he had been married in 1663 to a widow, Amy Markham, in St Bride's church; he was buried in the yard of another Anglican church, and according to the parish register was considered a 'Gentleman'.[67] This elevated status betrays his former radical rejection of personal property and social distinction, but it shows that he kept his vegetarian message alive in the wholly altered political environment of the Restoration.

Vegetarianism was a familiar expression of political and religious dissent in seventeenth-century England. It is unclear to what extent the Robins sect, the Diggers, the Family of Love, George Foster, Thomas Tany, Robert Norwood and Roger Crab were actively conspiring with each other. But diet was an integral part of a broadly cohesive radical agenda which they shared. Vegetarianism, for some, was an inherent part of the revolution. After their gory experience in the Civil War, veterans developed an aversion to blood so strong that they extended it to shedding animal blood. The rejection of violence, oppression and inequality went hand in hand with vegetarianism in a movement that aimed to achieve a bloodless revolution. Later, in the revolutionary 1780s and 1790s, vegetarianism re-emerged as part of a radical ideology. In the period between, vegetarianism survived by adapting to different cultural contexts, though often carrying with it traces of the old agenda. Roger Crab was the pioneer: lifting vegetarianism out of its Civil War context and refashioning it to new tastes laid the foundations for its continuation in Restoration England.

FOUR

Pythagoras and the Sages of India

Clown: What is the opinion of Pythagoras concerning wild fowl?
Malvolio: That the soul of our grandam might haply inhabit a
    bird.
Clown: What think'st thou of his opinion?
Malvolio: I think nobly of the soul, and no way approve his
    opinion.
Clown: Fare thee well. Remain thou still in darkness: thou shalt
    hold th' opinion of Pythagoras ere I will allow of thy wits;
    and fear to kill a woodcock, lest thou dispossess the soul of
    thy grandam. Fare thee well.

William Shakespeare, *Twelfth Night*, IV. ii

While meat-eating Christians fended off the vegetarian schism at home, another force was gathering strength that would assail them with even greater intensity. Having accustomed themselves to thinking of Europe as the pinnacle of humanity, travellers were shocked to find in India a thriving religion which had been sustained in a pristine form since well before – and virtually oblivious to – the invention of Christianity. The discovery of a people following an unbroken tradition of vegetarianism and exercising an extreme moral responsibility towards animals radically challenged European ideas about the relationship between man and nature. The stories of Indians living at peace with the animal kingdom were imaginatively merged with Christian traditions of prelapsarianism and Puritanism, and were a catalyst of Europe's seventeenth-century vegetarian renaissance. This neglected movement in European history profoundly affected some of the period's best-known figures and has had a lasting influence on Western concepts of nature.

On arrival in India, European travellers were astonished when they noticed that the modern 'Brahmins' – the Hindu priest caste, custodians of the Sanskrit scriptures – were the direct descendants of the ancient 'Brachmanes' encountered by Alexander the Great 2,000 years earlier. When the erudite Italian aristocrat, Pietro della Valle, encountered naked, dreadlocked, ash-smothered 'Yogis' with painted foreheads on his travels to India in the 1620s, he affirmed with confidence that 'There is no doubt but these are the ancient Gymnosophists so famous in the world . . . to whom *Alexander* the Great sent *Onesicritus* to consult with them'.[1] For travellers and readers alike – brought up on the primordial antiquity of the Bible – this was a disorientating realisation.

Merchants were excited by the trade in Indian diamonds, cotton and spices but thinkers all over Europe became obsessed with unlocking the jealously guarded secrets of India's strange and wonderful religions.[2] Missionaries were having a tough time getting Indians interested in Christianity, but Europeans at home were fascinated by Hinduism. Inevitably, Christian writing about India was distorted by religious bigotry and underwritten by Europe's nascent political agenda, but some seventeenth-century travellers examined Indian culture with remarkably open minds and even downright admiration. Enthusiastic descriptions were full of fantasies and projections too, but some aspects of Indian culture managed to penetrate the barriers of inter-cultural communication.[3] Readers at home developed such an insatiable craving for genuine Eastern knowledge that ideas taken from Indian philosophy were incorporated into debates about religion, science, history, human nature and ethics. At times, Hindu culture appeared so awesome that it shook Europe's self-centredness to its core.

The seventeenth-century 'discovery' of Indian vegetarianism was an astoundingly fertile cross-cultural encounter, but it was built upon an ancient history of passionate curiosity. Even before Alexander the Great reached India in 327 BC, its vegetarian philosophers were renowned in the ancient Greek world.[4] According to the historians whom Alexander took on his military expedition, the moment the Greek army arrived in the ancient university town of Taxila (now in Pakistan), Alexander despatched his messenger Onesicritus to find the famous 'gymnosophists', or 'naked philosophers'. In a legendary episode, which came to epitomise the meeting of East and West, Onesicritus came across a group of Brahmins sunning themselves on the outskirts of town. They burst into laughter at the sight of his hat and extravagant clothing, and derided his attempts to understand a translator's rendition of their transcendent wisdom with the caustic comment that it was like 'expecting water to flow through mud'.[5] Eventually one of them was prevailed upon to deliver a potted summary of Indian philosophy. Onesicritus was immediately struck by the similarities between Indian and Greek thought. In amazement, he told the Brahmins that like them Plato had taught the immortality of the soul and that their key doctrine of vegetarianism had been advocated in Greece by Pythagoras, Socrates, and even Onesicritus' own teacher, Diogenes.[6]

Although there are significant differences in their respective moral systems, it is nevertheless an extraordinary coincidence that roughly contemporaneous seminal Indian and Greek philosophers, the Buddha and Pythagoras, both taught that a soul's reincarnations depended on behaviour in previous lives, and that it was wrong for people to eat animals. Faced with this enthralling correlation, European match-makers fantasised about possible explanations for centuries; even today it remains one of the unsolved mysteries of world religion.[7] It was well known in ancient Greece and Rome that Pythagoras had travelled to Egypt and Persia in search of philosophical knowledge, and many, then and later, found it irresistible to imagine that he must have reached India.[8] Lucius Apuleius (AD 124–c.170), author of *The Golden Ass*, announced that the 'pre-eminent race called Gymnosophists' had indeed taught Pythagoras 'the greater part of his philosophy'.[9]

Pythagoras was believed to have launched Hellenistic philosophy, introducing the interlinked seminal concepts of the immortality of the soul through reincarnation or 'metempsychosis', the notion that all living things are kindred, and the corollary that it was wrong to cause suffering to animals.[10] Pythagoras wrote nothing down, but his doctrines became the basis of Plato's philosophy. It became a staple belief among Platonists that the Greek philosophical tradition owed its origins to India. Even those who thought the Egyptians were the first to invent philosophy could agree, since Egypt was widely believed to be an ancient Indian colony.[11]

Tracing Greek philosophy back to the Brahmins was a theory of inestimable significance. Despite cavils from Aristotle, it put the ideal of vegetarianism near the heart of ancient philosophy and enticed generations of travelling philosophers to drink at the original fountain of knowledge in India. Philostratus (AD 170–245) wrote a semi-fictional biography of Christ's first-century neo-Pythagorean rival, the legendary magical man-god and abolisher of sacrifices, Apollonius of Tyana.[12] Following in Alexander's footsteps to visit the Brahmins of Taxila, Apollonius defended vegetarianism, saying that the earth 'grows everything for mankind; and those who are pleased to live at peace with the brute creation want nothing', while carnivorous men, 'deaf to the cries of mother-earth, whet their knife against her children'. 'Here then,' explained Apollonius, 'is something which the Brahmins of India . . . taught the naked sages of Egypt also to condemn; and from them Pythagoras took his rule of life.'[13] Joining the dots between similar ethical systems, Apollonius posited Indian vegetarianism as a mandate for re-establishing harmony with the natural world. He was unambiguous: the basis of Pythagorean vegetarianism was Indian and the Brahmins were the fount of all true philosophy.

Plotinus (AD 205–70), the founder of Neoplatonism and principal Western proponent of metempsychosis, tried and failed to get to India to meet the Brahmins,[14] but his vegetarian star-pupil Porphyry (AD c.234–305) did the next best thing. Porphyry read the now lost account by the pagan convert to Christianity Bardesanes of Edessa (AD 154–c.222), who had interviewed a group of Indian ambassadors in Mesopotamia as they made their way to the court of the sun-worshipping homosexual-orgiast Emperor of Rome, Elagabalus.[15] In his seminal vegetarian treatise, *On Abstinence from Animal Food*, Porphyry championed the Brahmins for living on the natural products of the earth. 'To eat other food, or even to touch animate food,' explained Porphyry, 'is thought equivalent to the utmost impurity and impiety.' Eating meat was not technically against the law in India, Porphyry explained, but the Brahmins believed that abstinence from flesh was the purest diet (mirroring the arguments being made by ascetic flesh-abstaining Christians).[16]

Porphyry's vituperative detestation of the Christians, and Apollonius' stalwart rivalry with them, did not help to ingratiate the Brahmins or vegetarianism to Jerusalem's new religion. The Church fathers had much to say about abstinence from flesh, so the vegetarian Brahmins presented them with complex doctrinal questions. Was Indian vegetarianism a sign of prodigious spirituality, or was it blasphemous superstition? Worse still, could their diet give support to the contemporaneous vegetarian heresies breeding back home?

The Athenian pagan convert, St Clement of Alexandria (AD 150–c.215), was keen on flesh-free diets, which no doubt gave him a special interest in the Indian gymnosophists who, he said, 'feed on nuts, and drink water'. But the extremity of their abstinence, he insisted, made them dangerously similar to the heretical Gnostic Encratites, whom he called 'blockheads and atheists'.[17] St Hippolytus (*fl.* AD 234) also damned the Brahmins by suggesting in his *Refutation of all Heresies*, that it was from them that the Encratites originally derived their doctrines. Yet he grudgingly admitted that the Brahmins themselves appeared to live in a sort of Paradise, in which their food literally grew on trees. That the Brahmins did not have to cultivate the earth to get their bread implied that they somehow lived outside the remit of God's curse on Adam: 'In the sweat of thy face shalt thou eat bread.'[18] The pagan Greeks thought of the Indians living like the inhabitants of the Golden Age, the earth yielding fruit and grain to them without any labour.[19] Christians translated such fantasies into the belief that Eden had originally been situated in India.[20] On the other hand, lacking cultivation was sometimes construed as a sign of lack of 'culture', making the Indians uncivilised savages.[21]

But Bardesanes' enthusiasm for India was infectious. Bishop Eusebius of Caesarea, who wrote the *Ecclesiastical History* during the fourth-century Roman persecution, repeated Bardesanes' comment that the Brahmins 'neither commit murder, nor worship images, nor taste animal food, nor are ever intoxicated . . . but devote themselves to God'.[22] That they did not worship idols (which was true of some Hindus) suggested that they were Christians in spirit, even though they had not heard of Christ. The even more enthusiastic hermit St Jerome (AD *c.*347–420), in his defence of abstinence from flesh, declared that the Brahmins exemplified the spiritual benefits of fasting and were worthy of imitation by any Christian. He cited them alongside Diogenes and the Essenes, and even the unimpeachable biblical examples of Daniel the Prophet, Moses, John the Baptist and all the antediluvians including Adam and Eve. The Brahmins, said Jerome with admiration, 'are so rigidly self-restrained that they support themselves either with the fruit of trees which grow on the banks of the Ganges, or with common food of rice or flour'.[23] This ringing endorsement by one of the most revered Church fathers inspired Christian vegetarians for centuries.

Such willingness to identify points of contact between Hinduism and Christianity found its apotheosis in the monastic Bishop of Helenopolis, Palladius (AD *c.*363–431), who dramatised a dialogue between Alexander and Dandamis the Brahmin. Dandamis shuns

Alexander's splendid gifts, outsmarting the 'conqueror of many nations' with the rebuttal that, 'The earth supplies me with everything, even as a mother her child with milk,' and quips that it is better to be fed *to* beasts than to make oneself 'a grave for other creatures'.[24] Paraphrasing arguments from Palladius' own teacher, St John Chrysostom (AD 347–407), the Archbishop of Constantinople, and echoing Cynic philosophy, Dandamis says that even wolves were better than humans for at least they only ate meat because their nature compelled them to.

Palladius' account was incorporated into later versions of the hugely popular medieval *Alexander Romance* which spread throughout Europe, and possibly reached India in time to influence the sacred Buddhist text, the *Milindapanha*, a dialogue in which the vegetarian sage Nagasena converts Menander, the Greek King of Alexander's Bactrian kingdom. In the *Alexander Romance* the Brahmins claim to live in blissful harmony: 'When we are hungry, we go to the trees whose branches hang down here and eat the fruit they produce.' These Brahmins explicitly combine their vegetarianism with anti-monarchical sentiments; their role as entrenched critics of Western consumerism, tyranny and carnivorousness was growing apace.[25]

The extent to which medieval Christendom was ready for a new encounter with India was illustrated by Marco Polo's literary success on his arrival in Europe in the 1290s. After growing up at the court of Kublai Khan at Shang-tu (Xanadu) and travelling in Asia for more than twenty years, Marco Polo was captured by the Genoese and clapped in jail. Fortuitously, he was made to share a cell with the romance writer Rustichello. Polo whiled away the hours of imprisonment by dictating what he had seen in the East, and, between them, the two prisoners produced one of the most extraordinary travel adventures of all time, written like a medieval romance – except that this time nearly everything they said was true.[26]

Rather than simply ridiculing the outlandish cultures he had encountered, Polo made a striking leap towards cultural relativism. He recognised that by their own standards and even his own, the Brahmins were exceedingly virtuous. They were scrupulously honest, they bathed regularly (unlike Europeans), and they lived extraordinarily long and healthy lives during which, Polo explained, they would not eat or 'kill any creature or any living thing in the world, neither fly nor flea nor louse nor any other vermin, because they say that they have souls'.[27]

Marco Polo in Tartar attire

With such eye-witness reports, Europeans were quick to hold up the Brahmins as a quintessential embodiment of the 'virtuous pagan'.

Among the many other wonders Polo described was Adam's Peak on Ceylon (Sri Lanka) which was said by local Muslims to contain Adam's grave, and by 'idolaters' to hold a footprint of the Buddha.[28] Decades later, in 1338 the Pope's ambassador, John of Marignolli, was sent off to the East to examine the new Christian missions. He visited Ceylon to check up on Polo's fantastic reports about Adam's grave and was utterly astonished to discover that, as Polo had suggested, 'Paradise is a place that (really) exists upon the earth'.[29]

Back home, Marignolli wrote up his experiences for Emperor Charles IV whom he served as chaplain. He described how he had strolled through the garden that was once Adam's home, tasting mangoes, jackfruit, coconuts and bananas which, like the local spices, Marignolli surmised, were descended from the luscious trees of Paradise. On this mountain he found the remains of Adam's marble house, an imprint of Adam's foot, and – most amazing of all – a monastery populated by holy men (clearly Buddhists) who, he said, 'never eat flesh, because Adam and his successors till the flood did not do so'. These extremely holy, half-naked monks were as virtuous as any people on earth – despite not being Christians. They confounded Marignolli by arguing 'that they are not descended either from Cain or from Seth, but from other sons of Adam'. They claimed that the hill they lived on had protected them – and the original artefacts of Paradise – from the ravages of Noah's Flood. 'But as this is contrary to Holy Scripture', Marignolli added nervously, 'I will say no more, about it.' He could not resist the temptation of saying more, however, for he had found something that fulfilled Christians' wildest dreams: 'Our first parents,' he concluded, 'lived in Seyllan upon the fruits I have mentioned, and for drink had the milk of animals. They used no meat till after the deluge, nor to this day do those men use it who call themselves the children of Adam.'

Marignolli – perhaps with the misleading assistance of Muslim interpreters – readily incorporated vegetarian Buddhism into the biblical tradition. He claimed that the 'skins' Adam and Eve were given to wear after the Fall were actually coconut-fibre clothes (as modelled by the inhabitants of Ceylon). The vegetarian Buddhists and Brahmins of India, according to this dazed Christian, were continuing the prelapsarian vegetable diet. Having abandoned his initial caution, Marignolli doffed his European clothes, donned a coconut-fibre sarong, and joined the Buddhist fraternity until it was time for him to return. The Franciscan who set out to check up on the progress of the Eastern Catholic mission ended up using vegetarianism as a bridge between his religion and Buddhism.[30]

The Renaissance travellers who followed the missionaries to India reinforced expectations of finding remnants of Paradise. When the Venetian merchant Nicolò Conti returned from his Indian travels in 1448, the Pope sent his secretary, Poggio Bracciolini, to record what he had seen. The ancient Greek accounts of India – principally Strabo's *Geography* (AD 23) – had just been rediscovered, and Conti's new stories caused huge excitement. He spoke of 'Bachali' – presumably the descendants of the converts Bacchus had made on his mythical trip to India – who 'abstain from all animal food, in particular the ox'.[31] The Brahmins (whom Poggio differentiated from the Bachali) were great astrologers and prophets, living free from diseases to the age of 300, and their asceticism competed with anything practised in Europe.[32]

In 1520 the German cleric Joannes Boemus published his *Omnium gentium mores, leges & ritus*, a massive comparative ethnology which went through innumerable editions in French, Italian, Spanish and in English as *The Fardle of Facions* (1555). Boemus filled out what the classical sources did not provide with utopian fantasy: the 'unchristened Brahmanes', he said, put Europeans to shame by living a 'pure and simple life . . . content with suche foode as commeth to hande'.[33] This was hardly less fantastic than the part-fictional, part-plagiarised *Travels of Sir John Mandeville* written in the mid-1300s, which had imagined the 'Isle of Bragman' inhabited by pagans 'full of all virtue' living chaste and sober lives in 'perpetual peace'.[34] Sir Thomas More's *Utopia* (1516) was inspired by similar idealistic reports; More's Utopians, like the Indians, exercise temperance, are kind to animals and live in political harmony; there is even a cryptic suggestion that they are gymnosophists.[35]

This type of exotic idealism was elaborated by scores of other writers, such as Tommaso Campanella who wrote *The City of the Sun* in 1602, soon after being committed to twenty-five years' imprisonment for attempting to establish a Hermetic solar utopia in Calabria. The narrator of Campanella's story – a world-travelled sea captain – reports that the inhabitants of the City of the Sun rarely drink wine, never get the diseases of gluttonous Europe, live for up to 200 years, and derive their deistic* religion from the Brahmins.[36] Campanella was so aware that vegetarianism would be expected of his ideal community that he wittily took the issue face on: 'They were unwilling at first to slay animals, because it seemed cruel; but thinking afterward that it was also cruel to destroy herbs which have a share of sensitive feeling, they saw that they would perish from hunger . . . Nevertheless, they do not willingly kill useful animals, such as oxen and horses.'[37] More than a century later the theme was still very much alive, reappearing satirically in Jonathan Swift's *Gulliver's Travels* (1726) in which the barbarous flesh-eating Yahoos contrast with the idealised

---

* For an account of deism, see chapter 9.

Houyhnhnms who only eat herbivorous food (as does Gulliver during most of his residence with them).[38] Like the travel literature they were based on, these utopian works critiqued European manners by setting them against other cultures. It is little wonder that puritanical enthusiasts in Europe sought to recreate the ideal communities at home which they read about in both travel and utopian literature.

As the voyages of discovery fuelled a new wave of interest in India, travel literature became a subject of serious intellectual study. Renaissance scholars started interpreting Indian religions along similar lines as classical Greek and Roman paganism, forging the path for the late eighteenth-century Orientalism of Sir William Jones.[39] Some travellers were even bold enough to legitimise Indian customs by pointing out similarities with their own culture. In 1515, a Florentine envoy wrote from Cochin to tell Giuliano de Medici that he had encountered vegetarians who 'do not feed upon anything that contains blood, nor do they permit among them that any injury be done to any living thing, like our Leonardo da Vinci'.[40] Da Vinci – who was himself rumoured to have travelled in the Orient – had spent decades ranting against cruelty to animals and deploring how man had made himself their 'sepulchre', despite the plentiful vegetable food provided by nature. Like the Hindus, he even lamented that eating eggs deprived future beings of life. Contemporaries related how da Vinci used to buy caged birds to set them free – an act of charity long associated with Pythagoras, and a habit now being remarked upon by European travellers in India.[41]

Renaissance Neoplatonists had developed a method of syncretising the various pagan philosophies from Greece, Rome and Egypt and decoding them to find the hidden truths that lay behind their fantastic exterior. Some teachings of paganism were thus made compatible with Christianity. When new information became available on Indian 'gentiles' (or 'Gentoos' as they were often called), it was partially incorporated into this ready-made framework. But the Indians stood out, for unlike other bygone pagan peoples, they still existed. To some, this made them more threatening, but to anyone predisposed to learn from ancient Eastern sages, it made the Indians particularly sensational. Europeans were familiar with the vegetarian teachings of Pythagoras, and they had the biblical story of Eden engraved upon their hearts. But the Indian vegetarians stimulated an unparalleled renewal of interest, and the constant flow of varied reports about them encouraged a constant reappraisal of their significance. Europeans did project their own preconceptions onto Indian vegetarianism, but some tenets from Indian philosophy still managed to enter Europeans' consciousness. Indian culture exerted a powerful influence which altered Western understanding of the religious and ethical issues raised by the practice of abstaining from meat.

At the tail end of the fifteenth century, after years of trying to open the sea route to India, the Portuguese sea-captain Vasco da Gama and his crew limped round the Cape of Good Hope, and flopped – bedraggled and empty-handed – onto the Western coast of India. Da Gama's mission had a commercial goal: to find a means of importing Indian spices without using the expensive Muslim-dominated land route. But King Manuel of Portugal had also allegedly threatened da Gama that on pain of death he was not to return until he found the legendary Christian King of India, the perennial 'Prester John'. Almost the first people da Gama's men met on their arrival were dreadlocked Indians who seemed willing to worship the Portuguese images of the Virgin Mary, possibly seeing in the baby Christ a counterpart of their own baby Krishna. The Portuguese rejoiced at having linked up with their long-lost Christian brothers, and after an initial hesitation about the odd Indian 'churches', in a gush of enthusiasm, they knelt down and prayed in the Hindu temples.

The Portuguese soon realised that these 'Christians' were not entirely ordinary. They not only 'ate no beef', but when da Gama and his men arrived at the Calicut court for dinner they found that – in startling contrast to the lavish banquets of European royalty – the King 'eats neither meat nor fish nor anything that has been killed, nor do his barons, courtiers, or other persons of quality, for they say that Jesus Christ said in his law that he who kills shall die'. While the Portuguese remained under the delusion that the Indians were Christian, they were more than willing to integrate local vegetarianism into the biblical commandment against killing, and noted with amazement that it was actually perfectly possible for humans to live without eating meat.[42]

But da Gama and his men gradually realised that they had been mistaken about the Indians' Christianity and they became less tolerant about their vegetarian foibles. By this time, the other major European powers were eyeing with envy the Portuguese monopoly on Indian trade. At the end of the sixteenth century the Dutch finally muscled in on the game by sending armed galleons to back up their trading ventures. The British followed hot on their heels, promising the Great Mughal an alliance with Queen Elizabeth. They came in search of riches, but they knew there was also a market back home for tales of wonder and adventure, and each nation produced its own scribe of India.

Among the things that fascinated Europeans most were the vegetarians. In fact, only certain groups of Hindus were actually vegetarian. Most Brahmins upheld their caste purity laws by abstaining from meat, and to some Europeans this gave them an aura of austere sanctity. But still more surprising to Western travellers were the masses of ordinary people who lived on what in Europe was considered an exceptionally abstemious diet. Many Banians, the trading caste, were strict vegetarians especially on the Western coast in Gujarat, and some of these joined the all-vegetarian Jains.[43] Several Jain monks held prominent positions at the Mughal courts and Europeans were well-placed to observe them there and even interrogate them on their beliefs.[44] It should be noted that many of the ancient Sanskrit texts that applaud vegetarianism and *ahimsa* also list numerous exceptions under which meat-eating was allowed and even praised. These included cases of medical necessity; ritual sacrifice of animals; and hunting by the princely-warrior caste, the Ksatriyas.[45] Sanskrit texts such as the *Laws of Manu* (200 BC–AD 200) actually state (just like Aristotle) that it was *natural* for humans to be predators: 'animals without fangs are the food of those with fangs, those without hands of those who possess hands, and the timid of the bold.'[46] It was partly *because* eating animals was natural that abstaining was seen as a virtue. Thus the same text promises that 'He who does not seek to cause the sufferings of bonds and death to living creatures, but desires the good of all beings, obtains endless bliss.'[47] Europeans became fixated with the belief system underlying the Indians' vegetarianism and nearly every traveller marvelled at it, revealing in their responses their own prejudices and preoccupations: what was the proper relation between man and beast? What diet was suitable for the human body? What happened to people's temperament when they no longer committed daily violence to animals? Whatever the answers to these questions, one thing was certain: encountering Indian vegetarianism triggered a review of European morality. Hinduism became the arena in which these issues were fought out, and the travellers' varying responses produced a vocabulary for discussing the vegetarian question in the wider context.

The Indians' apparent animal worship was a massive hurdle for

Indian cow-worship from the frontispiece of Thomas Herbert's
A Relation of Some Yeares Travaile . . . (1634)

Christians to overcome.[48] Zoolatry was the ultimate degradation of God and humanity, and many took temple images of animals as proof that Hindus worshipped the devil.[49] The most prominent instance of 'animal worship' in India, which everyone commented on, was the reverence for the cow.[50] European Christians found the habit abominable – reminiscent as it was of the Israelites' golden calf and the Egyptian god Apis – and this made a great excuse for pillaging golden cows from temples.[51] The Franciscan missionary to India and China, Odoric of Pordenone (1286–1331), whose account was plagiarised in the widely successful *Mandeville's Travels*, wrote disparagingly of pagans who washed in cow dung and urine as if it were holy water.[52] Scatological details about Indians using cattle faeces as a cleansing agent for houses, bodies and souls became a staple of European writing about Hinduism.[53]

But alongside such stereotyping, Europeans as early as Marco Polo were prepared to see a utilitarian rationale behind cow worship. Cattle, they noticed, were the primary beasts of burden in India, responsible for cultivating the fields as well as providing milk, so any religious law that sought to protect the cow contributed to the agronomy and well-being of the country.[54] '[T]his superior regard for the cow,' wrote François Bernier in 1667, 'may more probably be owing to her extraordinary usefulness.'[55] In fact, there was already a long tradition of reading self-interested motives into cow-protection laws. St Thomas Aquinas, even while arguing against vegetarianism, allowed that some food taboos were rational, instancing Egypt where 'the eating of the

Brahmin with cow, from Henry Lord's
A Display of two forraigne sects in the East Indies (1630)

flesh of the ox was prohibited in olden times so that agriculture would not be hindered'.[56] St Jerome, likewise, commented that in Egypt and Palestine the killing of calves was prohibited in 'the interests of agriculture'. Even in sixteenth-century England, Queen Elizabeth had outlawed meat-eating during Lent to allow cattle stocks and grazing lands to be replenished.[57]

However, the protection of animals that were *not* useful flabbergasted even the most hardened travellers. The sixteenth-century Portuguese writer Duarte Barbosa was astounded by the 'marvellous' extreme to which the Indians took 'this law of not killing anything'. 'For it often happens,' he reported, 'that the Moors bring them some worms or little birds alive, saying they intend to kill them in their presence; and they ransom them, and buy them to set them flying, and save their lives for more money than they are worth.'[58] He was still more astonished – as future European travellers would be – to find that noxious insects like lice were looked after by special people allotted to the task of feeding them with their own blood.[59]

Christians thought that animals were made for humans, so an animal's value was dependent on its usefulness. The Hindus and Jains, they perceived, had a fundamentally different system which attributed value to animal life independent from, and even at the expense of, man. In the 1590s the Dutch traveller to India John Huygen van Linschoten articulated this in his internationally best-selling travelogue *Itinerario* (*The Journey*), by explaining that the Banians 'kill nothing in the world that has life, however small and useless it may be'. Despite his culture-shock, Linschoten rendered such morals comprehensible by giving them a Christian gloss: the Hindus, he explained, consider it 'a work of great charity, saying, it is don to their even neighbours'.[60] It became common for Europeans to regard the Hindu value of animal life not so much as something completely alien, but as an *extension* of laws compatible with Christianity such as 'loving thy neighbour'.[61] In that framework, Hindus were seen by some as more virtuous than Christians. As one English gentleman put in the 1680s, it was 'a sad thing' that in respect of their treatment of animals 'Christians, very many of them, may go to School, and learn of *Infidels* and *Heathens* to reform their Lives and Manners'.[62]

The ultimate surprise for the Europeans were the Indian 'animal hospitals'.[63] Again, Europeans were most challenged by the fact that such hospitals expended effort and money on animals that were past their usefulness. 'They have hospitals for sheepe, goates, dogs, cats, birds, and for all other living creatures,' wrote Ralph Fitch, the first Englishman to write a travelogue on India in 1594. 'When they be old and lame, they keepe them until they die.'[64] In Europe, sick animals or cattle past their productive age were automatically killed. The 'ingratitude' that this implied became a source of anxiety for Europeans.[65] Hindus appeared to be extraordinary exemplars of charity, which put some European noses out of joint. Many travellers responded to this with ridicule, but others were impressed by the workings of a moral system that was entirely neglected in the West.

In dealing with this challenge, Europeans projected onto the Indians the simplified Pythagorean idea that they abstained from killing animals for fear of hurting a reincarnated human soul. This implied that the Hindus were not valuing the life of the animal itself, but the soul of the human trapped within it. Since most Christians dismissed reincarnation as a preposterous theological error, interpreting Hindu vegetarianism in this way deflected the ethical challenge and amputated their principle of non-violence (*ahimsa*). It meant that writers could fall back on the long-standing Christian tradition of ridiculing the Pythagorean objection to eating flesh, as the Christian theologian Tertullian put it in the second century AD, 'lest by chance in his beef he eats of some ancestor of his'.[66] One author who assessed the scientific case for vegetarianism at the end of the seventeenth century, simply declared that the Pythagoreans didn't count as vegetarians because their diet was based on 'a Mistake in their Philosophy, and not a Law of Nature'.[67] Christians defused the moral strength of vegetarianism by reducing it to a comical superstition.

Having projected Pythagoreanism onto the Hindus, some Europeans explained the similarity by claiming that Pythagoras had *taught* the Indians their vegetarian doctrines, rather than the other way round.[68] This gave Pythagoras the European a superior status, and it also meant that Brahmins could be more readily assimilated into biblical history by claiming that they and their philosophy were descended from the Egyptians. By the time the clergyman Samuel Purchas published his enormous anthology of travel literature in 1625, the idea that the Indians were identical to Pythagoreans was already widespread. Purchas himself thought Pythagoras must have been to India and he printed several authors who had noticed, as King James I's ambassador to Jahangir, Sir Thomas Roe, put it in 1616, that the Indian 'Pythagorians' believe in 'the soules transmigration, and will not kyll any living creature, no, not the virmine that bites them, for feare of disseising the speiritt of some frend departed'.[69] Purchas made Indian vegetarianism part of common parlance and, inevitably, these ideas wove themselves into Europe's cultural fabric.

In the 1620s the humanist nobleman, Pietro della Valle (1586–1652), was astonished when a Brahmin called 'Beca Azarg' told him that Pythagoras was the same person as the Hindu god Brahma; that it was 'Pythagoras' who had taught metempsychosis and vegetarianism to the Brahmins and that they still revered his books.[70] It was, laughed della Valle, 'a curious notion indeed, and which perhaps would be news to hear in *Europe*, that *Pythagoras* is foolishly ador'd in *India* for a God'. 'But this,' concluded della Valle, 'with *Beca Azarg*'s good leave, I do not believe.'[71] Henry Lord, chaplain to the English trading post at Surat in Gujarat, did believe it. In the hope that Hinduism could be reconciled to Christianity by purging it of Pythagorean doctrines, in 1630 he set himself up as a latter-day heretic-hunting St Augustine, calling upon the Archbishop of Canterbury to reprimand the Hindus for disobeying God's instruction to eat flesh.[72] By contrast, the French editor of *The Open Door to Hidden Paganism* (1651), the most advanced account of the Hindus, by the Dutch missionary Abraham Rogerius, took the view that 'Plato and Pythagoras were not ashamed to learn the basic tenets of their philosophy from the Brahmans.'[73] In a conservative backlash against such liberal views in the *China illustrata* of 1667, the Jesuit scientist-missionary Athanasius Kircher retorted that metempsychosis had been carried to India by an execrable band of Egyptian priests and had subsequently been spread across the Eastern world (along with its corollary vegetarianism) by a 'deadly monster' called Buddha, 'a very sinful brahmin imbued with Pythagoreanism'. 'These are not tenets, but crimes,' concluded Kircher venomously. 'They are not doctrines, but abominations.'[74]

In 1665 Edward Bysshe dragged the debate into the forefront of modern politics by publishing an anthology of the ancient writings on India, including Palladius' dialogue, in which he presented the Brahmins as pure idealists who stood up to Alexander just as modern Puritans stood up to the tyranny of Charles II.[75] In the context of mid-century Puritanism, Sir Thomas Roe's chaplain, Edward Terry (1589/90–1660), gave a strikingly accurate account of the ancient doctrine of *ahimsa* – that an animal values its life just as humans value theirs, so destroying it manifestly against its will constitutes an act of violent injury (*himsa*). This was a remarkable moment of cross-cultural understanding which Terry appears to have accomplished by interviewing Jain monks, probably in Gujarat or while travelling with Jahangir's court. However, he did not want to give too much ground to the Indians; he drew attention away from the morally powerful doctrine of *ahimsa* by claiming that their *main* reasons for being vegetarian were the 'mad and groundlesse phansie' of Pythagorean metempsychosis and the false commandment *'Thou shalt not kill any living Creature'*. He castigated them for 'forbearing the lives of the Creatures made for mens use', but nevertheless acknowledged that they provided a better moral example than Christians who fought unrighteous wars and made riotous 'havock and spoil' with the animals. Going some way to meet them, Terry lauded their temperance and felt that their other 'excellent moralities' showed that the divine law of nature was 'ingraved upon [their] hearts'.[76]

As the seventeenth century matured, liberal philosophies started to compete more strongly with the Christian orthodoxies about man and nature. Over the heads of the Indian vegetarians, the great minds of the day fought out their disputes. Were Brahmins ignorant idolaters or ancient philosophers who could teach a thing or two to the Europeans?

The seminal analysis of Indian vegetarianism came from a most unlikely quarter, and showed how the association with Pythagoras could be a path towards assimilating Hinduism. François Bernier (1625–1688), who served as physician at the court of the Great Mughal Emperor Aurangzeb for eight years in the 1660s, had been trained in sceptical and Epicurean philosophy under Pierre Gassendi. With this enlightened background, Bernier attacked Indian culture not simply because Hindus were deluded idolaters who failed to see the obvious truth of Christianity; rather, his ridicules were aimed at the practice of superstitious rituals (many of which, he noted, were equivalent to the irrational beliefs of European Christians).[77] Bernier smiled wryly as he watched Hindus gathering en masse to bathe in sacred rivers, banging on cymbals and using incantations to ward off the evil influence of an eclipse. He recited all the 'monstrosities' of Hindu culture from widow-burning to sun worship. But there was one doctrine for which Bernier pulled his punches: their Pythagorean vegetarianism.

> Perhaps the first legislators in the *Indies* hoped that the interdiction of animal food would produce a beneficial effect upon the character of the people, and that they might be brought to exercise less cruelty toward one another when required by a positive precept to treat the brute creation with humanity. The doctrine of the transmigration of souls secured the kind treatment of animals ... It may also be that the *Brahmens* were influenced by the consideration that in their climate the flesh of cows or oxen is neither savoury nor wholesome.[78]

Bernier's willingness to recognise the health benefits of abstaining from meat may have been inspired by his master, Gassendi, who had himself been a staunch advocate of the vegetable diet (see chapter 11). But Bernier even rendered the doctrine of reincarnation comprehensible to Europeans by arguing that it was not designed to protect animals for their own sake, but ultimately for the benefit of humans. He was following a common tradition that had long been used to clear Pythagoras from imputations of superstition, exemplified by the third-century Epicurean biographer-philosopher Diogenes Laertius, who claimed that Pythagoras never believed in metempsychosis, but that 'his real reason for forbidding animal diet' was to give people 'a healthy body and keen mind'.[79] Indeed, this interpretative technique had been used by Christians on the Bible, for example when St Thomas Aquinas insisted that if Moses appeared to care for animals, he was really just trying 'to turn the mind of man away from cruelty which might be used on other men'.[80] Erasing from Hinduism the ethic of respect for animal life, and replacing it with European ideas of diet, agronomy and temperament, may seem like aggressive manipulation, but in doing so Bernier was treating Hinduism in much the same way as Christians treated the Bible. By transposing exegetical traditions onto Indian practice and regarding the Hindus as pseudo-Pythagoreans, Bernier developed a humanist interpretation of Indian culture that detected a reservoir of ancient sagacity behind their 'fables'.

Having identified its potential, Bernier was astonished by the advantages of vegetarianism, noticing in particular that it was India's greatest military asset. Whereas European armies were weighed down with barrels of salted beef and tankards of wine – without which the European soldier would absolutely refuse to fight – Indian armies were perfectly content with readily transportable dried food such as lentils and rice. He looked on with disbelief as Aurangzeb's immense army transported enough provisions for 'prodigious and almost incredible' numbers of people.[81]

Such concrete evidence of the benefits of vegetarianism made a sizeable dent in the typical European argument that meat-eating was essential for sustaining human life, or at least for strength and virility. It was commonly supposed that anyone who abstained from flesh must be effeminate, weak and lazy. This, Europeans said to themselves, was what made it so easy for meat-eating Muslims and Europeans to conquer Indian vegetarians.[82] This idea of Asian effeminacy, which dates back at least 2,500 years to Hippocratic medical ethnology, became one of the most pervasive means of denigrating Hindus, especially towards the end of the eighteenth century.[83] But it was counterbalanced by the recognition that the Hindus' frugality made them at least as long-lived as Europeans, and fuelled their admired industriousness and resilience to disease.[84]

The Europeans' idea that meat-eating was normal, or essential, was swiftly being demolished by the discovery of vegetarian peoples all over the world. Europeans gradually realised that instead of representing the norm, they were an exceptionally carnivorous society. In Africa and America travellers found people living in primitive simplicity 'before' the luxury of civilisation had corrupted them – a state with both

Edenic and barbaric connotations.[85] In the East vegetarianism had been preserved beyond the state of nature by virtuous temperance and the institution of sacred laws against killing animals.[86] Such discoveries were to provide grist to the mill of any European who wished to argue that eating meat was by no means a nutritional necessity.

Bernier's attempt to understand and even learn from this Hindu doctrine has to be considered as liberal, especially compared to the invectives of his European contemporaries at the Mughal court, such as the Venetian Niccolao Manucci who described the Indian vegetarians as 'a people who do not deserve the name of man'.[87]

Bernier's acquaintance Jean-Baptiste Tavernier was less vituperative than Manucci, but furnished plenty of sensationalist examples of Indian vegetarianism in his *Travels in India* (1676), warning prospective visitors with the story of a Persian merchant who was whipped to death for shooting a peacock, and noting the extreme lengths taken to ensure that relatives were not killed – in the form of ants in firewood. Tavernier praised the high morality of the Hindus, but he – like many others before and since – could not but see an absurd contradiction in preserving the life of vermin, and yet happily burning widows on the funeral pyres of their husbands.[88]

Surprisingly, the most enthusiastic seventeenth-century travel writer was an English clergyman, the Reverend John Ovington, who travelled to India in 1689. Ovington accepted Bernier's utilitarian rationale: vegetarianism clearly made the Indians less cruel, just as healthy, and spiritually and mentally 'more quick and nimble'. But Ovington even endorsed the Indians' animal protection practices on their own terms: '*India* of all the Regions of the Earth, is the only publick Theatre of Justice and Tenderness to Brutes, and all living Creatures,' he said, 'a Civil Regard . . . is enjoyn'd as a common Duty of Humanity'. Their innocence, said Ovington, made the Hindus comparable to 'the original Inhabitants of the World, whom Antiquity supposes not to have been Carnivorous, nor to have tasted Flesh in those first Ages, but only to have fed upon Fruits and Herbs'. Ovington concluded by giving Hinduism a *carte blanche* of philosophical integrity: 'there is not one of these Customs which are fasten'd upon them by the Rules of their Religion, but what comport very well, and highly contribute to the Health and Pleasure of their Lives.'[89]

The way was paved for Europeans to take Indian vegetarianism, if not as a lesson in philosophy and justice, then at least in medical health. The voyages of discovery and the new wave of early anthropology that followed in their wake impelled Europe towards a combination of cultural syncretism and relativism. Attempts to sustain the idea that European Christians had the best society often crumbled in the face of evident virtue and integrity in other peoples. International vegetarianism, which plugged directly into European discourses on diet and the relationship between man and nature, proved a serious challenge to Western norms. As readers back home assimilated the information in the travelogues, Indian vegetarianism started to exert influence on the course of European culture.

FIVE

'This proud and troublesome Thing, called Man': Thomas Tryon, the Brahmin of Britain

Thomas Tryon gazed out over the sugar plantations of Barbados. What he saw chilled his heart. With horror he watched lines of slaves labouring under the inhuman whip of their European masters. The cruelty of men claiming to be Christians surpassed all belief: the expatriated Africans were starved until they would eat putrefying horse meat; their limbs were crushed in the sugar mills; they died by thousands in the open fields. While Restoration England grew fat on their sweat and blood, Tryon complained, Barbados was perishing. The forests of the Americas were being depleted at a shocking rate; even the soil was suffering under the insatiable greed of the white man. After years of forcing the ground to produce the same cash crop, Barbados had gone from being 'the most Fertil'st Spot of all *America*', to 'become a kind of Rock' which grew nothing without dung fertiliser.[1] All this destruction was committed only to supply luxury goods back in London – that stinking heap of human corruption Tryon had left behind. Everything had gone horribly awry: America was supposed to be a New World in which laws of justice between man and beast would bring about a Golden Age of peace and harmony, not the ransacked sewerage of the Old World.[2] This was the opposite of what Tryon, in his youthful dreams, had imagined.

Born on 6 September 1634 in the Gloucestershire village of Bibury, Tryon had been sent out to spin wool at the age of six without an education. Working as a shepherd in his spare time he had accumulated enough capital by the age of thirteen to buy himself two sheep, and he swapped one of them for English lessons. Tryon loved his innocent flock and the contemplative life sleeping under the stars, but by the age of eighteen he 'began to grow weary of Shepherdizing, and had an earnest desire to travel'. Without telling his parents, he packed up his belongings, his life savings and his ideals, waved goodbye to his sheep, said good riddance to his father's plastering trade and set out for London.[3]

It was 1653 and the religious radicalism of Cromwell's interregnum was at fever pitch. Having paid all of his £3 apprenticing himself to a hat-maker near Fleet Street, Tryon soon joined his master's congregation of Anabaptists, attracted by their austerity, silence and periodic fasting from flesh.[4] Up in his apprentice's lodgings, he spent all his spare time and money delving into books on alchemy, herbal medicine and natural magic. In 1657, at the age of twenty-three, he had what he was waiting for – a divine visitation of his own: 'the Voice of Wisdom continually and most powerfully called upon me,' he wrote years later in his *Memoirs*; it told him to relinquish all luxuries and turn to vegetarianism: 'for then I took my self to Water only for Drink, and forbore eating any kind of Flesh or Fish, and confining my self to an abstemious self-denying Life.'[5]

This was the very year that Roger Crab started calling for followers, and Tryon's description of his conversion sounds so similar to Crab's that it could have been lifted straight out of *The English Hermite*.[6] So many of their interests are the same – Behmenist mysticism, astrological dietary medicine, vegan diet and even hat-making – that it is tempting to imagine Crab was Tryon's vegetarian guru.[7] Tryon called the Sabbath Mammon-worship, and the clergy '*Jockies* in the Art of Wiving'; he railed against upper-class exploitation and warned that private lands were 'the effects of Violence'.[8] Like Crab, he mastered the art of twisting the Bible into a vegetarian manifesto – enlisting Moses, Daniel, John the Baptist and Jesus as fellow vegetarians – and revealing that God's permission to eat meat after the Flood was really an act of 'Spite and Vengeance' tempting people into the spirit of wrath.[9] Humans were supposed to be 'faithful Stewards' of God's creatures, insisted Tryon, not murderous meat-eating tyrants.[10]

He joined a group of vegetarians whose doctrines sound similar to those of Crab's 'Rationals', Pordage's followers or even Winstanley's Diggers, for they '*would not eat Flesh*, because it could not be procured without breaking the Harmony and Unity of Nature, and doing what one would not be done unto'.[11] When Tryon heard the rumours of Indians living in harmony with the animals he was transfixed with joy:

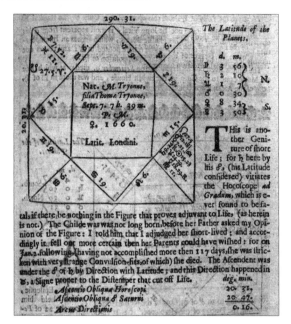

Horoscope of the nativity of Thomas Tryon's daughter (1661/1662)

vegetarianism was no longer relegated to the backwaters of English religious dissidence – it was the creed followed by entire nations of brother herb-eaters like himself.

Like many sectaries of the time, Tryon initially avoided persecution by keeping his head down and refraining from the provocative medium of print. Besides, he had a family to support: after marrying a childhood sweetheart who refused to give up eating meat, and fathering five children,[12] Tryon travelled to Holland and then Barbados where religious toleration was greater and commercial opportunities in the hat trade were lucrative. But after returning to London in 1669 he experienced his second epiphany. In 1682 his inner voice told him 'to Write and Publish something . . . recommending to the World Temperance, Cleanness, and Innocency of Living; and admonishing Mankind against Violence, Oppression, and Cruelty, either to their own Kind, or any inferior Creatures'.[13] Tryon fell to his new allotted task with ardour and over the next twenty years, until his death in 1703, he poured a total of twenty-seven works through the press. Many of them were popular enough to go into multiple editions, his *magnum opus, The Way to Health, Long Life and Happiness,* being reprinted five times in fifteen years. On average over the entirety of his writing career, Tryon went to press once every four months. Some of his works were circulated by the Quaker printer Andrew Sowle and his daughter Tace, and others were distributed by a dozen of England's most successful commercial booksellers including Elizabeth Harris, Thomas Bennet and Dorman Newman, and were advertised in works as popular as Daniel Defoe's.[14]

By now political radicalism had been stifled by its own failures and, with the accession of Charles II in 1660, Cromwell's interregnum had given way to the polite culture of Restoration England. In 1688 the Glorious Revolution (also called the Bloodless Revolution) saw an end to James II's whimsical reign and Parliament gave the crown to his daughter Mary and her husband William of Orange, ushering in a new era of constitutional democracy and relative social tolerance.[15] Tryon accordingly tempered his vegetarian philosophy with an element of compromise. His homely books with titles like *The Way to Make All People Rich, The Good Housewife made a Doctor* and *Healths Grand Preservative* were aimed at frugal householders. He encouraged people to forage for wild plants such as watercress, sorrel and dandelion, and lauded local, naturally produced vegetables from the 'brave noble' potato to the 'lively' leek. He helpfully furnished his readers with step-by-step guides on how best to cook cabbages, as well as his favourite meat-free recipes like 'Bonniclabber' which, he explained, 'is nothing else but Milk that has stood till it is sower, and become of a thick slippery substance' (try this at your own risk).[16]

He also cautioned against over-indulgence, especially in fatty meat, cream and fried foods, which, combined with lack of exercise, he repeatedly warned, cause obesity, obstruct the circulation of the blood and 'fur the Passages'.[17] But recognising that despite his warnings 'People will still gorge themselves with the Flesh of their *Fellow-Animals*', he deigned to supply his readers with instructions on how to prepare it (boiling rather than frying) so as to avoid the worst of its harmful qualities.[18]

In his lifetime Tryon was appreciated by a wide range of people, from recondite astrologers to the famous proto-feminist playwright, poet and novelist Aphra Behn. It is possible that Tryon met Behn in Barbados where his liberal attitudes appear to have influenced her slave-novel *Oronooko*. Behn described herself as Tryon's follower, claiming to have tried his vegetarian regime, and in 1685 wrote a laudatory poem about him which is so hyperbolic that it is hard to believe it was not penned with a hint of irony:[19]

> Hail Learned Bard! who dost thy power dispence
> And show'st us the first State of Innocence . . .
>
> Not he that bore th'Almighty Wand* cou'd give
> Diviner Dictates, how to eat, and live.
> And so essential was this cleanly Food,
> For Man's eternal health, eternal good,
> That God did for his first-lov'd Race provide,
> What thou, by God's example, hast prescrib'd:[20]

But any exaggeration would have been less evident then: by the end of his life, Tryon had accumulated such wealth from trading and writing that he purchased some land, bought the title of 'Gentleman' (as Roger Crab had done), and even took to wearing a long curly wig.[21] To some, this seemed like sheer hypocrisy – even the hats he sold were made from beaver-pelts (a fact he later came to regret) – but Tryon no doubt felt he had adapted his politics to fit in with the changing times.[22]

Tryon's works – forerunners of the modern self-help genre – continued to be anthologised for decades. He may not compare in intellectual rigour with his contemporaries John Locke and Isaac Newton, but he sold far more books than Newton did, appealing to a wide lay audience. Tryon's vegetarian philosophy – an eclectic concoction of notions culled from all over the world – was still being admired years after his death by the likes of Benjamin Franklin and Percy Bysshe Shelley. He was thus an important conduit, and the most powerful catalyst for Tryon's revamping of vegetarianism in the late seventeenth century, when radical vegetarians had dwindled, was the discovery of the Indian Brahmins. Having witnessed the challenge to man's rights over nature made by the radical pantheism of Winstanley and the Ranters, Tryon noticed the common ground with Hindu vegetarianism, and he embraced it with open arms. Above all, the Indians inspired Tryon with new conviction that a Golden Age of vegetarianism could still be achieved.

Eager to dispossess Western Europe of its monopoly over truth,

---

* Moses.

Thomas Tryon by Robert White (1703)

Tryon argued that the Indian wise men had devised their own 'natural religion' by studying nature and receiving divine revelations.[23] In addition, following the speculations of the travel writers (and some erroneous Renaissance translations of Philostratus), Tryon held that Pythagoras had travelled to India and taught the Brahmins his vegetarian philosophy. This contact with Pythagoras plugged the Brahmins into the network of ancient pagan philosophers, known to the Renaissance Neoplatonists as the *prisci theologi*, who were believed to have passed a pristine sacred theology between themselves and even, some thought, inherited doctrines from Moses.[24] Tryon intimated that Pythagoras had inherited his vegetarian philosophy from the antediluvians, so the Brahmins, who had inherited it from him, were the purest remnants of the paradisal tradition left on earth.[25]

He thought that the Brahmins and Moses essentially followed the one 'true Religion', which is 'the same in all places, and at all times'.[26] But whereas the Jews and Christians had corrupted their creed with schisms and wrathful appetites, the Brahmin priesthood – which stretched back millennia in a pure uninterrupted tradition – had preserved their sacred knowledge in its original form. Unenamoured of the malevolent Christian clergy of his own country, Tryon turned to the Brahmins and bowed down to them as the pre-eminent guardians of divine law.

Among the very first works Tryon published was the extraordinary pamphlet, *A Dialogue Between An East-Indian Brackmanny or Heathen-Philosopher, and a French Gentleman* (1683).[27] Reversing the stereotype of civilised Europeans and barbaric Indians, Tryon's Brahmin greets the Frenchman with ironic allusions to his acquisitive motives for venturing into India and questions him on the tenets and practices of Christians. The Brahmin's enlightened philosophy, his virtuous temperance, and his unassailable respect for animal life win a moral victory over the depraved and murderous European.[28]

Merging his voice entirely with the Brahmin's, Tryon rebuffs the arguments that had hitherto been used by others to denigrate Hinduism. He even defends the Indian practice of saving lice, for, as the Brahmin explains, if people were allowed to kill some animals they would soon believe they could go on to kill others 'and so by degrees come to kill men'.[29] The 'East-Indian Brackmanny' was Tryon's alter ego.[30] Although Tryon was trying to reconcile Indian vegetarianism to Judaeo-Christian beliefs, his ranking of Hindus above Christians was shocking and his anti-vegetarian enemy the Quaker controversialist John Field attacked him for having 'at once Unchristianed (as much as he can) all *Christendom*'.[31]

Abandoning some of the basic precepts of Christianity, Tryon espoused what he imagined to be the way of the Brahmins. Fusing the vegetarianism of his radical forebears with the Brahmins' concrete example, he announced with excitement that they have for 'many Ages ... led peaceable and harmless Lives, in *Unity* and *Amity* with the whole Creation; shewing all kind of *Friendship* and *Equality*, not only to those of their own *Species*, but to all other Creatures'.[32] They had achieved the very state that Robins, Crab, Winstanley and all the prelapsarians had dreamed of.

The travel literature about India emphasised that the Hindu diet was based on an ethical treatment of animals (indeed, the establishment of fearless harmony between man and the animals through the practice of non-violence was an ideal lauded in Sanskrit scriptures).[33] As George Sandys had commented in his translation of Pythagoras' speech in Ovid's *Metamorphoses* (1632), which Tryon read and quoted, the Indians had earned the trust of the animals by treating them with respect. Living in a social order reminiscent of the Golden Age, Sandys wrote excitedly, the Indians 'are so farre from eating of what ever had life, that they will not kill so much as a flea; so that the birds of the aire, and beasts of the Forrest, without feare frequent their habitations, as their fellow Cittisens'.[34] Tryon came to see the fair treatment of animals as the key to the restoration of Paradise. Tryon's Brahmin affirms that 'we hurt not any thing, therefore nothing hurts us, but live in perfect Unity and Amity with all the numberless Inhabitants of the four Worlds.'[35] By relinquishing flesh the vegetarian Hindus had attained physical and mental vigour and undone the Fall: 'We all drink Water, and the fragrant Herbs, wholsom Seeds, Fruits and Grains suffice us abundantly for Food,' declares Tryon's Brahmin, 'so we in the midst of a tempestuous troublesom World live Calm, and as it were in Paradise.'[36]

Inspired by Pythagoras' vegetarian conversion mission to India, Tryon began to imagine the state of 'perfect Love, Concord, and Harmony' he could institute in England – if only its citizens would convert to vegetarianism. Thinking of himself as a new Moses, or, even better, Pythagoras, Tryon told the English people that if they gave up eating meat like the Brahmins, they would achieve spiritual enlightenment, health and longevity, and their relationship with animals would transform from a state of perpetual war to one of Edenic peace.[37]

Tryon even looked to the Brahmins for a solution to the government's religious intolerance, by which he and his dissenting compatriots were routinely persecuted. Since the introduction of the Clarendon Code (1661–5) unlicensed religious meetings had been forcibly broken up, 2,000 Puritan ministers had been dismissed, 500 Quakers had been killed and 15,000 others suffered a variety of other punishments. Even after the Toleration Act of 1689 the problem persisted; Tryon's own publisher Andrew Sowle regularly had his printing shop smashed up and had even been threatened with death.[38] In arguments later echoed in John Locke's Letter Concerning Toleration (1689) Tryon called for universal religious tolerance. He recommended that England introduce the Indian Mughal's jezia system by which – as the Brahmin explains – anyone not adhering to the Islamic religion of the state simply paid an extra tax in return for 'unquestioned Liberty for the Exercise of our Religion'.[39] Dissenters meanwhile should emulate the Brahmins, he added, for as vegetarian pacifists they would avoid persecution because 'Governours would fear their Rising or Tumulting, no more than they do the Rebellion of *Sheep*, or *Lambs*, or an Insurrection of *Robin Red-Brests*'.[40] This was the pacifist philosophy of the Quakers and the Robins sect united with the vegetarian *ahimsa* of the Hindus and Jains.

Tryon fantasised that the Brahmins in India were the counterparts of the Puritans, Dissenters and religious radicals at home; this comparison had been made before, though often on less favourable terms. Pantheism, nudism, communism, sexual deviance, frugality and even the belief in reincarnation were all characteristics which contemporaries associated with both the Indian holy men and the home-grown religious dissidents.[41] In 1641 the Italian humanist Paganino Gaudenzio compared the vegetarian communist Pythagoreans and Brahmins with the Anabaptists.[42] Strabo's ancient Brahmins were pantheist apocalyptists and Alexander's Dandamis declared that anyone who followed nature 'would not be ashamed to go naked like himself, and live on frugal fare'.[43] Tryon himself was not inclined to nudism, but he did recommend the more socially acceptable practice of wearing as few clothes as possible.[44] But the resemblance to prelapsarian nudists was inescapable: 'their *Nakedness*', went one comparison of the Christian Adamite sect and the Indian fakirs in 1704, was their way of 'restoring themselves to the State of *Innocence*';[45] others, like Samuel Purchas, disbelieving their chastity, claimed that the Indian *yogis* were secretly just like the nudist orgiast '*Illuminate Elders of the Familists*, polluting themselves in all filthinesse'.[46] As early as the sixteenth century, the *Fardle of Facions* assumed that puritanical Indian women still enjoyed going 'buttoke banquetyng abrode' (shagging other men).[47] This accusation of hypocritical debauchery was a common slur made against suspect religious cults in Europe.

Tryon was not the first to try to turn the identification of Brahmins with puritanical Dissenters to advantage; others before him had seen the Brahmins as brothers-in-arms against a corrupt world. In 1671 the controversial Quaker George Keith and his co-author Benjamin Furly announced that the Brahmins were so virtuous that they 'rise up in judgment against the Christians of this age, and fill their faces with shame and confusion'.[48] They borrowed illustrative stories from Sir Edward Bysshe's version of Palladius,[49] and the Rotterdam Calvinist preacher Franciscus Ridderus whose writings anticipated Tryon's by giving his Brahmin character 'Barthrou Herri' lengthy 'Christlike' ser-

Naked Adamites from Bernard Picart, *Ceremonies et Coutumes Religieuses de Tous Les Peuples du Monde*

mons which he copied out of Rogerius' *Open Door*.[50] In 1683 Andrew Sowle presented the Brahmins as ideal vegetarian pacifists in *The Upright Lives of the Heathen*, an English selection of Bysshe's anthology of ancient writings, which Tryon may have helped produce (it ends by telling the reader to find out more in Tryon's *Brackmanny*, on sale in Sowle's shop for the bargain price of one penny).[51] And in 1687 one anonymous author, having read the travelogues of Henry Lord and Edward Terry, went nearly as far as Tryon by lamenting that the Hindus set a great example by 'extending their good Nature, Humanity and Pity, even to the very bruit Creatures' while shameful Christians were 'cruel and merciless towards our Beasts'.[52]

Hindu vegetarianism, as it was presented in the travelogues, had started to exert serious moral pressure on the conscience of Western Christians and Tryon rode this wave as far as it would go. His enthusiasm for the Brahmins peaked in his astonishing *Transcript Of Several Letters From Averroes . . . Also Several Letters from Pythagoras to the King of India* (1695), in which he had the nerve to fake an archival discovery of correspondence by Pythagoras and Averröes, the twelfth-century Spanish Islamic philosopher. Tryon appears to have seriously intended to convince the world that Pythagoras, Averröes and the Indian

Brahmins were all believers in the same divinely ordained vegetarian philosophy. So amusingly successful was his sham that the Sowle family reprinted it in the eighteenth century alongside *The Upright Lives of the Heathen*, but the work has more recently lain unidentified in library vaults.[53]

The *Transcript* climaxes in a dramatic reconstruction of Pythagoras' visit to the court of the Indian King, where he is ordered to defend his vegetarian philosophy against the cavils of the (as yet unconverted) Brahmins. The King has summonsed Pythagoras for illicitly spreading this new-fangled unorthodox doctrine of vegetarianism.[54] The King and the Brahmins throw at Pythagoras the same anti-vegetarian arguments that Tryon's contemporaries used against him, such as the God-given dominion over the animals and the heroic valour of hunting. But Pythagoras eventually wins the day, and thus India is converted to his doctrines.[55]

By making Pythagoras the original founder of Hinduism it may seem as if Tryon was imposing Western philosophy onto the East. But as it was to Hinduism that he turned to reconstruct Pythagoreanism – with the help of the Indian travelogues – Tryon was actually imposing what he knew of Eastern philosophy onto the West.

The travelogues, of course, are full of Orientalist projections – all European accounts of Hinduism were informed by the writers' Neo-platonist and Christian preconceptions – but they did also represent some genuine elements of Indian culture. At the very least, their report that there were people in India who taught and practised the principle of non-violence to all creatures was true. Were it not for the material existence of vegetarians in India, Thomas Tryon would never have developed his opinions and he certainly would not have been able to convey them with such clarity.

The vegetarian institutions Tryon's Pythagoras establishes in India come straight out of the Indian travelogues: animal hospitals,[56] the practice of saving animals destined for slaughter,[57] and special reverence for the cow on account of its usefulness.[58] Like the travel writers, Tryon's Pythagoras links pacifism and vegetarianism; he endorses the protection of vermin to clarify the total ban on violence and even institutes the taboo over sharing eating vessels with non-vegetarians.[59] He also recommends dubious practices such as the caste system[60] and the prohibition of widow remarriage.[61] These doctrines formed the backbone of Tryon's own edicts, some of which he set forth as

Studio of Jan Brueghel the Elder, *Adam and Eve in the Garden of Eden*, early 17th century.

Frans Snijders, *The Butcher's Shop*, c.1640–50.

Jan Brueghel the Elder and P.P. Rubens, *Adam and Eve in Paradise*, c.1615.
As Adam and Eve effect the Fall of man, the animals topple from herbivorous peace
into the predatory war of fallen nature: dogs prepare to pounce on a duck and the
leopard menacingly raises its paw.

RIGHT David Teniers the Younger, *In the Kitchen*, 1669.

The frontispiece of Christopher Plantin's Polyglot Bible (1569), in which the lion and wolf lie down in peace with the ox and lamb, symbolising the millennial harmony prophesied by Isaiah. Early Jesuit missionaries presented the Indian emperor, Akbar, (r. 1556–1605), with a copy and the motif was thereafter used frequently by the artists of the Mughal court.

This 17th-century ivory cabinet from Ceylon shows Adam and Eve in the Garden of Eden. Under European patronage, ivory carvers from South and East Asia produced devotional Christian objects for new churches in the East, as well as for export to Europe. Some early European travellers to Ceylon (now Sri Lanka) saw Buddhist vegetarianism as a vestige of Adam and Eve's harmonious vegetarian relation to the animals in Eden.

RIGHT *Iskandar* [Alexander] *meeting the Brahmins*, India, 1719. Alexander the Great's encounter with the Indian Brahmins (or 'gymnosophists' as the Greeks sometimes called them) in 327 BC was celebrated in both Europe and India as the quintessential clash of Eastern and Western culture.

BELOW 'Maître François', Alexander the Great meeting the Indian 'gymnosophists', or naked philosophers, Paris, c.1475-1480.

From a *Ragamala* (Garland of Melodies), Himachal Pradesh, India, 1685-1690.

OPPOSITE Banyans and Brahmins from Jan Huygen van Linschoten's *Itinerario*, 1596. 'The Brahmans are the most esteemed and most high-ranking among the Indians . . . They live on herbs, and abhor eating animals'. The Banyans 'do not eat or kill animals . . . an unmistakable influence of the Pythagorean notion of metempsychosis.'

Indian huts, country houses and villages near Goa from Jan Huygen van Linschoten's *Itinerario*, 1596. The 'Canarim' Indians 'abstain from the meat of cattle, pigs and oxen. These animals are held in particular veneration by them, because the people live under the same roof and eat the same food together with those animals'.

John Evelyn's *pietre dure* cabinet showing Orpheus charming the beasts.

School of Jan Brueghel the Elder, *Orpheus Charming the Animals, c.*1600-1610.

commandments for his followers, including the veiling of women after the age of seven.[62] He seems to have gathered some adherents around him, and may have been responsible for converting Robert Cook, the landowning 'Pythagorean philosopher' associated with the Quakers who 'neither eat fish, flesh, milk, butter, &c. nor drank any kind of fermented liquor, nor wore woollen clothes, or any other produce of animal, but linen', because, as he explained in 1691, his conscience told him 'I ought not to kill.'[63] In other words, as far as he was able, Tryon established a Brahminic vegetarian community in London.

It was with the help of Indian culture that Tryon freed himself from Christianity's anthropocentric value system and made a leap into another moral dimension. In the *Transcript* he did this with the figure of the Indian King. Dismissing the welfare of humans, the Indian King turns to the issue of animal rights, summarising it in starker terms than anyone in seventeenth-century England. Any argument against maltreating animals, he said, 'must proceed, either because they have a natural Right of being exempted from our Power, or from some mutual Contract and Stipulation agreed betwixt Man and them . . . if . . . the former, we must acknowledge our present Practise to be an Invasion; if the latter, Injustice'.[64] The idea that humans could make social contracts with animals had usually been discussed – by Thomas Hobbes among others – with derision.[65] The idea that animals had any right to be exempted from human power was an unorthodoxy of incomparable audacity. Animals were there for man's use; the most they could expect, according to Christian religious and philosophical legislators, as John Locke put it, was an exemption from cruel abuse. Tryon's Pythagoras, by contrast, argues that even without considering animal rights, it is vain to think that man 'has Right, because he has Power to Oppress'.[66] In this Tryon was answering Hobbes who had argued in 1651 that humans had rights over animals solely because they had the power to exert it (or 'might makes right').[67]

In complete contrast to the norms of his society, Tryon came firmly down on the side of attributing to animals a right to their lives regardless of human interests. He lobbied Parliament to defend the 'Rights and Properties of the helpless innocent creatures, who have no Advocates in this World'.[68] Where was the justification for killing animals, he demanded, when they were, in Tryon's radical deployment of political language, 'Fellow-Citizens of the World'?[69] They were God's children, created to live on earth and therefore 'have a Title by Nature's Charter to their Lives as well as you', he declaimed.[70] The 'True Intent and Meaning' of Christ's law to do unto others as we would be done by was, according to Tryon, 'to make all the Sensible Beings of the whole Creation easy, and that they might fully enjoy all the Rights and Priveleges granted them by the Grand Charter of the Creator'.[71] This spectacular piece of moral renegotiation was a radical step away from the orthodox Christian anthropocentric universe, and one that anticipates modern ecologists' value-laden claim for non-humans that 'they got here first'.

Tryon went even a step further. It was the animals' lack of language – according to Descartes among others – that signified their lack of reason. But Tryon artfully responded to this calumny by writing a series of striking ventriloquistic literary set-pieces, in which animals lament their plight in their own voice.[72] The animals, Tryon explained, never had a Tower of Babel so they all communicated perfectly even without articulate speech.[73] Cattle complain that 'we suffer many, and great Miseries, Oppression and Tyranny,'[74] while the birds protest that humans 'violate our part, and natural Rights'.[75] The animals point out that the reciprocal favours that pass between a domestic beast and its owner – food and shelter for milk, wool and labour – constitute a tacit contract, the breach of which is gross ingratitude and treachery. Once again, the ideal alternative is represented by the Hindus who allow animals 'all those Privileges and Freedoms that the Creator had given';[76] 'the People called *Bannians*,' said Tryon, 'are some of the strictest Observers of Gods Law, (*viz.*) doing unto those of their own kind, and to all inferior Animals and Creatures as they would be done unto.'[77]

Using the behaviour of the Hindus as a permanent backdrop to his enthused writings, Tryon extended his critique of man's treatment of animals into a wholesale attack on European degradation of the natural world. He observed that man was the only species so unclean that it irreparably defiled and polluted its own living quarters: 'even the very *Swine*, will keep their Styes and Kennels sweet and clean,' he exclaimed.[78] Like several of his contemporaries, he was disgusted by urban pollution. In 'The abundance of *Smoke* that the multitude of Chimnies send forth', he detected 'a keen sharp sulpherous Quality', which he blamed for increasing humidity in the air and causing '*Dis-*

eases of the *Breast'*. He deplored the peer pressure that had fuelled the spread of tobacco-smoking, correctly recognising the symptoms of addiction, some of the health impacts, and that children of smokers were more likely to pick up the habit. He even complained against passive smoking as it did 'so defile the common Air'.[79]

In a cycle that anticipates ecological thought, Tryon observed pollution escaping into *'Rivers* which receive the Excrements of Cities or Towns', enveloping the habitat of other species such as fish, and then returning – in the form of caught fish – to humans as polluted food.[80] In Tryon's 'The Complaints of the Birds', American birds protest against the destruction of forests by encroaching Europeans: 'thou takest liberty to cut them down . . . we are thereby disseized of our antient Freeholds and Habitations,' they cry.[81] The problem with this world, declaimed Tryon, was 'this proud and troublesome Thing, called *Man*, that fills the Earth with Blood, and the Air with mutherous Minerals and Sulphur'.[82]

Tryon warned that the excessive demand for animal products like wool was over-stretching natural resources, especially since intensive farming had turned animals into 'a grand Commodity, and (as it were) a Manufacture'.[83] He deplored the phenomenon of consumerism which 'causes great seeming Wants to be where there is not real or natural cause for it'.[84] People wouldn't pay a farthing for pointless luxuries like civet and coffee if they were available on Hampstead Heath, 'and if Hogs Dung were as scarce, its probable it might be as much in esteem'. He called on Europeans to stop 'ransack[ing] the furthest corners of the Earth for *Dainties'*, encouraging them instead to be satisfied with the produce of their own soil.[85] Meanwhile, Tryon imagined, the Hindus lived in total harmony with creation. Fruit and vegetables required less labour-intensive methods of production. By restricting themselves to the vegetable diet, the Hindus subsisted without needing to rape and pillage the planet as Westerners did.[86]

Even though his universe was essentially theocentric,[87] by putting man in the balance with the animals Tryon anticipated the shift from anthropocentrism to the biocentrism of modern ecological thought. While orthodox Christians tended to insist that all creatures had been made solely for man's use, Hinduism helped Tryon to develop a system that resembles, and would later be developed into, environmentalism. Surprising though it may seem, given modern history's usual emphasis on the West's overbearing influence on its colonies, the encounter with India in the seventeenth century opened the door to a different moral premise and this in turn stimulated a revision of European thought and practice.

Tryon, however, did not place all his eggs in one altruistic basket. He emphasised that vegetarianism was also in the interests of people themselves. Far more efficiently than alchemy, he said, vegetarianism profited mankind by giving them the secret to lifelong health and making them rich by saving money on food. But some of his 'self-interest' arguments were the most unconventional of all his ideas. So before leaving the image of Tryon as a prophet of modern environmentalism, we should delve a bit deeper into his philosophy.

It all goes back to the 1650s when Tryon's attention was first drawn to the Brahmins. Tryon's favourite book was the *Three Books of Occult Philosophy* by the sixteenth-century arch-magician from Cologne, Heinrich Cornelius Agrippa.[88] Tryon probably acquired the 1651 English translation when, as a hatter's apprentice in London, he was trying to train as a magician. This manual of demonic magic was Tryon's Bible and although he never once named Agrippa (no doubt wishing to avoid censure for having devoted himself to the work of a notorious heretic), he nevertheless built his ideas around Agrippa and frequently copied out whole gobbets from the *Occult Philosophy* into his own works.[89] In Agrippa's chapter 'Of abstinence . . . and ascent of the mind', Tryon came across the magician's recommendation that aspiring wizards and those who wished to communicate with God should pursue the vegetarian diet of Pythagoras and the Brahmins:

> We must therefore in taking of meats be pure, and abstinent, as the *Pythagorian* Philosophers, who keeping a holy and sober table, did protract their life in all temperance . . . So the *Bragmani* did admit none to their colledge, but those that were abstinent from wine, from flesh, and vices . . .[90]

Tryon was overawed by Agrippa's instruction and made it his favourite maxim, repeating it time and time again and adapting it to his own purposes. Shrewdly, he spliced these pagan practices into the mainstream of Western beliefs by claiming that this diet was pursued by all the 'Wise Ancients' including the biblical patriarchs.[91]

Agrippa's recipe of abstinence was famous among the mystics and magicians of the 1650s, and it may have been the inspiration behind the fasting techniques employed by Thomas Tany, John Pordage and even Roger Crab, who believed, like Agrippa, that ascetic purity was the path to making contact with the 'aerial spirits'.[92] Justice Durand Hotham, in his widely read *Life of Jacob Behmen* (1654) noted that many had tried Agrippa's dietary short cut to spiritual illumination.[93]

The ancient philosophers of Egypt, Babylon, Persia and Ethiopia held a legendary status as the most proficient adepts in magic, astrology and abstruse spiritual philosophy.[94] As one of Tryon's contemporaries wrote: 'all those who apply themselves to the Study of these *Ænigma's*, go into the *Indies*, to improve by their Skill, and to discover there the Secrets of *Natural Magick*'.[95] Even John Locke asked a friend in India to find out if the Indians really managed to work magic. Vegetarianism was seen as the key to the Brahmins' spiritual enlightenment and magical powers.[96]

It was from Agrippa that Tryon picked up the idea that the Brahmins were great wise men, and since they were the only surviving strain of the *prisci theologi* after the demise of the ancient Egyptians and Greeks, it was logical for anyone looking for vestiges to turn to them. It was also from Agrippa that Tryon absorbed the notion that man was a microcosm, or compact image, of the universe. Like the Renaissance Neoplatonist Pico della Mirandola, Tryon believed that both Pythagoras and Moses held this doctrine. But Tryon transformed this archaic idea by arguing that it was their fundamental rationale for vegetarianism.[97]

Since man and the universe were both created in the image of God it followed that everything in the universe had a corresponding miniature equivalent in man, and between these corresponding parts Tryon believed there was a hidden sympathetic affinity.[98] Agrippa taught that man could exert magical powers by exploiting these 'sympathetic' forces; but Tryon became much more worried about the influence they had *on* man.[99] If you ate an animal, he warned, the part of your nature that corresponded with its nature would be stirred up and you would become like the beast you had eaten. 'For all things have a sympathetical Operation,' he explained, and 'every thing does secretly awaken its like property'.[100]

Still worse, when an animal was killed, in its flesh welled up all the spirits of fury, hatred and revenge, 'for when any Creature perceives its Life in danger, there is such struggling and horror within, as none can imagine.'[101] The result of eating a plate of spiritual turmoil was obvious: 'those fierce, revengeful Spirits that proceed from the Creature, when the *painful Agonies of Death* are upon it . . . fail not to accompany the *Flesh*, and especially the *Blood*, and have their internal operation, and have their impression on those that eat it, by a secret, hidden way of *Simile*.[102] The furious spirits in dead animal flesh stirred up violent passions in the consumer, and by occult communication they could even bring down malign astrological influences causing famine, war and pestilence.[103] Herbs and seeds, on the other hand, did not lose their lively seminal virtues when harvested.[104] '*Vegetives*,' he explained (punning on the Latin *vegeto* – to live), are 'filled with Powerful Lively brisk Spirit and Vertue.'[105] Eating them made the eater so.

It may seem like a paradox that Tryon forbade eating animals out of both reverence for their life and disgust at the pollution they bring, but this was a dual ethic shared by Christian ascetics such as John Chrysostom and Hindu scriptures such as the *Laws of Manu* which regulated meat-eating because of both 'the disgusting origin of flesh and the cruelty of fettering and slaying corporeal beings'.[106] Tryon united them in his critique of meat-eating.

Tryon carried Agrippa's theories of sympathy into his ideas of the afterlife, and fused them with the belief in reincarnation that he read about in the Indian travelogues. In a complete reversal of orthodox priorities, Tryon gave greater weight to Pythagorean-Hindu doctrines than to Judaeo-Christian revelation and created his own hybrid metaphysical Neoplatonic-Christian-Hinduism. The idea of Christians converting to pagan beliefs was probably the most abhorrent scenario anyone could imagine. And yet Tryon did so with delight. Like Agrippa, he believed that after death badly behaved souls sympathetically attracted to themselves the form of the animal they had behaved most like during life. Agrippa himself had moulded this system by fusing ideas from Plato, Plotinus, the Kabbala, Hermeticism and the heretical Church father Origen. But Tryon added the vegetarian idea that it was flesh-eating that constituted the cardinal sin that made one take on the form of a vicious beast: 'such as have by continual Violence Oppressed and Killed the Unrevengeful Animals, their Souls and Spirits shall be precipitated and revolved into the most Savage and Brutish Bodies.'[107]

This was similar to the received wisdom about Hindu reincarnation – that immoral behaviour causes the soul to be reincarnated in an animal – but Tryon insisted that neither he nor the Hindus believed that animals had immortal souls.[108] Instead of reincarnating into animal bodies on earth, Tryon explained that the afterlife was more like an everlasting nightmare, which did not have material existence: 'These strange phansies,' he explained, 'put the captivated Soul into unexpressible fears & agonies . . . continuing forevermore in this doleful torture & perplexity, yea the predominating quality gives the form to the new Body, *viz.* of a Dog, Cat, Bear, Lion, Fox, Tyger, Bull, Goat, or other savage Beasts'.[109]

Tryon tried to reconcile this with the Christian belief in resurrection, pointing out that in the Bible it said that outside the gates of heaven 'are Dogs, Bears, Lyons and the like Beasts of Prey'; these, Tryon claimed, were the souls of wicked men.[110] He deftly used the powers of microcosmic sympathy to explain both the Christian and Hindu system, thus suggesting that they were branches of the same true religion. Needless to say, he did not fool his adversaries. John Field – ever on the lookout for chances to discredit Tryon – was appalled, demanding 'where doth the Scripture so say, or speak of being Cloathed with Hellish shapes in the next World?'[111]

By stepping outside the usual bounds prescribed by the religious authorities in Europe, Tryon developed a metaphysical rationale for vegetarianism which went hand in hand with his physical and ethical arguments. The breadth of his appeal must have been rooted in the diversity of his ideas, there being something in his philosophy for everyone, from the mundane methods of penny-pinching to the grander ideals of prelapsarianism. With remarkable cogency, Tryon treated the Hindus as his guide at every step of the way, reaching from hopeless utopianism down to serious suggestions for social and political reform. His principal accomplishment was welding the novel vegetarian philosophy attributed to the Brahmins with the familiar Neoplatonist and biblical traditions he had grown up with. He reduced this combination into a lifestyle philosophy, which would, he hoped, prevent the hellish degradation of man and nature that he had witnessed in Barbados.

SIX

John Evelyn: Salvation in a Salad

Theophilus: There's a superanuated Custom kept up among the
  Antients; that to gratify the Appetite violates the Creation . . .
Arnoldus: Was this the Primitive Practice of our former
  Ancestors?
Theophilus: I don't say it was, I discourse the *Brachmans* that
  offer this Argument. No Man has a Commission to create Life,
  no Man therefore by any Law or Custom ought to take Life
  away; which if he do, he makes himself an Instrument of
  unnatural Cruelty, and his Body a Sepulchre to bury dead
  Carcasses in . . . Were this Argument approv'd of, it would, I
  suspect, overthrow our design of Angling.

Richard Franck, *Northern Memoirs . . . The Contemplative
and Practical Angler* (1694)[1]

In the first comprehensive account of salmon- and trout-fishing in
Scotland, Richard Franck set out the opposition between the Brahmins'
and the Christians' value of animal life. Franck originally penned his
miscellaneous work in 1658 as a republican riposte to *The Compleat
Angler* (1653), in which the Royalist Izaak Walton had tactfully
submerged his attack on Cromwellian politics in scaly similes. As an
ex-Cromwellian soldier fusing Hinduism in the 1690s with his
outdated political Puritanism and mysticism, Franck had much in
common with (and may have been directing his dialogue at) Thomas
Tryon. Franck's character Theophilus, who takes the part of the Hindus,
transposes the elements of Tryon's *nom de plume* Philotheos.

Like Tryon, Franck was tempted by the dreamy similarity between
Indian vegetarianism and Edenic harmony, but ultimately he overrode
this by evoking the rival idea of Eden according to which animals
offered themselves up willingly to man – a notion backed up by the

Gospel's eradication of food taboos. But this was a bait to hook the unwary – for the vice Franck was trying to reel in was gluttony. Franck's most potent net was woven from the common threads of 'Hinduism' and Puritanism: their voices united in condemning *unnecessary* slaughter for the riotous gratification of excessive appetite. Under the influence of Hinduism – and particularly the account by Edward Terry – Franck shifted the Puritanical detestation of wasting God's gifts into his specific attack on wasting beings to whom God had given the inherently valuable property of life.[2] It was this absorption of Hindu vegetarianism that came to occupy the centre ground in social critiques of the late seventeenth century, espoused not just by political outsiders like Tryon and Franck, but by the most prominent thinkers of the intellectual world.

John Evelyn (1620–1706) is most famous for his diary, which, like that of his friend Samuel Pepys, records the quotidian minutiae of seventeenth-century society. A shining torch of the Enlightenment, Evelyn was one of the first members and secretary of the Royal Society, the internationally admired institution of empirical learning. He was a great friend of the eminent scientist Robert Boyle, and, as one of the trustees of the Boyle lectures, a bastion of the new orthodoxy of latitudinarian Anglicanism and Newtonian science. Though a Royalist sympathiser, Evelyn avoided active service during the Civil War by absenting himself on a Grand Tour of Europe. He made friends with the exiled royal family in Paris, and after the Restoration served in various philanthropic political posts until, dismayed by debauchery and intemperance at court,[3] he retired to Sayes Court in Deptford, the private estate of his father-in-law.

During his abdication from public service in Cromwell's era, Evelyn took up gardening, developing Sayes Court into a masterpiece of edible design. Thirty-eight beds of vegetables and a vast orchard of 300 fruit trees led into 'the apple-tree walk' which terminated in a moated island covered in waving swards of asparagus, raspberries, a mulberry tree and a blossoming enclosure of fruit bushes.[4] Later he moved on to the garden at his own home at Wotton in Surrey, where he supplied his wife and household with freshly grown produce, and his nation with advice on everything from tree-planting to city-planning.

As old age cast shadows over the garden of his soul, Evelyn drew together a lifetime's experience in horticulture to compose his *magnum opus*, the *Elysium Britannicum* or *Paradisium Revisitum*. He never

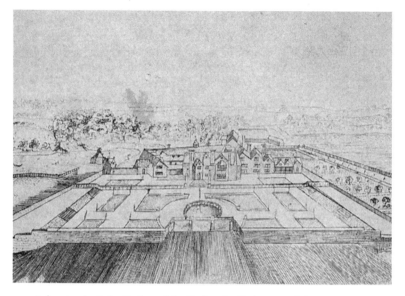

A drawing by John Evelyn of the Evelyn family house at Wotton, Surrey, from the terrace above the gardens, 1653

completed this compendious work, and it has only recently been edited from his surviving array of manuscripts. He did publish one chapter, however, as it blossomed into the full-length book, *Acetaria. A Discourse of Sallets* (1699). This was filled with instructions on how to grow, pick, prepare and eat salad, from the sight-enhancing, anti-flatulent fennel to the eighteen types of pain-quelling, lust-calming lettuce. In the seventeenth century eating a dish of raw leafy vegetables was something of a novelty, out of line with the predominant valorisation of red meat. But with the increasing interest in botany and the rise of gentlemanly vegetable gardening, to which Evelyn himself contributed, salads were to enjoy a vogue. Sowing seeds no longer needed be the sole prerogative of peasants – the most noble foot could grace a spade. On the face of it, *Acetaria* was designed, as other commentators have pointed out, to encourage the use of salads in the English diet.[5]

But, like Thomas Tryon, Evelyn also had a theological agenda. His Preface declared that he wished to 'recall the World, if not altogether to their Pristine *Diet*, yet to a much more *wholsome* and *temperate* than is now in Fashion'.[6] '*Adam*, and his yet innocent Spouse,' mused Evelyn, 'fed on Vegetables and other Hortulan Productions before the fatal

Lapse,' and even until the Flood God did not 'suffer them to slay the more innocent Animal'.[7] In the course of his work, Evelyn was carried away by the force of his own arguments and ended up writing one of the most scholarly panegyrics of vegetarianism.[8]

The belief that the prelapsarian diet was healthy and virtuous appears to have become almost an established norm by the end of the seventeenth century. In common with many of his gardening contemporaries – such as Ralph Austen and John Parkinson – Evelyn's botanical interests and lifelong practical and theoretical work on gardens aimed to recreate a garden like Eden.[9] The famous gardening expert in the generation before Evelyn, William Coles, displayed this artfully in his *Adam in Eden* (1657) and he too regarded the vegetable diet as a path to health and long life.[10] The garden, according to Evelyn, was 'A place of all terrestrial enjoyments the most resembling *Heaven*, and the best representation of our lost felicitie.'[11] Gardens were also like encyclopaedias. Knowing all about plants – and Evelyn's contemporaries did try to make their botanical knowledge as comprehensive as possible – was like knowing God's creation as Adam had known it in Paradise. Gardening was Adam's occupation before the Fall; therefore to garden was to relive the life of Adam. Gardening, said Evelyn, was 'the most innocent, laudable, and purest of earthly felicities, and such as does certainly make the neerest approaches to that *Blessed state*',[12] and he extended this common project into the realm of diet. Adam lived on raw vegetables and fruit in Eden, so if one wanted to live like Adam in Paradise, there was only one diet for it. Many herbs grew wild ('every hedge affords a Sallet'), and were therefore obtainable without labour, just like food before the Fall.[13] Composing salad was the original culinary art form: it was 'clean, innocent, sweet, and Natural . . . compar'd with the Shambles Filth and *Nidor*, Blood and Cruelty'.[14]

Evelyn complemented this dietary idealism by trying to establish a more harmonious relationship with animals. Just like collecting all plants together in one place, gathering animals to live in harmony was a potent symbol of primeval harmony. Like Pepys he condemned bear-, bull- and badger-baiting as 'butcherly sports or rather barbarous cruelties',[15] and he even tried to recreate Eden by setting up a zoo. Evelyn had been inspired by the big-cat menageries of the Turks, but he settled for a more modest collection of tortoises, squirrels and birds.[16] In an emblematic representation of his desire to live in harmony with nature, he personally commissioned an elaborate ebony cabinet, now held the Victoria and Albert Museum, decorated with hard stone and gilt-bronze plaques depicting the mythical Greek vegetarian, Orpheus, taming the animals with his music.[17]

As a Royalist, Evelyn was a long way from the republican vegetarians who retreated into hermetic solitude, but his retreat into gardening was no less political. He visited Thomas Bushell in his vegetarian cave, and wrote in 1658–9 to Sir Thomas Browne and Robert Boyle (who had also written a paper on salads[18]) that he thought gardening was an ideal around which the defeated Royalists could rally.[19] There in their little Edens, Englishmen could recreate the monarchy Adam enjoyed over the creation, living as 'a society of the *paradisi cultores*, persons of antient simplicity, Paradisean and Hortulan saints'.[20] As a collective community, Evelyn imagined they would live like the abstinent Carthusian friars, sheltered from the malign political world, but spearheading scientific investigation and progress. Although a naïve ideal, it was just such ideas, in line with Francis Bacon's *Solomon's House*, that led to the formation of the Royal Society.[21]

Sir Thomas Browne (1605–82), the famous Royalist physician and historian of gardens, was a particularly appropriate person for Evelyn to write to. In 1650, when vegetarianism was all the rage among the radicals, Browne reflected on its theological and medical implications in his famously witty collection of essays, *Pseudodoxia Epidemica* or *Vulgar Errors*. He hinted that God might have sent the Flood to punish people for eating flesh (a view he extrapolated from the natural-rights philosopher, Hugo Grotius) and suggested that God permitted flesh because the Flood 'had destroyed or infirmed the nature of vegetables'. The virtuous continued to abstain, however, and the Pythagoreans and the 'Bannyans' still did. All this showed that 'there is no absolute necessity to feed on any [animals]'; returning to the vegetarian diet, he concluded, might even 'prolong our days'.[22]

Evelyn was a respected gentleman and a family man; his position in the Royal Society ensured his adherence to social norms; even in his diary – in stark contrast to Pepys' frank confessions of fondling women's breasts and committing all sorts of peccadilloes – he maintained perpetual decorum, and 'never used its pages to reveal the secrets of the heart', as Virginia Woolf once complained.[23] So he avoided anything unseemly in his advocacy of vegetarianism, keeping his distance from mystic counterparts like Thomas Tryon by air-brushing them out of his anthology of herbivores. (Tryon requited this with mutual silence, either ignorant of Evelyn, or too much of an egotist to acknowledge his rival, except perhaps once in a miscellaneous work he might have edited.)[24] Evelyn's vegetarian idealism was a nostalgic grasp at human perfection, but it was always laced with stern-faced pragmatism. His lasting influence was inspiring a country-wide delight in gardening, and encouraging unrepentant carnivores, such as Pepys, to experiment more extensively with the bounty of fruit and vege-tables.[25]

For most of his life at least, Evelyn relished good dishes of flesh; about a third of the recipes in a manuscript cookbook he wrote for his wife contain meat products, and even some recipes in *Acetaria* acknowledge that the salad is to serve as an accompaniment to mutton broth or minced beef. His diary entries – recording his delectation of oysters and especially home-caught game – reveal that he did not worry too much about what he actually ate; indeed he insisted that there was 'no positive prohibition' on eating flesh.[26] Perhaps he considered himself vegetarian – indeed a vegetable! – even when he ate meat, for he observed that meat and men were made out of digested vegetation, so man 'becoming an *Incarnate Herb*, and Innocent *Cannibal*, may truly be said to devour himself'.[27] Only when he was staving off death in old age did Evelyn subject himself to a strict diet (which made his wife deeply anxious); this was apparently for the sake of his health, but perhaps the experience of writing *Acetaria* finally determined him to purify himself for the world that was to come.[28]

Beneath Evelyn's polite compromising surface, however, lay a true passion. With a literal-mindedness that it is difficult to comprehend today, Evelyn, like many of his contemporaries, fervently believed that Christ's second coming was on its way. His desire to reform the world to the conditions of Paradise was bound up with his preparation for Judgement Day. The idea of an establishment figure such as Evelyn espousing a religious theme usually associated with the radical mid-century may appear surprising, but many of his colleagues at the Royal Society were following Bacon's lead, trying to recover the universal knowledge enjoyed by Adam in preparation for the millennium.[29] Evelyn strove to differentiate himself from the radical Fifth Monarchy Men and other millenarian groups,[30] but his impulses have much in common with Tryon's yearning to recreate Paradise. Like Tryon, he quoted Isaiah's prophecy of the millennium and claimed that Christ's kingdom would be vegetarian: 'the *Hortulan* Provision of the *Golden*

Age,' he said, 'fitted all *Places, Times* and *Persons*; and when Man is restor'd to that State again, it will be as it was in the Beginning.'[31]

Like Tryon also, though the other way round, Evelyn transformed into a truth of immediate relevance the old legend that religious knowledge had been passed down from Adam to the nephews of Noah, through the British Druids, to the Brahmins and thence to Pythagoras and Plato. The pagans, he said, retained 'some opinions, agreeable to the primitive truth'. Evelyn did not regard the Brahmins as a superior authority to Christian priests, as Tryon did, but the genealogy he gave them illuminated them with a spark of divinity: 'it was from the people of God that they received their antient Traditions.'[32] Along with the Brahmins and Pythagoreans, Evelyn noted that the ancient Chaldaeans, Assyrians and Egyptians were vegetable-eaters, and that this had made them 'more Acute, Subtil, and of deeper Penetration'.[33] Such beliefs, then, were not confined to marginal eccentrics like Tryon; they appear to have been widespread. Evelyn's mentor John Beale joined with their friend and fellow fruit-enthusiast Samuel Hartlib in believing that the return of the Golden Age was about to be fulfilled, and added that the ancient knowledge recovered by the modern Europeans, Paracelsus and Robert Fludd had been passed down to them from the Eastern gymnosophists via the Druids.[34]

Given his belief in their common roots, Evelyn was particularly interested in the similarities between Christianity and Hinduism. In his own copy of John Marshall's account of 'the Heathen Priests commonly called Bramines' (published in the *Philosophical Transactions of the Royal Society*) he excitedly pencilled marginalia on the features of Hinduism that appeared to agree with Christianity. He was intrigued to discover that the Hindus believed in a supreme immaterial God, heaven, hell and eternal life, that they practised ascetic fasting, and had a story about the original man in a garden being tempted by a woman, and of a flood destroying the earth until it was repopulated by a small band of survivors.[35] Evelyn regarded the Hindus as distant relics of divine tradition, and this can only have spurred his interest in them. He was also an avid reader of the Indian travelogues; as well as the ancient Greek records on India and Bysshe's *Palladius*, Evelyn had pored over the modern descriptions of India by Garcia d'Orta, Jacob Bondt, Johann Albrecht von Mandelslo, Duarte Barbosa, Pietro della Valle and others.[36] Although he did not share Tryon's enthusiasm, the Indians nevertheless played a crucial role in his vegetarian argument.

The biggest obstacle to Evelyn's proselytisation of the 'herby-diet' was that most people thought it was not just ordinary to eat animals, but necessary for survival. While it may originally have been possible to live on vegetables, they thought that Noah's Flood had sapped the earth of all its goodness, leaving the vegetables less nutritious than they had been; and that the human constitution had been slowly degraded and was now so feeble it needed the stronger nourishment of animal flesh.

To combat this, Evelyn trawled through ancient, medieval, Renaissance and modern texts 'to shew how possible it is by so many Instances and Examples, to live on wholsome Vegetables, both long and happily'.[37] Unfortunately for Evelyn, nearly all the vegetarians he found existed only in ancient records. Pythagoras, Adam and Eve, the inhabitants of the Golden Age were all long gone, shrouded in aeons of dust and beyond the reach of empirical observation.

But the Brahmins saved the day. In a triumphant declaration (and trying to conceal that the Brahmins were the only living example he could name), Evelyn cited 'the *Indian Bramins*, Relicts of the ancient *Gymnosophists* to this Day, observing the Institutions of their Founder' 'who eat no Flesh at all'. These foreign vegetarians were not the unverifiable products of hearsay, but the extant people whose habits had frequently been recorded, as Evelyn proudly put it, in 'the Reports of such as are often conversant among many Nations and People', and 'who to this Day, living on *Herbs* and *Roots*, arrive to incredible Age, in constant Health and Vigour'.[38] He thought of India as a living Eden, a place 'the most pleasant & smiling of the World' where plants grew in their paradisiacal perfection, and he credited the travellers' reports that the Garden of Eden had been situated on 'Adam's hill' in Sri Lanka.[39] The Golden Age itself might not be achievable, but vegetarianism was the closest mankind could get.

The fact that the Hindus were still alive provided one of the few pieces of concrete empirical evidence that the vegetable diet was really viable. It was empirical evidence that his colleagues at the Royal Society demanded, rather than the heap of classical authorities he had accumulated. Evelyn envisaged a wholesale experimental investigation into this vegetarian people designed to determine what exactly made them capable of living solely on vegetables 'whether attributable to the *Air* and *Climate, Custom, Constitution,* &c.' It was his opinion that such an enquiry would prove that living on vegetables was something all humans could do.

Evelyn has been hailed as a forebear of modern environmentalism for his campaign against urban degradation and for encouraging forest conservation and replanting. He revered trees as sacred, especially ancient natural ones, 'such as were never prophaned by the inhumanity of edge tooles'. Evelyn harked back to the Druidic sacred groves and noticed that sylvan rites were scattered across the world – from Abraham's *Quercetum* to the Indians' holy Banian Tree.[40] His famous treatise *Sylva, or a Discourse of Forest Trees* (1664) successfully encouraged English landowners to plant much-needed timber trees, which had been consumed by the greedy furnaces of the iron industry and ravaged by desperate commoners during the interregnum. Forests provided shelter for game, and the trees themselves produced food such as chestnuts ('a lusty, and masculine food for Rustics'), beech-mast and acorns ('heretofore the Food of Men ... till their luxurious Palats were debauched'). Careful planting could provide country people with most of their food and drink 'even out of the Hedges and Mounds', making England more self-sufficient. Not only an act of political restoration, tree-planting, he concluded, was akin to God's foresting of Paradise.[41] Evelyn even lobbied Parliament to introduce laws to curb air pollution, revolted, like Tryon, by the 'horrid stinks, uiderous and unwholsome smells' emitted by the meat manufacturers, and the 'rotten Dung, loathsome and common Lay Stalls; whose noisome Steams, wafted by the Wind, poison and infect the ambient Air and vital Spirits, with those pernicious Exhalations'.[42]

But although many of these themes seem similar to Tryon, Evelyn's universe was fundamentally different. The existence of Hindus did help Evelyn to propose a more harmonious relationship with nature, and to reverse the artificial habits of urban society. But Hinduism did not make Evelyn step outside the confines of his religious orthodoxy. Nature did not have a value independent from mankind in the way it did for Tryon; nature, for Evelyn, was just part of God's man-centred Providence. For Evelyn, creating harmony in and with nature was just a part of the human spiritual quest and a prerequisite for the millennium.

Nevertheless, whether it was his original intention or not, Evelyn did formulate a new position for the status of man's relations with animals. Having empirically demonstrated that the vegetable diet was viable, Evelyn shifted the ground on which stood the usual justification for killing and eating animals. While most regarded meat-eating as a necessary cruelty – determined by the order of nature and the constitution of man – Evelyn had shown it to be nutritionally unnecessary. If meat-eating was unnecessary, the cruelty it entailed could be considered morally reprehensible. Evelyn did make emotional and moral appeals against 'the cruel Butcheries of so many harmless Creatures; some of which we put to merciless and needless Torment'. Now that he had shown that it was possible to live by the innocent sport of gardening without shedding a drop of blood, he could judge that meat-eating was cruelty and intemperance.[43]

A similar idea is suggested in Book XV of Ovid's *Metamorphoses* where Pythagoras points out that 'The prodigall Earth abounds with gentle food;/ Affording banquets without death or blood.'[44] But Evelyn made it relevant by transforming it from an ancient poetic ideal into a scientific observation. In that the Brahmins were a keystone in Evelyn's rational, empirically substantiated argument, Hinduism had a role in developing a new position with regard to animals.

The case for or against Brahmin vegetarianism became the subject of a much wider controversy at the end of the seventeenth century. The disagreement escalated into a pitched battle between the so-called 'Moderns' (who believed that modern science had advanced humanity to its highest pinnacle ever) and the 'Ancients' (who held that antique civilisations were superior). Evelyn, who had always tight-roped between the two, found that the Brahmins suited his compromise perfectly: they had the hallowed stamp of antiquity *and* stood up to modern empirical scrutiny. But others thought that simplistic conjectures about ancient vegetarians were outweighed by the statistical evidence on modern ascetic monks at home. 'There are many Monastical persons now that live abstemiously all their lives,' wrote Thomas Burnet, chaplain to William of Orange, in *The Sacred Theory of the Earth* (1684–91), 'and yet they think an hundred years a very great age amongst them.' Burnet concluded that vegetarianism 'might have some effect, but not possibly to that degree and measure that we speak of.'[45]

The ambassador to the Dutch, Sir William Temple (1628–99), picked up the gauntlet as principal protagonist of the Ancients and was later defended by his secretary Jonathan Swift in *A Tale of a Tub* and *The Battle of the Books* (1704).[46] Temple argued, like Evelyn (who admired Temple's garden estate), that conclusions based on modern Catholic monks were nugatory because people would have to be vegetarian for generations before purging themselves of the malignant effects of meat-eating. It was necessary instead to find examples who had sustained vegetarianism for many ages. The Brahmins, observed Temple, were the most ancient of all philosophers and he made them the heroes of his 'Essay upon the Ancient and Modern Learning' (1690). The Moderns were dwarves standing on the shoulders of giants and could see a long way, he conceded; but the Greek and Roman ancients had been standing on the shoulders of even greater giants – the Brahmins. These Indian philosophers were the originators of Greek ideas from vegetarianism to the eternity of matter and the four cardinal virtues, which, he said, 'seem all to be wholly *Indian*'. Their modern descendants, 'the present *Banians*', had preserved their secret to long life which had long since been lost in the West. They were the only people to have carried into a state of advanced civilisation the original laws of nature which were elsewhere only visible in primitive tribes. 'Their Justice, was exact and exemplary,' said Temple of the Brahmins, 'their Temperance so great, that they lived upon Rice or Herbs, and upon nothing, that had sensitive Life.' 'It may look like a Paradox to deduce Learning, from Regions accounted commonly, so barbarous and rude,' he declared, but it was only the bigoted Eurocentrism of the Moderns that had erased the fact that the West's greatest qualities were derived from the ancient East.[47] Temple's dressing up of the Brahmins in the garb of the Enlightenment was such a powerful spin that when the Modern chaplain William Wotton refuted Temple, he did so by going for Pythagoras' jugular and lambasting the Brahmins. Their vegetarianism, he argued, was based on nothing but the doctrine of transmigration – 'a precarious idle Notion, which these besotted *Indians* do so blindly believe, that they are afraid of killing a Flea or a Louse'. The Brahmins' chief employment for the last three thousand years, concluded Wotton derisively, has been depriving themselves of the lawful conveniences of life.[48]

Freed from its superstitious husk and recommended as a rational pursuit of nature's laws, Indian vegetarianism was championed by some of the most admired thinkers of the day. At exactly the same time that Tryon was flooding the popular market with his spiritual polemics, Evelyn and Temple were enshrining the Indian vegetarians in the mainstream of intellectual debate. The Brahmins were held up as torches lighting the way to a true understanding of health, nutrition and an ethical responsibility towards nature.

SEVEN

The Kabbala Stripped Naked

Baron Franciscus Mercurius van Helmont (1618–98) had never been comfortable with the settled life of a manorial lord. He had been persecuted by the Inquisition in his Catholic homeland of Louvain, near Brussels, and had, at an early age, escaped to become a 'wandering hermit' in more liberal countries. Filled with philosophical ardour, in 1670 he set out on a quest to England, determined to propagate a great theological discovery: that reincarnation was a true doctrine, compatible with the fundaments of Christianity. He hoped to find support in England because there had been a resurgence of interest in reincarnation there. Although widely criticised, his controversial arguments won the ear of some leading philosophers. John Locke, though deeply sceptical, spent many hours in conversation with Helmont and carefully studied his many books.[1] Gottfried Wilhelm Leibniz (1646–1716), the leading natural philosopher in Hanover, adapted his notions into the influential theory of Preformation according to which organisms grew from pre-existent microscopic life-forms. Helmont carved another inroad through which exotic sources influenced European ideas about the moral status of animals.

One of Helmont's first ports of call in England was Henry More (1614–87), the leading figure among the Cambridge Platonists. This band of academics had for decades sought to introduce into Christianity ideas drawn from the philosophies of Plato and Pythagoras, such as the existence of a world-soul which infused all of creation. Like his contemporary Gerrard Winstanley, More abhorred cruelty to animals and he thought that their souls – effluxes of the world soul – might be immortal, though he did not believe that they reincarnated into humans or vice versa.[2] However, he did argue that human souls had existed in a former state and incarnated on earth to live a life or two of atonement for a sin they had committed in a pre-existent state.[3] This doctrine of 'pre-existence' was similar enough to Helmont's beliefs for Helmont to hope that he could convert More to his cause.

Helmont had adopted the belief in reincarnation after studying the Kabbala – mystical Jewish texts written down from the twelfth century AD onwards. In early kabbalist writings reincarnation (called *gilgul* in Hebrew) only applied to humans,[4] but by the fourteenth century kabbalist texts such as the *Zohar* were claiming that human souls could descend into animals and even into inanimate objects for punishment and expiation until they were ready to return to God. In 1677 with the help of a team of Rabbis, Helmont and the Christian Hebrew scholar Knorr von Rosenroth published the first Latin translations of kabbalist texts. The title of their groundbreaking book was the *Kabbala Denudata*, or 'The Kabbala Stripped Naked' and it aimed to unite Christians, Jews and pagans into the one true faith. In it they included two texts on reincarnation by the sixteenth-century kabbalist cult-leader from the holy city of Zefat, Rabbi Isaac ben Solomon Luria (1534–72) and his follower Chaim Vital (1543–1620). Luria had taught that the earth was animated by sparks which had fallen from the primordial spiritual body of Adam and that in order to return from their fallen state these sparks, or souls, had to pass through an ascending cycle of reincarnations.[5] As Henry More explained in an essay which was printed in the *Kabbala Denudata*: 'Every spirit found in a bit of gravel is liable to be transformed into a plant, and from the plant into an animal, from the animal to a human being, and from the human being to an angel, and from the angel to God himself.'[6]

The belief that lower beings had souls did *not* necessarily mean it was wrong to kill animals. On the contrary, when an animal was ritually sacrificed its soul, or spark, was released from its bestial prison. But it did encourage the compassionate treatment of animals.[7] The cult of compassion that grew up among the kabbalists led to legends that Isaac Luria was a vegetarian and considered unkindness to animals (*tzaar baalei chaim*) a sin and a hindrance to the achievement of perfection. Vital apparently claimed that the ascetic Luria loved God's creatures so much that he never killed an insect, even an annoying one like a mosquito or fly.[8]

Helmont adapted Luria's system of reincarnation to accord with Christian doctrines like the resurrection, and in several of his own works he tried to convince others to follow his lead.[9] It may seem

Kabbalæ Denudatæ (1684)

mystical and slightly mad, but this optimistic theodicy was dangerously seductive for liberal Christians who were tired of fire and brimstone. Fitting reincarnation into the Christian world view justified God by giving sinners another stab at salvation.[10] According to orthodox Christian belief, souls born into tribes of cannibalistic savages had no chance of becoming Christian and no chance of getting to heaven. Instead of believing that such souls were plunged directly – and eternally – into hell, Helmont suggested that they would be progressively reincarnated until they were reborn as Christians.[11] Like Luria, Helmont believed that this held for all members of the creation, so that even the souls of wild animals, by 'an advance and melioration', would eventually incarnate in a Christian and be saved.[12] He even developed the kabbalists' notion that God carefully balanced the birth and death rates of animals and humans in order to ensure a steady flow up the chain of being.[13] Helmont was ashamed that Christians – who should have been the enlightened ones – were labouring under the mental tyranny of hell, while Jews (and even pagans!) were guided in their actions by the 'wise and solid Notion' of reincarnation.[14]

For most of Helmont's contemporaries it seemed obvious that the kabbalists' *gilgul* was just a rehashed version of the Pythagorean and Indian doctrine of metempsychosis.[15] This very accusation had always been levelled – perhaps correctly – at kabbalists within the Jewish community. Indeed, similar anxieties about importing pagan doctrines into Christianity can be traced back to the beginning of the Renaissance when the Byzantine theologian George Gemistos Pletho (1355–1450/52) first introduced Plato and Strabo's account of India to the Italian humanists. It was from these texts, as well as some recent accounts of India (perhaps by Marco Polo), that Pletho discovered that all wise men, from Zoroaster to the Brahmins, believed in reincarnation. In favour of these venerable authorities, Pletho abandoned Christianity's comparatively recent innovations, and converted to the ancient doctrine of metempsychosis.[16] In the ensuing uproar, Pletho's books were burned by the Patriarch of Constantinople and the chapters in which he addressed the issue of meat-eating are lost. But his works on metempsychosis survived and were reprinted in 1689 and 1718, just when there was a renewed interest in reincarnation in Europe.[17]

Helmont insisted, like More and many of their Jewish predecessors, that in fact it was Pythagoras and the Hindus who had learnt the doctrine from the Jews, not vice versa.[18] His aim, he explained, was to reinstate reincarnation 'corrected, reformed, and stripped of that disguised and deformed shape ... purged of those Mistakes, and reduced to the Primitive streightness and simplicity', 'and so accommodated to the Principles of Christian Religion'.[19] Initially, Helmont met with considerable success. A splinter group of Helmontians emerged, defending his claim that *gilgul* was a scriptural doctrine not a Platonic incursion. In the 1690s Reincarnationists were identified by one Anglican critic as being among the worst three dissenting movements of the age. Christians warned that the belief in reincarnation dissolved the fundamental difference between animals and humans.[20]

Surprisingly, Helmont converted the prominent Quaker George Keith, noted for his enthusiasm about the virtue of the Brahmins. Keith realised that Helmont's doctrines could reconcile the orthodox tenet that one had to believe in Christ, with his passionate feeling that people who had never heard of Christ could still get to heaven (by being reincarnated as Christians).[21] The entire Quaker community on both sides of the Atlantic was polarised by Keith's controversial kabbalistic reforms. When he gave a sermon in Philadelphia the crowd rioted and the magistrates smashed down his podium with axes. Keith's followers destroyed the podium of his opponents and he was eventually ejected from the Society of Friends because of his equivocation about transmigration.[22]

Christian believers in reincarnation were predisposed to be sympathetic to the suffering of animals. But they kept a strong arm between themselves and heretical vegetarianism. This was articulated in 1661 when an anonymous author from More's set (probably George Rust) championed the Platonic doctrines of the heretic Church father Origen in *A Letter of Resolution concerning Origen and the Chief of his Opinions*.[23] Origen was famous for being vegetarian, but Rust reiterated Origen's categorical denial (against the accusations of St Jerome) that this had anything to do with Pythagorean superstition. Origen did believe that animals' souls would be resurrected on the Day of Judgement, but Rust insisted that Origen never believed that humans could reincarnate into animals.[24] This ancient debate was resuscitated in a European-wide spate of Origenist works by several theologians, including the extraordinary Pierre-Daniel Huet (1630–1721). Huet later went on to argue that Pythagoras and the Brahmins had taken their doctrines from the Jews,[25] and apparently commissioned the Jesuit missionary in India, Father Bouchet, to compose a detailed essay distinguishing Origen's doctrines from Hindu and Pythagorean metempsychosis and vegetarianism.[26]

No one felt the tension between believing in reincarnation and maltreating animals more acutely than the 'Oxford Platonist', Joseph Glanvill. A cleric like More and Rust, Glanvill propounded an even more outspoken defence of transmigration, which he anonymously published in 1662 as *Lux Orientalis, Or An Enquiry into the Opinion of the Eastern Sages, Concerning the Præexistence of Souls*. The doctrine of transmigration, announced Glanvill, was attested by 'the *Indian Brachmans*, the *Persian Magi*, the *Ægyptian Gymnosophists*, the *Jewish Rabbins*, some of the *Græcian Philosophers*, and *Christian Fathers*'.[27] Taking his ideas from the Kabbala, Glanvill asserted that souls that had sinned before the creation of the earth were compressed into Adam's loins in Eden. But instead of behaving like good children trying to recompense for their former sin, the souls egged Adam on to sin for a *second* time, thus condemning themselves (that is, us) to a life of suffering on earth.[28] It took more than just one lifetime to atone for such heinous criminality, so each soul had to reincarnate until they had purged themselves and were ready to return to God.[29] In *Lux Orientalis*, Glanvill restricted his discussion of pre-existence to humans alone, but in the same year wrote privately to a fellow Origenist that their beliefs logically led to fully blown Pythagorean metempsychosis, 'for what account els can be given of the state of beasts who some of them are all their lives subject to the tyrannicall tastes of merciless man, except we suppose them to have deserv'd this severe discipline by some former delinquencyes.' The question of justice to animals was integral to the issue of reincarnation and it racked Glanvill with consternation. If animals had not sinned in a former life, how could one possibly justify treating them the way we do? Faced with this appalling conundrum, Glanvill argued that since God could not be so unjust as to make innocent animals suffer, it was necessary to believe that animals had deserved their suffering by being extremely sinful in former lives. The only alternative, he painfully conceded, was the Cartesian belief that they didn't suffer at all because they were just senseless machines.[30] But Glanvill's philosophical loophole was not the end of the discussion. Both More and Helmont were intimate friends with Lady Anne Conway, one of the most advanced women philosophers of her generation. During their walks in the woods and groves of her estate, Lady Conway became a convert to Helmont's creed and she realised that it had profound implications for the moral status of animals. Conway took ideas directly from Luria's Kabbala and devised an elaborate system that, like Glanvill's, argued that animals deserved the suffering to which they were fated, but that nevertheless humans ought to act responsibly towards them.[31] In her philosophical *Principles*, published anonymously by Helmont after her death in 1690, Conway held that animals – like all matter in the creation – were continually trying to improve and would eventually improve enough to become human and thence return to their spiritual origins. Thus 'a Horse may in length of Time be in some measure changed into a Man'. She seems to have been unclear whether this transformation happened by metamorphosis, metempsychosis or more prosaically by being eaten and raised up the food chain. Conversely, if a man led a brutish life, his spirit would 'enter into the Body of a beast, and there for a certain time be punished'.[32] Like Tryon (who may have heard of Conway through her friend George Keith), she maintained that 'if a Man hath lived . . . a Brutish [life] . . . he . . . should be changed into that *Species* of Beasts, to whom he was inwardly most like, in Qualities and Conditions of Mind.'[33]

Conway explained that it was in the interests of all creatures to unite in their effort to return to God. God created all species, explained Conway, to 'stand in a mutual Sympathy, and love each other; so hath he implanted a certain Universal Sympathy and mutual Love in Creatures, as being all Members of one Body, and (as I may so say), Brethren, having one common Father'.[34] If a man 'kills any of them, only to fulfil his own pleasure, he acts unjustly, and the same measure will again be measured unto him', she warned. Conway did not state whether she thought killing animals for food counted as unnecessary 'pleasure' and thus stopped short of advocating vegetarianism, but her philosophy provided a foundation for the ethical treatment of animals.[35]

This inclusion of animals in the process of *gilgul* captured the imagination of others and a flurry of Reincarnationist books stimulated a widespread theological debate. The anonymous author(s) of a tract called *Seder Olam: Or, The Order of Ages*, described a monist system of ascension almost identical to Conway's, explaining that 'even the basest Creature . . . may be changed, either into the noblest, or at least into some part of the noblest Creature'.[36]

Gilgul provided Christians with an alternative framework for understanding non-human life forms. Animals were striving in partnership with their fallen human brothers and sisters to improve and reclaim their lost divine status. It was everyone's responsibility to lend a helping hand in the common cause of mutual improvement. This did not necessarily mean desisting from killing animals (though it could), but it did mean treating them with due consideration for their plight. Although it never gained a foothold in the established Christian Churches, the kabbalist *gilgul* joined forces with the beliefs of Origen, Pythagoras and the Hindus, and became a persuasive doctrine that continued to inspire European minds for centuries. Some of the most prominent vegetarians in later decades owed something to the accommodation of *gilgul* into Christianity.

EIGHT

Men Should be Friends even to Brute Beasts: Isaac Newton and the Origins of Pagan Theology

One autumn day in 1665, while sheltering from plague-stricken Cambridge at his home in Woolsthorpe, the twenty-two-year-old Isaac Newton (1642–1727) sat pondering the fall of apples to the ground. He had always had a speculative turn of mind. His family had put him to work on the farm at the age of seventeen, but he was forever to be found reclining beneath a tree with a book instead of watching the cattle, and in the end they sent him back to grammar school. At the age of eighteen Newton became an undergraduate at Cambridge University, where he swiftly made his first major discovery simply by closing the curtains of his room to direct a shaft of sunlight onto a prism. Watching the familiar spectacle of white light refracting into all the colours of the spectrum, he hit upon an explanation which resolved a fundamental principle of light and colour. After graduating in the spring of 1665, and spending the autumn amongst the orchards at home, he extended his speculations in another direction. Since gravity exerted its power on objects such as apples even when they were high up in the air, he reflected, why should not this invisible power extend as far as the moon? By 1687, when Newton had established himself as a formidable scientist at the Royal Society, his calculations finally proved that the pull from the earth kept the moon in orbit, and ultimately that universal gravitation synchronised everything from the cycles of the largest planets to the tiniest particles bound together in matter. This single glorious manifestation of God's omnipotence was what kept the entire universe in harmonious motion.[1]

Newton is famous for his scientific discoveries with which, from his cloister in Trinity College, he revolutionised Europe's understanding of the physical laws of nature. But Newton did not limit his curiosity to physics: he was equally interested in discovering the moral laws of God's creation. Only by studying both the moral and physical laws could he come to understand God in His entirety. If God used the simple power of gravity to unite all things in the universe, might He not have used one moral law to bind together all His creatures, including animals?

Newton was renowned among his Cambridge colleagues for his extremely peculiar dietary habits. He rarely allowed his experiments to be interrupted by convivial eating hours and his friends noted that even those meals that were brought privately to his room he pushed around the plate in absent-minded disinterest.[2] His step-niece Catherine Conduitt, who lived with him when he moved to London to become Master of the Royal Mint, complained that 'his gruel or milk & eggs that was carried to him warm for his supper he would often eat cold for his breakfast.' Her husband John confirmed that 'His cat grew fat on the food he left standing,' and others joked that in Cambridge his meals were finished off by 'ye old Woman, his Bedmaker'. After Newton's death there was a flurry of anxious attempts to make sense of these prandial oddities and his modern biographer, Richard S. Westfall, wrote that 'No peculiarity of Newton's amazed his contemporaries more consistently.'[3] Newton's amanuensis, William Stukeley, tried to defuse gossip by explaining that Newton's temperate breakfasts of bread, butter and orange-peel infusion were the key to his self-control and long life.[4] So Newton, with his head in the skies, was remiss about meals, and the meals we do hear about were meagre, mainly fleshless – but not explicitly vegetarian.

Sir Isaac was 'a Lover of Apples, and sometimes at Night would eat a smal roasted Quince', reminisced his assistant and relative Humphrey Newton.[5] So passionate about apples was Newton that he applied his genius to encouraging the plantation of orchards in Cambridgeshire.[6] More than anything else, agreed John Conduitt, it was 'vegetables & fruit which he always eat very heartily of'. Did he choose to eat 'little flesh', as John Conduitt reported, to combat the chronic bladder condition of which he eventually died?[7] Was he dieting according to the rules for scholars set out in Luigi Cornaro's *Sure and Certain Methods of Attaining a Long and Healthful Life?*[8] Was he following the advice of his alchemical adviser, Michael Maier, that practitioners should eat plenty of fruit?[9] Or was there a more intimate connection between the apples he observed and those he ate?

The burgeoning vegetarian movement was quick to claim Newton as one of their own, triggering a debate that has raged ever since. Newton's personal acquaintance, the vegetarian doctor George Cheyne, often used him as a shining example of the benefits of a flesh-free diet: 'Sir Isaac Newton, when he studied or composed,' claimed Cheyne, 'had only a Loaf, a Bottle of Sack and Water, and took no Sustenance then but a Slice and a weak Draught as he found Failure of Spirits'.[10] Albrecht von Haller inserted this exciting data into his highly respected *Elementa Physiologiae*, and from then on it was repeated time and time again by vegetarians trying to prove that their diet enhanced mental acuity.[11] By 1860 the American vegetarians Sylvester Graham and Amos Bronson Alcott were making such capital out of this claim that their opponents, Andrew Combe and James Coxe, felt compelled to defend Newton from this slur on his character. With indignant bluster, they complained that 'Allusion is sometimes made to Sir Isaac Newton, as another example of the beneficial effects of a vegetable diet'; but, they continued, it was obvious that Newton ate meat because he 'occasionally suffered from gout', the classic ailment of carnivores.[12] Heedless of such remonstrances, scores of vegetarian societies around the world still list Newton among their favourite predecessors.

The denial that he was vegetarian seemed to have gained a sure footing when, in a bundle of household papers, a bill was found showing that one goose, two turkeys, two rabbits and one chicken were delivered to Newton's household in the space of a single week. In addition, at the time of his death Newton owed £10 16s 4d to a butcher and a total of £2 8s 9d to a poulterer and a fishmonger. This surely shows that Newton indiscriminately gorged on animals at a rate scarcely imaginable to modern appetites. Or does it? Newton certainly served his guests meat (they said so), and the other members of his household no doubt did not expect to go without.[13] But since Newton ate separately from his family, there is no guarantee that he ate these groceries himself, even if it seems probable.

Some saw a suspicious correlation between Newton's dietary habits and his renowned sympathy for animals. 'He had such a meekness & sweetness of temper,' wrote John Conduitt, 'that a melancholy story would often draw tears from him & he was exceedingly shocked at any sort of cruelty to man or beast, mercy to both being, the topick he loved to dwell upon'.[14] In the notebook Conduitt kept about Newton, there is one barely legible page that records both that 'He preferred' (or 'pursued'?) to 'live on vegetables' and that he could 'not bear sports that kill beasts – as hunting & shooting'.[15] Reading between the lines, it seems that Conduitt believed Newton preferred not to eat the objects of his pity.

It is to Voltaire – who did more than anyone to popularise Newton's philosophy in the decades following his death – that we owe the story of the falling apples. (Voltaire himself learned it from Catherine Conduitt, and the inspirational apple tree was visited as a shrine until it blew down in 1820.) The universe was bound together by one physical law, and, according to Voltaire, Newton believed that people were bound together by the universal law to 'do as you would be done unto' – the Golden Rule which every person was able to deduce with the natural faculty of sense. Voltaire extrapolated that Newton even extended the universal disposition of compassion to beasts. 'He acceded only with repugnance to the barbarous usage of feeding ourselves with the blood and flesh of beings similar to us,' declared Voltaire. 'He found it a truly awful contradiction to believe that animals feel, and to make them suffer. His morality accorded in this point with his philosophy.'[16] Voltaire would have gone to almost any lengths to promote Newton as the hero of natural religion and opponent of Descartes' ruthless theory about animals. But just how connected was Newton's philosophy with his morality?

In his quest to discover God's universal laws of morality, Newton undertook a massive project of biblical and historical scholarship, which he executed with the same intellectual rigour as he did his physical experiments.[17] He believed that 'in ye beginning' God revealed to mankind the laws upon which they were to base their religion. Since that time, mankind had corrupted God's original religion into all the idolatrous and superstitious cults that existed on earth. Even Moses, thought Newton, had introduced unnecessary and potentially schismatic doctrines. Christ himself had not revealed any new moral laws, and Christians had muffled the simple divine message with numerous elaborations and bodges.

Newton's mission – as important to him as discovering the laws of gravity – was to scrape away all these accretions and reconstruct the pure original religion. He tried to do this by comparing the world's different religious beliefs as they were recorded in ancient texts from Egypt, Babylon, Persia, Greece as well as in several modern travelogues.[18] Anything he found to be common to all or most cultures he took to be a remnant of mankind's shared heritage. (Claiming that universally held beliefs were 'innate' had become virtually untenable in the face of John Locke's 1690 *Essay Concerning Human Understanding*. Like Locke, Newton did think that some ideas – such as belief in God – were common all over the world because different peoples independently used their reason to come to the same conclusions, but Newton was more interested in showing that universal laws had been inherited from a shared cultural heritage.[19])

For Newton, the history of mankind's heritage hinged on the story of Noah. After the Flood was over, when the only surviving humans were those living in Shinar below Mount Ararat in Babylonia, God delivered to Noah a reiteration of the true religion. As Noah's community grew and divided into numerous satellite states, this original code was spread across the world, only to be corrupted in most places beyond recognition.[20] Newton's passionate desire was to lead the world back to the true source: 'tis not to be doubted but that ye religion wch Noah propagated down to his posterity was the true religion.'[21]

Newton completed most of his religious research in the 1680s and arranged it under the provisional title *Theologiae Gentilis Origines Philosophicae*, or *The Philosophical Origins of Gentile Theology*. Daunted by the unorthodoxy of his own conclusions, Newton realised that it would be perilous to publish them. Even after the Toleration Act of 1689, his disbelief in the Holy Trinity would alone have been punishable by severe fines, loss of position and even death. When faced with compulsory ordination into the 'corrupt' Anglican Church in 1675, Newton chose disgrace and dismissal from his Trinity fellowship. His position was saved at the last minute by a special royal dispensation, but it was at the price of silence.[22] Today, his theological work remains a confusion of Latin and English manuscripts scattered between the libraries of Jerusalem and Cambridge and is only now being gathered together and published online by the Newton Project. However, Newton did incorporate some of his findings into a subsequent book about his new technique of using astronomy to recalculate ancient historical events. This he left as a parting gift to the world and it was published as *The Chronology of Ancient Kingdoms Amended* within months of his refusal to take the Anglican sacrament on his deathbed.

From a careful study of this book and his unpublished manuscripts, it is clear that Newton felt he had discovered the fundamentals of the original religion, both its ceremonial form and its moral base. The ceremonial form of the original religion was solar. A fire was placed in the centre of a sacred space surrounded by seven flames, symbolising the sun encircled by the seven (pre-Copernican) planets. This ceremony had been designed by God to teach the first people the heliocentric mechanics of the universe, while simultaneously encouraging the worship of God through the magnificence of His creation. Newton found evidence of this religious rite among the biblical Patriarchs, the ancient Egyptians, the Greeks, Numa Pompilius' Pythagorean Romans, the Druids of Stonehenge and similar sacred circles in Denmark and Ireland; and in modern travel narratives he found the same among the Tartars and the Chinese; finally, he concluded that it had been the blueprint for the Second Temple in Jerusalem.[23] The universality of such formations convinced Newton that it must have been the form of the original religion revealed to Noah and spread by him to his descendants, 'For in ye first ages . . . I understand not how one & the same religion could so soon spread into them all had it not been propagated wth mankind in ye beginning.'[24]

This solar ceremony had been literally moved across the earth when Noah's descendants each took a coal from the original sacred fire with them on their travels. The fire-worshipping Zoroastrian Persians and the Brahmins, Newton thought, were still burning the same fires today.[25]

Along with the glowing embers, Newton believed that Noah's people carried with them the essential moral laws. Predictably, two of them were the key biblical commandments to love God and to 'love thy neighbour as thyself' (Leviticus 19:18; Matthew 22:36–40). But the third major law that Newton identified – much more controversially and unexpectedly – was the commandment of 'mercy to animals'. Newton's promotion of this notion as a cornerstone of religious morals has been overlooked by recent scholarship.

In a tortuous explanation of various biblical passages, Newton argued that God instituted mercy to animals when he prohibited Noah from eating blood: 'But flesh with the life thereof, which is the blood thereof, shall ye not eat' (Genesis 9:4).[26] The prohibition of blood-eating was so important to Newton that he wrote a separate essay entirely on the subject. Sadly, when Viscount Lymington sold off Newton's papers in the 1930s, this essay was purchased for £12 by an elusive Parisian called Emmanuel Fabius, and has never been seen since. However, Newton made the subject a central part of *The Philosophical Origins of Gentile Theology*, *The Chronology of Ancient Kingdoms Amended* and his condensed manuscript essay 'Irenicum'; he also worked it into his unfinished history of the Church and even envisaged making it the final conclusion of a new edition of *Opticks*, his groundbreaking work on the properties of light.[27]

The prohibition of blood is the basis of Jewish kosher and Islamic halal laws in use today, and of the Old Testament decree that blood was to be let out of sacrificial animals and offered to God. Unlike most Christians, Newton thought that the blood law was not a mere ceremonial taboo: it was a moral instruction of the most fundamental importance, designed to ensure that animals were killed in the least painful way, by slitting their throat and drawing out all their blood. This was, he believed, far preferable to the usual practice in Europe of throttling beasts or banging them on the head with a hammer before cutting their throats (indeed, seventeenth-century legislation stipulated that bulls should be baited by dogs before their meat was fit for sale in a butcher's shop).[28] 'Strangling', wrote Newton in a draft manuscript, 'is a painful death & therefore we are not to strangle things or eat them with their blood, but to let out their blood upon the earth. For we are to avoid all >unnecessary< acts of cruelty.' (He added 'unnecessary' as a qualifying afterthought: if people were going to define eating animals as a 'necessary cruelty' then the blood law would at least force them to do it in the most humane manner possible.)[29]

In his enthusiasm for the original laws, Newton was inspired by the Jewish rabbis who had always revered the 'seven laws of Noah' – the *sheva mizvoth b'ne Noah*. But the prevailing view among theologians, as John Selden (1584–1654) had recently shown, was that abstinence from blood was *not* one of the seven, and there was no question of it being a law for the protection of animals.[30] Yet Newton went out on a limb to adjust the traditional Noachic laws to fit in with his overall scheme. Newton was so sure of his interpretation that he claimed the law God actually established was 'mercy to animals' and that the prohibition of blood was just one euphemistic way of getting the message across. In his triumphant conclusion to chapter one of

Illustration of a slaughter-house (1751)

The Chronology of Ancient Kingdoms Amended he summarised the essential laws of the original religion; in the final condensed form he did not even mention the blood, instead replacing it with what he saw as its intended meaning: 'So then, *the believing that the world was framed by one supreme god, and is governed by him; and the loving and worshipping him, and honouring our parents, and loving our neighbour as our selves, and being merciful even to beasts,* is the oldest of all religions.' These few laws, he explained, were the basis of 'the primitive religion of both *Jews* and *Christians*, and ought to be the standing religion of all nations'.[31]

The prominence Newton gives to the law of mercy to animals is extremely unusual. But he went still further. Astonishingly, it transpires that Newton considered mercy to animals an integral adjunct of the central commandment 'love thy neighbour', rendering it – in other drafts of the same manifesto – 'all men should be friends to all men & even to bruit Beasts'. Newton's expansion of the sense of 'neighbour' to include animals was an unorthodoxy nearly as extreme as that of his contemporaries Tryon, Crab and Winstanley, and was, of course, said to be the belief of the vegetarian Indians.[32]

Loving one's neighbour was itself an extension of loving God (Matthew 22:36–40), so Newton appears to have deduced that in its purest form there was only one divine law which bound all beings together from God down to the smallest creature. This, it seems, was a moral analogy to the physical law of gravity which bound everything together from the sun to the smallest particle. The solar form of

Noah's original religion was an emblem of both the physical and the moral law.

In the moral, physical and ceremonial dimensions, Newton saw that God had repeatedly employed the formula of 'seven in one'. Just as the seven planets, represented by the seven flames around the sacred fire, were held around the sun by the one divine force of gravity, so Newton appears to have concluded that the seven Noachic laws were constituent parts of the one over-arching law of love and mutual respect. This septenary principle even applied to the laws of light, for Newton had analysed white light into the seven 'homogeneal' colours of the spectrum, just as the musical scale was composed of seven notes.[33] In its moral dimension, the law kept all God's creatures bound together by the love that bound them to God. No wonder Newton ushered animals into the fold of the moral law. As Newton himself explained, God's invisible presence was manifested in the workings of the universe and 'particularly in that of the bodies of animals'.[34]

Given that mercy to beasts was the only contentious commandment in Newton's universal religion, much of his work focused on proving its legitimacy. For Newton's contemporaries, this emphasis was so surprising that to some extent it eclipsed the astronomical subject of the *Chronology*. When dedicating the *Chronology* to Queen Caroline, who had always been friendly to Newton, John Conduitt (who was responsible for posthumously publishing it) passed over Newton's revolutionary chronological method, and instead called for her endorsement of Newton's discovery that banning '*cruelty, even to brute beasts*' ought to be part of '*the standing Religion of all Nations*'.[35] Newton's voice, echoing resoundingly after his death, reached the royal ears which during life he had sworn not to offend. It was probably after hearing about Newton's theory that John Clarke (the brother of Newton's friend Samuel Clarke) argued in his Boyle Lecture of 1719 that the law against eating blood was 'intended to prevent all Cruelty towards brute Creatures; and that . . . they should be put to the least Pain that is possible'.[36]

Newton no doubt felt supported in his beliefs by his favourite Jewish scholar, the twelfth-century Rabbi Moses ben Maimun (Maimonides), who had similarly tried to smash a conventional Jewish disregard for animals by insisting that some of Moses' laws were for the protection of animals (though conversely the prohibition of blood,

he believed, was instituted because Satanist pagans drank it to 'fraternize with the djinns').[37] Claiming that Moses instituted mercy to animals
was not unheard of in Christendom either. Francis Bacon said that
laws like abstaining from blood were 'not so meerely Ceremoniall,
as Institutions of Mercy' (though he was by no means calling for its
restitution);[38] and in a famous article against cruelty to animals in The
Guardian (1713), referred to by Conduitt in his notes on Newton,
Alexander Pope argued that Moses had instituted mercy to beasts.[39]
But the dominant Christian line, since St Thomas Aquinas and
St Clement of Alexandria, was to deny animals any moral status by
claiming that such laws were solely for the protection of humans.[40]
This was endorsed by both the Catholic commentators, such as Joannes
Mercerus, and by Reformers like John Calvin who said 'that God
intends to accustom men to gentleness, by abstinence from the blood
of animals . . . [because otherwise] they would at length not be sparing
of even human blood'.[41] Newton's contemporary, the theologian John
Edwards, agreed that eating blood made people cruel to each other:
'God therefore commanded those of Noah's Posterity to refrain wholly
from Blood, that they might not proceed from cruelty to Beasts, to
killing of Men. Besides,' added Edwards, 'this may seem partly to be a
natural Law, Blood being a gross Meat, and not fit for nourishment.'[42]
Newton probably agreed that eating blood inflamed men to cruelty,
but he stressed that the prohibition was also for the sake of the animals
themselves.[43]

Most Anglicans in any case believed that since Christ sacrificed his
own blood the law against eating blood had been dissolved.[44] But
Newton insisted that the Gospel did not have the power to abolish the
prohibition of blood as it did the Mosaic food taboos because the
blood law was a Noachic law and therefore universal and permanent.
Furthermore, he argued, the Acts of the Apostles clearly stated that
when the early Christians met at Antioch for a doctrinal convention
they explicitly decreed that the Gentile converts could ignore all the
Mosaic traditions except the prohibition of eating blood, strangled
animals, meat sacrificed to idols, and fornication (Acts 15:24, 29;
21:25).[45] This heavily disputed passage preyed on the conscience of
many a Christian blood-eater. As one Protestant Reformer put it in
1596: 'The Apostles commaunded to abstaine from bloud . . . What
Christian observes that this day? and if some few do feare to touch
such things, they are mocked of the rest.'[46] A few seventeenth-century

controversialists, like Newton, usually under the cover of anonymity, did brave the flak to warn fellow Christians of their peril. The author of *A Bloudy Tenent confuted, Or, Bloud Forbidden* (1646) argued that it was 'A cruell thing to eat life itself': eating the life-blood of an animal after it was dead was a token of more 'extreame crueltie, and unmercifulnesse' than killing the animal in the first place.[47] This conscientious pamphleteer was immediately lambasted by the author of *The Eating of Blood Vindicated*, who mockingly retorted that 'This mans charitie is more to the bloud of a dead beast, than it is either to the life itself of man or beast.'[48] In 1652 the controversy was reignited by the comically titled, *Triall Of A Black-Pudding. Or, The unlawfulness of Eating Blood*, which argued that 'God would not have Men eat the life and soul of Beasts, a thing barbarous and unnaturall.'[49] In the 1660s William Roe repudiated the blood-abstaining 'Hæmapesthites', calling the error a 'virulent Contagion' based on a false reading of Acts.[50] But the stain would not budge. In 1669 John Moore, a church minister on the Isle of Wight, attacked 'Blood-eaters' in *Moses Revived . . . Wherein the Unlawfulness of Eating Blood is clearly proved*, claiming that blood was the food of devils.[51] John Evelyn, Newton's colleague at the Royal Society, agreed that the prohibition had never been revoked – but recognised that trying to preach down the eating of hog's pudding was in vain;[52] and Thomas Tryon insisted that it was impossible to get a pound of flesh without a drop of blood, so even eating meat was a cardinal sin.[53] Newton was more extreme even than these critics (save Tryon); they emphasised that eating blood fostered cruelty towards humans; Newton was concerned with the welfare of the animals having their blood shed.

Despite the differences between Newton and these controversialists, association with them and the Judaists opened Newton to ridicule. Catherine Conduitt felt this keenly and leapt to defend Newton against the accusations levelled by his successor in the Lucasian Chair of Mathematics at Cambridge, William Whiston:

> Whiston has spread about that S[r] I[saac] abstained from eating rabbitts because strangled & from black puddings because made of blood, but he is mistaken S[r] I. did not – he often mentioned & followed the rule of St Paul Take & eat what comes from the shambles without asking questions for conscience sake[.] he said meats strangled were forbid because that was a painfull death & the letting out the blood the easiest & that animals should be

put to as little pain as possible, that the reason why eating blood
was forbid was because it was thought the eating blood inclined
men to be cruel.[54]

If Newton had followed his principles to the letter he would have had
to abstain from all butcher's meat – and this is what some contemporaries advocated.[55] But Whiston, who shared Newton's desire to revive
Primitive Christianity and also believed that vegetarianism was suitable
for lengthening life,[56] suggested that Newton was primarily concerned
with strangled animals like rabbits. Catherine Conduitt indicated that
he overcame his conscience by adhering to St Paul's instructions to put
social conformity first (1 Corinthians 10:25–7). But even this reveals
that Newton was in a constant state of moral conflict.[57] In the solitude
of his private rooms, perhaps Newton did avoid eating animals slaughtered in a manner contrary to God's fundamental laws. (Interestingly,
Descartes, who was a closet vegetarian, also preferred 'to be served
separately or to eat alone'.[58])

It was an odd leap of imagination for Newton to insist so categorically that the biblical prohibition of blood was really against cruelty to
animals. His aim had been to find fundamental principles that everyone could agree on – and yet he was willing to stake all on his contentious interpretation of the law against blood. How did he become so
convinced of it? No doubt personal sentiments predisposed him to
find in divine law something answering his own feelings of sympathy.
But equally crucial to his argument was the evidence from foreign
cultures.

Newton never said that the original religion banned eating animals,
but he was fascinated by the wide spread of vegetarianism in cultures all
over the world; he seems to have regarded such instances of superlative
clemency as vestiges of the original law of mercy to beasts.[59] He thought
that ancient Egypt had preserved the original religion in a strikingly
pristine form, and seems to have gone out of his way to show that
they were vegetarian. He read the histories of the fourth-century BC
Egyptian priest Manetho and the first-century BC Sicilian Diodorus,
who had said that the primitive Egyptians 'fed upon Herbs, and the
natural Fruit of the Trees'. Newton manipulated this evidence to make
it sound as if the Egyptians lived in a state of Golden-Age innocence
and that this led seamlessly into their (much later) religious abhorrence
of killing animals.[60] Eliding various sources and stories into one pithy

conclusion, Newton declared that 'The *Egyptians* originally lived on the fruits of the earth, and fared hardly, and abstained from animals.'[61]

When a band of French scholars sneakily laid their hands on a manuscript copy of Newton's work, they triggered a massive cross-Channel controversy by retorting that the real reason why the Egyptians abstained from eating meat was because they were abominable animal-worshippers. This, they argued, was obvious from the fact that when the Israelites went to live in Egypt, the Bible testifies that the Jewish custom of sacrificing bulls, sheep and goats was an affront to Egyptian zoolatry.[62] Newton explained this away and insisted that at that time the Egyptian religion was not idolatrous paganism but a slightly corrupted version of the original religion inherited from Noah; indeed, the Egyptian King Ammon, he sometimes thought, was no other than Ham, Noah's grandson.[63]

Why was Newton so eager to prove this? His most controversial argument was that Judaism was based on Egyptian religion. Moses had excised the errors that had crept into the original religion among the Egyptians but essentially, said Newton, 'Moses retained all ye religion of ye Egyptians concerning ye worship of ye true God.' Judaism, Newton concluded, was Moses' resuscitation of the Noachic religion as it had been propagated in an imperfect form *by the Egyptians*.[64] Nudging aside the Mosaic revelation in this way was an unspeakably radical move and turned the entire basis of the Judaeo-Christian belief system on its head.[65]

Though Newton did not specifically say it, he clearly thought that Egyptian vegetarianism was the counterpart – perhaps even the source – of Moses' law of mercy to beasts. This put pagan vegetarianism into the limelight. Rather than seeing it as a sign of satanic zoolatry, Newton regarded it as evidence that the Egyptians were following the original laws of God. Moving to still more exotic pastures, the vegetarians in India, he set about studying all the ancient sources and several travel narratives including Manucci, Chardin, Tavernier, Purchas and the best of all Indological studies, Abraham Rogerius.[66] He gleaned further information from Gerard Vossius, and from Eusebius who convinced him that the ancient Brahmins 'abstained from ye worship of Idols & lived virtuously'.[67] In his personal library, which survives in Trinity College, Cambridge, Newton folded the corner of the pages where Strabo, Philostratus and various humanist scholars described the similarity between Indian and Pythagorean vegetarianism.[68]

How did the ancient Brahmins manage to preserve the original religion in such a pure non-idolatrous state? Newton propounded the fantastic theory that the 'Brahmans' were descended from 'the *Abrahamans*, or sons of *Abraham*, born of his second wife *Keturah*, instructed by their father in the worship of ONE GOD without images, and sent into the east'. Genesis said that after Isaac was born Abraham packed off his children by Keturah and other concubines 'eastward, unto the east country', and so it seemed plausible that they were the original Brahmins. This enthusiastic dot-joining had been indulged in by many others, including the sixteenth-century savant Guillaume Postel (1510–81), who tried to recover a pristine Noachic religion like Newton's.[69] In addition, the alchemist Michael Maier connected this genealogy of the Brahmins with the theory, posited by Agrippa and Newton's favourite Jewish medieval astrological theologian Abraham ibn Ezra (1092–1167) (who had himself read genuine Hindu texts), that Enoch, Abraham's grandson by Keturah, was in fact the same person as the great Egyptian magus, Hermes Trismegistus.[70] The door was open to seeing Hinduism as a relic of the original religion.

According to Newton, one of the greatest religious reformations in world history occurred in 521 BC when Hystaspes, father of King Darius of Persia, returned from a crash-course in pure religion with the Brahmins, joined forces with Zoroaster and led the Reformation of the Persian magi. Between them, they abolished idolatry and instituted monotheism by importing the Egyptian wisdom preserved in Babylon and fusing it with 'the institutions of the ancient *Brachmans*'.[71] In a pincer movement with the Egyptians carrying the original religion eastwards,[72] and the Brahmins exporting it west, the whole of the ancient world enjoyed a restitution of some of the pristine elements of Noah's original religion.

Finally Europe enjoyed the fruits of the reform, because, as Apuleius and others said, Pythagoras travelled through Egypt to the Eastern philosophers, and brought their philosophy back to Greece.[73] Newton explained the ramifications of this in his sensational endorsement of pagan vegetarianism in the opening paragraph of his frequently redrafted manuscript essay, 'Irenicum, or Ecclesiastical Polyty tending to Peace':

> All Nations were originally of the Religion comprehended in the Precepts of the sons of Noah, the chief of wch were to have one God, & not to alienate his worship, nor prophane his name;

One of Isaac Newton's manuscript versions of the essay *Irenicum*

to abstain from murder, theft, fornication, & all injuries; not to feed on the flesh or drink the blood of a living animal, but to be mercifull even to bruit beasts ... Pythagoras one of the oldest Philosophers in Europe, after he had travelled among the Eastern nations for the sake of knowledge & conversed with their Priests & Judges & seen their manners, taught his scholars that all men should be friends to all men & even to bruit Beasts ... This was the religion of the sons of Noah established by Moses & Christ & is still in force.[74]

Newton clearly regarded Eastern and Pythagorean vegetarianism as a remnant of God's original law, and he made it a central pillar in the bridge between pagan religions and Judaeo-Christianity. It may look as if Newton just slipped his ideas into the old mould of the *prisci theologi*, but in fact he had gone much further. Unlike most contemporaries, Newton did not think that Pythagorean vegetarianism was based on the abhorrent belief in metempsychosis.[75] On the contrary, he suggested that the vegetarianism of Pythagoras and of 'the Eastern nations' was an extension to animals of the law 'love thy neighbour' which they inherited from Noah. When Pythagoras returned to Europe from his travels, what he brought with him was a secularised version of Noah's original religion, as well as all the heliocentric astronomic and mathematical knowledge the Eastern sages had preserved. Newton said that his own scientific work, like his religious research, was not so much discovery as *recovery*, for Pythagoras and the ancient inheritors of the original solar religion had known nearly everything that he had revealed in his *magnum opus*, the *Principia* of 1687.[76] In terms of religious and scientific reform, this put Pythagoras, Newton's fellow mathematician, scientist and moralist, in line with Moses, Christ and Newton himself.[77]

Interpreting pagan religions as corruptions of Judaeo-Christian theology was standard practice. The widely influential 'universal histories' of Newton's contemporaries, Pierre-Daniel Huet, Gerard Vossius and Ralph Cudworth, had all made this case.[78] John Selden and Joannes Mercerus both agreed with St Clement of Alexandria that Pythagoras (and the Brahmins) derived their 'mildness towards irrational creatures from the [Mosaic] law', even though they maintained that Moses himself didn't care about animals at all.[79] These ethnocentric speculations were provided with extra ballast when travellers suggested that Indian abstinence from flesh was basically the same as abstinence from blood. Sir Thomas Roe, for example, described Hindus 'that will not eate any thing wherin ever there was any blood,' and he strengthened the comparison to Judaism by referring to their temples as 'synagoags'.[80]

But Newton reversed the tide: rather than interpreting pagan doctrine solely through the lens of the Judaeo-Christian tradition, he allowed pagan religion to influence his interpretation of Judaeo-Christianity. It was pagan vegetarianism that helped to convince him that the Bible's law against blood was really a law against cruelty to animals. Europeans projected Pythagorean notions onto Indian culture, but it is also the case that Newton projected Indian values *back* onto Christianity. Rather than just seeing pagan vegetarianism as a corruption of the law against blood, he saw them both as branches from one original root – the law of mercy to animals. Newton may have thought that being vegetarian was taking the commandment further than was necessary, but pagan vegetarianism was clearly preferable to the Christians' total abandonment of any restraint on their consumption of blood, their methods of slaughter, and their cruel and neglectful treatment of animals. Europe was in universal breach of one of the most fundamental laws of God. Bizarre though it may seem, and heretical it would have appeared to his contemporaries, Newton considered that some pagan cultures were closer to the true religion in that respect than the Christian world he lived in.

Newton's attempts to reinstate a true understanding of the physical universe went hand in hand with his desire to re-establish the original laws of God.[81] If Westfall is right that 'he may even, in his innermost heart, have dreamed of himself as a prophet called to restore the true religion', then we must include in his reforms the readjustment of man's relationship with nature. For the sake of his peace and quiet, and for social conformity, Newton did not openly campaign for the restitution of the true religion. From his posthumous and unpublished legacy, however, it is clear that Newton passionately wanted his scientific revolution to be accompanied by a bloodless revolution.

So was he a vegetarian, or wasn't he? In practice, probably not – at least, not all the time – but there may have been periods in which he did adhere more strictly to his dietary principles. Along with the scientific and moral wisdom lost with the ancient world, Newton thought he could recover the forgotten art of alchemy. Closeted away in a special building in his garden, Newton often stayed up for several nights feverishly keeping his alchemical cauldron burning, sifting through ancient recipes, adding ingredients and trying to find real chemical processes in arcane formulae. This was Newton's main pursuit until the mid-1690s, at which point he suffered a severe nervous breakdown – explained by biographers variously as the effects of chemical poisoning or his acute religious crisis.[82]

In the user's guide to alchemy, Michael Maier told aspiring alchemists that the Egyptian priests, Orpheans, Samothracian Cabiri, Persian magi, Brahmins, Ethiopian gymnosophists, and Pythagoreans were all alchemists dedicated to the secrets of nature.[83] Maier had even read Jan Huygen van Linschoten's recent *Itinerario* and enthusiastically alerted the alchemical and Rosicrucian brotherhoods to the fact that the renowned, frugal Brahmins had survived into the modern world, representing an unbroken chain of alchemical and natural wisdom at least as old as Abraham.[84] Newton had read and marked up his copies of Porphyry and Philostratus and owned a copy of Agrippa's *Occult Philosophy*; he knew that the ancient philosophers purified themselves by abstaining from meat.[85] Modern alchemists all agreed that adepts had to be pure and temperate or their efforts would be wasted.[86] Even Newton's favourite prophet Daniel had, according to Josephus (AD 37–100), acquired the occult skill of the Chaldaeans by forbearing 'to eat of all living creatures'.[87] Newton once told Conduitt that 'They who search after the Philosopher's Stone by their own rules [are] obliged to a strict & religious life,' and Conduitt commented that 'Sr I excelled in both.'[88] Perhaps when attempting alchemical feats, Newton followed in the footsteps of the ancient wise men, keeping himself pure by refusing to eat animals.[89]

Newton shared many opinions more usually associated with retrospectively marginalised characters like Thomas Tryon.[90] But although by Newton's contemporaries' standards such beliefs were far out, his religious opinions can be seen as pushing an Enlightenment agenda. His faith was founded on an empirical observation of the universe (the power of gravity alone was enough to prove the existence of God), and his religion was based on a comparative examination of world cultures. Not only did he challenge entrenched orthodoxies about man's relationship with nature, he also threw aside the millennia-old detestation of 'pagans' and established that they had the same origins as European Christianity.

NINE

Atheists, Deists and the Turkish Spy

By the end of the seventeenth century, a band of secretive philosophers were taking the inquisitive principles of the early Enlightenment to a logical extreme. Some proponents of the radical Enlightenment merely doubted a few biblical tenets; others rejected religion outright. At the heart of the movement were the deists, who accepted that the world had been divinely created but regarded all other religious doctrines as highly suspect human fabrications. Bundled together by contemporaries and invariably misrepresented in the press, the 'deists and atheists' were regarded as the epoch's greatest threat. At the head of this supposedly demonic alliance stood the apostate Jew Benedict de Spinoza (1632–77) whose philosophy spread across Europe in clandestine manuscripts and books, triggering a new wave of thinkers for whom it often seemed – shockingly to Christians – that 'God' meant little more than 'nature'.[1] Because they rejected tradition as a basis for morality, they were commonly portrayed as amoral, Godless rakes. But many of these 'libertines' believed they were simply ringing the death knell for an outdated system of oppression.

Under the scrutiny of their unflinching gaze, customary treatment of non-Europeans and the natural world came in for a dramatic reappraisal. This effort reached a pinnacle in the incredible eight volumes of *Letters Writ by a Turkish Spy*, purportedly a cache of personal papers penned in Arabic by an Ottoman spy called Mahmut operating in Paris from 1637 to 1682. The letters unfold Mahmut's story as he lives through this fraught period of Christian–Muslim relations preceding Europe's final defeat of the Ottoman army in 1683 after narrowly escaping humiliation in the final siege of Vienna. Mahmut's intelligence despatches to his political masters in Constantinople concerning the European courts' military actions and political intrigues are inter-

Mahmut The Turkiſh ſpy Ætais suæ 72

woven with gripping stories about his escapes from assassination, his failed affair with a married Greek woman, his culture shock and psychological turmoil as a Muslim in Europe. The *Turkish Spy* is a deeply sympathetic political romance.

The first volume was in fact written by the Francophile Genoan journalist Giovanni Paolo Marana (1642–93) after his release from an Italian jail for sedition, and the subsequent seven anonymous volumes may have been the work of a coterie of British authors (with an aberrational sequel added in 1718 by Daniel Defoe).[2] From the moment of its first publication, the *Turkish Spy* was a literary sensation throughout Europe. Among the most popular works of the period, read by adults and children alike, it was published in Italian, French, English, German and Russian; reissued at least thirty times and was still being read more than a century later, not least by Samuel Taylor Coleridge.[3]

Part of its popularity was due to its position at the vanguard of a new literary genre: the novel. Widely imitated, the *Turkish Spy* spawned a rash of fabricated collections of letters such as Charles Gildon's *The Post-boy rob'd of his Mail: or, the Pacquet Broke Open* (1692), and was a forerunner of Samuel Richardson's novels. Numerous other copy-cat spy thrillers rolled off the press, including the *Golden Spy, Jewish Spy, German Spy, London Spy, York Spy,* and *Agent of the King of Persia.* Mahmut's role as an outsider in Europe also mirrored that of della Valle and Bernier in their travel narratives which were themselves written in the form of letters and from which the *Turkish Spy* occasionally copied whole chunks verbatim. Indeed, the *Turkish Spy*'s sceptical comparison of different cultures was a logical progression from the voice Bernier developed in his travelogues. From this point on, the satirical foreign observer became a standard figure of European literature, perfected, for example, in Montesquieu's *Persian Letters* (1721), Voltaire's *Letters of Amabed* (1769) and Eliza Hamilton's *Letters of a Hindoo Rajah* (1796).[4]

Particularly curious given its popularity is the fact that the *Turkish Spy* is one of the most radical assaults on established religion to have made it past the censors into print – apparently providing a rare glimpse of the openness to scepticism and even closet deism in Europe.[5] In the interests of the plot, Mahmut himself vacillates between the extremes of devout mystical enthusiasm and Epicurean atheism,[6] going so far as to suggest that the world is no more than a random conglomeration of atoms 'Tack'd, and Stitch'd, and Glew'd together, by the Bird-lime of *Chance*'.[7] But the most sustained philosophical position constructed by the *Turkish Spy* as a whole is revealed when Mahmut declares his allegiance to 'a Sort of People here in the *West,* whom they call *Deists,* that is, Men professing the *Belief* of a *God, Creator* of the *World,* but *Scepticks* in all Things else'. In a remarkable display of the authors' knowledge of Islamic history, Mahmut aligns himself and the European deists with the tenth-century coterie of irenic Neoplatonist Muslims based in Basra and Baghdad, the Ikhwan al-Safa. Mahmut says correctly that the 'Sincere Fraternity' (as he calls them) made inviolable pacts and met in secret clubs to discuss all topics 'with an Unrestrained Freedom . . . without regarding the *Legends* and *Harangues* of the *Mollahs*'.[8]

The *Turkish Spy* evaded prosecution for irreligion partly by dis-avowing its most execrable opinions as belonging to the 'Muslim' writer.[9] But even the moments when Mahmut professes pious adher-ence to Islam – despite his denials that there is any solid basis for doing so – are surreptitious rhetorical devices used by the authors to show that dogmatic faith in any religion (including Christianity) is absurd. His argument for the authenticity of the Qur'an is a mirror image of the Christian defence of the Bible; if European readers were to dismiss one, they had to dismiss the other. Likewise, his withering demolition of Judaeo-Christian mythology, his fears of the Inquisition's lethal persecution, and his passionate yearning to share his religious doubts, are neatly consistent both with Mahmut's Muslim identity and with the anonymous free-thinking authors who spoke through him.[10]

Religions are human inventions, and ceremonial prayers, declares Mahmut, are nothing but '*Hocus-Pocus-Whispers*'.[11] 'What signifies it,' he asks in a classic statement of indifferentism, 'whether we believe the *Written Law* or the *Alcoran*; whether we are Disciples of *Moses, Jesus,* or *Mahomet*; Followers of *Aristotle, Plato, Pythagoras, Epicurus,* or *Ilch Rend Hu* the *Indian Brahmin?*'[12] With its liberal Muslim hero arguing that religious affiliation was little more than social conformity,[13] the *Turkish Spy* opened the door to an unusually favourable view of Ottoman Islamic culture (which, it showed, was no more or less legitimate than European Christianity).[14]

Having cleared the ground with the bulldozer of scepticism, Mahmut proceeds to display an astonishingly fervent admiration for one particular religious group: the Indian Brahmins.[15] An ardent reader of Indian travelogues, and frustrated with the biased accounts of Jesuit missionaries, he begs his masters to send him as their agent to the Great Mughal so he can interview the Brahmins himself. 'There is nothing that I have a greater Passion for these many Years,' he declares, 'than . . . to converse with the *Bramins*, and pry into the Mysteries of their Unknown Wisdom, which occasions so much Discourse in the *World*. I know not what ails me, but I promise my self more Satisfaction from their *Books* . . . or from the Lips of those *Priests* . . . than from all the *Prophets* and *Sages* in the *World*.'[16]

Indeed, it transpires that the Brahmins are a linchpin in the *Turkish Spy*'s attack on Christianity, for Mahmut snidely points out that their ancient Sanskrit scriptures – as the recent travelogues had revealed to the discombobulation of Christians – described events that happened many thousands of years before the biblical beginning of the world. The realisation that Indian history pre-dated everything in the Bible struck a blow to Christianity, and it gave powerful ammunition to the sceptics' argument that religions were products of history's tangled thicket and not transcendent truths.[17]

Having loosened Christianity's stranglehold over moral norms, and also established India as an alternative moral platform, the seven anonymous volumes of the *Turkish Spy* then launch into an attack on one of Europe's most basic tenets: man's right over nature.[18]

Putting Europeans to shame by contrasting them to the humane Indians, Mahmut declares that '*India* is at Present the onely Publick Theatre of Justice toward all Living Creatures.' The idea of applying justice to animals flew in the face of all expected norms. And yet, Mahmut intends to convert his readers to this cause: 'I have been long an Advocate for the *Brutes*, and have endeavour'd to abstain from injuring them my self, and to inculcate this Fundamental Point of Justice to others.'[19] Mahmut's effusions about Indian vegetarianism often replicate passages in John Ovington's *Voyage to Suratt* (which, strangely, was not published until 1696); but the *Turkish Spy* transformed the dreamy utopian tradition of prelapsarian harmony into the much more radical demand for real legislative or moral reform.[20]

In Mahmut's opinion, Hinduism had preserved what was once a universal law of nature to which all cultures bear vestigial testimony.[21] Beginning with Islam, Mahmut claims that Muhammad the Holy Prophet charmed animals and discoursed with them just like Orpheus, Apollonius or St Jerome. In repayment for his kindness, wild animals listened to Muhammad's preaching and a leopard guarded his cave 'and did all the Offices of a kind and faithful Servant'.[22] Mahmut concedes that the Prophet 'did not positively enjoin Abstinence from *Flesh*', but insists that he recommended it and that his first disciples refrained 'from Murdering the Brutes'. Transposing onto Islam arguments familiar from vegetarian Bible glosses, Mahmut adds that the Qur'anic food laws were designed to make it as difficult as possible to eat flesh.[23]

Turkish 'charity' to animals was by then a familiar trope: Francis Bacon compared the Turks to Pythagoras and the Brahmins for bestowing 'almes upon Bruit Creatures', while George Sandys described their universal 'charitie' of which Samuel Purchas had commented that 'Mahometans may in this be examples to Christians.'[24] Other commentators were more critical of their soft-heartedness, and, as a Turk himself, Mahmut lamented that bigoted Europeans 'censure the *Mussulmans*, for extending their Charity to Beasts, Birds and Fishes . . . who, in their Opinion, have neither Souls nor Reason'.[25] Mahmut's aim is to isolate Western Christians with regard to their rapacious treatment of animals.

Next, Mahmut enrols Judaism to the cause, writing to his Jewish confederate that the Mosaic law 'obliges all of thy *Nation* to certain specifick Tendernesses towards the Dumb Animals'. (That the law contradicts itself by also instituting barbaric sacrifices, argues Mahmut, only shows that the Bible is a hopelessly unreliable 'Collection of Fragments patch'd up'.[26]) The true original law, explains Mahmut, having heard the story from the legendary 'wandering Jew', was still maintained by the descendants of the ten lost tribes of Israel. This isolated stock, he says, reside beyond a mountain range in northern Asia living off the fruit of the land, adhering to the common oath: 'I will not taste of the *Flesh* of any *Animal*, but in all things observe the Abstinence commanded by *Allah* to *Moses* on the Mount.' While the Christians and Jews had debased their Bible so much that they believed that the law '*Thou shalt not Kill*' only applied to humans, the lost tribes (and to some extent the modern Muslims) had not forgotten that 'This Prohibition . . . extends to all *Living Creatures*.'[27] At the heart of Judaism, Christianity and Islam, Mahmut identifies a long-lost vegetarian dictate.

Christianity too, ventures Mahmut, was originally vegetarian. Like Thomas Tryon and Roger Crab, he invokes John the Baptist (who did not eat 'locusts' as the translations of the Bible stated, but, as a true rendering of the Greek revealed, 'plant buds' like asparagus[28]), Jesus' brother James, and even Jesus himself, who 'was the most Temperate and Abstemious Man in the World'.[29] Jesus, he claims, was a member of the Essenes, the ascetic Jewish sect who 'would rather suffer *Martyrdom*, than be prevail'd on to taste of any Thing that had *Life* in it'.[30]

Mahmut doesn't stop there. He finds vegetarianism in all cultures: ancient Egyptian, Persian, Athenian, Druidic, Lacedemonian, Spartan, Manichean and 'almost all Nations of the East'. His taxonomic collation of the world's civilisations is a stepping stone between the Renaissance *prisci theologi* and eighteenth-century Orientalism. Making Neoplatonism and deism bedfellows, he fervently declares that he is 'inflam'd afresh with *Pythagorism, Platonism*, and *Indianism*'.[31]

For the most part, Mahmut recognises that cultural values are arbitrary; but if something occurred universally, it was reasonable to suggest that it was natural (a deduction not so far from those of modern sociobiology). In comparing world cultures, the *Turkish Spy* came to the same conclusion as Isaac Newton, Thomas Tryon and no doubt numerous other contemporaries: that the universal law of nature 'to do as you would be done by' applied to animals as well as humans. Vegetarianism, he concludes, is based on 'the *Fundamental Law* of *Nature*, the *Original Justice* of the *World*, which teaches us, *Not to do that to another, which we wou'd not have another do to us*. Now, since 'tis evident, That no Man wou'd willingly become the Food of Beasts; therefore, by the same Rule, he ought not to prey on them.'[32] 'In a Word,' Mahmut declares, 'let us love all of [the] *Human Race*, and shew Justice and Mercy to the *Brutes*.'[33]

Thomas Hobbes had argued in *Leviathan* (1651) that 'doing as one would be done by' was a mutual contract which it was impossible to make with the beasts because they did not understand human speech. The *Turkish Spy* used its empirical analysis of world cultures and its ethnographic description of Hinduism to challenge the basis of Hobbes' argument. In a scene reminiscent of Michel de Montaigne's affectionate sport with his cat, Mahmut pointedly explains how the social contract can be undersigned without the use of verbal language: 'I contract Familiarities with the Harmless *Animals*,' he explains. 'I study like a Lover to oblige and win their Hearts, by all the tender Offices I can perform . . . Then when we once begin to understand each other aright, they make me a Thousand sweet Returns of Gratitude according to their Kind.'[34] Identifying the reciprocal agreement as a natural law meant that the social contract was embedded in nature, and thus animals were bound by it too.

Western Christians, by contrast, had manipulated the Bible to give them authority for their abhorrent behaviour: 'They assert, That all Things were made for Man, and style him *Lord* of his *Fellow-Creatures*; as if . . . [they] were Created onely to serve his Appetite.'[35] The Bible itself was not at fault. It had been wilfully co-opted to justify Christians' gluttony, cruelty and pride, providing a mandate for the '*Epicurism* of those, who ransack all the *Elements* for Dainties'.[36] The true Christian message, argued Mahmut, was encapsulated in the harmony of Paradise which was an image of the original state of the world when man and beast did as they would be done by. By decoding the prelapsarian myth as anthropological data, the *Turkish Spy* showed that even Christianity enshrined a mandate for the natural law regarding animals.

To show that adherence to nature's laws was still a viable option, the authors of the *Turkish Spy* put Mahmut into regular correspondence with five living vegetarians. Most prominent of them is Mahmut's spiritual guru, Mahummed the Hermit, who lives in a cave on Mount

Uriel and has recreated harmony with the animal kingdom – just like the Prophet – converting the idea of saintly kindness to animals into a manifesto for interspecific egalitarianism.[37] Others include a Christian hermit, a Muslim monk and Mirmadolin the mendicant who 'suck'd the Milk' of Mother Earth like the first inhabitants of the world.[38] Mahmut writes to them about other vegetarian hermits such as 'Ilch Rend Hu', the centenarian miracle-working hermit of Kashmir described by François Bernier.[39]

Mahmut repeatedly (about thirteen times) expresses his ardent desire to become a vegetarian hermit too, but in practice his 'Voracious Appetite' always tempts him back into eating flesh. He is perpetually racked by a crisis of conscience, 'self-condemn'd for living contrary to my Knowledge'.[40] This is the subject of frequent lamentation:

> the *Divine Providence* has scatter'd up and down the Surface of this Globe, an Infinite Variety of Roots, Herbs, Fruits, Seeds . . . as in a most pleasant Garden or *Paradise* of Health. But alas, instead we break the Rules of Hospitality; and rushing violently on the Creatures under his Protection, we kill and slay at Pleasure, turning the Banquet to a Cruel Massacre: being transform'd into a Temper wholly Brutal and Voracious, we glut our selves with Flesh and Blood of Slaughter'd *Animals*. Oh! happy he that can content himself with Herbs and other Genuine Products of the Earth.[41]

Even with the added incentive that meat in Paris is not halal, Mahmut's resolution to 'taste of Nothing, that has Breath'd the Common Air' is almost certainly short-lived, like his miserable attempt to abstain from alcohol.[42]

Mahmut also thinks that ascetic abstinence from flesh elevates the intellect and is the path to spiritual restoration.[43] However, in moments of disillusionment, he sardonically reflects that his experiences of religious ecstasy while abstaining from flesh are really the physiological effect of fasting and hyperventilation induced by repeatedly saying prayers (a sceptical critique of asceticism that Bernier deployed in his comments on Indian *yogis*).[44] But despite these scoffs at monasticism, Mahmut remains committed to the morality of vegetarianism and sees it as 'the way of perfection' and the route to Paradise.[45]

His tumultuous wrestling between ethics and appetite is designed as a manual on how to become a vegetarian in real life. Addressing the social difficulties any aspiring vegetarian would have to contend with, Mahmut acknowledges that were his vegetarian sentiments publicly known, his neighbours 'would censure me as a *Heretick*, a *Fool*, or a *Madman*'.[46] Turning away from authorities and reasons, Mahmut ultimately appeals to his human instincts: 'am I not obliged to obey the Inspirations of my *Nature*, or *Better Genius*, which tells me, 'Tis a Butcherly and Inhuman Life, to feed on slaughtered Animals?'[47] At the same time as being an emotional appeal, this also makes the subtle claim that the law of nature is inscribed in every human: this is the voice of nature speaking. There is no doubt that the *Turkish Spy* promoted the cause of vegetarianism across Europe; it opened the minds of its readers to the far-flung ethics of the Brahmins and recommended treating animals with high standards of justice. Unlike their mystical contemporary Thomas Tryon, the authors of the *Turkish Spy* advanced their case in a finely tuned voice which blended cool rationality with heartfelt human sympathy.

The *Turkish Spy* showed what could happen when European norms were abandoned for a fresh examination of man's relationship with nature, especially when they were held up against the moral example of Indian vegetarianism. But the *Turkish Spy* was not an isolated case. The scriptural sanction for killing animals was the mainstay for justifying meat-eating. Indeed, one of the principal functions of religion was to create a fundamental distinction between man and beast. Once faith in Scripture was shaken, and people started turning to other ways of codifying behaviour, the ethics of meat-eating became more problematic. Even the defenders of meat-eating in the past had acknowledged that without the express permission from God in Genesis, the idea of eating animals would be repellent and one would do it, as Calvin said, with a 'doubtful and trembling conscience'.[48] One critic of the deists, John Reynolds, realised that one of the worst aspects of dismissing Scripture was that it undermined man's right to kill animals. He argued that everyone who denied revealed religion should logically be vegetarian. The intelligence of animals, our sympathy for them, the inferior nutritional quality of meat, and the practice of the Indian vegetarians, all suggested that it was wrong to eat flesh: if the Bible and with it God's permission to kill animals was just a mythical invention, he said, then everyone would have to 'let the Butcher's Trade be cashier'd from off the Face of the Earth; let the Shambles be converted into Fruiterer's Shops, and Herb-Markets . . . [and] have done with their

Ragous, with their Fricassies, and Hashes, made of broken Limbs of dismember'd Brother-Animals.'[49] The Bible was the meat-eaters' greatest bulwark, and the foes of religion were also the biggest enemies of meat.

Man's dominion and superiority over nature had for millennia been framed by theology. When deists and free-thinkers came to challenge this framework, the distinct boundary between man and nature, which the Judaeo-Christian tradition had reinforced, either vanished or had to be redrawn. Contemplating vegetarianism became a fashionable way of articulating a rejection of orthodox Christianity as a whole. This trend was often coupled with interest in Eastern culture and the use of that perspective in attacking European norms. At the time of the *Turkish Spy's* publication, there was a coterie of free-thinkers in Britain who were clearly willing to scrutinise the practice of meat-eating from a radical perspective.

Even before the *Turkish Spy*, those who questioned religious orthodoxy also often questioned dietary norms. The heretical sixteenth-century ex-Jesuit Guillaume Postel and his followers were among the first ever people to be accused of being '*Deites*'.[50] The Inquisition imprisoned Postel for trying to prepare for the second coming by uniting all the world's religions under his humanist banner and joining forces with the Family of Love. Postel influenced the heretic Isaac La Peyrère (1596–1676) whose challenge to Christian orthodoxy in turn inspired the *Turkish Spy*.[51] Postel, like the *Turkish Spy*, was particularly interested in the vegetarian Indians. Poring over the travel accounts of Marco Polo and Ludovico de Varthema among others, Postel was overwhelmed by the virtue of the Indian Brahmins, who, he remarked, 'abstain from everything that has life like the Pythagoreans'. The Buddhist holy men of Japan, he noted admiringly, also 'never eat flesh, nor any animals, from fear that the flesh would make them unruly.' This, he said, was a universal practice 'approved of from all times', in which, like the Pythagoreans, the Buddhists exceeded even the purest Christians. He concluded that the Buddhists had originally been Christians who had 'bit by bit converted the truth of Jesus into the fable of Shiaca [Buddha]'; they and the Brahmins still held divine secrets that had been lost to the West and had constructed these into a perfectly adequate religion through their own superior reasoning faculties.[52] Even though skewed by idealism, such syncretic impulses were like porous inlets through which Asian culture influenced the West's construction of man's relationship with nature. Renaissance Neoplatonists, India-loving deists and eighteenth-century Orientalists all contributed to changing European culture by importing the Indian perspective.

Most people holding radical anti-Christian views concealed themselves in anonymity, circulating their ideas in clandestine manuscripts, or using ruses like the *Turkish Spy* to air their ideas in print. Foremost in the British network of deists were Charles Blount (1654–93) and Charles Gildon (1665–1724) and it may be that these two even had a hand in writing the *Turkish Spy*. (If Charles Blount was involved, his decision to escape government spies and the harangues of his detractors by stoically hanging himself in 1693 would help to explain the embarrassing two-year delay between the publication of the *Turkish Spy*'s fifth and sixth volumes.[53])

In 1680 Blount had used his study of paganism – particularly the writing on Hinduism by Rogerius, Bernier, Tavernier, Roth and Kircher – to assault Christian orthodoxy.[54] Blount translated and copiously annotated Philostratus' biography of the legendary vegetarian, Apollonius. But his critics quickly realised that his book was no simple reservoir of erudition, for beneath its placid surface lurked the serpent of sardonic scepticism.[55] There was also a broadside critique of society's bloodthirsty practices.

In his notes on Apollonius' attempts to abolish sacrifice, Blount propounded a popular conspiracy theory which blamed the superstitious practice of sacrificing animals on the priesthood who 'grew so covetous, that nothing but the Blood of Beasts could satiate them'. As well as ensuring a constant supply of 'Rost-meat to the Priests', Blount went on, 'The other concern, *viz.* of the State in those great Sanguinary Sacrifices, was by inuring the People to such horrid and bloudy Sights . . . rendring them fitter for the Wars, and thereby more capable either of defending or enlarging their Empire.' Meat-eating, Blount showed, was a sinister instrument that the state and its conspiratorial allies, the priesthood, had used to tax the people and make them submit to killing each other for the amelioration of their masters' estates. The people were still suffering under the yoke of this legacy, said Blount, for 'at the Battel of *Edgehill* it was generally observ'd, that one Foot-Regiment of Butchers, behaved themselves more stoutly than any other Regiment of either side.'[56]

In this context, the ancient vegetarians, Orpheus, Pythagoras and Plato, were elevated as heroic rebels against an oppressive priesthood.

They had always rejected sacrifices, said Blount, considering it 'a great crime to kill any harmless innocent Beasts, they being intercommoners with men on Earth'.[57] As well as condemning the 'detestable Recreation' of hunting, which, as Agrippa had said, consisted in making 'War against the poor Beasts; a Pastime cruel, and altogether tragical, chiefly delighting in bloud and death', Blount showed that the Pythagoreans' vegetarianism, far from being superstitious, was a rational decision based on the preservation of health and the political subversion of tyranny.[58]

It would be jumping the gun to suggest on the basis of his sardonic writings that Blount really advocated vegetarianism. He knew that all creatures lived by 'devouring and destroying one another'. 'Nay,' he conceded, 'we cannot walk one step, but probably we crush many Insects creeping under our feet'.[59] But his attack on gluttony was a sincere aspect of his social critique, and he did carry it into his personal life by claiming that 'For my own part, I ever eat rather out of necessity, than pleasure'.[60]

Radicals like Blount felt they had much in common with Pythagoras and the Brahmins. They even reinterpreted the doctrines of reincarnation and pantheism to suit their materialist agenda. Reincarnation, they explained, really referred to the *recycling* of matter in the universe. As Blount's contemporary, John Toland (1670–1722) explained, 'Vegetables and Animals become part of us, we become part of them, and both become parts of a thousand other things in the Universe.'[61] If matter was perpetually recycling from one thing to another, then all living beings were basically made of the same stuff. There was no essential difference between a man and an oyster.[62] The Turkish spy, who at times felt he was 'a profess'd *Pythagorean*, a *Disciple* of the *Indian Brachmans*, *Champion* for the *Transmigration* of *Souls*', even suggested that the sympathetic force of 'Magnetick *Transmigration*' ensured that 'souls' were attracted to locations that matched their nature.[63]

These arguments provided a notion of eternal life through the perpetuity of matter and of cosmic justice which worked by natural laws without the need for divine intervention. They also provided a basis for ethical equity between all life forms, and a kind of karmic incentive to moral behaviour. Thus Pythagoras and the Indians, traditionally regarded as the arch-pedlars of superstition, were refashioned as the founding fathers of non-religious ethics, and this in turn encouraged the deists to espouse their vegetarian ideals.[64] It was not long before critics claimed that '*Pythagoras* was a *Deist*' and that Buddhism and Hinduism were 'nothing but Pantheism or Spinozism'.[65]

Charles Gildon, a shady figure in the literary world, used the oriental perspective to attack orthodoxy in his *Golden Spy* (1709).[66] In *The Oracles of Reason* (1693), which he compiled with Charles Blount, he used the antiquity of Chinese and Indian culture, just as the *Turkish Spy* had done, to undermine faith in the absurdly dwarfish history in the Bible.[67]

Gildon's anonymously published *The Post-boy rob'd of his Mail* (1692), as the title suggests, is a miscellany of letters like the *Turkish Spy*, and one of the letters contains a rare account of Thomas Tryon's followers. Gildon co-opted Tryon's vegetarianism into an anti-Christian political statement by emphasising that Tryon derived his beliefs from the Hindus, not from Christian Scripture, and that he thought eating 'our Brethren and Fellow-Creatures' was 'Opression' and 'qualifies Men to be sordid, surly, and Soldiers, Hunters, Pirates, Tories, and such as wou'd have the bestial Nature fortify'd; that they might act like Lions, and Devils, over their own kind as well as over all other Creatures'.[68] So it seems that Gildon, Blount, and possibly the authors of the *Turkish Spy*, recognised some common ground between their own views and Tryon's vegetarianism. Gildon may have been encouraged to do this by their mutual friend Aphra Behn. Perhaps the vegetarian ideas in the *Turkish Spy* were inspired by or even supposed to be a mockery of Tryon.[69]

Although Tryon subscribed to all sorts of mystical inventions, he shared with the radical sceptics a desire to erode traditional orthodoxies. His 'East-Indian Brackmanny' is a precursor of Mahmut as an Oriental vegetarian critic of Western society, and his *Letters From Averroes* (1695) combines this Oriental critique with the letter format which slyly uses a Muslim character to challenge Christian dogmatism.[70]

At the end of the seventeenth century the vegetarian question was as prominent as it ever has been in Western intellectual debate. The parameters of culture were shifting radically. The exclusive powers of the Church were giving way to unorthodoxy, empiricism and relativism. Political turmoil and monarchy in Britain were replaced, in the Glorious Revolution of 1688, by liberties that fostered open-minded debate. Enlightened intellectual movements combined with new access to information on foreign cultures to challenge traditional values. Fundamental assumptions were under constant review, and the right to eat meat was one of them. With the flood of information on the vegetarian Indians, more and more people were questioning their long-held belief that eating animals was a natural, necessary part of human life. There were so many prominent thinkers from widely different intellectual backgrounds who were challenging the practice of killing animals that it is hardly an exaggeration to say that the late seventeenth century harboured a vegetarian renaissance. In many minds at least, there had been a bloodless revolution.

PART TWO

Meatless Medicine

TEN

Dieting with Dr Descartes

René Descartes was born in La Haye in 1596, and when he was one his mother died of a lung disease which he inherited. He was a sickly baby and was not thought likely to survive, but survive he did, and in combating his own weak constitution he came to believe that he had found the secret to long life. His blend of solitary reflection and stead-fast adherence to mathematical reasoning created a new climate in European philosophy which, by the end of the seventeenth century, had flourished into the Natural Philosophy of the Enlightenment. Rather than relying on second-hand religious doctrines, Descartes showed how to establish truth firmly on the principle of 'Reason'. This breach with religious tradition created a need to reconstitute the mandate for man's superiority over the rest of creation. But Descartes' legacy was an enduring schism in European thought, the remnants of which can still be felt today.

At the Jesuit school of La Flèche, he had been raised from the age of eight on the old school theories of Aristotelian philosophy and Augustinian theology according to which the world was divided into matter, immaterial spirit and an 'intermediate substance'. When Des-cartes came to scrutinise his education with his rigorous method of sceptical reasoning, he agreed with the Aristotelians that humans had an immaterial rational soul: as he explained in his *Meditations* (1641), the fact that he could say 'I think, therefore I am' proved this beyond doubt. He also agreed with the Aristotelians that animals lacked the rational soul – their inability to speak languages was proof enough of that. But he thought that the Aristotelians' claim that animals were animated by an intermediate sensitive soul was meaningless mumbo-jumbo. If animals had no soul, they had to be made purely of matter, and as Descartes believed that matter by itself could not think, he concluded that animals were just like soulless machines. All their actions were the result of automatic material cause and effect; they did not even have feelings or sensations as humans did. They were only alive in so far as the heat of their heart pumped blood around their bodies.[1] As Descartes' chief disciple, the Jesuit Father Nicolas Malebranche, explained in his *Search after Truth* (1674-5), 'The Cartesians do not think that Beasts feel Pain or Pleasure, or that they love or hate any thing; because they admit nothing but what is material in Beasts, and they do not believe that Sensations or Passions are Properties of Matter'; 'the Principal of a Dog's Life,' wrote Malebranche provocatively, 'differs very little, if at all, from that of the Motion of a Watch.'[2] This, rather than Scripture, was the rational justification for killing animals: they did not suffer; indeed, given the mechanical nature of their life, they hardly even 'died'.

Descartes' ability to explain the operation of a body in mechanistic terms – as the great intricate clockwork of God – provided the foundation for a powerful school of physicians in the eighteenth century, and insofar as he showed how 'life' worked without the need for 'soul' he led the way to a modern scientific understanding of living things.[3] But although he won many followers, his rigid dualism – dividing everything so starkly into matter and spirit – and particularly his relegation of animals to the status of insensible lumps of dirt, became the focus of widespread protest all over Europe, notably in England.

People found it hard to accept his contention that animals had no sensation as it contradicted a common-sense view of animal behaviour and made a nonsense of their sentimental attachment to pet dogs. In the intellectual backlash, many philosophers preferred to think that animals had souls *and* reason rather than concede that they were mere machines.[4]

The English philosopher Thomas Hobbes agreed with Descartes that animals lacked reason, but he suggested that mind *was* made of matter and therefore animals could think to some extent.[5] Hobbes did not think this accrued to animals any sort of moral protection from humans, even though, like Descartes, he thought the scriptural permission to Noah an insufficient basis for eating them. For Hobbes, *might* made right: all beings had the right to kill for their own preservation, and humans – by forming alliances with the use of their reason and language – had become powerful enough to kill any animal they chose (while beasts, lacking reason and language, were incapable of entering into the contract of forbearance from conflict enjoyed by human beings).[6]

The philosophical Duchess of Newcastle, Margaret Cavendish (1624–74), sustained a lengthy correspondence about animals with Descartes and voiced her dissent in her striking poetry:

> As if that God made Creatures for Mans meat,
> To give them Life, and Sense, for Man to eat; . . .
> Making their Stomacks, Graves, which full they fill
> With murther'd Bodies, that in sport they kill . . .
> And that all Creatures for his sake alone,
> Was made for him, to Tyrannize upon.[7]

Descartes' new philosophical view of animals, it seemed to many, was still worse than the disdain fostered by Aristotle and Augustine. Most of the earlier seventeenth-century radical vegetarians, whose main inspiration was the Bible, ignored or remained ignorant of the debate Descartes had triggered.[8] But the vegetarian-oriented deists – Blount, Gildon, the *Turkish Spy* and Simon Tyssot de Patot – identified Descartes as their common enemy, and embraced instead the more conducive animal-friendly philosophy of his rival, Pierre Gassendi.[9] If Reason proved that humans had souls, declaimed Mahmut in the *Turkish Spy*, then the fact that animals were clearly intelligent showed 'the *Brute Animals* to have *Souls* as well as We'; if it did not, he warned, then ' 'tis as easie to defend, That Humane Nature it self is but Matter'.[10] (As the traveller to India, John Ovington, had said, even the Pythagoreans and Indians knew *that*.)[11]

Descartes felt he had established man's superiority on the firmest foundations, but because he based it on rational argument rather than Scripture, he opened the door to opposite deductions. Reversing both Descartes' and Hobbes' rationale for eating animals, the *Turkish Spy* concluded that 'it is little less Injustice to Kill and Eat them, because they cannot speak and converse with us, than it would be for a *Cannibal* to murder and devour thee or me, because we understood not his *Language* nor he ours'.[12] It was precisely this sort of grotesque logical deduction from Hobbes' theory of the 'War of Nature' that the German philosopher Samuel Freiherr von Pufendorf sought to clear up with his monumental counter-vegetarian article in *The Law of Nature and Nations* (1672). Pufendorf gave the vegetarians a great deal of space; he was liberally uncritical of Brahmins and other vegetarian peoples and he even endorsed the vegetarians' argument that meat made people vicious and that humans were better suited to a herbivorous diet. But he explained that men had an indissoluble right to kill because the hostility and competition between them and animals was (in contrast to the occasional conflicts between men) acute and irreparable. Nevertheless, he insisted that the vegetarians were right in so far as 'foolish Cruelty and Barbarity' to animals was indisputably reprehensible.[13]

Members of the public were appalled to hear that Cartesians kicked and stabbed animals to make the point that their cries had no more significance than the squeak of a door. As one horrified witness testified, 'They administered beatings to dogs with perfect indifference, and made fun of those who pitied the creatures as if they had felt pain.' Descartes himself was renowned for having cut open his own dog to show exactly how the animal machine operated. Cartesians became indelibly marked as the most inhumane of philosophers. Even Descartes' contemporary Henry More the Platonist, who admired Descartes to the extent of keeping a portrait of him in his closet, could not accept the doctrine of the beast-machine: 'my spirit,' pleaded More to Descartes in a letter, 'through sensitivity and tenderness, turns not with abhorrence from any of your opinions so much as from that deadly and murderous sentiment . . . the sharp and cruel blade which in one blow, so to speak, dared to despoil of life and sense practically the whole race of animals, metamorphosing them into marble statues and machines.' It was better to be a Pythagorean and believe animals had immortal souls than to be so cruel to the creatures, he said.

Descartes, however, urged that far from being cruel, his philosophy was the only just system. If animals could feel pain then man and God were guilty of the most horrendous crimes. Humans (as Augustine explained) deserved to suffer because they had sinned, and had the promise of heaven to look forward to. But innocent animals had never sinned, so how could one justify allowing them to suffer? The only way of excusing mankind's treatment of animals was to insist that animals were incapable of sensation. 'And thus,' announced Descartes, 'my opinion is not so much cruel to wild beasts as favourable to men, whom it absolves, at least those not bound by the superstition of the Pythagoreans, of any suspicion of crime, however often they may eat or kill animals.'[14] Descartes, in his own opinion, had come up with the *only* viable justification for eating meat. Deny what he said was true, he implied, and morally you would be obliged to take up vegetarianism. As one later vegetarian cynic commented, 'One must either be a Cartesian, or allow that man is very vile.'[15]

The extraordinary irony is that Descartes was in any case free from the suspicion of committing crimes to animals because he was, by preference, a vegetarian. According to his friend and biographer Father Adrien Baillet, Descartes lived on an 'anchoritic regime' of home-grown vegetables. He did not manage to live like this consistently, but at his own table he served 'vegetables and herbs all the time, such as turnips, coleworts, panado, salads from his garden, potatoes with wholemeal bread'. On this Lenten diet he shunned flesh, though he 'did not absolutely forbid himself the use of eggs'. Baillet explained that this was because Descartes believed that roots and fruits were 'much more proper to prolong human life, than the flesh of animals'.

It is often forgotten that Descartes conceived of himself as a physician as much as a rationalist philosopher. Descartes claimed that improving human health 'has been at all times the principal goal of my studies', and he vowed in the *Discourse on the Method* (1637) to dedicate himself to 'no other occupation' than freeing mankind from sickness 'and perhaps also even from the debility of age'. Descartes conducted dietary experiments upon himself and concluded that meat was unsuited to the mechanism of the human body, whereas the vegetable diet could, in the words of his friend Sir Kenelm Digby, 'lengthen out his life span to equal that of the Patriarchs'.

Like the mystical Rosicrucians he so admired, Descartes dispensed free medical advice throughout his career, and shared his secret about the efficacy of vegetables with other 'friends of his character'. His companion the Abbé Claude Picot was so impressed that after spending three months at Descartes' hermit-like retreat in Egmond, 'he wanted to reduce himself to the institute of Mr Descartes, believing that this was the only way to make a success of the secret which he claimed our Philosopher had discovered, to make men live for *four or five hundred years.*' When in 1650 Descartes died at the pitiful age of fifty-four, Picot – after all the claims he made for his diet – was understandably discomposed, and insisted that without a freak accident 'it would have been impossible'; others even suspected that Descartes had been poisoned.[16]

Descartes' mechanistic physiology convinced him both that it was morally acceptable to eat meat and, simultaneously, that it was healthier not to. This reasoning placed him at the crossroads of the vegetarian debate of the eighteenth century. Ethical vegetarianism was built on a refutation of Descartes' 'beast-machine'; medical vegetarians used his mechanistic system of the body to explain the benefits of the vegetable diet. The fact that Descartes himself saw no contradiction between refusing one and embracing the other could be viewed as demonstrating the absolute distinction between the medical and ethical motives for vegetarianism – but that is not how some eighteenth-century doctors saw it. When they argued that the body's hydraulic mechanism was clogged and damaged by meat, they almost invariably acknowledged that this implied that God never intended humans to eat animals.

Descartes' diet ostensibly had nothing to do with ethical objections to killing animals. Indeed, his *Discourse on the Method* directed a specific attack against the cult of loving animals inaugurated by Michel de Montaigne's *Apology for Raymond Sebond* (1585). Descartes' dualist theory of the beast-machine seems to have been devised partly *in order* to extinguish these feelings of compassion. This is borne out by Descartes' early manuscripts which show that he first devised the idea of the animal automata in 1619–20 after his friend and superior brother at the Jesuit college, Father Molitor, presented him with the animal-friendly *Treatise on Wisdom* (1601) by Montaigne's disciple Pierre Charron.[17]

Following Descartes' lead, Malebranche also attacked the 'dangerous' Montaigne for being 'angry with Men; *because they separate themselves from . . . Beasts,* which he calls *our Fellow Brethren,* and *our Companions'*.[18] Malebranche explained that sympathy was just a mechanical process in the body – like blood circulation, an animal function as bestial as a sexual urge – and should therefore be subjugated like other carnal appetites to the superior power of reason: and reason indicated that animals were not really feeling pain in any case.[19] This lesson was lost on 'Persons of a fine and delicate Constitution, who have a lively Imagination, and very soft tender Flesh', especially women and children who, he said, 'are Mechanically dispos'd to be very Pitiful and Compassionate'.[20] But Malebranche recognised that even being as convinced as he and Descartes were that animals did not feel pain was no protection against this corporal *feeling* of sympathy. For this inescapable automatic compassion, he said, 'often prevents those Persons from Butchering Beasts, who are the most convincingly perswaded they are meer Machines'. He warned that failing to realise that the body was sending misleading signals was 'a prejudice that is very dangerous in view of its consequences'.[21]

Though tantalisingly unverifiable, it would be most surprising if Descartes' medical decision to abstain from meat also made him feel better because it avoided the irrepressible sensation of sympathy for animal suffering. But by the end of the eighteenth century at least, that is precisely what some commentators believed was the case. One author even implied that it was *because* of his humanity that, 'in imitation of the good natured Plutarch, [Descartes] always preferred fruits and vegetables to the bleeding flesh of animals.'[22]

Regardless of Descartes' own feelings, it is superlatively ironic that this Cartesian mechanistic explanation of sympathy was turned into an argument *for* ethical vegetarianism in the eighteenth century. The fact that sympathy was an innate function of human anatomy convinced many that it was an embodiment of natural or divine law – especially since most people believed God had personally designed the human body. This came to underwrite the argument that sympathy was an innate source of moral and social principles, formulated by the 'moral sense' philosophers from the 3rd Earl of Shaftesbury (1671–1713) to Francis Hutcheson (1694–1746) and David Hume (1711–76), until it was finally revised by Immanuel Kant (1724–1804).[23] It became common to extrapolate the same argument onto sympathy for animals and for Jean-Jacques Rousseau this constituted a basis for animal rights. As the Dutch physician-philosopher Bernard Mandeville (1670–1733) expressed it in 1714, because sympathy 'proceeds from a real Passion inherent in our Nature, it is sufficient to demonstrate that we are born with a Repugnancy to the killing, and consequently the eating of Animals'.[24] At a time when natural observations carried as much force as biblical strictures, this deduction of natural law became one of the most potent arguments for vegetarianism. Anti-vegetarians fiercely responded by adopting the neo-Cartesian argument that sympathy should be subjugated to reason and to the scriptural permission to kill animals.

Even if Descartes was not one of those described by Malebranche, who knew animals were machines but still could not bring themselves to kill them, his extraordinary legacy influenced both sides of the medical and ethical vegetarian debate which flourished throughout the eighteenth century.

ELEVEN

Tooth and Nail: Pierre Gassendi and the Human Appendix

In 1699 the anatomy lecturer at Surgeon's Hall in London, Edward Tyson, made a breakthrough in the understanding of humanity's relationship to beasts. For the first time in Western science, Tyson dissected the body of an ape, and to the fascination of all found that in nearly every way it resembled a human. He called it the 'Orang-Outang' – Malayan for 'Man of the Woods' – or in Latin, *Homo sylvestris*, and his specimen still stands in the upright posture of a human in the British Museum. The 'Orang-Outang' was in fact a young chimpanzee, but Tyson's observations were nevertheless sensational and were still being consulted 150 years later when Charles Darwin (1809–82) devised his theory on the 'missing link'.

Tyson's chimp shed new light on the perennial question about the distinction between humans and animals: this 'pygmie', said Tyson, was 'no man, nor yet a common ape but a sort of animal between both'. As far as he could see there was no difference between the two, even 'the *Brain* in all Respects, exactly resembling a Man's'. Contrary to expectations, Tyson believed this *disproved* the ancient atheist idea that man was just a sophisticated ape. In accordance with Descartes' philosophy, Tyson argued that if there was no *physical* difference and yet animals still couldn't speak or reason, man's pre-eminence must reside in the 'Higher principle' of a rational soul. However, in the longer term, Tyson's observations did lend force to the argument that humans were not essentially different from animals.

Tyson's dissection has gone down as a landmark in the history of human self-knowledge, but its immediate impact is less well known. If the ape was corporally identical to humans, Tyson's contemporaries began to wonder, mightn't its habits tell us something about human nature? As one anxious reader (perhaps John Evelyn) scribbled in the

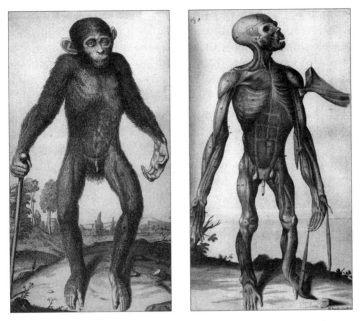

Edward Tyson's chimpanzee, before and after dissection (1699)

margin of Tyson's book *Orang-Outang*, King Charles I had to put down his court ape for being disturbingly lecherous.

What about other natural appetites? Before he cut the poor chimp open, Tyson had been charmed by its virtuous temperance: it had got extremely drunk the first time someone gave it a jug of wine, but subsequently it restricted itself to just one glass with every meal, which proved, said Tyson, that the '*Instinct* of *Nature* teaches Brutes *Temperance*; and *Intemperance* is a Crime not only against the *Laws* of *Morality*, but of *Nature* too.' The chimp also seemed to show that St Paul's commandment against food taboos was a natural law, for it ate anything that was set before it, which – in the absence of any information on its natural feeding habits – led Tyson to suggest tentatively that 'I can't but think, (like a Man) that they are *omnivorous.*'

It is true that chimps do occasionally prey on monkeys but the ape we now call the orang-utan is exclusively herbivorous. Tyson and his contemporaries were confused about the difference between the great apes which made it difficult to collate behavioural observations with anatomical studies made back home. Travel books that Tyson quoted described other apes which 'feed upon Fruits that they find in the

Woods, and upon Nuts; for they eat no kind of Flesh'. If it was true that the apes were herbivorous and if their bodies were identical to man's, wouldn't that imply that humans were naturally designed to be herbivorous too? This set the stage for one of the most enduring and heated debates of the century: if man was an animal, what sort of an animal was he: carnivore or herbivore? What implications did this have for human nature: vicious or benign?[1]

Immediately after dissecting the ape, Tyson released a series of articles 'On Man's feeding on Flesh' in the *Philosophical Transactions of the Royal Society*. These were written in response to the enquiries of the ex-medical student, now Oxford Professor of Geometry and founder member of the Royal Society, John Wallis (1616–1703). As if the turn of the century demanded a new direction in thinking, Wallis and Tyson formally set out the new agenda: that man's eating of meat was to be scrutinised on an empirical, rather than scriptural, basis. 'Without disputing it as a Point of Divinity,' declared Wallis, 'I shall consider it (with *Gassendus*) as a Question in Natural Philosophy, whether it be proper Food for Man.'[2]

As Wallis noted, the empirical vegetarian tradition had in fact been inaugurated seventy years earlier by the philosopher 'Gassendus', or as he is known today, Pierre Gassendi. Gassendi shared Descartes' detestation of the fusty old Aristotelian scholasticism, but rejected Descartes' excessively speculative rationalism, and emphasised instead that human knowledge is based on empirical sensory experience. Though less well known than his adversary today, Gassendi's resuscitation of Epicurean atomism spawned one of the most important philosophical movements in Europe. He taught such writers as Cyrano de Bergerac (1619–55), the big-nosed *libertin érudit*, and influenced a whole school of eighteenth-century materialists, ultimately paving the way for modern atomic theories.[3]

Given Epicurus' reputation as an arch-atheist and hedonist, Gassendi was sailing close to the wind by espousing his materialist philosophy and he was constantly fending off accusations of being an atheist and drunken libertine himself.[4] But Gassendi insisted that Epicurus was misunderstood: his ethic of attaining pleasure meant avoiding pain by *detaching* oneself from fleshly appetites, and Epicurus proved this by living a heroically sober and temperate life. The Epicurean diet, said Gassendi, far from being a gluttonous feast, was more like that of peasants and Pythagoreans 'who live on nothing but bread, fruit and water, and who maintain themselves to a marvel, without hardly ever having need of doctors'.[5] Epicurus took his temperance so far that he allegedly maintained 'a total abstinence from Flesh'.[6]

With regard to the allegations of atheism, Gassendi was a Catholic abbot and professed an implicit faith in man's immortal soul; but in opposition to Descartes' impassable line between spirit and matter, Gassendi thought of the soul as a rarefied substance like a flame which pervaded and animated the body. Descartes' definition of animals as soulless, mindless and thoughtless machines was consequently fallacious, since they too had an animating soul even if it was not immortal.

Developing his objections to Descartes in unison with Hobbes, Gassendi suggested that as everything in the human mind came there only by the senses, and as animals had the same organs of sense as humans, it seemed clear that animals would think just like humans. Gassendi claimed that animal thoughts were not essentially different from 'reason' and differed only in the degree of their perfection: 'though animals do not reason so perfectly and about so many things as man, they still do reason,' Gassendi wrote to Descartes in 1641, 'though they do not utter human expressions (as is natural seeing they are not man) yet they emit their own peculiar cries, and employ them just as we do our vocal sounds.'[7]

By this time Gassendi's dispute with Descartes on behalf of the animals was more than a decade old. In 1629, soon after leaving the company of Descartes' friends in Paris, Gassendi travelled to northern Europe where he met another of the greatest intellectuals of the period, the chemist Jan Baptista van Helmont (1579–1644), father of Franciscus Mercurius the kabbalist. Of all subjects they could have chosen, Helmont and Gassendi engaged in a debate about vegetarianism which they later pursued in letters to each other, and which Gassendi finally built into one of the most influential philosophical works of the seventeenth century, the *Syntagma Philosophicum* (posthumously published in 1658).

Like Tyson and Wallis decades later, Gassendi's principal argument was based on comparative anatomy, a discipline as old as Aristotle. Gassendi adapted this part of his argument from Plutarch's essay 'On the Eating of Flesh' (1st century AD). Man, Plutarch had argued, 'has no hooked beak or sharp nails or jagged teeth, no strong stomach or warmth of vital fluids able to digest and assimilate a heavy diet of flesh.'[8] For Plutarch, the corporal design of the human body indicated that nature intended humans to be herbivorous.

A millennium and a half later, Gassendi produced the mandate for philosophical vegetarianism, by proclaiming that 'The entire purpose of philosophy ought to consist in leading men back to the paths of nature.' He gave new precision to Plutarch's anatomical argument by pointing out that carnivores had sharp, pointed, unevenly spaced teeth, whereas the teeth of herbivores were short, broad, blunt, and closely packed in jaws that joined perfectly for effective grinding. Human teeth, with their prominent molars and incisors, he said, were most like the herbivores. Gassendi concluded that 'Nature intended [men] to follow, in the selection of their food, not the first, namely the carnivorous, but the latter, which graze on the simple gifts of the Earth.' This observation, he said, was corroborated by the herbivorous diet instituted by God in Eden and by the myths of the classical Golden Age: 'in this time of innocence,' Gassendi speculated, 'man did not want to drench his hands in the blood of animals.' Because our teeth weren't properly designed for chewing flesh, he said, they couldn't cope with all the membranes, tendons and sticky fibres, leaving too much work for our stomachs, overcharging the system with succulent juices and clouding the spirits. Fruit and vegetables, on the other hand were easy to break down into pulp.

Helmont's interpretation of the facts was totally different. He insisted that man was a microcosmic combination of all the animals: he had the canine teeth of carnivores and the molar teeth of herbivores, and could be nourished by the flesh of them all. That flesh also *tasted* delicious and nourished the human body was clear proof that 'it was permitted to man by his nature, to eat the flesh of animals'.[9]

Gassendi retorted that the similarities between ourselves and animals – rather than being a mandate for eating them – should teach us to recognise our consanguinity. Taking a sideswipe at 'a celebrated man' (presumably Descartes), Gassendi argued that in terms of anatomy 'monkeys can pride themselves on having the same as us'; 'notwithstanding they are earthly, they are coeval with us, however much we are used to despising them.'

'So how come you do not abstain from eating meat?' Gassendi imagined his opponent asking, to which he replied that his nature had been depraved by being brought up a carnivore, and that it would be dangerous to change his diet all of a sudden (a pervasive assumption rooted in ancient medicine[10]). But nevertheless, he conceded, 'I admit that if I were wise, I would abandon this food bit by bit, and nourish myself solely on the gifts of the earth: I do not doubt that I would be happier for longer and more constantly in better health.'[11]

It was ironic that Gassendi framed some of his arguments in opposition to Descartes, for this was just the sort of conclusion that Descartes appears to have come to. Perhaps when Descartes and Gassendi had their famous reconciliatory meeting in 1647, this was one of the topics they agreed upon. If the opinion of Descartes' disciple, Antoine le Grand, is anything to go by, the Gassendists and Cartesians both agreed that humans were naturally herbivorous. In the *Entire Body of Philosophy, According to the Principles of the Famous Renate des Cartes* (1672), le Grand endorsed every point of Gassendi's vegetarian argument. The fact that eating *raw* meat was instinctively repellent, he insisted, shows 'that *Flesh* is not our Natural *food*, being only introduc'd by *Lust*, which hath quite changed our Nature from its Primigenial Inclination and Temper'. If a boy were raised on a natural fruitarian diet, le Grand speculated, he might 'not be inferiour to *Stags* in running, nor to *Apes* in climbing of *Trees*'.[12]

Gassendi's medical arguments developed into a long-lasting scientific tradition. This received a massive boost in 1678 when his major works were abridged and translated from Latin into French by an ex-pupil who had just returned from travelling in India and was now at the medical faculty of Montpellier.[13] This vital redactor of Gassendi's theories was no other than François Bernier, the most influential interpreter of Indian vegetarianism in seventeenth-century Europe – who suggested that abstaining from meat had originally been a rational practice based on the preservation of health and the inculcation of good morals. Although Bernier never said so in his travel writing, he had probably been predisposed to the medical arguments for vegetarianism by Gassendi, his friend and mentor.

In Bernier's hands, Gassendi's vegetarian arguments underwent a fascinating transformation. Gassendi had little empirical evidence that the vegetable diet really was as healthy as he hypothesised, but Bernier used his experience in India to show that vegetarians really were at least as healthy as meat-eaters. So, in Bernier's *Abrégé de la Philosophie de Gassendi*, where Gassendi noted that ancient pagan philosophers and Christian ascetics lived on the vegetable diet, Bernier updated this information with the crucial contemporary fact that 'even now many people of the East Indies still do'. Where Gassendi argued that the fortitude of herbivorous animals suggested that plants were very nourishing, Bernier inserted the comment that 'the Indians who live on nothing else are just as strong, and at least as healthy as us'.[14] And when Gassendi wrote that Diogenes, Seneca and Lucretius were exemplars of Epicurean frugality, Bernier appended an entire essay on the living 'Indian Diogenes', in order, he explained, 'to shew that all these fine things we have spoken of, are not only bare Philosophical Speculations, but that there are whole Nations, who lead as sparing a Life'. The Brahmins, Banians and naked Indian fakirs eat hardly anything but lentils and rice, never eat flesh, and yet, said Bernier, 'they live as contented, as quiet, and pleasant as we do, and far more Healthy, at least full as strong and lusty as we are.'[15]

Most intriguing of all – given his professional status as an academic physician – is Bernier's attention to Indian medicine. Although he did not think much of their anatomical knowledge – and ridiculed them for fleeing every time he cut open an animal alive to demonstrate the circulation of the blood – he did think their medical *practice* could teach Europeans something, even though it 'differs essentially from ours'. In his travelogue, Bernier noted that for Indians 'the sovereign remedy for sickness is abstinence; nothing is worse for a sick body than meat broth.' This went against the prevailing practice in France where feeble patients were considered in need of 'strengthening' with rich meat broths. And yet, Bernier noted that the Indian practice of abstinence from flesh seemed like an effective remedy, used by both Hindus and Muslims alike.[16] In the *Abrégé* Bernier converted this into a full-blown defence of vegetarianism, arguing that meat broths did more harm than good and that 'a great part of Asia believe them to be mortal to fever patients, and that this was, apparently, Hippocrates' opinion, since he usually prescribes them nothing but oat broth'.[17]

Bernier adopted the Indian method of treatment by abstinence from flesh in his own medical practice: 'I might mention also a Person of great Eminency, who was severely tormented with the Gout, but by my Advice, yielding to live one Year very abstemiously, and scarce to Eat any Flesh (according to the Custom of the *Indians*, who nevertheless are very healthy and strong, and are rarely troubled with such Distempers) was perfectly cured.'[18] Indeed, Bernier had cured himself of such ailments as soon as he arrived in India. This, he extrapolated, was proof that vegetarianism was a healthy diet for anyone.

Not only did Bernier's experience in India turn him away from the use of meat broths in medicine, it even seems to have convinced him that flesh-eating itself was bad for the health. Bernier, who despised Hinduism as a whole, ended up converting – at least on an intellectual plane – to what he saw as one of its principal doctrines.

Bernier forcefully injected the teaching of Indian medicine into the European tradition at exactly the time that other doctors were starting to revive the ancient Hippocratic use of therapeutic dieting. This was a medical reform that profoundly affected the understanding of life-style and which can be seen as the beginning of modern notions about balanced diets, the requirement of fresh vegetables and the nutritional viability of vegetarianism. Bernier thought the Indian doctors were leading the way.

In the 1670s the English philosopher John Locke (1632–1704), a doctor himself, spent fifteen months curing his own ailments among medical colleagues in Montpellier. He befriended Bernier, frequently quizzed him about India, avidly making notes in his diary on Indian physiology and metempsychosis; he read his travel narratives, which inspired him to study the other major works on Hinduism by della Valle, Lord, Roe, Ovington and Rogerius, and these provided the variety of cultural perspectives Locke employed in his *Essay Concerning Human Understanding* (1690).[19] Locke agreed with Gassendi that animals could think, and he even seems to have been influenced by the 'Hindu' doctrine (reported by Rogerius) that humans were only more intelligent than animals because their brains (not their souls) were better constructed.[20]

It may also have been thanks to Bernier that, in his widely used educational guidebook *Thoughts Concerning Education* (1692), Locke joined Gassendi in criticising the custom of weaning children onto meat, suggesting that they would be much healthier if they 'were kept wholly from flesh the first three or four years of their lives' – a practice he recognised was hardly likely to catch on among parents who were 'misled by the custom of eating too much flesh themselves'. Like Bernier, Locke also recommended that most children's ailments should be cured by 'abstinence from flesh', and in a conclusion that fore-shadowed the social critiques of later vegetarian doctors, Locke attributed 'a great part of our diseases in England, to our eating too much flesh, and too little bread'.[21] The anatomical vegetarianism of Gassendi merged with the Indian example observed by Bernier and became a serious foundation for a reassessment of man's natural diet.

Gassendi stressed that sensory observation was the means by which people acquired knowledge, and this Epicurean methodology underpinned the early Enlightenment's emphasis on empirical observation. The similarity to Locke's philosophical mantra has led many to suggest that Locke was deeply indebted to Gassendi, an assumption backed up by the fact that Locke spent hours in conversation with Bernier and owned a copy of the *Abrégé*.[22] In the hands of Gassendi, Bernier and the members of the Royal Society in London, the vegetarian debate was shifted into this new empirical arena.

Bernier's observations in India and his trials on his patients provided a new set of empirical data that appeared to substantiate Gassendi's anatomical argument. Decades later, when John Wallis read about Tyson's recent meticulous dissection of animals, he remembered Gassendi's vegetarian treatise, and realised that here was yet another set of data that might shed light on the question. While Gassendi had focused on the morphology of the teeth, Tyson and Wallis extended the enquiry to the shape and function of animals' guts. Wallis pointed out that herbivores tended to have intestines designed for slow digestion with a large colon and 'caecum' (a pouch between the small and large intestine). Carnivores, on the other hand, had little or no colon and the caecum was reduced to a small appendix or was completely absent, indicating a rapid digestion of food.

Wallis agreed that the human caecum was small and shrivelled but this was not necessarily natural, since the human foetus had a much larger, healthy caecum. Overall, the human intestines, Wallis and Tyson agreed, fell in line with the herbivores. So did those of the monkeys, baboons, apes and, as Tyson had shown, the *Homo sylvestris* whose guts were proportionately exactly the same dimensions as man's.[23] On the basis of the evidence, Tyson grudgingly – but decisively – agreed with Gassendi, 'that Nature never designed [Man] to live on Flesh; but, that the Wantonness of his Appetite, and a depraved Custom, has inured him to it.' This was exactly the claim of the radical vegetarians. If Thomas Tryon had been in the habit of reading scientific papers he might have been enthralled to find his religious and moral theories so clearly backed up by the latest scientific research. But Tyson and Wallis were not ready to part with their 'depraved' meat dinners. Despite their recognition of the very strong evidence, they refused to endorse a return to the natural diet. 'I am not fond of advancing a New Hypothesis, contrary to the common sense of mankind,' said

Wallis. 'And I should not have ventured so far, if *Gassendus* had not first broken the ice.'[24] Wallis couldn't face relinquishing meat, and instead he claimed that because meat-eating was universally practised it must be natural after all. Rather than accept the unpalatable conclusion that God intended he should be herbivorous, Tyson scuppered the entire basis of comparative anatomy and pointed out exceptions to the rule, such as the hedgehog and the opossum, the latter of which he had recently shown to have the gut of a herbivore but was carnivorous.[25]

Paradoxically, the papers published by Wallis and Tyson presented evidence in favour of the herbivorous nature of man, but argued for the opposite. It was therefore used by both vegetarians and anti-vegetarians to support both sides of the debate for decades to come. John Evelyn read and marked up his copy of these papers, finding it most surprising, for example, that both Wallis and Tyson made the blunder of asserting that there were no vegetarian people on earth.[26] The eighteenth-century medical lecturers Boerhaave and Haller cited the articles to support their view that man was naturally omnivorous;[27] John Arbuthnot claimed that they proved man was 'a carnivorous Animal';[28] while the Italian vegetarian Antonio Cocchi, on the other hand, used the evidence to argue that the human gut showed we were supposed to be herbivores.[29]

When naturalists started to divide all creatures on earth into a taxonomical system, Gassendi's anatomical arguments remained profoundly influential.[30] In his seminal *Historia Plantarum* (1686–1704), the eminent botanist John Ray (1627–1705) asserted conclusively that 'Certainly man by nature was never made to be a carnivorous animal, nor is he armed at all for prey and rapine, with jagged and pointed teeth and crooked claws sharpened to render and tear, but with gentle hands to gather fruit and vegetables, and with teeth to chew and eat them.' The scientific evidence had obvious moral implications and he exclaimed against the unnatural consumption of 'the reeking flesh of butchered and slaughtered animals'.[31]

Ray's taxonomical research provided the foundations for the definitive work of Carl Linnaeus, whose 'binomial system' of classification is still in use today. In the first edition of the *Systema naturae* (1735), Linnaeus placed humans and apes in the same order, *Anthropomorpha* (Ray's term which Linnaeus later changed to 'Primates'), partly on the basis that man shared the four (distinctly herbivorous) incisors of apes, monkeys and sloths.[32] Even this shocking decision – which still cordoned humans off into a genus (*Homo*) and even a whole family of their own – was nothing like as radical as what Linnaeus privately entertained; he wrote to a zoological colleague with the challenge: 'I demand of you, and of the whole world, that you show me a generic character . . . by which to distinguish between Man and Ape. I myself most assuredly know of none. I wish somebody would indicate one to me. But, if I had called man an ape, or vice-versa, I would have fallen under the ban of all ecclesiastics. It may be that as a naturalist I ought to have done so.'[33] This epoch-making recognition of human proximity to animals had a lesser-known corollary: in the same year Linnaeus – a physician by training – wrote his doctoral dissertation in which he argued that a comparison of the structure of the mouth, stomach and hands of the *Homo sylvestris* and other mammals demonstrated that fruit was the natural food for mankind and should therefore always be prescribed to patients whose bodies had been weakened by fever.[34] As royal physician and medical professor, Linnaeus kept Gassendi's scientific vegetarian tradition alive in the Swedish university of Uppsala by encouraging his students to combine medical dietetics with anatomical analysis. For example, in 1757 the young Isaac Svensson submitted to Linnaeus a doctoral dissertation in which he argued that the most natural food for man was fruit, as was exhibited by children's natural inclinations, the structure of the teeth, the Persians who fed on nothing but the fruit of palm trees and by the fruitarian 'Gymnosophists, the wise men of India'.[35] By this time in European universities, the Indian vegetarians had taken on the mantle of the greatest adherers to the laws of human nature. While the Western world had long ago abandoned the vegetarian laws of nature, the Indians remained a constant reminder of what they had left behind.[36] These three sets of data – human anatomy, the Indian vegetarians, and the effects of the vegetable diet on ailing patients – were repeated time and time again by medical practitioners throughout the eighteenth century and beyond.

Enlightenment scientists were fixated on the concept of natural origins; in a divinely designed world, the narrative of 'in the beginning' held enormous sway. Even in the nineteenth century the radical Darwinist, Ernst Haeckel (1834–1919), noted that the human appendix was a 'relic of an organ that was much larger and was of great service in our vegetarian ancestors.'[37] Still today scientists employ callipers to determine whether human teeth betray a herbivorous or carnivorous evolutionary origin and archaeologists examine prehistoric remains to discover when *Homo sapiens* first started hunting. Despite the recognition that 'nature' consists in continual flux, there still remains in Western culture a paradigm of the 'natural' which is supposed to define the fixed essence of our being.

At the same moment as Wallis and Tyson's announcements in London, a similar gesture of turning to empirical evidence to shed light on the old vegetarian debate was made in the French academy by Louis Lémery (1677–1743) in his university textbook, the *Traité des Aliments* (1702), translated into English as *A Treatise of Foods* (1704). Lémery opened his entire discussion of food by addressing the formidable school of Gassendist vegetarians in the French academies who argued that because human anatomy was designed to be herbivorous, meat causes excessive fermentations and tends to 'corrupt our Humours, and occasion divers Diseases'.[38] Rather than contradicting them in theory, Lémery acknowledged that man had lost touch with nature: 'it looks as if the Food which the God of Nature designed for us, and what best agreed with us should be Plants, seeing that Mankind were never so hail and vigorous as in those first Ages, wherein they made use of them.' But after a detailed discussion of all the issues, Lémery's final conclusion, like that of Wallis and Tyson, was pragmatic:

> it may be, if [meat] had never been used, and that Men had been content to feed upon a certain number of Plants only, it would have been never the worse for them: But it's no longer a question to be disputed, and if it be an abuse, it has so long obtained by Custom in the World, that it is become necessary.[39]

Though in practice few could imagine a world without chicken fricassée, on the theoretical front the vegetarians were making serious headway. So astonishingly widespread were views like these that one might reasonably see a coalescing intellectual orthodoxy. Scientists had 'proved' the old claim that man was originally a herbivore and meat-eating was an unnatural deviation from his intended diet. Academics across the board assented to Gassendi's arguments – even those affiliated to rival schools of thought, including Cartesians such as Antoine le Grand and Hobbesians such as Pufendorf. That man was originally designed as a herbivore became a controversial medical fact accepted by scientists from all parts of Europe. But one question remained – was it feasible or desirable to bring man back from the path of corruption and return him to his natural diet? In the wake of the scientific case, a wave of practising doctors dedicated their careers to achieving just this. In the course of promoting vegetables as nutritious and meat as potentially damaging, this growing school of vegetarian medics laid the foundations for the modern understanding of diet and lifestyle.

TWELVE

The Mitre and the Microscope: Philippe Hecquet's Catholic Fast Food

At the beginning of the eighteenth century vegetarianism emerged as a powerful voice in France and other Catholic countries, by knitting scientific discoveries to the Church's traditional teaching on abstinence. Many of the early Church fathers had been penitent ascetics, believing that luxury corrupted and abstinence was the key to purification. St Clement of Alexandria, Tertullian and St John Cassian concurred that meat was a lust-inducing luxury.[1] Good Christians did not have 'unpleasing smells of meat amongst them', said St John Chrysostom: 'The increase of luxury is but the multiplication of dung!'[2] St Peter, St Matthew and St James were said to have lived entirely upon vegetables, and even the anti-vegetarian St Augustine maintained that Christ 'allowed no animal food to his own disciples'.[3]

But while they agreed that abstinence was a virtue, the Church fathers equally insisted that it was not a *sin* to eat flesh.[4] One of the principal purposes of religion was to show that the world had been made for man's use. Even abstinence-endorsing texts like the *Clementine Homilies* assented to the orthodoxy that God made animals for man 'to make fishes, birds, and beasts his prey'.[5] Claiming otherwise was dangerously subversive and was indelibly associated with the pagan Pythagoreans and the heretic Manicheans and Cathars.[6] '[Pythagoreans] abstain on account of the fable about the transmigration of souls,' insisted Origen. 'We, however, when we do abstain, do so because "we keep under our body, and bring it into subjection".'[7] Animals had no rational soul, insisted St Augustine, and were a matter of indifference to humans. Hurling the Gadarene swine off a cliff, he said, twisting the meaning of the Gospels, was Christ's way of showing 'that to refrain from the killing of animals and the destroying of plants is the height of superstition'.[8]

Keeping heretical vegetarianism at bay, the Catholic Church instituted its own laws on periodical fasting that emphasised the virtues of abstinence. Eating flesh inflamed fleshly passions and was a luxury, so it was forbidden on fast days. The medieval Church banned flesh and even dairy products on half the days of the year; even in the comparatively lax seventeenth century, flesh was forbidden for the forty days of Lent as well as every Friday and other holy days. Fish, a cold sexless animal, did not contain the sanguine humours that stirred desires, so it was a permitted accompaniment to Lenten bread and vegetables (an interesting source of modern 'piscatarian vegetarianism'). For most people, who could not afford fish or substitutes such as almond milk, the Lent diet was a meagre affair. For members of the strictest monastic orders such as the Carthusians and Capuchins, the same restrictions applied all the year round.[9]

It was partly this very institutionalisation of abstinence from flesh which meant that 'vegetarianism' as a separate religious position did not take hold as much in Catholic countries as it did in Protestant regions after the Reformation. Any Catholic who did branch out and make abstinence from flesh a doctrinal issue would be liable to immediate condemnation as a heretic. Contrariwise, during the Reformation, Protestants rejected Catholic fast laws, claiming that outlawing flesh constituted a blasphemous rejection of God's gifts to man and was thus indistinguishable from heretical vegetarianism. John Calvin called the Catholic proscription of flesh a 'sacrilegious opinion'.[10] The humanist Erasmus of Rotterdam, in his *Epystell concerning the forbedynge of eatynge of fleshe* (1534), suggested that Catholic fast police were unwise for punishing peasants who dared nibble on a dry bacon rind while the rich supped on sturgeon and hot spicy rocket 'and such other thynges which kyndleth the genitales'.[11] It was missing the point of the fast to focus so particularly on the issue of meat-eating.

In England, Henry Holland, vicar of St Bride's in London, proclaimed the Catholic fast a 'doctrine of devils' passed down to them from the Satanically inspired vegetarian Egyptian priests, the Persian magi and the 'wizards of India'.[12] In *Lenten Stuffe* (1599), the satirist Thomas Nashe dismissed the ichthyic diet as useless 'flegmatique' food and depicted abstinent monks as 'Rhomish rotten *Pithagoreans* or *Carthusian* friers, that mumpe on nothing but fishe'. He even implied that the continental temperance writers Luigi Cornaro and Leonard Lessius were part of a counter-Reformation conspiracy attempting to infiltrate

Protestant countries with superstitious abstinence.[13] Even John Donne snidely equated salad-eating with madness and Papism, 'Like Nebuchadnezar perchance with grass and flowers,/ A sallet worse than Spanish dieting'.[14] In the political arena, Queen Elizabeth trod the knife-edge of compromise. Though it remained illegal to eat flesh on fast days, the Acts of Parliament insisted that this was in order to alleviate the pressure on livestock, boost the fish trade, stimulate shipbuilding and thus support the navy – and 'not for any superstition'.[15] Some Protestants thought that watering down the Lenten fast was a bad idea. Sir William Vaughan, the American colonist, felt that the Elizabethan Acts failed to bridle the appetites of libertines, and suggested that a healthy dose of vegetarianism would do them good. But like Bacon and Bushell, he was at pains to insist that his dietary convictions were not a sign of Catholic superstition.[16]

While in England critics of meat-eating had to demarcate themselves from Catholicism, in France vegetarianism was often absorbed into the religious establishment. Whereas Bushell and Crab withdrew from society in order to pursue their vegetarian beliefs, across the Channel Armand-Jean de Rancé (1626–1700) used the monastic system as a means of publicly championing abstinence from flesh.

Rancé lived a worldly existence as a youth at the Parisian court until 1657 when the lady of scandalous reputation whom he adored and with whom he probably had a passionate affair, Marie, Duchess of Montbazon, died of scarlet fever. Renouncing his former life, Rancé turned to the revival of severe asceticism, bringing the Cistercian monastic order back to the rule of St Benedict which had forbidden 'the eating of the flesh of quadrupeds'.[17] Basing his popular movement at the monastery of La Trappe, he insisted on hard physical labour and absolutely forbade meat, cheese, eggs, butter and even fish. The order thrived throughout the eighteenth century and escaped suppression after the French Revolution in 1791 by fleeing to Geneva; it still survives, though they now permit themselves fish, eggs and dairy products.[18]

Rancé's numerous pamphlets on abstinence and the thousands of proclamations about the fast laws published by the Catholic diocese all lauded the physical and spiritual benefits of the Lenten diet. So when vegetarians appeared in the eighteenth century claiming that abstinence was healthy, they had a strong ground-rock of endorsement from the state religion.[19] For example, in 1700 the French medic

Barthelemy Linand, in his *Abstinence from Flesh made Easy*, suggested that the fleshless Lenten diet was beneficial even when practised 365 days a year. Linand's medical colleagues applauded his aggregation of 'medical precepts' with 'good advice on Christian morality, & hygiene', and his book stayed on university reading lists across the Continent for over half a century.[20]

Foremost in the marriage between Catholic fast laws and advances in natural philosophy was the Parisian physician Philippe Hecquet (1661–1737). In 1709 Hecquet introduced his *oeuvres* with a manifesto reminiscent of Wallis, Tyson and Lémery, that he would 'examine by the principles of Medicine & Physics, which is the most natural diet for man; if the use of meat is suitable & absolutely necessary to him'.[21] His scientific findings, he hoped, would shore up morality and theology, in a school of thought which he dubbed 'Theological Medicine'. Publishing his major works in French for the burgeoning educated classes rather than in Latin (which was swiftly falling out of fashion), Hecquet provided the public and particularly the poor with a cheap self-help method of preserving health.[22] Although he has been almost completely ignored by modern scholarship, and his virulent Catholic slant prevented his works from ever being translated into English, Hecquet was a pioneer of the widespread movement of dietary medicine and vegetarianism in Europe.

After graduating in medicine from the University of Reims, Hecquet established himself as a practising doctor in Paris. In 1688, at the age of twenty-seven, he was offered the prestigious post of personal physician to the noblewoman Catherine-Françoise de Bretagne, who was retiring to the convent of Port-Royal-des-Champs a few leagues south of Paris. Port-Royal (nerve-centre of the highly controversial Jansenist movement, famous for converts such as Blaise Pascal) was dedicated to the mortification of human flesh and Hecquet plunged himself into their harsh ascetic regime.

On the most basic level this proved to him that he could live on meagre foods even while sustaining rigorous study and zealous charity work for the poor, whom he travelled miles on foot to visit, scorning the luxury of coaches. Within a year, though still only twenty-eight years old, his health started to trouble him and his friends, who blamed it on the deprivations of monastic life, exhorted him to leave Port-Royal and return to Paris. But Hecquet declined, and spent the rest of his life insisting that the monastic diet was, on the contrary, exceptionally invigorating.[23]

Following the death of his patroness in 1693, Hecquet established a successful medical practice in Paris, serving both the nobility – including the Prince of Condé – and the poor in the Hospital of Charity.[24] Hecquet united his role as doctor with those of preacher and lay social reformer by attacking both the medical and moral evils of modern urban luxury, and principally the unnecessary consumption of flesh. The pinnacle of decadence, felt Hecquet, was the laxity that people of his generation were now showing with regard to the Lent fast.

Traditionally individuals had been able to gain exemption from the fast if they could show that they were so ill they needed meat to strengthen their bodies. An exemption certificate had to be endorsed by a doctor, countersigned by a priest, and then taken to the one licensed Lent butcher in Paris at the Hôtel-Dieu. This system, Hecquet proclaimed in his *Traité des Dispenses du Carême* (1709) (*Treatise on Exemptions from the Lent Fast*), was now being widely abused. Whereas eighty years ago only 450 people obtained fast-exemption certificates, there were now 37,000 people buying beef during Lent, using 'specious pretexts' and even bribery, while still more got it on the black market. Tobacco was widely smoked, and, still worse, the definition of fish was extended to include any aquatic animal including ducks, otters and porpoises! As a litmus test to society as a whole, this indicated that Paris was eighty-three times more decadent than just one lifetime ago. Strict fasting, Hecquet felt, was a matter of urgent nationalist resistance to the infiltration of Protestant laxity. Using Lenten indulgence as a sign of the general carnivorous malaise in society, Hecquet began his wholesale campaign against flesh.[25]

Hecquet joined the new wave of Cartesian doctors who were reforming the understanding of animal physiology. Descartes had based his system on the discoveries of the English physician William Harvey, who demonstrated at the beginning of the seventeenth century that the pulse of the heart pumped blood round the body in a circuit of vessels.[26] Descartes used this as a linchpin in his argument that animal life consisted in the heat of the heart, which caused the circulation of the blood, which in turn drove all the other mechanics of the body. Taking Descartes' lead, the Italian physiologists Lorenzo Bellini (1643–1704) and Giovanni Borelli (1608–79) instituted what would become the dominant physiological theory of 'iatromechanics' (from the Greek *iatros* meaning physician), which conceived of the human body as a complicated hydraulic machine made of pipes, pumps, levers, fibres, vibrations and forces.

This school was developed further by the Scottish professor Archibald Pitcairne who fused the mechanism of the Italian Cartesians with Isaac Newton's latest observations in physics and mathematics.[27] With such a sturdy scientific base, Pitcairne and his followers were confident that medical research could yield the same degree of certainty as a mathematical equation.[28] Animal life and health, said Pitcairne, depended on the free and regular circulation of the blood.[29] Sickness, by contrast, was caused by an excessive or diminished circulation, a blockage or rupture in the body's pipework, or an over-thickness or -thinness of the blood.[30] Pitcairne spawned a school of mathematically minded iatromechanists in Britain, which included Newton's personal doctor Richard Mead, who also read Hecquet's books.[31]

William Harvey had realised that the blood flowed away from the heart through the arteries and returned through the veins, but how exactly the blood got from one to the other remained a matter of speculation until Marcello Malpighi of Bologna (in 1661) and the keen-eyed Dutchman Antoni van Leeuwenhoek (in 1680) independently used primitive microscopes to watch blood globules (which we now know to be haemoglobin) passing through capillaries between the arteries and the veins. These microscopic vessels were the missing link which completed the jigsaw of the body's hydraulic system. Leeuwenhoek noticed that the globules only just managed to squeeze their way through the capillaries, and observed blockages hindering the flow.[32]

Latching his vegetarian critique onto these recent findings, Hecquet extrapolated that when people ate flesh, the 'cumbersome' globules therein entered the body's hydraulic system and 'diminish[ed] its ability to circulate'. He warned that globules also agglomerated in the lymph vessels and in the gut, hindering digestion, producing bad blood and fattening people more than it nourished them. Besides, as his friend, the leading German iatromechanist Friedrich Hoffman (1660–1743), observed, people tended to have too much of the globular part of the blood, so the last thing they needed was an extra dose from flesh. This, explained Hecquet, was why the Bible forbade the eating of blood.[33]

Hecquet also said that animal fat blocked the lymph and clogged the porosity of the body's membranes. Bellini had emphasised the necessity of maintaining the ductility of the body's fibres – especially those of the nerves and the blood vessels – and Hecquet warned that eating too much flesh caused the fibres to stiffen, hindering circulation. Feed your body on flesh (or wine), warned Hecquet, and the disruption to the flow of vital fluids would be sure to result in 'inflammatory diseases'.[34]

The mechanical school also revolutionised the understanding of the digestive system. Whereas the traditional school of iatro*chemists* held that foods were 'fermented' by acids in the stomach, the mechanists argued that digestion was conducted by grinding and crushing. In his lectures at the prestigious University of Leiden, Pitcairne instigated a European-wide controversy by adopting this new theory of digestion. Hecquet stuck his neck out by publishing a paper defending Pitcairne's theory, earning himself numerous enemies but also many friends who hailed him as the greatest medic in France and the 'Reliever of Mankind'.[35] His private correspondence with Pitcairne and numerous other medics of the day demonstrates how embroiled he became in the European-wide dispute.[36]

Hecquet explained that the process of grinding began in the mouth where the jaws acted like two natural millstones. In the stomach, food was crushed by the surrounding muscles, a force that Pitcairne had calculated to total an incredible 461,219 pounds. This grinding was assisted by villi on the inside of the gut, the 'million motorised fibres', which crushed and kneaded the food like so many kitchen hands, making it 'dissolve, melt, & pass into a fine & delicate cream'. This creamy substance, called 'chyle', entered the lymphatic system where it was distilled and used to create new blood.

The food that could be ground most easily into smooth, homogeneous pulp was, declared Hecquet, 'man's most natural diet'. Fat, unctuous, fibrous, globular flesh was clearly resistant, and thus, Hecquet considered, the matter rested: 'From this without doubt one perceives already what sort of foods are preferable to man; they will not be the flesh of animals, but . . . seeds and grains,' which have a 'tendency to melt into a milky juice'.[37]

Having placed the action of grinding at the centre of the body's health, the old argument about comparative anatomy took on new significance. Needless to say, Hecquet sided with Gassendi in concluding that 'The disposition of [men's] teeth have destined them to crush nothing but fruits, grains, or plants.' It was therefore 'beyond doubt that man was made to live and nourish himself from the fruits of the earth'.[38]

Not only was eating meat unhealthy, immoral and unnatural, said Hecquet, it was also disgusting and inefficient. Vegetables were the primary source of nutrition, 'like virgin juices', so why eat animals, he demanded, when they were just made up of 'second-hand' pre-digested vegetables, coming 'as if with a stain of prostitution . . . by the different uses which they have had to suffer before arriving at the human body'?[39]

If, on all this evidence, Hecquet could not get the whole world to relinquish flesh absolutely, like François Bernier, at the very least he wanted doctors to stop trying to 'feed up' the sick on concentrated meat broths. Convalescent foods should be as similar to chyle as possible, he said, which meant nothing stronger than oat broths and moistened bread.[40]

In regarding abstinent dieting as the key to treating sickness, Hecquet was resurrecting the therapeutic tradition of the ancient medics Hippocrates, Galen and Asclepiades, who had consistently prescribed the cooling, fleshless diet to allay the heat of fever and restore humoural imbalances. The first-century AD physician Galen had dedicated entire works to the *ptisan*, or barley broth: every disease had its own special diet, and it was the duty of the physician to prescribe and enforce it.

According to Hecquet, a core of sixteenth-century French physicians had begun to revive ancient dietary medicine, but it was still only used for a few diseases; he earned himself the title 'l'Hippocrate de France', by wishing to bring diet back to the heart of medical practice. But it was perhaps more of a hijack than a renaissance, because Hecquet's main point was to extrapolate (as St Jerome had) that if the 'slender diet' was good for the sick, it must also be good for the healthy.[41]

Eleven years after Hecquet first published a full-length diatribe against eating flesh, a Scottish doctor based in England started to publish his own ideas about the utility of the fleshless diet in medicine. This man, Dr George Cheyne, was swiftly becoming a prodigy in the British medical world, and by 1724, with the publication of his *Essay of Health and Long Life*, Cheyne had established himself as the authority on the prophylactic vegetable diet. His work went through three French translations and circulated in Latin as well.

Hecquet came upon Cheyne's work and immediately recognised a brother-in-arms. Cheyne, like Hecquet, was an avid iatromechanist, who had in fact been taught by (and was a personal friend of) Pitcairne. Hecquet's major work, *La Médecine Théologique*, was filled with enthusiastic allusions to 'the savant Mr *Cheyne*' and in 1733, the year of Cheyne's next major work, *The English Malady*, Hecquet formally hailed Cheyne as his own English counterpart. While Hecquet cast himself as the foremost promulgator of Hippocratic dietary medicine in France, he said that the neglected art 'has just been skilfully resuscitated in the Medicine of England, by the excellent Work of one of their illustrious Masters [Dr Cheyne]'. Despite his pointed priority claim, Hecquet followed everything 'this skilful Doctor' had to say, and even adapted his own physiological system at the tail end of his career to incorporate Cheyne's focus on the effect of meat on the nervous system. He even began to clamp down on fish-eating, which his Catholic bias had always caused him to regard as harmless.[42]

The recognition of their joint aims constitutes something of a medical vegetarian movement in Europe, dating from the 1730s. It was the aim of this loosely connected brotherhood to promote vegetarianism through the discourse of dietary medicine, and, it was phenomenally successful. Most doctors who thought that the vegetable diet was a useful medical therapy did not agree that vegetarianism was the best diet for everyone, but a number – sometimes inadvertently – adopted elements of the vegetarian ideology.

Joining forces with Cheyne, Hecquet envisaged an international research project that would prove once and for all that abstaining from flesh increased health and longevity. Cheyne was already cataloguing statistical evidence that vegetarians lived to ages of well over a hundred, a project that had been crystallised in 1635 when William Harvey conducted the autopsy of a celebrated farmer called Thomas Parr, and concluded that he had lived for 152 years and 9 months largely thanks to his Pythagorean frugality.[43] In addition to such local instances, Hecquet felt that the innumerable vegetarian peoples all over the world were living empirical proof. The Tartars, the Irish, the Scottish, 'and all the Northerners who eat little or no meat' were just the beginning:

> if one joins to them most of the Orientals, who live on hardly more than rice, and a quantity of peoples, even our neighbours, like the Spanish, the Italians, and those who live in Languedoc and Provence, among whom the use of meat is just about only

used by the privileged, who besides eat it very soberly: one will acknowledge that this custom is not at all so natural to man, nor so necessary as we usually claim, because so much of the world do without it . . . even among the nations where meat is more common, most of the girls, women, children, poor, artisans and all the country people hardly ever eat it, and they prefer fruits, milk foods & pastries. If one remarks finally . . . that all the reformers of paganism, legislators, priests, philosophers, without counting the Brahmins of today, who are the priests of the Indians, so many thousands of monks, hermits, holy men and women, and people of every sex and condition, who strictly abstain from meat: we will admit without trouble that there are at least as many people who live and maintain themselves well without living on meat, as there are who believe it necessary.[44]

The obvious deduction to make from this welter of evidence, Hecquet concluded, was that 'A sentiment so universally received, cannot but come from the foundation of nature itself.' Following a similar line of thought to Newton, though in a more cavalier fashion, Hecquet claimed that vegetarianism had spread out culturally with the migration of peoples ever since Noah's Flood, and *also* that God had imprinted it as an innate part of human nature: *'une impression* innée *& universellement répanduë dans les esprits'.*[45]

And yet the best was still to come. A new group of healthy herb-eaters were forming a groundswell of vegetarianism. Triumphantly, Hecquet announced that 'either by virtue, or by natural disposition, or by indisposition caused & and brought on by infirmity, there are today even more persons who eat nothing but meagre foods.' Among these he included patients such as his own, suffering from diseases that could only be cured by abstaining *'totalement de viande & du vin'*, and, best of all, those who voluntarily shunned meat for 'the love of health'.[46] Hecquet was the pastoral physician guiding mankind back to the natural diet.

Hecquet believed that his physiological evidence that meat was unhealthy *proved* that all the old theological arguments for vegetarianism were true. That meat clogged the system surely implied that God made man to live on fruit and herbs? The microscope had revealed the truth of St Jerome's claim that God's permission to eat meat was a grudging concession, and even substantiated Cheyne's novel theory that God allowed people meat on purpose to shorten their lives. Thus, it was not just more healthy to abstain from meat, it was also more virtuous.[47]

Many of Hecquet's colleagues at the Faculty of Medicine were delighted that he had 'solidly established & proved' that Lenten food was suitable to human nature. Others in the medical establishment were less impressed and accused him of heresy, scandal and blinkered science.[48] He was clearly one of the Gassendist vegetarians addressed by Louis Lémery.[49] Nicolas Andry de Boisregard, Master of the Faculty of Medicine, published a tract which lamented that many people held views like Hecquet, and answered him point by point. Andry cast doubt over Hecquet's biblical interpretations and, as a dedicated iatrochemist, refuted the scientific basis of Hecquet's mechanical theory of digestion.

Hecquet was wrong for two reasons, argued Andry. First because tender meat was much easier to crush and grind 'than cod, salmon, oysters, roots, and many other similar foods which the Author recommends so forcibly in his Treatise. Second, because it is not in the slightest bit true that digestion is carried out by crushing.' How, asked Andry, could the thin wall of a snake's stomach digest the bones of a frog by crushing and grinding? How could berries pass whole through the guts of a man if such a lot of pressure were being exerted on the stomach? How could inhalation and exhalation occur if the muscles of the diaphragm and belly were squeezing the stomach simultaneously? No, said Andry, the old model of digestion by fermentation was the only way to explain these anomalies and it made a nonsense of Hecquet's claims about the difficulty of digesting meat.

Hecquet's comparative anatomy was likewise flawed, Andry argued; for as Aristotle had observed, humans had the universal organ, the hand, with which they made knives and performed the art of cooking. And besides, human teeth were *not* capable of grinding grains – hence the use of flour mills and ovens to make bread.[50]

Like other vegetarians, Hecquet was also open to satire for his moral extremism. In 1715 the playwright and novelist Alain-René Lesage satirised Hecquet in his picaresque novel *The Adventures of Gil Blas*. The Hecquet caricature, Dr Sangrado, is called upon to treat the gouty gourmand Canon Sedillo:

> 'Pray, what is your ordinary diet?' asked Sangrado; 'My usual food,' replied the Canon, 'is broth and juicy meat.' 'Broth and juicy meat!' cried the doctor, alarmed. 'I do not wonder to find you sick; such dainty dishes are poisoned pleasure and snares that luxury spreads for mankind, so as to ruin them the more effectually ... What an irregularity is here! what a frightful

regimen! You ought to have been dead long ago. How old are you, pray?' 'I am in my sixty-ninth year,' replied the Canon. 'Exactly,' said the physician; 'an early old age is always the fruits of intemperance. If you had drunk nothing else than pure water all your life, and had been satisfied with simple nourishment – such as boiled apples, for example – you would not now be tormented with the gout, and all your limbs would perform their functions with ease.'[51]

In 1726, at the age of sixty-five, Hecquet was yearning once again to retire from the fleshly world and he accepted accommodation with the religious Carmelites of Faubourg Saint-Jacques, where he had been a practising doctor for thirty years. He continued writing up to his death, never retreating from his vegetarian idealism, and corresponding with the most prestigious doctors of Europe. He died in 1737 and was buried in the church of the Carmelites where a Latin epitaph testified to his success in unifying theology and medicine.[52]

THIRTEEN

Dr Cheyne's Sensible Diet

George Cheyne (1671–1743) was the most influential vegetarian in eighteenth-century Britain. He provided a novel scientific explanation for the effects of food on the body that shaped much eighteenth-century dietary medicine and contributed to modern ideas of diet. Unlike his censorious French counterpart, Philippe Hecquet, however, Cheyne brilliantly concocted his medical arguments into an appealing recipe which pandered to the tastes of his clientele. Combined with his notorious Scottish wit, this allowed him to push his reforms while remaining widely popular. He treated a variety of establishment figures, including Alexander Pope, and converted many others – notably the novelist Samuel Richardson – to his vegetarian creed. By the end of the century King George III (1738–1820) was lampooned as Cheyne's frugal follower and the Prime Minister had come under his sway. Astoundingly, this evangelist of abstinence was also a behemoth of obesity. His bulky frame was recognised by everyone in society and it was the target of many a satirical dart.

One can picture Cheyne occupying his corner in the coffee-house, ranting against gluttony. The paradox of this puritanical Falstaff provided sheer amusement to his contemporaries: his friend and patron Lord Bolingbroke wrote comically that the portly Dr Cheyne, 'with a gallon of milk coffee, and five pounds of Biscuit before him at Breakfast, declaimed to [Alexander] Pope, and me, against the enormous immorality of using exercise to promote an appetite'.[1] The poet and dramatist Edward Young laughed at the contradictions in Cheyne's comportment in his 'Epistle to Mr Pope':

> 'Who's this with nonsense would restrain?
> Who's this', they say, 'so vainly schools the vain?
> Who damns our trash, with so much trash replete?'
> As, three ells[2] round, huge Cheyne rails at meat.

George Cheyne (1671–1743)

One satirist taunted Cheyne as a Pharisaic bellygod: 'oh rare Doctor – I would fain learn, if Bag-Pipe Cheeks . . . Double Tripe Chin or Pot-Gut Belly, are the consequences of this regulated Diet?' Even his friends, like Pope, who said, 'There was not an honester man nor a truer philosopher,' joked about the swelling of Cheyne's girth; John Gay, author of *The Beggar's Opera* (1728), commemorated him as 'Cheney huge of size'; and the poet James Thomson chimed in with the proverbial 'Great fat Doctor of Bath'.[3]

But to Cheyne – who spent his life fighting desire with self-denial – his size was anything but hilarious. He had come to London from Scotland in 1701, a fresh-faced twenty-nine-year-old, confident that he would establish his fame as a Newtonian mathematician and Pitcairnian physician. But in the metropolis, where consumer goods were available in an abundance virtually unknown elsewhere in the world, the 'great *Temperance*' he claimed to have pursued in his youth was replaced with gut-expanding excess and debauchery: 'and thus,' he related years later, 'constantly Dineing and Supping in *Taverns*, and in the Houses of my Acquaintances of *Taste* and *Delicacy*, my Health was in a few Years brought into great Distress . . . I grew excessively *fat, short-breath'd, Lethargic* and *Listless.*'[4]

In fact, Cheyne was renowned as a drunken fatso before he even left Scotland: his rival, Charles Oliphant, who knew him as a personal tutor, maligned his character with stories of his 'unwieldy Carcass' reeling home after nightly binges, full of 'nauseous Loads . . . which he often, to the scandal of the Whole family, disgorged in his Pupil's Bosom'.[5] But Cheyne's fable about the horrendous effects of London luxury (which he wrote about in his autobiographical essay 'The Case of the Author') was not just exaggeration or excuse: Cheyne was translating his physical demise into a moral-medical theory of which his own suffering body was the prime clinical example.

He described himself as 'a putrified overgrown Body from Luxury and perpetual Laziness, scorbutical all over'. The corruption visited on his body was a symptom of wider society's sickness. The faecal build-up in urban spaces seemed to be mapped onto his legs as they erupted in pus-oozing ulcers; grocer's shops were stuffed with cognac and pâté, clogging his veins with morbid matter; the capital swollen with imported delicacies reflected his ever growing paunch. His body grew and grew, reaching at its maximum an incredible thirty-four stone. He dubbed himself the fattest man in Europe.[6]

As the fat built up, Cheyne's hopes of fame started to crumble. After a catastrophic falling-out with Isaac Newton over their work on the calculus, which ended in furious mutual accusations of plagiarism, Cheyne's nerves began to falter.[7] Within a few years of arriving in London, he was suffering from an intermittent fever, a permanent headache, trembling and morbid anxiety. Eventually, he wrote in his clinical autobiography, 'I was suddenly seized with a *vertiginous Paroxysm*, so extreamly frightful and terrible, as to approach near to a *Fit* of an *Apoplexy*, and I was forced in it to lay hold on the Posts of my Bed, for fear of tumbling out.'[8] His sickness and moroseness drove away his old 'Bottle-Companions', and Cheyne, left in loneliness, plunged headlong into physical and mental collapse.[9]

It was in the very depths of his sickness, however, that Cheyne discovered the vital combination of physical and spiritual regeneration that would mark the turning point in his life. Under the guidance of the Anglican priest George Garden, he found solace in the spiritual writings of the primitive Christians and European mystics.[10] Pacifying his soul with a course of healthy reading, Cheyne found the strength to placate his body with a primitive abstinent diet.[11]

In 'The Case of the Author', which became his user's guide to vegetarianism, Cheyne claimed that as soon as he took up a 'low diet' he started 'melting away like a *Snow-ball* in Summer'. The truly miraculous cure took effect, he wrote, when, in around 1708, God intervened and guided a sequence of events that ended in his conversion to vegetarianism. Cheyne happened to meet a clergyman who 'accidentally' dropped a hint about a man in Croydon – one Dr Taylor – who had cured himself of epilepsy by sticking exclusively to a diet of milk. For Cheyne, this was nothing short of an epiphany. Despite his sickness, he rode out from London in the middle of winter to meet Dr Taylor, and, as if by divine ordination, Cheyne arrived panting with anticipation and 'found him at home, at his full Quart of Cow's Milk (which was all his Dinner)'.[12]

As a dedicated disciple of Pitcairne's mathematical-hydraulic physiology, Cheyne was certain that epilepsy was caused by the same hydraulic blockages in the blood and nerves as all other nervous illnesses. So if abstaining from meat and living on milk cured the one, he deduced, it ought to cure all the others. Furthermore, since milk was just semi-digested vegetables, the milk and vegetable diet should theoretically be the universal remedy.[13]

Cheyne immediately relinquished flesh and restricted himself to a diet of milk with '*Seeds, Bread, mealy Roots,* and *Fruit*'. The effect was instantaneous. He lost sixteeen or eighteen stone, and in a matter of months was cured of his crippling nervous distempers. With miraculous speed, said Cheyne, 'I had been extremely reduced in my Flesh, and was become Lank, Fleet and Nimble.'[14] The efficacy of Cheyne's milk, seed and vegetable diet was proved not just on paper, but on his own body in full view of British society. With such a substantial, corporeal demonstration before them – the archetype of before-and-after weight-loss advertising – Cheyne's miracle diet was guaranteed a starry future.[15]

His conversion to vegetarianism became a legendary event. After his death in 1743, and for the rest of the century, scores of biographical dictionaries reported that the vegetable diet had cut two-thirds off Cheyne's bulk, brought him back from the brink of death, and allowed him to live to the ripe old age of seventy-two. Even commentators who pointed out that Cheyne was still immense by ordinary standards acknowledged that he had been effectively cured of his malaise.[16] A playful obituary-epitaph 'On the death of Dr Cheyne' commemorated his dietary success:

> Once hypochondriac, of portentous Size:
> Since, lively, slender, by his Milk's Supplies . . .
> For, while on Earth, from Carnage and from Wine
> Abstaining, he on harmless Milk would dine.[17]

The benefit of the vegetable diet was mechanically demonstrable, but Cheyne believed that it was God who had revealed it to him. In the climactic sentence of 'The Case of the Author', he suggested that God, through *'casual Hints'* (like the one about Dr Taylor) had deliberately transformed him into the world's vegetarian guru.[18] With his divine mandate, Cheyne fused the role of spiritual priest and physical doctor to promote his complete dietary regimen. The vegetable diet was no longer just a set of food regulations, it was, as he put it in the final words of *The English Malady*, 'an *Eminence* of *Light* and *Tranquility*'. Skirting the divide between Enlightenment rhetoric, illuminist revelation and the benefits of the 'light' diet, Cheyne presented his dietary cure as the quintessential medical, spiritual and moral Enlightenment.[19]

Like today's lifestyle gurus, Cheyne claimed to resolve the turmoil of mind and body in one holistic method and his promises were greeted by followers with reverential enthusiasm. His works were widely read by both medical and lay audiences, selling more copies than any medical book of the period; the *Essay of Health and Long Life* (1724) went through at least twenty-four editions and *The English Malady* (1733) was reprinted six times within two years.[20] His fame quickly spread to Italy, France, Holland, Germany, Ireland and America and sufferers of nervous disorders wrote to him from all over the kingdom. His books warned people they needed personal guidance, so Cheyne was inundated by patients demanding one-to-one consultations in which they confessed to their dietary peccadilloes and received remedial absolution. With a successful practice in London, Cheyne also set up shop in the fashionable spa town of Bath (where crowds flocked every year to drink mineral water and bathe in the therapeutic springs – and to dance at society balls). There he helped found what is now the Royal National Hospital for Rheumatic Diseases, and became the celebrity doctor to a spectacular array of political and literary icons. Using his own 'crazy Carcase' as a vivid example to others, Cheyne achieved the cultic status of society's greatest diet doctor.[21]

Samuel Johnson's companion Mrs Thrale characterised the height of devotion his followers attained: 'when I read Cheyne,' she declared, 'I feel disposed to retire to *Arruchar* in the Highlands of Scotland – live on oat bread and Milk, and bathe in the Frithe of Clyde for seven years.'[22] John Wesley, founder of the thriving Methodist movement, adored Cheyne's tocsin for temperance, built it into his own preaching on the *Primitive Physic*, and attributed his longevity to following Cheyne's vegetarian rules.[23] Samuel Richardson reported that 'more and more' people were giving up meat and following his dietary method.[24] Cheyne was frequently anthologised in the popular medical self-help books, while poetic eulogies about him are scattered through the literature of the period. The rebel laird Hon. Alexander Robertson praised the 'inspir'd, divinely just' Dr Cheyne and elsewhere claimed that he too 'ne'er could see [animals] bleed, / Ev'n to subsist himself, whom they were born to feed'.[25]

Needless to say, there were as many who found Cheyne's advice preposterous. One satirist lampooned Cheyne with the title 'Dr Diet', commenting that 'the Trick of making Men Immortal upon *Asparagus* and *Parsnips*, will not deserve a Patent.'[26] A macho pro-meat poem in the *Grub Street Journal* refuted Cheyne's 'silly books' by appealing to the evidence of anatomy: 'Were the brave grinders in my head, / Plac'd only to crack nuts: champ bread?'[27] In his biography of the great wit Richard 'Beau' Nash, Oliver Goldsmith reported that 'When *Cheney* recommended his vegetable diet, *Nash* would swear, that his design was to send half the world grazing like *Nebuchadnezzar*.'[28]

In the medical profession, Cheyne's work spawned numerous copy-cat volumes and as many vehement refutations.[29] When his dietary extremism was attacked by 'the Beef eating Doctor', David Bayne-Kinnier, Cheyne had a hard time convincing Pope's friend Lady Murray that her sister, Lady Grisell Baillie (his 'Disciple'), was under no danger from her vegetable diet. Opposition to Cheyne was so aggressive he once wrote in fear to Lady Selina Huntingdon that 'I have been threatened with being mobbed.'[30] John Arbuthnot, probably the most esteemed doctor of the age, remarked that Cheyne 'became the subject of Conversation, and produc'd even Sects in the dietetick Philosophy'. Arbuthnot orchestrated a systematic counter-vegetarian movement to challenge the claims of Cheyne and his medical followers. 'Man', he insisted, 'is by his Frame as well as his Appetite a carnivorous Animal.' But despite his opposition, Arbuthnot admitted that 'I know of more than one Instance of irascible Passions being much subdu'd by a vegetable Diet'.[31] Other colleagues who repudiated the dietary extremism of the 'fat-headed Scot' – like Thomas Morgan, John Wynter and Richard Mead – conceded that people should eat more vegetables and less meat, and should avoid meat altogether when suffering from certain ailments.[32]

At a safe distance from the corrupt Babylon that he perceived London to be (ignoring the fact that Bath itself was a major centre of conspicuous consumption), Cheyne launched one of the most severe attacks on luxury in Georgian Britain. As a Tory – possibly even a Jacobite (a supporter of the Stuart succession) – Cheyne saved a special dart for the tyrannical 'Roman' luxury associated with Robert Walpole's corrupt Whig government.[33] Adopting the political language of Crab and Tryon, he offered to lead his patients from the oppressive 'flesh Pots of Egypt' and prescribed them food laws to guide them to the 'Promised Land' of milk and honey.[34] Although Cheyne tended to avoid the customary language of enthused vegetarians, sometimes he could not resist: 'these *Pythagoreans*, these Milk and Vegetable Eaters', he declared at the end of *The English Malady*, 'were the *longest liv'd, and honestest of Men. Milk* and *Honey* was the Complexion of the *Land* of *Promise*, and *Vegetables* the *Diet* of the *Paradisiacal State.*'[35]

Using such loaded rhetoric, it was little surprise that Cheyne's contemporaries saw him as a new Roger Crab. He was presented by Thomas Tryon's old publisher, George Conyers, as even more radical than Tryon himself,[36] and he was remembered this way for generations.[37] One satirical sketch apparently cast Cheyne as a primitivist bent on emulating the herbivorous feral children recently discovered in the forests of Europe: 'I am told that the new sect of herb-eaters intend to follow him into the fields, or to beg him for a clerk of their kitchen; and that there are many of them now thinking of turning their children into woods to graze with the cattle, in hopes to raise a healthy and moral race, refined from the corruptions of this luxurious world.'[38] Cheyne felt such characterisation was wholly unjust; he was horrified by the rumour that he was 'at Bottom a mere *Leveller*, and for destroying *Order, Ranks* and *Property*' and that he had 'turn'd mere *Enthusiast*, and ... advis'd People to turn *Monks*, to run into Desarts, and to live on *Roots, Herbs* and *wild Fruits*'.[39] Instead, he strenuously promoted his image as a moderate scientist advising temperance on the basis of empirical evidence. Onlookers readily lumped vegetable-toting doctors with all the other vegetarians, but Cheyne stressed that medically motivated abstinence from meat had nothing to do with the radical tradition of former decades.

Cheyne's vegetarianism was indeed backed up by a rigorous physiological theory at the cutting edge of contemporaneous neural science. In the 1660s the Oxford anatomist Thomas Willis had dissected innumerable human and animal corpses and come to the conclusion that the soul – contrary to all previous speculations – resided around the cerebellum in the brain, and it operated by pumping animal spirits into the latticework of hollow nerves. His pupil, John Locke, later demonstrated that the senses were the source of every notion in the human mind.[40] By the eighteenth century, every educated person had some idea of the nervous system, and it became the dominant means of explaining everything from feelings to character.

In the course of Cheyne's career, the theory of neural function gradually changed. In early life Cheyne believed that nerves pulsed fluid around the body with the help of adjacent vibrating fibres.[41] But after 1722 Cheyne stopped thinking about nerves as hollow tubes and claimed instead that they were solid springy fibres resonating like the strings of an instrument, and he tentatively added Newton's idea that an omnipresent 'etherial substance' might pervade them, creating 'the Cement between the human Soul and the Body'.[42]

Eighteenth-century society was obsessed with nerves. They were the sensitive interchange between mind and body and held a position equivalent to that which genes have acquired today as an explanation of inherited predispositions that could be triggered or mollified by lifestyle. A sensitive nervous system was an essential attribute for any genteel man or woman. Sensitive – or 'sensible' – nerves ensured a fine sentiment and a morality underwritten by the divinely ordered anatomy. God had created the human body with organs of sense: what better tool for moral judgement and social conduct? 'Feeling' demonstrated both refined manners and fidelity to nature.

But sensitive nerves were also dangerously susceptible to nervous disorders, and Cheyne diagnosed the English as suffering from a nervous epidemic. Society was plagued with the 'English Malady' – a psychosomatic disorder Cheyne himself helped to invent with innumerable symptoms from mild trembling to fainting and paralysis.

Cheyne's most successful medical coup was making everyone believe that being susceptible to nervous distempers was a sign of superior sensitivity.[43] He was in a prime position to sympathise with his 'fellow-sufferers', for he felt that he too had been born with tender, oversensitive nerves: 'my Senses and Sensibility were rather too acute', he declared, causing 'a Disposition to be easily ruffled on a *Surprize*'.[44] His theories spawned fictional characters like Oliver Goldsmith's hero in *The Vicar of Wakefield* (1766) who likewise suffered (or claimed to) from 'a disorder in which the whole body is so exquisitely sensible, that the slightest touch gives pain'.[45] By the beginning of the nineteenth century Jane Austen was mocking the perilous excesses of 'Sense and Sensibility', but despite these sardonic jabs, sensibility remained a social code with very wide appeal.[46]

Those born with sensitive nervous systems were vulnerable to severe disorders if they committed even a slight degree of dietary intemperance, especially in meat and alcohol. Cheyne combined the tradition of Cartesian mechanistic physiology with Isaac Newton's latest theories on the gravitational properties of different substances to develop his rigorous physiological explanation of how meat attacked the nervous system. By the standards of modern science Cheyne's theories are inaccurate, but the dangers of meat and alcohol which he highlighted have nevertheless remained a preoccupation up to the present day. Cheyne inherited his moral concern about eating too much meat from his predecessors while revising the medical explanation of its harmful effects; we have done the same in turn. Cheyne's belief that meat and alcohol clogged the body's hydraulic system, for example, foreshadows the modern idea that consuming too much meat and alcohol blocks blood vessels with cholesterol. Claims by modern dieticians tend to be founded on direct scientific observation – but the questions that motivated those observations and the conceptual framework through which they are made are influenced by inherited cultural traditions. Men like Cheyne can shed light on why we think as we do today.[47]

Cheyne reported that meat was high in 'urinous' salts, which were visible when one distilled meat and examined the residue after burning it.[48] He knew that salts accumulated into sharp-pointed crystals, and had read in Newton that these particles 'unite the most firmly of any Bodies whatsoever'.[49] Meat was also high in fatty oils, he said, and these gathered together into deposits which also could not be broken down because they 'attract one another, and unite more strongly than other Substances do, (except Salts) as Sir *Isaac Newton* observes'. Furthermore, animal flesh was composed of smaller particles than vegetables (because they had already been filtered by one digestive system) and thus they stuck together more strongly and so were even harder to digest.

If you came to Cheyne with a nervous complaint, the first thing he would do was take a sample of your blood and leave it aside to settle. If you had too much glutinous red globular blood compared to clear fluid serum he would warn you that it was too thick and sticky. Your capillaries were in danger of blocking up, bursting open and forming ulcerated swellings which would squeeze on nearby nerves and thus 'stop and intercept their *Vibrations* or *Tremors*'.[50] This interruption of the nervous system caused fainting, melancholy and apoplexy.

Next he would take a drop of blood and taste it on his tongue. The serum, he remarked like a true connoisseur, ought to be 'almost insipid, or, at least, not biting saltish': if there was too much salt in your blood, hard crystals could form and wedge themselves in small blood vessels. Then, 'like a *Lancet* or *Razor*', each sharp crystal would pierce through the vessels, ram up against nerve fibres and thus, 'by twitching and vellicating the *Nerves* or nervous Fibres, produce Convulsions, Spasms, and all the terrible Symptoms of that Tribe of nervous Distempers'.[51] In addition, he would probably suggest that your bodily fibres had become too lax (through insufficient exercise and too much eating). This reduced the body's ability to break down tough particles, which exacerbated the other problems and could cause trembling, lethargy, numbness and even paralysis.[52]

Nervous disorders, then, were mainly the *symptoms* of having 'bad blood' as a result of eating too much of the wrong sort of food – a condition Cheyne often referred to by the amorphous term 'scurvy'. Diagnosing nervous distempers in this way, Cheyne was able to bring under his remit a whole host of ailments, from hypochondria, hysteria, asthma and 'the Vapours' to the classic disorders of intemperance – gout, rheumatism and scrofula. The scientific analysis gave him the platform from which to bellow his moral censures on intemperate meat-eating:

> The *Scurvy* is the *Root* of most *chronical* Diseases of the *British* Nation; and is a necessary Consequence of their Way of *living* almost wholly on *animal Food*, and drinking so much *strong Liquors* . . . Nothing less than a very moderate Use of *animal Food*

... and a more moderate use of *spiritous Liquors, due Labour* and *Exercise* ... can keep this *Hydra* under. And nothing else than a *total Abstinence* from *animal Foods,* and *strong fermented Liquors,* can totally extirpate it.[53]

Meat, considered by most of his contemporaries to be the most desirable and nourishing of all foods, Cheyne perceived as harbouring a richness verging on excess. The poor saved meagre wages to buy the occasional joint of flesh; the rich consumed it in staggering quantities. In Britain especially, beef-eating was becoming synonymous with national pride and the annual consumption of 208 pounds of meat per head consumed by the British navy was seen as crucial to the nation's military prowess.[54] Cheyne's admonition that people should avoid meat and drink water flew in the face of common opinion.[55] But Cheyne stuck to his mechanical arguments and showed that the flesh-free vegetable diet was perfectly suited to prevent and cure nervous distempers. '*Milk* and *Vegetables* have but little saline Matter,' he observed; they diluted the blood and refreshed the body's fibres.[56]

In addition to regulating people's diet, Cheyne administered purges of vomiting and diarrhoea to cleanse the body, astringents to tighten up fibres and mercury to blast the obstructions in the vessels.[57] Bathing and drinking in mineral springs helped to cleanse the body, and physical exercise cleared out all the glands and pores. With its inculcation of virtuous self-restraint and its mechanical logic, the vegetable diet became for Cheyne the perfect purification for both his glutted body and corrupt society as a whole.[58]

Cheyne was not the first to use dieting to cure the nation's sorry medical record. In the 1670s Gideon Harvey recommended milk and vegetables as an antidote to England's plague of scurvy and consumption caused by 'flesh greediness' among the populace.[59] Alongside his discovery of nerves, Thomas Willis described the nervous disorders caused by laziness, gluttony and too much sex which blocked the nerves with 'dregs or filthiness ... [causing] Convulsions and painful wrinklings' and recommended abstinent diets – including Cheyne's favourite milk diet – as cures for them all.[60] Much of Cheyne's dietary autobiography even appears to have been plagiarised from a friend's account of 'the Milk Doctor of Croydon' and Francis Fuller's 'account of my own distemper' which concluded that many people 'are by their Constitutions condemn'd to an Antediluvian Diet of Roots and Vegetables'.[61] Cheyne was spearheading a widespread resuscitation of ancient dietary medicine, and like Hecquet he was hailed as the modern Hippocrates.[62] But in contrast to most colleagues, Cheyne manipulated the ancients' therapeutic dietetics and their warnings against intemperance into a specific stigmatisation of meat, which he then carried over from medicine into a vegetarian prophylactic guide to lifestyle.[63]

Although Cheyne sustained a base of scientific authority, many of his contemporaries lost patience with his equivocal claim that most people would be all right if they just ate a little less meat, and that they should only consider the vegetable diet as a last resort. They suspected that this was just a pose to conceal his dedication to vegetarianism, particularly as he invariably ended up pushing his patients into it anyway. Sick patients who read Cheyne's works tended to assume that they were in need of the last resort and relinquished flesh of their own accord.[64]

Cheyne was certainly very persuasive. The Essex surgeon Silvanus Bevan, for example, read *The English Malady* and immediately considered taking up the milk diet to treat his chronic bouts of drowsiness. When he wrote to tell Cheyne that he found milk indigestible, Cheyne replied that he should try fruit and vegetables instead.[65] When John Wesley stopped following Cheyne's vegetable diet in order to avoid accusations of vegetarian heresy, Cheyne insisted that if he continued to eat meat he would be condemned to a plague of fevers for the rest of his life. Wesley fearfully obeyed and two years later told the Bishop of London that 'since I have taken his advice, I have been free (blessed be God) from all bodily disorders.'[66] Indeed, every one of Cheyne's patients whose consultations with Cheyne have survived in manuscript letters were eventually reduced to the vegetable diet. Despite all his concessions to moderation, Cheyne was evidently committed to total vegetarianism.

Cheyne's milk diet itself was a vegetarian 'adaptation' of an ancient remedy. In the first century AD Galen lauded the invigorating powers of drinking milk directly from a woman's breasts, claiming that old men had been resuscitated by copulating with and 'sucking a beautiful young nurse'.[67] Suckling breast milk was still advocated by many in the medical profession, and the use of the animal milk diet had become popular – if controversial – by the 1660s.[68] Thomas Sydenham, the most respected English doctor of the previous generation, recognised that the fad for the milk diet had been remarkably efficacious against hysterical women and gout, but warned that it was usually 'much more injurious than beneficial'. It weakened the patient so much that they were no longer able to digest anything else, leaving them with the option of either worsening their condition, or sticking to the milk diet for the rest of their lives.[69]

But Cheyne had reinvented the milk diet as just another version of vegetarianism, and he skilfully turned these warnings to his own advantage. Having coerced his patients into adopting the milk and vegetable diet, he then forced them to stay on it on pain of death.[70] He warned Selina Hastings, Countess of Huntingdon (1707–91) against apostatising from her milk and vegetable regimen by reminding her that his friend Dr Taylor had 'perished miserably' when he succumbed after twenty-five years to eating meat.[71] He used the same technique on Ann Hervey, the sickly daughter of the Earl of Bristol and god-daughter to the Princess of Wales (later Queen Caroline), who came to Bath in 1727 suffering from chronic fits, a paralysed right leg and arm, constant pain in the head, and slurred speech. Cheyne put her onto a milk and vegetable diet and terrified her so much that despite the entreaties of her family and their physician she absolutely refused to break his prescriptions. 'She dares not think of changing anything in her present method,' her mother lamented, 'lest some relapse or check should happen by such alteration.' Lady Bristol knew exactly who to blame: 'The whole world is ready to pull [Cheyne] to pieces for so many miserable creatures that he has brought to death's door,' she raged.[72]

But Cheyne did not stop with Ann: he was already inflicting the same fate on Lord Hervey, her flamboyant brother. Hervey – with his frilly waistcoats, scarlet lipstick and face powder – was the darling of fashionable society. He shared a mistress with the Prince of Wales and lived openly with his homosexual partner in London, despite already being married. But his riotous life was beginning to take its toll: in addition to his chronic headaches, fever, fits and nervous delirium, he was slipping into a punishing addiction to opium.[73] When Hervey read the *Essay of Health and Long Life* and came to purify himself at Bath in 1726, he and Cheyne formed an intimate friendship, both enjoying overt displays of their mutual sentimental dependence. Cheyne encouraged Hervey to treat him like a priest, and his patient responded by submitting himself entirely to Cheyne's 'sensible' dietary religion.

Initially Cheyne assured Hervey that he would only have to abstain from meat for a few months, during which time he was 'to eat no meat; and at the end of it to go into a total milk diet for two months'. But three years later, Cheyne had revealed his true colours by keeping poor Hervey from the tiniest morsel of flesh: 'From the time of my first putting myself into his hands, to this hour,' Hervey reported, 'I ate neither flesh, fish, nor eggs, but lived entirely upon herbs, root, pulse, grains, fruits, legumes and all those sorts of foods.'[74]

Years later, when Hervey finally felt well enough to downgrade himself to Cheyne's intermediate 'trimming diet' with its allowance of white tender meat, Cheyne felt utterly betrayed and erupted in wounded fury. Hervey rose to the occasion with paralleled melodrama, detailing in a letter to Cheyne his daily food intake precisely, claiming that he had overcome a sickness in a few days 'that would have stuck by a true beef and pork-eater as many months', and assuring Cheyne that he was still 'one of your most pious votaries':

> If you were as just to *my* practice as I am to your doctrine, it would be impossible for you, whilst I always acknowledge and revere you as the great Aesculapius* of this age and country, to speak of me as an apostate, a heretic or even a schismatic in your medical religion . . . After this account of myself, I expect you should compare me no more to *Mahomet's Tomb*, because I think my rigid perseverance in this faith entitles me, in the Heaven of Health, to the place immediately next to the Angel Gabriel.[75]

Cheyne's contemporaries suspected that there was something going on beneath the surface of his 'objective' scientific call for vegetarianism. They were right, and towards the end of his career in 1740, Cheyne let down his guard, overcame his 'Dread of the odious Designation of *Enthusiasm* or Superstition', and revealed the theology behind his vegetarianism. Cheyne had always said that abstaining from meat was the cure for disease; but it transpired that it also worked the other way round: disease was really the cure for meat-eating. Cheyne believed that vegetarianism reconnected people with nature. By renovating the nervous system and thus revitalising the neural function of 'sympathy', Cheyne thought that vegetarianism was a route to heaven. Alongside his role as dietician, Cheyne conceived of his entire professional life as a mission to save people's souls through abstinence from flesh. His

---

* The god of medicine.

theological beliefs never took precedence over his scientific rationale, for he insisted, perfectly credibly, that it was his science that had led him to his theological deductions. If it was true that meat was bad for the health and vegetables good for it, God must necessarily have had reasons for making it so.[76] Cheyne simply believed that he had discovered what God's reasons were.

Cheyne believed that meat damaged the nervous system and the vegetable diet cleansed it. But nerves were not just physiological: they were also the vessels of morality. 'Sympathy' was a natural function of the nervous system which caused people to experience 'the Misery of their Fellow Creatures' and this was the physiological basis of social harmony.[77]

It did not take much imagination to extend this same principle to animals. In 1672 Thomas Willis showed that 'four-footed Beasts' had exactly the same nervous system as man – even their brains were only different in size.[78] Bernard Mandeville noticed in the *Fable of the Bees* (1714) that this physiological similarity was why man naturally sympathised with terrestrial mammals 'in whom the Heart, the Brain, and Nerves . . . the Organs of Sense, and consequently Feeling it self, are the same as they are in Human Creatures'.[79] Even Nicolas Malebranche the Cartesian agreed that this was why inflicting pain on animals mechanically rebounded in 'a Repurcussive stroke of Compassion', making tender-hearted (and foolish) people 'unable to see a Beast beaten, or hear it cry, without some disturbance of Mind'.[80]

For Cheyne, this natural propensity in the nerves to 'sympathise' with animal suffering was anatomical evidence that man was not designed to kill and eat them. Not only did humans lack carnivorous claws, teeth and guts, their entire nervous system was repulsed by killing. God gave man verbal permission to kill animals, but He also gave them the nervous organs and the sense of natural justice to tell them it was wrong. Cheyne took a radical step in allowing the physiological fact of sympathy to overrule the scriptural authority for eating meat. In this prioritisation of feeling in moral decision-making, Cheyne provided an anatomical basis for the claims of the 'moral-sense' philosophers Francis Hutcheson (1694–1746) and his one-time nervous patient David Hume (1711–76).[81]

Cheyne acknowledged that the 'Custom' of meat-eating had blunted natural human sensibilities:

> To see the Convulsions, Agonies and Tortures of a poor *Fellow-Creature*, whom they cannot restore nor recompense, dying to gratify *Luxury* . . . must require a rocky Heart, and a great Degree of Cruelty and Ferocity. I cannot find on the Foot of natural Reason and *Equity* only, between feeding on *human Flesh*, and feeding on brute animal Flesh, except *Custom* and *Example*.[82]

Cheyne showed that eating meat physically stifled nervous sensations and thus apparently prevented the experience of sympathy. Meat built a wall – hardened by salts and oil – between man and his natural repulsion to flesh-eating. Cheyne's vegetarian diet psychosomatically broke down that wall and reconnected man with his innate sympathy. 'Custom', or civilisation, had caused a breach between man and his nature: it was Cheyne's aim to reunite them and show that meat-eating was a horrific contravention of natural sensibility. And sympathy, as he had always explained, was more than a matter of mere physical health: it was the body's inbuilt mechanism for spiritual salvation.[83]

This prompted Cheyne to develop a bizarre reinterpretation of the Bible. He explained that God permitted meat after the Flood as a means of sorting the sheep from the goats. The voluptuous would gorge on it and consequently die quickly, clearing the world of their evil souls.[84] The virtuous, however, would realise that meat caused disease and thus redeem themselves by abstaining.[85] Whenever Cheyne's patients became sick he told them that this was their 'particular *Call*' sent by God to initiate them 'into a Low Diet'.[86]

This pious conviction made Cheyne's friends chuckle into their sleeves. The poet and statesman Lord George Lyttelton wrote to Alexander Pope that Cheyne insisted that the sickness afflicting Lord George Grenville (who was to become George III's Prime Minister) was 'nothing but a fillip which Providence gave him, for his Good to make him temperate, and put him under the care of Doctor Cheyney. When we tell the Doctor, that he always has been temperate, a water Drinker; and eater of Whitemeats, he Roars like a Bull, and says we are all liars; for had he been so, he cou'd not have had an Inflammation, which he is ready to prove by all the Rules of Philosophy, mathematicks and religion.'[87]

Still more extraordinarily, Cheyne surmised that only those born with the highest 'Degree of *Sensibility*' ever suffered from nervous disorders, and thus only they would ever embrace the vegetable diet, 'this (as it were) material *Metaphysicks* of a *Regimen*'.[88] Others, in Cheyne's words, were 'unfit' for the role.[89] His insistence that an ordinary omnivorous diet was best for most people, especially '*Ideots*, *Peasants* and *Mechanicks*', takes on a more sinister aspect as it appears that according to Cheyne's semi-Calvinist vegetarian predestination, this essentially excluded them from virtue and even from heaven.[90] No wonder Cheyne said that before his conversion to vegetarianism, he felt like a '*Malefactor* condemn'd'.[91]

According to Cheyne's idiosyncratic system of salvation, which was very similar to that of the kabbalists and Platonists, all beings had committed a primeval sin of rebellion in a former existence.[92] In punishment, they had been imprisoned as microscopic organisms in the testicles of the first male of each species.[93] Those who failed to purify themselves would leave planet earth when they died and reincarnate in a 'more gross, miserable and dark' planet – perhaps even a burning hellish comet – until they were fully purged of all their wickedness.[94] But those who took up Cheyne's vegetarian ascetic principles made their bodies 'lighter' and detached their souls from the material world so that when they died their soul and its ethereal body would float up to a higher planet (by the power of electro-magnetic attraction) until eventually gravitating back to God.[95] Indeed, Cheyne told his patients that the dietary purification was helping to purge the whole world's '*Load of Corruption, Deteriority*, and *Lapse*', thus paving the way towards the ultimate Golden Age of '*Perfection*' or 'universal Gaol delivery' when all creatures would be released and return to God.[96] Vegetarianism was a key to unclogging the human body as well as the whole universe's system of spiritual purification.

This interplanetary cycle of reincarnation even included animals, which he tentatively suggested might be intelligent beings like humans on a lower rung of the purificatory ladder. Animals experienced pain and suffering and, he explained, 'to me it seems utterly incredible, that any Creature, whether *sentient* or *intelligent*, should come into this *State* of Being and Suffering, for no other Purpose than we see them attain here . . . There must be some infinitely beautiful, wise and good *Scene* remaining for all *sentient* and *intelligent* Beings, the Discovery of which will ravish and astonish us one Day.'[97] (According to Cheyne's logic, this meant that God was not unjust for letting animals suffer and be killed, because it helped to 'advance these *Victims* to a higher State of Being and Happiness'.[98]) Cheyne had devised the rudiments of this belief system right back in 1705 when he explained that sympathy was the principle by which all creatures in the interplanetary salvation system were united, and the means by which souls were attracted back to union with God.[99]

Cheyne's system might look like a half-lunatic regression into kabbalistic mysticism, but in fact he could have taken half of it from the widely respected doctrine of Preformation devised by the leading German philosopher, Gottfried Wilhelm Leibniz, who had rationalised the kabbalism of his friend Franciscus Mercurius van Helmont. According to Leibniz, a sperm was a miniature version of the human body which 'unfolded' in the womb and grew into an adult organism. When a person died, their bodies folded up again into their original microscopic size and awaited their turn for another birth.[100] As for Cheyne's belief in extra-terrestrial life, this was common among scientists and theologians at the time and there were even several others who believed in animal heaven.[101] The bastion of the Newtonian-Anglican orthodoxy Samuel Clarke, for example, considered it possible that animal souls might be resurrected onto the planets.[102] Cheyne was probably also encouraged by the French theosophist Charles Hector Marquis St George de Marsay, who, like Cheyne, thought suffering was a process of purification and that souls were guided to suitable planets or stars by mechanical attraction. Both of them in turn were probably influenced by the Chevalier Andrew Michael Ramsay (1686–1743), founder of French Freemasonry, who reputedly believed that 'there's an eternal pre-existence of souls; that the bad supply the world of brutes'.[103] Such beliefs might seem strange, but the status of animals and how to make sense of God allowing them to suffer simply for our pleasure was a serious problem for Christians.

Although for Cheyne this eschatological theory always simmered beneath the surface of his dietary prescriptions, he knew better than to divulge it at all times. Instead he stuck for the most part to the physical rationale for vegetarianism. His ideas about man's natural sympathy for creatures spread by means of his own books, and those of his illustrious patients and readers, providing scientific backing for Europe's ensuing 'back-to-nature' movement. His belief that abstaining from flesh cleansed the nerves, reawakened the innate force of sympathy, absolved the stricken conscience and facilitated the sympathetic attraction of the soul back to God, may seem alien today. But much of Enlightenment science was originally backed up and motivated by such beliefs, and they have thus, surprisingly, contributed to modern notions about the moral and physiological implications of meat.

FOURTEEN

Clarissa's Calories

Long before the founding father of the novel, Samuel Richardson (1689–1761), embarked on his glittering literary career he was a printer of books, and among his most valued clients was the eminent nerve doctor, George Cheyne. In the course of their business correspondence, Cheyne encouraged his printer to confide in him about his ailments, and there developed a friendship which lasted to the day Cheyne died. Richardson valued Cheyne's letters so much that he had them transcribed into a note book and bound them into a volume with his old doctor's obituaries – though he honoured Cheyne's demand that they should never be published. Over the years Cheyne taught Richardson about the link between diet and nervous sensibility; his ideas made their way into Richardson's novels and thus trickled into the mainstream of eighteenth-century emotional, literary and domestic culture.

Cheyne quickly diagnosed Richardson as having been 'born originally of weak *Nerves*', making him acutely intelligent, imaginative, spiritual and subject to intense emotional experience. He asked Richardson to write to him uninhibitedly about the troubles of his body and soul – to 'open your Heart frankly and unreservedly' and write 'without Restraint in a running Manner'.[1]

The 'running Manner' which Richardson developed in his letters to Cheyne became the distinguishing feature of his novels, *Pamela* and *Clarissa* (still the longest novel in the English language), in which his heroines suffer all the anatomical-emotional symptoms of acute nervous sensibility while callous, hard-hearted rakes who assault them display all the disorders of intemperance. Richardson's novels outstripped even Cheyne's books with their popularity; Pamela and Clarissa became the defining characters of the culture of sensibility, uniting society in sympathy for their plight.

Before examining Richardson's novels, I want to reveal the shocking means by which Cheyne secured his power over Richardson. The diet doctor poisoned his patient with mercury.

When Richardson first complained to Cheyne that he was ill, he was suffering from 'a mere Cold'. To unblock Richardson's clogged system, Cheyne prescribed him with ten daily pills of his favourite deobstruent, Aethiop's Mineral, a highly potent mercury composition pounded up with other ingredients to maximise absorption in the gut.[2] Similar pills have been found to contain around 9,000 times the level of mercury considered safe today.[3] The secrets of Cheyne's prescriptions are hidden away at the end of his letters in medical notes written in a specialised form of abbreviated Latin for the information of Richardson's apothecary.

Mercury had long been used as a cure for syphilis, but Cheyne, who thought it a '*Divine Antidote*', told his readers that 'There is nothing I could more earnestly wish were brought into the common Practice of *Physick*, than the more free and general (but cautious) Use of the Preparations of *Mercury*.' The round particles of mercury, he explained, were like 'so many little Bullets, shot against a mud Wall', making it the most efficient method of unblocking the body's hydraulic system.[4] Cheyne even devised a special formula for increasing absorption by constipating the patient so that the mercury could not be evacuated in diarrhoea.[5]

Mercury, as we now know, is a virulent neurotoxin. It seems hardly surprising, therefore, that within months of beginning his course of mercurial medicines Richardson was suffering from fits of trembling, twitching, temporary and local paralysis, giddiness, nausea, anxiety, depression, hypersensitivity (erethism) and a tendency to withdraw from social contact.[6] This was exactly what Cheyne would have expected, since they were all manifestations of what he called 'nervous disorders'. Each one of these symptoms, however, as well as Richardson's micrographia and festinating gait (resulting from damage to the neural heel–toe coordination mechanism), are classic symptoms of mercury poisoning. Cheyne's response to Richardson's increasing 'nervous' ailments was to prescribe him even more mercury.[7]

In 1940, during the blitz of London, St Bride's Church in Fleet Street, took a direct hit from a Nazi bomb and the crypt was blown open exposing 200 lead coffins, among them Samuel Richardson's. On the basis of his skeletal remains, a group of scientists in the 1990s diagnosed Richardson's chronic stiff neck as diffuse idiopathic skeletal

hyperostosis (DISH), and although they knew about his nervous problems, they did not look beyond the old speculation that he suffered
from Parkinson's disease, which is unverifiable since it leaves no trace
on the skeleton.[8]

If one accepted that chronic trembling was a sign of Parkinson's
disease then one would be faced with the awkward problem of explaining an apparently massive outbreak of that non-infectious disorder
during the eighteenth century affecting probably many thousands of
people all over Europe. Contemporaries, including Cheyne, reported
that trembling and symptoms as extreme as paralysis reached epidemic
proportions in middle- and upper-class society.[9] It is common to treat
this phenomenon as a cultural construction in which biological reality
is of secondary importance. But it has also become common to diag-
nose retrospectively Parkinson's, epilepsy and 'psychiatric disorders'.
Any of these might be true, but it is almost certain that the plague of
nervous disorders recorded in eighteenth-century Europe was caused
in substantial part by the widespread medical use of mercury, of which
Cheyne and Richardson were both unfortunate victims.

From 1733 until late 1741 Cheyne made light of Richardson's
ailments saying they were 'vapourish and nervous, of no Manner of
Danger, but extremely frightful and lowering'.[10] He explained that it
was a 'scorbutic nervous case', which meant that corrupt blood and
blocked capillaries were causing Richardson's nervous symptoms. His
weak nerves had been wasted and relaxed by his sedentary life, thinking
too hard and – Cheyne insisted despite Richardson's denials – intemperance.[11] Richardson's nerves and other fibres had become so lax that
his guts were no longer able to grind animal food,[12] so Cheyne prescribed Richardson a temperate, 'trimming' diet, with reduced quantities of flesh and wine, and gave him extra doses of mercury.[13]

When Richardson continued to report that his symptoms were
getting worse, and none of Cheyne's methods was helping, Cheyne –
following his usual practice – told Richardson that there was no option
left but to give up meat entirely and resort to the pure vegetable diet.
The startling thing is that at exactly the same moment as prescribing
the vegetable diet for the first time – in late November 1741 – Cheyne
stopped the mercurial medicines:[14]

> you have already gone through too tedious a Course of Apothe-
> caries' Stuff, and if you were my Brother and could have Patience

and Perseverance, you should have done both with Apothecaries and Doctors, and trust to God and Providence under the lowest, thinnest, and coolest Diet . . . In a Word, a Milk and Vegetable Diet with sole Water Beverage is your only certain Defence from a Fit of Apoplexy or Palsy, and I have no Peace till I propose it. Consider of it and let me hear your Resolution.[15]

The significance of this letter has been overlooked partly because it is placed in the wrong order in Richardson's letter book, but it reveals an extremely important fact about Cheyne's medical technique. Unsurprisingly, with the cessation of the mercury pills, Richardson's health did improve, and Cheyne immediately claimed another success for the vegetable diet.[16] This was no accident. Indeed, it was Cheyne's usual practice. In *The English Malady*, for example, he reported that he had treated a lady with high doses of mercury until she was so desperately ill that she accepted his proposal of stopping all medicine and turning instead to the milk and vegetable diet – which inevitably (miraculously) produced a total cure within six months.[17]

It is hard to believe that Cheyne knowingly poisoned people with mercury until they succumbed to his vegetable diet. But he did know that mercury could cause nervous disorders and paralysis; he publicly admitted this in his books and he experienced its effects himself. He once treated his ulcerated legs with so much mercury that he was overcome by giddiness and convulsions and his shirt buttons were discoloured by the mercury coming out in his sweat.[18] Richardson himself, when he started taking Cheyne's medicines, complained that they were making him ill.[19] The harmful effects of mercury were well known.[20] Thomas Willis, for example, warned that mercury damaged the nerves, causing convulsions, vomiting, blindness, comatosis, anxiety and bloody stools. Willis was so 'terrified' of these side effects that when he treated Lady Anne Conway for her chronic headaches he was too scared to use it and declared that it was only appropriate as a punitive medicine for syphilis: 'that evil Remedy', he said, 'ought to be applyed to that evil Distemper'.[21]

Cheyne probably regarded mercury as a part of the retributive purgation of his patients' corrupt bodies – a necessary precursor to the purifying vegetable diet. But whether deliberately or simply through his cavalier attitude, Cheyne's mercury medicines were a crucial instrument in his 'providentially-guided' promotion of vegetarianism. By causing Richardson's nervous ailments and teaching him how to articulate them, Cheyne was a formative influence on the development of Richardson's novels of sensibility.

Richardson was even more worried about giving up meat than he was about taking mercury, and in the first weeks and months of the vegetable diet, 'perplexed and puzzled', he found it extremely hard going.[22] Cheyne responded to Richardson's 'doubts' with a barrage of firebrand conversion letters, bullying and terrorising him, just as he did with other patients.[23] Abandoning his soothing assurances that Richardson's malady was minor, Cheyne suddenly insisted, on his authority as world-class physician, that if Richardson did not adopt the vegetable diet he would certainly die in extreme pain and suffering, a death threat he repeated on several occasions. Eating meat, said Cheyne with more than a hint of moral blackmail, was an act of selfish concupiscence which would leave his children fatherless, and would even constitute the damnable sin of suicide.[24]

Cheyne warned Richardson that friends, family and other doctors would try to get him to eat meat. He contemptuously lumped all those tempters together as 'free-livers', 'Beef-eaters', 'cannibals', 'Voluptuous and Flesh-eaters', likening them to carnivorous beasts eating 'Dog's meat', and outrageously suggesting that they were in cahoots with the devil himself.[25] Resisting them would be like re-enacting Christ's passion: Richardson was to respond with the prayer, 'Father forgive them for they know not what they say or do.'[26]

In militant opposition to these satanic carnivores, Cheyne gave Richardson the sense of belonging to a vegetarian brotherhood, or 'Lovers of Virtue' who had a special means of salvation. He introduced Richardson to other 'Vegetable Patients' and encouraged them to correspond between themselves.[27] These included Cheyne's own family whom he had also coaxed into the vegetable diet, especially his daughter Peggy, Richardson's favourite. The teetotal vegetable regimen was not just a cure, it was an identity, a lifestyle he called 'living strictly aqueously and vegetably'.[28] And as soon as Richardson adopted the diet, Cheyne slammed the door behind him and announced that he must stick to it indefinitely: 'for when the Stomac and Constitution is once habituated to this Diet it is certain Death to change it at your Time of Life'. Cheyne imagined himself as the priest marrying his patient to the vegetable diet which must be pursued 'like Matrimony for better and for worse'.[29]

By the end of the first month Cheyne was bubbling excitedly:

'I could no longer delay congratulating you upon your entering upon your State of Rejuvinescence.'[30] Cheyne told him that the milk and vegetable diet was analogous to spiritual 'Purification and Regeneration . . . Repentance, Self-Denial', and that it inculcated 'Innocence' and 'Simplicity'. It was, furthermore, one of the keys to salvation: living on milk, he preached, 'is like becoming little Children. Without becoming such our Master tells us we can not enter into the Kingdom of Heaven.'[31] He assured Richardson that God had providentially afflicted him with illness and was coaxing him away from the carnivorous diet.[32] Richardson felt his health improve under Cheyne's regimen, and was so convinced that, although Cheyne died sixteen months after his conversion, he persisted with it for at least another five or six years, until 1748 or 1749.[33] As he wrote to his friend Lady Bradshaigh in 1748, he had been '*forced* . . . to go into a Regimen, not a Cure to be expected, but merely as a Palliative; and for Seven Years past have forborn Wine, Flesh, and Fish'.[34] Although he may eventually have given it up, in the course of their relationship Richardson had been indoctrinated into Cheyne's vegetarian ideology.

Constantly receiving encouragement from his physico-spiritual doctor, Richardson wrote parts I and II of *Pamela* in the years running up to 1741 while Cheyne was limiting his flesh intake and telling him to follow 'Not only a temperate but an abstemious Diet'.[35] *Clarissa*, published in 1747–8, was written while Richardson was rigorously pursuing the vegetable regimen. It is little surprise, therefore, that Pamela and Clarissa are the archetypal heroines of sensibility and obey all Cheyne's physiological theories of dietary abstinence.

Their foods of choice are bread, butter, water, tea, milk, salad, toast and chocolate.[36] More often than not they refuse to eat anything at all, and signify their dissent from the tyrannical patriarchy that oppresses them by refusing to share their predominantly carnivorous meals. Some contemporaries even criticised *Pamela* for encouraging young ladies to be too weight-conscious – Pamela's waist is so thin a man could encompass it with his two hands.[37] Both Pamela and Clarissa think of themselves as Plutarch's proverbial 'old Roman and his lentils' – a symbol of parsnip-eating protest against luxury.[38] Pamela – a servant girl who has been abducted by her master, Mr B. – frequently threatens to escape from his decadent world and return to innocent poverty, living on bread and water, 'and if I can't get me Bread,' she says, 'I will live like a Bird in Winter upon Hips and Haws, and at other times upon Pig-nuts, and Potatoes, Turneps, or any thing.'[39] Clarissa meanwhile makes the classic Cheynian comment that her own peasant-like frugality will be rewarded with health, while her greedy oppressors are repaid with the distempers of luxury.[40]

Clarissa, like Pamela, is abducted by a young gallant; but whereas Pamela ends up marrying her assailant, Clarissa is raped by Lovelace, precipitating her into a nervous illness and an inability to eat anything 'nourishing' at all. In other words, just like Richardson and Cheyne (whose disorders were also exacerbated by grief), the fibres of her body had become so weak that her stomach could no longer digest strong food like meat.[41] To resolve this critical juncture in the novel, Richardson brings in an apothecary who may as well have been George Cheyne himself, for instead of prescribing 'Apothecaries' Stuff' he announces to Clarissa: 'I'll give you a regimen, madam . . . which . . . will make physic unnecessary . . . Let your breakfast be water-gruel, or milk-pottage, or weak broths: your dinner anything you like, so you will *but* eat: a dish of tea with milk in the afternoon; and sago for your supper: and my life for yours, this diet and a month's country air will set you up.'[42] Cheyne regularly prescribed his patients sago, milk-pottage, water-gruel, weak broths and country air, and, indeed, Richardson's novels are populated by a network of sympathetic characters on abstinent regimens.[43] Even the wording in *Clarissa* echoes Cheyne's letter to Richardson while he was writing the novel: 'Your new Regimen,' he wrote, is to 'Breakfast on Tea, Milk with little thin Bread and Butter, at Noon have Asparagus, roasted Potatoes, Tarts and the like, at Night a Porridge of Bread and Milk.'[44]

But instead of getting better under her Cheynian regimen, Clarissa wastes away and dies. The exact 'cause' of Clarissa's death has been a matter of intense speculation by literary critics ever since it was first published – anorexia being the favourite retrospective diagnosis of recent years. In the light of the similarities between her diet and her author's, it seems that Richardson was airing his own anxieties about starving to death on Cheyne's vegetable diet. Richardson's friends had scared him with stories about vegetarians who had perished, and he wrote to Cheyne naming Lord Cadogan and Lord Barclay as examples. Cheyne was outraged and rebuked Richardson, insisting that Lord Cadogan was not on a vegetable diet and wasn't dead in any case and Lord Barclay had only died because his doctor, Hermann Boerhaave, was a novice in the use of the vegetable diet, and anyway

Barclay had not followed the rules closely enough (a firm warning to Richardson).[45]

A similar death hit the headlines in 1744 while Richardson was writing *Clarissa*. Cheyne was already dead, but when the hunchbacked Bath poetess Mary Chandler died everyone attributed it to her strict adherence to Cheyne's vegetable regimen. As the historian David Shuttleton has pointed out, Richardson knew Mary: he had printed her works, quoted from them in his novels, and had been introduced by Cheyne to her brother Samuel Chandler, the prominent nonconformist divine who ran a bookshop and was another of Cheyne's vegetarian followers.[46]

Samuel Chandler explained his sister's death as a result of the weakening effect of the vegetable diet, but scandalised contemporaries suggested that Mary's starvation amounted to suicide, and this was also a concern voiced by critics about Clarissa's apparently voluntary demise. Like Mary Chandler, however, Clarissa composed her own epitaph revealing the true spiritual meaning of her asceticism and death. Just as Samuel Chandler defended his sister from ignominy by emphasising that her diet was a virtuous attempt to suppress fleshly passions in order to raise her spirit, so Richardson indicated that Clarissa's abstinence freed her soul from her body, preparing it for a higher place in heaven. It seems that Richardson resolved the crisis in his novel by portraying Clarissa as an exemplar of Cheyne's principles of physical and spiritual purification.[47]

Just as Cheyne did, Richardson linked his dietary motifs with the principle of sympathy for animals. Where Cheyne compared sensitive people to gentle birds and hard-hearted meat-eaters to beasts of prey,[48] so Richardson represented his herbivorous heroines as innocent lambs and doves and their male assailants as meat-gorging predators.[49] While Pamela and Clarissa are constantly compared to chickens (for 'daughters are chickens brought up for the tables of other men'), their abductors frequently eat chicken, especially their freedom-symbolising wings.[50] Even from his sick-bed Lovelace cannot forbear sardonic comparisons, writing that he is 'as patient and passive as the chickens that are brought me in broth' – a sadistic allusion to his power to destroy helpless creatures laced with a pun on the chicks that are brought to him in broth[el]s.[51]

Clarissa affectionately cares for her poultry and Pamela exhibits her sympathy for animals by releasing a carp and sowing the horse beans she has been using as fish bait in a flowerbed: 'I will plant life,' she tells her indignant carp-killing guardian, 'while you are destroying it.'[52] Lovelace, by contrast, proudly acknowledges the continuity between his abuse of animals and women: 'We begin with birds as boys, and as men go on to ladies; and both perhaps, in turns, experience our sportive cruelty'[53]. In one of the crowning observations of the novel, Belford (Lovelace's repentant accomplice) has a moment of clarity when he understands that chauvinism, anthropocentrism and class tyranny all stem from the same human impulse. 'Lords of the creation!' he exclaims sardonically:

> Who can forbear indignant laughter! When . . . [he] is obliged not only for the ornaments, but for the necessaries of life (that is to say, for food as well as raiment) to all the other creatures; strutting with their blood and spirits in his veins, and with their plumage on his back . . . thinks himself at liberty to kick and cuff, and elbow out every worthier creature: and when he has none of the animal creation to hunt down and abuse, will make use of his power, his strength, or his wealth, to oppress the less powerful and weaker of his own species![54]

In this Montaigne-like attack,[55] Belford realises that humans are inexorably connected to the rest of creation: indeed, they practically *are* the other animals and thus ought to sympathise with them. Richardson was not taking a radical stance against killing animals, nor advocating the demolition of social hierarchy, perhaps not even calling for the equality of the sexes. But with the recognition of likeness, Richardson did hope that sympathy would bridge the rupture in the moral responsibility that had arisen between the powerful and the weak.[56]

Just as Cheyne showed that having meat coursing round your veins made you sick, so Richardson strikes his predatory rakes down with providentially perpetrated distempers. As Cheyne explained, illness triggers an awakening of sympathy in the sufferer and initiates their reform.[57] The *Medicinal Dictionary* (1743–5), which Richardson and Samuel Johnson helped to write, said of Hermann Boerhaave, 'his own pain taught him to compassionate others.'[58] With Cheyne's explicit encouragement, Richardson translated this medical schema into the didactic model of the reformation of the rake,[59] and he applied it, without a single exception, to every rake and malevolent female accomplice in *Clarissa* and *Pamela*.[60]

According to Cheyne's medical theory, sickness could force

Stage One from William Hogarth, 'The Four Stages of Cruelty'

carnivorous patients to feel sympathy for their animal victims. In
Richardson's novels the rakes' debauchery of women is figured as preying on animals. When the rake is finally struck down by a providential
illness, they learn to sympathise for their victims and reform their
sexual diet. In the case of Lovelace, reform comes too late and he is
struck down by an illness which he pictures as an animal coming
back to take revenge on its predator.[61] Cheyne had often spoken to
Richardson about the pangs of 'remorse' that followed a bout of over-

eating; Richardson harnessed the etymology of remorse (re-*mordere*, to bite): the prey literally bites its predator back.[62] On his sick-bed Lovelace cries out that 'Remorse *has* broken in upon me . . . A thousand vultures in turn are preying upon my heart!'[63] When Lovelace survives his sickness, he is finally killed by Clarissa's cousin Morden (who shares his etymology with *re*-morde-*re*).

The parallel between sexual concupiscence and meat-eating is explicit, and the role of reconnecting people with their own natural sympathy is the same in Richardson as it was in Cheyne. When Lovelace's hirelings' sympathies are finally reawakened they still receive pecuniary benefits from Clarissa's plight and do nothing to save her.[64] This, Richardson indicates, is the equivalent of claiming to sympathise for animals but continuing to eat them. 'A pitiful fellow!' exclaims Lovelace of one of them. 'Such a ridiculous kind of pity *his*, as those silly souls have, who would not kill an innocent chicken for the world; but when killed to their hands, are always the most greedy devourers of it.'[65] Richardson's image here comes from the *Fable of the Bees* in which Bernard Mandeville pointed out the hypocrisy of people who could not bear to kill their own poultry, and yet happily ate meat by getting as far as they could from the site of slaughter.[66] Cheyne and Richardson both wanted to rejuvenate people's natural moral feeling by reconnecting the sympathiser with the sympathised.

Belford starts off as one of these hypocrites who fail to see the connection between their own purported morality and their complicity in immoral acts. His desire to dissociate himself from Clarissa's fate is, declares Lovelace, 'the palliating consolation of an Hottentot heart, determined rather to gluttonize on the garbage of other foul feeders, than to reform'.[67] In the end, however, Belford does reform, and once again Richardson used Cheyne's dietary model to express it. After suffering a 'consumptive cough' and witnessing the demise of his fellow debauchees, his sensibilities are awakened; he becomes 'a man of sense', turns away from 'a life of sense and appetite' and converts to the 'palatable' 'regular' diet of married life.[68]

The medical-metaphorical motifs that Richardson developed in all his novels became standard fare in eighteenth-century fiction. In Tobias Smollett's novel *Ferdinand Count Fathom* (1753), the heroine Monimia, like Richardson's Clarissa, is kept in an isolated London residence guarded by a malicious woman collaborating with the rapacious anti-hero, Fathom. Like Clarissa, she languishes under her ordeal and ends up on a severe ascetic diet which threatens her life: 'Her sustenance was barely such as exempted her from the guilt of being accessory to her own death.'[69] As in *Clarissa*, the novel's predatory villains, who are figured as carnivorous beasts, are eventually reformed. In Fathom's case this is precipitated by a distemper which softens his heart and teaches him to feel for his victims. In the case of the murderous Castilian, Don Diego de Zelos, it is represented with the Promethean image of vultures preying on his insides, and modulated through the play on the word remorse. Their consequent reformation, as in Richardson, is adumbrated in their change of diet. Fathom vows to adopt the life of a penitent hermit, and Zelos turns from his bloody past of revenge and violence to adopt a vegetarian ascetic life of penitence: 'the fields shall furnish herbage for my food; the stream shall quench my thirst,' vows Zelos zealously.[70]

Like Cheyne, Smollett studied medicine at Marischal College in Aberdeen, and became a physician-author in Bath. He almost certainly knew about Cheyne and the vegetarian doctor James Graham. Smollett ridiculed dietary faddism by comparing the fervent 'abstinence' of some health-conscious gamblers in *Fathom* with the superstitious 'abhorrence' of Brahmins and Pythagoreans.[71] He reused this satire in his presentation of the Cheyne-like regimen pursued by Matthew Bramble in *Humphrey Clinker*, and in *Peregrine Pickle*, where an old officer manifests his detestation of the Bath medical profession by treating himself for gout by 'pursuing a regimen quite contrary to that which he knew they prescribed to others'.[72] In *Roderick Random* Smollett rubbished frugal fleshless diets and referred contemptuously to the navy's so-called 'banyan-days' when the meat ration was withdrawn.[73] When Smollett's own poor health forced him to take up a herbivorous diet, he mocked himself, saying 'I . . . eat like a Horse.'[74]

By the end of the eighteenth century, although the literary motifs of Cheynian sensibility were still widely employed, they were as often ridiculed. Jane Austen (1775–1817) extended her satire on the culture of sensibility to its dietary excesses, which she had read about in her favourite novel – Richardson's *Sir Charles Grandison* – and to which her own parents had been subjected during their residence in Bath.[75] In *Emma* (1815) Mr Woodhouse, father of the eponymous heroine, is the archetype of the hypersensitive hypochondriac who is so particular about food that he consults his apothecary on the dangers of eating wedding cake.[76] In accordance with Cheynian dietary principles, Woodhouse's 'conviction of suppers being very unwholesome' forces him to dissuade his guests from eating the food laid before them: 'Such another small basin of thin gruel as his own, was all that he could, with thorough self-approbation, recommend.' With hilarious fastidiousness, he says to one guest, 'let me propose your venturing on one of these eggs. An egg boiled very soft is not unwholesome. Serle understands boiling an egg better than any body. I would not recommend an egg boiled by any body else ... I do not advise the custard.'[77] But for all the mockery, Austen's personal letters reveal that she was not immune to dietary doctrines herself when, for example, she betrays her assumption that full meals clog the brain: 'Composition seems to me Impossible, with a head full of Joints of Mutton.'[78]

Despite such taunts, the medical theories of which Cheyne was an architect had a profound effect on the figuration of morality in the eighteenth century. Nervous disorders and their moral implications provided one of the era's most pervasive representations of the reformation of manners. It became an accepted doctrine that flesh-eating, or at least cruelty to animals, signified and exacerbated a savage disposition which was best dealt with by the natural retributive justice of bodily disorders, which in turn stimulated moral reformation. It was a literary form of Richardson's creation which could be termed 'dietary didacticism'.

FIFTEEN

Rousseau and the Bosoms of Nature

In the 1780s the French court was overcome by a fad for rustic chic. In place of heavy jewels, Marie-Antoinette and her intimates sported flowers and grasses in their hair; their breasts sat proudly open to view like Mother Nature's herself as they affected the simplicity of milkmaids and shepherdesses.[1] The Queen's favourite painter, Elisabeth Vigée-Lebrun, caused scandal by depicting the ladies scantily dressed.[2] Courtiers indulged in romances with unheard-of freedom, and even the disapprobation they elicited was balanced with a reverential awe for the natural passion that they claimed as their moral sanction. Even in religion people broke from the shackles of church services and went looking for God in pristine natural forests and wild mountain landscapes.

This popular, back-to-nature cult was initiated by Jean-Jacques Rousseau (1712–78). His call for a liberation from convention was a primary catalyst for Romanticism, and by the end of the 1780s his staunch avocation of political freedom spilled over into the French masses and helped to inspire real shepherds to overthrow the ruling elite of the *ancien régime*. Aristocrats who had embraced his call for emotional freedom lost their heads on the guillotine, while others joined the rebels at the barricades to bring down the fabric of their own power in the name of liberty, equality and fraternity.

Rousseau detonated the first of his explosive arguments in the *First Discourse* of 1750, which upended conventional presumptions by arguing that civilisation and culture – far from being the lights that liberated humanity from savage stupidity – had become a ball and chain that fettered human nature. Following his initial success (the essay won the prize at the Academy of Dijon), Rousseau spent the rest of his life trying to goad society down a path that would reunite people with their inner humanity. Essential to his case was his insistence that man was naturally benevolent and that vice was an artificial, avoidable corruption of society. The noble savage, living solitarily in a pre-social state of nature, Rousseau contended, had the instinctive capacity for benevolence built into his very anatomy. Rousseau's arguments altered the course of European history, inspired some of the greatest thinkers of the nineteenth and twentieth centuries, and are still being grappled with by modern social thinkers. What few people know – though everyone saw it at the time – is that Rousseau's social philosophy had a fundamental grounding in the vegetarian debate. In his second catatonic essay, the *Discourse on Inequality* (1755), man's herbivorous origin underpinned his main argument.

In the very first paragraph of the *Discourse on Inequality* Rousseau acknowledged, like Edward Tyson, that comparative anatomy had yet to determine conclusively man's original nature, and announced ironically that he would forgo 'the supernatural knowledge we have on this point' (i.e. he would not rely on spurious documents like Genesis for his evidence). In their current state, Rousseau acknowledged, humans were uniquely free from any binding natural instinct and had adapted to become omnivorous: 'Each species has but its own instinct,' he wrote, 'while man perhaps having none that belongs to him, appropriates them all, feeds equally [*également*] on most of the various foods which the other animals divide among themselves.'[3]

But in his extraordinary footnotes to the discourse, Rousseau dug deeper into human pre-history and gave full rein to his suspicion that the human animal, 'in the first Embryo of his species', had been herbivorous – and this became a building block for his central contention about humanity. Rousseau set out the full scientific case for primitive vegetarianism, from the fleshless diet of orang-utans to the ancient testimony of the Golden Age. But most prominently of all, he introduced new sensational evidence to the old anatomical debate about teeth and guts, which reflected his own, and his era's, fascination with breasts.[4]

Rousseau had long been obsessed by the female bosom, perhaps partly because of the death of his mother in the act of giving birth to him. After running away from his home in Geneva at the age of fifteen, he fell into the maternal bosom of the Baronne de Warens who educated him, eventually became his lover and nurtured him in ill health on a diet of milk; he spoke rapturously in his *Confessions* of his passion for girls' bosoms. Now, in the *Discourse on Inequality*, he announced that mammaries constituted a 'general System of Nature . . . which provides a new reason for removing man from the Class of carnivorous animals and placing him among the frugivorous species.'[5]

Rousseau had studied anatomy at Montpellier until he quit because he found it too appalling to dissect animals and 'delve into their palpitating entrails'.[6] But he read the vegetarian anatomy arguments in Plutarch, the Italian physician Antonio Cocchi, and possibly also in Gassendi, Hecquet, Pufendorf and the Tyson–Wallis debate. He was also no doubt influenced by Linnaeus who – as the feminist historian Londa Schiebinger pointed out – used the number of teats as a way of classifying different species, and in 1758 glorified the breast by naming the entire class *mammalia* (mammals) after the female organ *'mammae'* – a word derived from noises made by infants suckling at the breast, and in some cultures developed into the name for the mother.[7]

With bosom-toting enthusiasm, Rousseau observed that carnivores (such as cats and dogs) have numerous nipples and large litters for which they could easily provide enough food because it only took them an instant to catch their prey. By contrast, herbivores (such as goats, horses and sheep) have only one pair of teats and a maximum of two offspring, he claimed, because they had to graze all day long to produce enough milk for their young. Therefore, said Rousseau, 'a woman's having only two teats and rarely giving birth to more than one child at a time is one more strong reason for doubting that the human species is naturally Carnivorous'. Even though Rousseau claimed that he was forgoing the case for human herbivorous origins, he nevertheless claimed that the single pair of human bosoms was a primary piece of anatomical evidence in his favour. Breasts were not just symbols of gentle nourishment and innocence, they bore scientific testimony to humanity's original herbivorous nature.

The significance of this lay in the fact that carnivores fight over their prey, whereas 'Frugivores live in constant peace with one another.' If humans were naturally herbivores, then logically they should be innately peaceful and benevolent. This was Rousseau's fundamental contention about humanity and the guiding principle of his moral crusade. Women's breasts – testimony of our herbivorous past – were anatomical evidence in favour of Rousseau's belief that mankind was naturally good.[8]

No wonder Rousseau encouraged women to bare their breasts with pride, and spoke of the euphemistic 'breast' (*sein*) as the source of human emotion. The front page of the *Discourse on Inequality* – as if symbolising his manifesto – depicted a woman, broken free from her chains, with one breast fully exposed.[9] This enthusiasm caught on. By 1783 the first portrait of a woman breast-feeding was displayed in public; in 1794 Prussia legally required every fit woman to breast-feed her baby; and the bared breast of Liberty – symbol of egalitarian sympathy freed from its misguided social fetters – became the mascot of the French revolutionary republic.[10]

In making the argument that man was born good and virtuous, Rousseau was pitting himself against Thomas Hobbes who had argued, a century before, that man's basic instinct was selfish and the original state of nature was a perpetual war ('nasty, brutish and short') in which every creature had a natural right to use its power for its own preservation. In a civilised state, humans divested themselves of their natural rights and obeyed the natural law to do unto others as they would be done by. Animals, however, being irrational, were unable to agree to divest themselves of their natural right and thus could not be protected by mutual covenants of forbearance. Rousseau was appalled by Hobbes' violent pessimism and insisted (like Shaftesbury and the moral-sense philosophers) that in addition to the instinct of self-preservation, man also had a natural impulse of sympathy: 'an innate repugnance at seeing a fellow-creature suffer'. This 'pure emotion of nature' was, according to Rousseau, 'the force of natural compassion, which the greatest depravity of morals has as yet hardly been able to destroy!' Before cultivated civility or social contracts governed mankind, it was raw sympathy that moderated people's self-interest: 'from this single attribute flow all those social virtues . . . generosity, Clemency, Humanity . . . Benevolence and friendship'.[11]

Absorbing and revising Bernard Mandeville and David Hume's observations, Rousseau pointed out that animals had the same neural mechanism for sympathy as humans.[12] Sometimes the human instinct of self-preservation (*amour de soi-même*) would drive humans to kill animals (or humans). But if you adhered to nature, Rousseau insisted, the instinctive power of sympathy would normally restrain you from destroying another sentient creature. This fact of human and animal nature in itself constituted a natural *right*. By basing animal rights simply on the sentience they shared with humans, Rousseau swept aside the millennia-old assumption, which Hobbes had cleverly adjusted and which Hugo Grotius had expressed in his *Rights of War and Peace* (1625), that 'no beings, except those that can form general maxims [i.e. that can "reason"], are capable of possessing a right.'[13] Rousseau's account of how human and animal *feelings* were a basis for animal rights was the most significant renegotiation of man's relationship with animals in the period:

> so long as [a man] does not resist the internal impulse of compassion, he will never hurt another man, nor even any sentient being, except on those legitimate occasions on which his own preservation [*conservation*] is concerned and he is obliged to give himself the preference. By this means also we put an end to the time-honoured disputes concerning the participation of animals in natural law: for it is clear that, being destitute of intelligence and liberty, they cannot recognise that law; but since they in some measure partake in our nature through the sentience with which they are endowed, they must partake of natural right; so that mankind is subjected to a kind of obligation even toward the brutes. It appears, in fact, that if I am bound to do no injury to my fellow-creatures, this is less because they are rational than because they are sentient beings: and this quality, being common both to men and beasts, must at least give the beast the right not to be needlessly [*inutilement*] maltreated by man.[14]

Unlike Hobbes, who rigorously defined his terms, Rousseau referred only vaguely to conditions in which it was permissible for a human to kill animals: 'those legitimate occasions on which his own preservation is concerned'. Rousseau may have had in mind the ancient allowance – widely accepted by vegetarians – that humans were entitled to kill animals such as wolves which endangered human life, a view expressed in Ovid's Pythagorean speech: 'To kill Man-killers,/ Man has lawful Pow'r,/ But not th' extended Licence, to devour.'[15] But Rousseau's '*conservation*' which answers Hobbes' 'preservation' (Latin, *conservatio*) could also allow for meat-eating on the grounds that one ate animals to preserve oneself.[16] However, Rousseau elsewhere stressed that eating meat was unnecessary for self-preservation because nature provided enough vegetable food for human nourishment.[17] Furthermore, his point that 'needless' ill-treatment was the *least* that animals were exempted from implies that he considered it possible that even *useful* ill-treatment (such as meat-eating) might be unlawful (especially if one thought that meat-eating was a useless superfluity in

Joseph Highmore, *The Harlowe Family* from the illustrations of Samuel Richardson's *Clarissa*, 1747-8. Clarissa's oppressive father, Mr Harlowe, is reclining with his foot raised on a foot stool to alleviate the symptoms of gout, the classic ailment of cholic and intemperance.

LEFT Jean-Baptiste Greuze, *Girl Weeping over her Dead Canary*, c.1765.

Elisabeth Vigée le Brun, autograph copy of *Self Portrait (with a straw hat)*, 1782. Representative of the 'rustic chic' fashionable in 1780s Paris, as encouraged by Jean-Jacques Rousseau's classic novel *Julie*.

BELOW Jean-Baptiste Greuze, *The Milkmaid*, before 1784.

DISCOURS

SUR L'ORIGINE ET LES FONDEMENS DE L'INEGALITÉ PARMI LES HOMMES.

Par JEAN JAQUES ROUSSEAU

CITOYEN DE GENÈVE.

Non in depravatis, fed in his quæ bene fecundum naturam fe habent, confiderandum eft quid fit naturale. ARISTOT. Politic. L. 2.

A AMSTERDAM,

Chez MARC MICHEL REY.

M D C C L V.

The frontispiece of Jean-Jacques Rousseau's *Discours sur l'Inégalité*, 1755. The exposed breast, which became a symbol of natural simplicity as well as revolutionary fervour, was, according to Rousseau, also anatomical evidence of humanity's herbivorous origins; for like goats and sheep (and unlike cats and dogs), women had only one pair of teats.

ABOVE Jean-Baptiste
Greuze, *The White Hat*,
c.1780.

RIGHT Attributed to
Marie Victoire Lemoine
(earlier attributed to
Elisabeth Vigée le Brun),
Young Woman with a Dog,
c.1796.

LEFT Jean Laurent Mosnier, *The Young Mother*, c.1770-80. Following a campaign by Rousseau and others against the use of wet-nurses, it became fashionable for high- and middle-class women to breast-feed their own babies .

BELOW Eugène Delacroix, *Liberty Leading the People, 28 July 1830*.

SINGULAR EFFECTS OF THE UNIVERSAL <u>VEGETABLE</u> PILLS ON A GREEN GROCER! *A FACT!*

Who <u>Green'un</u> like was order'd to live for the space of one Month upon <u>Vegetable</u> Diet & to Take during that time 132 Boxes of <u>Vegetable</u> Pills for the Cure of a Gan<u>green</u>, & being caught in a Shower of Rain in the Green Fields in the evening of the 1st of April last, was put to Bed 'midst <u>Shooting</u> pains, & in the Morning presented the above Phenomenon of a Moving Kitchen Garden !!!

Query ___ Is he not one of the Productive Classes

C.J. Grant, *The Singular Effects of the Universal Vegetable Pills on a Green Grocer!*, 1841.

LEFT 'The Mansion of Bliss: A New Game for the Amusement of Youth', from 1822, was designed 'to promote the progressive improvement of the juvenile mind' including the prevention of vices such as 'Cruelty to Animals'.

BELOW Thomas Daniell, The Old Fort, Playhouse and Holwell's Monument in Calcutta, 1786.

RIGHT Attributed to Johann Zoffany, *Portrait of John Zephaniah Holwell*, c.1765.

BELOW Marquis de Valady (1766-1793) and his wife, daughter of the Comte de Vaudreuil.

any case). Rousseau was not vegetarian and he never stuck his neck out as far as to argue explicitly that meat-eating was a violation of animal rights. Indeed, it is difficult to see – in his 'mitigated Hobbesian' allowance that self-preservation could still be a basis for killing animals – where exactly Rousseau thought people's compassion ought to outweigh their self-interest. But Rousseau had provided a foundation for others to argue that his idea of being obliged 'to do no injury to my fellow-creatures' was a rights-based defence of vegetarianism.

Despite Rousseau's caveats and discreet relegation of the argument about bosoms to his footnotes, its centrality to his argument is demonstrated by the fact that much of the backlash against the *Discourse on Inequality* was directed at his ideas about the herbivorous anatomy of man, especially its mammary manifestations. Not the least of these counter-attacks came from Georges-Louis Leclerc, Comte de Buffon (1707–88), the greatest naturalist in eighteenth-century France. When Rousseau's *Discourse on Inequality* came out, Buffon was mid-flow in his mind-bogglingly massive *Histoire Naturelle*, the definitive study of natural history which he pursued for twelve hours each day over a period of fifty years. With such a broad topic, Buffon necessarily barged into everyone's intellectual territory. Friends with the clandestine encyclopaedists Diderot and d'Alembert, Buffon enjoyed irritating theologians with his geological theories, but there was no one whose toes he liked treading on more than Rousseau's – and it was a double-whammy if he could simultaneously repudiate the nipple-centric classification system of his major rival in natural history, the pro-vegetarian Carl Linnaeus. (Buffon thought it was stupid to name mammals after an organ that some members of the group – stallions, for example – did not possess, and he strongly objected to Linnaeus' blasphemous taxonomical decision to herd humans into the same zoo as sloths.)[18]

In 1753, just before the *Discourse on Inequality*, Buffon had published his fourth volume in which he argued that by bringing domestic animals into existence man 'seems to have acquired a right to sacrifice them'.[19] But Buffon felt that people overreached their right to kill animals by hunting wild animals and by eating unsustainable quantities of meat: 'Man alone consumes and engulfs more flesh than all other animals put together,' exclaimed Buffon. 'He is, then, the greatest destroyer, and he is so more by abuse than by necessity.' Abusing this right was even more appalling, he said, because people could survive on vegetables alone – as proved by the vegetarian Hindus. However,

Buffon insisted that this did not mean that humans were *naturally* herbivorous: with their comparatively small stomachs, people were best designed to eat the concentrated nourishment found only in meat and suffered malnourishment when confined to peasant foods. The Pythagoreans and vegetarian doctors, he concluded, were totally incorrect to claim that giving up flesh was beneficial.[20]

Buffon was riled by Rousseau's idealism, his biased presentation of the anatomical facts, and his cheeky ignoring of the *Histoire Naturelle*'s authoritative conclusions. He began his counter-attack by apparently contributing to the refutation posted to Rousseau by Charles-Georges Le Roy (1723–89), Master of the King's Hunt, which argued that Rousseau had based his arguments on a false generalisation about female breasts. Contrary to Rousseau's claims, it was in fact the case that many herbivores, like rabbits, had several nipples and large litters; and some carnivores had few, like weasels. It was equally fallacious, they said, to claim that herbivores took longer to gather food, since carnivores often spent the whole night without catching anything. In any case, humans could never have survived on vegetables alone because they would have starved during winter.

Rousseau's scientific opponents thought that he sustained his idea about harmonious laws in nature only by ignoring the facts. But in his response to the letter – which survives in manuscript form – Rousseau stuck to his vegetarian arguments, countering that carnivores only had difficulty finding their prey because man had destroyed their hunting grounds, and that the point about harsh winters only applied to a few corners of the earth like Paris and London, which were irrelevant to the origins of humanity.[21]

In another footnote to the *Discourse on Inequality*, Rousseau had used female breasts to explicate the non-committal sexual relations in the state of nature. John Locke had claimed that human males, like carnivores, remain in conjugal union with their mates to help raise the offspring, whereas among herbivores 'the Conjunction between Male and Female lasts no longer than the very Act of Copulation; because the Teat of the Dam [is] sufficient to nourish the Young.' Rousseau retorted that Locke had got his facts mixed up and that the opposite was more like the case: in the state of nature humans copulate and then return to their natural solitary existence. This provides an interesting perspective to Rousseau's notoriety for polygamous affairs and abandoning his five illegitimate children to orphanages, and it opened him up to Le Roy and Buffon's lacerating parodic quip that the only true correlation between humans and herbivores was that deer, like humans, 'are the biggest whores on earth, which might lead one to believe that we indeed are frugivorous'.[22]

At the next opportunity – the seventh volume of his *Histoire Naturelle* (1758) – Buffon launched his campaign against Rousseau into print and turned against vegetarianism with greater vehemence than before. In his article on 'Carnivorous Animals', Buffon declared 'that man, in the state of nature, was never destined to live upon herbs, grain, or fruits'. 'Certain austere and savage philosophers,' said Buffon, alluding to Rousseau and the vegetarians, had invented the idea of vegetarian harmony as an attack on human civilisation solely for 'the humiliation of the whole species'.

Buffon acknowledged that 'the motives which have raised doubts concerning this matter [of killing animals], do honour to humanity . . . To sacrifice unnecessarily those animals . . . who, like man, exhibit symptoms of pain when injured, indicates a cruel insensibility'. But it was precisely by conceding that 'the sentiment of pity belongs more to the body than to the mind' that Buffon turned the point against Rousseau. By defining sympathy as a corporal phenomenon, shared even by the animals, Buffon implied (as had Malebranche the Cartesian) that succumbing to it was a sub-human subjugation of reason to animal instincts. Contrary to the vegetarians' usual claim, it was sentimentality that was bestial, not meat-eating.

Reason indicated that killing animals was only superficially destructive; in fact, explained Buffon, life was renewed as fast as it could be destroyed, permitting both carnivorous and lower species to exist, thus producing the greatest number and the greatest variety of life possible. 'Hence the killing of animals is both a lawful and an innocent practice,' Buffon concluded, 'because it is founded in nature, and they hold their existence under that seemingly hard condition.'[23] Eating meat fulfilled the human niche in the ecological system, whereas vegetarianism was anti-ecological in its attempt to set humans apart by making them forgo their natural power over the animals.

Buffon knew perfectly well that he was kicking out a keystone of Rousseau's anatomisation of the noble savage. The battle lines were drawn between the Rousseauists who believed humans were fundamentally gentle, and the anti-Rousseauists who believed they were born aggressive hunters.

Le Roy's childhood friend and fellow *philosophe* Claude-Adrien Helvétius (1715–71) joined the attack against Rousseau by arguing that humans had teeth designed for cutting meat and were clearly supposed to be omnivorous. He thought that although Bernard Mandeville was right that people unused to killing felt pity, their ability to overcome pity through habit was just as natural as pity itself. Delisle de Sales backed Rousseau against Helvétius by repeating that human teeth were herbivorous and that Asian vegetarians proved the healthiness of the vegetarian diet.[24] Linnaeus' disciple, the traveller Sparrman, likewise joined the vegetarians by insisting that Buffon's men had totally misunderstood human anatomy.[25] The ancient question of man's nature came to be predicated on the equally ancient question of man's natural food. In an attempt to find an explanation for human behaviour, eighteenth-century philosophers looked to human origins, much as we in the twenty-first century still search for evolutionary traits that make us behave the way we do. These strong echoes of the prelapsarian myth and the scriptural mandate for human dominion illustrate the inescapable continuities in the West's cultural heritage.

Such arguments dominated the intellectual scene, but Rousseau knew that they would only ever affect a tiny proportion of society. In order to engineer a widespread cultural movement he had to appeal to people's sentiment as much as to their reason. Turning his back on Parisian society, Rousseau went back to nature and took up residence in a solitary cottage close to the country estate of his friend Madame d'Épinay near Montmorency. There he produced his works of sentimental fiction, the epistolary novel *Julie, ou La Nouvelle Héloïse* (1761), and the educational treatise *Émile, ou de l'Éducation* (1762) – and it was these as much as his philosophical treatises that shaped the course of European history in the ensuing tumultuous decades. The radically unorthodox religious agenda of *Émile* ensured that Catholics in Paris called for the incineration of the book and the incarceration of the author; *Julie* guaranteed that Rousseau attained celebrity status, especially among the women of the reading classes whom he personally idolised in his passionate admiration for the noblewoman Sophie d'Houdetot. Thanks to his sympathetic connections, Rousseau was provided with a carriage and, immediately after the publication of *Émile* escaped from France to remain forever a fugitive *cause célèbre*, dodging his way through Switzerland before eventually landing in the lap of the Scottish philosopher David Hume.

Rousseau had read Richardson's *Pamela* and *Clarissa*, vastly popular in France, and felt that their championing of emotion in intimate personal letters provided the perfect literary form for inspiring European society *en masse* with a new zeal for the pure principles of nature. Rousseau's heroine Julie's passionate love affair with her tutor, Saint-Preux, and her eventual death at the mercy of her own acute sensibility pushed Richardson's principles of sensibility to a Romantic extreme.[26] Rousseau also admired Richardson's dietary didacticism; he made Julie a model of abstinent virtue; and in a deliberate allusion to *Clarissa*, Julie refuses a chicken breast offered to her by a man as she wastes away on her deathbed.[27] But where Richardson merely hinted at Clarissa's abstemiousness, Rousseau radicalised the topos by turning his own heroine into a (piscatarian) vegetarian:

> she likes neither meat, nor stews, nor salt, and has never tasted wine straight. Excellent vegetables, eggs, cream, fruit; those are her daily fare, and were it not for fish of which she also is very fond, she would be a true Pythagorean.[28]

The profusion of milk-based sweets that Julie concocts bears testimony to the bounty of her maternal benevolence, becoming in turn a symbol of 'egalitarian hierarchy' as she shares them equally with the peasants on her estate. It is a theme that draws on the milky innocence in Richardson's *Pamela* where Mr B.'s illegitimate daughter is treated with cream and butter on visits to a dairy. In *Émile*, Rousseau's heroine, Sophie, conforms to the same feminine model: 'She loves dairy products and sugared things. She loves pastry and sweets but has very little taste for meat. She has never tasted either wine or hard liquor.'[29] These symbolic connections between milk-food, breasts and the natural impulses of vegetarianism are the narrative equivalents of Rousseau's footnotes to the *Origins of Inequality*. Where in his academic work Rousseau had to couch his principles in sceptical empiricism, in his novels his characters imbibe the principles of innocent morality at the provident bosom of nature.

Julie's lover, Saint-Preux, explains that 'Milk products and sugar are one of the sex's natural tastes and as it were the symbol of innocence and sweetness that constitute its most endearing ornament.' Saint-Preux's attempt to confine these impulses to femininity conforms to the traditional association of meat with masculinity – a mould that Cheyne and others tried to break but which was widely endorsed by the likes of Philippe Hecquet, who thought that women 'prefer to eat patisseries, milk-foods, fruits and similar meagre foods rather than meat'.[30] But Saint-Preux learns that there is more to Julie's diet than feminine sweetness: it is a product of her radical adherence to sympathy.

Rousseau recognised that the power of sympathy relied on the proximity of the sympathiser and the sympathised. Creating a distance between these two agents – a distance that had been introduced into human society by the invention and division of labour and other innovations of 'cultivation' – was the origin of inequality. It was the chasm that disconnected man from his own nature, the Fall that tumbled him into modern depravity. To a more extreme degree than Richardson or Cheyne, it was Rousseau's mission to close up this gap.

Nearly everything Julie eats is home-grown on her Alpine estate, keeping her in direct contact with all the people and processes involved in their production. Even the meat that comes to table for the household's male carnivores is locally hunted game (which, in contrast to Buffon, Rousseau considered a more natural source of food than agriculture).[31]

In the philosophical mode of the *Discourse on Inequality*, Rousseau did not state where compassion for animals should outweigh the self-interested desire to kill them; but in his literary works it seems that in the ideal woman, at least, the balance fell towards vegetarianism. In the letter that immediately follows the description of Julie's diet, Saint-Preux reveals the radical extent of her attribution of rights to nature. Whereas Richardson's Clarissa kept captive birds in her aviary and chicken house, Julie and her husband, M. Wolmar, maintain a sanctuary for wild birds and animals which have become so trusting of humans that they gather to eat scattered corn 'like hens'. When Saint-Preux remarks with admiration that Julie keeps her birds as 'guests' rather than 'prisoners', Julie is quick to point out that he has not understood the extent of her restitution of natural order: '"Who are you calling guests . . .?" answered Julie. "It is we who are theirs. They are the masters here, and we pay them tribute so they will put up with us occasionally."'[32]

By giving priority to animals, Julie's sanctuary went beyond the stock notion of prelapsarian harmony. Such a reversal of man's dominion was as radical as Thomas Tryon's 'Complaint of the Birds'; its closest relatives were the idealised sacred groves of ancient Greece and the Indian sanctuaries or animal hospitals, like those described by the *Turkish Spy*.[33] It was a motif that became a staple of the sentimental novel.

Saint-Preux's re-education continues on a fishing trip with Julie: 'I had brought along a rifle to shoot sea-swallows,' writes Saint-Preux, 'but she shamed me for killing birds wantonly and for the sole pleasure of doing harm' (which, as Rousseau had shown in the *Discourse on Inequality*, was an unambiguous infringement of their natural rights). The lesson is not over: 'The fishing was good;' writes Saint-Preux, 'but except for a trout that had been struck by an oar, Julie had them all thrown back into the water. These are, she said, suffering animals, let us set them free; let us enjoy their pleasure at having escaped the danger.' Julie uses the situation – reminiscent of tales about Pythagoras and the Hindus saving doomed animals as well as Pamela's release of the carp – to demonstrate how compassion can outweigh self-interest.[34]

Émile was a fictionalised treatise designed to show how to bring up a child according to the laws of nature, free from the corrupting influences of society. Here Rousseau showed that his vegetarian principles did not apply to females alone, for he guides the male pupil, Émile, down Pierre Gassendi's clearly marked vegetarian path of nature. Once again, Rousseau's inspiration was the maternal breast.

Rousseau knew that the ninety or so per cent of Parisian babies sent off to be wet-nursed in the country stood a much lower chance of survival than those raised on the fresh milk of their own mothers. So instead of abandoning infants to lower-class wet-nurses, Rousseau encouraged middle- and upper-class mothers to nurse their own infants, liberating them from taboos about uncovering bosoms (though shackling them to no less onerous a life centred on child-rearing in the home, and, to the dismay of husbands, ruining the perceived attractiveness of their pert virginal breasts).[35] Rousseau thus redressed the injustice in *Pamela* when Mr B. resorted to his patriarchal prerogative by forbidding Pamela from marring her figure by breast-feeding their baby, despite her conviction that it was an indispensable moral duty. This was key to the regeneration of virtue in society. 'Let mothers deign to nurse their children,' Rousseau pleaded, 'morals will reform themselves, nature's sentiments will be awakened in every heart, the state will be repeopled.'[36]

It was still more important, Rousseau explained, that whoever was nursing the infant preserve the purity of their milky nourishment by keeping meat entirely out of their diet.[37] Having nursed the child on healthy vegetarian milk, mothers were then responsible for ensuring that the child kept to their natural herbivorous impulses for as long as possible.

Rousseau agreed with Gassendi that children's instinctive preference for vegetable foods proved that 'meat is not natural to man',[38] and he warned that 'It is, above all, important not to denature this primitive taste and make children carnivorous.' As well as protecting the child from physical ailments like worms, Rousseau believed that abstaining from flesh preserved the innate principle of sympathy – the essential ingredient to moral virtue. The brutalising effect of meat-eating was all too visible in carnivorous societies like the English, who were 'more cruel and ferocious', whereas vegetarian peoples like the Banians and Zoroastrians were 'the gentlest of men'.[39]

So long as these rules were observed, the child would grow naturally into a benevolent being. 'He will begin to have gut reactions at the sounds of complaints and cries, the sight of blood flowing will make him avert his eyes; the convulsions of a dying animal will cause him an ineffable distress.' From this natural tendency, Rousseau explained, all the human virtues could be cultivated.[40]

Still using Gassendi as a template for his argument, Rousseau paraphrased Plutarch's graphic challenge to anyone who claimed that meat-eating was natural:

> Kill the animals yourself – I mean with your own hands, without iron tools, without knives. Tear them apart with your nails, as do lions and bears. Bite this cow and rip him to pieces; plunge your claws in its skin. Eat this lamb alive; devour its still warm flesh; drink its soul with its blood. You shudder? You do not dare to feel living flesh palpitating in your teeth?[41]

Rousseau went on to list all the five senses, showing how each one was repulsed by killing: what more scientific proof did one need that predation was unnatural? Even when the time came to harden the adolescent pupil against the extremes of sympathy (though Rousseau doubted if this was entirely necessary), it was to be accomplished by sending him hunting where the killer and the killed came into direct contact.[42]

Modern society had bypassed the natural relation between man and his prey by distancing the consumer from the consumed, employing butchers to kill and cooks to disguise the flesh. This spatial distance – as Plutarch, Gassendi, Richardson, Cheyne and Mandeville had pointed out – created a hypocritical moral distance. Rousseau argued – in the economic critique that inspired Marx and Lenin – that the division between the sympathiser and the sympathised facilitated inequality in society. Rousseau had faith that the principles of nature held the solution, if only people would realise the ethical ramifications latent in their consumption.[43]

Rousseau did not try to push the whole of society back into a pre-human state of herbivorousness. In his *Confessions* he unabashedly admitted to eating meat.[44] Looking back to the days of his youth, when, as a runaway watchmaker's son, he was given sanctuary by the buxom Baronne de Warens, he remembered her lessons about natural good-ness and the healthy fleshless meals she provided: 'I did not know and I still do not know of better fare than a rustic meal,' he said. 'With dairy-foods, eggs, herbs, cheese, brown bread and tolerable wine, one is always sure to regale me well.'[45] He recalled the happy day when he enjoyed a polyamorous country adventure with two women and – replaying the foraging instincts of his fruitarian ancestors – he clam-bered up cherry trees collecting the dessert to their frugal meal. Uniting breasts, polygamy and frugivorousness into one unified symbol, he dropped cherries into their bosoms and fantasised, 'Why are not my lips cherries? how gladly would I throw them there likewise!'[46]

Rousseau's principles of pure food became a national craze in France. From the 1760s frugality was fervently embraced by high and middle society and, as the historian Rebecca Spang has shown, the nascent restaurant industry jumped on the bandwagon. Calling them-selves *maisons de santé* and touting their *nouvelle cuisine*, instead of lavish feasts they served light meals which claimed to 'restore' natural balance in the body of the consumer. Tailored to fastidious patrons on delicate regimens, whole menus were carved from the pages of Rousseau's novels: semolina, fresh eggs, seasonal vegetables, fresh butter and cream cheese.[47] The court artist Elisabeth Vigée-Lebrun – who painted stunning images of ladies with the trademark one breast exposed – accompanied her new artistic movement by serving Arcadian suppers of honey cake and raisins.

The implications of Rousseau's herbivorous breast were destined to overspill the nature-adoring enthusiasm of the French court. For by 1789 the populace had become inflamed with desire to try out Rousseau's 'general will', and in place of milk, the bosom-baring French *Liberty* – memorably depicted by Eugène Delacroix – was to shed rivers of blood before the egalitarian principles of sympathy could be restored to ailing mankind.

Revolutionaries later in the century pushed Rousseau's equivocations on sympathy and primitivism to an even further extreme (see Part III). Herbivorousness became a byword in the French republic and *Émile* spawned a generation of Rousseauist children educated in the vegetarian laws of nature.[48] The meat-free education became such a distinctive mark of 'natural' morality that the cynical Marquis de Sade (1740–1814) attacked it in his anti-moralist novel *Eugénie de Franval* where Eugénie's fleshless vegetable regimen is part of the routine her father employs to ensure the success of his incestuous seduction.[49]

This legacy of Rousseauist vegetarianism – which went beyond what Rousseau himself espoused – was very largely thanks to Rousseau's young friend Jacques-Henri Bernardin de Saint-Pierre (1737–1814) who developed his own nature philosophy and carried it over into the era of the French Revolution, this time with an explicit endorsement of vegetarianism. Saint-Pierre was an unrepentant idealist. As a child he ran away from school to live as a hermit with the plants and animals in the woods. After renouncing an official job in France and going to work for the beautiful Tsarina Catherine II, he set his heart on establishing a Rousseauist-cum-Platonic community on the banks of the Caspian Sea. Later he imagined that the island of Madagascar would be more appropriate and took a job on Mauritius, the French island in the Indian Ocean, where he formulated his theories about the tropics which became a central part of his thinking. Eventually he gained enough expertise to succeed Buffon, on the eve of the overthrow of King Louis XVI, to the prestigious post of *Intendant* of the Cabinet of Natural History and the Jardin des Plantes (where he oversaw the creation of an animal menagerie).[50]

On his initial return to France in 1771, Saint-Pierre made friends with Rousseau and followed his technique of using both popular fiction and learned philosophy to propagate his ideas. Saint-Pierre's novel *Paul et Virginie* (1788) was met with unprecedented rapture throughout

Egalité, engraved by L. Gautier, c.1793–94
after Antoine Boizot (c.1702–82)

Europe and became one of the most frequently reprinted and imitated works ever. By the end of the nineteenth century this quintessence of the sentimental genre had become known as the archetype of slush, and Gustave Flaubert affectionately debunked it in his tale 'Novembre' by putting it in the hands of the prostitute Marie who read it a hundred times; and in *Un Cœur Simple* by giving Madame Aubin's children the names Paul and Virginie. But in the Romantic period the eponymous hero and heroine were idolised as true representations of pure benevolent humanity.

Growing up in an isolated community on Mauritius, the pair live in harmony with nature. Virginie has a special grove in the woods where she feeds birds that have become so tame that (just as in Julie's grove) they come 'up to her feet like domestic hens'. 'Paul and she delighted themselves with their transports of joy, with their eager appetites, and with their loves.' 'Never has the murderous gun terrified these peaceful children of nature. Sounds of joy alone are heard,' enthused Saint-Pierre of his island Paradise.[51] Into these sentimental themes, Saint-Pierre infused the ethics of Hinduism: after Virginie dies in a shipwreck Hindu girls 'brought cages full of small birds, to whom they gave freedom over her coffin'. The novel celebrates Paul and Virginie's 'Indian repasts', 'those delicate rural repasts, which cost no animal its life! Gourds filled with milk, new-laid eggs, cakes of rice served up on banana leaves, baskets filled with potatoes, mangoes, oranges, pomegranates, bananas, dates, and pineapples; affording at once, nutriment the most salutary, colours of the most delightful hues, and juices the most delicious.'[52]

In his next novel, *La Chaumière Indienne* (*The Indian Cottage*) (1790), Saint-Pierre depicted a Western scientist's search for wisdom in the East. (Saint-Pierre had read the works of Linschoten, Roe, Kircher, Tavernier, Bernier and the more recent Orientalism of Sir William Jones.) The scientist realises that the Brahmins take their vegetarian taboos to excessively superstitious extremes, but he eventually finds wisdom in the poor cottage of an Indian pariah who lives happily on the original diet of nature. The pariah entertains his European guest with a meal of 'mangoes, custard apples, yams, potatoes roasted under the embers, grilled bananas, and a pot of rice dressed with sugar and coconut milk'; his wife, as she was represented in all the contemporary illustrations, bared her maternal breasts, and in the hearth of the cottage a cat and a dog lie down together in symbolic realisation of the Golden Age.[53]

Saint-Pierre revealed the significance of these meals of tropical fruit in his monumental works *Études de la Nature* (1784) and *Harmonies de la Nature* (1815). He explained that the tropics must have been the birthplace of mankind because only there did nature supply all human needs without requiring labour or technology: 'the banana tree could have sufficed alone for all the needs of the first man. It produces the most healthy foods in its farinaceous, succulent, sweet, unctuous and aromatic fruits . . . under its delicious shade, and amidst its fruits . . . the bramine prolongs often over a century the course of a life without inquietude.' Saint-Pierre translated the Judaeo-Christian Garden of Eden into a deistic-Rousseauist notion of the origins of mankind. This was a stepping stone between biblical and modern evolutionary history.[54] His Orientalist notion of man's union with nature became a vital stimulus to Romanticism and informed the early philosophies of environmentalism. As far as he was concerned, the tropical civilisations still provided a model for environmental harmony which the whole world should pursue:[55]

A. Colin, *The Interior of a Native Hut*, 1832

It is from [India] also that our arts, sciences, laws, games and religions originated. It is there that Pythagoras, the father of philosophy, went to search among the wise brachmanes the elements of physics and morality. It is from there that he brought back to Europe the vegetable regimen [*le régime végétal*] which carries his name, and which causes health, beauty and life to flourish, and, in calming the passions, increases wisdom and intelligence. Some enemies of the human race have claimed that this diet enfeebles courage and the vigour of the body . . . But is it necessary to be a carnivore or murderer to brave dangers and death?

Having refuted the idea that vegetarianism caused effeminacy, Saint-Pierre explained the main advantage of the vegetable diet. In the wake of grain shortages and ecological degradation, the French physiocrats were searching for the most efficient methods of food production. Saint-Pierre suggested turning to the chestnut tree, for it provided 'a great deal more substantial fruit than a field of corn' and supplied a bonus crop of useful timber. This, Rousseau had argued, was the only way of reversing the transformation of the earth into desert under the pressure from the increasing consumption habits of urban populations. Buffon had noticed that plants put more back into the soil than they take out of it, whereas animals – including humans – did the opposite. Fruit trees, Rousseau proved in a practical land-use experiment, produced enough to feed animals while still returning enough nutrients to the soil.

Alongside the Indians with their banana tree, the Japanese delectation of seaweed provided another solution. Locked away on their isolated rocky island, the 'Pythagorean' Japanese had solved most of the problems associated with limited resources. Not only were they a flesh-abstaining martial nation – disproving the idea that vegetarianism effeminates – they had also discovered the use of seaweeds, an abundant food source edible without complex preparation, which, Saint-Pierre lamented, 'we neglect because most of them are unknown to us, even to our botanists'. (The shellfish consumed by the Japanese alongside their seaweed was another ecologically efficient resource, which may explain why they were the only animals Saint-Pierre allowed Paul and Virginie to eat.) Saint-Pierre wished that Europeans would learn a lesson from these enlightened Eastern nations, but even without resorting to seaweed, he insisted, it was perfectly possible 'right now, to lead a very agreeable pythagorean life'.[56]

In *Études de la Nature*, Saint-Pierre developed Rousseau's maxim that children should be brought up on the vegetable diet: 'Inasmuch as the non-flesh diet introduces many virtues and excludes none, it will be well to bring up the young upon it, since it has so happy an influence upon the beauty of the body and upon the tranquillity of the mind.' 'The peoples living upon vegetable foods,' he concluded, 'are, of all men, the handsomest, the most vigorous, the least exposed to diseases and to passions, and they whose lives last longest.'[57]

Saint-Pierre was not just a theorist: he practised what he preached. 'Do you use the *régime végétal*?' he wrote to his friend Monsieur Hennin. 'I am persuaded that this diet suffices to cure all illnesses.'[58] Though he did not permanently abjure meat, he brought up his own daughter, whom he called Virginie, on the vegetable regimen. While away from home during the French smallpox outbreaks, he anxiously urged his first wife to 'keep, as far as you are able, our Virginie from all animal food, whose juices augment alkalescency and the putrefaction of the humours'.[59] Saint-Pierre regarded vegetarianism as a solution to moral, physiological and agronomic problems, and he transformed Rousseau's philosophy into a manifesto that French revolutionaries took to the barricades.

In Germany, Romanticism was swiftly germinating from Rousseau's fertile seedbed. The great literary icon Johann Wolfgang von Goethe (1749–1832) elusively referred to a phase in his life during which he and his companions adopted a rigorously simple lifestyle of cold baths, hard beds and 'an unfortunate diet [which] destroyed the powers of my digestion'. That Goethe was pursuing a vegetarian diet under the illusion that this is what Rousseau recommended seems to be supported by his explanation that 'These and other follies, the consequence of some misunderstood suggestion of Rousseau, would, as was promised, lead us nearer to Nature and deliver us from the corruption of morals.'[60] Like Saint-Pierre, his sympathy for animals, his quasi-pantheist idea of the unity of nature, and his belief that all living things experienced 'joy and pain', was inspired by Indian culture which he read about in Rogerius and in Jones' new translations of Sanskrit texts.[61] In his novels *The Sorrows of Young Werther* (1774) and *Wilhelm Meister's Travels* (1821–9), Goethe treated his characters to a dose of Rousseau and Richardson's dietary didacticism. Werther, for example, rejoices in a dinner of home-grown peas and butter, declaring how happy he is 'that my heart is capable of feeling the same simple and innocent pleasure as the peasant whose table is covered with food of his own rearing'.[62]

Goethe's contemporary Jean Paul (Richter), who had nicknamed himself 'Jean' after Rousseau, was echoing *Émile* when he wrote that 'The child learns to regard all animal life as sacred,' and that animals in turn 'impart to him the feeling of a Hindu in place of the heart of a Cartesian philosopher'. Their companion, Johann Gottfried von Herder (1744–1803), enquired about vegetarianism from the Scottish Rousseauist James Burnett, Lord Monboddo, who had suggested that since orang-utans (which he considered to be primitive people) were herbivorous, humans must originally have evolved with a diet based entirely on vegetation.[63] These figures were probably encouraged by another friend, the Weimar court physician Christian Wilhelm Hufeland, whose enthusiasm for the 'natural way of life' echoed that of Goethe. His correlation of human longevity and vegetarianism continued the project of Cheyne and Hecquet and lent scientific force to the more emotional appeals against flesh-eating: 'We frequently find a very advanced old age amongst men who from youth upwards have lived, for the most part, upon the vegetable diet, and perhaps, have never tasted flesh.'[64]

In the wake of Rousseau and Saint-Pierre's vegetarian educational reforms, a generation of children were raised by parents hoping to preserve the innate sympathy that would flourish into natural virtue. The Napoleonic poet Alphonse de Lamartine (1790–1869) was one of them, brought up by his mother according to the philosophy of 'les philosophes du sentiment', Rousseau and Bernardin de Saint-Pierre, and the laws of Pythagoras and Émile:

> My mother was convinced, as I myself am, that killing animals for the sake of nourishment . . . is one of those curses imposed upon man either by his fall, or by the obduracy of his own perversity. She believed, as I do still, that the habit of hardening the heart towards the most gentle animals . . . brutalise[s] and harden[s] the instincts of the heart. She believed, as I do still, that such nourishment, much more succulent and much more energised in appearance, contains in itself irritating and putrid principles which embitter the blood and shorten the days of men. She cited, to support these ideas of abstinence, the numberless gentle, pious populations of India who forbid themselves everything that has had life.

Lamartine said that, despite his convictions, in adulthood he conformed to society by eating meat. But contemporaries recall that later in life Lamartine reconverted to vegetarianism after travelling through India, and lived in Paris like a Hindu vegetarian, giving all the best food to his pets.[65]

Rousseau championed the natural feeling of sympathy, and this provided a serious challenge to the long-held complacency about man's natural right to kill animals. Exactly how many people relinquished flesh or changed their behaviour towards animals can never be known, but if literature and art are anything to go by, Rousseau changed the face of European culture forever.

SIXTEEN

The Counter-Vegetarian Mascot: Pope's Happy Lamb

The poet and wit Alexander Pope (1688–1744) was laughed at by contemporaries for his Horatian frugality. His weak digestive system buckled when exposed to the arduous carnivorous feasts occasionally imposed upon it by social conformity, and as a friend of Cheyne he knew that the remedy was to try to restrict himself to dinners of spinach and eggs.[1] Lines in the poetic *Essay on Man* (1733–4) might lead one to suppose that Pope himself endorsed vegetarianism – and that is certainly how he has been read by later scholars and vegetarians.[2] But Pope, and many other writers like him, was in fact using sympathy for animals as a deliberate subterfuge *against* the moral case for vegetarianism.

The purpose of this chapter is to dispel the claim, pervasive not least among scholars, that 'James Thomson's *The Seasons* argues in favor of vegetarianism and against hunting, as does Cowper's *The Task*', when exactly the opposite is the case.[3] These poems – and innumerable other literary works including Pope's – expressed sympathy for animals and horror at their death, and they gave enormous currency to vegetarian ideas. But they invariably overrode these expressions of sympathy by appealing to man's God-given right to kill animals, or by resorting to notions of the 'painless death' and the 'happy lamb' by which meat could be procured without causing suffering. The mistaken belief that this reactionary literature was *pro*-vegetarian originates with the eighteenth- and nineteenth-century vegetarian anthologists John Oswald, George Nicholson, Joseph Ritson and Howard Williams – all of whom quote sentimental poetry as if it supported their case. They could only do so, however, by selecting the lines that encouraged sympathy for animals, and deliberately excising those that overrode that sympathy in favour of the right to eat meat.

The real aim of this literature was to shore up the right to eat meat against the claims of vegetarianism. Such works drew a distinct line between an acceptable degree of sympathy for animals, and the unacceptable, irrational and blasphemous challenge to man's right to kill them for food. They were designed to navigate readers along the 'true path' of sympathy, avoiding on the one side the Scylla of vegetarianism and on the other the Charybdis of insensibility. The poems of Thomson, Pope and Cowper are, in this sense, not 'vegetarian', but *counter-vegetarian*, and they represent the fiercely fought battle lines entrenched in European culture between dominant norms and marginal fanaticism.

Cheyne (and later Rousseau) were the most obvious enemies, but the counter-vegetarians were also marshalling themselves against the battalions of Hindus whose ethics seemed dangerously allied to the cult of sensibility. Much energy also went into undermining Ovid's 'Pythagorean Philosophy', greatly popularised by John Dryden's 1700 translation, into which he had sneaked an extra argument possibly recruited from the Indian travelogues: 'Take not away the Life you cannot give:/ For all Things have an equal right to live.'[4]

In his epoch-making nature poem, *The Seasons* (1726–30), James Thomson – patriotic author of 'Rule, Britannia' – appears to make the case for vegetarianism. Emulating Ovid, he appeals to the state of innocence when man, 'unfleshed in blood', was 'The Lord, and not the Tyrant of the World'.[5] Carnivorous beasts do not have the capacity for sympathy, he says:

> But *Man*, whom Nature form'd of milder Clay,
> With every kind Emotion in his Heart,
> And taught alone to weep; while from her Lap
> She pours ten thousand Delicacies, Herbs,
> And Fruits as numerous as the Drops of Rain
> Or Beams that give them Birth: shall he, fair Form!
> Who wears sweet Smiles, and looks erect on Heaven,
> E'er stoop to mingle with the prowling Herd,
> And dip his Tongue in Gore? The Beast of Prey,
> Blood-stain'd deserves to bleed: but you, ye Flocks,
> What have ye done; ye peaceful People, What,
> To merit Death? You, who have given us Milk
> In luscious Streams, and lent us your own Coat
> Against the Winter's Cold? And the plain Ox,
> That harmless, honest, guileless Animal,

In What has he offended? He, whose Toil,
Patient and ever-ready clothes the Land
With all the Pomp of Harvest; shall he bleed,
And struggling groan beneath the cruel Hands,
Even of the Clowns he feeds?[6]

Thomson gave Ovid's objections to meat-eating a contemporary resonance by highlighting man's sympathetic anatomy, which could be
taken – as Thomson's friend Cheyne took it – as evidence that eating
meat was unnatural. But Thomson's sentimental verses were a ruse.[7] It
turns out that all these appeals against eating animals are just what a
typical, sentimental 'feeling Heart/ Would tenderly suggest'. This is a
natural and worthy instinct if taken lightly, says Thomson patronis-
ingly, 'but', he emphatically interjects, God has 'fix'd us' in the state
of being carnivorous and thus tacitly 'forbids' such 'presumptuous'
objections: we 'must not' try to subvert the decree of heaven. The
'Perfection' aimed at by the prelapsarian vegetarians, says Thomson, is
blasphemously audacious.[8] Vegetarianism was not an unachievable
ideal: it was an undesirable extreme.

In his later poem *Liberty* (1735–6), Thomson used a similar ploy
by professing admiration for Pythagoras' 'tender System' which valued
'Whatever shares the Brotherhood of Life'. But just as in *The Seasons*,
Thomson subsumes this sentimental egalitarianism into the Christian
hierarchy of the Chain of Being and – apparently alluding to Cheyne's
theory of reincarnation – quips that killing animals might actually
send them to a 'higher Life'.[9]

In one of the first editions of *The Guardian* (1713), Alexander Pope
wrote an essay in imitation of Seneca and Plutarch, which argued that
'Humanity may be extended thro' the whole Order of Creatures, even
to the meanest.'[10] But Pope deliberately diluted the arguments that
Plutarch used against eating flesh *per se* into a mere critique of over-
indulgence and excessively cruel methods of slaughter: '*Lobsters roasted
alive, Pigs whipt to Death, Fowls sowed up,** are Testimonies to our out-
rageous Luxury.' Pope showed that pitying and killing could indeed be
harmonious bed-fellows by adopting Plutarch's fall-back position: 'If
we kill an Animal for our Provision, let us do it with the Meltings of
Compassion, and without tormenting it.'[11] The idea of cruel slaughter
became a straw man which diverted sentimental arguments against

---

* Sewing up their eyes in fattening chambers. Plutarch complains about this.

killing animals: society felt itself acting justly, while doing nothing to curtail its culinary demands.

This means of self-righteously assuaging guilt became standard fare in British periodicals like the *Tatler* and the *Gentleman's Magazine*, those newly fledged mouthpieces of civil society.[12] In 1731 the *Universal Spectator* ran an article just like Pope's, which concluded that although humans were anatomically herbivorous, abstinence from meat was off the cards: 'Let us eat it then;' but just try not to 'imbitter Death itself by the most excruciating Torments'. Meat-eaters were absolved from guilt by transposing the crime of cruelty onto the producers (butchers and farmers) rather than the consumers.[13]

Pope came up with the perfect solution. In *An Essay on Man* he celebrated the Indians' reverence for animals and the vegetarian harmony of the Golden Age when 'Man walk'd with beast, joint tenant of the shade . . . No murder cloath'd him, and no murder fed.'[14] He gave voice to the Cheynian (and Senecan) idea of providential distempers avenging the victims of the dinner plate, and pointed out that by becoming a predator man had made himself a murderer of his own species too:

> But just disease to luxury succeeds,
> And ev'ry death its own avenger breeds;
> The fury-passions from that blood began,
> And turn'd on Man a fiercer savage, Man.[15]

At first one might think that Pope yearned to undo the cycle of violence and return man to the peaceful 'state of nature'. But, like Buffon, he argued that since people bred and fed domestic animals, it was only fair that they should eat them. Challenging meat-eating, he showed, was like trying to stem the flow of nature: 'Say, will the falcon, stooping from above,/ Smit with her varying plumage, spare the dove?'[16]

Humans – as everyone knew – had the sympathetic hearts that falcons lacked; so how did Pope answer that? He did so by masterfully reversing a scene from Ovid into the myth of the Happy Lamb:

> The lamb thy riot dooms to bleed to-day,
> Had he thy reason, would he skip and play?
> Pleased to the last, he crops the flowery food,
> And licks the hand just raised to shed his blood.[17]

It is easy to construe this passage as an indictment of the treachery of killing domestic animals – and vegetarians have often done so. But

Pope coolly undercut the pathos by arguing that nature had benevolently kept the lamb devoid of foresight and therefore ignorant of its death until the fatal blow is struck. This was the ideal 'painless death'. The lamb is alive one moment and dead the next: the transition from one state to the other occurs without even a twinge of suffering. Since sentimentalists only cared about causing pain, rather than valuing life *per se*, if they could be convinced that animals felt no pain they could eat guilt-free meat. The legacy remains today: 'sympathetic' objections to cruelty are fired against the grotesque practices of the animal industry (battery hens, farrowing crates, stall-reared veal), and people sit down to a Sunday lunch of 'happy' chickens/pigs/bullocks *et cetera*.

The counter-vegetarian role of Pope's lamb was illustrated explicitly by Richard Graves (1715–1804) in his sentimental novel *The Spiritual Quixote* (1773). Graves was part of Cheyne's social circle and tried his ascetic diet, but in his later novel satirises soppy sentimentality through the character of Mr Graham, a pseudo-Pythagorean who calls for legislation against cruelty to animals and has Cheyne- and Rousseau-like associates.[18] 'My compassion for dumb animals,' says Graham, 'is so excessive, that it often makes me quite miserable.' Graves' hero, Geoffrey Wildgoose, desperately tries to argue Graham out of his 'strange effeminacy' by quoting Pope's idyllic picture of the unwary lamb. Alluding to Shakespeare's *Measure for Measure*, Wildgoose explains that 'I can easily reconcile myself to their fate: as the pain of death consists, I believe, chiefly in the apprehension':

> 'And when it is instantaneous (as in those cases it is or ought to be) they enjoy themselves, and feel nothing till the stroke arrives; and the moment it does so, the violence of it either deprives them of life, or at least of the sense of pain.'[19]

Without pain, animal slaughter no longer needed to excite compassion. Pope's happy lamb assumed iconic status for the counter-vegetarian tradition. In 1767 John Brückner, one of Buffon's followers, used the ignorance of Pope's lamb as the justification for meat-eating, arguing that sympathy only dictated that we should 'shorten, as much as possible, the pains necessarily inflicted'.[20] Some vegetarians, on the other hand, accurately perceived Pope's insensible lamb as an obstacle to their cause. Both John Wolcot (alias Peter Pindar) and Percy Bysshe Shelley rebuffed Pope's idea of guiltless killing, and when the vegetarian revolutionary John Oswald – who had read *The Spiritual Quixote*

– rewrote Pope's scene in his *Cry of Nature*, he turned from the pathos of the lamb to its mother who suffers agony at its death.[21]

These counter-vegetarian sentimental works were literary renditions of arguments made by theologians who tried to dispel qualms about killing animals. The Newtonian John Clarke had pointed out in his *Enquiry into the Cause and Origin of Evil* (1720) that the principal objections to killing animals were 'the depriving the Creature of Life, and of all that Pleasure it was capable of enjoying in the right Use of its Faculties and Senses; *and also* the putting it to all that Pain and Misery; which a violent and unnatural Death is unavoidably attended with.'[22] Pope's ovine response was a poetic illustration of the arguments that his favourite theodicist, the Archbishop of Dublin William King, had spelled out in order to calm the conscience of troubled souls in 1702. With his authority as an Archbishop, he explained that animals

> ought, if they had Sense enough, to praise their Creator . . . because it is better to enjoy Life and Sense for some Time, than to be always a Lump of Matter, and void of all Perception. Besides, Beasts enjoy present Satisfaction always, without remembering what is past, or disquieting themselves with what is to come; and, after all, they suffer less by being kill'd, than they would if they died of a Disease, or old Age.

Using animals for food did not injure them; it actually made them happier: they were bred in prodigious numbers, looked after by assiduous farmers, and then painlessly despatched shortly before becoming too old to enjoy their life in any case.[23] In other words, the counter-vegetarian argument was based on the recognition of what would now be called the mutualistic symbiosis between humans and domesticated animals.

Philosophers continued to develop these arguments throughout the eighteenth century. It is usual to trace an ameliorative 'progression' of enlightened moral responsibility towards animals in this period. But the authors who made this 'progression' also saw their task as a rearguard action against the vegetarian challenge. They gave ground to the vegetarians, but in many cases their principal concern was fortifying the fundamental bulwark around man's right to eat meat. Between 1742 and his death in 1746, the moral-sense philosopher Francis Hutcheson moved from condemning unnecessary cruelty as 'highly blameable' to actually acknowledging that animals had an absolute 'right' to be exempt from 'useless pain or misery'. But he emphasised – in contrast to Rousseau's *Discourse of Inequality* which was published in the same year as Hutcheson's posthumous papers – that rearing and killing animals for food *was* necessary and, reiterating William King's argument, that it actually increased the greater common happiness of both man and beasts. When Hutcheson made his universally lauded demarcation of animal rights, defending animals from abuse seems to have been a secondary consideration: his primary concern was defending man's right to kill animals against the challenge posed by the 'many great sects and nations, at this day, [who] deny this right of mankind', and simultaneously the 'great names among ourselves' who alleged that meat-eating could not be defended by natural reason so 'that without revelation, or an express grant from God, we would have had no such right.'[24]

Meanwhile, Hutcheson's pupil, David Hume, had acknowledged in 1739 that the mechanical 'springs and principles' of sympathy 'takes place among animals, no less than among men'.[25] Whether rational or not, he said that they should be indulged with 'compassion and kindness'. But in contrast to Rousseau's subsequent arguments and Hutcheson's own conclusion, Hume denied that they could be treated with 'justice'.[26]

The philosopher David Hartley (1705–57) – a friend of Cheyne and tentative believer in animal heaven – took the emerging philosophies a step towards fully-blown Utilitarianism in his seminal *Observations on Man* (1749). He agreed with Bernard Mandeville's *Fable of the Bees* that killing animals 'does great Violence to the Principles of Benevolence and Compassion'. But although he came close, he did not – as has been claimed – provide an intellectual defence of vegetarianism. Hartley observed that no matter what people ate, innumerable microscopic animals would be destroyed, and trying to prevent that would simply mean starving to death. This pragmatism was backed by God's explicit permission to eat flesh and therefore, he concluded, 'Abstinence from Flesh-meats seems left to each Person's Choice, and not necessary, unless in peculiar Circumstances.'[27]

Philip Dormer Stanhope, Earl of Chesterfield (1694–1773), the celebrity of aristocratic literary London life and another of Cheyne's clients, briefly became a vegetarian as an undergraduate after reading Ovid's *Metamorphoses*, but by 1756 he looked back on this as youthful, misguided folly. Nature, he reflected, 'has instituted the universal preying upon the weaker as one of her first principles' and thus we are only 'under indelible obligations to prevent their suffering any degree of pain more than is absolutely unavoidable'. In a flourish of aristocratic arrogance (and emulating the periodicals), he cynically concluded that since only the educated felt pity and only the lower classes worked as butchers, no animal would benefit from sympathetic morals.[28] The theological essayist Soame Jenyns (1704–87), meanwhile, defended middle-class meat-eaters by offloading the guilt of animal cruelty onto the upper-class grouse-hunter and the plebeian butcher who 'knocks down the stately ox with no more compassion than the black-smith hammers a horse-shoe'. Thus he defended the tastes and sensibilities of the metropolitan bourgeoisie which comprised his readership by dissociating their consumption from the cruelty involved in supplying them with food.[29]

Even the poet William Cowper (1731–1800), adored by Romantic nature-lovers and called vegetarian by modern scholars,[30] really belongs with the counter-vegetarians. His lengthy masterpiece, *The Task* (1785), which became one of the most popular poems in England, is replete with imprecations against cruelty, empathy for wild animals, and appeals to the primeval law of 'universal love'. With typical sentimentality, Cowper wrote:

> I would not enter on my list of friends
> (Though grac'd with polish'd manners and fine sense
> Yet wanting sensibility) the man
> Who needlessly sets foot upon a worm.[31]

His private letters, meanwhile, testify to the intensity of his sympathy for animals. When Cowper's mental health declined into total breakdown, it was to his pet birds, hares, cats and dogs that he turned in his convalescence.[32] He idealised the frugal meals of the peasantry, occasionally dieted on milk to combat his illness,[33] and translated John Milton's Latin *Ode to Christ's Nativity*, which recommended that divine poets should live on a Pythagorean diet.[34] But there is no evidence in his letters that he ever abstained from meat on moral principle, and like the others he directed his protest not against death but on adding 'tenfold bitterness to death by pangs/ Needless':

> On Noah, and in him on all mankind,
> The charter was conferr'd by which we hold
> The flesh of animals in fee, and claim

O'er all we feed on, pow'r of life and death.

  . . .

The sum is this: if man's convenience, health,
Or safety interfere, his rights and claims
Are paramount, and must extinguish theirs.[35]

The anti-slavery poet Samuel Jackson Pratt (1749–1814) has like-wise been hailed as an advocate of vegetarianism. Emulating Cowper, he celebrated the vegetarian benevolence of the great prison-reformer John Howard, and in his poem *Humanity, or the Rights of Nature* (1788) he praised the uncultured Brahmins who 'refuse the worm to kill'. But he emphatically denied that Indian vegetarianism suited Europe's 'cultur'd state', and echoing Cowper and Pope he restricted himself to criticism of the '*ling'ring* death':

Live, tho' thou do'st on blood, ah! still refrain,
To load thy victims with *superfluous* pain;[36]

It has also been claimed that the eighteenth-century women poets – in particular Ann Yearsley 'the Bristol Milkwoman', Anna Seward, Ann Finch and Anna Laetitia Barbauld – teamed up in sympathy for animals against male oppressors in a defiant and exclusively female way. Perhaps the men poets Thomson, Pope and Cowper had these women in mind when they marshalled their sentimental backlash against excessive sympathy for animals – and it is no doubt true that women, who were seen as pertaining more to the body and less to the spirit, were believed to experience the corporal function of sympathy more intensely. But even the women poets avoid the extreme of vege-tarianism or attributing to animals an absolute right to life. Yearsley lamented the wanton murder of a robin, but (entirely in line with male authors) she had nothing to say about the sheep and cows destined for slaughter; Barbauld objected to the unnecessary cruelty wreaked on a mouse, not its execution as such; and Seward's cat dreamed of its own cat heaven – but it was a heaven that explicitly endorsed the killing of weaker animals. The line they drew between legitimate and illegitimate killing seems to be much the same as that of their male contem-poraries.[37]

The sentimental novelists Sarah Scott and Lady Barbara Montagu emulated Rousseau and Richardson in many ways, but subverted Rous-seau's radical stance on animals. The utopian community of women in their co-authored novel *Millenium Hall* (1762) is furnished with an animal sanctuary just like Rousseau's *Julie*, where animals 'live so unmolested, that they seem to have forgot all fear, and rather to welcome than flee from those who come amongst them'. However, the heroine, Mrs Maynard, insists that 'I imagine man has a right to use the animal race for his own preservation, perhaps for his convenience, but certainly not to treat them with wanton cruelty.' Their sanctuary is a purely sentimental evocation of Thomson's Golden Age when man and beast 'walked joint tenant of the shade', for in another part of the estate they have poultry, pigeons, deer, fish, hares and rabbits destined to supply their table with 'as much venison as we can use'. The women tick the box of sensibility towards animals without giving up eating flesh.[38]

A young lady in Mary Deverell's *Miscellanies* (1781) also adopts the moral high ground against luxury when a doctor prescribes her an abstemious vegetable diet; but she denies she has ethical motives, and doubts she will keep up vegetarianism once her health recovers. It is her young male acquaintance who has confined 'himself to a vegetable Diet, on Pythagoric Principles':

> Humanely wise, abhorring bloody feasts,
> Where useful are devoure'd by useless beasts . . .
> Nor shall the sightly view of butter'd veal,
> Make him his abstemious resolution reel;

But the tone is cajoling and even this panegyric literature could undermine the viability of vegetarianism by confining it to Ovidian fantasy rather than practical reality.[39]

It seems that most women, at least, followed the rules laid down by their society. Enforcing this was the purpose of many educational treatises of the period. Erasmus Darwin's *Plan for the Conduct of Female Education* (Derby, 1797), for example, explained that sympathy was the foundation of the law 'to do as you would be done by'. 'This compassion, or sympathy with the pains of others, ought also to extend to the brute creation,' said Darwin. But, he insisted (clearing up any lingering misunderstanding of Rousseau's animal rights theories), it should only be taken 'as far as our necessities will permit; for we cannot exist long without the destruction of other animal or vegetable beings . . . Hence, from the preservation of our existence we may be supposed to have a natural right to kill those brute creatures, which we want to eat'.[40] As he had already warned in *Zoonomia; or, the Laws of Organic Life* (1794–6), 'This sympathy, with all sensitive beings, has been carried so far by some individuals, and even by whole tribes, as the Gentoos, as not only to restrain them from killing animals for their support, but even to induce them to permit insects to prey upon their bodies.' People had to be taught to balance the law of sympathy with the knowledge that 'the first law of nature is, "Eat or be eaten."' [41]

In the sentimental society of the eighteenth century (just like today's) there was nothing unusual about making elaborate displays of sympathy for animals – fawning over rabbits, lambs or pigeons – and in the next moment devouring the same species of animal at table. As the Brahmin-loving Chinese character Lien Chi Altangi in Oliver Goldsmith's *Citizen of the World* (1762) exclaims of his European hosts, 'Strange contrariety of conduct! They pity, and they eat the objects of their compassion!' [42]

As pets – from mollycoddled poodles to caged canaries – became part of popular culture in the eighteenth century, so farm animals became industrialised as the demand for them burgeoned with affluence. Cruelty exercised in the production of food continued and even increased. Georgians had their abattoirs in the open air, right at the point of retail. The sight of slaughter, the smell of blood and the shrieking of animals in their dying moments were familiar experiences to city-dwellers. As professions of sympathy for animals escalated, so pressure grew for slaughterhouses to move indoors and out of town. Eventually this is what happened (also thanks to economic industrialisation and urban hygiene initiatives), thus pushing the unpleasant aspect of the meat industry out of sight and mind.

Cheyne had tried and Rousseau was desperately trying to force people to realise that their sentimental feelings were at odds with the processes of production behind the items they consumed. But most of culture's inscribers were quite happy with the consumer's distance from the producer and vehemently protected themselves from inconvenient moral injunctions. Because most consumers were the sort of 'silly soul' whom Mandeville, Richardson and Coleridge reviled, sentimentalism had little beneficial effect for animals. Inflicting pain on animals for the sake of amusement (rather than gastronomic pleasure) was eventually outlawed in 1822, and the working-class blood sports, cock-fighting, dog-fighting, and bear- and badger-baiting, were suppressed (though the upper-class stag- and fox-hunting were to enjoy a reprieve until 2004). [43] But then as now, the anti-cruelty movement was largely a distraction from the fundamental issue of meat consumption. Urban dwellers were vehement critics of cruelty inflicted for the sake of entertainment, but quite happy for animals to suffer for the pleasures of the table. Meat-eaters drew attention away from the moral implications of their consumption by protesting against what they deemed to be 'unnecessary' suffering. The potential challenge to meat-eating posed by sympathy was effectively averted. This situation survives intact today and has its roots in the sentimental culture of the eighteenth century.

SEVENTEEN

Antonio Cocchi and the Cure
for Scurvy

The Florentine physician Antonio Cocchi (1695–1758) was the highest-standing professional advocate of vegetarianism in eighteenth-century Europe, and he avoided censure by grounding his arguments in nutritional evidence. Professor of Medicine at Pisa and of Anatomy at Florence, court antiquarian to Francis I of Tuscany, innovative curator of the Uffizi Gallery, member of both the Florentine College of Physicians and the Royal Society of London, Cocchi was in a prime position to propagate his views.[1] His most famous work, *Del Vitto Pitagorico per uso della Medicina* (Florence, 1743), was reprinted several times in Italy, translated into English as *The Pythagorean Diet, of Vegetables Only* (1745), into French in 1750, and later into German. Jean-Jacques Rousseau considered Cocchi the greatest authority on vegetarianism, and in *Émile* he referred his readers to the *Vitto Pitagorico* and the counter-vegetarian work of Cocchi's opponent, Giovanni Bianchi.[2]

After making friends with the 9th and 10th Earls of Huntingdon in Florence, Cocchi returned with them to England where he remained for three or four years from 1723. Falling in love with the country, in 1727 he wrote to the Marchese Scaramuccia Visconti in the typical vein of European Anglomania, saying that 'A man who has spent some time there is spoilt for ever, unless he settles there.' During his residence in England Cocchi cultivated contacts with the elderly Isaac Newton and with the prominent iatromechanists John Freind and Richard Mead, both of whom knew George Cheyne. Cocchi was corresponding with the Earls of Huntingdon at the same time that Cheyne was treating Selina, the Countess of Huntingdon, and Cheyne's *Essay of Health and Long Life* came out in 1724 while Cocchi was in the country. Cocchi became convinced of the powers of vegetarianism when, in 1727, he cured a gouty patient in London by instructing him to keep the 'indestructible' salts of flesh out of his diet. From that moment on Cocchi became a proselyte of the medical vegetarian movement initiated by Cheyne and Hecquet.[3] In his treatise *Eccessiva Grassezza* (Excessive Fatness) Cocchi championed Cheyne who had, he said, *'una corpulenza che lo rendeva immobile'* (a corpulence that rendered him immobile) until he adopted the diet *'totalmente vegetabile'*.[4]

As a medical mechanist, Cocchi considered himself a follower of Cheyne's tutor, Archibald Pitcairne, and he edited the works of the Italian iatromechanical master, Lorenzo Bellini.[5] Like his forebears in dietary medicine, Cocchi put a new spin on the vegetable diet to legitimise it by the rigorous standards of contemporary science. He wished to dissociate vegetarianism from the shady recesses of eccentricity, radicalism and superstition, and to reconstitute it as an Enlightenment ideal. He therefore completely ignored the biblical basis for vegetarianism and established his arguments on the firmest scientific observations. Despite the anti-vegetarian conclusions of Tyson and Wallis, Cocchi claimed that they had demonstrated that the human gut was herbivorous: 'such Animals as feed on vegetable Diet,' he reiterated, 'are furnish'd with a Gut *Colon*, whereof most of the Carnivorous are destitute.' Drawing on the chemical school of medicine, Cocchi explained that vegetables were rich in 'fixed' acid salts – so called because they did not evaporate when heated; meat, by contrast, was high in 'volatile' alkaline salts which, Cocchi warned, turned into venomous vapour when heated in the body. Acidity made vegetables a great solvent and therefore easy to digest, whereas the oily 'saponaceous' substance in meat could create glutinous blockages and separation in the blood. Taking a cue from Cheyne, Cocchi claimed that vegetables could cure nervous disorders from rheumatism to melancholy as well as being effective against consumption, aneurisms, clogging of the vessels and scurvy.[6]

For someone who was trying to free vegetarianism from the stigma of superstition, *The Pythagorean Diet* may seem like an odd title. But Cocchi's premise was that Pythagoras had never believed any of the 'false' superstitions about reincarnation. On the contrary, Pythagoras' vegetarianism had been motivated by the most enlightened scientific understanding of diet and nutrition: 'His Doctrine of the Transmigration of Souls was only a specious Reason to make his medical Advice go down with the People,' Cocchi declared, citing the ancient testimony of Diogenes Laertius to back up his opinion. Vegetables were easy to grow, suppressed noxious desires when eaten, created tranquillity of mind and harmonised the body's humours: Pythagoras, Cocchi insisted, 'had Health principally in View'.[7]

Vegetarians throughout the world bore testimony to the healthiness of vegetarianism. Countering the assumption that vegetables did not supply enough strength (and ignoring the Indians who had acquired a reputation for feebleness), Cocchi attributed the health of the Tuscan poor to the ready availability of fresh Mediterranean vegetables.[8] The vigorous mountain-dwelling people of Europe, he added, live only on milk and herbs 'and the *Japanese* (who are very resolute in despising Dangers, and even Death itself) abstain from all animal Food'.[9] As the crowning proof of these generalisations, he presented himself, his wife, his daughter and son, Raimondo, who all allegedly lived according to Cocchi's Pythagorean Diet and were perpetually in good health.[10]

Vegetarianism was the result of the most enlightened scientific knowledge. It was also, Cocchi insisted, in line with the most enlightened morality. Pythagoras' protection of animals, he said, was motivated by the innocent curiosity of a 'true Naturalist' and by humane principles 'so contrary to the childish, restless, and destructive Inclination . . . of pulling to Pieces and spoiling, for the most trifling Purposes, the beautiful and useful Productions of Nature'.[11] Cocchi imagined that vegetarianism would physiologically purify the human faculty of sense: 'any one who restrains himself, for a long time from Wine, and season'd Meats, will acquire a most exquisite Delicacy and distinguishing Sense of Tasting.' Echoing Cheyne's idea that vegetarians were part of a sensible elite, Cocchi claimed that they were the most enlightened, educated, 'ingenious' beings at the summit of European society.[12]

In England Cocchi was initiated into the Freemasons, and in 1732 helped to establish the first Masonic Lodge in Florence. Freemasonry was widespread in Enlightenment Europe, and many of the prominent thinkers of the period counted themselves members of this antique society. Priding themselves on modern principles of open-mindedness and liberty, the Freemasons also venerated the ancient learning of Pythagoras and the Egyptians.

Most Masonic history remains shrouded in secrecy, but Cocchi left to posterity a unique manuscript diary called 'Effemeridi', the first document written in defence of Masonry by an Italian. Cocchi traced an inheritance of Pythagorean philosophy from ancient Egypt through to the Pythagorean colony in Italy and ultimately to Galileo's revival of heliocentrism and his own vegetarianism. This line of thinking (shared by his associate Isaac Newton) was typical of the Masonic belief that the ancients held pristine wisdom which it was modern man's duty to rediscover. It seems that vegetarianism, for Cocchi, was part of a fusion between ancient knowledge, modern science and enlightened morality, which were all part of one syncretic episteme. There are tantalising scraps of evidence which suggest that many Free-masons shared Cocchi's view on their vegetarian heritage.[13]

Cocchi (renowned as a classical scholar as well as a physician[14]) conceived of himself, like Hecquet and Cheyne, as participating in a Europe-wide revival of ancient dietary medicine. To advance the cause he wrote a biography of Asclepiades, the first-century BC Greek phys-ician of Rome who frequently prescribed abstinence from flesh to his patients.[15] Citing Hippocrates, Pliny, Aretaeus and Celsus as intermedi-aries, Cocchi traced the medical use of the vegetable diet right back to Pythagoras. It had 'remain'd neglected for so many Ages, thro' a fatal Inadvertency', he announced in his *Pythagorean Diet*, 'till in this happy Age it was at last again brought into the Use of philosophical Medi-cine'.[16] He attributed the modern revival of medical vegetarianism to the discovery that the milk diet cured gout and rheumatism in 'about the Middle of last Century, by the Sagacity and Experience of a gouty Physician of Paris' (possibly François Bernier). This discovery had been substantiated by Johann Georg Greisel's *Tractatus medicus de Cura lactis in Arthritide* (1670), and had been confirmed by Dr Francis Slare's experiments in England. Making the same extrapolation as Cheyne, he explained that it was thanks to the esteem for the milk diet that 'the like Reputation was there at last extended to all Sorts of vegetable Diet'.[17]

But there was one factor that set Cocchi out from the rest. Cheyne and Hecquet encouraged an abstinence verging on asceticism, some-times limiting themselves and their patients to meagre diets of milk and seeds or even bread and water. Their focus was on the harmful qualities of meat rather than the beneficial effects of vegetables. This may have been attractive to a society burdened with consumer guilt and searching for means of purifying bodies and souls, but Cocchi wanted to appeal to the palate and the imagination as well as morality. Laying before his readers a kitchen-garden feast, Cocchi announced that nature provided not just necessities but 'even splendid Luxury'.[18] Indeed, Cocchi insisted that fresh vegetables were an *essential* nutritional requirement. In this lay the seed of the modern ideas about diet, and it was the path to discovering the cause and cure of scurvy.

In January 1740 Commodore George Anson led an attack on the Spanish trade ships in South America. This state-funded act of piracy met undreamed-of success: the Spanish treasure galleon they captured was laden with golden booty from the Mexican port of Acapulco and Anson's fame was assured. But by the time the fleet docked in England, three of Anson's ships were lost and of his 1,000-strong crew only 145 returned alive. Most of the rest had perished, not in fighting with the Spanish, or in shipwrecks, but slowly and painfully from a sickness with the simplest of cures. Scurvy, wrote one lieutenant in Anson's fleet, 'expresses itself in such dreadful symptoms as are scarce credible'. Gums went black and decayed, oozing blood and breeding foul breath; teeth started to drop out and the skin erupted into large purple blotches and raw ulcers. Legs swelled and an extraordinary lassitude seized every limb. Weakness eventually degenerated into an inability to move at all, breathing became difficult, fevers, tremors and 'violent terrors at the slightest accident' would take hold and eventually all would end in a ghastly death. With men dying all the way across the Pacific, Anson's fleet finally reached the Mariana (Ladrone) Islands. Knowing that 'vegetables and fruit are his only physic', the lieutenant recorded the crew's relief on finding fresh meat, lemons and oranges, 'the only treasure which we then wanted'.[19]

Grim tales such as these punctuate the history of navigation from its inception right up to the nineteenth century. On land, diets were often nearly as nutrient-deficient and scurvy was considered the root cause of epidemic diseases suffered by thousands of city-dwellers across Europe – as Cheyne had noted.[20] Scurvy had been dubbed the Proteus of diseases: it appeared in innumerable shapes, constantly throwing up new symptoms like the many-headed Hydra.[21] Several of the disorders gathered under the name would not today be diagnosed as scurvy, the condition deriving from vitamin C deficiency and easily cured by eating citrus fruit or fresh greens. But with little accurate knowledge of nutritional requirements and limited access to fresh vegetables, scurvy and other deficiency disorders were common in Europe on land and at sea.[22]

Until the causes and cure of scurvy were universally accepted, sailors continued to die in their hundreds.[23] It was an inhibiting factor to voyages of discovery; and once the new lands had been discovered, the colonists left behind to promote international trade dropped off like flies, some of them from the dreaded scurvy.[24] Finding the cause and the cure was one of the most pressing international questions of Enlightenment medicine.

Ironically – as Anson showed – the citrus cure for scurvy was widely known among sailors. As early as 1498 Vasco da Gama's men were struck with scurvy on their way to India and were saved by a fortuitous encounter with an orange-laden Arab ship. Da Gama himself attributed the sickness to bad air, but when thirty men died on the way home and only seven or eight were fit enough to navigate each ship, the crew themselves knew what they needed and cried out for more oranges.[25] Francis Drake carried citrus fruit on his voyages; Francis Bacon had mentioned blood oranges as 'an assured remedy for sickness taken at sea';[26] and in 1603 François Pyrard asserted confidently that 'There is no better or more certain cure than citrons and oranges and their juice.' The Dutch planted citrus orchards on Mauritius and St Helena to supply east-bound traders, and even tried constructing vegetable gardens on the decks of their ships.

Recognition of the citrus secret was hampered by the deficient technology for preserving fruit juice. The juice went bad and every time poorly stored juice failed to take effect it looked like evidence that citrus did not hold the answer. Besides, learned doctors were always reluctant to accept the testimonies of mere sailors. Old-school physicians floundered around blaming the disease on melancholic humours, raw wheat and even cold water and fruit, and they prescribed quackish apothecaries' pills to cure it.[27] Chemists thought scurvy was caused by the corrosive effects of vitriolic salts in preserved meat and recommended abstaining from sex and taking laxatives.[28] Medical mechanists like Pitcairne thought it was caused by dilation in the blood and advised patients to drink water and milk.[29] Others said laziness, tobacco and intemperance were responsible and thought mercury or ground millipedes held the cure.[30] The British navy – acting under the recommendation of the Royal College of Physicians – customarily treated scurvy with an elixir of sulphuric acid, alcohol, sugar and flavourings.[31]

To others, who noted that sailors ate a lot of meat preserved in salt, it seemed obvious that therein lay the cause of their malady. Cheyne had been sure that excessive alcohol and salt meat were the cause – and he was not the first to build this into an argument for vegetarianism. Evelyn argued that 'raw *Sallets* and *Herbs* have experimentally been found to be the most soveraign Diet in that *Endemical* (and indeed with us, *Epidemical* and almost universal) Contagion.'[32] Tryon blamed flesh for causing scurvy and delightedly pointed out that regularly eating green vegetables prevented it.[33] None of them conceived of scurvy as a deficiency disease; even those who knew the effectiveness of oranges, fresh greens and 'scurvy grass' (*Cochlearia curiosa* and *officinalis*) regarded these as a herbal remedy rather than a dietary requirement.[34]

In 1734 Johann Bachstrom made a breakthrough by establishing that scurvy was a disease caused by the deficiency of fruit and vegetables. His conclusion was drawn from observations made in India, and in Greenland, where victims of scurvy were treated with nothing but herbs and acid fruit and experienced a 'miraculous convalescence'. This led Bachstrom to 'conclude with mathematical certainty' that 'Since herbs and fruit manifestly remove the sickness, *therefore* it is caused by a withdrawal from them.'[35]

Cocchi latched on to Bachstrom's theory and realised that it held the only reasonable solution. Usually a supporter of Cheyne's, Cocchi made it clear that on this matter he was a step ahead. Systematically refuting all the competing theories about scurvy – including Cheyne's – Cocchi insisted that 'It is not a Northern Climate, not the Air of the Sea, nor the Salts of Flesh, but only an Abstinence from Vegetables which produces it.' Withdrawal symptoms, he insisted, occurred among sailors and land-dwellers who did not eat enough vegetation. This constitutes an unambiguous recognition that scurvy was a nutrient-deficiency disease which could be easily relieved by supplying those foods that were wanting. It was not just lime juice acting as a specific remedy, Cocchi noted, but any fresh vegetable, even leaves off a tree, would do the trick.[36] In the ensuing decades, many physicians hailed Cocchi as the saviour of scurvy.[37]

One French physician, apparently Jean-Baptiste Sénac (1693– 1770), doctor to the King of France and member of the Académie Royale des Sciences, was so impressed that when he edited the French translation of Cocchi's *Vivre Pythagoricien* he appended the account of Anson's dreadful voyage and added his own notes which endorsed Cocchi's claims for vegetarianism. Vegetable food, observed Sénac, 'totally disdained as it had been on every other occasion, was devoured [by Anson's men] with the utmost avidity'. Scurvy, he concluded, struck 'in proportion to the degree of deprivation from simple and soft vegetable food'. Eating vegetables was so potent that it could 'bring back to life nearly dead and suffering men'; it seemed to Sénac entirely logical that vegetables must also be the best food for people in good health.[38] Anson's men were a microcosm of society as a whole, deprived of what their bodies needed and naturally craved: the answer, he agreed with Cocchi, was to return to the natural vegetable diet.[39]

The discovery of the cure for scurvy is usually attributed to the Edinburgh naval surgeon James Lind whose *Treatise of the Scurvy* was published in 1753, ten years after Cocchi's work. Lind's groundbreaking achievement was to conduct a controlled experiment on twelve sailors suffering from scurvy on a ship under his care. Dividing them into six pairs, he gave each pair one of six trial remedies: cider, elixir-vitriol, vinegar, sea water, citrus fruits, and a potion containing mustard and garlic. The citrus pair were back on duty after six days; those on cider and vitriol seemed slightly better; and the others were as bad as patients who had not been treated at all. With his outstandingly careful experiment, Lind had proved, once and for all, 'that oranges and lemons were the most effectual remedies for this distemper at sea'. Anson was so delighted that he made Lind physician to the naval hospital in Portsmouth where he remained until 1783.

The remarkable thing is that twentieth-century medical histories – and even the *Encyclopaedia Britannica*[40] – have given Lind the credit not just for finding the cure but also for showing that scurvy was *caused* by dietary deficiency. But Lind thought scurvy was more to do with bad, moist air and blocked perspiration than the vegetable-free diet of sailors. He had no idea why lemon juice cured scurvy and insisted that warm dry air or vinegar could cure it without any help from vegetables.[41] Although Lind quoted Cocchi's conclusion that it was caused by a lack of vegetables and repeated the idea about balancing alkalescency with vegetable acids, he emphatically rejected the argument, made by Bachstrom, that 'the constitution of the human body, is such that health and life cannot be preserved long, without the use of green herbage, vegetables, and fruits; and that a long abstinence from these, is alone the cause of the disease.'[42] Cocchi was incensed that his discovery had been rebuffed once again and he replied to Lind by publishing a new edition of Bachstrom's treatise in 1757.

Despite Cocchi's efforts and even Lind's demonstrations, it was decades before the cure was universally accepted. Captain Cook helped the cause by successfully using sauerkraut (rich in vitamin C if well preserved) and encouraging his men to eat fresh vegetables whenever they could. By the time Nelson was fighting Napoleon, the British navy had gained a military advantage by reducing scurvy with the help of lemon juice, but even then provisions were often inadequate.[43]

Cocchi was instrumental in the final recognition that scurvy was a deficiency disease, and thus he contributed to the modern understanding that fruit and vegetables contain nutrients that are essential for a healthy diet. This in turn played into the hands of the vegetarians: these hitherto despised foods were a dietary necessity. The fetid body of the scurvied sailor crying out for fresh vegetables came to stand as an epitome for corrupt society thirsting for their long-forgotten natural diet.

EIGHTEEN

The Sparing Diet:
Scotland's Vegetarian Dynasty

It has been said that after George Cheyne's death, vegetarianism retreated to the 'irrational fringe' of animal-loving revolutionaries.[1] But in fact the late eighteenth century was the heyday of medical vegetarianism and it flourished in the most prestigious medical faculties of Europe.

Several leading physicians believed that vegetarianism was simply the healthiest diet, and many more accepted that abstinence from flesh was an effective cure for a range of diseases.[2] Some practitioners and their patients drew a line between their diet and the ethical questions of vegetarianism, but for others there was a moral aspect to abstinence. Patients trying to cure their physical malaise could be drawn into the ethical ideology of vegetarianism; with a hotbed of dieticians, moralists and eccentrics preaching the same dietary code, there was bound to be a substantial cross-over in their ideas. In the late eighteenth century Scotland in particular was home to numerous advocates of the 'sparing' diet – sparing both to animals and sparing in its sparse frugality. A dynasty of medical professors at the universities of Leiden and Edinburgh lectured their students and patients on the dangers of eating meat, while radical Pythagoreans stalked the surrounding countryside preaching the moral implications of vegetarian science. It was just another part of the Scottish scenery when Johnson and Boswell found themselves face to face with a nudist Scottish laird insisting that men should learn to live like orang-utans.

Standing before packed lecture houses in Leiden and Germany, quietening the buzz of black-clad students who thronged to hear the world's foremost medical lecturer, Hermann Boerhaave (1668–1738) struck a blow to the counter-vegetarian claim that it was unhealthy to live solely on vegetables. At the beginning of the first lecture of each academic year at the greatest medical faculty in Europe, in the very first words each successive wave of students heard him speak, Boerhaave reminded his audience that 'in the first Ages of Mankind . . . our Species liv'd entirely upon the Fruits of the Earth.'[3] Boerhaave explained that the biblical and classical records – such as Pythagoras' command 'to abstain from Flesh' – were fully exonerated by the herbivorous human origins exhibited in 'the Nature of Things'.[4] Boerhaave was not trying to convert his students to vegetarianism, but he did want them to understand that all foods were chemically the same, and all animal bodies were essentially built from a digested 'aggregate of vegetable Substances', and thus it made little difference whether one lived on meat or vegetables.[5]

That vegetables were perfectly adequate to sustain life, he announced, was proven by the Greek philosophers, pre-colonial Brazilians and the ancient and modern Brahmins whose 'Lives were . . . of the greatest Extent, and their Minds fitted for Meditation, and the Culture of every thing curious and learned'.[6] Boerhaave's empirical data was inextricably bound up with theology; his information on the Brahmins, for example, was partly derived from the Dutch botanist Joannes Bodæus Stapel who had collated a mass of evidence that the naked 'sages of India' still lived on the banana which 'the Protoplasts in Paradise tasted'.[7] Indian and prelapsarian vegetarianism was still a serious topic for the medical practitioners of the Enlightenment.

Boerhaave also noted that the contemporaneous relevance of man's original diet had recently been exhibited in a shocking form, in the extraordinary discovery of feral children, one of whom had grown up with sheep and cattle, bleated like a cow and 'lived upon nothing but Grass and Hay'.[8] The healthiness of vegetarianism, he added, was testified by several finer examples: a famous magnate in Holland lived only on peas, while an unfortunate German tourist, arrested in France, had been forced to survive on horse beans and now 'often declared in Company . . . that he hardly ever enjoy'd better Health and Spirits than when he lived under Confinement upon that Diet'. The salubrity of living without flesh was absolutely proven, said Boerhaave, by the fact that it was 'a common thing for People to live many Years upon nothing but a Milk-diet, for fear of the Gout'.[9] It transpires from his personal correspondence that Boerhaave prescribed the milk diet to patients with smallpox, ulcers and gout, and in his medical textbook he declared that 'I myself have lived a considerable Time upon the poorest Whey and Biscuit, without the least Prejudice to the Strength and Action of my digestive Organs.'[10] Boerhaave's opinion provided an authoritative rejection of the stubborn notion that the vegetable diet was unnatural or unhealthy.

Boerhaave's star pupil, the neurologist Albrecht von Haller (1708– 77), continued his master's legacy at the University of Göttingen. Like Boerhaave he was influenced by Pitcairne's hydraulic model, which he adapted to his ground-breaking discovery of the 'irritability' of muscular fibres and nerves. Haller agreed that humans originally 'lived contentedly on the tender roots and plants';[11] he thought that eating too much flesh caused hyper-alkalinity in the blood and that the acidity of vegetables was the only antidote.[12] Like Cocchi, he traced Hippocratic dietary medicine back to Pythagoras, who 'seems deserving of much praise, for having endeavoured to reduce the quantity of animal food in a hot climate'.[13] He even encouraged benevolence to animals in his popular sentimental novel, *Usong* (1772), in which the Oriental heroine, Liosua, 'took pleasure in providing for the happiness even of the dumb creation'.[14]

But surprisingly, Haller twisted Boerhaave's thesis round into the counter-vegetarian argument that living on vegetables alone could be extremely dangerous and that the gelatinous lymph in animal flesh was an indispensable nutritional requirement. The vehemence with which Haller launched his refutation of vegetarianism illustrates just how powerful an idea it had become. The constant tussle between the vegetarians and their antagonists split medical departments asunder, and Haller was determined to make the case against it as strong as possible. He noted that eating animals was an economic necessity, for, as many had pointed out before him, if we did not they would overpopulate the earth. Besides, human guts and teeth were carnivorous not herbivorous, and furthermore, 'abstinence from animal food . . . generally causes great weakness to the body and the stomach, being perpetually attended with a troublesome diarrhoea or purging.'[15]

Yet Haller's hostility to and bad experiences with vegetarianism did not stop him instructing his students to read the canon of vegetarian authors – Porphyry, Plutarch, Hecquet, Linand, J. Samuel Carl, Lémery, Cocchi and Cheyne, who, he said, 'seems to me to excel among all the writers on diet'. Most astonishing of all, he included on his reading list six works by Thomas Tryon, including the *Way to Health*.[16] Radical vegetarians had achieved a substantial coup by persuading the most serious intellectuals of the period to consider their arguments; the dietary mainstream, on the other hand, had taken the sting out of their critiques by absorbing them into the curriculum of the scientific Enlightenment. Haller saw no fixed boundary between the ethical, scientific and religious debates, and clearly recognised that vegetarianism was still a major player in the open questions about diet and health.

By the early eighteenth century Britons were tired of travelling all the way to Germany for a decent medical education, and in 1726 Edinburgh University finally opened the doors of its new medical faculty, destined to become the centre of academic medicine in Britain. Originally dreamed of in 1705 by Cheyne and Pitcairne as part of their abortive ambition to reform medicine,[17] the Edinburgh medical school self-consciously founded its curriculum on Boerhaave's Leiden model. The lecturers used his and Haller's textbooks as guides to their own teaching and, despite Haller's apostasy from Boerhaave's credo, Edinburgh became the headquarters of medical vegetarianism.

The first Lecturer in Anatomy, Alexander Monro (who had been sent to train under Boerhaave in Leiden by his father John, himself a Leiden graduate), announced his allegiance to the vegetarian side of the debate in his seminal *Essay on Comparative Anatomy* (1744). To the dismay of Buffon's counter-vegetarian followers on the Continent, Monro declared that 'Man, from this Form of his *Intestines* and that of the *Teeth*, seems to have been originally designed for feeding on Vegetables.' Monro explained that carnivores had shorter intestines because just as meat rotted quicker than vegetables, so it was easier to digest (not harder as his forebears like Hecquet had argued). The carnivores' short gut was designed to evacuate digested meat swiftly before it became dangerously fetid. This could mean that man's long herbivorous gut – which was made especially large in order to delay the unbecoming 'ignoble Exercises' of defecation – was *not* able to get rid of putrid meat faeces fast enough, thus exposing people to 'the worst Consequences'.[18] When his son, Alexander Monro II, Professor of Medicine, Anatomy and Surgery at Edinburgh, came to reissue his father's treatise nearly forty years later 'with Considerable Improvements and Additions, By other Hands', he and his co-editors kept his father's herbivorous design perfectly intact.[19] Among the hundreds of eminent scientists who emerged from the Monro dynasty – which occupied the Chair of Anatomy continuously for 126 years – was

Charles Darwin, who studied medicine at Edinburgh in 1825–7 while Alexander Monro III was continuing his father and grandfather's lecture course. Darwin showed that even after the radical break from Creationism, the herbivorous argument could be sustained by replacing God's design with evolutionary origins: 'We now know that man inhabited warm areas, allowing the favourable conditions for a fruit regimen, which according to the Anatomic laws, is his natural diet.'[20]

The Monros' teachings in the Anatomy department were consistently backed up in other lecture courses at the university. In the thirty-four-year period that William Cullen (1710–90) dominated the Edinburgh medical faculty – holding the Chairs of Chemistry (1755–66), Theory of Medicine (1766–73), Practice of Medicine (1773–89), and simultaneously giving clinical classes in the Edinburgh Royal Infirmary (1755–76) – vegetarianism became nothing less than a medical orthodoxy. Cullen lectured to thousands of pupils over the years; he was regarded as one of the greatest authorities in the United Kingdom and was a substantial contributor to European medicine. He was an intellectual celebrity, and he spread his moralised dietary advice to a wide audience. Thanks to the survival of his manuscripts at the Royal College of Physicians in Edinburgh it has been possible to gain a unique insight into the relation between Cullen's theory and practice. Both his lecture notes and his hitherto unexamined twenty-one volumes of consultation correspondence testify to his moral and medical dedication to vegetarianism.

Cullen, like most other people, agreed with Monro that 'There is not so much nourishment in a certain quantity of turnip as in a like Quantity of Beef or mutton.' But many people already ate too much, he argued, so eating meat risked causing a 'plethora' in the body and ultimately obesity and a plague of other ailments. Because meat rotted faster, as Monro had explained, it could not be excreted in time and 'from these stagnations taking place a corruption will insue which will produce ye most fatal Diseases'. Cullen was particularly concerned that meat 'over-stimulated' or irritated the nerves, causing fevers and hypertension;[21] and a sample of his medical consultation notes indicates that he prescribed a vegetable diet to at least one-fifth of all patients who came his way. Recommendations such as 'Nothing seems more useful in such Cases than avoiding irritation by a diet entirely of milk & Vegetables' are scattered throughout his letters, and he often insisted on the strictest Cheynian 'milk and seed' diet.[22] A further one-seventh of patients are cautioned to reduce their meat intake to a minimum, while others are allowed some meat with a few limitations. It is also worthy of notice, that Cullen laid nearly as many restrictions on vegetables, many of which he considered too flatulent or cooling, such as roots and cucumber.[23]

Cullen's medical theory led him to the conclusion that meat was pathologically rich and nutritionally superfluous. This was backed up by the anthropological data that had always proved so useful to vegetarians: that the majority of the world's population survived perfectly happily without ever eating meat. Indeed, Cullen went a step further than most by claiming in his lectures that he could statistically prove that vegetarianism improved health by comparing the meat-eating Muslims in India with their Hindu neighbours: 'Amounting to above 40,000,000 of People, who live without Animal Food, & seem to enjoy as perfect health as ye Europeans, & more health than ye Mahumetans their Neighbours, who indulge in animal food'. This controlled population survey showed that it could not be the climate, for example, that gave Hindus their long healthy lives.

Cullen disliked making rash statements, and one can detect his hesitancy about his explosive conclusions: 'This would tend to say that Animal Food is not necessary, but I dare not say so . . . But I would observe that where hard labour is not required in all persons of a sedentary & indolent life it is not Necessary.' In cases of extremely hard labour and cold climates where housing and heating were not sufficient, he allowed that meat might be beneficial. But then he countered that all over the world 'the lower Class of People . . . live almost entirely upon Vegetable food, & undergo a great deal of labour, without any inconveniency, & from this Circumstance they are probably free from many Diseases that those who indulge in Animal Food are liable to.' Breaking through his fear of censure, Cullen eventually came out with it: 'In short I cannot perceive that animal food is any where necessary to health . . . & Milk joined with the Farinacia* are probably sufficient for every Duty that Human Life requires.'[24] His final conclusion was unambiguous: meat was a dangerous, poisonous superfluity and everyone would be better off without it.

The irritation that meat-eating caused to the nerves disordered the body; but Cullen also warned that tampering with the nerves also

---

* Mealy grains.

corrupted human morals by disrupting self-control. Loss of self-control in turn led to still more gastronomic indulgence: in a vicious cycle of vice and disease, Cullen showed that intemperate meat-eating was both the cause and effect of diseased morality.[25]

Cullen's theory on the nutritional viability of vegetarianism had ramifications well beyond the realm of medicine. As the historian Rosalie Stott has pointed out, Cullen's neurological explanation of morality had an important influence on the philosophers of the Scottish Enlightenment including David Hume. Their friend Adam Smith, the philosopher of the free market, agreed that Stoical self-command (of which temperance and frugality were a part) lay at the heart of human morals and he thought that it was a key principle in the market economy.[26] In his seminal work, *The Wealth of Nations* (1776), Smith noted that Irish prostitutes sustained their incomparable beauty on a diet of potatoes, while Scottish and French labourers hardly ever ate meat, and he thus concluded like Cullen that a diet of grain, vegetables and dairy products 'can, without any butchers' meat, afford the most plentiful, the most wholesome, the most nourishing, and the most invigorating diet'. Thus he rationalised the taxation of meat as a luxury by proposing that 'It may indeed be doubted whether butchers' meat is anywhere a necessary of life.'[27]

With such prominent members of Edinburgh University promoting a flesh-free existence, the number of vegetarians began to proliferate. Joseph Black (1728–99), the physician and chemist who discovered 'latent heat', was one of Cullen's keenest students and became his assistant before eventually succeeding him in the Chair of Anatomy and Chemistry in Glasgow and then as Professor of Medicine and Chemistry in Edinburgh. In accordance with Cullen's principles, Black regarded meat as highly stimulating, and when he started suffering from blood-spitting and rheumatic problems himself, he relinquished flesh. Later in life he moved to a house next to the Edinburgh Meadows in order to live almost exclusively on the milk produced on his doorstep. He felt that his diet of 'fresh air and grass milk' was insipid but, as he wrote to a friend, it 'is necessary for me on account of my lungs and it is fortunate that my stomach can bear it. I do feel however sometimes the want of something more stimulating.' Nevertheless, he thought that his health improved and the rheumatic symptoms disappeared.

Black treated Hume in his last illness and he became close friends with Adam Smith and other major figures in the Scottish philosophical circle, including James Hutton, the anti-Creationist founder of modern geology, who also 'ate sparingly' and is said to have given up meat. When the famous proponent of 'common sense' philosophy Adam Ferguson (1723–1816) came to Edinburgh to win the Chair of Philosophy, he became friends with Cullen, moved in with Black and eventually married his niece. Ferguson had been a hearty eater until a 'paralytic attack' nearly killed him at the age of fifty. Black put him on a vegetable diet and claimed that this cured his hemiplegia. Ferguson was allowed animal stock in broths but he never ate meat itself: 'Wine and animal food besought his appetite in vain;' wrote his friend Lord Cockburn, 'but huge messes of milk and vegetables disappeared before him.'

Strengthened by their shared experiences, Black and Ferguson each wrote eulogistic accounts of the other's vegetarian diets, and they became a renowned pair of vegetable eaters; Ferguson's son Adam described how 'it was delightful to see the two philosophers rioting over a boiled turnip.' Ferguson witnessed Black's death and wrote admiringly that at the final moment he was sitting calmly 'at table, with his usual fare, some bread, a few prunes, and a measured quantity of milk diluted with water'. Ferguson himself lived on his rigorous abstinence to the age of ninety-three and 'never once tasted animal food, or any fermented liquor' until a few years before his death. Between them they became specimens of considerable curiosity and their medical case-studies were printed in the major journals of the day.[28]

Cullen's theories had a less successful reception in the tragic saga of William Stark, who graduated under Smith and Black in Glasgow and became a dedicatee of the vegetable diet when he joined Monro and Cullen in Edinburgh.[29] With the encouragement and guidance of Dr Benjamin Franklin (a renowned scientist as well as a revolutionary American statesman), in June 1769 Stark began to experiment on himself to discover the minimum nourishment a human body required. He limited himself to a measured daily intake of bread and water, apparently emulating the recommendations of Thomas Tryon whose books had inspired Franklin himself to take up vegetarianism. Stark systematically tested the effects of adding portions of flesh to his diet, but he quickly developed the swollen gums of scurvy, and by February of the following year the ardent thirty-year-old had inflicted on himself such severe malnutrition that he perished – a conspicuous death that damaged the vegetarian cause. Here was proof that living on a few ounces of flour was not just deranged but positively lethal, and Franklin wrote to his friends desperately trying to clear up the mess. James Carmichael Smyth, physician extraordinary to the King, published a defensive introduction to the *Works of the late William Stark* insisting that his diet cannot have been solely responsible for his death. To back up this claim, he printed Stark's notes on the vegetarians Mr Slingsby and Dr Knight, and Franklin's own assurance that when he lived on bread and water he found himself as 'stout and hearty' as ever.[30]

Franklin showed that it was impossible to dissect the medical, economic and ethical motives of vegetarianism. Originally taking up a frugal diet of bread after discovering Tryon's *Way to Health* when working as a printer at the age of sixteen, Franklin soon turned his sparing economics into a full-blown endorsement of sparing animals, and this merged easily with his sympathy-based arguments on anti-slavery and political rights. It was the weakness of the humanitarian argument, however, that eventually led him to indulge his appetite after some cod were caught on a ship he was travelling in: 'on this Occasion, I consider'd with my Master Tryon, the taking every Fish as a kind of unprovok'd Murder . . . I balanc'd some time between Principle & Inclination: till I recollected, that when the Fish were opened, I saw smaller Fish taken out of their Stomachs: Then thought I, if you eat one another, I don't see why we mayn't eat you.'[31] Although Franklin's commitment to vegetarianism was sporadic, the account of his frugality in his autobiography, and the living example he presented, became the inspiration for many vegetarians in the late eighteenth century.

Dr James Gregory (1753–1821), another of Cullen's junior colleagues, carried the tradition of medical vegetarianism into the nineteenth century. Thanks to the survival of the letters of his regular patient, John Ramsay of Ochtertyre (1736–1814), it is possible to chart the trickle-down effect from Cullen's vegetarian medical school to wider society as patients were routinely instructed to forgo the dangerous luxury of meat. Ramsay's letters reveal how prominent medical vegetarianism became in the higher circles of the Scottish gentry. From 1797, when Gregory first diagnosed him with a potentially terminal illness, Ramsay regularly resorted to a diet of home-grown vegetables[32] to treat heavy colds, stomach complaints, a chronic eye condition and the incipient apoplexy that threatened his life.[33] After ten years in this state, he told his cousin Elizabeth Graham that Gregory's diet had saved him: 'vegetables and fruit, strange remedies you will say, for such complaints! It is one of the secrets which good Dr Gregory disclosed to me.'[34] Following the inclinations of his appetite – and encouraged by the moderate counter-vegetarian advice in Sir John Sinclair's *Essay on Longevity* (1802) and *Code of Health and Longevity* (1807) – Ramsay did allow himself to break Gregory's strictures from time to time.[35] He was no dedicated vegetarian and – as a bull-baiting enthusiast – clearly did not care about the fate of animals. But even in this strictly medical context the vegetable diet carried moral connotations. Ramsay's abstinence gave him a sense of superiority and he used it as a lever with which to criticise the luxury he saw around him. He refused invitations to dinner with friends whom he considered too lavish, except when he saw it as an opportunity to exhibit 'my temperance at Dives's table'*.[36] Mixing the role of priest and physician, he imagined prescribing his self-indulgent contemporaries a diet of *'water, kaill, and sowins*† . . . by way of penance'.[37] Damning the party-goers of Stirling, Glasgow and Edinburgh, he commented satirically that 'A little fasting and prayer or, in other words, a little of Dr Gregory's regimen, would be good for the purses, persons and souls of those bourgeois-gentlehommes.'[38]

Ramsay's private correspondence reveals a network of humble pursuers of the vegetable regimen in his locality. Ramsay himself was censorious of the too-strict diet of his close friend and fellow sufferer James Stirling of Keir, warning that 'he is highly culpable in eating nothing but milk and vegetables whereas a mixture of them with animal food would assimilate best.'[39] As well as Keir, there was John Francis, restored Earl of Mar (1741–1825) who was, recorded Ramsay, 'also a patient of Gregory and may be exhibited in the Doctor's lectures as a strong proof of the effects of temperance and regimen'.[40] Another friend, one Mr Edmonstoune, Ramsay predicted would go on a 'perpetual regimen and abstinence for fat things and strong liquors'.[41] And then of course there was Dr Gregory himself who fought a lifelong battle with his own ill health.[42]

Ramsay regularly conferred with his fellow vegetable-eaters, just as Cheyne's converts had communicated as part of a vegetarian clique. There were, no doubt, comparable client networks among the patients

---

* '*Dives*', literally 'the opulent man'.
† Kaill: cabbage or any brassica broth; perhaps it should read 'water-kaill', 'broth made without meat or fat' (*OED*). Sowins: boiled oatmeal.

of dietary doctors all over Europe. If one considers how many of the foremost medical academics of the age advocated the vegetable diet, and then extrapolate to the impact they had on their students, the hundreds of practising doctors who followed their lead, and the very wide general readership of their books; then extend again to all the patients who were prescribed this vegetable course, the number of people in eighteenth-century Europe who followed a vegetable diet starts to look incalculably large. Categorising temporary abstinence from flesh as vegetarianism would be going too far, but it engaged the public with the experience and some of the theories concerning the salubrity of meat and the nourishing qualities of vegetables, and in many cases it brought them towards the moral position occupied by the vegetarians. Far from being confined to the 'irrational fringe', vegetarianism had come to occupy the moral and intellectual high ground of European culture.

Ramsay's perspective on the ethics of vegetarianism may have been further developed by his much beloved cousin Maria Graham (née Dundas, later Lady Calcott) who spent years travelling across India in search of the vegetarian idyll she had been led to expect by the travel literature.[43] Ramsay was deeply worried that she would become so absorbed in Indian religion that she would 'forget her Catechism' and lose her Christian roots altogether.[44] Ramsay already knew at least one man who had done this and become a raving vegetarian Indophile. In fact, Graham was quickly disillusioned, as she registered in her *Journal of a Residence in India* (1812) and *Letters on India* (1814): 'very few Hindoos abstain entirely from animal food,'[45] she lamented, 'My expectations of Hindoo innocence and virtue are fast giving way, and I fear that, even among the Pariahs, I shall not find anything like St Pierre's Chaumiere Indienne.'[46] Graham's sceptical response to Indian vegetarianism was no doubt representative of most people in society. But there were others who still regarded the Indians as the prime exemplars of the truth of the vegetarian theories propounded in the university medical faculties. One of these was Ramsay's old acquaintance, John Williamson of Moffat.

While Scottish patients consulted doctors in Edinburgh's austere medical faculty, for their treatment they were sent to Moffat, the fashionable lowland spa town where mineral springs soothed their ailing bodies. Awaiting their arrival – ready to prey upon their hypochondriac fears – was John Williamson, Moffat's resident vegetarian. Williamson had no medical training, and he never achieved the intellectual stature or national fame of George Cheyne, but, like the fat doctor in Bath, he did manage to convert some high-standing members of Europe's literary world to his animal-friendly creed.

Williamson started life as a shepherd and allegedly lost the tenancy when he refused to sell his sheep for slaughter. His landlord John Hope, 2nd Earl of Hopetoun – who himself published treatises on the wisdom of animals and the carnivorous extreme of the 'Englishman's food'[47] – took a liking to Williamson's eccentric manners and bestowed upon him a small annual pension. Known to his friends as 'Pythagoras', Williamson wandered the hills prospecting for minerals, attracting the attention of landowners and mining magnates who encouraged him to trace (from medieval manuscripts) seams of silver and cinnabar on their lands. On one of his rambles he discovered the medicinal spring at Hartfell near Moffat: the Earl of Hopetoun built a road to the spring for invalids and awarded Williamson the profits from the highly esteemed bottled water.

Williamson shocked his neighbours by absconding from church and worshipping God (like the 'oriental theologists') among the mountains and grand scenery of nature. He became something of a local character and his unconventional views on sex provided endless amusement to the lairds. It was rumoured that despite being a bachelor Williamson thought that every fit man should keep at least three wives. When asked why he resisted his own amorous recommendations he is reported to have answered that 'the women of this age and country are such abominable flesh-eaters that I cannot think of any serious connection with them.' His friends introduced him to a girl who, they claimed, abstained from animal food; Williamson was initially charmed, but his heart was soon broken when 'Jenny' having 'a strong hankering after *flesh*' ran off with the soldiers.

When John Ramsay visited Moffat to treat his stomach complaints in 1757, decades before becoming a vegetarian patient of James Gregory, Williamson latched onto him and took the opportunity, in the course of a country walk, to divulge to him 'with great enthusiasm the doctrines of the Pythagoreans and Brahmins'. Despite his opinion that 'John had a mist in his brain', Ramsay became so fascinated with Williamson that he ended up writing a short biography of him. After encountering him on a number of occasions, Ramsay recalled that the

Indian travel books had made Williamson embrace 'with all the ardour of a new convert the opinions of Pythagoras and the Brahmins with regard to the transmigration of souls and the duty of abstaining from animal food, as conducing to the health of the body and the soul'.[48] Williamson's enthusiasm for the Indian vegetarians earned him the nickname 'Brachman', and, emulating their peaceful example, he preached a message of non-violence and kindness to animals to the bemusement of his Scottish audience.

But Williamson did not expect his listeners to take his convictions on trust. The fact that eating meat made people sick, he argued, was proof that killing animals was contrary to the laws of God and nature. Ramsay was aware of the medical aspect of Williamson's arguments, and he acknowledged that 'His Brahminical diet had not impaired his health or strength.' Even the moral aspects of Williamson's diet struck a chord with Ramsay's own tendencies. Ramsay gleefully described dinner parties in which Williamson played the anti-luxury critic – just as Ramsay himself did when he later took up the vegetable diet. At the home of Baron Erskine, Williamson once watched the local aristocrat Harry St Clair munching his way through a huge heap of meat, and 'with equal scorn and indignation . . . declaimed against flesh-eaters'. St Clair later fell ill and was forced – just like Ramsay – to live on nothing but 'prayers and porridge'.[49]

New light has been shed on this dimension of Williamson's vegetarianism thanks to David Allen's recent discovery of Williamson's manuscript, 'A Just Complaint on Mankind for Injuring, Killing and Eating Animals' (c.1765).[50] This extraordinary treatise suggests that Williamson did not believe in reincarnation as Ramsay claimed; rather, his views were broadly compatible with the medical case for vegetarianism propounded by the professors of Edinburgh University. Indeed, he presented the moral case for vegetarianism as an extrapolation from their scientific theories.

Williamson argued that man's herbivorous anatomy was not designed for 'bloody' carnage,[51] so meat-eating spoiled people's 'blood & Juices, with Acid humours Causing Rheumatisms, Scurvys, pains, fevers &c. and with Gluey humours, causing obstructions Asthmas Coughs decays &c.'. In line with Cullen, he warned that these physiological disorders had a knock-on effect on the mind, stimulating 'Anger, & Melancholy, Madness &c. distempering the mind'.[52] Just like Ramsay, Williamson said of himself that since becoming a vegetarian, 'he enjoys a better state of health, than in flesh eating Wherein he had fevers scurvys violent head achs Tooth achs &c . . . He also now finds his passions more easily moderated & ruled by reason than in his former way of living.'[53]

Williamson took these medical observations to their theological conclusion. If God made meat poisonous to the human body, it followed that He did not want humans to kill and eat animals. The sickness caused by meat-eating was nature's way of punishing humans for murdering creatures.[54] This was a logical extrapolation from the medical case for vegetarianism, not an entirely alien viewpoint.

Williamson's almost deist system of divine justice being wreaked by the forces of nature had one principal source: the works of Thomas Tryon. Exactly like Tryon, Williamson taught that the furious spirits of a violently slaughtered animal remained in its flesh and incited the consumer to wrathful acts of murder, and thence caused 'famine & pestilence the Common Consequences of War'.[55] Williamson excised Tryon's outdated ideas about the occult power of sympathy and replaced them with a credible process of mechanical cause and effect. This providential mechanism, he thought, was manifested in events such as the late seventeenth-century Anglo-Dutch war, which started over a fight about fishing rights, and in the recent war with the French (1754–63) in America which, he said, 'arose about fishing and the fur Trade of Deer & Beaver Skins'.[56] Justice had been done when humans killed each other in their avaricious competition for the profits derived from animal murders.

Williamson recommended Tryon's *Way to Health* – which he appears to have asked the book-collecting Earl of Hopetoun to purchase on his behalf[57] – and he even claimed that there were other communities of 'Tyronians' (*sic*) still living in England and Pennsylvania. In addition to a comprehensive list of early flesh-shunning ascetics – from the seventh-century Glaswegian bishop St Mungo to the twelfth-century Waldensians – Williamson produced an impressive catalogue of modern vegetarians. He tracked down the 1745 edition of Roger Crab's *English Hermit*, Robert Cook's defence of Pythagorean vegetarianism, an account of the Pennsylvanian Dunkards in the *Royal Magazine* (1759), and George Cheyne's *The English Malady* and *Essay on Regimen*.[58] Williamson successfully forged a unity out of the ideas gleaned from all these authors, from Cook's vegan proscription on wearing animal products to Crab's vegetarian Bible exegesis (which he embellished with the observation that Jesus ordered His disciples to stop being fishermen).[59]

Above all, Williamson was enamoured of the Indian Brahmins and Banians, and he read about them in every ancient and modern source he could lay his hands on: Strabo, Arrian, Porphyry, Clement of Alexandria, Palladius, the travel collections of John Churchill and John Harris, as well as Chevalier Andrew Michael Ramsay's syncretic histories of world religion.[60] Follow the Indians' example, said Williamson, and humans could restore their original happiness as far 'as possible in the present State'.[61] Rather like the enlightened self-interest arguments of modern ecological and permacultural philosophies, Williamson insisted that wild animals could be more useful alive than dead. Even those traditionally considered pests, like moles, were actually beneficial, for they cultivated the soil.[62] The art of camouflage and even the technology of flight could be learned from the animals, and tamed rats would eat less food than the cats and dogs employed to catch them. The animals – according to Williamson's interpretation of the Fall – only became wild and savage because of man's violence and murder. If only humans would 'reclaim & reconcile them' by reverting to vegetarian pacifism, they would grow tame and helpful.[63] Williamson even thought we should emulate the beasts' natural mating patterns (seasonal copulation limited by sustainable birth control), a habit he said the ancient Brahmins employed, which was also the kind of naturalist model for human behaviour advocated by Rousseau and by Tryon's 'Complaint of the Cow and the Oxen'.[64]

He mediated this idealism through a serious engagement with current socio-political developments, such as the clearance of Scottish communities from the land for the sake of animal grazing. Williamson appears to have been one of the first (if not the first) to work out a thorough critique of meat-eating on the basis of its resource inefficiency. It was an idea that, within a few decades, all the greatest economic and philosophical authors – including Adam Smith, Bernardin de Saint-Pierre and Thomas Malthus – would heed. Vegetable subsistence, he claimed, is

> the most innocent and profitable Moral & Political method for society, as it wou'd not only remove the great Grass farms feeding Cattle to the Slaughter, which now in many places depopulate the Country: But by multiplying the people & improving the ground to the best advantage to bear fruits and grains greens

&c. this method would make the most wholesom necessarys of life so plentifull & easy to be got, that they would relieve all the Indigents distresses;[65]

This is not very different from the view of modern demographers who warn that it will only be possible to feed the world's growing population if we limit the resource-inefficient business of animal-grazing and use the land to produce arable crops for human consumption instead.[66] In the bleak era of the Highland Clearances, when crofters' survival was pushed to the brink by powerful landowners seeking profits from grazing, Williamson caught a glimpse of the threat to world food-security posed by competition for limited resources. Even though this did not readily fit into his providential scheme – because these victims of meat-eating were not the consumers – Williamson appealed to egalitarian justice against the interests of a few.

In 1787, about twenty years after Williamson's death, the *Gentleman's Magazine* ran a eulogy on him which claimed that his vegetable diet had preserved his health to the age of over ninety (twenty years older than Ramsay's more objective account suggests). This report also mentioned the epitaph and obelisk erected by his friend Sir George Clerk of Penicuik above his burial spot in Moffat churchyard 'at a distance from the other burying places'.[67] This obituary was reproduced by the Scottish antiquarian Joseph Ritson in his vegetarian anthology in 1802; it seems possible that Ritson knew Williamson or Ramsay and he may even have read Williamson's manuscript.[68] By giving voice to a range of vegetarian arguments and compiling numerous abstruse references to others, Williamson contributed to the formation of the 'vegetarian' tradition.

Despite his humble beginnings, Williamson's principles reached the highest rungs of society. As a young man James Boswell (1740–95) was sent to Moffat from his home in Edinburgh to treat a scorbutic nervous illness with the salubrious mineral waters. He strolled over the hills with Williamson and embraced his call for a return to nature – no doubt as impressed by the idea of emulating the animals' mating habits as he was by his vegetarianism. Boswell always retained a primitivist streak – idealising Williamson and Rousseau in turn and yearning to flee to the woods himself – for which he was frequently reprimanded by his more conventional father-figure, Samuel Johnson.[69] If you wish to regress to the desert, said Johnson drily, return to Scotland for they have plenty of desert there. Johnson's suggestion that Scotland was a breeding ground of primitivism was a sardonic quip; nevertheless, it seems that abstemiousness, and in particular vegetarianism, since at least the days of George Cheyne, struck a special resonance north of the border, if only as an attempt to distance Scottish identity from the luxurious roast beef of England.

Later in life Boswell wrote to Jean-Jacques Rousseau in the hope of obtaining a blessing from this revered guru of nature. In a confessional account of his own life Boswell told Rousseau about meeting Williamson in his youth: 'I met an old Pythagorean,' wrote Boswell, 'I attached myself to him. I made an obstinate resolve never to eat any flesh, and I was resolved to suffer everything as a martyr to humanity.' He told Rousseau that although he had never completely renounced these moral principles, they had dropped out of his life, and he conformed to convention.[70] But the sensitivities remained latent, surfacing in his guilty conscience on killing birds for sport,[71] and feeling pity for fighting cocks.[72]

Ironically, Boswell was continually forced to return to a flesh-free diet in his lifelong struggle with recurring bouts of gonorrhoea (contracted during his enthusiastic adoption of the polygamous sexual practices of deer).[73] In using diet for health, Boswell was encouraged by George Cheyne's prescriptions, which he and Johnson mutually enthused about in The Life of Samuel Johnson. Both Boswell and Johnson diagnosed themselves with Cheyne's 'English Malady', and felt that Cheyne was their physiological advocate and guide. Indeed, Johnson was so impressed by Cheyne's theories that – tortured by hypochondria, eye disorders and frequent colds – he suppressed his notorious appetite and adopted what he called 'a semivegetable diet', which Cheyne had recommended for mild nervous disorders. Writing often to Mrs Thrale about the details of his diet, he assured her that while he indulged occasionally, for the most part he exercised rigorous abstinence, living often on nothing but potatoes, spinach or peas.[74]

Johnson insisted that his diet was based on the most rigorous medical considerations, but he also questioned man's moral right to kill, and vehemently objected to the cruelty of vivisection.[75] Launching a full-frontal assault on the standard defence of eating meat employed by William King, Buffon and Soame Jenyns among others,[76] Johnson argued that the important question was not whether farm animals owed their lives to the people who bred them but 'whether animals who endure such sufferings of various kinds, for the service and entertainment of man, would accept of existence upon the terms on which they have it'.[77]

When Boswell finally managed to drag Johnson away from the comforts of London on their famous journey to the Hebrides in 1773, he sneaked onto their itinerary a quick visit to his old friend the notorious Scottish judge, James Burnett, Lord Monboddo (1714–99). Monboddo had recently published his opinion that the great apes – gorillas, chimpanzees and orang-utans – were races of primitive people who had not yet learned to speak. Although not so far from modern evolutionary theories, this seemed ridiculous to his contemporaries and Johnson frequently had a laugh at Monboddo's expense – but he readily agreed to lunch with the eccentric laird on their way to Aberdeen.

Monboddo was a striking figure in the history of primitivism, a stepping stone between Rousseau's idealisation of the noble savage and the Romantics' attempt to realign culture with the wild 'state of nature'. For Monboddo, no less than for Rousseau, the evolutionary origin of the human species – particularly its natural diet – was of paramount importance in determining man's innate characteristics. Monboddo inherited the paradox of Rousseau's *Origins of Inequality* in acknowledging that man had the 'amphibious' capacity to be either a solitary carnivore or a herding herbivore. But, like Rousseau, he insisted that 'by nature, and in his original state, he is a frugivorous animal, and that he only becomes an animal of prey by acquired habit'. Human populations turned to hunting and agriculture when they grew too numerous to be fed by the fruits of nature, and the transition from herbivore to carnivore, Monboddo thought, produced 'a great change of character':

> While man continued to feed upon the fruits of the earth, he was an innocuous animal . . . But as soon as he became a hunter, the wild beast, which is part of his composition, became predominant in him. He grew fierce and bold, delighting in blood and slaughter. War soon succeeded to hunting; and the necessary consequence of war was the victors eating the vanquished, when they could kill or catch them. In this state, man, if not tamed, or subdued by laws or manners, is the most dangerous and most mischevous of all the creatures that God has made;

Monboddo thus carved out a position between Rousseau and Hobbes. He contradicted Rousseau by insisting that the 'ties of love and sympathy which bind us so fast together' were acquired, not instinctive;

but neither was man the exclusively selfish animal Hobbes imagined. Monboddo answered Buffon's objections to the antisocial aspects of Rousseau's so-called 'primitivism' by insisting that social affections and the human intellect *did* have to be cultivated, but the *body* should be kept as close to the state of nature as possible.[78] Monboddo thus resolved the timeworn clash between nature and culture, by arguing that it was possible to follow both simultaneously. Europeans, he argued, should emulate the Indians, who had cultivated their intellects for longer than any nation, but whose vegetarian regimen 'is as natural as any diet can be'. Although they took their respect for animal life 'too far' by feeding lice with their own blood, Monboddo complained that 'we in Europe go to the other extreme, and abuse very much that dominion which God has given us over the animals.'

Monboddo thought that meat was hard to digest and caused diseases, whereas the vegetable diet had the power to save people from fatal sickness. 'Now,' he concluded, 'any diet that is good for restoring health when lost, must be at least as good for preserving it.' It was best to return the body to its herbivorous origin. At the very least Monboddo recommended mixing vegetables with meat and avoiding alcohol as far as possible – and this was the course he followed himself.

The orang-utans' herbivorous diet was no less informative than their natural dress sense. The artificial invention of clothes, Monboddo explained, prevented the pores of the skin from being exposed to the fresh air, and thus he recommended 'being naked as much as conveniently may be'. It was particularly important to work off meals by exercising in the nude: this was the custom of the ancient Greeks, and his illustrious acquaintance and founder of the state of Georgia, General James Oglethorpe, kept himself alive to the age of one hundred with the help of a daily dose of naked star-jumps.[79]

Monboddo had been Boswell's guide and mentor – no doubt building on Boswell's early exposure to both Williamson's and Rousseau's creed.[80] Johnson, however, regarded Monboddo as an eccentric primitivist and he did not relish Boswell's tales of Monboddo prancing around naked in front of his open window every morning.[81] As they drove in the rain over the bleak moors to visit the loony laird, Boswell got cold feet; Johnson, wry as ever, merely recited Macbeth's speech on meeting the witches. 'Monboddo is a wretched place, wild and naked, with a poor old house,' reflected Boswell with foreboding.

The moment 'Farmer Burnett' appeared on his doorstep to greet his guests dressed in rustic clothing holding a prize stalk of corn, the altercation began, Monboddo championing the strength of our primitive ancestors, Johnson insisting that modern humans were as strong as them and wiser: 'This was an assault upon one of Lord Monboddo's capital dogmas,' commented Boswell morosely. When they sat down to dinner, Johnson was dismayed by the 'farmer's dinner', grumbling that 'I have done greater feats with my knife than this'; Monboddo, for his part 'affects or believes he follows an abstemious system, [and] seemed struck with Dr Johnson's manner of living'. But after clashing over 'whether the Savage or the London Shopkeeper had the best existence', Johnson and Monboddo warmed to each other. The idea of tracing man back to monkeys amused Johnson and he started reading Monboddo's six-volume work, frequently quipping on the topic of men having tails and discussing the subject in his letters to Mrs Thrale.[82] Back in Edinburgh, Boswell hosted a dinner for Johnson with the medical vegetarians William Cullen and Adam Ferguson, where they jocularly discussed Monboddo's theory that orang-utans could be taught to speak; and Monboddo himself turned up for another meeting with the travelling pair.[83]

Vegetarianism circled the full gamut of eighteenth-century society; it was espoused by puritanical jesters, landowning aristocrats and metropolitan university lecturers. Distinctions could be drawn between the medical motives and the ethical ones, but the divergent traditions invariably ended up reverting to their shared assumptions about man and nature. It had become increasingly difficult to enjoy a beefsteak without at least considering the ethical implications. People connected their food with morality and they had mechanisms for dealing with the theological context of sympathy and the health impacts of meat. In the era before the French Revolution, the landscape was already dotted with wild men seeking for a union with nature which the Romantics would take to new extremes. From the anatomical observations of the scientists to the social anthropology of the Rousseauists, man's nature as herbivore or carnivore had become a central preoccupation of European culture.

PART THREE

Romantic Dinners

NINETEEN

Diet and Diplomacy: Eating Beef in the Land of the Holy Cow

In 1602 the young Italian aristocrat Roberto de Nobili (1577–1656) arrived in south India to begin his vocation as a Jesuit missionary. Swiftly realising that his colleagues in the mission were reviled by the Brahmin priests for eating meat and consorting with low-caste Hindus, de Nobili decided to infiltrate the higher castes of Indian society. He perfected his Sanskrit and Tamil, and after a brief spell posing as a raja discarded his European black cassock and leather shoes to robe himself in the ochre cloth of a Hindu *sanyassin*, a renouncing holy man. Shaving his head, smearing a rectangle of sandalwood paste on his brow, and donning a Brahmin sacred thread, de Nobili passed himself off as an ascetic by the name of Tattuva Podagar Swami (The Teacher of Reality).

Aware that Hindus – especially in the Tamil south – believed that eating flesh or eggs was violent and bestial, de Nobili relinquished all animal food and vowed to live like a vegetarian *sanyassin* forever. 'My food consists of a little rice,' he reported, 'with some herbs and fruit; neither meat nor eggs ever cross my threshold. It is necessary to observe all this, for if these people did not see me do such penance, they would not receive me as one who can teach them the way to heaven.' Decamping from the European settlements to dissociate himself from their polluting influence, de Nobili moved into his private mud hut, learned to sit cross-legged on the ground and to eat from a banana leaf with the fingertips of his right hand. His senior missionary colleague Gonçalo Fernandez, a comparatively ill-educated ex-soldier from Portugal, was having none of these new-fangled integrationist techniques. Like many of his compatriots, Fernandez preferred to ridicule pagan follies such as vegetarianism in the hope of undermining the Hindus' attachment to them – or even to convert Hindus forcibly by

Robert de Nobili in *sanyassin* dress,
from an original picture by Baltazar da Costa

military conquest.[1] So while de Nobili crouched on the floor in the corner eating a fleshless meal served by exclusively Brahmin servants, Fernandez continued to sit nonchalantly at table cutting up plates of meat with a knife and fork.

These two figures symbolise the two radically divergent ways in which Europeans in India responded to the strange and novel culture around them. Riven by these alternatives, the Christian mission split down the middle and continued in tumult for more than two centuries. The pattern carried over into the domain of mercantile colonialism with the disagreement between de Nobili and Fernandez being replayed time and time again by East India Company servants. By the end of the eighteenth century, the stereotypical European 'nabob' in India would don Indian clothes, eat Indian food, and enjoy sexual relations – even marriage – with Indian women. Some really did bring Fernandez's warnings to pass by losing their grip on Christianity and adopting not just the vegetarian *practice* of the Indians but their principles too. As well as enjoying exotic forays into an experience of 'the Other', this trend for 'Indianisation' allowed the British to step seamlessly into the shoes of the indigenous ruling classes. It was only during the nineteenth century, after the Wellesleys had made their mark and especially after the Indian Mutiny of 1857, that stringent racial boundaries were erected by bigoted scientists and administrators and Europeans were officially and effectively instructed to resist such temptations and like Fernandez to assert their European superiority by wearing impractical woollen broadcloth and importing food – at great expense – from back home.

Fernandez took de Nobili's refusal to eat with him as a slap in the face, and he was appalled that his new partner had apparently gone native. Nobili 'behaves in everything as a man of another religion', complained Fernandez to the missionary inspector from Rome in 1610. 'The dress of the Father is that worn by the pagan Sanyassins,' he wrote. 'The serving and the food are according to Brahmin usage, which is everything except meat, fish and eggs.' As far as Fernandez was concerned de Nobili had been swallowed up by the dark continent. Indian vegetarianism was the ultimate sign of pagan superstition and animal worship; it put man on a level with animals and denied his unique place in the universe. It literally turned the world upside down. By giving way to Indian customs, de Nobili seemed to undermine the superiority of European culture and the very purpose of the Christian mission itself.

De Nobili – who read Sanskrit scriptures a century and a half before the famed English Orientalists – did respect ancient Indian culture and believed that it contained distant revelations of divine truth. Following detailed discussions with Hindu teachers, he wrote one of the most profound comparative studies of Hindu metempsychosis. He was happy to see the similarities between their culture and his own, and pointed out that his vegetarianism was just like Christian asceticism. Even those who disapproved of de Nobili's methods acknowledged that 'no Carthusian monastery is more strict . . . no anchoret or hermit of Thebais* more abstemious'.[2] But in 1613 de Nobili's provincial superior in India, Father Pero Francisco, ordered him and his followers to let up on vegetarianism for the sake of their health: 'The abstinence from meat and fish etc., must not be observed so strictly and rigorously that, even in case of necessity, sickness, disgust or natural weakness,

---

* Monastic followers of the Egyptian Desert Fathers.

they do not touch meat, for experience has shown that on such occasion it is absolutely necessary to yield to nature and help it by eating meat, and this must be done.'

The dispute reached Rome, and before he knew it de Nobili was spearheading a doctrinal dispute. He explained in his vehement defence that his behaviour was in line with the Apostles: St Timothy circumcised himself to adapt to the Jews and thus convert them; even St Augustine of Canterbury had allowed the Brits to continue sacrificing oxen; as St Paul had said, be 'all things to all men'. The founding father of the Asian mission, St Francis Xavier (1506–52), as well as de Nobili's immediate predecessor, the educated Neapolitan aristocrat Alessandro Valignano (1539–1606), had fully developed this into the technique of 'accommodation' which was now widely used all over the East. In Japan, Valignano had controversially ordered the Jesuits to dress like Buddhist monks and learn how to eat with chopsticks squatting at low Japanese dining tables. In order to win converts, Valignano had said, it was imperative that missionaries overcome their 'initial repugnance' and follow the Japanese diet of 'salted raw fish, limes, sea snails and such bitter or salty things', for the Buddhists had an equally 'great revulsion from eating any kind of meat'.[3]

De Nobili won a resounding success when, in 1623, Pope Gregory XV issued a bull endorsing almost all his points. But the dispute raged on and spilled over into the 'Malabar rites' controversy about whether converts could keep their native customs. Despite the claim that de Nobili's techniques had won tens of thousands of converts, in 1704 the apostolic delegate for India overruled the papal allowances and insisted that Christianity in India should be practised just as it was in Rome – beef, pork and all.[4]

But he could not squash the practice. There were obvious advantages to acquiring high caste status – and it was clearly impossible to demolish the local culture of vegetarianism. If Europeans were to take on the mantle of teachers or even rulers, they would have to make some concessions to local customs. In 1710, when Joseph Constantius Beschi joined the mission founded by de Nobili in Madura, he took to wearing the luxurious purple gown and pearl earrings of an *acarya*, a Saivite or Vaishnavite raja-guru. Members of the vegetarian Tamil Pillai castes flocked to him, and later in the century the convert A. Muttusami Pillai eulogised the fact that 'From the time of his arrival in this country, he abstained from the use of flesh, fish, etc.'[5]

Eating anything else, many realised, was literally a recipe for disaster. The seventeenth-century Venetian freebooter Niccolao Manucci claimed that there was a riot when locals discovered that the Portuguese Jesuits at Tanjor were not 'Roman Brahmins' as they claimed, but beef-eating *feringhis* (foreigners) and the Christians had been persecuted ever since. One Jesuit was caught cooking up a beef stew by another member of the mission who flung it outside in fear, exclaiming that 'the Jesuit fathers were not *pariahs* and low caste; they did not eat cow's flesh.'[6]

In Protestant missions also, Hindus stuck to their vegetarian customs after converting to Christianity. 'If you tell them of the christian liberty in victuals and drinks,' reported the Protestant missionary Philippus Baldaeus in 1672, 'they reply, that they are not ignorant of it, but as the essence of christianity does not consist in eating and drinking, so they did not think themselves obliged to feed upon such things as are contrary to their nature and education, being from their infancy used to much tender food, which agrees best with their constitution, and makes them generally live to great age.' Baldaeus' report gives an exceptional insight into the contribution the Indians themselves were making to the debate, and he was evidently impressed, for he concluded that these Christian Brahmins 'are for the most part men of great morality, sober, clean, industrious, civil, obliging, and very moderate in eating and drinking'.[7] He made their diet more palatable by reconceiving it as an expression of the Christian ethic of temperance.

The tradition of dietary accommodation was by no means unique to European visitors. Indeed, it seems to have been a widespread – even common-sense – response. Europeans were intrigued to find that the Syrian Christian community, established in Kerala and Cochin from at least the sixth century, used many Hindu rites and accommodated itself to the Nayar Brahmins by 'abstaining from animal food'.[8] In 1630 Henry Lord noted that the Zoroastrian Parsis – who fled from Persia to India as early as the eighth century AD – abstained from beef 'because they will not give offence to the *Banians*', and another traveller reported that they were granted asylum on the condition that they did not 'Kill any Beasts or living Creatures'.[9]

Indeed, these diplomatic agreements bear much resemblance to the ancient Indian practice by which non-vegetarian Hindu castes adopted vegetarianism in order to ingratiate themselves with, and even attain the status of, higher castes. Ruling Rajputs and Jats often relinquished their traditional meat-eating warrior customs to legitimise themselves in the eyes of the Brahmin priesthood.[10] This was an indigenous model which the early Mughal emperors adopted, and pre-imperialist Europeans probably took a pragmatic cue from these predecessors.

When the Afghan Muslim leader Muhammad bin Ghur invaded northern India in the twelfth century he was characterised in Hindu texts as a beef-eating *mleccha*, or barbarian. Punning on his name (Ghur), the word for foreigner (*Gori*), and cow (*go-*), a Kashmiri poet called the invader 'the evil Gori – him who was given to eating foul foods, the enemy [*ari*] of cows [*go-*], from whence he got his very name'.[11] The culture clash continued to pose serious problems for Muslim – Hindu integration, and the Mughals soon realised the benefits of deploying dietary diplomacy.[12]

The Emperor Akbar the Great (r. 1556–1605) went further than merely being polite about local mores. He took Hindu wives and was immensely impressed by Jainism, especially the doctrine of *ahimsa*. Throughout his reign he issued numerous *farmans* (imperial orders) forbidding the killing of animals and fish and discouraging meat-eating for up to six months in the year. Such far-reaching legislation against animal-killing had hardly been seen in India since the Buddhist King Ashoka issued his rock edicts in the third century BC. Akbar's Jain subjects expressed their gratitude in abundance.[13] His official chronicler Abu 'l-Fazl 'Allami (himself friends with high-standing Jains) made an astonishing announcement in the *Ain-e Akbari*, which reveals that Indian vegetarianism produced a powerful impression on the Mughals, just as it did on Europeans:

> His majesty has a great disinclination for flesh: and he frequently says, 'Providence has prepared a variety of food for man, but, thro' ignorance and gluttony, none seems to have an eye for the beauty inherent in the prevention of cruelty, he destroys living creatures, and makes his body a tomb for beasts. If I were not a king, I would leave off eating flesh at once, and now it is my intention to quit it by degrees.'[14]

Akbar's articulation of the case for vegetarianism is particularly remarkable for its similarity to ancient European arguments familiar from Plutarch and Ovid. He also adapted Indian vegetarianism to make it compatible with the Semitic proscription of blood-eating, just as Sir Thomas Roe did after visiting the Mughal court: 'Blood is the principal of life,' said Akbar, 'To avoid eating thereof is to honour life.' According to Akbar's favourite Jain courtier, the revered monk Shantichandra, Akbar adopted these arguments for vegetarianism after Shantichandra requested permission to leave court the day before the Muslim festival of 'Eid because so many animals were going to be slaughtered; he explained to Akbar, on the basis of Islamic doctrine as well as Jain, that *'ahimsa* is the only way to God'. Akbar horrified his fellow Muslims by fusing Indian religions and Sufism into his own eclectic sun-worshipping cult Din-i-Ilahi, in which he stipulated that beef should be forbidden (while pork, blasphemously, was allowed).[15]

Akbar's son and successor Jahangir (r. 1605–27), born of a Hindu mother, eulogised his father for confining himself to vegetarian 'Sufi food' for nine months of the year. Jahangir issued his own Jain-influenced *farmans* and in 1618 made a shocking break with court tradition by vowing (in penitence for having murdered Abu 'l-Fazl) to forbear his passion for hunting and 'injure no living thing with my own hand'. In his *Memoirs*, he claimed that wild beasts had become so tame during his reign that they wandered harmlessly amongst people.[16]

When Shah Jahan (r. 1628–58) came to power, he rejected Jahangir's receptiveness to local religions and strove to purify Islam in India. But even he broke the Islamic rule against representing human and animal figures in art by having his throne in the Red Fort in Delhi embellished with inlaid semi-precious stones depicting Orpheus charming animals with his music. Shah Jahan was almost certainly evoking the figure of King Solomon who extended his fabled power over the animals, like Kayumarth the first king of mankind in the Golden Age. As the art historian Ebba Koch has illustrated, these images were frequently used to express part of the Mughal imperial ideology. They were also closely linked to the numerous depictions of the fictional character, Majnun, in the desert with the animals, and even the Christian icon of the wolf lying down with the lamb which had been popular in Mughal art since the time of Akbar. It is also possible that the Orpheus image was chosen to appeal to Shah Jahan's Hindu and Jain subjects who had comparable artistic traditions, including the depiction of musicians charming wild animals.[17] The artists who prepared Shah Jahan's throne may have been unaware of Orpheus' standing as Greek antiquity's pre-eminent vegetarian cult-leader, though the idea that his follower, Pythagoras, had taught the Indians their philosophy was widely disseminated by Muslim Neoplatonists. At the very least, the appearance of Orpheus on the throne of an Islamic Indian ruler remains a striking irony and a testimony to the fusion of Eastern and Western traditions.

Later Indian artists came to see the Orphic musician as a bridge between European and Indian ideas. A school of late seventeenth-century artists from the Deccan produced a number of paintings showing figures in European dress charming animals and placed them alongside traditional Indian paintings of women surrounded by animals.[18] Perhaps unintentionally, these remarkable paintings represent the European encounter with, and assimilation into, the Indian practice of kindness to animals.

Even Shah Jahan's son Aurangzeb (r. 1658–1707) – renowned for his orthodox Islamic practice and distaste of his forebears' openness to local religions – signified his penance for murdering his brothers by eating (to the astonishment of European onlookers) 'nothing which has enjoyed life. As he lives upon vegetables and sweetmeats only.'[19] The last Mughal emperor Bahadur Shah II (r. 1837–58) was eulogised for taking after Akbar in his treatment of his Hindu subjects. Born of a Rajput mother in 1775, Bahadur Shah sometimes dressed as a Brahmin, visited Hindu temples, wore the sacred thread and a hallowed mark on his forehead. He abstained from beef as a concession to both Hinduism and Sufism, and banned cow-slaughter in 1857 in an attempt to cement Hindu–Muslim concord during the Indian Mutiny.[20]

This royal dynasty of vegetarian advocates provides a fascinating insight into the attitude of Mughals to the culture they conquered. The *Ain-e Akbari* was one of the first Indian texts to be translated by the English Orientalists and it gave useful tips for the new phase of European colonialism.[21] Several Englishmen followed Akbar's example and gave up eating meat, but there were many more who ignored such accommodating efforts. Indeed, as meat was much cheaper in India than in Britain, colonists took the opportunity of gorging themselves in a manner impossible at home.[22] Some administrators did intermittently ban cow slaughter but, with beef as the British national dish, and bigotry now ingrained in the empire-building exercise, disregard for local traditions gradually prevailed.

The result of British insouciance about native food taboos was cataclysmic. In 1857 it transpired that Indian sepoys were being supplied by their colonial masters with a new sort of rifle cartridge which had been greased with beef and pork fat. As cartridges needed to be bitten before use, it was impossible for the sepoys to do so without defiling themselves. It was even whispered in camp that the British were adulterating flour rations with bone-dust. No Indian – Hindu or Muslim – was safe, for such religious defilement was believed to be a preparation for forcible mass-conversion, an idea some missionaries did espouse and express (and for which the missions in general were later severely blamed). Grievances against the British colonial power had been building up for years. This new development was used to fan the flames of rebellion. When the army predictably started punishing anyone who resisted, resentment flared: the sepoys killed their officers and triggered the greatest ever Indian rebellion against British power – the Sepoys' Revolt, or Indian Mutiny – which almost toppled the Raj and convulsed the region in over a year of bloodshed. Well into the twentieth century riots were sparked by British attempts to legalise cow slaughter, and sharing meals with Hindus remained a tortuous minefield of misunderstanding.[23]

As many commentators pointed out at the time, such misadventures could have been avoided if the British had learned to be more sensitive to local dietary taboos. The revered Jesuit missionary Abbé Jean-Antoine Dubois (1765–1848) had anticipated the trouble to come in his authoritative *Hindu Manners, Customs, and Ceremonies*, in which he recommended extending the missionaries' use of 'accommodation' into a wider approach to diplomatic relations. When the Liberal Governor-General of Bengal Lord William Bentinck (1774–1839) received a copy, he immediately recognised its potential as handbook for Europeans in India and announced that it 'might be of the greatest benefit in aiding the servants of the Government in conducting themselves more in unison with the customs and prejudices of the natives'.

Dubois sarcastically observed that 'the Europeans do not seem disposed to adopt the same rules of abstinence as are followed by the people among whom they live, and that, without paying any attention to the disgust which they cause, they continue to eat beef openly. It is certain that this conduct estranges them from all the better classes of Hindus, who, consequently, in this respect place them far below the Pariahs.' Europeans should not be lulled into a false sense of security by the apparent passivity with which Hindus allowed these slaughters to continue, he warned prophetically, for insurrection was bubbling beneath the surface. Such was the Hindu abhorrence, he said, that 'to offer meat at a meal with a guest with whom one is not intimate, would be the height of rudeness'.

Taking after de Nobili, Dubois had adopted the white turban, Indian robe and bamboo staff of a Hindu pilgrim the moment he arrived in India. He preached under the name Doddhaswâ-miayavaru (Great Lord), 'Embracing,' as he put it, 'in many respects, the prejudices of the natives; living like them, and becoming all but a Hindu myself'. Even eating meat in secret, he cautioned, was not advisable, for 'People who abstain entirely from animal food acquire such an acute sense of smell that they can perceive in a moment from a person's breath, or from the exudation of the skin, whether that person has eaten meat or not.'[24]

Dubois' text illustrates the continuities between the theology of accommodation from the time of its nurture by the Renaissance humanists, de Nobili and Valignano, through to the early colonial practice of Indianisation. But Dubois was not just a diplomatic master of strange table manners. His theoretical apparatus for the interpretation of Hinduism actually led him to identify within it a concealed kernel of truth.

Demolishing the persistent myth that Hindu vegetarianism was based on the belief in reincarnation, Dubois insisted that when Pythagoras came and learned about vegetarianism and metempsychosis from the Indians he had muddled or deliberately exaggerated their principles. 'As a matter of fact,' announced Dubois, 'everything induces us to believe that the Hindus, though foolish enough in many respects, are not so foolish as to believe, when they show repugnance to feeding on anything which has had life, that they might be swallowing the limbs of their ancestors.' The religious doctrines used by the priests to enforce vegetarianism were not reincarnation, he explained, but the deity of the cow, the 'fear of pollution', the horror 'of feeding on the remains of a dead body' and 'the horror of murder'. Dubois thus rightfully reinstated the doctrine of *ahimsa* at the heart of Indian vegetarian philosophy.

Just like previous Europeans, however, Dubois refused to see the legitimacy of *ahimsa*, portraying it as a cowardly and effeminate doctrine. But he went on to explain that the real historical origin (as opposed to the more recent religious rationale) for vegetarianism and cow protection was that cattle were essential for local agriculture, and meat was indigestible and putrid in a tropical climate. 'There is no doubt,' he concluded, 'that it was for the sake of health and cleanliness, in the first instance, that Hindu lawgivers inculcated these principles of defilement and purification.' Dubois' immediate inspiration for this influential utilitarian interpretation (which anthropologists still partially maintain) was Montesquieu's notorious *De l'Esprit des Lois* (1748), but both authors were ultimately drawing from Bernier's use of an ancient empirical method. The idea that vegetarianism had really been imposed because of the hot Indian climate meant that it had little validity as a universal moral stricture; nevertheless, Europeans in India were encouraged to learn from local example. In direct agreement with the original sanitary intentions of the 'Hindu lawgivers', Dubois declared that 'I have known many Europeans who entirely left off eating meat for this reason, because they found that they could not eat it without suffering afterwards from indigestion.' The implication for the European reader was clear: if you don't give up meat for the sake of your host, then give it up for your health.[25]

Dubois' suggestion was endorsed by a widespread tradition of European tropical medicine. From at least the seventeenth century European medics had been warning that meat was a 'heating' food and was therefore particularly dangerous when consumed in a hot climate. God, they pointed out, had benevolently ensured that humans everywhere were supplied with just the right sort of food: and in the tropics this was clearly indicated in the lavish quantities of cooling fruit.

Other Europeans, by contrast, persisted in believing that consuming meat and liquor while in India was essential if one was to avoid melting into the feeble 'effeminacy' of the natives.[26] Several medics pointed out that it was because of such ignorant prejudices that thousands of Europeans – especially 'ignorant' sailors and soldiers – perished soon after arriving in India. In 1680 John Fryer noted that while the debauched English died in Bombay like exotic plants transplanted from their native soil, 'the Country People and naturalised *Portugals* live to a good Old Age, supposed to be the Reward of their Temperance; indulging themselves neither in Strong Drinks, nor devouring Flesh as we do.'[27] Vegetarians like Thomas Tryon, who had personal experience of living in the tropics, built these medical prescriptions into their critiques, arguing that only 'idle sottish People that understood Nature no more than Swine' failed to realise that the fruitarian 'Natives of most hot Countrys might be our Examples'.[28]

Taking their cue from the travellers who noted just how healthy and long-lived the Hindus were,[29] by the end of the eighteenth century it had become standard advice that Europeans should give up or severely limit their flesh intake on arrival in India.[30] As the medical historian Mark Harrison has observed, learning how to survive in the tropics was important to a people who aimed to colonise the world.[31]

In the authoritative *Influence of Tropical Climates, more Especially the Climate of India, on European Constitutions* (1813), the naval surgeon James Johnson exported European dietary medicine to the Indian context. He was perfectly aware of how his ideas merged with the ethics of Pythagoreanism, and he interspersed his medical advice with poetic renditions of George Cheyne's principles and playful allusions to Erasmus Darwin's Pythagorean edict that man 'Should eye with tenderness all living forms,/ His brother-emmets,* and his sister-worms'.[32]

Johnson was a follower of William Cullen and he frequently warned that many disorders suffered in Europe, especially in England, were caused by the 'irritating', over-stimulating qualities of meat. In India's warm climate in particular, he advised that 'vegetable food, generally speaking, is better', although having acclimatised he allowed that Europeans could safely transfer from 'the Hindoo model' to 'adopt the Mahomedan manners'. He was no fan of Hinduism, but he acknowledged that Hindu vegetarianism contained sound medical knowledge and (like Montesquieu) that it helped to 'diffuse a more humane disposition among the people'. Finally, in his *Economy of Health* (1837), he reluctantly declared that 'although Brahma and Pythagoras greatly overrated the salutary influence of their dietic systems on health, they were not totally in error.' Living on the 'slender and unirritating food of the Hindoo', he admitted, could be healthier for Europeans not just in India but even at home. Observations on the healthiness of Indian vegetarians reaffirmed the tradition of medical vegetarianism in India; but now it seems that medical vegetarianism in turn allowed Europeans to see Hinduism in a new and more positive light.[33]

European records were full of reports about how much Hindus were revolted by meat-eating Europeans. Well-worn yarns circulated about Indians pulling down their own houses if a European so much as

* Ants.

stepped on their porch.[34] Europeans had an incentive to exaggerate as they often wished to portray Hindus as irrational fanatics. But finding records *written by Hindus* expressing this abhorrence for early European settlers is a much harder task.

One such rare source is the twelve-volume personal diary written in Tamil between 1736 and 1761 by Ananda Ranga Pillai, the chief dubash (a personal assistant dealing with 'native' affairs) of the most powerful Frenchman ever to have ruled in India, the Governor of Pondicherry, Joseph François Dupleix. Stuffed with fascinating detail about historical and social events, religious practice and day-to-day life in this crucial period, this diary provides one of the best insights into early European colonialism written by an Indian.

As chief dubash, Ananda Ranga was locally known as the 'head of the Tamils' and he wielded exceptional powers.[35] It was Ananda Ranga who helped to reverse the Jesuit influence that had dominated earlier in the century. He was so successful that a Jesuit priest – vainly trying to convert him – complained that, thanks to his patronage, Hindus thrived while Christian converts were ailing.[36] Ananda Ranga was highly censorious of European misdemeanours, taking the rank-and-file to task for 'feeling the breasts of, and otherwise shaming and molesting women', raping them and killing their men.[37] He furnished Dupleix with horoscopes prepared by Brahmin astrologers,[38] and was honoured with being the only native allowed to wear shoes in front of the governor.[39] But there remained, nonetheless, a significant point of friction which both he and his European friends spent a great deal of energy trying to overcome – their dietary differences. As Ananda Ranga makes clear, it was a diplomatic *impasse*.

Being a Pillai – a subset of the south Indian Vellala/Idaiyan caste – Ananda Ranga was a staunch vegetarian, and like most of his compatriots he could not eat at table with his European or Muslim colleagues.[40] He watched others consume sumptuous feasts of mutton, pork and fowl, but he himself could not partake.[41] Instead, each day at lunchtime, he would retire to a specially made godown – or to his home when he had time – bathe himself according to Hindu ritual, and eat his home-cooked rice, dhal and ghee alone.[42] He noted that even prisoners had to be permitted to do so.[43] On a few special occasions he entertained Europeans, counting among his guests the Comte de Montmorency, a director of the East India Company. In such situations he would usually offer rice, dhal, fruit, sweets, milk or coffee,[44] but at least once he arranged for others to supply his guests lavishly with goat, deer, hare, partridge, poultry and fish. The implication was that they could eat what they wished – as long as his personal purity was not impugned.

Europeans were extremely solicitous that Ananda Ranga should return their visits, and took the extraordinary measure of having 'their food prepared by a Brâhman that I might partake of it'.[45] With so much focus on Ananda Ranga's need to avoid being defiled by Europeans, these experiments in reciprocal hospitality had mixed results. After cumulative tensions such as these, the governor Dupleix finally lost his temper and subjected Ananda Ranga – with whom he was usually very cordial – to a lengthy tirade of insults. As Ananda Ranga himself recalled, Dupleix shouted:

> Tamil food is not worth eating. They eat animal fodder. What else is their vegetables and curry stuffs? It is not food fit for men. Now a Muhammadan *pilaû* is something; but there is nothing like our food in the world, either for cooking or ingredients; and it is served at a well-laid table, where wives, husbands, relations and friends all sit round and eat at their leisure in social enjoyment. The Muhammadans and Tamils always want our food but we don't want theirs. We don't like their vegetable food . . . Tamils have long lived with us, still they say it is against their custom, and speak ill of us, comparing us, in their brutal ignorance, to Pariahs.[46]

Ananda Ranga recorded these comments in his usual careful manner, merely stating with a measure of cool diffidence that Dupleix 'thus depreciated our food, dwelling on its defects'. But he made no rejoinder to Dupleix, even in private, and nowhere does he explicitly criticise the European diet.[47] Ananda Ranga was not shy of criticising European behaviour when he did feel appalled; for example he was triumphant when Dupleix had an officer fined and imprisoned for committing the 'outrage' of shooting and eating a stray bullock.[48] While Ananda Ranga was vociferous in his censure of Christian blasphemy against Hinduism, his highest praises were reserved for the British Governor of Madras, Thomas Saunders, who in contrast to Dupleix 'used to eat Tamil food – rice, dhall, ghee, pepper, pepper water, pachadi, etc – and now he never comes to table', preferring to eat alone like a Hindu.[49]

It is ironic that Ananda Ranga's Hindu perspective on European behaviour in India does not endorse the commonly held view in contemporaneous English and French circles that Indians found the *feringhi* diet inherently abhorrent. Nevertheless it does illustrate a range of problems that Hindus experienced in their relations to Europeans, which played a significant part in the diplomacy of empire-building.

What happened when people tried to pick their way through this diplomatic minefield the other way round – when a vegetarian Hindu came to the land of roast beef? The first official visit from a high-caste Hindu to Britain appears to have taken place in 1781 when Humund Rao, a vegetarian Brahmin, came uninvited to England on behalf of Ragunath Rao, the deposed Peshwa (sovereign) of Maratha, to ask George III for military assistance. Accompanied by an English-speaking Parsi, Manuar Ratanji and his son Cursetji Manuar, Humund Rao was at first unceremoniously ignored by the East India Company. Rao and his cortège were sent to reside outside the city of London in Islington until they were asked to leave Britain without even being informed of the Company's decision.

By this time, the Whig politician Edmund Burke – self-appointed champion of victims of British colonialism who brought Warren Hastings to trial for corruption and despotism in Bengal – had caught wind of the situation. He was outraged: the Maratha Peshwa was one of Britain's most important allies, responsible for ceding to the East India Company highly valuable territories, and the fight to restore him was at a critical stage. Having failed to force the Company to treat them decently, Burke insisted, against entrenched opposition, that he should be allowed to entertain these Indian ambassadors at his house, and thus fulfil his perpetual preoccupation, to demonstrate to Indians 'the decency of the English character' and the 'National honor'. Burke managed to get King George to agree that the conduct of the Company directors had been 'shameful' and to authorise Burke to spend £200 on gifts for the agents.

Within a few days, Humund Rao had become a *cause célèbre* and was visited by a train of intellectuals and dignitaries such as the artist and critic Sir Joshua Reynolds. His visit became the topic of conversation and it was Burke's sensitive accommodation of his eating habits that impressed most of all. Burke's friend Mary Shackleton confirmed that Rao prepared his dinner on a flagstone in a greenhouse because 'he would eat in no house which was not his own'. He refused to eat 'animal food or wine, eating off the ground stripped from his waist up, and throwing away his dinner if any one came within a certain distance from him'.

When the time came for his departure, Burke wrote to the deposed Peshwa to testify that his ambassador had done nothing in England to jeopardise his purity. 'I endeavoured to make my place as convenient, as any of us are able to do,' Burke asserted. But 'for a person so faithfully strictly observant as he was, of all the rules and ceremonies of the religion, to which he was born, and to which he strictly conformed often at the manifest hazard of his Life', there were inevitable teething troubles. 'The sufferings this Gentleman underwent at first,' Burke apologetically assured him, 'was owing to the ignorance not to the unkindness of this Nation.'

He assured the Peshwa that now the British had the

> benefit from the instructions he has given us relative to your Ways of Living, that whenever it shall be thought necessary to send Gentûs of an high Cast to transact any business in this Kingdom, on giving proper Notice and on obtaining proper License from authority for their coming we shall be enabled to provide for them in such a manner as greatly to lessen the difficulties in our intercourse and to render [England] as tolerable as possible to them.[50]

Dietary diplomacy, Burke realised, was the oil of Anglo-Indian relations.

Although political interests were Burke's primary incentive, his willingness to accommodate Rao's vegetarianism was no doubt accentuated by the fact that he had an 'awe bordering on devotion' for Hinduism, particularly because they 'extend their benevolence to the whole animal creation'. In a letter to a friend, Burke expressly denied being a 'Pythagorean' vegetarian himself, but he sincerely wished to make the world 'think more favourably' of animals.[51] In the second half of the eighteenth century, enthusiasm about Indian religion – especially the Hindus' humane attitude to animals – reached such fever pitch it is difficult to discern what was mere diplomacy and what was genuine dedication to vegetarian principles.

TWENTY

John Zephaniah Holwell: Voltaire's Hindu Prophet

John Zephaniah Holwell was the archetypal nabob. He left England a surgeon's mate on an East Indiaman bound for Calcutta in 1732 and came back thirty years later a fantastically wealthy man.[1] He built himself an extravagant mansion in Steynton near Milford Haven, called it Castle Hall, and later retired to one of the finest residences in Bath. While the Bath house still stands overlooking a peaceful valley – a classic statement of Georgian pomp – Castle Hall testifies to his zealous Indophilia: it was said to be the first country house built in the 'Hindu style' and rumour has it that there was an Indian-influenced outbuilding – something like a pagoda – at the far end of the estate. Sadly, although his sweeping landscape garden is still extant, surrounded by forbidding twelve-foot walls and coastal cliffs, the house itself was demolished by the Ministry of Defence in the 1950s, and all that is left of the nabob's enigmatic outbuilding is a small pile of stones. Holwell may or may not have owned a private Hindu temple, but he was not ashamed to let everyone know that he prayed to Hindu deities and regarded Hinduism as the greatest religion on earth.

For the startled British public, these unpalatable facts were made worse by Holwell's otherwise conservative demeanour. An upstanding member of the establishment, he had long been regarded as a hero of British colonialism.[2] Born in Dublin in 1711, Holwell had trained for medicine in London before joining the East India Company. After a few years following armed trading ventures around the subcontinent, he was made assistant surgeon to Calcutta Hospital and from there worked his way up the administrative ranks of the Company. In 1736 he became an alderman, and in 1748 on a visit to England sent proposals for the reform of the Zamindar's court (which dealt with the native population) to the directors of the Company. They enthusiastically adopted his recommendations and Holwell was appointed to the twelfth high-est position in the governing council and perpetual Zamindar of Calcutta.

As Zamindar, which literally means 'landlord', Holwell was respon-sible for governing the native courts and collecting land taxes and trade tariffs which had supposedly been ceded to the Company by the Mughal ruler, the Nawab of Bengal, in 1698.[3] Holwell quickly realised that the Company could make far more money by taxing local popu-lations than it ever would on trade, and thus he laid the foundations for the transition of the East India Company from a commercial partner to a colonial power.[4] He promised to double the Company's annual income of 60,000 rupees, and after five years he had been so phenom-enally successful that the directors tripled his salary and made him seventh in the council, applauding the fact that he had 'greatly en-creased' their revenues, without, they assumed, 'imposing any new duties or oppressing the poor'. Indeed, Holwell was said to have allevi-ated 'Mughal tyranny' over Hindus; he commuted most corporal pun-ishments into fines and set in motion the Company's realignment of their court system in accordance with ancient Hindu customs. Holwell convinced himself that he could be a philanthropic Indophile at the same time as filling the coffers of the Company.[5]

But in June 1756 disaster struck when the new Nawab of Bengal, Siraj-ud-Daula, sent an army to lay siege to Calcutta after the British had illegally fortified their settlements and reneged on other agree-ments. Most of the pitifully unprepared British residents made a hap-hazard and ignominious retreat by ship down the Hooghly River. Holwell and a few soldiers were stranded in Fort William, which after a brief resistance led by Holwell, the Nawab promptly sacked and had the prisoners herded into a tiny airless dungeon that would become infamous as the Black Hole of Calcutta. According to Holwell's trau-matic report, 123 of them stifled to death, while the remaining 23 survived by drinking sweat from their own clothing and fighting for air at the only window. Later scholars have argued that the number of dead was no more than 69, and even that it never happened; but as far as the British were concerned, Holwell was a living martyr to the British imperial mission against Mughal despotism and his story became a justification for British territorial conquest in India. Within months the British had despatched a force led by General Robert Clive, which defeated the Nawab's army at Plassey and set the precedent for

Britain's future imperial expansion. Even in the twentieth century, the viceroy of India, Lord Curzon, totemised the Black Hole and hailed Holwell as a founding father of British India. In memory of those who died, or rather as a dark reminder of the British right to conquer, Holwell erected a monument which became the focus for rising tides of Indian national protests and was destroyed, rebuilt by Curzon and finally removed after Indian independence. In gratitude for his heroism he was offered the governorship of Bengal, which he apparently refused, but when Clive returned to England Holwell took the post of governor for a few months until he was nudged aside by a coterie of opponents who accused him of giving and taking bribes, having an affair with another man's wife and generally being wholly untrust-worthy.[6]

Having rebuffed the charges, he returned to Britain with his honour officially intact and immediately set about publishing an array of polit-ical and historical books on India. Holwell's variegated writings reveal that he had spent much of his spare time in India collecting sacred Hindu texts and having them explained to him by Hindu pandits. All his papers had been lost in the siege of Calcutta, but this was perhaps a blessing in disguise, for with the help of his memory and fertile imagination, Holwell set about reconstructing a Hinduism tailored to his tastes.

His initial publications – supposedly translations from scraps of the Hindu Shastah, or scripture – did not reveal the extent of his devotion for Hinduism. But in 1771, after much delay and a change of publisher, Holwell finally released the third part of his *Interesting Historical Events* under the extraordinary title 'A Dissertation on the Metempsychosis of the Bramins, or Transmigrations of the fallen Angelic Spirits; with a Defence of the original Scriptures of Bramah, and an occasional comparison between them and the Christian Doc-trines'. This was the first full-scale defence of Hinduism in Europe, and Holwell its pioneering evangelist. At the top of his agenda, needless to say, was the institution of a worldwide vegetarian reform.

Holwell's attempt to convince Europe that he had finally unlocked the secrets of ancient Hinduism would seem laughable if it were not the case that his work was among the most influential sources on Indian religion for decades. Monboddo drew his knowledge of Indian vegetarianism from Holwell; and Voltaire applauded him as the first to have 'revealed for us what has been hidden for so many centuries'.

The French Revolution sympathiser and unorthodox clergyman Joseph Priestley (1733–1804) – most famous for his discovery of oxygen – built his demonstration that Christianity was full of fictional doctrines on Holwell's translation of the Shastah in his *Comparison of the institutions of Moses with those of the Hindoos* (1799).[7] Through Voltaire and Priestley, Holwell provided an arsenal of information for the radical deists and their epoch-making assault on the Christian hegemon.

Like the seventeenth-century travellers, Holwell was struck by the similarity between Hindu doctrines and those of the Chinese, the Zoroastrians and the ancient Greeks, notably Pythagoras and Plato.[8] Holwell noticed, as Sir William Jones later proved, that some Sanskrit words bore a close resemblance to European equivalents and that Greek mythology and cosmogony were related to Sanskrit myths.[9] He discerned that Hindu scriptures told the story of a vegetarian Golden Age and three subsequent ages of decay and decline,[10] and he showed that they even contained the fundamental Christian tenets – the unity of the Godhead, the immortality of the soul, and a future state of rewards and punishments. To explain this mind-boggling coincidence, he jumped to the logical conclusion that Hinduism was the oldest religion, and the source of all the others.

Holwell allowed that Moses' revelation was genuine, but he stressed that it had occurred at a much later date than the scriptures of the prophet Bramah.[11] Indeed, Moses was a reincarnation of the prophet Bramah, and Jesus Christ, according to Holwell's audacious interpretation of world religion, was an avatar of the Hindu god Birmah who had incarnated in various forms to remind man of his obligations at various points in human history.[12] The warlike archangel Michael was in fact the destroyer god Siva, and Gabriel was the benevolent Vishnu. These three divine beings, created by one supreme God, were the original trinity – of which the Christian Trinity was an idolatrous corruption.

Quirky though this may seem, Holwell's decision to credit Hindu scriptures over Christianity was based on his reasonable supposition that, as they contained many of the same doctrines as the Bible and yet pre-dated it by hundreds of years (he credulously dated the Shastah back to 3100 BC), they had to be the original revelation from God. Gazing into the vast, unknown abyss of global history, Holwell found he could no longer believe that Christianity had a monopoly over truth. That all other world religions seemed also to bear otherwise inexplicable resemblance to Hindu doctrines confirmed to him that they too were derived from the ancient Indian revelation delivered to the prophet Bramah.

In addition to the doctrine of reincarnation – which he found replicated in faiths all over the world – Holwell was fascinated to discover that Hindus believed the story told in various Sanskrit texts that the demons (*asuras*) rebelled in heaven and were cast down to hell by the gods (*devas*). This struck him as undeniably similar to the Greek and Christian myth of the war in heaven and the fall of the angels. He concluded that God created the world as a place of punishment and purgation for Moisasoor (Maha-asura, Great-demon) – or Lucifer as he was known in Christendom – and his rebel angels, or Debtah (*deva*). Each spirit was imprisoned in the body of an animal – the worst into carnivores, the best into herbivores – and were forced to reincarnate eighty-eight times, ending up in the divine form of the *Ghoij*, or cow, before finally passing into *Mhurd* (man). If, in this main phase of trial and probation, the spirit showed itself to be truly repentant for its primeval sin of rebellion, it would pass up the ladder of fifteen planets, or Boboons (Sanskrit, *bhavana*), to be purified before finally returning to heaven.[13] Spirits that sinned in their lives as humans would be plunged into the hellish *Onderah* and begin the whole cycle again.

Having established the identical nature of human and animal souls, Holwell felt that it was clear that the consumption of meat was an unnatural sin. How could we justify murdering animals when they were animated with exactly the same sort of soul as our own, and with whom we had once joined in sinful rebellion? 'The mortal forms wherewith I shall encompass the delinquent Debtah are the work of my hand,' God declared in Brahmah's scripture, 'they shall not be destroyed.' The delinquent Debtah, it instructed, 'shall not eat of the Ghoij, nor of the flesh of any of the mortal bodies . . . whether it creepeth on Murto [earth], or swimmeth in Jhoale [water], or flyeth in Oustmaan [the air], for their food shall be the milk of the Ghoij, and the fruits of Murto'.

The sin of meat-eating, Holwell explained, had been introduced on earth by the arch-demon Moisasoor who tricked the early priests into believing that sacrificing an animal shortened its punishment and sent it up a rung in the chain of reincarnations.[14] Any human who ate flesh was condemned to start the cycle of punishment all over again.

Meat-eating bred further violence and curtailed human life by causing disease.[15] In this way Moisasoor kept his kingdom on earth well populated, while completely cutting off the flow of purified spirits returning to God. Alcohol, too, was a principal weapon in the devil's arsenal, for it induced such inebriation that humans wilfully murdered their fellow creatures. 'To give the devil his due,' wrote Holwell with his characteristic alacrity of phrase, 'it must in justice be acknowledged, that the introduction of these two first-rate vices was a master-piece of politics.'[16]

Having set out the theological background, Holwell launched into a full-scale vegetarian diatribe that posited the most extreme of animal rights philosophies. He gave an Indian gloss to arguments from the Western vegetarian tradition, pointing out that eating meat was 'in opposition to the natural and obvious construction of the mouth and digestive faculties of Mhurd'. Trained in medicine in the era of George Cheyne and once treated in Leiden by Hermann Boerhaave, Holwell had also been impressed by the Indian prescription of vegetable diets to prepare patients for smallpox inoculation – a procedure he described in 1767 which eventually became the standard practice in Europe.[17] He pointed out that Hinduism endorsed all the sanitary and agronomic arguments for vegetarianism and cow protection, for the cow not only yielded 'delectable food, but was otherways essentially serviceable in the cultivation of their lands; on which depended their vegetable subsistence'. But contrary to the claim of commentators since Bernier, Holwell insisted that these utilitarian arguments were secondary to the original religious reasons.

The theological question about the status of animals, he pointed out, was still not resolved in Western philosophy, though some, such as Richard Dean, had given it their best shot by arguing that animals had souls and could get to heaven. Holwell felt that he had come up with the conclusive answer to Descartes' troubling query about the misery animals experienced on earth: they were undergoing punishment for their primeval sin.[18] However, the Bible was wrong to endorse man's 'use and abuse' of the creatures, for as Hinduism showed 'the world was made for the fly, as much as for him'.

Europeans did not just study Hinduism as a means of extending their power over Hindu subjects. As Edward Said pointed out, early Orientalists were often searching for solutions to their own theological problems.[19] Ever since the Renaissance, theologians had been obsessed with the origins of mankind and civilisation, and ancient Hinduism now presented a raft of possible answers. Although Holwell's belief that humans were animated by the souls of the fallen angels seemed bizarre to many, he felt that it solved a number of inconsistencies in Christianity, such as the 'horrid incestuous union' of Adam and Eve's children.

The extent to which Holwell's research into Hinduism was motivated by a sincere desire to resolve unsettled questions in Western religious debate is illustrated by his interest in the Christian Reincarnationists.[20] Holwell engaged with this long tradition of unorthodox theologians and considered that they were all groping towards the original truth which he had finally uncovered in Hinduism.

Holwell had read the works of the printer Jacob Ilive (1705–63), famously imprisoned in the 1750s for writing 'a most blasphemous book', who had argued that human souls (not those of animals) were the spirits of the rebel angels which were condemned to reincarnate on earth until they had worked off their sins and rose to a heavenly planet.[21] Holwell was also inspired by the highly unorthodox Anglican cleric, Capel Berrow (1715–82), who had extended Ilive's logic to include animals by fusing Hinduism with the beliefs of Henry More, Joseph Glanvill, the seventeenth-century Origenists and kabbalists, the *Turkish Spy* and 'the very sensible and acute Dr *Cheyne*'. Berrow had explained that since God would not let 'either *sentient*, or *intelligent* beings, suffer, merely for suffering sake', all souls on earth must be the spirits who rebelled with the apostate angels and were now reincarnating from the level of microbes up to humans on their long journey back to heaven. Though not an advocate of vegetarianism, Berrow was appalled by unnecessary cruelty to animals: 'What exquisite, what affecting tortures do many of these animals endure,' he lamented, 'from some merciless, callous-hearted monster of a master!'[22]

Holwell also learned a great deal from Cheyne's friend, the Chevalier Andrew Michael Ramsay,[23] who had argued that the Greeks, Persians and Chaldaeans all derived their philosophies from the Brahmins and that the souls of the rebellious angels were imprisoned in animals on earth.[24] Ramsay dismissed reincarnation as a pagan corruption of the true doctrine of pre-existence,[25] but his recognition that it existed in an astonishing number of ancient religions nevertheless provided Holwell with an excuse for arguing that it was a true doctrine that Christianity alone had forgotten.

More recently, the Jesuit Father Guillaume Hyacinthe Bougeant had been imprisoned for jocularly suggesting that animals (not humans) were animated by the souls of the fallen angels which meant that even though they deserved their suffering, animal souls were 'more perfect than ours'. He also added provocatively that, though illegal, it was reasonable to believe that they reincarnated according to the Pythagorean and Indian system. (As Voltaire later said, Bougeant had inadvertently uncovered 'an article of the faith of the most ancient oriental priests'.) The rector of Wath in Yorkshire, John Hildrop, had modified Bougeant's theories by arguing that animal souls had only been condemned to suffer because of the Fall of man, and therefore ought to be 'the unhappy Objects of our Care and Compassion'.[26]

Holwell was keen on all these writers – especially the *Turkish Spy* – but with recourse to genuine Hindu doctrines he showed how their theodicies (contrary to most of their own conclusions) meant that it was a sin to kill animals. Holwell thus used the venerable antiquity of Hinduism to resolve a long-standing Christian debate, and simultaneously showed how easy it was to reconcile the two religions.

The Christian and kabbalist Reincarnationists no doubt coloured his interpretation of Hindu doctrines, but Holwell was most unusual in the extent to which he gave priority to Hinduism. His eighty-eight reincarnations obviously came from Hinduism, as did the idea that cow killing was punished by being pushed back to the beginning of the cycle. His idea that envy and jealousy precipitated Moisasoor's original fall accords with Christianity, but Holwell may equally have derived this from Hindu scriptures which blame it on pride and anger. Even Holwell's conflation of the three types of being – *devas, asuras* and humans – is justified by a Hindu myth in which all three fall from heaven together. In Hinduism, too, the demons gradually regain their former influence, just as Holwell's Debtah do. Holwell's notion of the world being overburdened by sinners – unable to escape from *samsara* (the cycle of reincarnations) because of the predominance of vice – also has an equivalent in classical Hinduism. The Hindu and Christian myths really are so similar that – as the Indologist Wendy Doniger has shown – some Indians who heard about the Christian version fused it with their own beliefs about the Fall. Holwell's idea that infections were spread by microscopic organisms inhabited by the worst of the fallen spirits – first hinted at in his medical *Account of the Small Pox* (1767) – also seems to be derived from the classical Jaina belief that souls that have committed extreme crimes in previous lives are incarnated into airborne microscopic *nigoda,* which parasitically colonise other beings. Just as Holwell said, certain foods are abstained from because they contain high concentrations of *nigoda.* Even Holwell's point that wine induces men to commit violence without hesitation occurs in Sanskrit texts.[27]

The similarities between Western and Indian traditions – on any explanation of which scholars still disagree – made Holwell conclude that Hinduism must have been based on a true revelation from God. His recognition that modern Hinduism had been altered since the original writing of the scriptures also meant that he felt able to determine better than Hindus themselves what the original revelation to Bramah contained. Holwell made a brilliant and in many respects unique fusion of Christianity and Hinduism; cracks and seams of instability were cemented over by his imagination and commitment to systematising a workable eschatology, and with the help of his affable character, colourful rhetoric and integral humanity, he pushed his new system into the consciousness of Europe.

Holwell's early writings on the Hindu scriptures – before he plainly announced that he was a vegetarian proselyte – received more attention than any previous Indological work. Magazines and pamphlets ran extracts and reviews and his work was immediately translated into German and French.[28] The *Gentleman's Magazine* reproduced long excerpts from his 'translation' of the Shastah, and considered that it 'abounds with curious particulars, and is well worthy the attention of learning and curiosity'.[29] In 1770, when Denis Diderot and the anti-clerical Abbé Guillaume-Thomas Raynal (1713–96) published their six-volume critique of European imperialism – which went through more than thirty editions before 1789, despite being banned – they copied out Holwell's account and agreed that the Hindus' 'sublime morality, deep philosophy, and refined policy' had been successful in inducing sobriety and strict laws against 'the effusion of blood'.[30] Johann Rudolph Sinner, who wrote one of the most serious studies of metempsychosis in the eighteenth century, applauded Holwell for having 'vindicated the Brahmans of the charge of idolatry, of polytheism, and of the absurd doctrines which have been imputed to them up to today'. As late as 1826 the Professor of History at the University of Heidelberg, Friedrich Schlosser (1776–1861), affirmed that 'The best essay on the religion of Brahma is to be found in Holwell's work.' Holwell had succeeded in making Hinduism a legitimate – even essential – study for Christian intellectuals.[31]

To those less keen on acrediting pagan Indians with a philosophy comparable to any in Europe, Holwell's enthusiastic vindication appeared preposterous. William Julius Mickle, a careful student of Indian culture, saw in Holwell's endorsement of Hinduism a hurdle in the way of British imperialism, and took the view that India was desperately in need of illumination by the rational and democratic forces of European culture. Hindu vegetarianism, with its stupid Pythagorean philosophy, was, he thought, the ultimate demonstration of benighted Indian ignorance. If it was damnable to eat animals, as Holwell had claimed, then even the most assiduous Brahmin would end up in hell for accidentally killing 'innumerable living creatures' while drinking a glass of water or eating a salad.[32]

The Conservative *Critical Review*, meanwhile, accused Holwell of being a renegade, rebuffed his critique of colonialism and slandered his personal character – and that was only after he published the first two parts of *Interesting Historical Events*, which only hinted at his enthusiasm for Hinduism. Instead of doubting the authenticity of Holwell's 'Shaster', they argued that it confirmed that Hinduism was a recent 'compound of Manicheism, vitiated Christianity, pagan idolatry, superstitious rites, and unintelligible jargon'.[33]

When Holwell finally unveiled, in his third volume, the extent of his conversion to Hinduism, he was met with an embarrassed silence. Here was a man who had been governor of the country's most prestigious colonial outpost. He was a respected public figure, a magistrate in Wales, and even after his death officially remembered as one 'in whom brilliancy of talents, benignity of spirit, social vivacity, and suavity of manners were so united as to render him the most amiable of men'. His portrait by Sir Joshua Reynolds, in full British uniform, hung in the Company's halls. And now, to the dismay of all conservative Christians, he had thrown the fundamentals of his religion to the wind, and clung to the monstrously sensual pillars of pagan India. Indians were supposed to be subordinate – raw material waiting to be utilised – not the inheritors of the pristine word of God. Vegetarianism, in particular, was a direct blow to the British constitution. In the character of John Bull, beef-eating had become the insignia of British national pride – by the time of the Napoleonic Wars the French nickname for British forces had become 'rosbifs' – and here was Holwell calling the cow a sacred animal, the killing of which carried a cosmic punishment!

In contrast to the chorus of reviews that greeted his early scholarly works, reviewers now looked the other way: the sooner this was hushed up the better. Even his obituarist in the *Gentleman's Magazine*, who dug up his most obscure paper on a new species of oak tree, quietly passed over *Interesting Historical Events* part three, and politely excused his unfortunate belief in reincarnation by mourning that 'Mr H. being then 77, was advancing fast into dotage, or the second childhood.' Apart from getting Holwell's age wrong by two years, this deliberately omitted the fact that by the time of his death Holwell had been propounding the same doctrines for at least twenty-seven years, since the age of sixty.[34] This pointed silence was replicated by subsequent biographical notices. The nineteenth-century nostalgic historian of British India, H. E. Busteed, who communicated with Holwell's grandson and inheritor of his lost papers, cut his account of Holwell short, avoiding the later developments. Until the most recent edition, the *Dictionary of National Biography* recounted uncritically Holwell's version of the Black Hole saga but said nothing about his conversion to Hindu vegetarianism.[35]

It took the *Monthly Review* in 1771 to state what the whole of decent society must have been thinking: that Holwell's latest work was akin to the mystic visions of the Behmenists.[36] This evident disapproval, however, did not stop Holwell reissuing his work in more editions. Nor did it stop him writing two more books which, if anything, were more outlandish than before. The hitherto unattributed *Primitive Religion Elucidated, and Restored . . . By a Divine, of No Church* (1776) was supposedly penned by a member of the public who approved of Holwell's doctrines, but was certainly by Holwell himself, and although he laconically confessed his authorship later on, no one blew his cover. *Primitive Religion* propounded Hindu doctrines, but under the cover of palatably unaffiliated deism. Holwell's final book, the *Dissertation on the Origin, Nature, and Pursuits of Intelligent Beings* (1786), used the same trick. By this time, Holwell no longer believed in active divine Providence, and he argued that it was blasphemous to think that atrocities such as imperialist massacres happened with God's direct consent. Instead, he reverted to the ancient idea of a 'kind of *sympathetic movement*' – espoused by Henry More, Thomas Tryon and the *Turkish Spy* – which automatically forced each spirit to enter the appropriate species of animal according to its deserts.[37] 'Extravagant as the foregoing doctrine may appear to some,' concluded Holwell at the twilight of his public life,

> Forty years meditation, study and reasoning, have brought me a full conviction, that there is no other *hypothesis* which can, consistent with piety, reason or philosophy, reconcile the *creation* of that miserable being *Man*, with the wisdom, justice, or benign attributes of God; or afford any probable cause, why? and to what end or purpose, the material universe was created and constructed.[38]

By now, Holwell's incessant ranting had become impossible to ignore. The assiduous anti-Indophile William Julius Mickle quickly identified Holwell as the author of this last work, and immediately denounced the sly attempt to disguise as rational deductions the 'transmigration of souls, and the other principles of the Gentoo religion'. The public had borne with Holwell's absurdities long enough; it was time to drop the hushed respect and tell Holwell that his work was 'risible entertainment':

> When an author narrates the religious madness and absurdities of a country in which he has travelled, it is proper and fair. But when he becomes a zealous convert to, and enthusiast in such inconsistent and unphilosophical doctrines as Mr H. ascribes to his favourite Gentoos, we are lost in surprize at the weakness of human nature; and cannot refrain the wish, that our eastern travellers would employ themselves better than in obtruding on their native country, as the most sacred and sublime truths, the wild dreams and incoherent crudities of Indian superstition and contemptible folly.[39]

Mickle was no doubt as concerned by the likes of Alexander Dow, who had slowly lost his grip on Christian orthodoxy as he delved into the 'Platonic' splendour of Hinduism;[40] or Colonel Antoine Polier who had gone native in 1758, married Indian women, and ended up promising a raja that he would never bind his copy of the Vedas in animal skins;[41] or even Anquetil Duperron who went to India in 1754 and became a disciple of 'the sages of Asia' when he found that the Upanishads expressed the same universal religion as Christianity and on his return to France joined the vegetarian community of Antoine Gleïzes.[42] But Mickle's desperate backlash would not stem the tide. Later there would be Major General Charles 'Hindoo' Stuart (1757–1828), a Bengal officer who offered puja to idols and was, in the words of one shocked onlooker, 'an Englishman, born and educated in a Christian land, who was become the wretched and degraded partaker in this heathen worship'. William Fraser, assistant to the Resident in Delhi (1806–11) who wore Indian clothes, had Indian mistresses and lived on the vegetarian food of his hosts. And Thomas Medwin (1788–1869), whose literary representation of a nabob seemed more than a little autobiographical, as 'a person neither English nor Indian, Christian nor Hindu. In diet he was a rigid disciple of Brama' and looked 'upon the slaughter of a cow as only next to the murder of a human being.'[43] Over the coming years more and more Christians came back from their travels with an enthusiasm for Hinduism which they unleashed on the European public.

Voltaire – or François-Marie Arouet (1694–1778) – was not so daunted by Holwell's Indophilia. When Holwell's translation of the Shastah came out, Voltaire had already fled from Paris, Prussia and Geneva to avoid persecution for his aggressive promotion of religious tolerance and deism, and had taken refuge on his private estate which straddled the French and Swiss border in order to escape the police of both countries. Holwell's dating of the Shastah before the Bible provided fuel to the fire of Voltaire's crusade against Christianity, and vegetarianism was a particularly powerful perspective from which he could critique the cruelty innate in European culture.

Voltaire had already presented the ancient Brahmins in his *Essai sur les Moeurs* (1756) as exemplars of religious tolerance and he highlighted the pure monotheism that underlay their polytheistic customs. Like Montesquieu, Voltaire argued that the doctrine of metempsychosis made the Hindus 'lovers and arbiters of peace' and thus had been the only successful means of suppressing viciousness and instilling instead 'a horror at shedding blood, constant charity towards human beings and animals'. With his irrepressible irony he added that 'Their religion and the temperature of their climate made these peoples entirely resemble those peaceful animals whom we bring up in our sheep pens and our dove cotes for the purpose of cutting their throats.'[44] Their harmlessness accentuated the savageness of European culture: 'The Indian books announce only peace and gentleness; they forbid the killing of animals: the Hebrew books speak only of killing, of the massacre of men and beasts; everything is slaughtered in the name of the Lord; it is quite another order of things.'

In his entry under 'Viande' in the famous Dictionnaire Philosophique (1764), Voltaire had extolled the Brahmins – so excessively it is difficult to imagine that he was being entirely sincere – alongside the ancient Greek philosophers, the monks of La Trappe and the medical vegetarian Philippe Hecquet. These enlightened advocates, he announced, had shown that vegetarians were 'notoriously the most free from disease and most long-lived of their countrymen'. In his entry on 'Animals' he launched into a sharp anti-Cartesian tirade:

> There are barbarians who seize this dog, who so prodigiously surpasses man in friendship, and nail him down to a table, and dissect him alive to show you the mezaraic veins. You discover in him all the same organs of feeling which are in you. Answer me, mechanist; has Nature arranged all these springs of feeling in this animal, so that it does not feel? Has it nerves in order to be insensible? Do not even imply this impertinent contradiction in nature.

In subsequent publications Voltaire showed how the Hindu doctrines endorsed his own enlightened view of animals.[45] Holwell's Hindu Shastah exonerated everything he had said, and thus Voltaire hailed Holwell as a new Pythagoras and 'the only European who has understood the beliefs of the Brahmins'.[46] Despite his doubts that everything in the Shastah was authentic, Voltaire championed Holwell in a mass of essays on a range of different subjects and rewrote whole chunks of his own works to incorporate Holwell's new information. In later editions of the Essai sur les Moeurs he thanked Holwell for his thirty-year-long selfless quest for knowledge (this compliment, too, was probably tongue-in-cheek), and portrayed the original Brahmins as the ideal king-priests presiding over a pure deistic religion. The fact that the modern Brahmins also held preposterous superstitions showed how religions corrupted over time and that Christianity too was just as full of fictions as any other. With stunning audacity, Voltaire argued that the whole of Christianity was based on the Brahmins' doctrine of the fall of the angels. 'Our religion was hidden deep in India,' he asserted, and it 'incontestably comes to us from the Brahmans'. In ironic contrast to Holwell, of course, Voltaire did not think the similarities corroborated each other; both were mythologies invented by avaricious priests to maintain their power over the people. Joseph Priestley developed this argument in his extremely provocative assault on Christian orthodoxy. Even though Holwell was an enthusiastic devotee of Hinduism himself, his comparative approach to demonstrating that the Bible was ahistoric helped to create the Enlightened, liberal secular outlook in modern society.

As a towering figure in the Enlightenment of European culture, Voltaire plugged Hinduism into the mainstream of intellectual debate and he rightly congratulated himself for spreading Holwell's account of Indian scriptures to the whole of literate Europe. His comments on vegetarianism greatly increased the attention given to the subject in European intellectual circles inspiring numerous copycat works, and strengthening the bond between radical liberal thinking and vegetarianism.[47]

The points that he made in his philosophical and critical works he reintroduced in his fictional *contes* with an even freer pen. In a farcical scene in *The Princess of Babylon* (1768), a phoenix explains to the eponymous princess that his fellow animals no longer speak to humans because 'men have accustomed themselves to eat us' and declares uncompromisingly that 'Men who are fed with carnivorous aliments, and drenched with spirituous liquors, have a sharp, acrid blood, which turns their brains a hundred different ways. Their chief rage is a fury to spill their brother's blood.'[48] But Voltaire also attempted to present Hindu vegetarianism in a reasonable, utilitarian light. Focusing on the anatomical similarity between man and beasts, the phoenix concludes his teaching with a delectable meal lavishly consisting of 'a hundred delicious foods, among which was seen no disguised corpse. The feast was of rice, of sago, of semolina, of vermicelli, of maccaroni, of omelets, of eggs in milk, of cream-cheese, of pastries of every kind, of vegetables, of fruits.' Voltaire's Indophilia added new spice to the fashionable appetite for simple vegetarian food which had just been launched by his intellectual rival, Jean-Jacques Rousseau.

In his *Lettres d'Amabed à Shastasid* (1769) Voltaire developed the mock-travel genre which turned the tables on the ethnocentricity of European travel-writing. Amabed, a young Hindu traveller to England, expresses his shock at the contrast of civility and barbarity even in this 'citadel of faith':

> The dining-hall was clean, grand, and tidy . . . gaiety and wit animated the guests; but in the kitchens blood and grease were flowing. Skins of quadrupeds, feathers of birds and their entrails piled up pell-mell, oppressing the heart, and spreading contagion.

In the fictional setting, Voltaire let the superstition of metempsychosis take a back seat and instead emphasised that meat-eating was at odds with refined manners and inflamed people with cruelty.[49] Through Voltaire, Holwell provided a bridge between the seventeenth-century deists' use of Hinduism and the later eighteenth-century radicals who embraced India as an alternative to the brutal oppression they saw in European culture. With the blood-abhorring Hindus as his foot-soldiers, Voltaire helped to engineer the – albeit hypothetical and impossible – bloodless revolution.

Sir William Jones (1746–94) is remembered as the greatest pioneer of Orientalism in the eighteenth century. Under his aegis the Asiatic Society of Bengal was founded and for the first time translations of whole Sanskrit texts were made available to the stunned admiration of European audiences. It would be normal to contrast Jones' diligent mastery of Indian languages and his careful historical methodology with the half-crazed fulminations of John Zephaniah Holwell – and before Jones travelled to India he had the opportunity to make that distinction himself. Acting as attorney in the Pembrokeshire courts in 1780 he successfully defended a man accused by Holwell of panic-mongering, and Jones took the opportunity to ridicule Holwell as a nabob-magistrate attempting 'to import the Indian laws into England, by imprisoning and indicting an honest man'. Vegetarianism must have seemed an abomination to Jones; he wrote to his friend Viscount Althorp in a vein typical of the bloodthirsty English gentleman about his longing to go stag-hunting, and he fantasised that 'I should prefer the more violent sport of the Asiaticks, who enclose a whole district with toils, and then attack the tigers and leopards with javelins.'[50] When Jones finally arrived in India, however, it was not the hunting that impressed him, but the doctrine of *ahimsa*.

In 1783 Jones was knighted and sent out to Bengal as a judge of the Supreme Court, and he immediately set about translating *The Laws of Manu* or, as he called it, the *Institutes of Hindu Law*. It is often pointed out that the primary motive of this endeavour was the establishment of a legal framework for effectively governing the Hindus. But Jones' exploration of Indian culture also had other, less sinister, aims. When Jones finally managed to get a Hindu to teach him Sanskrit – having worked his way around the objection that he was an untouchable *feringhi* (foreigner) – he was delighted by what he found. Casting himself as the new Pythagoras, he gloated that he understood Sanskrit and thus had 'an advantage, which neither Pythagoras nor Solon possessed, though they must ardently have wished it'. 'Nor is it possible to read the *Védánta*,' he announced, 'without believing, that Pythagoras and Plato derived their sublime theories from the same fountain with the sages of India.' Even Christianity, he acknowledged, bore great resemblance to Hinduism: 'The Hindus,' he wrote, 'would have less difficulty in admitting the Thirty-Nine articles; because if those articles were written in Sanscrit, they might pass well enough for the composition of a Brahman.'[51]

However, in stark contrast to – and conservative reaction against – the likes of Holwell, Jones was absolutely committed to the authenticity of the Bible and he could not concede that Sanskrit scriptures pre-dated it. Instead, he insisted that the Hindu scriptures were much younger than Holwell had claimed, and he spent his entire career constructing the case that the similarities between Indian, Greek and Hebrew cultures could all be traced back to one antecedent common source. In his famous anniversary lectures to the Asiatic Society, he gradually revealed that this original source was the settlement in Iran of Noah and his three sons. The descendants of Noah's son Ham colonised India, Italy and Greece, and they carried their particular culture with them. Pythagoras and Plato might have learned certain doctrines from the Hindus at a much later date, but well before that direct contact they already shared a common Noachic heritage. Jones picked out episodes in the Hindu scriptures and twisted them to corroborate the Bible's history – and even its dating – of the universal Flood, the peopling of the earth and the tower of Babel. In this stubborn adherence to the presumptions of his own culture – no matter how seemingly objective the arguments he adduced to prove it – he can hardly be seen as exhibiting a more advanced methodology than Holwell's. Holwell was ridiculed by his contemporaries principally because he admitted what most others would not: that the Bible was younger than Indian scriptures and therefore if any of their doctrines were true, the Indians had had the true religion first.

Jones' proposition that Indian and Greek culture were linked by a common origin was superior to (though not exclusive of) the crude stories about Pythagoras' travels, and he thus brilliantly constructed the basis for the modern secular understanding of the Indo-European language group. But when people laud Jones for his spectacularly modern achievements, they often do not realise that he was operating within an ancient model of biblical exegesis. In tracing similarities between diverse cultures back to Noah, Jones was self-consciously extending the work of Sir Isaac Newton's *Chronology of Ancient Kingdoms Amended* (1727). However, even though Jones fixedly prioritised the Bible, whether he liked it or not, his reconstruction of the ur-religion was strongly influenced – just like Newton's – by the Indian doctrine of *ahimsa*.

The *Laws of Manu* in Jones' 1794 translation stated that 'Fleshmeat cannot be procured without injury to animals, and the slaughter of animals obstructs the path to beatitude; from fleshmeat, therefore, let man abstain.' In response to such passages (and despite others that enjoin ritual animal sacrifice), Jones acknowledged in his Preface that 'a spirit of sublime devotion, of benevolence to mankind, and of amiable tenderness to all sentient creatures, pervades the whole work.'[52]

Jones even considered the doctrine of metempsychosis more 'benevolent' than the Christian doctrine of eternal damnation. 'I am no Hindu,' he insisted to his friend and former pupil, the 2nd Earl Spencer, 'but I hold the doctrine of the Hindus concerning a future state to be incomparably more rational, more pious, and more likely to deter men from vice, than the horrid opinions inculcated by Christians on punishments *without end*.' Even though Jones turned away from reincarnation, he brought Hinduism into theological debate on a serious level with Christianity. Just as he manipulated Indian scriptures to fit in with his idea of the Noachic origin of the world, so when his interest lay in the other direction, he twisted the Bible's statement about 'eternal' punishment into meaning '*of a long but limited duration*'.[53]

Just like Newton, Jones claimed that the Indian doctrine of non-violence to animals had its roots in the original laws of Noah. In 1787 he told Earl Spencer that 'kindness to all living creatures' was 'one great article of the primitive religion delivered by God to man'. Jones became so convinced of the fundamental importance of this doctrine that he took up the protection of animals as one of his pet subjects. He now upbraided Earl Spencer for enjoying hunting and quoted his translation of his favourite couplet from Firdausi: 'Ah! spare yon emmet, rich in hoarded grain:/ He lives with pleasure, and he dies with pain.' Making a dramatic break with his English hunting past, he claimed that 'I cannot reconcile to my notions of humanity the idea of making *innocent* beasts miserable and mangling *harmless* birds. I should be laughed at in many companies for this sentiment.' Yet far from reserving such 'laughable' statements to private correspondence, in his Tenth Anniversary Discourse to the Asiatic Society (1793) he pointed the same accusing finger at naturalists who shoot animals in order to study them:

> I never could learn by what right, nor conceive with what feelings, a naturalist can occasion the misery of an innocent bird and leave its young, perhaps, to perish in a cold nest, because it has gay plumage . . . or deprive even a butterfly of its natural enjoyments, because it has the misfortune to be rare or beautiful.

The mandate of the Asiatic Society was to study both man and nature in the region, but Jones made one extraordinary caveat on the extension of research into India's fauna: 'though rare animals may be found in all Asia, yet I can only recommend an examination of them with this condition, that they be left, as much as possible, in a state of natural freedom, or made as happy as possible, if it be necessary to keep them confined.'[54] India had turned Jones into a prototype of the animal welfare campaigner.

On his own idyllic Indian estate, Jones forbade the killing of animals for the sake of science, and he even extended kindness to his domestic animals including a tame tiger cub. He spoke of his home in Krishnagar as 'my Indian Arcadia', reminiscent of 'what the poets tell us of the golden age; for, not to mention our flocks and herds that eat bread out of our hands, you might see a kid and a tiger playing together'.[55] In the *Laws of Manu*, Jones had found the ancient medical injunctions for abstinence: 'The man, who forsakes not the law, and eats not fleshmeat, like a bloodthirsty demon, shall attain good will in this world, and shall not be afflicted with maladies.'[56] Jones – afflicted with 'bad digestion' in India – followed the concordant advice of the tropical medics by observing 'extreme temperance', eating a 'light and sparing' diet rich in home-grown vegetables and citrus juice, and avoiding 'solid food' (i.e. flesh-meat).[57] To all intents and purposes, this one-time bloodthirsty English huntsman had been transformed into a proponent of the Hindu doctrine of *ahimsa*.

As Professor Nigel Leask explored in his *Anxieties of Empire*, the colonialist tendency to 'reverse acculturation' (i.e. 'going native') could be used as a way of demonstrating national splendour, so long as the Self was not threatened by absorption by the Other. Jones did not go as far as Holwell; rather, he clung even more tenaciously to the fundamentals of biblical doctrine. But the effects of reverse acculturation worked on a spectrum, and Hinduism not only transformed Jones himself, it altered his whole interpretation of the original religion to which he clung.[58] Holwell's conversion was definitely beyond the pale, but in the era of early colonialism even the most revered figures shifted within received traditions of European doctrinal, philosophical, social and political anthropocentrism towards the Indian philosophy of harmlessness. While Europe was spreading its wave of technological and mercantile power on the subcontinent, an undertow of cultural influence was flowing back to the European heartland and threatening to overturn its cherished predatory principles.

TWENTY-ONE

The Cry of Nature:
Killing in the Name of Animal Rights
in the French Revolution

In 1782 John Oswald, the son of an Edinburgh goldsmith, arrived in Bombay as an officer in the Black Watch. His regiment was to fight Britain's foes – Hyder Ali, the ruler of Mysore, and his son Tipu Sultan who had made a hostile alliance with the French. Oswald was an unruly young man in his early twenties and he had, as legend has it, nearly killed his commanding officer in a duel on the journey out. After only a few months in active service, his rebelliousness crystallised into ideological dissent. Witnessing massacre and rape perpetrated by the avaricious British, he perceived that the Indians were exploited by the same imperial machine as the pre-Independence Americans had been, and as the British working masses still were.[1] The oppressed of the world, he concluded, must unite to throw off the tyrannous yoke. Oswald dissociated himself from his colonial masters, resigned his commission in the army and went on a walkabout among the Hindu populace.[2]

Having switched political allegiance, Oswald adopted the identity of his new associates: 'he imitated the Gentoos, abstained from animal food, and regularly performed the usual ablutions,' explained one contemporary. '[H]e lived a considerable time with some Brahmins, who turned his head,' wrote another. 'From that period he never tasted flesh meat, from what he called a principle of humanity.'[3] Oswald's sympathy with the political cause of the Indians merged into acceptance of their sympathy for all members of oppressed species.

After wandering among the holy men of India, Oswald made an epic journey through Persia and the territory of the Central Asian Kurds, all the way overland to Britain, where he soon appeared, in the words of one onlooker:

so changed by the manners and dress he assumed, as to be unknown to his friends. He became a convert so much to the Hindoo faith, that the ferocity of the young soldier of fortune sunk into the mild philosophic manners of the Hindoo Brachman. During his stay in England he uniformly abstained from eating animal food, that rather than pass through a *Butcher*'s Market, he would go any distance round about.[4]

Such eccentric figures were becoming familiar in Britain and critics immediately tried to dismiss him as a faint-hearted fool like Holwell, whose reason had clearly been addled in India. In an editorial note to a defence of meat-eating in Philip Doddridge's *Lectures on Pneumatology, Ethics, and Divinity*, the dissenting minister, Andrew Kippis, commented that 'Mr Holwell and Mr Oswald, both of whom have resided in the East-Indies, have embraced the principles of the Hindoos, and written against the use of animal food.'[5] The mention of this pair of cultural vagrants was bound to raise a titter among readers. When William Julius Mickle published his attack on Holwell and other converts to Hinduism in the *European Magazine* in 1787, he may have had his sights also set on Oswald, with whose employer in Grub Street, William Thomson, Mickle often worked. Within three years, the same magazine made a similar swipe directly against Oswald:

> The religious and philosophic opinions of this gentleman are said to be extremely singular. He adheres to the doctrines of the Hindoo system of worship, and turns with an abhorrence truly Braminical from every species of animal food. To a gentleman who urged him to assign reasons for an aversion so singular, he replied, 'that he thought it cruel to deprive of life an innocent animal, and filthy to feed upon a corpse.'[6]

It was disingenuous of the *European Magazine* to claim that Oswald had converted to 'the Hindoo system of worship', for everyone knew that despite his admiration for Hindu ethics, as the quotation from Oswald actually implies, and as one friend later clarified: 'He did not, however, enter into the whole theology of the Brahmins, for he was a professed atheist and denied the Metempsychosis.'[7] For Oswald, Hinduism embodied a natural law of humanity to which the religious doctrines were merely auxiliary. The claim that he had followed in Holwell's footsteps was an attempt to push Oswald further beyond the pale than he had really gone. Critics wished to distort Oswald's statement in this way partly because they knew he represented a growing and threatening political voice in Britain. It was not vegetarianism *per se* that journals like the *European Magazine* had a problem with: the very same edition of the magazine gave a respectful account of the vegetarian advocate Lord Monboddo and a eulogistic interview with the late philanthropist John Howard, who lived so long and healthily because 'for many years he had not tasted animal food'; in other issues it praised the toast-eating teetotal asceticism of the highly esteemed atheist American revolutionary Thomas Hollis; gave a rave review of Saint-Pierre's fruitarian *Paul et Virginie*; and described the novel *Hartly House* whose heroine converts to Brahminical sympathy for animals as 'virtuous' (albeit 'uninteresting'); it even ran four long articles that defended the intelligence of animals and condemned anyone 'who can hear, without being moved, the plaintive cries of an animal'. What set Oswald out from the rest – what really led contemporaries to try to anaesthetise the threat he posed – was the anti-imperialist implications of identifying with the Hindus, and more generally the revolutionary politics for which he was by now notorious.[8] As the publisher Thomas Rickman reported, Oswald was one of the 'select few' friends of Thomas Paine, architect of the American revolution and foremost advocate of republican revolution in Britain.[9]

Oswald's combination of vegetarianism and aggressive revolution-peddling was both scary and puzzling. His hypersensitivity about animals was matched with an equally extreme aptness for revolutionary violence, and this extraordinary paradox of aversion to shedding animal blood and eager bloodthirstiness remained the image that shocked and amused both his friends and enemies. 'Here is to be remarked the contrariety of the human character,' wrote the literary critic Joseph Haslewood. 'He whose mildness of disposition could not behold a drop of blood without shuddering with horror – he who could call a Soldier by no milder epithet than that of *Butcher!* – even he instantaneously fled from one extreme to the other.'[10]

After Oswald had moved to France to use his military expertise to further the ambitions of the French revolutionary National Convention, a compatriot, Henry Redhead Yorke, remembered the perplexity with which most contemporaries received him:

> He dined on his roots one day at a party of some members of the Convention, at which I was present, and in the course of the conversation, very coolly proposed, as the most effectual method of averting civil war, to put to death every suspected

man in France ... The expression was not suffered to pass unnoticed; and from the famous Thomas Paine he received a short but cutting reprimand; 'Oswald,' said he, 'you have lived so long without tasting flesh, that you now have a most voracious appetite for blood.'[11]

William Wordsworth – who David Erdman suggests may have befriended Oswald during his secretive phase of revolutionary activism in Paris – immortalised this image of Oswald in his poem *The Excursion* (1814), portraying the character 'Oswald' as a 'modest comrade' who opposes the shooting of wild animals but serves as a valiant military instructor and dies a hero. As a whole the poem gives a sympathetic hearing to the case for animal rights in the figure of 'The Wanderer'. In the final draft of Wordsworth's *The Borderers* (1842) Oswald reappears as a mutinous, duelling revolutionary who is interested in herbs and has imbibed 'certain curious beliefs' among the Brahmins.[12] Amusement tinged with horror was the usual tone in which Oswald was discussed by Englishmen as they observed his progress through the ranks of the French revolutionary machine.

Oswald was by no means unaware of the apparent paradox in his character, and he strenuously set out to explain how both sides sprang from the same heart. His sympathy for all beings convinced him that killing was an evil, but equally that it was necessary to get rid of killers. Peace and equality in society could not be achieved without first purging the world of tyrants. Weapons were a regrettable invention, but he argued that it was necessary to take bitter remedies to cure the greater evil. We cannot 'arrive at the age of gold without passing through an age of iron', he said; 'let us use it like those poisons which, taken in copious draughts, are said to defeat the fatal effects of a smaller dose.' Armed with this rationale for ruthlessness, Oswald knitted together the philosophy of militant vegetarianism.

Responding to misrepresentation in the press, in 1791 Oswald published the copious and rhetorically charged treatise, *The Cry of Nature; Or, an Appeal to Mercy and to Justice, on Behalf of the Persecuted Animals*. Rousseau had elevated 'sympathy' into the philosophical basis for both human and animal rights: Oswald took this to its radical extreme, transforming sympathy into a mandate for democratic revolution and vegetarianism. On the title page Oswald declared his allegiance to Rousseau by quoting the lines from Juvenal's fifteenth satire which Rousseau had used in the *Discourse on Inequality*: 'Nature avows she gave the human race the softest hearts, who gave them tears.' Sympathy, declared Oswald, was 'that kindly principle of union which nature has infused into our bosoms'; it was 'that sentiment of brotherhood which united mankind from the beginning, and which was taught as the base of morals by Plato, Brimha, Confucius, Jesus Christ'. Sympathy was nature's voice crying out the eternal law that humans should exist in egalitarian brotherhood.[13]

In the same year, 1791, Thomas Paine published the seminal republican treatise *The Rights of Man*, which used Rousseauist principles to defend manhood suffrage; others were using the rhetoric of sympathy to promote the emancipation of slaves and political rights for all sectors of the human race. The French Revolution had inspired Oswald with the belief that 'the barbarous governments of Europe [were] giving way to a better system of things'. Now he hoped that this 'growing sentiment of peace and good-will towards men will also embrace, in a wide circle of benevolence, the lower orders of life'.[14]

Hinduism, he felt, had instituted the law of universal sympathy that justified both vegetarianism and violent revolution. All other religions, he said, had been 'Satisfied with extending to man alone the moral scheme', leaving 'every other species of animal . . . unfeelingly abandoned'. By contrast, the merciful Hindu, 'Diffusing over every order of life his affections', considered every creature a kinsman, and thus on the basis of secular justice Hinduism deserved a place 'above all religions on the face of the earth'. Hindu pantheism instilled a worthy respect for the natural world, and even animal worship, Oswald explained, ensured that all creatures were treated with care.[15] He argued, in line with his favourite author Lord Monboddo, that Indian civilisation had faithfully reinforced the natural law of universal sympathy, while anthropocentric Judaeo-Christianity had suppressed it under the influence of the misled Jewish sacerdotalists, St Augustine and latterly Descartes who promulgated 'unfeeling dogmas, which, early instilled into the mind, induce a callous insensibility, foreign to the native texture of the heart'.[16] But nevertheless, like Monboddo, Oswald had faith that progressive cultural enlightenment had the power to overcome these malign influences until eventually peace and harmony would reign again on earth. Despite his atheistic detestation of Judaeo-Christianity, Oswald clung to the promise of future perfection, which he believed the human race, rather than God, would achieve.[17]

Oswald felt that the physiological capacity for sympathy proved that killing animals was unnatural. But whereas George Cheyne and Bernard Mandeville (whose views on this he quoted) had always been forced to acknowledge the Bible's explicit permission to eat animals, Oswald had no such difficulties, for he had dismissed Christianity to the slag heap of human credulity and delusion. He took up the gauntlet cast down against Rousseau and the vegetarians by the Comte de Buffon, who argued that human intestines were carnivorous, and replied: 'holding up the entrails of man, ye exclaim; behold the bowels of a carnivorous animal! . . . Barbarians! to these very bowels I appeal . . . to these bowels . . . entwined with compassion.' It is a striking image – the scientist holding the guts of a human cadaver in mid-air; and in doing so demonstrating, so Oswald pointed out, that by cutting open human bodies scientists had become hardened to the most unnatural activity: 'in quest for your nefarious science, the fibres of agonizing animals delight to scrutinize'. Reclaiming the bowels from the domain of scientific investigation and returning them to their traditional role as the source of tenderness, Oswald appealed: 'Vainly planted in our breast, is this abhorrence of cruelty, this sympathetic affection for every animal?'

Despite this Rousseauist anti-rational assault on science, Oswald himself backed up his visceral appeal to sentiment with the old arguments about human anatomy. He quoted the Plutarchian passage from Cheyne's *Essay of Health and Long Life*: humans, he said, do not have the speed, fangs, sense of smell, digestive organs, rapacious appetite, or insensible heart of predators. We only manage to kill and eat animals by making sure that 'the dying struggles of the butchered creatures are secluded from our sight'. Without this distance, the senses would irrepressibly recoil 'to devour the funeral of other creatures, to load, with cadaverous rottenness, a wretched stomach'. '[L]isten to the voice of nature!' he declaimed: it is audible in 'the combined evidence of your senses, to the testimony of conscience and common sense'. Whether Cheyne and other Enlightenment scientists intended it or not, they had laid the foundations for a radical assault on Western mores.[18]

Oswald's belief that vegetarianism was a suppressed human instinct gave him a free hand to interpret eighteenth-century sentimental literature as testimony to this primeval truth, despite the fact that this literature actually tended to repudiate vegetarianism. Oswald insisted that the ignorance of Pope's 'happy lamb' heightened the pathos, and he illustrated this on the front page of *The Cry of Nature* with the cartoon by James Gillray (who made several pictures for Oswald's works) in which a fawn lies slaughtered, and the mother – universalised into the multi-breasted classical goddess, Mother Nature – experiences it as a woeful violation. Oswald did archaeology on European culture, finding in the expressions of sympathy for animals in Thomson's *Seasons* and Dryden's Ovid the remnants of a suppressed nature bursting out. 'The vestiges of that amiable sympathy, even in this degenerate age are still visible, [and] strongly indicate the cordial harmony which, in the age of innocence, subsisted between man and the lower orders of life.' Instinctive sympathy, he wrote, was the 'cry of nature' calling for democratic revolution and the recognition of animal rights.[19]

Predation was symbolic of social inequality, and most people could not afford to eat meat, so for Oswald vegetarianism was also an act of solidarity. Indeed, like John Williamson of Moffat, Oswald recognised that the meat industry was a principal *cause* of economic oppression. Enclosing land for animal grazing displaced the poor, and once again it was in the crisis of limited resources manifested in the infamous Highland Clearances that Oswald saw a microcosm of the effects of human consumption: 'Shall the field support no living thing except the victims of your gluttony? . . . This is literally the case in the north of Scotland, where large tracts of land that formerly supported a hardy happy race of men, are now converted to grazing ground for cattle.' Vegetarianism, Oswald demonstrated, was a consumer choice that directly reduced social injustice.[20]

Oswald's promotion of more sustainable means of food production owes something to the French physiocrats who tried to reform agriculture by changing people's diets. In the years before the Revolution, France had the largest population in Europe and it was constantly struggling to stave off famine. Louis XVI's reforming minister Anne-Robert Turgot (1727–81) had tried to convince Limousin peasants to increase output by cultivating potatoes instead of their staples of chestnuts (which they boiled) and buckwheat (cooked up as gruel). In 1764 the pre-revolutionary apocalyptic Simon Linguet, who later chafed under the bit of Turgot's physiocratic ministry, proposed that the solution to France's perennial bread crisis was to change the French diet from grains to potatoes, fish, maize, vegetables and rice. He also argued that chestnuts, the food of the ancient Gauls, *could* be made into civilised nourishment – as Rousseau himself advised in the *Discourse on*

The frontispiece of John Oswald's *The Cry of Nature*, by James Gillray

Inequality. In the climate of growing discontent among the French peasantry, frugality had been embraced by reformers as a way of distinguishing their own civic responsibility from the distasteful conspicuous consumption of the French court, grotesquely epitomised by Louis XVI's ever growing addiction to hunting and feasting as political troubles mounted around him.[21]

When the revolutionary government took over in France, simplicity became a sign of egalitarian patriotism and many leaders harked back to the austere Spartan principles of the early Roman republicans. The vegetarian American revolutionary hero, Benjamin Franklin, who was ambassador to France, had set the trend in the 1770s and '80s by modelling himself on the simplicity of Rousseau's fictional characters.[22] He promoted vegetarianism, for example, in his comical essay on flatulence, in which he observed that 'He that dines on stale Flesh, especially with much Addition of Onions, shall be able to afford a Stink that no Company can tolerate; while he that has lived for some Time on Vegetables only, shall have that Breath so pure as to be insensible to the most delicate Noses.'[23] His frugal example was quickly followed by leaders such as Jacques-Pierre Brissot de Warville (1754–93) with whom Oswald was in constant collaboration. The revolutionary statesman Charles Talleyrand (1754–1838) was renowned for nibbling on only one mouse-like meal of biscuit, peach and cheese each day; patriotic leaders like Bertrand Barère called on all citizens to give up meat, and others tried to impose a 'civic Lent' to ensure egalitarian food distribution and to prevent depletion of animal stocks. The down-at-heel clothing of the common-man revolutionary, dubbed the *'sans-culotte'* (literally 'without' the fashionable upper-class 'knee-breeches'), was elevated as a sartorial badge of ultra-radical political allegiance; so also the fleshless existence of the lower classes became the ultimate sign of revolutionary fervour. Vegetarianism was not exactly an entry requirement for the hard core of the Revolution, but for the first time in European culture it became a definite status symbol among the new ruling elite. 'A glass of wine and a crust, that's all that true sans-culottes need,' declared the radical journal *Père Duchesne.* In truly Rousseauist style, idealists imagined that nature provided everything for her children – from wild nuts to raw vegetables – as long as all gifts were shared equally. Oswald cultivated this image of Rousseauist frugality in his translation of *The Almanach of Goodman Gérard,* which championed Michel Gérard, a political delegate who used to turn up at the meetings of the Estates-General, not in the traditional black and white costume of the Third Estate, but in a suit of brown fustian as if he had just stepped out from the pages of Rousseau's novel *Julie*. This was no doubt in Oswald's mind when living in Paris, where his family, recalled one contemporary, were 'truly reduced to *Sans-Culottes* in their clothing, he turned out both his sons to feed on what they could pick up in the neighbouring gardens and forests, for they possessed an equal antipathy with the Father to animal food.'[24]

The politicisation of gastronomy played into the hands of British counter-revolutionaries who claimed that French idealism led to nothing but starvation. The English caricaturists Thomas Rowlandson and James Gillray showed what would happen to the corpulent John Bull – the mascot figure of patriotic England – if forced to exchange his roast beef for the meagre bread of Liberty. Refined French cuisine, typified by *soupe maigre*, onions and frog's legs, had always been juxtaposed to the hearty meat diet of the British.[25] In *The Adventures of Ferdinand Count Fathom* (1753) Tobias Smollett voiced the emerging antipathy to the Frenchified 'macaroni' (a long-wigged dandy, named after the exotic refined pasta, who displayed exquisite continental manners). His character of a fat landlady whose 'corporation is made up of good, wholesome English fat' berates France, where she tells Fathom, 'you have been learning to cabbage* . . . you have been living upon rye bread and soup maigre, and now . . . pretend to find fault with a sur-loin of roast beef.' These xenophobic images were magnified by the British reaction to revolution; the typical *sans-culotte* was depicted in the British press as a half-starved onion- and snail-eater. Gillray's ironic *French Liberty: British Slavery* (1792) presents the emaciated French revolutionary imagining himself in the millennial utopia of 'Milk & Honey' while nibbling on radical roots flanked by a chamber pot filled with live snails, while John Bull's constitution is preserved by a massive joint of roast beef.[26]

Oswald twisted these images round to reveal that the fat beef-eater was the oppressive tyrant of Britain, not the common man, while the frugal Frenchman represented sympathetic egalitarianism. He managed to direct his critique of beef-eating against the political establishment

---

* 'To pilfer' (*OED*); Smollett is probably also punning on the other meaning, 'To grow a head like a cabbage' (*OED*), alluding to Fathom's wig; as well as on the idea of eating cabbage.

'John Bull's Sacrifice to Janus' by James Sayers, 1794

while also presenting himself as a radical British patriot. For Oswald, the true John Bull was no longer the beef-*eater*, but the labouring, free, *living* bull. Most beef was eaten by comparatively few people, so beef-eating was a sign of unjust privilege. Raising beef-cattle meant herding people off their land and laying waste the healthy constitution of the nation: the true Briton was the bull being sacrificed for the gratification of the rich.

In *John Bull's Sacrifice* (1794), the cartoonist James Sayers depicted the threat that the French Revolution posed to Britain by representing John Bull as a bull with his head in a guillotine. Oswald had the same image in mind, except that he was arguing that the sacrifice of John Bull was being committed by the beef-eating British ruling classes, rather than the revolutionary French. Oswald turned the idea that cattle were protected for their usefulness into an elaborate political metaphor: sacrificing John Bull stood for exploiting the labouring poor of Britain.[27]

In his early operatic farce, *The Humours of John Bull* (1789), Oswald attacked the British for selling themselves – in the form of beef exports – to the decadent *ancien régime*.[28] The innkeeper Timothy Pimpleface is complicit in this unpatriotic sell-out, and consequently does not see the irony of his own garbled misinformation which he addresses to one Mr Worthy who has just returned from India (in whose worthiness one can detect traces of the author):

> 'without doubt, you have seen the elephants, the rhinoceroses, and those savage cannibals, the Gintoos, who eat nothing but herbs, and entertain a most treasonable antipathy to roast beef, the glory of Old England.'[29]

Oswald transformed Indian vegetarianism into a political opposition to the tyrannical British establishment. The bull was no less useful and deserving of protection in Britain than in India: it should be conserved for economic reasons; figuratively John Bull had to be saved from the predatory rapacity of the country's current leaders. Vegetarianism opposed carnivorous exploitation both figuratively and literally. In that sense, Pimpleface was right: vegetarianism *was* treason, but treason against an illegitimate and corrupt monarchy and oligarchy.[30]

Oswald's espousal of Indian vegetarianism united radical politics and animal rights: symbolic opposition to a blood-sucking elite, literal opposition to their greedy appropriation of material goods, solidarity with the undernourished poor, and the enfranchisement of all sentient life. It was with this manifesto that Oswald took himself and unnumbered other followers to the battle-front of the French Revolution. Social revolution and animal rights flowed from the same source, and Oswald was prepared to lay down his life in their name.

Despite his most unusual views, Oswald carved out for himself an impressive literary and political career. His early works gained him a spot in the *Five Hundred Celebrated Authors of Great Britain Now Living* and later among the *Lives of the Scottish Poets*. Collaborating with Thomas Paine and John Horne-Tooke, the radical parliamentary reformer, Oswald counted himself among the principal instigators of Europe's revolutionary movement. At a time when the vote was still in the hands of a few propertied men and could be literally bought and sold by unscrupulous politicians, Oswald called for the democratisation of British politics. Renowned for scathing commentaries in his own journal, the *London Mercury*, and his columns in others like the *London Gazetteer* and the *Star*, Oswald outraged Parliament with his incendiarism, and Edmund Burke singled out his theory of the sovereignty of the people as 'the most false, wicked, and mischievous doctrine'.[31]

Oswald argued that the corrupt House of Commons had become a 'mock-representation of the people'; the Lords were unelected and could only represent their own interests; and the King was the greatest 'devourer of the people'. He called for universal enfranchisement (a more extreme position than the limited enfranchisement endorsed by most French revolutionaries) and even claimed that representation itself was a flawed concept. Oswald imagined that true democracy could only operate if everyone had a chance to voice their views directly: they should gather in masses to discuss political issues and all vote with their own voices. Laws should only be established if ninety per cent of each region assented. This would be a far better way of spending time than being forced to attend obsolete church services on Sundays. One of Oswald's ex-comrades once sardonically mocked this ideal democratic 'cry of nature', recalling that 'I have often endeavoured to persuade him, that his plan was not sufficiently extensive, as he had excluded from this grand assembly of the animated world the most populous portion of his fellow-creatures, namely, cats, dogs, horses, chickens, &c.'[32]

Aware that the British government were never going to assent to his plebiscitary system of direct democracy, Oswald turned his attention to France. In 1789 the French populace revolted against the privileged tax-breaks granted to the richest of France's nobility. They succeeded in forcing Louis XVI to allow the Estates-General – the body of nobles, clergy and the democratically elected Third Estate (the commoners) – to abolish the feudal system and form a new constitution based on the redistribution of land and the Declaration of the Rights of Man and of the Citizen. Oswald, committed to the end of monarchy and the establishment of a republic, formed an alliance with the Rousseauist primitivist Nicolas de Bonneville (an advocate of the communal sharing of sexual partners), with whom he became an important leader in the proto-communist Cercle Sociale.

As hostilities began between the two main factions of the Revolution – the moderate republican Girondins and the ultra-radical followers of Maximilien Robespierre, later called the Montagnards, who presided over the Reign of Terror – Oswald collaborated closely with the leader of the Girondins, Jacques-Pierre Brissot, impoverished son of a pastry cook to whom the keys of the fallen Bastille were delivered in 1789 and who controlled the political situation from late 1791 to September 1792. For his services to the revolutionary cause Brissot nominated Oswald – along with Paine, Horne-Tooke and Jeremy Bentham – for honorary French citizenship, and Oswald was possibly the first British man to join the Jacobin Club,* the principal revolutionary political society.

Under intense observation from British spies, Oswald acted as a middleman for the burgeoning radical societies in Britain, supplying money and weapons to the French revolutionary government. In turn, he called on the Jacobin Club to help export revolution to England and thence to spread democracy to 'the human race in general'.[33] The English, claimed Oswald's followers, had produced the theoretical framework of democratic revolution: they should now be helped to bring their own ideals to fruition. Letters of encouragement from the French would, said Oswald, 'revive the courage of our English brothers and patriots, shackled by royal proclamations and tyrannized by all the odious arts of a conspiratorial minister'. England would then help France 'to achieve with you the revolution of Europe, of the human race'. During the heated months of 1792 at the Jacobin Club, he warned that without pre-emptive action George III would soon declare war against the French: 'Scarcely having escaped the madhouse, where he should have spent the rest of his days, this mad king wishes to hurl the thunderbolts of war and shed the blood of the two fraternal peoples.' And he warned, too, against monarchy itself: 'Frenchmen, you have driven from your own house the monster royalty; but as long as this ferocious beast crouches in your neighbours' field, can you live with out alarms?'[34]

Robespierre urged caution, warning that Oswald's suggestions would precipitate a premature war with an already aggravated Britain and distract from the important work of radical reform at home. Oswald succeeded in passing his motion to send letters of encourage-

* Not to be confused with the Jacobites, supporters of the Stuart succession.

ment, but he did not stop there. He took the most extreme step, advocated by Brissot – one that was inevitably construed as high treason in Britain. He called on the French to send a detachment of 60,000 volunteers who 'knew how to die' to lay siege to the Tower of London and bring it down just as they had the Bastille. Political agitation was spreading throughout Britain, and Oswald insisted that the disenfranchised English workers would welcome the French revolutionaries with open arms as liberators and together they would 'form a single republic'. 'It is in London,' Oswald predicted, 'you must attack him; it is in London, amid an immense population, oppressed, miserable, agitated, that it will be quite easy to topple the tyrant . . . George the sanguinary will soon suffer the fate of Louis the traitor.' The French did finally declare war on Britain and Holland – or rather, on their monarchs – on 1 February 1793, and they planned a 100,000- strong invasion of England; but by then they no longer believed in Oswald's promise of an enthusiastic reception.[35]

Unflinching in his belief that violence was an essential tool for overthrowing the tyrants of the people, Oswald was intimately involved in the process that transformed the French Revolution from a mainly peaceful process into a bloodbath. On 10 August 1792 the Parisian masses stormed the royal palace and arrested the King and his family; in September they broke into prisons and in a four-day orgy of bloodshed they massacred the detained aristocrats, dragging their bodies through the streets with their heads stuck on spits. At this critical turning point in the Revolution, many previously sympathetic British onlookers turned away in horror, and the French leaders themselves did their best to deny responsibility. But Oswald was among those who found it encouraging that the people were ready to use violence against the oppressors.

In January 1793, after vigorous strife between the Girondins and Robespierre's Montagnards (also called the Jacobins since their successful takeover of the Jacobin Club), the National Convention voted to replicate the regicide of the English Cromwellians: they condemned King Louis XVI for treason and gave him a 'painless death' with the efficient killing-machine recently invented by Monsieur Guillotin. Although many Girondins opposed the execution of the King, Oswald no doubt applauded the final end to monarchy. One uncorroborated report claimed that

He is said to have commanded at those unspeakably horrid massacres at Paris . . . He also at the head of his infernal pikemen formed the guard which closely surrounded the scaffold on which the late King of France was guillotined. Immediately after the head of the unfortunate monarch fell into the basket, he and his whole troops struck up a hymn he had composed for the occasion, and danced and sung, like so many Savages, round and round the scaffold![36]

Oswald became a cherished figure in revolutionary circles, continuing to publish and to draw attention to himself as a result of his unusual living habits. His vegetarianism became a legendary manifestation of his radical reappraisal of humanity, and he was not alone in dragging Rousseau's animal rights arguments into the ideology of the Revolution. Not least among his notorieties was his unabashed practice of polygamy. In France he lived with two wives, and, it seems, succeeded in impressing his contemporaries with the viability of such a course. 'They were extremely handsome,' wrote one with tickled curiosity, 'and he had brought his domestic economy to such a perfect state of discipline, that they lived together in the greatest friendship and harmony. A singular fact! which has, I believe, no parallel in the history of the fair sex.'[37]

Oswald's gruesome fate was sealed when he devised the military deployment of the infamous killing instrument, the pike – to be thrust into the body of the opponent at close quarters, thus maximising total exposure to the bloody act of murder. If hundreds of thousands of impassioned voluntary citizens were trained in Oswald's 'simple, easy, and natural' strategies, to advance according to their own natural instinct, following absolute necessity, in an egalitarian 'line of science' they would become 'a powerful means of destroying all the despotisms and all the aristocracies on earth'. They would represent the natural power of the people over the powerful elites, and could not fail to succeed. This was Oswald's masterminding of the pikemen, and in the words of one companion, he 'had under tuition an immense concourse of both sexes, to instruct in the use of that instrument'.

It was this bloodthirstiness that shocked his contemporaries. In the liberal *Edinburgh Review*, Henry Brougham accused Oswald of 'an incongruity unexampled':

Retaining his unparalharm'd humanity of disposition, and abhorrence at the sight of animal blood, this abstinent sage was the first who proposed to the Convention the introduction of the pike, both for the use of the army and the mob . . . A maniac who fought the massacres of Paris, and was zealous to avoid even the sight of blood: a wretch who would not kill a tyger, but died unsated in his thirst for human blood![38]

Weapons were in extremely short supply in the early years of the Revolution, and Oswald's military expertise made an important contribution to the victories of the unprecedentedly massive million-strong revolutionary army. Although Oswald's troops did receive guns when they went to battle, his theoretical application of the Revolution's favourite weapon proved successful. Oswald was elected Colonel Commandant of the First Battalion of Volunteer Pikemen, the Piquiers, and in 1793 – rather than risk sending him at the head of an army to his homeland – he was sent to suppress the royalist uprisings in La Vendée. He was applauded as a hero for expressing his man-of-the-people solidarity by wearing ordinary soldier's garb and eating austerely: 'He was exceedingly admired for the plainness of his dress and manners, and above all for the simplicity of his life. He had eaten no meat for the last twelve years, and scarce ever drank more than half a dozen glasses of wine,' remembered one contemporary.

Oswald led to battle his men and women (the revolutionary government had allowed women to be soldiers for the first time, and this remained the case in Oswald's regiment until his fellow officers concluded that they were 'the mothers of all vices', and in Oswald's absence banished them from the battle zone). We can imagine Oswald trudging out to La Vendée to quash the army led by royalist aristocrats backed by thousands of peasants who had risen against compulsory conscription and restrictions on religious freedom. His determination that democracy would not be defeated made warfare appear justified. His words of a few years earlier must have come back to him: we cannot 'arrive at the age of gold without passing through an age of iron'. Blood must be shed to establish the universal, bloodless peace.

After Oswald's army had marched west across France and engaged in months of desperate fighting, on 14 September 1793, in a day of fierce battle at Thouars, they were totally defeated by the royalist insurgents. A massacre ensued, only a few being allowed to escape. As his old friend Henry Redhead Yorke recounted, following his final meeting with Oswald, while bravely leading on his men at the battle of Pont-de-Cé, he was killed by a cannon ball, and at the same instant, a discharge of grape shot laid both his sons, who served as drummers in the corps of which he was colonel, breathless on their father's corpse.

So Oswald was killed in action, fighting to defend egalitarian vegetarianism. By a remarkable coincidence, the historian David Erdman discovered that Oswald's was the only unit in the republican army for which an almost complete minute book of officers' meetings has survived. As a result we know that Oswald's two sons, William and John, did not in fact die with their father: they survived as dedicated drummers and fighters in the pike corps: they were killed years later in further battles with the royalists. Oswald himself was not forgotten, and rumours persisted that he had not died but continued to perpetrate military ravages in the name of universal fraternity. When Paine was imprisoned at the end of 1793 for having tried to save the life of King Louis, in fear of execution and unaware of Oswald's death, he sent a letter to England promising that Oswald would carry it home.[39] His old hack-master at Grub Street, William Thomson, became convinced that Oswald had invented a new pseudonym and was in fact Napoleon Bonaparte himself. (After all, both were small of stature, militaristic and humane, revolutionary ideologues and lovers of Ossian.)

By dying, Oswald escaped the persecution of Revolution sympathisers that followed his British colleagues: Thomas Paine had already been condemned *in absentia* for seditious libel and Horne-Tooke was narrowly acquitted of high treason by a jury in 1794. But Oswald's theories of direct democracy – among the first advocates of that system – filtered into the radical milieu of his time and had a lasting influence on the history of socialism.[40] His 'Cry of Nature' left a resounding echo in the radical vegetarian movements that spread across Europe.

TWENTY-TWO

The Marquis de Valady faces the Guillotine

The Marquis de Valady was only twenty-seven years old when he was forced to reconcile himself to death. His vegetarian comrade, John Oswald, had died three months earlier; Valady's end was to prove at least as bloody. The bloodless revolution to which these men dedicated their lives had become as bloody as a slaughterhouse.

Jacques-Godefroy-Charles-Sébastien-Francois-Xavier   Jean-Joseph d'Yzarn de Freissenet, Marquis de Valady – to give him his full aristocratic name – was born in the Auvergne in 1766. Although he has been almost entirely neglected by Anglophone historians, Valady's letters, preserved in an extraordinarily rich archive at his ancestral chateau, provide a fascinating insight into some of the most important episodes in the French Revolution.

Educated according to his station, Valady 'imbibed from the ancient authors a love of philosophy, an ardent passion for liberty'. His father's great friend the Comte de Vaudreuil had fought zealously alongside the Americans in their struggle for independence, and Valady grew up surrounded by men committed to the great cause of freedom. His domestic life, however, embodied all the opposite values. His authoritarian father – opposed to French republicanism – subjected him to all the usual disciplines of an aristocratic household and, at the age of barely sixteen, betrothed him without his consent to the even younger daughter of the Comte de Vaudreuil. According to their mutual American friend Samuel Breck, 'a more bewitching girl was seldom seen'. But Valady could not abide the arbitrary use of paternal power: marriage without love was null and immoral and he refused to consummate their marriage, despite his mother-in-law forcing him to spend a night in his wife's room. His battle for personal freedom fuelled a burning desire to fight for political liberty.[1]

Escaping his domestic nightmare, Valady gained the privileged post of an ensign at the Gardes Françaises. He moved to Paris and immediately fell in with a clique of friends from whom he imbibed the spirit of radicalism: Samuel Breck, Saint-Jean de Crèvecoeur, the liberal *Encyclopédistes* and, most importantly for Valady's future, Jacques-Pierre Brissot, the friend and collaborator of John Oswald. Breck remembered Valady at this time as 'a wild enthusiast in matters of political freedom', and counted him among the disinterested worshippers of liberty who 'were ready to lay down their lives and their all for the good of France'.[2]

Disgruntled with the French government and opposed to warfare, in June 1786 Valady quitted his post in the army, repudiated his former life of luxury, and refashioned himself – like Oswald – as a model of Spartan austerity. There was no mistaking that, in the words of one contemporaneous history, this was 'in consequence of sentiments of simplicity he had imbibed from Brissot'. Brissot had been a great admirer of Benjamin Franklin; he saw his own fight for liberty in France as a continuation of the struggle for independence that Franklin had led in America, and he emulated Franklin's Quaker-like simplicity as a potent and charismatic ethical statement. Drawing on Franklin's *Autobiography*, Brissot dedicated pages of his own *Mémoires* to Franklin's frugality: 'Benjamin had read a treatise of doctor Trion, on the Pythagorean regimen; strongly convinced by his reasonings, he abstained from meat for a long time . . . This Pythagorean diet economised the money of the printer's apprentice; and he used it to buy books.'[3] Plainness and Liberty formed a united front against Luxury and Tyranny, and Valady dramatically transferred his allegiance from the court life of his upbringing to the new idiom of unadorned egalitarianism. The budding revolutionary took hold of his curly locks of hair and ceremoniously cut them off; he renounced the title of marquis; sold his watch because 'it is not appropriate for men to wear jewellery'; laid aside his elegant military costume and donned the Quaker-like clothes of simplicity.[4]

Wishing to escape the shackles of his background, he decided to travel to England, 'the only spot in Europe where liberty dwelt'. In London, Valady took lodgings with John Bell (the publisher of David Williams, the Welsh republican druid-priest). He met many of the leading British republican agitators, studied law at an academy in Fulham and formed an intimate friendship with Thomas Paine. But then he became disillusioned with the British government for committing the 'foulest encroachments upon our national rights', and decided to move to America, the real land of democracy.[5]

This extraordinary behaviour threatened to disgrace the houses of Valady and Vaudreuil, and his friends used all their aristocratic networks to cover up the young man's follies. But none of his family friends could persuade him from his new-found life, until finally his unfortunate wife and her mother made the journey to London with their cousin the Comte de Parroy. On hearing that Valady had embarked for America two days earlier the delegation despaired, but the news turned out to be false and they made contact with the miscreant marquis. Valady at first invited his wife to emigrate to America with him, but, overcome by their pleas, he agreed to return to France only once they had signed a bizarre contract stipulating that Valady would retain his personal freedom and would be allowed to travel according to his desire.[6]

Only two months after departing to England, he arrived back in France. These were the years building up to the Revolution of 1789 when King Louis XVI had gathered the Assembly of Notables to try to appease the grievances of the French people. Valady continued to ignore his military duties and spent all his energy trying to convince the aristocrats and ecclesiastics to alleviate France's fiscal crisis by relinquishing their exemption from the taxes that currently burdened the Third Estate (the commoners). Alarmed by Valady's continual intransigence, his friends won him a pardon for his desertion from the army and arranged for the young marquis to take a long vacation. Away from the political stirrings in Paris, his family hoped he would reflect on his follies, and return to his national duties and the wife whom he had spurned. But Valady ignored the imprecations of his father and remained at Paris with the pretext of poor health, until January 1787 when he grudgingly made the journey first to his spouse's home and then to his father.

By springtime he was expected back in the army, but instead Valady returned to England from where he wrote to Samuel Breck: 'I am here on my way to America, where I mean to delve the earth for a subsistence, rather than be beholden to any of my proud connexions. They form the clan of oppressors, and being the enemies of liberty I hold them in enmity myself.' Just as he was about to depart for America he heard that the Dutch Patriots had started a new democratic revolution in Holland and he immediately returned to Paris to assist them. This time his family used financial coercion to thwart his plans and deprived him of his annual allowance. But Valady persisted and joined the Duc d'Orléans and Lafayette in offering protection to the defeated Dutch Patriots, promising to join with them in arms as soon as a new campaign could be launched.[7]

Once again, his family stepped in. His uncle, the Baron de Castelnau, obtained a new holiday for him and invited Valady to stay with him in Geneva for the summer.[8] There, in Valady's words, Castelnau had 'the design of curing me of my eccentricity, of my wildness, and my philosophic and republican manner, and to make a man of the world of his poor day-dreamer of a cousin'. But the plan blew up in his family's faces. For, as Valady wrote to his sister, in Geneva, instead of cooling off, he became still more immersed in radical idealism. He made 'acquaintance of a great man, of a sage around whom I found refuge, the port so desired. He put me in the path of the true wisdom and which is that of Nature and the only one which leads man to the sovereign good.'[9] This 'great man' was Robert Pigott (1736–94) and the path of nature he showed Valady was radical vegetarianism.

Their meeting became a legend in the histories of the Revolution. The *Biographical Anecdotes of the Founders of the French Republic* (1797), published by the republican vegetarian Richard Phillips (1767–1840), elaborated that Valady met 'an English Pythagorean, well known by the name of *Black Pigot*, who confined himself entirely to eating vegetable fare. Valady immediately adopted this gentleman's dietetic system, and for several years after never tasted animal food.'[10] Five years later, Phillips' friend, the revolutionary vegetarian Joseph Ritson, correctly affirmed that this was Robert Pigott, once high sheriff of Shropshire and inheritor of the ancient and extremely valuable estate of Chetwynd.[11] Originally emigrating to the Continent after selling his English estates because he thought the American war would ruin England, Pigott became acquainted with Voltaire, Franklin, Brissot and the leading hostess of the revolutionary Girondins, Madame Roland, who called him the '*franc original*' (alluding to the fact that like Oswald he had been granted honorary French citizenship). Pigott had immediately set about promulgating his vegetarian solution to France's chronic food shortages by calling for the populace to revert to a diet of potatoes, lentils, maize, barley and cabbage.[12] In Brissot's republican journal *Le Patriot François*, he announced that prisoners in particular should have their hard natures softened by 'that wholesome and natural regimen of bread, water and vegetables'.[13] Brissot mentioned his friendship with Pigott in his *Mémoires*, and promised a full discussion of him which unfortunately he never got round to completing.[14]

From 1790 Pigott was trying to purchase one of the 'nationalised' ecclesiastical estates in order to establish a model Rousseauist agricultural commune with Brissot and other prominent Girondins, François Lanthenas, Bancal des Issarts, Champagneux de Blot, François Buzot, the Rolands and possibly Valady. Pigott had promised to fund the project with the vast sum of 100,000 francs, but Madame Roland rightly put little faith in 'this inconstant Pythagorean' and the dream never came true. The few of this confederacy who survived Robespierre's Reign of Terror ended up buying private retirement estates and lived their shattered dreams in solitude.[15]

After meeting Pigott, Valady became an evangelist of vegetarianism and ardently wished to convert his fellow revolutionaries to the same cause, seeing in it the only hope for a future of peace. He took to wearing the signature white linen gown of the ancient Pythagoreans, and he still yearned to travel to America and establish a Pythagorean community of vegetarian harmony: 'a school of Temperance and Love, in order to preserve so many men from the prevailing disgraceful vices of brutal intemperance and selfish cupidity'.[16]

Valady even impertinently tried to convert the far senior Jacques-Henri Bernardin de Saint-Pierre, co-designer, with Rousseau, of the Revolution's rhetoric of nature. As Saint-Pierre wrote to Brissot with amused indulgence for their junior comrade:

> M. de Valady, full of zeal for the well-being of the human race and without experience of men . . . wants to reduce me to the diet of the Pythagoreans and, which is more, to their costume. I give my best wishes for his success in America and if ever he forms there a society which has his virtues, his mores, as much as your wisdom, I will endeavour to go there to end my days: there will be nothing missing for the satisfaction of my heart and my spirit.[17]

Despite his irony, Saint-Pierre was genuinely attracted to Valady's callow conversion to the vegetarian ideas he was himself publishing in the *Études de Nature* and *Paul et Virginie*.* One of their mutual

---

* See chapter 15.

associates expressed the emotion of listening to Valady's impassioned diatribes: 'Never have we experienced the enchantment, the amazement which he caused us. It was truly a divine gift . . . Bernardin de Saint-Pierre, who loved him much, after having listened to him one day in our presence, cried "You are a man of the time of Orpheus, you are Orpheus himself resuscitated to train men by the charm of the word."'[18] It may have been thanks to Saint-Pierre that Valady had visited Robert Pigott in the first place, for Saint-Pierre commemorated Pigott in his sincere approbation of vegetarianism in the *Études de Nature*:

> Under an improved system of education children will be brought up to a vegetable regimen, as being the most natural to man . . . I have seen an instance of it in a young Englishman aged fifteen . . . He was of a most interesting figure, of the most robust health, and of the most sweet disposition . . . His father, Mr Pigott, told me that he had brought him up entirely upon the Pythagorean regimen, the good effects of which he had known by his own experience. He had formed a project of . . . establishing in English America a society of dietary reformers . . . Would that this educational scheme, worthy of the best and happiest times of Antiquity might succeed![19]

Pigott's hopes of establishing a vegetarian community in America were clearly dreamed in collaboration with Valady, and even Saint-Pierre wrote of his own desire to 'establish a happy colony' in America.[20] Valady's American dreams had been fired by his friend, Saint-Jean de Crèvecoeur, the French consul in New York, whose *Letters from an American Farmer* (1782–4) inspired generations with its bucolic images of the log-cabin rural life and America's 'melting pot' society.[21]

In the passion of his recent conversion under Pigott, Valady wrote to his sister the Comtesse de Freissinet La Guépie in the summer of 1788, explaining in stunning rhetoric his new Rousseauist vegetarian convictions. All the evils that man encountered, he told his sister, all illnesses and weaknesses 'which make nothing but a scene of sadness of his whole life' were due to 'his improper and anti-natural' habit of eating flesh. Records of a healthy vegetarian Golden Age existed in 'all the nations which have covered and inhabited this earth', and all ills 'come from the corruption of our humours, which is produced entirely by the use of meat and its pernicious effects'.[22] If men relinquished meat-eating, he insisted, their health would improve infinitely, they could extend their life threefold and would 'taste the happiness destined to their species'. But people were so accustomed to poisoning themselves that their nature had been suffocated, and they no longer even felt the horror that should accompany eating animals. So much so, predicted Valady, that if someone rose up against the error, he would be treated like a madman:

> How will such a one be received – in this age of wild luxury, where all the vices mount with undisguised effrontery, this real age of iron – who will raise his voice to say to men that they ought not to feed on flesh, that it is criminal to take life from God's creatures in order to devour them and that all the ills which they suffer here on earth are the just punishment of their voracious cruelty . . . I am convinced that I would render the most considerable service to men if I could . . . return them to the path of their all beneficent mother, nature.

To turn back the effects of this terrible social malaise one would have to start early, with the new generation of children: it was on them that the future happiness of the human race depended. Valady felt that his vegetarian insights which he gleaned from Pigott could even improve on the educational scheme set out in Rousseau's *Émile*, and he planned to write a commentary on this work.[23]

His sister was bringing up her own children, and he warned that meat was particularly pernicious for the weak organs of the young. In England and Scotland, he said, 'one sees the most beautiful children of the world, because, even though the parents eat a lot of meat, they feed them entirely on vegetables and milk'. The children of vegetarian parents, he averred, were immune to smallpox, measles and toothache and always had 'a soft, animated humour', because 'It is an irrevocable fact that the nature of our food determines our humours and our moral dispositions.'[24]

Pigott first converted Valady to vegetarianism, but an earlier account, *The History of Robespierre* (1794), attributed Valady's conversion to another member of Brissot's gang of collaborators, John Oswald:

> Among his friends, he counted an Englishman* (Oswald), who was eccentric in his mode of thinking, and who had adopted the dietetic principles of the Bramins. So much had Oswald prevailed with him against the custom of eating portions of a

* Oswald was, of course, Scottish.

corpse, that Valady, for a considerable time, abstained from animal food. These sentiments, and others, which he had imbibed from books, induced him to write a system of philosophy, so romantic and chimerical, that some attributed it to a derangement of mind.[25]

It is perfectly plausible that Oswald was involved in inspiring Valady's vegetarianism; many of their ideas and rhetorical phrases are similar, and Valady had certainly been well primed in Rousseauist ideals of radical simplicity before he met Pigott. Since Oswald was working alongside Pigott, Lanthenas and Brissot – writing in the same journals and campaigning for the export of revolution to Britain – it seems probable that Oswald and Valady at least encountered each other.[26]

It appears that Pigott, Oswald and Valady – along with Saint-Pierre – knew each other and formed an important, highly conspicuous if loosely united attempt to build a vegetarian republic. Their idealism touched many prominent figures, particularly those close to Brissot, the most powerful leader in the early years of the Revolution. Even Alphonse de Lamartine, author of the multi-volume hagiography the *History of the Girondins*, and inheritor of Brissot's political legacy, was himself a follower of Saint-Pierre's vegetarian creed. The philosophy of the revolutionary vegetarians had its roots in Rousseau and Saint-Pierre who were – more than anyone else – the central figures of revolutionary culture. Brissot himself admired vegetarianism and cultivated the image of simplicity in self-conscious emulation of Benjamin Franklin. Through Franklin and Brissot, the puritanical philosophy of Thomas Tryon converged with Rousseauism in the era of the French Revolution. There was a tradition of radical vegetarianism stretching from the English Civil War of the 1640s through to the revolutionary 1780s and '90s. In periods of war, food shortages accentuated the need to economise on food and the luxury of meat was associated with the predatory injustice of ruling classes. Radical vegetarians sought to enfranchise animals within the wider circles of democratic fraternity. Even those who regarded meat-eating as a necessary evil, like the revolutionary statesmen Ludot and Coupé, called for legislation to force people to 'strive to render life pleasant to all that breathes', while other revolutionaries instituted a festival in honour of domestic animals, 'the companions of man'.[27] Radical vegetarianism was not an isolated extreme; it was a flourishing branch on the main trunk of revolutionary philosophy.

*

(which he said 'is remarkable for the purity of life which it inculcates'), Iamblichus' *Life of Pythagoras* (the author of which he eulogised for having 'imitated in his diet the frugal simplicity of the most ancient times'), and parts of Plutarch's essays on animal sagacity (which he considered 'ingenious').[42] Whether Taylor intended it or not, his works had a lasting impact on the future of vegetarianism: Mary and Percy Shelley avidly read his works; he influenced the poetry – and perhaps the reverence for animals – of William Blake and John Flaxman; Ralph Waldo Emerson became Taylor's disciple; and he inspired Thomas M. Johnson, American editor of the *Platonist*, whose associate, Bronson Alcott, became a founder member of the Vegetarian Society and planned to deploy Taylor's works in establishing a 'Second Eden'.[43]

But Taylor himself had a torn conscience over the vegetarian diet: intellectually he knew it was right, but in practice he did not keep to it. He agreed with Porphyry that it was the best diet for a man of pure spirit and philosophy, but he insisted that it was not appropriate '*to those who lead an active life*'. In an apologetic note, Taylor explained that he 'has been obliged to mingle the active with the contemplative life' and therefore that he 'has also found it expedient to make use of a fleshy diet. Nothing, however, but an imperious necessity, from causes which it would be superfluous to detail at present, could have induced him to adopt animal, instead of vegetable nutriment.'[44]

Valady must have been disappointed with his new tutor, who did not even follow the diet instigated by the founder of his philosophy – and certainly Taylor was no less exasperated by his disciple. A few years after their meeting, Taylor anonymously published the satirical *Vindication of the Rights of Brutes* (1792), which mockingly claimed that if everyone accepted that animals were equal to humans, one could expect 'that beautiful period be realized . . . when "Man walk'd with beast joint tenant of the shade."'[45] As a marginalised, dissenting member of society himself, Taylor had become friends with radicals such as Paine, Thomas Brand Hollis and Mary Wollstonecraft. But he did not share their egalitarian idealism. The title of his work was clearly sending up Paine's *Rights of Man* (1790–1) and Wollstonecraft's *Vindication of the Rights of Woman* (1792); both authors had also advocated kindness to animals.[46] The logical conclusion of their politics he laughingly suggested was that 'government may be entirely subverted, subordination abolished, and all things every where, and in every respect, be common to all'.[47] He had obviously found Valady's exten-

Such was the result of Valady's fateful summer of 1787. Taken to Geneva by a concerned but conventional uncle, Valady was now even thicker with the radicals than he had been before. Until equality and tranquillity were established in France, he wrote to Breck in February 1788, he would dedicate himself to the 'destruction of that fatal and wretched order of beings called kings'.[28]

In the same month he helped Brissot found the infamous Société des Amis des Noirs, or the Blacks, modelled on similar English societies run by David Williams and Granville Sharpe, ostensibly campaigning for the abolition of the slave trade, but simultaneously operating as a secret circle of revolutionary activism. Among its members were many of the most prominent revolutionaries of the coming years, including Constantin Volney, the Girondist republican, atheist, Napoleonic empire-building Orientalist, who, like Valady, argued that the tender human heart was naturally sensible to animal suffering. 'The habit of shedding blood, or even seeing it shed, corrupts all sentiment of humanity,' Volney concluded in his *Voyages*, and only vegetarian peoples had 'preserv'd a humane and sensible heart' which shrank from human and animal slaughter.[29]

Valady was one of the Blacks' most enthusiastic members, and with his persuasive enthusiasm he swelled its numbers by bringing in the Marquis de Pastoret, Pierre-Paul-Sylvain Lucas de Blaire, the Marquis de Pampelune, and at one meeting in May he introduced a number of his friends and comrades in the Gardes Françaises: d'Arnaud, d'Aubusson, the Comte de Dampierre, the Marquis de Mons, the Comtes Coustard de St-Lô and d'Avaux, and Louis-Sébastien Mercier. At this meeting Brissot also brought his own friends, among whom was Robert Pigott, explaining the meaning of his nickname 'Black Pigott'.[30]

Valady also added Saint-Pierre to the membership list, but Saint-Pierre curtly turned down the offer and sent an article to Brissot claiming that although he approved of the principles of the meeting, he wasn't well enough, lived too far away, preferred solitude, and did not in principle join confederations. Brissot, embarrassed by the rejection, felt let down: Saint-Pierre had, with Rousseau, taught a generation to love nature, liberty and virtue, but now would not exert himself to advance their progress.[31]

When Brissot travelled to America to further the aims of the society – also with idyllic notions of settling there – he wrote letters of introduction to Lafayette so that Valady could join him later. Valady became an assistant to Lafayette who in turn gave Valady letters of recommendation to George Washington, Henry Knox and General Mifflius. (Lafayette's other aide, Chastel de Boinville, married Harriet Collins who later formed a nudist vegetarian community with Percy Bysshe Shelley.)[32]

Valady never did join Brissot in America, and instead hung around at his house irritating Brissot's wife. She wrote to Brissot and her brother warning them that association with Valady could 'be dangerous or at least onerous'. She thought his 'pythagorean' diet was motivated 'more from singularity than austerity' and that his claims for its healthiness did not add up, as he would be 'eating all day even though he insists that vegetables are very nutritious'. She complained that Valady said he didn't want to create difficulties but he was always asking for vegetable food that one did not have in the house, and would be astonished if one did not have milk at all times of the day. He believed 'that everything ought to be communal' and did not know 'the boundaries at which one ought to stop'.[33] It seems possible that Valady had offended Madame Brissot by proffering his notorious conviction that sharing between communal brethren ought to extend to their wives.

In pursuit of his dreams, Valady once again ditched his post in the Gardes Françaises which had, in Valady's eyes, become an instrument of 'injustice and despotism'.[34] He returned to England where, according to the *Biographical Anecdotes of the Founders of the French Republic*, 'one of his first cares, on arriving in the capital, was to visit a gentleman of eminence in the literary world, and to propose to him the station of chief of the Pythagorean sect. Followers, he assured him, he could not fail to find in every quarter of the globe.'[35] Who this potential leader of a global vegetarian sect was, is not stated: it could have been John Oswald, or any of the other British vegetarians – David Williams, James Graham, John Stewart or Joseph Ritson. In any case, the gentleman turned down Valady's optimistic offer and 'Upon his refusal, Valadi intimated some intention of assuming the honourable post himself.' The unnamed man suggested that if Valady was to become a true Pythagorean, he should learn Greek and advised him to travel to Edinburgh and study there.

In the autumn Valady returned from Edinburgh to London, but by this time his father had succeeded in making his financial affairs extremely complicated, and again Valady forestalled his journey to America.[36] He had still not departed by winter when he came across the

most prominent resuscitator of Pythagorean philosophy in [Thomas Taylor, who had just started translating Platonic and orean texts and had recently published *The History of the Resto the Platonic Theology*, which focused on the vegetarian Neoplat(Most of Taylor's contemporaries surmised that Taylor actually I in a polytheistic universe, and it was rumoured that he poured li and even sacrificed sheep and cattle to the statues of pagan Dubbed 'the modern Pletho', 'the apostle of paganism', 'the priest of England', and 'the great apostle of the Heathen gods', attracted the attention of Valady, who had also relinquished Ch ity.[39] Valady realised that the Rousseauist return to nature co united with the Pythagorean idea of natural harmony and Gold vegetarianism. The moment Valady heard of Taylor, he wrote hi extraordinary letter of introduction:

> O Thomas Taylor! mayst thou welcome a brother Pythagorea ... My good fortune was, that I met, eighteen months ago, a English gentleman of the name of Pigott, who is a Pythagorea Philosopher, and who easily converted me to the diet an manners agreeable to that most rich and beneficent Deity . Mother Earth; and to that heaven inspired change I owe perfec health and tranquillity of mind ... I would more cheerfully depart from my present habitation on this Themis-forsaker earth, than defile myself evermore with animal food, stolen either on earth, in air or water.
>
> I met with thy works but two days past. O divine man! a prodigy in this iron age![40]

The following day Valady threw himself at Taylor's feet demandir remain in the household as a disciple. After some reluctance, T relented and Valady moved in.[41]

But it was an ill-fated match. Taylor was indeed a renowned anir lover, and many suspected that he believed his many pet anir were inhabited with human souls. This is how he is represented Disraeli's novel *Vaurien*, and for this reason he was compared in *Fra: Magazine* (1875) to Percy Bysshe Shelley and to John Fransh another 'pagan' who 'was greatly in advance of his age in advocat humanity to the lower animals'. Some even suggested that Tay was vegetarian – William Blake called him 'Sipsop the Pythagorean and modern scholars have assumed he was. Taylor did translate t ancient vegetarian works: Porphyry's *Abstinence from Animal Fo*

sion of radical politics to the rights of animals preposterous, and he jestingly used the same ancient vegetarian arguments that Oswald had included in his *Cry of Nature* (1791), as well as those in Herman Daggett's *The Rights of Animals* (1792).[48] He probably also had in mind his associate, the vegetarian John Stewart, when he commented ironically that since 'it is an ancient opinion, that all things are endued with sense . . . there is some reason to hope, that this Essay will soon be followed by treatises on the rights of *vegetables* and *minerals*', 'and even the most apparently contemptible clod of earth'. Although Taylor was mocking his friends' extremism, there was a sincere element to his writing. It was the idea of attributing *equal* rights to animals that he found so risible, but he nevertheless believed, with Plato, that *respect* for the many rungs in the great Chain of Being was the best mechanism for hierarchical harmony.[49]

It was not long before Valady realised his mistake, and he seriously stretched Taylor's indulgence when he suggested that since 'a community of possessions in every thing was perfectly Pythagoric', should not a man also share his wife with his friends?[50] Taylor was not amused by the hint and the restless Valady resolved to move on once again. Hearing of the growing political tumults in France, he prepared to return home and take part in the Revolution. 'I came here Diogenes,' he told Taylor on departing, 'and I return Alexander.'[51]

At the beginning of 1789, Valady was back in France and in June he arrived in Paris when rumours were spreading that the King was about to disband the National Assembly forcefully (the monarchy's earlier gesture towards democratic reform). Discontent was growing among the soldiers of the Gardes Françaises, many of whom were drawn from the same social classes as the mobs they were increasingly being mobilised to put down, and some had been punished for refusing to fire on the people. The King's employment of the Swiss Guards and the Gardes du Corps to protect his person fuelled more acute suspicion and resentment.

Valady seized his chance and, according to several contemporary reports, became a key player in precipitating the Revolution. 'In one point, he may be considered as the chief promoter of the vicissitudes which have caracterized the eventful history of France,' said one impartial source. He returned to his former regiment and spread the spirit of sedition. The *Secret History of the French Revolution* (1797) by François Xavier Pagès related that Valady, 'one of the most zealous apostles of liberty, perhaps also paid by Orleans,* went from barrack to barrack to enlighten the soldiers with regard to the real duties of men, and what they owed to their country and to humanity.' Thomas Carlyle, in his narrative reconstruction *The French Revolution* (1837), wrote that thanks to 'Valadi the Pythagorean', the Gardes Françaises promised not to march against the National Assembly or against the people.[52] The anxious officers commanded the troops to remain closed in their barracks, but on 25 and 26 June whole battalions defected and joined the people gathering at the Palais Royal. There they were met with applause and refreshments and joined in the chanting of 'Long Live the Third Estate'. It was the knowledge that the Gardes Françaises would not stop them – and might even help – that gave the people confidence to storm the Bastille.

Recognised as an instigator, Valady was said to have been arrested and condemned to a private death by the King. But he escaped and, apparently with the help of his father-in-law, was helped onto a ship at Nantes bound for America. Contrary winds kept the ship in port long enough for Valady to hear news of the taking of the Bastille. He raced back to Paris and was cheered by the Gardes Françaises and elected as their leader. Vaudreuil wrote to Valady's father bewailing the latest twist in Valady's career and remarking remorsefully that 'It would be much better that he had gone to America for your tranquillity and ours.'

Hailed as a hero of the Revolution in Paris, Valady's fame spread back to his home town where, on 2 September, a prominent band of bourgeoisie and thirty other armed youths visited Valady's father, offering to march with the flag of national liberty to congratulate Valady on 'his talents, his virtues and his devout patriotism' and even to join this 'hero of National Liberty . . . if the case requires it'. With insurrection spreading through the country, however, in January 1790 the peasants of Golinhac and of Vernhettes stormed his chateau and were only quelled when Valady himself appeared to settle the situation.

Valady spent most of 1790 and 1791 stoking revolutionary sentiment in Villefranche, preparing his candidature for the next national election. In the first months of 1792 he was back in Paris, where, despite his 'sobriety, wisdom, philosophy, economy, simplicity', the debts he incurred for his own upkeep and in arming the Revolution

---

* Duc D'Orléans, nicknamed 'Philippe Égalité' for his leading role in the Revolution.

became overwhelming. His clothes had become shabby, and he sported scruffy cropped hair and a long beard. Under financial duress, to his lasting shame, he sold the birthright to his mother's family home, Montjésieu, for 30,000 livres.

In 1792 his friends were startled to find that Valady was building an arsenal in his Parisian lodgings, apparently to support the seizure of the royal family, which occurred on 10 August, forcing the Legislative Assembly to suspend the monarchy and dissolve itself in favour of a new 'National Convention', to which Valady was elected deputy for Aveyron. Republican though he was, Valady was not in favour of executing the King, and in January 1793 sided with many of the Girondins. He proposed that Louis should be kept in honourable confinement until the end of the war currently raging against the Queen's nephew and his Austrian and Prussian army, and afterwards to banish the royal family with a large pension.[53]

Hostility between Brissot's Girondins and Robespierre's Jacobins descended into violence, and Valady helped to instigate the Girondins' practice of carrying pistols into the hall of the Convention: on 20 January 1793, the day before the execution, it was said that Valady sent a note around declaring: 'Tomorrow in arms to the Convention – he is a coward who does not appear there.'[54] But the execution went ahead; on 1 February France declared war on Britain and Holland; and in March the *sans-culottes* rioted against the Girondins; by May it was rumoured that the Girondins were part of a nationwide royalist conspiracy. Jean-Baptiste Louvet de Couvray, one of the prominent Girondins, recommended fleeing to the Girondist provinces and leading an army against Robespierre's Paris-based Jacobins. Others, balking at the prospect of civil war, placed their confidence in the new democratic institutions.

On 31 May Robespierre helped to gather an 80,000-strong armed mob baying for the blood of the Girondins who were, they believed, trying to fragment the unity of the republic into a federal state; on 2 June they surrounded the National Convention claiming that they – rather than the elected representatives – were the voice of the people. They demanded, among other things, that the twenty-two Girondin deputies who had become the focus of their ire – Valady among them – be handed over. When the President of the Convention demanded respect from the mob, their leader François Hanriot replied: 'Tell your fucking President that he and his Assembly can go fuck themselves, and if within one hour the Twenty-two are not delivered, we will blow them all up.'[55] Cannon were aimed at the doors of the assembly hall; deputies tried to escape through the perimeter fence in the garden but were thwarted; the mob invaded the hall waving pikes, shouting and sitting on the benches with the Jacobin deputies. Faced with the prospect of another bloody massacre, the Convention succumbed, obeyed the mob, and the unfortunate twenty-two were offered up to the hungry fury of post-revolutionary dissatisfaction: they were all put under house arrest to await condemnation.

This was the beginning of Robespierre's Reign of Terror and there followed a purge of moderate voices from the National Convention. On 28 July the twenty-two were pronounced outlaws and traitors 'to be led to the scaffold without trial as soon as they can be got hold of'.[56] Brissot was pained, in the months before his inevitable execution, to think of 'the young and unfortunate Valady, who shares today the proscription of the most virtuous and the most faithful friends of the motherland'.[57] After the fugitive ex-minister Jean-Marie Roland committed suicide on hearing that his wife had been guillotined, a number of others took their own lives to deprive the Jacobins of their bloodthirsty satisfaction. And yet, on 31 October the full original quota of twenty-two men were guillotined with a flourish of sacrificial finality in the chillingly efficient time of thirty-six minutes. But the completeness of this iconic sacrifice – as the purge's only survivor Louvet de Couvray pointed out – was a sham, for, apart from the suicides, several of the original twenty-two had already escaped Paris and were fleeing across France.[58]

Valady had managed to get through the city gates incognito with a friend, and joined up with Louvet, Barbaroux and four others. With the help of loyal supporters they fled to Normandy and tried to raise an army; but Jacobin propaganda preceded them everywhere and whole towns were on the lookout for strangers. Protected for a while in Caen, they eventually broke cover and headed for the coast, marching in disguise in a regiment of Bretons who had been fighting against the royalists in La Vendée. They reached a ship to take them to Bordeaux – the heartland of the Girondins – and after several narrow escapes chanced upon the house of a sympathetic curate who gave them shelter. Valady's friend departed to find relatives near Périgueux, but was immediately caught and executed on the following day. A search party was sent out and Valady, Barbaroux and Louvet had to move to a hay barn. Hungry, exhausted and despairing, Valady's friends raised pistols to each other's heads in a suicide bid; the crisis was only averted by Valady's pleas and the moment of tension dissolved into tears. The Revolution, the ideal for which they had risked their lives and engaged all their passions, had now turned on them like a ferocious beast. These men, shattered by hardship and persecution, receiving news every day of new horrors – friends executed and imprisoned, massacres in the fighting at La Vendée, military losses in the war against Prussia and Austria – could do nothing but listen as they heard their hopes crashing to the ground under the ascendance of Robespierre. Having fought for freedom each of them faced the bleak realisation, in Louvet's words, that they 'could no longer doubt the enslavement of his country'.

That night they heard the voice of their provider calling them to come down. Fearing they had been discovered, Barbaroux and Louvet prepared to fight to the last, while Valady in terror refused to believe that their captors would kill them in cold blood. It turned out to be a false alarm, but they were turned out into the rain until they were installed in an underground hideout with their comrades Jérôme Pétion, Louvet's childhood friend, and François Buzot, both of whom later committed suicide. As suspicion in the area grew, the friends were forced to disband. 'What a look did he give us when we quitted him!' recalled Louvet – perhaps the last sympathetic face Valady saw – 'Never shall I lose the sad remembrance of it; he had death in his eye.'[59]

In a desperate attempt to pass through Périgueux, Valady was recognised on 5 December 'by the ferocious agents of Robespierre' and arrested at Rivaux, near Montpon.[60] He was briefly tried before a criminal tribunal; as an outlaw he stood no chance and he was immediately sentenced to death. In the official report sent to the National Convention, the officer, Roux-Fazillac, was frustrated to confess that 'I saw with regret, on the occasion of this judgement, that the republican spirit is not as strengthened in this district as I had convinced myself. Even though the conspirator had demonstrated great weakness in his interrogation, he nevertheless moved the spectators, and even some of his judges shed tears.'[61]

In the few days before his execution, Valady poured out his '*derniers sentiments*' in a string of breathtaking letters to his family. Like a true martyr, Valady steadfastly reconciled himself to dying for a cause in which he passionately believed. 'I loved the people like you taught me to,' he told his aunt, 'I threw myself headlong into the Revolution which I regarded as a necessary remedy, directed by Providence against the excessive ills of the people and the oppression of a corrupt government.' If he had lived, he could have fulfilled even more of his patriotic dreams and consummated 'my true vocation, that of letters and moral philosophy'. The noble circumstances of his death, he reassured her, should be a consolation for 'the blow which is going to strike you'. His brave example, he said, ought to provide inspiration for his young nephews whom he hoped would be brought up according to his vegetarian principles.

But alongside his valour, Valady also had aching regrets. Abandoning his wife stung him with remorse; his loss of faith in God now filled him with sorrow; his unpaid debts lacerated his pride; and worst of all he had sold his mother's home. Addressing his father (who at that time was imprisoned in the citadel of Montpellier) as 'citizen Izarn-Valady', he begged forgiveness for being a recalcitrant son and, in true filial style, asked him to settle his debts; and in a message directed to Boudon-Laroquette, to whom he had sold his birthright, he begged him 'in the name of friendship, to sell back to my sister the natal home that I turned her out of' and the 'maternal bed where we were all born'.

Finally, at the thought of his beloved grandfather, Valady burst into words of weeping sorrow: 'Alas! If I had adhered to his repeated demands to live near him with my wife to be the staff of his old age, I would be living unknown but tranquil, and I would have fulfilled my domestic duties.'[62] So, on 11 December, with pangs of remorse mixed with steadfast pride in the noble-mindedness of his deeds, Valady ascended the scaffold. Placing his head in the neck-shaped groove of the guillotine, he sent a last prayer to 'his God', heard the command to release, the sound of the blade hurtling down towards him, the whistle of the ascending rope, and felt the impact before his head thudded, bloodily, to the ground.

TWENTY-THREE

Bloodless Brothers

In France the vegetarian radicals came close to the centre ground of revolutionary politics. In Britain the authorities – horrified by the scenes of decapitation and civil war over the Channel – were determined to stamp out the rebels before it was too late. Many radicals were fomenting revolution in Britain, the monarchy of George III was in almost perpetual crisis, and by the time of Valady's execution the thought police were poised for a vigorous crackdown. The British revolutionaries – with a thriving network of vegetarians among them – had become a force to be reckoned with.

Jacques-Pierre Brissot, the French revolutionary leader who patronised Oswald and Valady, regularly visited London to cultivate political alliances. As a frequent guest at the London household of 'the Pythagorean Pigott', Brissot became friends with several others who extended their 'fraternity' to animals, and he made detailed comments about them in his *Mémoires*. Prominent among these was the Welsh druid-priest David Williams, notorious for disseminating his pagan-influenced pantheism from the Temple of Nature in Cavendish Square. Influential in Bonneville and Oswald's Masonic Social Circle, Williams agitated in France and England and he set up a Literary Fund which subsidised Oswald's activities.[1] His *Lectures on Education* revived the principles of Rousseau's *Émile*, including the Pythagorean attention to dietary temperance, and Brissot referred to Williams cordially as an 'apostle' of vegetarianism.[2]

Williams in fact ended up turning against vegetarianism, but his Utilitarian argument proving 'the false humanity of the Pythagorean system' was nevertheless emphatically animal-friendly – like the arguments of Francis Hutcheson and William King on which it was based.[3] If farm animals were made happy through careful husbandry, he explained in his *Lectures on the Universal Principles and Duties of Religion and Morality* (1789), then cultivating as many animals as possible for human consumption would create *more* happy creatures than if we all just ate vegetables. Thus, he concluded, 'humanity pleads in conjunction with reason; and thereby encreasing the general sum of happiness in the world, it is reconciled to what at first appears inhuman, submitting the life of one animal to another.' Vegetarianism, he explained, was one of those 'excesses of tender passions, [which] delight and fascinate, while they mislead and injure us'. Without these reasons, he insisted, 'I should certainly have continued, what I once was, a thorough Pythagorean.' Despite his apostasy from vegetarianism, however, Williams held on to his conviction that evil could be eradicated on earth if everyone emulated the Hindus in exercising *compassion* to 'all living creatures', and this helped many radicals to see why the 'social circle' should be widened beyond the confines of the human race.[4]

At Pigott's London house, Brissot also became closely acquainted with the arch-quack James Graham (1745–94), 'so famous for his electric bed, his earth baths, his Pythagoreanism,' commented Brissot, 'and by twenty other systems not less bizarre that he had preached in the American continent'.[5] At his incredibly well-frequented Temple of Health in London's Adelphi and the Temple of Hymen in Pall Mall, Graham hired out his notorious electro-magnetic bed which purportedly enhanced sexual vigour by stimulating the nervous impulses in the body, and he counted the likes of Georgiana, Duchess of Devonshire, among his patients. Like Lord Monboddo and John Stewart, Graham was convinced that humanity's sexual capacity was being eroded by decadent lifestyles, and he sought to remedy this with a holistic treatment of raw food (rather than cooked 'dead' food), plenty of fresh air, hard beds, early hours, and puritanical washing of the body, especially the genitalia – ideally in one of his special mud baths.[6]

Graham peddled an extraordinary brand of physical and spiritual regeneration which would, he claimed, ensure 'felicity in the eternal spiritual worlds' and help to bring about a millenarian 'New Jerusalem' of perfection. This revival of millenarianism was typical of extremists at the end of the eighteenth century, who fused their hopes of democratic reform with the expectation of a utopian future.

Sympathy and sensibility lay at the heart of Graham's philosophy. When residing in America he followed Benjamin Franklin in backing the rebels, and he called for the extension of 'universal benevolence' to the victims of war, colonialism and slavery.[7] To animals also, Graham stretched the circle of sympathy: 'your bounties and benevolences,' he told his readers, 'must not be confined to your own family and friends, nor even to your own species; – no, you must . . . shew mercy to all the dumb animals, or brute creation (as they are called) about you.'[8]

Graham was an avid reader of Thomas Tryon, and he revived many maxims from that seventeenth-century brahminical prophet of prelapsarian purity. In works with titles borrowed from Tryon, such as *The Guardian of Health, Long-Life, and Happiness*, Graham adopted Tryon's belief in karmic resonance: 'Nourish, protect, and cultivate a friendship as it were, with every fowl, beast, and fish that belongs to you, or that you come near: Those poor, sweet, innocent, and wonderfully intelligent creatures will all as it were, bless you with their whole hearts, and they will implore and draw down blessings on you and yours, from the common father of the Universe!'[9]

Although Graham kept the temple of his own body pure from the taint of dead animals, he was not such a fool as to think he could convince everyone else to do the same; and in most of his works he did not actually insist on vegetarianism. Instead, like Tryon and George Cheyne, he explained how to minimise the deadly effects of meat – by avoiding battery-farmed animals fed on unnatural food and those suffering torturous deaths:

> If you must eat flesh, let it be that of the clean, young animals . . . Do not degrade and bestialize your body, by making it a church-yard, or burial-place for the corpses of vile unclean animals . . . In regard to myself; if foul and filthy animals must be murdered and put out of the way, for fear, as is pretended, that they should be too numerous, I beg that some other executioner than me may be found to butcher them, and some other burying places for their inflamed, maddened, and mangled corpses to rot in than in my body.[10]

Educated in Edinburgh (though he did not graduate), and resident in Bath, Graham acknowledged his debt to the great progenitors of vegetarian medicine, Cullen and Monro.[11] Like Cullen, he believed that nervous disorders were caused by the irritating qualities of luxurious diets and lifestyles. 'The ground of all our diseases, and the shortening of life,' he said, echoing Cheyne, 'is from the excessive eating of flesh and other meats, and from drinking inflammable and inflammatory liquors.'[12] In this respect, Graham's advice differed very little from many of his contemporary doctors; but Graham radicalised the medical tradition into a revolutionary critique of modern corruption and a holistic vision for the rejuvenation of the cosmos (though this, of course, was only marginally more extreme than Cheyne's outlandish theories).

Considering the scientific support Graham had on his side, Brissot was perplexed by the doctor's failure to acquire a larger following for his diet. 'Graham had a beautiful figure, an admirable form, a noble and majestic countenance, and looks which seemed to command respect,' wrote Brissot in his *Mémoires*. Graham followed 'with the most rigorous scruple the abstinence from flesh ordered by the reformer of Crotona [Pythagoras]. It was to this regime, proved and undertaken during twelve years, that he attributed his brilliant health; I do not know how, with so many means of succeeding, he made so few proselytes.' Brissot sympathetically concluded that it was not because his vegetarian arguments were intrinsically nonsensical; on the contrary, they were extremely virtuous and people only failed to heed them because society was already so irreparably corrupt. In London, Scotland and the United States, where people were too habituated to 'the most succulent substances, and where Pythagoreanism is nearly treated as a fable', Brissot explained, Graham was inevitably treated as a charlatan rather than a philosopher. Repeated imprisonment for debt had not improved Graham's reputation, but even this provided Brissot (who had himself been jailed for debt in England) with an excuse to eulogise him. While in prison, Brissot proclaimed, Graham continued to deliver lectures through the bars of his cell – not to accrue profit to himself, but solely to repay his creditors.

Graham's doorway to fame had been opened wide in 1778 when his brother William (aged twenty-one) shocked the world by marrying Brissot's friend, the eminent republican historian Catherine Macaulay (aged forty-seven). Macaulay – who was also friends with Benjamin Franklin – consulted Graham for his healing powers and she in turn advocated compassion to animals in her widely read treatises on radical social reform.[13] Macaulay's *Letters on Education*, published in 1790, a year before her death, opened by castigating the clergy for having failed to inculcate 'the necessity of extending our benevolence to the dumb animals', which, she argued, God had created with souls in order to be happy. She warned that bringing up children as 'devourers of animal substances' – especially rare bloody meat – could 'tend to weaken that sympathy which Nature has given to man', and that rather 'Milk, fruit, eggs, and almost every kind of vegetable aliment, ought to be the principal part of the nourishment of children.' Anxious to appeal to as wide an audience as possible, she was less extreme than Rousseau, and allowed that children could be fed meat up to three times a week; but she went beyond the usual stance by presenting the avoidance of animal suffering as a motive for reducing meat-eating 'within as moderate limits as the present state of things will admit'.[14]

Through Macaulay, these sentiments were incorporated in a diluted form into one of the most influential radical works of the era, Mary Wollstonecraft's *Vindication of the Rights of Woman* (1792). Wollstonecraft, who called Macaulay 'the woman of the greatest abilities that this country has ever produced', also avoided the vegetarian position: she denied animals reason and she seems to have considered unscientific Rousseau's denial that man is 'a carnivorous animal'. But she nevertheless took the robust stance, in line with Graham and Williams, that 'Humanity to animals should be particularly inculcated as a part of national education' because 'Justice, or even benevolence, will not be a powerful spring of action unless it extend to the whole creation.'[15]

That Brissot – de facto leader of France for a few critical years – gave such a sympathetic assessment of Graham and collaborated with several other vegetarians, indicates how centralised the movement was in the years of the Revolution. Pythagoras' legendary opposition to tyranny appealed to revolutionaries (just as it had to the seventeenth-century republican deists), and it was easy for the likes of Brissot to read into Pythagoreanism their own ideas of extending the 'social circle' to include all of humanity and even other species.[16] Graham, Williams, Oswald, Valady and Pigott no doubt represent the tip of an iceberg now hidden by the passage of time. Many revolutionaries, without actually practising it, could see the point of a diet that claimed to cleanse the corruption of the modern age. It was a harmless opinion in itself, and if it instituted a gentle temperament and was based on principles of egalitarian sympathy, what could be said against it?

Even Robert Southey, soon to be poet laureate, who had been a sympathiser of the Revolution but turned into a vehement Tory, did not have a problem with vegetarianism *per se*. In his fictionalised

Letters from England (1807), he expressed his detestation for the radical vegetarian Joseph Ritson; but this was for Ritson's shameless blasphemies rather than for actually abstaining from meat. He had also found Valady ridiculous when he came over to England during the Revolution 'dressed in white like an aspirant'. Southey wasn't particularly impressed by Graham either; but again, this was for his eccentric antics rather than his diet. 'This man,' said Southey, 'lived upon vegetables, and delighted in declaiming against the sin of being carnivorous, and the dreadful effects of making the stomach a grave and charnel-house for slaughtered bodies. Latterly he became wholly an enthusiast, would madden himself with ether, run out into the streets, and strip himself to clothe the first beggar whom he met.' It was Graham's involvement in the subversive tradition of millenarian radicalism that raised Southey's deeper suspicions of his character.[17]

While the mature Southey was very keen to distance himself from the radicals with whom he had happily associated in the 1790s, he acknowledged that 'The principle of abstaining from animal food is not in itself either culpable or ridiculous, if decently discussed ... There is therefore nothing irreligious in the opinion, and certainly it is favourable in some of its consequences of morality.' Indeed, back in the 1790s, Southey had written several poems about sympathising with animals. The problem, he mused in agreement with Brissot, was not the principle of vegetarianism in itself, but with modern society's addiction to meat, and, even more importantly, the political significance of beef as a symbol of British patriotism. 'A certain Thomas Tryon attempted to form a sect of such about a century ago,' but he was bound to fail, said Southey, because the idea of living on lentils 'would hardly become popular in a country where Beef-eater is a title of honour, where the soldiers march to battle with a song about roast-beef in their mouths, instead of prayer, and where the whole nation personify themselves by the name of John the Bull'. Meat-eating was a litmus test of political affiliation, and Southey deftly implied that hesitating even for a moment over a plate of beef could be construed as a deeply suspect assault on the nation. In the role of his imaginary Portuguese interlocutor, he remarked drily that 'I have more than once been asked at table my opinion of the roast beef of Old England with a sort of smile, and in a tone as if the national honour were concerned in my reply.'[18]

It was the national honour with which the anxious state authorities were concerned: and they had had enough of the likes of Oswald starting with murmurings against roast beef and ending up trying to invade England with 60,000 demented Frenchmen. The government was determined to put the leading radicals behind bars and in the 1790s scores of them were imprisoned, some of them on their way to the scaffold or Botany Bay, and many of those who survived the judicial process were conveniently picked off by jail typhus and other delights of prison life. Somewhat unwisely, groups of them were locked up together in London's Newgate Prison where they could socialise with each other and the outside world. As the historian Iain McCalman has shown, this had the counter-productive effect of bringing together numerous disparate figures and uniting them in their plight. *Causes célèbres* would be an understatement for the status that the Newgate martyrs of freedom attained; they became a hive of dissenting activism and a pilgrimage for all budding radicals. Incarceration at Newgate became a more or less mandatory entry on the curriculum vitae of anyone wishing to be admitted into the hard core of the radical networks. In the light of the new material on Brissot and Pigott's vegetarian fraternity and on the prominence of vegetarianism in revolutionary France, it is worth revisiting the Newgate experience to see how it helped to form a more cohesive radical vegetarian tradition than might otherwise have emerged. In particular, it fostered the construction of a tradition that linked them with their radical forebears in the seventeenth century, who had similarly been crushed by a powerful state determined to block the universal suffrage and land redistribution demanded by the radicals.

At the end of the eighteenth century many movements that had flourished in the seventeenth century were revived. Radicals harked back to the republicanism and democracy of the Cromwellian era. Catherine Macaulay saw her own republicanism as a parallel to that advocated by the radical parliamentarian opponents of Oliver Cromwell. The French regicide had only one precedent – the execution of Charles I; the communism of the Cercle Sociale echoed earlier experiments in communalism; the utopian agrarian communities dreamed of by Brissot, Pigott, Valady and Saint-Pierre resembled the digging communities of the 1640s and 1650s. The battle of democracy against tyranny was seen as an attempt to instate what the radicals had tried and failed to accomplish 150 years earlier.

Just as in the seventeenth century, violent turmoil was imagined to augur the coming of a new global epoch. On both sides of the political spectrum, the cataclysmic events in France were seen as portents of apocalyptic proportions. To the radicals it promised the coming of perfect egalitarianism; to the conservatives it seemed like a coming of the kingdom of Satan – personified by Robespierre and later Napoleon. Just as in the seventeenth century, these patterns of thought were not restricted to religious extremists. Radical atheists had their own utopian equivalents to the Christian myth of the millennium and they looked forward to a world of harmony built on the progressive achievements of mankind.

Intriguingly, these developments were coupled with a new wave of Indophilia. In the seventeenth century mystics like Tryon had been mirrored by Indophile deists like the *Turkish Spy*; in the eighteenth century religious fanatics believed that Indian scriptures revealed hidden secrets about the cosmos, while to unbelievers like Oswald, Hinduism represented a secular natural law of mutual respect.

It seems less surprising, therefore, that there was a resurgence of vegetarianism along with these other movements. As in the seventeenth century, vegetarianism was part of a radical critique of mainstream culture, and it latched onto the multifarious significances of diet. Luxury was a sign of inequality and a cause of economic oppression; killing animals was a symbol of cruelty in society; and anthropocentrism was the legacy of a power-hungry Judaeo-Christian priesthood – all of which the vegetarians of both periods claimed they could resolve.

Many of the precedents from the previous century were well known: Thomas Tryon, for example, enjoyed a revival. His attack on slavery struck a chord with the new liberals; his puritanical edicts shared a common pedigree with later temperance movements; even some of his wackier ideas survived a hundred years of Enlightenment science. Other parallels with the seventeenth century were not the result of direct debt or deliberate revivalism; they seem rather to point to shared impulses and more pervasive cultural continuities. Both eras saw a reshuffling of constitutional affairs, wider democracy and pluralism, and a surge of expansion in Britain's exposure to global cultures (in the 1770s to 1790s Britain was gaining decisive ascendancy over the major European powers in India and other colonies). Radicals were keen to see their struggles as the latest chapter in an eternal, *natural* fight for freedom, and differences between their times and the past were often deliberately ignored.

Just as in the seventeenth century, the radicals did not constitute a total break from the rest of their social milieu. Sympathy – a universally espoused virtue – was now radicalised into a mandate for rights-based national constitutions, and the relevance to animals was inescapable. Moderate Indophilia and even abstinence from meat were endorsed by mainstream figures, like William Cullen, who did their best to keep the radicals nervously at arm's length. But, in the end, the extremists had to be suppressed.

In the 1790s Southey was still an enthusiastic republican and it was no doubt as a pilgrim to the Newgate radicals that he first encountered some of the newly allied vegetarians he later mocked. It was in Newgate that James Graham became involved with the millenarian radicals, particularly the infamous convert to Judaism, Lord George Gordon, whose libels against the Queen of France and the British legal system had earned him a long-held place behind bars. Gordon's followers were convinced that he was Moses risen from the dead, and like the seventeenth-century philo-Semites Traske and Tany, he took his Judaism to the extent of cutting off his foreskin and exhibiting it in his prison cell, and abominating non-kosher food. Gordon styled himself as a biblical prophet living on an ascetic diet, and this gained him the esteem of medical purification-enthusiasts like Graham. Gordon formed a partnership with the notorious continental heretic-healer Count Cagliostro (1743–95) who shared Gordon's interest in mystical Judaism and rejuvenation through ascetic fasting. The dietary strictures would have been an extra attraction for Gordon's disciple and visitor at Newgate, Martin van Butchell, a revolutionary vegetarian healer who also hooked up with Count Cagliostro by publishing extracts from the vegetarian *Turkish Spy* on the wandering Jew, whom Cagliostro – originally a street urchin from Palermo – claimed to be. When Gordon perished in prison in 1793, van Butchell – who had by then been incarcerated for hailing Thomas Paine as a prophet-healer – used his prophetic powers to assist a wholesale shift of allegiance from Gordon to another Newgate inmate, Richard Brothers (1757– 1824), who pronounced himself the 'nephew of the Almighty' and promised to restore the lost Hebrews to a 'New Jerusalem'. The comparison with seventeenth-century radicals was irresistible and van Butchell drew a direct line from the Fifth-Monarchy Men through to Gordon and Brothers.[19]

Brothers dismantled Gordon's Jewish food laws, and supplanted them with a revival of the paradisian diet enjoined by seventeenth-century prelapsarian millenarians.[20] Although Brothers did not uniformly call for vegetarianism,[21] in his utopian *Description of Jerusalem . . . with the Garden of Eden in the Centre* (1801), he declared that 'To eat also of fish, flesh, or fowl, clean and unclean, ever was and ever will be lawful, when distress or hunger requires it for human preservation. But if there was, or is, not any necessity to do such things, then indeed the crime becomes presumptuous and the sin of the blackest nature.'[22]

This no doubt helped to attract Brothers' most prominent disciple, the eminent Orientalist Nathaniel Brassey Halhed (1751–1830). Halhed had started off like Holwell, a respected pioneer in the discovery of Hindu culture, and his *Code of Gentoo Laws*, which endorsed Holwell's discoveries, was used by the colonial administration in Bengal. But like Holwell (whose famously beautiful daughter, Elizabeth, he fell in love with while staying with her and her husband in Calcutta), Halhed drifted further and further from the scholarly mainstream, until he had convinced himself that the Hindu epic, the *Mahabharata*, revealed the same prophetic truths as the Bible. Halhed was a Member of Parliament and in 1795 he defended Brothers from the charge of treason, and tried to convince the House that his prophecies were of national importance. Amid hoots of laughter and outraged sensibilities, Halhed resigned his seat; his political career was over and there were moves to have him sectioned in the mad hospital at Bedlam.[23] Southey had a jibe at this pair, though his claim that Brothers believed in a kabbalistic system of reincarnation seems to be belied by Brothers' derisive comments about the doctrine.[24]

Newgate served as a melting pot for these millenarian radicals, and gave them greater opportunities to make alliances. The prison diet, however, put the cat among the pigeons. The jailers' masterstroke was giving these prisoners a choice: eat beef or starve. Brothers' resolve broke immediately: he claimed that the remainder penny loaf was not enough to live on, and this no doubt informed the starvation get-out clause in his vegetarian edict. If Gordon was as strict an adherer to kosher laws as everyone claimed, he too, like the Traskes a century and a half earlier, was presumably not eating prison meat. Graham, however, rose in triumph: he was quite content to forgo eating beef and let everyone know it; Brissot recalled with admiration that a few potatoes was all Graham required.[25]

The principal medium for political dissent was the printed word, and thus when the authorities started imprisoning publishers with the radical authors, new publishing deals were struck. When the republican Daniel Isaac Eaton was locked up he had the opportunity to spend some time with Robert Pigott's revolutionary brother Charles (who died in 1794 within months of Robert's demise). In the following year, Eaton published Charles' *Political Dictionary*, which defined 'Adam' as 'a true *Sans Culottes*, and the first revolutionist'; the East India Company as 'chartered robbers, licensed murderers'; and reaffirmed the links between oppression of humans and animals in his provocative definition of 'Brutality'.[26]

James Ridgway (who published the works of John Oswald and the vegetarian John Stewart) was incarcerated in Newgate with another radical publisher, Henry Symonds. Working in close collaboration, these two operated with Brissot, Bonneville and the Cercle Sociale; they printed van Butchell's prophecies on Gordon and Brothers and other works espousing the polygamous practices of certain Indian Brahmins. The radical Sampson Perry joined them for a two-year stint in Newgate, where he no doubt took the opportunity to reminisce with Ridgway over their mutual friends, Stewart and the recently killed Oswald. The liberal writer, actor and ex-stable boy Thomas Holcroft (1745–1809) (who represented his friend Joseph Ritson as a hopelessly idealistic Jain-like guardian of injured creatures in his novel *Alwyn* (1780)) joined the Newgate coterie on a treason charge in 1794, which earned him a job doing translations for Symonds. Symonds' and Ridgway's association with the anarchist William Godwin – a devout pilgrim to Newgate – helped to bring Ritson's and Oswald's vegetarianism to the attention of Mary and Percy Bysshe Shelley, thus ensuring that their legacy stretched well beyond the end of the eighteenth century. Another of Holcroft and Godwin's radical friends, John Tweddell (1769–99) became a vegetarian after travelling through revolutionary France in 1798.[27]

Symonds extended his portfolio of nature-loving literature by publishing *A Philosophical and Practical Treatise on Horses and on the Moral Duties of Man towards the Brute Creation* (1796–8) by the revolution-sympathiser John Lawrence (1753–1839). By no means a vegetarian, Lawrence held the counter-vegetarian position that it was possible to kill animals without causing suffering, but he dedicated his life to 'zoo-ethiology', or the prevention of 'unnecessary' cruelty to animals.

A woodcut from George Nicholson's
On the Conduct of Man to Inferior Animals (1797)

Lawrence was keen to distinguish himself from Indophile vegetarians like Oswald: 'I am aware of a small sect of *Bramins* among us who are disposed to take a step beyond me,' he said dismissively. He tarred them with the same brush as Lord Gordon's kosher followers who 'were for / abolishing black-pudding / And eating nothing with blood in'.[28]

An important step in broadening the radical vegetarian movement across the nation occurred when Symonds linked up with the Manchester-based vegetarian pro-democracy publisher George Nicholson (1760–1825), by publishing his anthology of vegetarian writing, *On Food* (1803), later subtitled *Cookery without Flesh*. Nicholson's many vegetarian anthologies, which he started publishing in 1797, forced unity on the disparate vegetarians in Britain – and indeed the rest of the world – by binding them all together between the covers of a single volume. Exhibiting a prodigious capacity for research, Nicholson incorporated extracts and adaptations from Franklin, Tryon, John Stewart, Rousseau, Cheyne, Gassendi, Graham, David Williams, John Wolcot (alias Peter Pindar – another Newgate inmate and author of a poetic defence of vegetarianism), and a virtually entire reprint of

Oswald's *Cry of Nature*, as well as scores of other animal-loving writers.[29]

Despite this connection with the north, it was apparently not until 1815 that the London radicals linked up with the hundreds of 'Bible Christians' in Salford who gave up eating meat in 1809 at the instigation of their radical Painite minister William Cowherd (1763– 1816).[30] Other individuals, at a distance from the metropolitan radical networks, continued to come up with variant brands of vegetarianism, like the physician Benjamin Moseley (1742–1819) who lived in Jamaica and suggested that if Europeans ate sugar instead of meat, it would sweeten their savage temperament and might fulfil Pythagoras' dream that 'the earth would cease to represent a grazing ground, for slaughter; and its bloody inhabitants a mass of canibals!' (This, it seems, was his riposte to the opinion of most vegetarian radicals, that consuming slave-produced sugar was itself vicarious cannibalism).[31] One such anti-slavery vegetarian was the Reverend Gilbert Wakefield (1756–1801) who was imprisoned in 1799 after claiming that the lower orders who lived on 'cheese-parings and candles' ends' were so cruelly oppressed that they might welcome an invasion from the revolutionary French. He spent two years in Dorchester jail corresponding with fellow political activists, including Charles James Fox whom he encouraged to give up hunting and adopt vegetarianism, and died at the age of 45 after contracting typhus in jail.[32]

As the vegetarians gathered force and cohesion, there was a backlash of beef-eating among conservatives which articulated patriotic opposition to the onion-eating French and their radical allies in Britain. John Bull was represented as the British bulldog: bull-baiting was held up as a backbone of British working-class vigour and the best means of toughening men up for war against the French republicans.[33] In the early 1800s when repeated attempts were made in Parliament to introduce laws banning cruelty to animals, the whiff of radicalism doomed them to initial failure. In 1794 the Hon. John Byng defended his class's right to blood sports against the animal-rights fanaticism of the *sans culottes*, and in 1802 William Windham MP led the resistance against the Jacobins' attempts to curb bull-baiting. Condemning excessive cruelty to animals had occupied the centre ground of social commentary for over a century, but when the bill enforcing this familiar ethic was put before the House it was met with guffaws of laughter. The proponents of the various bills, meanwhile, leant over backwards to dissociate themselves from the radical vegetarians. When trying to push through the bill in 1809, Thomas Lord Erskine (who had defended Horne-Tooke and others in the treason trials of 1794) quoted the counter-vegetarian passage in Cowper's *The Task* to illustrate that he was only seeking to eliminate 'wilful and wanton cruelty' not man's right to kill and eat animals. It was no coincidence that when Richard Martin MP was working on the bill that finally passed through Parliament in 1822, it was to John Lawrence he turned for advice – for at least Lawrence had made it abundantly clear that he was not in favour of vegetarianism and even approved of ethically conducted field sports.[34]

The irony was that the radical vegetarians derived many ideas from mainstream medical, agronomic and ethical theories. Indeed King George III, in whose name the suppression of the radicals took place, was himself lambasted as an enemy to roast beef. One of James Gillray's finest caricatures, *Temperance Enjoying a Frugal Meal* (July 1792), showed George III and Queen Charlotte enjoying a vegetarian meal of eggs and salad or sauerkraut, flanked by numerous emblems of their frugality – including Cheyne's 'On the benefits of a Spare Diet', an invented title which probably also alludes to the King's nervous breakdown (1788), a condition for which Cheyne had always prescribed the vegetable diet.[35] The King too is associated with the seventeenth century in the framed miniature hanging on the wall: the profile is of the King but it is titled *The Man of Ross*, the nickname of John Kyrle, a seventeenth-century ascetic philanthropist. Apart from satirising the reputed miserliness of the royal pair, Gillray was expressing national anxiety that the King was not eating his portion of patriotic roast beef, and that his German wife, with her propensity for sauerkraut, was weakening the King's constitution. Gillray, as a great satirist, was not one for taking sides, and he was equally ruthless in his depiction of the opposite end of the gastronomic-political spectrum, represented by George's dissolute son, the Prince of Wales (or the Prince of Whales as he was known) in *A Voluptuary under the horrors of Digestion*.

Gillray often worked with John Oswald and produced many prints for his works, including *The Cry of Nature* in the previous year, so he was well aware of the radical implications of diet. Oswald, meanwhile, in the years before the Anglo-French war, observed that the King 'is said to delight in the story of the frugality of Spartan royalty' and suggested that this might mean that he approved of the French Revo-

Richard Newton, *A Blow-Up at Breakfast!*, (1792)

lution and would become a noble patron of egalitarian reform in Britain.[36]

Gillray's theme was widely used, and Newton's *A Blow-Up at Breakfast!* has the King mistaking his own flatulence – no doubt caused by his diet of vegetables and crumpets – for a bomb plot to assassinate him. In that the King's diet seemed dangerously close to that of the radical vegetarians, the equation between eating gaseous vegetables and political terrorism was not entirely a joke. As Southey had warned, rejecting roast beef was taken as a threat to national honour.

In its lasting political anxieties, radical vegetarianism had an impact on the political vocabulary in Europe. It crystallised a widely recognisable political statement, detested by conservatives and embraced by radicals as a pre-formed mould for them to articulate their opposition to the prevailing government. The networks that arose, partly because of the crackdown in the 1790s, left a cohesive legacy of radical vegetarianism which aimed to tackle society's flaws through a combination of dietary purification, universal benevolence and also rights-based democracy. By pooling their knowledge, they constructed a tradition of vegetarianism reaching back to the seventeenth century which gave them a sense that they had eternal truth and natural law on their side. These ideas were carried over into the fringe Victorian movements of Theosophy and the Vegetarian Society, but they also had a striking impact on mainstream social discourse.

TWENTY-FOUR

John 'Walking' Stewart and the Utility of Death

In the years immediately after the 1789 Revolution, the eccentric figure of John Stewart (1749–1822) could be seen strolling the streets of Paris. Tall, strong and fabulously dressed, he gained a reputation for his extraordinary speeches. Determined that France should heed his plans for the future organisation of the human race, he liaised with other British men involved in the Revolution, and became with John Oswald one of the eighteen 'select few' friends of Thomas Paine.[1] He also met the young William Wordsworth who, many years later, reminisced about Stewart's formidable eloquence, telling a friend that he 'had been equally struck, when he had met him at Paris between the years of 1790 and 1792, during the early storms of the French Revolution'.[2]

Although Stewart and Oswald ended up in intractable political disagreement, their lives followed remarkably similar paths – and they were both philosophical proselytes of Indian vegetarianism. In 1767, at the age of eighteen, Stewart had travelled to India to seek his fortune. As the black sheep of an eminent Scottish family of drapers based in London, he had been a reluctant pupil at Harrow and Charterhouse, and was keen to break the shackles of European education. Through the influence of an ex-Prime Minister, his fellow Scot Lord Bute, he attained a post as a writer for the East India Company's Presidency and, with high expectations of glory, he was despatched to Madras.[3] After barely two years in the service, however, Stewart was fed up with the low pay and drudgery; he quit his post at the factory of Masulipatam and wrote a vicious letter of protest to the Madras Council – entered in their minutes as a specimen of 'juvenile insolence and audacity'.[4] As with Oswald's disaffected anti-imperialism, it was later said that 'suddenly, some strong scruples of conscience seized him,

John Stewart by Henry Hoppner Meyer

with regard to the tenure of the Company's Indian empire, and to the mode in which it was administered.'[5] Stewart became a rebel freebooter and set off across India to find adventure among the native kingdoms.

Treading the knife-edge of treason, Stewart made his way to the Hindu state of the infamous Muslim ruler Hyder Ali, who had recently inflicted a humiliating defeat on the British in the first Mysore war and had forced them to agree to help him crush the Marathas. In 1771 the Maratha army attacked Hyder Ali – but the British failed to help, a tacit declaration of their continued antagonism to Hyder Ali which ultimately resulted in the second Mysore war of 1780–4 (the one that Oswald fought in). On his arrival at Hyder Ali's court, Stewart was made a captain in the army and reportedly led four battalions against the Marathas in the Battle of Chinakurali on 5 March 1771. He left a unique manuscript account of the battle that gives an unusual insight into a European's service under an Indian ruler. He describes how, during the night, Hyder Ali's soldiers tried to slip past the superior Maratha army to retreat to their fort at Seringapatam, but in the morning they were charged by the enemy cavalry. Faced with almost certain defeat, many of Hyder Ali's sepoys tried to desert, and when Stewart responded with the order to execute them they 'swore they would murder us Hat fellows (as they call'd Us)* & would have kep'd their Oath but were prevented by the Cavalry who killed 8 or 10 of the most turbulent which quieted their Mutiny'. Eventually Hyder Ali fled with his cavalry, leaving the foot soldiers to be massacred, and Stewart – depending on which account you believe – was either left for dead with a serious wound, or taken prisoner and escaped.[6] Decades later when he eventually died, it was reported of Stewart that 'his body bore marks of several desperate wounds by sword and bullet, and the crown of his head was indented nearly an inch in depth with a blow from some warlike instrument.'[7]

With the excuse of needing medical attention – but in truth in outrage at Hyder Ali's conduct – Stewart handed in his resignation and set off again on his travels. According to his own thrilling account, Hyder Ali sent assassins after him to prevent Stewart divulging confidential information to his enemies, but Stewart escaped by diving into a river and fleeing through the forests of south India. Arriving back in British territory, Stewart was accused of treachery, but he insisted that he had been forced on pain of death to work for Hyder Ali, and in any case had assisted the British ambassadors while he was there. He was eventually granted amnesty, but as he was on his way out of Cuddalore a band of Company sepoys under George Dawson shot and wounded him, allegedly fired his pistol to make it look like Stewart had attacked them, and imprisoned him in Madras. Stewart pressed charges against them but lost his case in court and was deported on the next ship home.[8]

Thriving on mishaps, Stewart appears to have either escaped or returned to India, for he apparently ended up in the service of the Nabob of Arcot, before setting off on an epic peregrination through the Middle East and North Africa and finally travelling back to Britain overland in 1783 – exactly the same year that Oswald undertook the same journey. Stewart, however, claimed to have gone the whole way on foot. In Ispahan he sent a spy-missive warning Warren Hastings that the French were secretly trying to instigate the Persians to attack the Russians, and complaining that the British hostilites with the Nabob of Oudh prevented him from travelling back to India and 'of making

---

* Europeans; so called for their unwonted headgear.

such discoveries as might be useful to the Interests of the Honble Company & worthy of your Patronage'. Instead, Stewart resolved to amble through 'Georgia & Circassia', and he was said to be the only European other than Oswald to have visited the northern Turkish Kurds.[9]

For this legendary journey, along with several other pedestrian ventures in Germany, Russia, Lapland, Canada, Scotland and France, he earned the nickname 'Walking Stewart'. In London he became a celebrity, shuffling through the streets in full Armenian costume, and peddling his bizarre ideas hammered together from a range of Eastern and Western philosophies. Contemporaries remembered him standing on Westminster Bridge, studying humanity as it passed by, dressed in a massive overcoat, his clothes and boots dusty and travel-stained, or sitting in St James' Park inhaling the breath of the cows.[10]

At the time of the French Revolution, he moved to Paris where, like Oswald, he was said to have applied his Indian military experience to the revolutionary cause by supplying tactics for the arming of the people.[11] But as the Revolution descended into sectarian aggression, Stewart was repulsed and later excoriated Robespierre's 'ephemeral and bloody despotism' which would, he predicted, be followed by 'a more desperate and durable anarchy'. In mid-1791, just as Robespierre was emerging as a dominant voice in the Jacobin Club against the moderate constitutional revolutionists, Stewart fled the country, leaving half his fortune behind him. In July he arrived at New York on an evangelical mission to persuade Americans to avoid the extremes of tyranny and anarchy. But they 'refused his mental gas', as one contemporary put it, and he returned to England embittered against Paine for his incendiary radicalism and for having 'seduced America to a disastrous separation from its metropolitan empire, (cutting the sçion from its parent stock, before it had acquired its full sap)'.[12]

After years of pecuniary difficulties, Stewart won the enormous sum of between £10,000 and £16,000 in a suit against the East India Company in lieu of debts owed to him by the Nabob of Arcot.[13] Freed from his dreary London lodgings, he took lavish 'Epicurean apartments' in Cockspur Street and had them decorated in fashionable gaudy Chinoiserie and mirrors (to match his elaborate Oriental philosophy). From 1789 to his death in 1822 (allegedly from a laudanum overdose), he produced reams of poetic and polemic work with extraordinary titles like *The Apocalypse of Nature, The Revolution of Reason,* and *The Sophiometer; or, Regulator of Mental Power*. Published in England, France and the United States, they were idiosyncratically dated according to a chronological system in which 1795 was 'the fifth year of intellectual existence, or the publication of *The Apocalypse of Nature*' and 1818 was 'the 7000th year of Astronomical History, from the Chinese Tables'. Keen to spread his ideas far and wide, he held cultured musical soirées frequented by many of London's literary elite: the socialist industrial reformer Robert Owen, Thomas Taylor the Platonist, the publishers Thomas 'Clio' Rickman and Henry George Bohn, all of whom seem to have tolerated Stewart's notoriously egotistic disquisitions in which he declared himself 'the universal self, or man-god'.[14]

In pragmatic terms Stewart had become convinced that the masses were debauched by commercial interests and poor education, and thus needed to be governed by an educated aristocracy whose power should be balanced by Parliament and a powerful monarchy. But he still maintained a profound Rousseauistic faith that mankind was naturally benevolent. In an ideal world, he declared to his audiences, he would abolish the nation-states and replace them with a forum of global governance embracing the entire human race. Like Oswald, he envisaged a direct democracy where the world's populations would gather in councils of 100,000 and send out deputies to represent their views, 'And thus succeeding take in all the globe,/ Till one vast hall collects deputed world'.[15]

Everyone, he fantasised, should move into communal barracks where food, ideas, passions and bodies could all be shared. These hot-houses of sexual and mental intercourse would swap their pubescent youth with each other to ensure 'the improvement of the species', would institute peace, wisdom and, of course, vegetarianism. Although in favour of promiscuity, Stewart was also an early advocate of birth control and natural contraception, arguing that inflated populations only caused famine and helped tyrants to build larger armies.[16] Stewart never married, but he admitted coyly 'that self-denial of the fair sex was not rigorously practised by him', and he defended a system of regulated prostitution.[17]

He had no religious qualms about sex. Like his friend Oswald – many of whose views he shared – Stewart was an outspoken atheist (still very unusual in British society, not to mention illegal). He conceded that religions provided a temporary bulwark against immorality, but he wished to replace their God-derived rules with an ethical system based on the idea that all beings were connected parts of the universe, a fact he liked to highlight by addressing his friends as 'Dear fellow part of our common integer, Nature'.[18] Stewart only escaped being prosecuted, suggested one friend, because his views were so outlandish they were regarded as obscure oddities rather than a threat.[19]

Despite his shocking opinions, which won him several enemies, Stewart maintained cordial relations with an array of British literary figures. The dissenter John Taylor, who was intimately acquainted with Stewart for many years, recalled that 'I never knew a man with more diffusive benevolence, for he not only felt an interest in the welfare of mankind but of all sensitive nature.' In Vienna, Michael Kelly (who also shared a mistress with Oswald) 'had the pleasure to find the eccentric Walking Stewart' arriving on foot from Calais, and remembered him as a highly accomplished man, an 'enthusiast about music, although not about beef steaks; for, of the most tender . . . he would not touch a morsel; he lived entirely on vegetables.'[20]

In 1798-9 Stewart was spreading his revelations to innocent bystanders in Bath when he met the thirteen-year-old Thomas De Quincey (1785-1859), later to become the great friend of Wordsworth and author of the *Confessions of an English Opium Eater* (1821). De Quincey was overwhelmed by Stewart, and ten years later when he came to London as a young man he sought him out again. They formed a lasting friendship and De Quincey remained Stewart's most outspoken advocate, keeping his memory alive in fashionable literary magazines for the next fifty years. For the twenty-year course of their friendship, he said, Stewart was 'the most interesting by far of all my friends', and 'the most eloquent man . . . that I have ever known', despite the 'hybrid tincture to his diction' picked up on his multitudinous travels. De Quincey acknowledged that Stewart caused great offence from 'the uniform spirit of contempt which he manifests for all creeds alike', but he insisted that he was 'comprehensively benign' with a 'true grandeur of mind' and a 'very extraordinary genius'. 'Animal food or wine he never allowed himself to use; or, in fact, anything but the Brahminical diet of milk, fruit and bread'; this in itself was perfectly harmless, and it kept him healthy, for he was 'a fine specimen of the animal Man'. Stewart entertained a megalomaniac notion that the rulers of the world would conspire to destroy his works, so he instructed people to bury them for future generations, and asked De

Quincey to translate them into Latin (who thankfully never fulfilled his promise). De Quincey compared his extraordinary walking feats with Wordsworth's 175,000 miles of rambling in the Lake District, and he made a rather pathetic attempt to emulate them by walking round his garden.[21]

Stewart was a fellow opium-eater, and his vivid philosophical visions of tangible connections between all life forms seem to bear testimony to this fact. He claimed that travelling the globe had emancipated his mind from the fetters of national prejudices. The personal philosophy he developed during his survey of world cultures was an impressive fusion, drawing on common ideals from an eclectic mix of philosophies which aimed to propel humanity towards universal happiness.[22]

As an avowed Spinozist, Stewart revived the claim of the various seventeenth-century free-thinkers – Blount, Toland and the *Turkish Spy* – that the Pythagorean-Hindu doctrine of metempsychosis actually referred to the recycling of matter in the universe, according to which all beings were parts of one interconnected whole.[23] Poring over the works of Sir William Jones and other Orientalists, Stewart absorbed the vital Hindu idea of oneness with the universe. Enlightenment was achieved, he said, when man learned 'to identify self with all nature'.[24] To this he added a materialist Epicurean explanation of karma according to which atoms participated in the sensations of the organism of which they were a part, and they carried the impression of those sensations even after leaving the body. This meant that any sort of violence, whether it be whipping a horse, oppressing farm-workers or picking flowers, contributed to universal suffering which would persist in an endless cycle of bad karma. Suffering in another being was really suffering in another part of our own 'universal-self'. The atoms of a tyrant would one day join the bodies of his victimised subjects, and the atoms in a farmer would eventually experience the suffering of his slaughtered animals. Individuality was dissolved into the unity of nature and any violence increased suffering in the whole. Man, 'though his mode may dissolve and disperse the eternal particles of matter, that composed it . . . live eternally in all surrounding nature'. Killing animals, he suggested, was not only cruel, but against our own interests; it was a violation of common sense.[25]

It was not just after death that organisms diffused their sensible atomic substance. Even in this life matter was always passing from one body to the next. 'The human body emits every hour half a pound of matter ... which ... must attach itself to millions of beings, and participate in their sensation.'[26] By the continuous flux of atomic effluvia, Stewart reckoned that the atoms in a hand that struck an animal could be absorbed into the victim and participate in the very suffering it inflicted; the atoms in a horsewhip could incorporate into the body of the horse it whipped. This, he claimed, was the true reason why human sympathy should spread from self, to family, to nation, to species, and finally to all living beings.

The Chinese, he said, had first discovered this cycle 5,000 years ago; it was adopted by the Egyptians, communicated to the Greeks under the title of *To Pan*, and thence to the Romans; it had recently been revived by Lord Bolingbroke (1678–1751) and received a vivid expression in Alexander Pope's image of widening ripples on a lake in his *Essay on Man*: 'See matter next, with various life endued,/ Press to one centre still, the general good.' Or, as Stewart put it:

> Nature, matter, essence, being's whole,
> Whose parts are join'd in body and in soul;
> Now king, now subjects, slaves, now cattle, sod,
> Now riding man, now million horses rod;
> Matter besieging to besieged turn'd,
> Now soldier burning, and now peasants burn'd;
> The hunted hare transmutes to hunting dogs,
> And whipping driver into slaves he flogs;
> And though no agent memory remain,
> The patient atoms feel augmented pain.[27]

The solution to suffering in the universe was to teach everyone 'to liberate the brute creation, to fraternize man, and identify self with the whole of existence'. This was the answer to cruelty to animals, not the legislation that Lord Erskine was attempting to bring before Parliament. 'The homo-ousiast, or man of nature,' he explained, 'who fears to communicate pain to the crust he eats, what tenderness, what benevolence must he ever feel for a sensitive fellow being; he would lift the worm from the path, lest some heedless fool might crush it, and save the drowning fly from his tea-cup.'[28]

In Stewart's interconnected universe, the medical reasons for vegetarianism were not separate from the humanitarian reasons. Damaging oneself and causing suffering in one's own body by eating a vitiated diet created bad karma just like killing animals. Stewart combined

Cullen's opinion that meat caused irritation and plethora with Cheyne's theory that it caused blockages, impeding physical and mental activity and inflaming ferocious passions. He also followed the radical quack James Graham in recommending purificatory mud baths and washing the penis with soap to combat venereal disease. If such measures failed, opined the tripped-out traveller, then flee the 'excremental air' of cities and take up opium.[29]

Stewart had a fetishistic concern with teeth: fibres of flesh, he warned, caught in their interstices and engendered caries. But it was equally pernicious to use toothpicks to dislodge them, for this tore the gums and allowed pestilential cold air into the body. Indeed, a vegetable diet was the only means by which the human race could survive. This was an urgent matter: for women, Stewart claimed, were so cursed with menstrual disorders and pain at childbirth, that when human nature reached the point at which reason overcame instinct, they would refuse to be mothers and 'the species must be extinguished.' The only remedy for this imminent catastrophe was the universal adoption of vegetarianism, for as his 'travels, over various parts of the eastern world' had demonstrated to him, 'air, exercise, and vegitable diet' spared Eastern women the pain they suffer in the West.[30]

Bizarre as Stewart's ideas seem, they formed a meaningful part of a wider debate then raging about how to create the greatest possible amount of happiness in the world. This was the age of Utilitarianism, and most Utilitarians agreed that non-human sentient beings should be included in the sum of overall happiness – though opinions differed on how much weight to allow them. Indeed, Stewart frequently articulated his view in exactly the terminology of the Utilitarians as he advocated the 'maxim of *effecting the greatest possible good to the whole of nature*', and 'the augmentation of good and the diminution of evil, to all sensitive life'.[31] His karmic theory was an attempt to equalise the value attributed to human and non-human suffering, and thus fully enfranchise animals within the greater common good.

In essence, Stewart's notion of interconnectedness was not so radically different from the ideas of many Utilitarians, who had themselves been influenced by the same Epicurean 'pleasure principle' and Pythagorean interconnectedness that inspired Stewart. As with Stewart, it was the Hindu consideration for animals that helped the nominal founder of Utilitarianism and philosophical radicalism, Jeremy

Bentham (1748–1832), to identify the lacuna in Western legislation. 'Under the Gentoo and Mahometan religions,' wrote Bentham in his seminal *Introduction to the Principle of Morals and Legislation* (1789), 'the interests of the rest of the animal creation seem to have met with some attention.' Thus he observed:

> The day *may* come, when the rest of the animal creation may acquire those rights which never could have been withholden from them but by the hand of tyranny. The French have already discovered that the blackness of the skin is no reason why a human being should be abandoned without redress to the caprice of a tormentor. It may come one day to be recognized, that the number of the legs, the villosity of the skin, or the termination of the *os sacrum*,* are reasons equally insufficient for abandoning a sensitive being to the same fate.

To the delight of all future animal liberationists, Bentham swept aside the age-old question of animal reason, and insisted that 'the question is not, Can they *reason?* nor, Can they *talk?* but, Can they *suffer?*'[32] This central contention, which reframed Rousseau's argument in the *Discourse on Inequality*, showed that the capacity for sensation was enough to gain consideration in a moral code that was based on happiness. This remains one of the cornerstones of the current animal-rights debate, and it is the basis of the Utilitarian philosophy of the most eminent animal liberationist, Peter Singer, Professor of Bioethics at Princeton University.[33]

However, contrary to the misleading statements peddled by historians eager to enrol him to the vegetarian cause, Bentham was emphatically *not* suggesting that it was wrong to kill animals.[34] On the contrary, his argument was geared towards *refuting* the idea that animal sensation was a basis for vegetarianism; he joined the catalogue of counter-vegetarian sensibility writers and divine apologists, like Archbishop William King, who believed that the death meted out in the slaughterhouse was, or could theoretically be, painless. If death occurred without suffering, then it was no longer a bad thing for an animal to be killed. Life itself had no value, only pain and pleasure. Bentham even went as far as to argue that an animal could be *better off* being killed: 'The death they suffer in our hands commonly is, and always may be, a

---

* The wedge-shaped triangular bone at the base of the vertebral column; Bentham means having a tail or not.

speedier, and by that means a less painful one, than that which would await them in the inevitable course of nature,' and therefore 'they are never the worse for being dead.' So, he concluded, 'there is very good reason why we should be suffered to eat such of them as we like to eat: we are the better for it, and they are never the worse.' The furthest he was willing to go – just like all the other counter-vegetarians – was that we should not wilfully torment animals.

Such thinking proved infectious. Bentham's Utilitarian godson John Stuart Mill (1806–1873) also thought the happiness of animals was a considerable part of the common good, but did not advocate vegetarianism. David Williams, who published his *Lectures* in the same year as Bentham, also agreed with his calculation. Before Bentham, Philip Doddridge, in his *Lectures on Pneumatology, Ethics, and Divinity* (1763), had elaborated that as well as meat making people happier by giving them 'brisker spirits', one should also add the happiness of all the people employed in the meat industry (an argument still very much in force today). Arthur Schopenhauer (1788–1860), who was also impressed by Hinduism and Buddhism, echoed Bentham in concluding that it was unnecessary for Europeans to be vegetarian like the Brahmins, because in the colder climate people would suffer more from the lack of meat than animals suffered 'through quick and always unforeseen death'.[35] Stewart differed from them in his decision that the pleasure of eating meat *was* outweighed by the suffering animals experienced on being eaten (and he thought meat wasn't good for you anyway); and, second, he went a lot further in his definition of sensitive life.

Stewart's extension of sense beyond the animal kingdom was by no means unheard of, however: the idea that all life was endued with sensitivity captivated the Romantics with enthusiastic love for the interconnected harmony of the natural world (an enthusiasm reinforced by their interest in Indian culture). The mimosa, a plant that retracts its leaves on being touched, fascinated Romantic writers, stimulating poems such as Percy Shelley's 'The Sensitive Plant', and leading some to conclude that plants' capacity for pleasure and pain was comparable to that of animals.[36]

The greatest progenitor of these ideas was Erasmus Darwin (1731–1802), the radical free-thinking physician and grandfather of Charles. His works provide an insight into Stewart's: they agreed on many things, but their moral conclusions on meat-eating were directly opposed. Darwin enjoyed his hearty meals and grew so fat that he had a concave salient carved into his dining table to accommodate his belly: he was not going to let the greater common good squeeze him out from his meat-eating niche (though he did ultimately provide the vegetarians with their strongest Utilitarian argument).[37]

Darwin's 'Loves of the Plants' (1794–5) – a lengthy poem with extensive discursive notes – proposed that flowers had sex lives very similar to our own, committing intentional acts of love-making and even adultery. In *The Temple of Nature* (1803) Darwin portrayed a whole universe animated by pleasure, and, as the scholar Ashton Nichols has shown, this provided an underpinning for the love of nature expressed in Keats' nightingale and Wordsworth's poems about daffodils: 'every flower/ Enjoys the air it breathes'. Darwin injected this principle into the Utilitarian mandate: every living thing experiences 'pains and pleasures', he said, and the aim of everything was to 'increase the sum total of organic happiness'.

Darwin's concept of nature as an interconnected ecological cycle of pleasure creation was very close to Stewart's: 'every part of organic matter from the recrements of dead vegetable or animal bodies,' wrote Darwin, 'becomes again presently re-animated; which by increasing the number and quantity of living organisms . . . adds to the sum total of terrestrial happiness.' Darwin's pleasure principle enfranchised even microscopic organisms into the system of moral value. Indeed, the underlying measure of value was no longer confined to particular species. Once the value of life had been reduced to a unit of pleasure it no longer mattered to whom or what that pleasure belonged: 'The sum total of the happiness of organized nature is probably increased rather than diminished, when one large old animal dies, and is converted into many thousand young ones.' This was in line with Bentham's argument that the death of one creature can be justified by the amount of pleasure its death could bring to others. This was essentially an ecological value system, which subsumed the value of individual organisms into the wider picture of the whole ecosystem.

Darwin, like Stewart, regarded Pythagorean metempsychosis as a representation of this 'perpetual transmigration of matter from one body to another'. Like Stewart also, he regarded this as the basis of a universal 'system of morality and benevolence, as all creatures thus became related to each other'. With a philosophy so close to Stewart's, Darwin's poetry inevitably sounded very similar:

LEFT Akbar ordering the slaughter to cease, from Abul Fazl's *Akbarnama*, *c.*1590. During a hunt in 1578 Akbar experienced divine revelations; some of his attendants told him 'that the beasts of the forest had with a tongue-less tongue imparted Divine secrets to him . . . he in thanksgiving for this great boon set free many thousands of animals. Active men made every endeavour that no one should touch the feather of a finch and that they should allow all the animals to depart according to their habit.'

Silsila al-Zahab, 'Majnun and the Hunter', Akbar's court, India, 1613. 'Every wild animal which was in the desert/ Rushed to his service,/ . . . The sheep was freed from the violence of the wolf,/ The lion withdrew his claws from the wild ass,/ The dog made peace with the hare,/ The calf of the deer suckled milk from the lion'.

King Solomon and the animals, from the *Iyar-i-Danish*, *c.*1595.

LEFT Top-cover of a pen box signed by Manohar, late 17th century.

ABOVE (*Top*) Detail of lady holding a tree from a jewel casket from India, attributed to Rahim Deccani, late 17th century.

(*Bottom*) Further detail from the same casket. Manohar and Rahim Deccani, whose painting also appears on the front cover, combined European and Indian motifs; in this case the image of a European, playing music to animals like Orpheus, blends seamlessly with the traditional Indian Ragamala illustrations of female musicians surrounded by animals.

ABOVE The *pietre dure* Orpheus on Shah Jahan's Throne in the Hall of Public Audiences in the Red Fort, New Delhi.

RIGHT From a *Ragamala* (Garland of Melodies), Jaipur, India, *c.*1750.

LEFT The Buddhist scribe Amrtanda delivers a copy of the *Lalitavistara (Sutra of Great Magnificence)* to Captain Knox, an officer of the East India Company's army, resident in Nepal, 1803.

ABOVE James Fraser, *A Street Scene in the Village of Raniya*, 1816-1820.

OPPOSITE Detail of an illustrated *vijnaptipatra* by the eye-witness Ustad Salivahana, 1610. The Jain monk Vivekaharsha is shown receiving emperor Jahangir's *farman* (imperial order) that no animals should be slaughtered in all the kingdom during the twelve-day Jain festival of Paryushana. From the outer perimeter of the court in Agra, two Europeans, probably Father Conti and William Hawkins, observe this typical instance of Mughal diplomacy towards Jain vegetarianism.

James Gillray, *French Liberty: British Slavery*, 1792

James Gillray, *Consequences of a Successful French Invasion, or We teach de English Republicans to Work*, 1798. The French revolutionaries force the English to exchange their national dish of roast beef for the cultivation of turnips and onions.

James Gillray, *Temperance Enjoying a Frugal Meal*, 1792. One of James Gillray's most audacious satires, this shows George III and Queen Charlotte enjoying a meal of eggs and sauerkraut or salad, flanked by emblems of their frugality. Dr Cheyne's *On the Benefits of a Spare Diet* lies on the locked chest in the bottom right. On the wall hangs an empty frame titled *The Triumph of Benevolence*, a quip at the royal misers but also the title of Gillray's portrait of the vegetarian prison reformer John Howard.

James Gillray, *A Voluptuary under the Horrors of Digestion*, 1792. The Prince of Wales (or Whales), bloated after polishing off a joint of meat, reclines beneath a portrait of the 16th-century temperance writer, Luigi Cornaro.

James Gillray, *New Morality; – or – The Promis'd Installment of the High-priest of the Theophilanthropes, with the homage of Leviathan in his suite,* including caricatures of David Williams and William Godwin, 1798.

Edward Hicks, *The Peaceable Kingdom, c.*1848. Hicks, a Quaker, produced about a hundred versions of this theme.

With ceaseless change, how restless atoms pass,
From life to life, a transmigrating mass;
How the same organs, which to day compose
The poisonous henbane, or the fragrant rose,
May, with to morrow's sun, new forms compile,
Frown in the Hero, in the Beauty smile.
Whence drew the enlighten'd Sage,* the moral plan,
[That] man should ever be the friend of man;
Should eye with tenderness all living forms,
His brother-emmets, and his sister-worms.

Darwin did not endorse Stewart's idea that suffering could be carried by particles of inorganic matter from one being to another, and thus he emphatically did not conclude that this moral-material interconnectedness was a reason to refrain from eating animals. It was precisely because all life was united, in Darwin's view, that the loss of one animal did not impinge on universal happiness. He believed, on the contrary, that the natural processes of death and renewal were perpetually increasing happiness. This emphasis on interconnected natural life cycles was a vigorous counterpoint to the 'sentimental' ethic which focused all its concerns on individual suffering.[38]

This unsentimental ecological view of nature had been developed decades earlier by Georges-Louis Leclerc, Comte de Buffon, in his *Histoire Naturelle*, and had recently been redacted in Oliver Goldsmith's *A History of the Earth and Animated Nature*. Buffon was part of a long tradition going back to the theodicists Leibniz and the Archbishop William King, who argued that the apparent brutality of natural predation and human carnivorism can be reconciled to the idea of universal benevolence. Buffon saw death as the mother of life: the potential for life simply transferred from one form to another. To explain this transfer of life, Buffon proposed that the life capacity of all beings consisted of a special sort of 'animate atoms' (a theory similar to Leibniz's idea that animated 'monads' constantly 'transformed' into new life forms). Buffon explained that if the living being they were in died or was eaten, they would simply dissolve, circulate and be absorbed into other living beings. 'These particles pass from body to body,' said Buffon, creating 'a perpetual renovation of beings'.

Buffon, too, saw metempsychosis as a fabular rendition of this true Lucretian-Epicurean material life cycle. Among the Hindus, he said, it

* Pythagoras.

was known 'long before the present aera, that all animated beings contained indestructible living particles, which passed from one body into another'. It was this belief, he noted, that made the Hindus conclude that 'they ought to abstain from every thing endowed with life.' However, according to Buffon this vegetarian position put far too much emphasis on the preservation of an individual organism and ignored the fact that 'a succession of beings cannot otherwise be effected than by mutual destruction'.[39] Buffon's dedication to the principle of 'plenitude' – valuing the maximum quantity and variety of life – was a forebear of Erasmus Darwin's 'greater common good' principle. It was essentially a *laissez-faire* attitude to the Hobbesian war in nature. Although Buffon believed that the quantity of animate atoms in the universe was a fixed constant, whereas Darwin believed that life and happiness were on the increase, they both agreed that death was a desirable part of the life cycle, for it facilitated the greatest number and variety of organisms. In this, Buffon and Darwin formed a united front against the unscientific, hyper-sentimental vegetarians who saw only the suffering of individuals rather than the system of which they were a part.

This was the crux between two brands of philosophy whose disputes still rage today between the biocentric 'tree-huggers' who focus value on ecosystems, and the animal-welfare 'bambi-lovers' who care more for individual organisms' experience of pain or pleasure. Just as they do today, those who valued ecosystems as a whole, like Darwin and Buffon, claimed that vegetarians blindly concentrated on the loss of individual animals while ignoring the wider benefit of meat-eating and the natural basis for a *laissez-faire* attitude to carnivorism. However, Stewart's karmic idea that suffering was retained by matter even after death added a new variable to these calculations: matter incorporated into new life, but it carried with it previous sensations, which could make future life miserable, rather than 'happy'. Since his aim, like Darwin's, was to increase universal happiness, the principle of persistent suffering inserted a new integer which made the moral equation – even from the ecosystemic point of view – show that killing animals was wrong. In the Romantic era elements of the modern environmental debate were in full swing, and the conflicts were expressed acutely in the reactions to Stewart, whom many dismissed as a 'madman', while others embraced him as the embodiment of universal benevolence.[40]

TWENTY-FIVE

To Kill a Cat:
Joseph Ritson's Politics of Atheism

Among John Stewart's London acquaintances was the radical vegetarian Joseph Ritson (1752–1803). Ritson was a renowned antiquarian, famous for his valuable collections of folk-ballads about Robin Hood, and for providing Sir Walter Scott (1771–1832) with background information for his bestselling historical novels. Despite his public eminence Ritson was a vigorously anti-establishment republican; he visited France in 1791, and looked forward to the revolution spreading to Britain.[1] During the government crackdown on republicans in 1792, Ritson feared for his life as he watched his friends being picked off one by one. He cowered behind his desk at the bailiff's office where he worked, as government agents prowled around collecting information, and he warned his friends that 'I find it prudent to say as little as possible upon political subjects, in order to keep myself out of Newgate.'[2] Anyone convicted of 'speculating in his closet upon the title of tyrants', Ritson reflected morosely, would be dragged to the scaffold, hanged, 'cut down alive, his privy members cut off, and his heart and bowels ripped out, and thrown into the fire before his face; then his head is to be cut off, and his body divided into four quarters, which are to be *at the King's disposal*: The execrable tyrant who first devised, ordained and permitted this horrid butchery,' wrote Ritson, 'would probably eat them raw.'

Fear of his own horrible demise, however, did not stop Ritson privately indoctrinating his friends and family with republicanism and trying to wean them from the 'unnatural and diabolical practice of devouring your *fellow creatures*'. He devised an egalitarian system of universal rights which opposed the hierarchical structure of both human society and natural ecologies. Ritson had shunned meat since reading Bernard Mandeville's *Fable of the Bees* at the age of nineteen, and after thirty years of being the most famous vegetarian public figure in London, he published *An Essay on Abstinence from Animal Food, As A Moral Duty* (1802). The *Essay* was an anthology of vegetarian writing which his acerbic commentary marshalled into a formidable attack on man's presumptuous idea of his place in nature. By lacing his material together in a more analytical and aggressive way than his fellow vegetarian anthologist George Nicholson, Ritson's *Essay* became a flagship for the emergence of a cohesive tradition, and it showed how vegetarianism ought to be an essential part of the revolutionary agenda.

Ritson was a great admirer of Stewart's robust individuality, and he warmly dubbed him 'citizen Bruin'; they obviously shared a great deal – both republican, atheist and vegetarian. They were also bound together by their mutual friend, the architect of anarchy and communism, William Godwin (1756–1836), Percy Shelley's father-in-law, who endorsed political reasons for limiting the consumption of flesh, though he refused to eat the insipid vegetable food of his many vegetarian friends until chronic piles, constipation and delirium eventually made him all but give up meat.[3] Stewart himself saw his own works as the fruition of Godwin's idealism, and for a while Stewart, Ritson and Godwin enjoyed each other's company. By 1793, however, Ritson was fed up with Stewart's arrogant posturing, his sell-out to bourgeois culture, and the blithering karmic mumbo-jumbo he produced to defend their vegetarian principles. Sending one of Stewart's books to a mutual friend, Ritson declared contemptuously that 'he does not deserve the name of citizen', adding with finality that 'I am so disgusted with his bigotted prejudices and absurd opinions, that the continuation of our acquaintance will be owing rather to ceremony than to esteem.'[4]

While Stewart was busy speculating on incredible doctrines of universal sentience, Ritson was intent on nurturing a rationale for vegetarianism that would avoid the flaws of sentimentalism. Defending vegetarianism on the basis of avoiding animal suffering looked shaky in the light of the counter-vegetarian notion of the painless death, and the ecological argument – espoused by Buffon and Darwin – that ecosystems as a whole gained more 'pleasure' from an individual animal's death than the animal lost in dying. Instead of using animal *suffering* as a basis for vegetarianism, therefore, Ritson constructed an animal rights argument based on the inherent value of *life*, which gave animals a natural right to their existence. Furthermore, he showed that humanity's claim to have an inalienable right to kill any animal they chose was built on a baseless religious myth. Thus Ritson provided an important perspective to the emerging debate about animal rights and an answer to the ecological defence of meat-eating.

Whereas Stewart had been content to regard humanity as the world's principal moral agent, Ritson was determined to kick *Homo sapiens* from his self-made supernatural pedestal. Religion was responsible for giving humans the idea that they transcended the rest of the universe, and so in his *Essay on Abstinence* it was on religion that Ritson turned with fury.

Humans, insisted Ritson, were not essentially different from the monkeys to whom they were so manifestly related. Whatever rights humans had to life, animals had them too, and eating them was as good as cannibalism.[5] God was an invention designed to flatter humans into believing that they were half divine while the rest of nature was a quagmire of pure dirt. Religion was not so much God-worship as self-worship; and it was time this super-elevated ape was taught where he belonged in the scheme of things.[6]

Ritson dragged man down to earth, stripped him of his divine soul and shoved him into the zoo with all the other animals. Inviting his readers to re-examine this curious animal, he declared on the strength of all the anatomical evidence that he was clearly formed like a herbivore and 'in a state of nature, would, at least, be as harmless as an ourang-outang'.[7] In any case, whether meat-eating was natural or not it was this carnivorous practice – first introduced by malevolent sacrificial priests[8] – that had turned man from a docile herbivore into 'the most universal destroyer'.[9] As things stood, he said in a fit of pessimistic fury, humans and other predators were perpetrating such horrific 'murder, bloodshed, cruelty, malignance, and mischief', that it might well 'be better that such diabolical monsters should cease to exist'.[10] If eco-systems required murder to sustain themselves, they had a negative overall value. If nature was a constant war, it could not create the greatest possible happiness; it merely contributed to universal misery.

In order to rectify this dire situation, Ritson proposed that Europeans should emulate the Hindus. He was contemptuous of the Brahmin priesthood and their hypocritical doctrines, but, like Rousseau, Oswald, Stewart and Volney, he nevertheless admired the qualities of their vegetarian philosophy. They demonstrated that the vicious cycle of flesh-eating was the cause and the effect of human cruelty, whereas vegetarianism instilled egalitarian relations between people and 'the exercise of gentleness and humanity toward the minuteëst objects of creation'.[11] Furthermore, meat-eating was the preserve of the rich, so any self-respecting democrat should be vegetarian.[12] Atheism was the ground-rock for demolishing the idea of man's violent supremacy over animals, and thus Ritson redrew the battle lines for the debate over animal rights and ecology.

Ritson quickly converted his widowed sister to vegetarianism: 'You will certainly find yourself healthier,' he told her in 1782, 'and if you have either conscience or humanity, happier, in abstaining from animal food than you could possibly be in depriving, by the indulgence of an unnatural appetite and the adherence to a barbarous custom, hundreds, if not thousands, of innocent creatures of their lives, to the enjoyment of which they have as good a right as yourself.'[13] But his first major problems emerged when training her son, Joe Frank, to become an upstanding radical republican vegetarian. In the face of Frank's boyish knack for revealing inherent paradoxes, Ritson found it difficult to define the reasonable limits of his life-preserving principles. First there was the questionable ethical status of eggs: '*eggs* are henceforward to be considered as animal food,' wrote Ritson to Frank in 1782, 'and consequently prohibited to be eaten. You will take notice of this, and act accordingly.' Frank's response to this unsavoury deprivation was 'refractory and *obstropulous*' so Ritson agreed to allow that 'if a pudding stand before you, you are not obliged to refuse it on account of the eggs, I do not myself. But I should never *direct* a pudding to be made for me with eggs in it.'[14] These occasional indulgences were permitted, Ritson explained in 1802, because it 'deprives no animal of life, though it may prevent some from comeing into the world to be murder'd and devour'd by others'.[15]

If preventing death was the aim, Frank perceived, surely the first place to start was with the bloodthirsty animal predators. Indeed, Ritson did speak as viciously against 'sanguinary and ferocious' feline predators as he did against humans.[16] Taking this logic to its extreme, the young lad murdered his neighbour's cat: 'I rather think he went a little too far, in putting his friend Mrs Wiseman's cat to death for killing a mouse, which perhaps nature, certainly education, had taught her to look upon as a duty,' wrote Ritson apologetically to his sister. But to Frank himself he played another tune: 'Far from desiring to reprove you for what I learn you actually did, you receive my warmest approbation of your humanity.'[17] As all animals had the right to life, this had to apply to those murdered by carnivorous animals as well as by carnivorous humans. It was surely as worthy to interfere on behalf of a cat's prey as it was on that of a human – a problem with the animal rights basis for vegetarianism that is still posed in academic debates today.[18]

When the cartoonist James Sayers satirised Ritson in 1803, this was one of the logical implications he ridiculed. The emaciated cat in the top of Sayers' picture is chained to the wall, allowing the rats to run amok. This alludes to Ritson's radical politics: chain up those at the top of the hierarchy so that the lower orders can play in liberty. But Sayers' point is that trying to prevent predation, and by extension political hierarchies, is unnatural. The cat starves and rats perpetuate the cycle of violence by gnawing on a bundle of candles made of whale tallow. Hierarchies, Sayers implied, are a natural part of social harmony, just as they are in natural ecologies. Republicanism and vegetarianism are presented as unnatural ideals misguidedly attempting to eradicate inequality in nature. Ecology could be used to defend political hierarchies; no surprise that in the twentieth century Fascists used ecology to present their ideology as 'natural'.

Ritson had implied to his sister that cats were perversely trained to catch mice by their inhumane owners (as John Williamson of Moffat once claimed). Perhaps they could be reformed into peaceful herbivores – a hope strengthened by Ritson's suspicion that animals were capable of language. Accordingly, in Sayers' cartoon Ritson has placed a copy of his *Essay on Abstinence* open in front of the cat, presumably in the hope that it would read and reform its vicious ways.

Republicanism, vegetarianism and atheism formed a three-pronged attempt to level the hierarchies of politics, nature and religion. Naturally, therefore, the *Essay on Abstinence* evoked more negative press than any previous vegetarian treatise, and Ritson, already a famous literary figure, became the most notorious vegetarian of his time. Unsurprisingly, most people were not so keen on seeing humanity tumbled into the mud, and the reaction to Ritson's ungodly assault on religion and monarchy was outrage. Robert Southey reviled the *Essay*, 'every page and almost every line of which teems with blasphemy'.[19] Critics were delighted when, in the following year, Ritson apparently went mad – allegedly in the process of writing a paper claiming Jesus Christ was an impostor. He was discovered in the act of setting fire to his papers,

Joseph Ritson by James Sayers (1803)

whereupon he chased concerned onlookers away with a knife and
started hurling his furniture about and breaking his windows. His
apoplexy finally brought on his miserable death. Reviewers already
hostile to Ritson did not hesitate to damn him as well. In the *British
Critic*, Robert Nares called the *Essay* 'ineffable nonsense':

> mischievous in its design, detestable in its conduct, impious,
> and even daringly atheistical, in its principles and avowed

deductions . . . The fool, who, in the pride of his no-knowledge . . . aspired to pull the Almighty from his throne, sunk, in the twinkling of an eye, beneath the level of the lowest and most contemptible of the beasts that perish! It is said that he was found naked, at midnight, in the court of his inn, with a large clasp-knife in one hand, and a copper kettle in the other, on which he was exercising his impotent fury.

Refusing to relent even in the wake of an adversary's death was most unusual, and publishing humiliating details of his last hours was seen as distasteful in any circumstances. Sir Walter Scott, ever an advocate of Ritson's integrity, wrote to Robert Spence that 'I was very indignant at the insult offered to his memory, in one of the periodical publications . . . imputing the unfortunate malady with which he was afflicted to providential vengeance and retribution, for which the editor, in exact retributive justice, deserved to be damned for a brutal scoundrel.'[20] But the slur stuck: it was rumoured that Ritson's vegetarian principles had been the product of madness – a common slur on vegetarians with which Crab, Robins, Stewart, Oswald, Holwell, Valady, Graham and Brothers had all been tarred. The original article in the *Dictionary of National Biography* maintained this position, even though Ritson had been a practising vegetarian for thirty years before he went mad, and even the recent edition suggests that the inchoate format of Ritson's *Essay* was the product of 'incipient insanity'.[21]

Despite such defamatory remarks, however, Ritson's moral philosophy was seriously challenging, and it clearly seemed important enough for his contemporaries to spend a great deal of energy refuting it. If it did nothing else, Ritson's case for moral abstinence from meat injected another direction into the debate about humanity's relationship with nature. In the *Edinburgh Review*, Henry Brougham called his republicanism and atheism 'nauseous and contemptible'; but he nevertheless agreed to tackle Ritson's arguments on their own secular terms. Like Southey, Brougham did not have a problem with reasonable arguments in favour of vegetarianism – its improvement of human health and enlightening of morality – but Ritson's claim that man's consanguinity with animals made it a *crime* to kill them was an untenable position. Brougham dedicated his review to showing that Ritson's animal rights argument defeated itself when viewed from the wider ecological point. Irrespective of his benevolent intentions, Ritson would never be able to extract himself from the ecological war in nature of which every human is a part. Ritson was himself guilty, Brougham pointed out, of starving calves by drinking milk, aborting chickens by eating eggs, and murdering whole ecologies of microscopic organisms every time he washed his armpits. Even while Ritson was in the act of writing his vegetarian arguments, he was using a quill from a plucked goose, ink made from crushed insects, and even the whale-tallow candle he used to light his study 'is a damning proof of the long-protracted torments and inhuman butchery of the great leviathan, the lord of the deep'. 'His harangues against destroying animal life,' concluded Brougham, 'are ushered into the world on the spoils of the slain.'

Even if Ritson were able to disentangle himself from the animal products that compose the fabric of human existence, Brougham showed, he would still not be able to avoid the crime of killing his 'fellow-creatures':

> Every drop of water that quenches our thirst, or laves our bodies, contains innumerable insects, who are sacrificed to our necessities or comforts; each simple that forms a part of the most humane and scrupulous Pythagorean or Brahmin's vegetable fare, conveys to a cruel and inevitable destruction thousands of the most beautiful and harmless of created beings. The ground on which we press to succour a wounded animal, or to adore the God of tender mercy, is by those actions necessarily turned into a scene of torture and carnage. From the first to the last gasp of our lives, we never inhale the air of heaven, without butchering myriads of sentient and innocent creatures.[22]

By killing animals to eat them, said Brougham, we merely 'swell, by an imperceptible voluntary addition, the catalogue of necessary enormities'. As Buffon and Darwin pointed out, living inextricably within the great chain of life also meant submitting to the great chain of death. This argument had frequently been used against Eastern vegetarians:[23] it was a lethal criticism. Not only was it unnatural to try to prevent killing, it was actually impossible.

There remained another essential element to Ritson's vegetarian argument which Brougham and other critics of Ritson's vegetarianism were also keen to refute: the idea that eating meat made men savage. Brougham himself acknowledged that killing animals accidentally was different from those murders that we commit *voluntarily*. As George Cheyne had pointed out in 1724, it was *intentional* slaughter of animals that made men violent, rather than inadvertent mass-murder of micro-scopic organisms.[24]

But this again did not stand up to the facts, and Brougham pre-sented Ritson and Oswald as prime examples: they were both vege-tarian, but both total savages. Ritson was renownedly irascible, venomous and intractable with anyone who disagreed with him. Like Oswald, his gentleness to animals was contrasted to his truculence to humans. Nares mocked this by sardonically remarking that Ritson's *'tranquility of soul,* which has led him to maintain a restless and envenomed warfare with the whole human race, and chiefly with the most respectable part of it, cannot be too strongly pressed on the reader's notice, as one of the happy effects flowing from a total abstin-ence from animal food'.[25] Ritson was being framed as the archetypal misanthropic animal-lover; he had sided with the animals, making it easy to portray him as a beast himself. As early as 1783 Sir Harris Nicholas had satirised Ritson in his poem 'The Pythagorean Critic', which pointed out his incongruous cannibalistic viciousness towards his intellectual rivals:

> By wise Pythagoras taught, young Ritson's meals
> With bloody viands never are defil'd;
> For quadruped, for bird, for fish he feels,
> His board ne're smoaks with roast meat, or with boil'd.
> In this one instance pious, mild, and tame,
> He's surely in another a great sinner,
> For man, cries Ritson, man's alone my game!
> On him I make a most delicious dinner![26]

Sayers likewise made this a central part of his satirical cartoon of Ritson. The inkpot Ritson is dipping his (feather) pen into is labelled 'Gall', evoking his notoriously vituperative controversies and punning on his allegiance to revolutionary France – his 'Gallican frenzy' – also indicated by the frog and onions hanging near the window. His political tendencies are no doubt being alluded to with the numerous radical roots that surround him. Sayers might have known that Ritson was working on a system of etymology (more roots) in his massive dictionary which aimed to return the English language to its original purity, a system that he was confident would be adopted when the Revolution finally reached England. (The dictionary, which was never published, defined Carrion as 'The flesh of animals, naturally dead, or, at least, not artificially murdered by man', while a Lobster was 'A shel-fish, which is boiled alive, by people of nice feelings & great humanity'.[27])

Ritson's friends used to insist that he was not as vitriolic as everyone claimed. Walter Scott made a jocular couplet about Ritson – 'As bitter as gall, and as sharp as a razor,/ And feeding on herbs as a Nebuchad-nezzar' – but he was cordially tolerant when Ritson came to stay with him at Lasswade and abused his housekeeper for offering him a slice of beef and viciously clashed with his guests for their mockery of his scruples. Scott was no fan of vegetarianism itself – he had been repeat-edly constrained to a 'severe regimen' of boiled rice for his health – but he admired Ritson nonetheless, and he insisted that 'he had an honesty of principle about him which, if it went to ridiculous extremi-ties, was still respectable from the soundness of the foundation.'[28]

This teasing respect manifested itself in a number of Scott's novels. Ritson himself is named in *The Antiquary*, in which the Catholic Earl of Glenallan refuses a decent dinner in preference for 'a small mess of vegetables . . . arranged with the most minute and scrupulous neatness'. Sir John Oldbuck, the eponymous antiquary, 'attacked his noble guest without scruple on the severity of his regimen . . . "A few half-cold greens and potatoes – a glass of ice-cold water to wash them down – antiquity gives no warrant for it, my lord."' One can hear the echoes of Scott's reaction to Ritson's strict adherence to his system while a guest at Lasswade. Again, in *St Ronan's Well*, the character Cargill offers 'a Pythagorean entertainment' of bread and milk to his guest, while Dr Gregory, the Edinburgh physician, appears alongside Dr Cullen, as the 'starving doctor', Macgregor.[29]

Ritson's animal rights argument had little chance of gaining wide acceptance in early nineteenth-century Britain. His assault on God made him unacceptable to the majority, and even in secular debate the ecological rationale for hierarchy and human predation had clear pre-eminence over his egalitarian alternatives. However, Ritson's an-thology remained an important inspiration for vegetarians, and it was precisely his republican atheism that attracted the radicals. Ritson moved away from the sentimental culture that focused on the suffering of animals, and evolved an argument based on atheism: without the scriptural mandate, or even an eternal soul marking him out from the rest of the animals, what right did an intelligent ape have to claim mastery over all his fellow creatures? Despite the flaws in the rights-based argument, Ritson's vision that humans should see themselves as equal members of the animal kingdom proved a magnet to the next generation of vegetarians. His proposition that humans could live like a tribe of peaceful herbivores, and the massive body of travelogue anthropology he provided to showcase other cultures that had already achieved this, set the agenda for the following decades. His hope for the regeneration of humanity propelled the tradition of eighteenth-century vegetarianism into the era of Romanticism. Even among those political radicals, like Godwin, who had not joined the vegetarians by the beginning of the nineteenth century, it became *de rigueur* to give at least some ground to their perfect idealism. Living in harmony with nature – whether it was a contingent secular world or one governed by a benevolent creator – became an obsession among those early nineteenth-century thinkers eager to solve the world's problems with one quick and easy dietary reformation.

TWENTY-SIX

Shelley and the Return to Nature

When Percy Bysshe Shelley (1792–1822) first brought his university friend Thomas Jefferson Hogg to the home of his vegetarian companions, Shelley thrust him forward as the door opened. Hogg, who ended up writing Shelley's biography, described what he saw as 'a strange spectacle': there were 'five naked figures in the passage advancing rapidly to meet us'. 'As soon as they saw me,' he wrote, 'they uttered a piercing cry, turned round and ran wildly upstairs, screaming aloud.' These nudist enthusiasts were the children of John Frank Newton, author of *The Return to Nature* (1811), who was trying to return his whole family to nature by practising a combination of 'nakedism' and vegetarianism. 'The custom of flesh-eating as much as that of covering our persons with clothes,' preached Newton, was an accidental feature of human development which 'appears to have arisen from the migration of man to the northern climates'.[1]

The beneficial effects of Newton's Rousseauist educational experiment were apparent to all who encountered his offspring. Newton's vegetarian ally Dr William Lambe (1765–1847) opined that 'For clearness and beauty of complexion, muscular strength, fulness of habit free from grossness, hardiness, healthiness, and ripeness of intellect, these children are unparalleled.'[2] Lambe's membership of the Royal Society of Physicians and fellowship at St John's College, Cambridge lent such claims scientific clout. Shelley agreed that 'His are the most beautiful and healthy creatures it is possible to conceive; the girls are perfect models for a sculptor; their dispositions are also the most gentle and conciliating.'[3] They were, it seemed, perfect specimens of the uncorrupted human animal: fit, healthy, clever and temperamentally gentle. In this cult of physical perfection, vegetarianism, teetotalism and nudism formed a united front in freeing mankind from the unnatural elements of civilised life.

Newton's wife Cornelia and her sister Harriet de Boinville also liked to 'nakedise' occasionally, and their men associates responded with candid appreciation. Shelley passionately confided to his friend Thomas Love Peacock that he thought Mrs Boinville 'the most admirable specimen of a human being I had ever seen'; his lamentation that the 'extreme subtlety & delicacy' of her affections made it impossible for her to be 'quite sincere & constant' could imply an emotional involvement.[4] Lambe's daughter and Boinville's son Alfred fell in love and retreated to the country to live a bucolic dream, in Hogg's words, 'tilling the earth, the innocent occupation of our first parents'.[5]

This group of nature-loving purists also flirted with the idea of free love, seeing wild animals as exemplars of natural procreation. Among their close friends they counted the Chevalier James Henry Lawrence, who notoriously suggested that European ladies should emulate the Nair Brahmin women by winning the right to inherit property, liberating themselves from the shackles of monogamy, choosing their own lovers and shedding all their clothes. Once women had thrown aside their sexual and sartorial inhibitions, Lawrence fantasised, 'Love . . . would rekindle that open and generous fire that would make the world a paradise.'

This sort of 'peace and love' nudist perfectibilism was exactly what Shelley had been yearning for. He was an idealistic youth – growing his long straggling hair in the fashion of radical activists, and keeping 'the temple of his body' pure by abstaining from sex and grazing on frugal fare like raisins and dry bread which he carried around in his pocket. Born to an ennobled family in Sussex, he had the leisure to espouse radical liberal causes. A shy, sickly child, Shelley's experience of being bullied at school inspired him to sharpen his pen against oppression, which he came to believe was rooted in people's oppression of their own bodies under the burden of an unnatural diet. Purifying his own body, he hoped, would liberate his mind for the higher pursuit of poetry. In March 1812 Shelley, along with his first wife Harriet Westbrook, officially renounced meat. Apart from a few reported lapses, he remained a vegetarian for most of the rest of his brief adult life. In November 1812 he met Newton campaigning for a working-class land reclamation project in North Wales, and soon afterwards Harriet and he moved in with Newton's budding vegetarian community at Bracknell in Berkshire.[6] Over their meals of vegetables, washed down with distilled water, the families of Newton, Lambe and

Shelley forged a broadly cohesive ideology in which diet played a central role.

Hogg joined them in 1813 and recalled that Shelley's 'Pythagorean, or Brahminical, existence, and his intimate association with the amiable and accomplished votaries of a Return to Nature was perhaps the prettiest and most pleasing portion of his poetical, philosophical, and lovely life'. As late as 1832 – a decade after Shelley's drowned body had been washed up on the Italian coast – Hogg was still nostalgically reminiscing with the elderly Newton over their shared 'bloodless dinner'.[7] Although Hogg maintained an ironic distance, while he was at Bracknell he adhered to the canons of 'the bloodless regimen' and dubbed their community 'the gentle, tolerant, bloodless church', or 'the vegetable church of Nature', casting Newton as its great patriarch leading the way to 'the true Eden, the earthly Paradise'.[8] During this period, Shelley was writing his famous radical poem *Queen Mab* to which he appended an adapted version of his polemic, *A Vindication of Natural Diet* (1813). Shelley's charged works brought rhetorical concision and political insight to the collaborative manifesto of his vegetarian community.[9]

In the same year that he converted to vegetarianism, Shelley adopted Lawrence's anti-marital principle of Nairism, and this no doubt influenced his callous decision in 1814 to break off the marriage with his heavily pregnant wife, Harriet, and elope with Mary, the daughter of William Godwin and Mary Wollstonecraft.[10] While Harriet later drowned herself in the Serpentine, Percy and Mary evaded ostracism by travelling to Switzerland, where they continued their domestic vegetarian experiment in the Alpine heartland of Rousseauist rusticity.[11] On a later journey in 1816 they joined Lord Byron near Lake Geneva (bringing with them Mary's half-sister Claire Clairmont, who had just become Byron's lover). Decades later, their friend the Hinduphile phrenologist, Thomas Forster (1789–1860), wrote to Thomas Love Peacock, reminiscing that 'You will recollect than in or about 1814 Shelley, Byron, Lawrence & myself began the *Cibo di latti et del frutto* [Diet of milk and fruits]'. This recently discovered letter shows that Byron adopted vegetarianism, albeit temporarily, along with Shelley's physician Sir William Lawrence (1783–1867).[12]

Following this period of conviviality and intellectual stimulation, all five authors inscribed vegetarianism into their works. In the summer of 1816 in Geneva, Mary started *Frankenstein: or the modern Prometheus*, which climaxes with the monster vainly pleading for his life, assuring Frankenstein that he and his mate would be rendered 'peaceful' and harmless by their primitive herbivorous diet: 'My food is not that of man; I do not destroy the lamb and the kid to glut my appetite; acorns and berries afford me sufficient nourishment. My companion will be of the same nature as myself and will be content with the same fare. We shall make our bed of dried leaves; the sun will shine on us as on man and will ripen our food.'[13] The idea of stripping humanity down to its primeval natural origins – benevolent, harmless and herbivorous – remained a constant point of reference for writers in the Romantic era. Byron later mocked both the windy vegetable diet of his companions and simultaneously the savage implications of counter-vegetarian arguments by employing Buffon's anatomical opinions to justify the cannibalistic instincts of shipwrecked sailors in *Don Juan* (1819): 'man is a carnivorous production . . . like the shark and tiger, must have prey:/ Although his anatomical construction/ Bears vegetables in a grumbling way'.[14] For Byron, the flatulent and political 'grumbling' of peasants forced to live on vegetables drowned out the cry of nature articulated by his naïve young friend Shelley. Sir William Lawrence likewise turned against Shelley's vegetarianism with a vengeance. Forster, by contrast, went on to found the Animals' Friend Society with Lewis Gompertz and remained a convinced Pythagorean for the rest of his life. He had only one lapse into meat-eating in the aftermath of which he said that the 'cursed animal Food acted like a slow poison and brought on a vitiated state of the nervous system, dyspepsia & melancholy . . . double Vision, headache, giddiness & debility'.[15]

Newton and Lambe, meanwhile, had been publishing the results of their own experiment in alternative living. Newton originally converted to vegetarianism in 1806 after successfully using a vegetable diet to alleviate his lifelong asthmatic complaint; and this had convinced him, Dr Lambe and both their families that vegetables were man's natural diet.[16] After a three-year trial, Lambe declared in his *Reports on The Effects of a Peculiar Regimen* (1809) that 'I am at length convinced, that man is in his proper nature strictly to be ranked among the herbivorous animals; and that the use of flesh of animals is a deviation from the laws of his nature, and is universally a cause of disease and premature death.'[17] This became the medical mantra of Shelley's vegetarian community. By 1815 Lambe had compiled the most extensive defence of vegetarianism yet written, using his medical notes on numerous patients to substantiate the long tradition of medical vegetarianism which he traced back from Cheyne and Cocchi through to Sir William Temple in the seventeenth century.[18] Since the natural physiological state of all animals was health, it followed that diseases were caused by unnatural habits. Thus Lambe explained that diseases as acute as cancer could be cured or prevented by avoiding meat and other impurities such as lead deposits in water. Returning to the natural diet, he promised, could extend human life by one-sixth or even double it.[19] New statistical evidence that abstinent monks had a longer than average life expectancy lent extra credit to the traditional claim that 'the Bramins, who abstain most scrupulously from the flesh of animals, attain to the greatest longevity.'[20] Lambe warned that, at the very least, it was essential to eat a daily portion of fruit and vegetables, preferably lightly cooked or raw.

Newton agreed with Lambe's findings, and in *The Return to Nature* he too emphasised that his convictions were based on empirical medical evidence. He also identified echoes of this muffled 'voice of nature' in historical instances of vegetarian advocates – from Hippocrates and Homer to Evelyn, Cheyne and Isaac Newton. Finding a kindred spirit in Pierre Gassendi, he championed the latter's declaration that 'the doctrines of morality and philosophy are directed to no other object than to recall mankind to the paths of nature which they have abandoned' (see chapter 12). According to Newton's specialised analysis (which Shelley unquestioningly repeated in his own works), ancient myths also revealed the truth of man's natural diet. Adam and Eve's eating of the forbidden apple was really an allegory for the beginning of meat-eating, which condemned mankind to a future plagued by disease and premature death. The Greeks' story of the demigod Prometheus giving humans the use of fire and medicine was a version of the same historical event: what else were fire and medicine for than cooking meat and curing the diseases it caused? Natural man fed only on raw vegetation – a fact Newton famously tried to prove by eating a raw potato (though he judiciously decided not to make it a staple of his diet).[21] Unnatural customs like cooking and wearing clothes created barriers between humans and nature, and Newton was determined to strip them away.

Newton was most fascinated by Indian mythology, and here too Shelley seems to have followed his lead. Endorsing Sir William Temple and Voltaire's Indophilia, Newton claimed that the 'peaceful and respectable' Brahmins were 'the most ancient priests of whom we have any knowledge' and that they quite possibly held the secrets of the world's past and future.[22] Newton specified exactly what those secrets were ten years later in his *Three Enigmas* (1821). Like his namesake Sir Isaac Newton, and more recently the eminent Orientalists Sir William Jones and George Faber, Newton argued that all pagan mythologies were branches of the divine body of knowledge passed down by the descendants of Noah immediately after the Flood.[23] All ancient cultures from Druidic Europe through Egypt and Iran to India testified to the primeval truth that man originally lived on vegetables and that reverting to this natural diet would hasten the return of the Golden Age. Newton saw this manifested most clearly in the corresponding iconography of Indian theogony and the twelve signs of the Greek zodiac. By tortuously collating their hidden messages he found that they both signified the four ages of the world. Brahma stood for the first age of creation; Vishnu stood for the second age of balanced bliss, represented in the zodiac by Libra, the scales. The Hindu destroyer-god Siva typified the third dark age when man started hunting the animals, corroborated in the zodiac by Sagittarius the archer chasing Capricorn the goat. The arrival of Krishna and Danwantaree (god of medicine) signified the future fourth age, 'the Satya-yuga, or Age of Happiness', represented by the water-drinking Aquarius and Aries, the gentle herbivorous sheep. Until the coming of this prophesied Golden Age, Newton recommended that individuals should emulate the Brahmins, the Persian magi, the Druids and Daniel the prophet, whose vegetarian diets improved their physical health, illuminated their minds and helped to establish peace on earth: 'live solely on fruit,' Newton affirmed, 'and you will be innocuous as the sheep.'[24]

Although Newton published this latter work after Shelley had written most of his 'vegetarian' poems, he had clearly been developing the theory over many years. It is therefore little surprise to find that Shelley, his enthusiastic young disciple, likewise proposed that 'the mythology of nearly all religions' testified that humans were originally vegetarian; that their consumption of meat precipitated global disjunction; and that one day they would re-establish harmony by returning to the natural diet. In the meantime, Shelley suggested, individuals could achieve this in their own domestic sphere.[25]

Although Newton clearly developed an arcane faith in mythologies

Title illustration of Mary Shelley's *Frankenstein: or the modern Prometheus*.
Frankenstein's monster was created with an unadulterated human nature
corrupted only by a hostile human environment. He started life eating
berries and drinking water; he learns to cook offal, but finally declares
that he will live on acorns and berries and thus live a life that is 'peaceful
and human'.

similar to John Zephaniah Holwell, for Shelley, at least, the mythological data principally confirmed the empirical evidence. Newton, Lambe and Shelley all emphasised that the effect of meat on social dispositions was materially demonstrable. 'In Physiological discussions,' Newton insisted, 'the moral and intellectual faculties should never be disjoined from the physical and organic.' Damaging the body with a diet for which it was not suited had an inevitable impact on the moral character. Newton claimed that meat-eating depraved the physical constitution, perverting mankind from cool rationality to heated insanity, firing up 'illiberal feelings, quarrelsome inclinations; thirst for power; inflamed eagerness to have one's way'. By contrast, he reported that if children were protected from eating meat, 'their irritability, and consequently their objugatory propensities will gradually subside'.[26] Lambe agreed that the vegetable diet gave people a 'milder character, dispositions more benevolent, and morals more pure'.[27]

Shelley extended this physiological explanation of moral depravity into a political vision in which he identified meat-eating as the principal cause of violence. Without eliminating the primary ingress of violence into society, there was no hope of social reform, let alone utopian perfection. Like the disappointed Cromwellian vegetarians, Shelley claimed that revolutions in France and elsewhere in the world had always failed because the people had continued to make themselves into ferocious beasts by eating meat. In the *Vindication of Natural Diet* Shelley argued that the only solution was a vegetarian revolution:

> Who will assert that, had the populace of Paris satisfied their hunger at the ever-furnished table of vegetable nature, they would have lent their brutal suffrage to the proscription-list of Robespierre? ... It is impossible, had Buonaparte descended from a race of vegetable feeders, that he could have had either the inclination or the power to ascend the throne of the Bourbons.

Shelley also introduced a parallel economic theory that eating meat and drinking alcohol increased the demand for international luxury goods: 'On a natural system of diet we should require ... none of those multitudinous articles of luxury, for which every corner of the globe is rifled, and which are the causes of so much individual rivalship, such calamitous and sanguinary national disputes.'[28] Echoing the seventeenth-century Diggers, he suggested that if the poor stopped aspiring to the luxuries of the rich and lived instead on the products of a garden, they would be free from the enforced labour that currently maintained social inequalities. Shelley carried these convictions into his poems with such sweeping rhetoric that, more than a century later, Mahatma Gandhi found in them an inspiration for a real bloodless revolution which combined vegetarianism and pacifism in the successful eviction of the British from India.

Shelley's belief in the power of his vegetarian lifestyle therefore revolved around a medical and economic social theory which was not entirely at odds with the dominant scientific understanding of his period. He used scientific theories to defend himself from the accusation of being romantically deluded by unrealistic ideals. The fact that Shelley grounded his arguments on this anthropocentric foundation, rather than an altruistic animal rights basis, is significant and has not been fully appreciated. The anthropocentric argument constituted one of the main thrusts of Shelley's and his friends' articulation of their position, and ensured that their ideology could be used by generations of environmentalists within the framework of 'enlightened self-interest'. To illustrate their point, Lambe, Newton and Shelley emphatically distanced themselves from the radical animal rights arguments of Joseph Ritson. Shelley and the Bracknell vegetarians were well aware of Ritson; he was a close friend of their regular visitor, Shelley's father-in-law, William Godwin, and they shamelessly plundered material from his *Essay on Abstinence* without ever mentioning his name.[29] The scholar David Clark has demonstrated that Shelley based the overarching structure of his *Vindication of Natural Diet* on Ritson's work; still more revealing, however, are those aspects of Ritson's work that Shelley chose to leave out. The Bracknell vegetarians had seen how unpopular Ritson had made himself with his embittered attack on humanity in defence of animals – and how easily the animal rights argument could be refuted. It was far more effective, they realised, to defend vegetarianism from an anthropocentric viewpoint; even if they did think an animal had a right to life, they had reasons to play this down.

The Romantic poets have been held up as the pioneers of the modern sensibility to nature; Wordsworth, Byron, Shelley, Coleridge and many others were gripped with awe for the natural world. This chapter and the next will re-examine this theme, analysing what exactly Shelley's idea of 'nature' was, and questioning some of the assumptions made by recent scholars. In his groundbreaking book, *Shelley and the Revolution in Taste*, Professor Timothy Morton showed how Shelley's figuration of the body as an interface with the natural world embodied economic and social ideals. But despite Morton's engaging discussion about Shelley's interest in ecosystems, the extent to which Shelley's thoughts can be considered 'ecological' remains unclear. Where did Shelley position himself in the furious debate between Ritson's attempt to bring humans down to the level of equality with animals, and Erasmus Darwin and Buffon's argument that predation was a desirable dynamic in the system of nature? Did he credit natural ecosystems with intrinsic value like modern 'deep ecologists', as some recent scholars have suggested, or was he interested in ecosystems mainly insofar as they provided a context for social harmony? Was his vegetarianism an altruistic forbearance towards animals, or was it based on human self-interest; indeed, to what extent was human agency involved in establishing what he claimed to be a law of nature?

Lambe, Newton and Shelley all appealed to sympathy for animals in their defence of vegetarianism, but they presented this sympathy not so much as a moral reason for abstinence in itself, but rather as a piece of anatomical evidence that killing animals was repulsive to man's herbivorous nature. Lambe even pronounced that it was an 'error' to abstain on 'a principle of humanity, and a conscientious feeling'. Hogg explicitly contrasted the Bracknell vegetarians' dietary experiments with those of Ritson, who had, he said:

> some reputation as an antiquary; but as a feeder on vegetable substances, he put forward his theories with such vehemance and wild extravagance, as to be stigmatised, perhaps unjustly, as a wretched maniac. He called sheep, oxen, and pigs 'our fellow creatures,' as undeniably they are in a certain sense; and he inferred from that appellation, that we ought not to eat their flesh, or put them to death. A flea, a bug, a louse, or a tapeworm, is a fellow creature; and what then? So likewise is the cabbage.

Hogg explained that Shelley, by contrast, took up vegetarianism as a 'calm, deliberate choice, and a sincere conviction of the propriety and superior salubrity of such food'.[30]

Shelley was renownedly sympathetic to animals; he once hurled himself into a dispute in defence of an abused ass like Mr Graham in Richard Graves' *Spiritual Quixote*, and he famously attacked Wordsworth for including in *The Excursion* a 'description of the beautiful colours produced during the agonising death of a number of trout'.[31] But Shelley conceded that the counter-vegetarians were right to suggest that if eating meat benefited humans, this would outweigh the suffering inflicted on the animal. However, he always insisted that meat-eating was harmful to humans, not beneficial. Furthermore, he repudiated the idea – articulated by Archbishop William King, Francis Hutcheson, David Williams and Jeremy Bentham – that animals profited from being eaten because their assiduous human husbandmen looked after them so nicely. Echoing Ritson, Lambe, Newton and indeed Samuel Johnson, Shelley pointed out that the common practice of castration deprived farm animals of everything worth living for, and concluded that 'It were much better that a sentient being should never have existed than that it should have existed only to endure unmitigated misery.'[32] Thus, while the theodicists and Utilitarians had seen animal husbandry as a win–win situation enjoyed by both consumer and consumed, Shelley recast the equation as a lose–lose scenario in which both man and animal suffered. In the closing paragraph of his unpublished essay 'On the Vegetable System of Diet', Shelley explained that subjecting animals to misery was 'unwarrantable' *because* meat-eating was 'subversive to the peace of human society':

> The mere destruction of any sentient being abstractly considered, is perhaps an event of exceedingly minute importance . . . It is because a malevolent and ferocious disposition is generated by the commission of murder that this crime is so tremendous and detestable.[33]

Shelley was deliberately aligning himself with the traditional anthropocentric objection, articulated by Locke, Hogarth, St Clement of Alexandria and innumerable others, that wanton cruelty to animals was objectionable because it nurtured a vicious temperament. This dovetailed neatly with the notion that meat-eating made men courageous, assertive and even aggressive – a sentiment that was widely accepted at the time, and still remains a common preconception today.[34] Shelley merely pointed out that meat-eating was the most obvious source of cruelty in society. Shelley's contemporaries strenuously emphasised that this anthropocentric perspective made his views more acceptable than Ritson's. When Horace Smith met Shelley in 1817, he reported favourably that Shelley objected to meat-eating 'not upon the Pythagorean or Brahminical doctrine that such a diet necessitates a wanton, and, therefore, a cruel destruction of God's creatures, but from an impression that to . . . chew their flesh and drink their blood, tends to fiercen and animalize both the slaughterer and the devourer'.[35]

Despite the anthropocentric motives, however, Shelley imagined that taking up vegetarianism would re-establish 'equality' between man and the animals, which has led some commentators to suggest that Shelley sought to replace Judaeo-Christian anthropocentrism with a more 'biocentric' value system.[36] A closer examination of the poetic scenes of harmony with animals reveals the dynamics of Shelley's struggle with contemporaneous ecological debates, and provides insight into some of the assumptions that underlie modern conceptions of nature and the place of humanity within it.

In a string of early poems, Shelley developed his fantasy that converting to vegetarianism would reverse malignancy throughout the world. *Queen Mab* (1813) portrays the earth in three ages – past, present and future. During the first two, the 'Earth groans beneath religion's iron age . . . Making the earth a slaughter-house!' But the future promises a 'bloodless victory' in which a social revolution ushers in an age of harmony so profound it extends to all creatures and the whole of the universe:[37]

> no longer now
> He slays the lamb that looks him in the face,
> And horribly devours his mangled flesh,
> Which, still avenging Nature's broken law,
> Kindled all putrid humours in his frame,
> All evil passions, and all vain belief,
> Hatred, despair, and loathing in his mind,
> The germs of misery, death, disease, and crime.
> No longer now the winged habitants,
> That in the woods their sweet lives sing away,–
> Flee from the form of man; but gather round,
> And prune their sunny feathers on the hands
> Which little children stretch in friendly sport
> Towards these dreadless partners of their play.
> All things are void of terror: Man has lost
> His terrible prerogative, and stands
> An equal amidst equals:[38]

The first part of this passage shows how 'no longer' eating meat physiologically reverses nature's retributive cycle by re-establishing natural health and freeing humanity from the cause of disease, violence and crime. This was a dramatic claim, but by this time Shelley felt he had sound empirical evidence to support his prognosis. In 1812–13, while writing *Queen Mab*, Shelley and his then wife Harriet convinced themselves that, despite an initial sense of lassitude which made them temporarily revert to meat-eating, their health was 'much improved' by the vegetable diet. In the *Vindication of Natural Diet*, which Shelley inserted as a footnote to this passage, he reported that 'Seventeen persons of all ages (the families of Dr. Lambe and Mr. Newton) have lived for seven years on this diet without a death, and almost without the slightest illness.' He confidently asserted that by the following year this number would be augmented to 'sixty persons' all having lived healthily for three years;[39] and when Dr Lambe later heard about William Cowherd's vegetarian Bible Christians in Salford, the specimens jumped to over 400 who 'enjoy at least as good, if not better health than their fellow townsmen'. Six years earlier, Robert Southey had challenged the vegetarians to provide empirical evidence for the healthiness of their diet: 'It is to be wished that the Pythagoreans in England were numerous and philosophical enough to carry on a series of experiments . . . upon the physical effects of their system.' Shelley, who read Southey's challenge with close attention, believed that he was fulfilling those requirements to the letter.[40]

In *Queen Mab*, Shelley then turns to how the animal kingdom would respond if man 'no longer' acted like their bloodthirsty tyrant. Shelley's fantasy about the cessation of treachery between humans and their animal victims echoes the proclamation of an earlier poem by the radical poet John Wolcot, alias Peter Pindar (1738–1819):

> I cannot meet the lambkin's asking eye,
> Pat her soft cheek, and fill her mouth with food
> Then say, 'Ere evening cometh, thou shalt die,
> And drench the knives of butchers with thy blood.'

As in Shelley, this 'abdication' from violence makes wild and domestic animals miraculously gather round the human with a 'fearless eye'.[41] In his prose works, where he focused on the anthropocentric motives for vegetarianism, Shelley did not discuss precisely how this aspect of his vegetarian vision would be achieved; but in his poems it is a revealing refrain.

Despite the fact that he professed to be an atheist at this time,

Shelley's imagery in *Queen Mab* and other poems is explicitly modelled on the millennial restitution of paradisal harmony. Like the *Turkish Spy* more than a century earlier, Shelley was deliberately reclaiming Judaeo-Christian salvation and recreating it as a secularised image of future perfection. He once explained to a friend that '*my* golden age . . . will be the millennium [*sic*] of the Xtians "when the lion shall lay down with the lamb"'.[42] In *Queen Mab*, Shelley recycled that very image from Isaiah:

> The lion now forgets to thirst for blood:
> There might you see him sporting in the sun
> Beside the dreadless kid; his claws are sheathed,
> His teeth are harmless, custom's force has made
> His nature as the nature of a lamb.[43]

Shelley believed that it was custom that had perverted man's herbivorous nature into unnatural meat-eating; here he suggests that through 'custom' the carnivores' predatory nature could be transformed into that of a 'harmless' herbivore. It may seem like a contradiction that Shelley argued that humans should be vegetarian because they were naturally herbivores, and yet that 'natural' carnivores would ideally turn into herbivores. But in fact it reveals Shelley's belief in the emerging proto-evolutionary theory that species could change their nature over time.[44] Although ferocity might have become 'natural' to the lion, Shelley's basic assumption was that ferocity was not in fact natural to nature. Thus, according to Shelley, eradicating predation would not be a *reformation* of nature's laws, but a *restoration* of them. He was convinced, like Lambe, Newton and his father-in-law William Godwin, that nature was solely good and therefore anything evil was artificial and unnecessary. For Shelley, nature did not mean 'everything that is', nor even 'everything that is non-human'; it meant 'everything that is good': anything that did not fit his own aesthetic ideal of nature was by definition 'unnatural'. Shelley could not reconcile anything poisonous or predatory, anything barren like deserts or winter, with his quasi-prelapsarian idea of nature and thus he classified them, along with social injustice, as extraneous and aberrational. As his second wife, Mary, explained: 'The prominent feature of Shelley's theory of the destiny of the human species was that evil is not inherent in the system of the creation, but an accident that might be expelled . . . That man could be so perfectionized as to be able to expel evil from his own nature, and from the greater part of the creation, was the cardinal point of his system.'[45] Like his friend Newton who had a predilection for Zoroastrianism, Shelley envisaged a Manichean struggle in which good was striving to expunge unnatural corruption from the universe.

In dividing the world thus, Shelley was adopting an alternative to the orthodox claim that 'evil' was part of a benevolent grand plan, as articulated by theodicists like Archbishop William King and John Clarke in their works *On the Origin of Evil* (1702 and 1720 respectively), and by Buffon and Darwin in their quasi-materialist apologia for nature. In their attempt to show that there was nothing absolutely evil in the world, they had argued that the apparent evil of predation was in fact a necessary and desirable part of nature's system. Shelley agreed that there was no evil in the system of nature, but he rejected the theodicists' explanation of predation as sophistical attempts to excuse the ways of God to man. William Godwin and the highly influential Reverend William Paley conceded that predation seemed to be at odds with the idea of universal benevolence, and Ritson had argued that it was enough to prove that there *was* no benevolent design in nature.[46] Shelley agreed with Ritson that predation was irreconcilable to the notion of benevolence, but his solution was to suggest that such things were not really part of nature.

For Shelley, meat-eating was the Pandora's box that introduced savagery into the world, and vegetarianism was the key with which it could be locked away again. Eating animals was the equivalent of the Fall; it turned man into the tyrant of the world and introduced inequality into both natural ecologies and human society. By ceasing to eat animals, man would return to his natural place as 'An equal amidst equals'. This 'egalitarianism' may suggest that Shelley was against anthropocentrism *per se*; but in fact there were still important elements in his thinking that kept men at the centre of the world even after being dethroned from their unnatural despotism. Shelley's anthropocentrism is more subtle and complicated than it at first appears.

The idea that converting to vegetarianism could rectify cosmic imbalance and re-establish harmony between all the animals seems to attribute to man an extraordinary transcendent power, traditionally associated with the Christian notion that animals and the rest of the universe had 'fallen' into a corrupted state, and were awaiting man's millennial regeneration.[47] It seems also that Shelley entertained an arbitrarily sanitised ideal of nature (though it is no more or less absurd from a modern perspective than the dominant contemporaneous theory, expounded by the theodocists, that mosquitoes, disease and poisonous berries were among God's benevolent gifts to mankind). Shelley's idea that man and nature could be cleansed of all viciousness sounds similar to the optimistic prophecies of the radical quack James Graham or the mystical visions of Thomas Tryon – and it is customary to read Shelley's faith in this as hyperbolic poetic licence or faddish naïvety.[48] But in fact there had been a convergence of circumstances in the late eighteenth century which made the possibility of re-establishing harmony with animals look distinctly plausible. Shelley, who followed developments in science with care, knew that some of the most eminent scientists of the age agreed.

In 1764 the French circumnavigator Louis-Antoine, Comte de Bougainville, had landed on the little known island of Malouine (in the Falkland Islands) and was greeted with an awesome sight. The wildlife on the island, which had no experience of human beings, approached his men 'without fear': 'The birds suffered themselves to be taken with the hand, and some would come and settle upon the people that stood still.' Some Christians saw this as a vestige of the animals' prelapsarian instinct to proffer themselves to their rightful human lords; but to others it implied a natural state of mutual trust. To Bougainville this touching scene seemed to prove 'that man does not bear a characteristic mark of ferocity'. It was a captivating image, and a flood of similar stories emerged in the ensuing decades – indeed, they are still evoked today in serious discussions of human relations to the environment. Lord Monboddo recited Bougainville's story to back up his argument that humans were naturally herbivorous, vividly imagining that 'all the animals came about him and his men; the fowls perching upon their heads and shoulders, and the fourfooted animals running among their feet.' He too observed that 'if man had been naturally an animal of prey, their instinct would have directed them to avoid him.' Erasmus Darwin copied this description out of Monboddo and added to it instances of similar experiences reported by Professor Johann Gmelin about foxes in Siberia 'that expressed no fear of himself or companions, but permitted him to come quite near them, having never seen the human creature before'. According to Darwin this suggested that 'the fear, [animals] all conceive at the sight of mankind, is an acquired article of knowledge,' and thus that humans might be able to re-establish a trusting relationship with animals by being kind to them 'if they were not already apprized of our general malevolence to them'. Darwin implied that even carnivores could overcome their ferocity and related the story told by his contemporary Gilbert White, the famous naturalist revered by modern environmentalists, about a cat who nursed an orphan hare with gentle maternal kindness. Even tigers, according to the sugar-enthusiast Benjamin Moseley, could be rendered utterly harmless by being raised on a vegetarian regime.[49]

Such observations corroborated the millennial fantasy indulged by the animal advocate Humphry Primatt, in 1776, that if people obeyed God's law to be merciful to animals, 'All would be peace, harmony, and love. Men would become merciful; Savage Brutes, would become tame; and the tame Brutes would no more groan under the lash . . . all, both Men and Brutes, would experience the blessing of the renovating change.'[50] It seemed that the idealistic dreams of David Graham, John Williamson and Thomas Tryon were being substantiated by empirical evidence. The vegetarian anthologist George Nicholson seized on Darwin's concatenation of such material, and added the still more sensational report contained in Georg Forster's account of Captain Cook's *Voyage Round the World*. On their arrival at Dusky Bay, New Zealand in 1773, Cook's crew found that 'Numbers of small birds which dwelt in the woods were so little acquainted with men, that they familiarly hopped upon the nearest branches, nay on the ends of our fowling-pieces . . . This little boldness in reality at first protected them from harm, since it was impossible to shoot them when they approached so near.'[51] It did not take the animals long to learn that humans were best avoided, however. As Bougainville reported sinisterly: 'This confidence was not of long duration with them; for they soon learnt to mistrust their most cruel enemies.'[52]

To Shelley, Lambe and Newton, these momentous events confirmed the claim made by Plutarch, Gassendi and innumerable others that humans did not have a carnivorous anatomy. Were mankind predatory in appearance, then animals would instinctively know to avoid them: but man, observed Shelley, 'has neither the fangs of a lion nor the claws of a tiger'. If being afraid of man was learned rather than instinctive, as scientists seemed to agree, it followed that if man stopped teaching the animals he was dangerous – that is, if he stopped killing them – they would lose their fear of him and join with him in trusting community. In *Queen Mab* Shelley pointed specifically to this anatomical aspect: the birds no longer 'Flee from the *form* of man'. They have become 'dreadless' and just like the Falklands birds they gather round and settle on people's arms.[53]

Still more categorically, Captain Cook's report from New Zealand disproved Buffon and others' claims that predation was essential for maintaining balanced ecologies. The Cook report had accurately observed that, aside from the few comparatively recently arrived Maoris, there were no terrestrial predators in New Zealand – and yet there was a thriving ecology apparently living in total harmony. The birds in Dusky Bay were not even afraid of the ship's cat, said the report, for they 'were not aware of such an insidious enemy'. Here, as far as Shelley was concerned, was a natural ecology in which even predation between animals was unknown. It seemed to embody the true egalitarian state of nature on which the myths of Eden and the Golden Age had been originally based – and it was this image he recycled in *Queen Mab*. To Shelley, it may even have seemed a logical conclusion that humans were responsible for introducing predation into the natural world, for it was in the places untouched by human interference that predators were absent. Ecologies which 'had not yet undergone any changes from the hands of mankind', as the Cook report put it, appeared to be non-hierarchical and non-predatorial.[54] If humans stopped being predators, animals would learn to trust them and a harmonious predation-free social ecology could be re-established all over the earth.

Dr Lambe followed Shelley in his enthusiasm:

> There is no antipathy between man and other animals, which indicates that nature has intended them for acts of mutual hostility. Numerous observations of travellers and voyagers have proved, that in uninhabited islands, or in countries, where animals are not disturbed or hunted, they betray no fear of men: the birds will suffer themselves to be taken by the hand; the foxes will approach him like a dog. These are no feeble indications, that nature intended him to live in peace with the other tribes of animals.[55]

Lambe's argument introduced a subtle new scenario to the theme of the uninhabited island, for he included inhabited 'countries, where animals are not disturbed or hunted'. These were more relevant to the cause of vegetarian reform because rather than being islands where humans were unknown, they were places where animals had developed a harmonious relationship with humans *in response* to people's benign behaviour. The most obvious example of where this was believed to have happened was India. Ever since the seventeenth century, travellers had spoken about extraordinary relations between Indians and their animals, and these images began to take on new vividness in the second half of the eighteenth century. Joseph Ritson picked up on them, and alongside his extracts from the voyages of Cook and Bougainville he reproduced a section of Pierre Marie François de Pagès' *Travels Round the World* (undertaken in 1767–71), which elevated the fantasy to another order. In the region around Surat, Pagès claimed that the Hindus were so humane that animals – even predators – had become docile:

> The birds of the air, undismayed by our approach, perch on the trees and swarm among the branches, as if they conceived man to be of a nature equally quiet and inoffensive with themselves ... Even the more formidable quadrupeds seem to have lost their natural ferocity in the same harmless dispositions; and hence the apprehensions commonly occasioned by the proximity of such neighbours, no longer disquiet the minds of the natives. Happy the effect of those mild and innocent manners, whence have arised peace and protection to all the inferior animals![56]

This 'empirical' evidence provided for Shelley one element which the 'pristine' ecologies of New Zealand and the Falklands did not: in those remote islands there had been no predatory species, whereas here the people's vegetarianism has transformed the predators' nature from 'ferocious' to 'harmless' (the very word Shelley used in *Queen Mab*). These stories followed in the wake of Rousseau's *Julie* – which Shelley described as 'an overflowing of sublimest genius, and more than mortal sensibility' – and thus they joined with Julie's animal sanctuary and *Paul et Virginie*'s tropical Eden into Romanticism's web of beliefs about the possibilities for man's relationship with nature.[57]

Despite his contempt for the Brahmin priestcraft,[58] like Ritson, Shelley nevertheless saw the Hindus as prime exemplars of how vegetarianism made people gentle and re-established natural harmony, without the *deus ex machina* of orthodox Christianity. Indian vegetarianism allowed Shelley to reclaim the millennial myth from transcendental religion, and replace it into the natural law from which he believed it had originally been culled. Bloodless ecologies provided a materialist aesthetic still more ancient than religious myth.

Ever since his undergraduate days at Oxford (before he was expelled for atheism), Shelley had studied the works of the 'Eastern travellers' and the Orientalists, Sir William Jones, Edward Moor and William Robertson. He had, of course, also read Monboddo and thus absorbed second-hand the work of John Zephaniah Holwell.[59] He was friends with Thomas Forster who was so impressed after studying Hindu and Pythagorean philosophy that he published numerous works arguing that animals had immortal souls and humans were not naturally carnivorous.[60] Shelley was so enamoured of India that he wanted to go there to see for himself and – perhaps inspired by his father-in-law's friend John Stewart – he once wrote to Thomas Love Peacock at his office in East India House asking for advice on how to find employment in the court of an Indian maharajah.[61]

Shelley was particularly inspired by Sydney Owenson's *The Missionary, an Indian Tale* (2nd edition, 1811) which told the story of Luxima, a 'Priestess of Brahma', and her platonic affair with Hilarion, a Christian missionary living as an Indian *sanyassin* like Roberto de Nobili. By being gentle to all around her, Luxima has tamed the animals in her sacred grove, and she is first attracted to Hilarion when he acts towards her favourite faun 'as a Hindu would have acted'. As the scholar John Drew has shown, *The Missionary* contained genuine Indological insights gleaned from the works of William Jones, and in particular, the character Luxima is based on the eponymous heroine of Jones' translation of the Sanskrit drama *Sakuntala* in which King Dusyanta renounces hunting after encountering Sakuntala's forest haven of tame wild animals. These stories – of which there was another version in Robert Southey's *The Curse of Kehama* – no doubt had a profound influence on Shelley's belief that vegetarianism could re-establish universal harmony. Indeed, even the diction in *Queen Mab* manifests this influence: Shelley's 'terrible prerogative' (which he argues man must lose) echoes Hilarion's phrase 'dreadful prerogative'.[62]

These stories were particularly pertinent for Shelley's belief that *individuals* had the power to change their environment – an essential element to his faith in Newton's nudist vegetarian community at Bracknell. Shelley called vegetarianism 'the Orphic and Pythagoric system of diet' and he believed that his own vegetarian poetry could help to restore harmony in nature just as the mythical Greek vegetarian

Orpheus charmed animals and humans with his music.[63] Several of Shelley's poems focus on solitary characters whose 'natural diets', like those of the perfect hermits in the *Turkish Spy*, restore harmony with animals. These were clearly part autobiographical fantasy, for Shelley considered himself a beleaguered individual, in Mary Shelley's words, 'warring with the Evil Principle'.[64] They expressed John Frank Newton's theories about the coming Golden Age and they make sense of Shelley's claim in *A Vindication of Natural Diet* that vegetarianism 'strikes at the root of all evil, and is an experiment which may be tried with success, not alone by nations, but by small societies, families, and even individuals'.[65]

As discussed by Timothy Morton, the isolated poet-character in Shelley's *Alastor* (1816) enjoys an Orphic relation with animals, and relives the experience of Bougainville's men on the Falklands: 'the doves and squirrels would partake/ From his innocuous hand his bloodless food,/ Lured by the gentle meaning of his looks'.[66] In Shelley's fragmentary poem 'Mazenghi' (1818), the eponymous Florentine hero similarly achieves the kind of union with nature encouraged by the Indophile John Stewart, as he 'Communed with the immeasurable world;/ And felt his life beyond his limbs dilated,/ Till his mind grew like that it contemplated.'

> His food was the wild fig and strawberry;
> The milky pine-nuts which the autumn-blast
> Shakes into the tall grass; or such small fry
> As from the sea by winter-storms are cast;
> And the coarse bulbs of iris-flowers he found
> Knotted in clumps under the spongy ground.[67]

The only animals Mazenghi eats are those that are already dead by natural causes; he thereby converts death into life. Similarly, he tames not just docile animals, but even those 'things whose nature is at war with life' (Shelley's squeamish euphemism for the amphibian inhabitants of a hellish swamp), which come and 'talk and play' around him.[68] (Shelley may have been thinking of the story related by George Nicholson of a man who, by kindness to animals, claimed that even poisonous reptiles made friends with him.)[69] The evil that Shelley conceived as an aberration of nature is disarmed by Mazenghi's union with natural laws: the food he eats is that which nature yields of its own accord. As Shelley explained in the *Vindication of Natural Diet*, echoing the pragmatism anciently attributed to Pythagoras, the vegetable diet is that which is simplest to procure. Isolated from the complications of urban life, Mazenghi's only choice is to feed on readily available food; he is not so much making a self-conscious moral choice about what to eat, he just eats the 'milky' food provided by Mother Nature (rather like the hypothetical solitary primitive man in Rousseau's *Discourse on Inequality*). The pine nuts are blown down by the wind, and even the fish are delivered for Mazenghi's consumption by the waves, a symbolic power of nature, manifesting an alternative to Buffon's insistence that fish populations should be controlled by being preyed upon.

The power of such individuals to instil harmony in the world around them may appear to suggest that Shelley believed humans had a transcendent power to control nature. But it would be a paradox if Shelley imagined that man would reconcile himself to nature by exerting a will that transcended it. The key to understanding how Shelley imagined man could be reconciled with nature lies in the language of *Queen Mab*. Man does not so much abdicate his predatory power over the animals, he *loses* it: 'Man has lost/ His terrible prerogative'. Shelley believed that reverting to herbivorousness was not so much an idealistic act of altruism; he thought it was a necessary obedience to natural forces. Man's hand is forced. In both his essays on the vegetable diet, Shelly stated that in the face of the scientific evidence 'the world will be *compelled* to regard animal flesh and fermented liquors as slow but certain poisons' and thus that 'it is scarcely possible that abstinence from aliments demonstrably pernicious should not become universal.'[70] Man could not escape the natural physical laws that made meat so pernicious, and thus a universal reversion to vegetarianism was as necessary an event as the ebb and flow of the sea. Shelley thought his vegetarian arguments were merely instruments, or linguistic facets, of nature's edicts; they did not speak of transcending nature's laws: they were merely a product of them. By following his instructions, people would be acting under nature's physical determination of their actions.

The Romanticist Onno Oerlemans has shown that Shelley did not think of himself as a radical crying in the wind: he and his poetry were leaves being blown along by it. In *Queen Mab* Shelley compares man's utopian reformation to the propulsion of planets orbiting under the power of nature: 'Man, like these passive things,/ Thy will unconsciously fulfilleth:/ Like theirs, his age of endless peace,/ Which time is fast maturing,/ Will swiftly, surely come.' In the 'Ode to the West

Wind' (1820) Shelley envisages himself as a messiah, prostrate before the will of nature: 'Oh, lift me as a wave, a leaf, a cloud!/ I fall upon the thorns of life! I bleed!' His poems had the power to reform mankind only insofar as they too were passive instruments of nature:

> Drive my dead thoughts over the universe
> Like withered leaves to quicken a new birth!
> And, by the incantation of this verse,
>
> Scatter, as from an unextinguished heart
> Ashes and sparks, my words among mankind!

Oerlemans curiously asserts that 'Shelley wrote no poetry about vegetarianism (though he occasionally refers to it in poetry written throughout his life)'.[71] But vegetarianism plays a crucial role in Shelley's major poetry, and it is the prime example of the observation that Shelley believed that his moral injunctions were merely passive instruments of nature's laws. Indeed, realising this untangles how Shelley managed to appear both a delusional megalomaniac and simultaneously prostrate in humility before the awesome power of nature; how he seemed to sustain an archaic anthropocentrism while also battling for man to dissolve his dreadful prerogative in order to become 'An equal amidst equals'. Humans did not need to take a moral stance that transcended nature. Under the ineluctable power of nature's laws, mankind would be forced one day to relinquish their unnatural habits and go with the flow.

In his next 'vegetarian' poem, *The Revolt of Islam* (1817–18), Shelley elaborated on how social and ecological revolution would be propelled by nature. The revolutionary forces (which the title implies are Hindu masses rising up against a Muslim tyrant) led by the messianic character, Laon, are compared to forces of nature like waves and river flows. In the face of their unstoppable power, the bloodthirsty tyrant, like man in *Queen Mab*, has no choice but to lose his tyrannical prerogative. Laon's revolutionary forces erect an 'Altar of the Federation' whose pyramidical structure symbolically alludes (according to the iconography of the contemporaneous Orientalist, George Faber) to the primeval mountain from which all mankind was said to have descended – the real Eden and Ararat – and thus points to the peaceful gathering of all humans and animals in the original state of nature.[72] Beneath this pyramid, the revolutionaries celebrate with a 'banquet of the free', modelled on the civic feasts of the French Republic, except that theirs is a vegetarian feast to which all creatures are invited to feed at the same board. Laon's Eve-like partner, Cythna, declares:

> My brethren, we are free! The fruits are glowing
> Beneath the stars, and the night-winds are flowing
> O'er the ripe corn, the birds and beasts are dreaming –
> Never again may blood of bird or beast
> Stain with its venomous stream a human feast,
> To the pure skies in accusation steaming;
> Avenging poisons shall have ceased
> To feed disease and fear and madness,
> The dwellers of the earth and air
> Shall throng around our steps in gladness,
> Seeking their food or refuge there.[73]

In the seventeenth century Thomas Hobbes identified mutual fear as a driving force in the war of nature. Here Shelley suggests (echoing Wordsworth) that fear results from transgressing nature's laws, and could thus be eradicated by reverting to the diet that nature willingly 'Pours from her fairest bosom'.[74] The force of nature is not antipathy, as Hobbes averred, but harmony.

In *The Revolt of Islam*, this triumphal idyll is ultimately drowned in a hideous massacre at the hands of the gathered forces of world tyranny while Laon and Cythna escape to mystical Paradise by being burnt on a pyramidical funeral pyre.[75] In the following year, however, Shelley revisited similar themes in his poetic drama *Prometheus Unbound*, and this time the messianic individual successfully redeems the fallen world.

By this time Shelley's doctors had warned that his declining health would never recover if he did not abandon the vegetable diet; in humiliation Shelley conceded that his experiment had gone awry. Friends had always believed that his faith in the vegetable diet was illusory. His cousin Thomas Medwin, who also wrote a biography of Shelley and himself appears to have converted to vegetarianism while resident in India, claimed that along with his 'immoderate use of laudanum', the Pythagorean diet crushed Shelley's health. Thomas Love Peacock, who frequently visited the Bracknell vegetarians, thought Shelley's vegetable diet 'made him weak and nervous, and exaggerated the sensitiveness of his imagination'. In 1817 Shelley even asked the radical journalist Leigh Hunt and his wife Marianne to cover up his illness 'for the advocate of a new system of diet is held bound to be invulnerable by disease, in the same manner . . . as a reformed parliament must at least be assumed as the remedy of all political evils. No one will change the diet . . . or reform parliament else.' By 1821 Leigh Hunt referred jocularly to Shelley's 'downfall from the angelic state' once he started eating 'veal cutlets'. Shelley had become, in his own Indian idiom, a 'pariah' from the vegetarian community.[76]

Correspondingly, vegetarianism plays a quieter part in *Prometheus Unbound* than in his earlier writing. In *A Vindication of Natural Diet* Shelley had followed Newton's theory that the myth of Prometheus was an allegory for man's fall into meat-eating. The Prometheus in *Prometheus Unbound* is a more complicated figure, but he nevertheless represents humanity's Manichean struggle with the power of tyranny and corruption. By realigning his thoughts with pure nature, Prometheus, like Mazenghi, achieves an Orphic power to charm nature back into harmony.[77] The rejuvenation of the earth triggered by his successful struggle climaxes in a scene of natural feeding in which all creatures live on earth's natural bounty in a harmonious ecological cycle. The character 'Earth' herself declares:

> Henceforth the many children fair
> Folded in my sustaining arms; all plants,
> And creeping forms, and insects rainbow-winged,
> And birds, and beasts, and fish, and human shapes,
> Which drew disease and pain from my wan bosom,
> Draining the poison of despair, shall take
> And interchange sweet nutriment;
>   . . .
> And death shall be the last embrace of her
> Who takes the life she gave, even as a mother,
> Folding her child, says, 'Leave me not again.'[78]

Violent death has been replaced with 'natural' death of reassimilation into the ecological cycle. Buffon and Darwin had argued that perishing naturally was worse than suffering 'painless' slaughter; Shelley reconceived natural death as a maternal embrace. The distinction between it and predation is the difference between sucking milk from the breast, and devouring the nurse (an image with which Shelley repeatedly toyed). Just as in *Queen Mab* and 'Mazenghi', 'malicious beasts' become herbivorous, 'loathly' reptiles become 'mild and lovely', and poisonous plants become sweet; kingfishers leave their prey in peace and feed on the once poisonous fruit of the deadly nightshade.[79]

Once again, Prometheus' agency in this transformation consists in aligning himself with natural forces. Mary Shelley explained that Shelley's Prometheus 'used knowledge as a weapon to defeat evil, by leading mankind, beyond the state wherein they are sinless through ignorance, to that in which they are virtuous through wisdom'.[80] Prometheus' cultivation of the civilised arts to drag mankind from the mire of oppressed slavery mirrors Shelley's own belief that spreading the knowledge of scientific facts would necessarily cause people to reform their own ways. The Promethean reformer appears to have extraordinary anthropocentric power over the outer world, but he achieves this only as an instrument of necessary physical laws.

By placing earth in the centre of the vision in *Prometheus Unbound*, Shelley indicates that man's agency in global transformation is secondary to nature's self-propelling powers. Nevertheless, the transformation requires human consent, so man is still a principal protagonist and beneficiary. Man loses his tyrannical relation to nature, but he does not lose his *centrality* within the ecological system. Even after making man 'An equal amidst equals', Shelley fantasised that animals would gather and play *'round'* him, come to him as a protector, and dance to his music. Part of Shelley's fear of eating meat was that it 'animalised' humans: his vegetarianism served the function of distancing humanity from animals – a motive that the anthropologist Claude Lévi-Strauss attributed to vegetarian cultures across the world. By keeping humans on an elevated level, Shelley avoided the attacks suffered by Joseph Ritson, and he protected himself from Buffon's accusation that the Rousseauist vegetarians were trying to achieve 'the humiliation of the whole [human] species' by propounding their fable of 'entire abstinence from flesh, of perfect tranquillity, of profound peace'.[81]

Shelley's thought was 'ecological' in the sense that he was interested in the relations between species, and the human place in natural cycles. But in discussions of Shelley it is vital to distinguish this from the other definition of 'ecological' as a synonym for a 'biocentric' value system which values non-human ecosystems for their own sake, in contrast to anthropocentrism. Applying the term 'biocentric' to Shelley unduly fades the extent to which Shelley kept humanity in the centre of his vision.[82]

Mary Shelley said that Shelley responded to his failure to reform the world by walling himself into a world of poetry. Shelley himself repudiated reading his poems as didactic or providing a theoretical model for social reform. Shelley has thus been criticised for retreating into 'interior' radicalism, manifested in his focus on the individual and the domestic sphere. But for Shelley the 'domestic' was a symbol of the wider 'dome' of the world, and Shelley's personal practice was supposed to exhibit to mankind the harmonious law of nature. He hoped that through him natural forces would still reform the world into a harmonious utopia. As Mary Shelley put it with a gloss of humility, 'he hoped to induce some one or two to believe that the earth might become such, did mankind themselves consent.' Shelley's vegetarian poetry did indeed continue to wield an influence on radical working-class movements in the nineteenth century.[83] In fulfilment of his desire expressed in the 'Ode to the West Wind', Shelley's 'dead thoughts' were indeed driven across the world like leaves, when Mahatma Gandhi re-exported them to India and scattered them as inspirational ashes and sparks in the largest non-violent movement of radical liberation the world has ever seen.

TWENTY-SEVEN

The Malthusian Tragedy: Feeding the World

Nature and culture are not necessarily opposed: this was the fundamental premise of Shelley and his Bracknell friends, John Frank Newton and William Lambe. Humans could return to nature without uncivilising themselves; culture should follow natural laws. In practical terms, this meant giving up meat and returning to the natural diet. But it was the civilised arts of science and education – as Shelley's Prometheus revealed – that would make such a change possible. In making the case for naturalising culture, the Bracknell vegetarians were following Lord Monboddo, who had shown that Rousseau's attack on the corrupting influence of civilisation did not require humanity to return to a savage state. Monboddo thus provided the nineteenth-century vegetarians with the framework for claiming that vegetarianism was both the natural diet and the logical next step in the advance of civilisation. Society needed more cultivation, not less; in particular, argued the vegetarians, more *agri*culture.

It was often assumed that humans had evolved from being fruitarian gatherers into hunters, then into shepherds and had finally invented agriculture. In the *Origins of Inequality*, Rousseau argued that the shift to agriculture was the ambivalent 'great revolution' which introduced inequality to human society: 'property was introduced, work became indispensable, and vast forests became smiling fields, which man had to water with the sweat of his brow, and where slavery and misery were soon seen to germinate and grow up with the crops.' The Bracknell vegetarians broadly accepted Rousseau's theory of social evolution, although Lambe pointed out that it was also this 'great revolution' that enabled people to leave meat-eating behind them and cultivate enough vegetable food to return to their original herbivorous diet. '[T]he adherence to the use of animal food,' said Lambe, 'is no more than a persistence in the gross customs of savage life.' Vegetables were the most civilised foods and the most natural.[1]

Lambe's enthusiasm for agriculture – which he shared with Shelley and Newton – grew out of an epoch-making realisation that had recently struck Europeans with deep consternation. Mushrooming populations were threatening to outstrip food production. Britain had doubled in the eighteenth century from about five million to nearly ten million people. When food shortages struck in Europe during the 1790s and 1800s, concern became all the more intense.[2] Was misery and starvation the future of humanity? Had human progress reached the end of the road?

In the quest to resolve this crisis, improving land-use efficiency became a national obsession. Robert Southey's critique of vegetarianism was again undoubtedly instrumental in providing a focus for Lambe, Newton and Shelley: 'The principle of abstaining from animal food is not in itself either culpable or ridiculous, if decently discussed,' Southey conceded. 'But ultimately it resolves itself into the political question, *Whether the greater population can be maintained upon animal or vegetable diet?*' If eating vegetables was a more efficient way of using available agricultural land then there was a new and urgent reason to re-examine the practice of meat-eating.[3]

Large populations were regarded as desirable in themselves. A nation's strength and honour depended on its economic, demographic and military size. The Utilitarians put a new gloss on the ancient ethic of 'peopling the earth' by pointing out that since each person was a potential unit of happiness, sustaining the greatest number of people was an essential ingredient to achieving the greatest possible happiness. The agricultural system that produced the largest amount of food was clearly the best. Vegetarians argued – with a significant body of agronomists, economists and demographers backing them up – that arable agriculture sustained far more people per acre than rearing animals or hunting.

The most important proponent of the moral implications of population growth was the Reverend William Paley (1743–1805), whose *View of the Evidence of Christianity* (1794) remained on the Cambridge University reading list right up to the twentieth century. In his *Elements of Moral and Political Philosophy* (1785), Paley argued that the scriptural permission to Noah was the only way of defending man's moral right to kill animals. He acknowledged that some animals had to be eaten in order to prevent them becoming overpopulated and competing for resources with humans, and that others we had the right to kill because we had reared them. But he pointed out that these familiar counter-vegetarian arguments did not apply to fish, for example, and therefore could not comprehensively justify human habits without recourse to Scripture.

However, Paley did not think that the divinely ordained moral right constituted a justification in itself for acting on that right. This was a classic illustration of the major philosophical shift in Britain, from Hume and Hutcheson's metaethics, which aimed to identify the nature of morality as a whole, to the Utilitarians' normative ethics which focused on identifying what people actually ought to *do*. Meat-eating may not have been a sin against animals, but was it reconcilable with the good of humanity? In his chapter 'Of Population and Provision', Paley pointed out that the principal aim of politics was to nurture the greatest population; and herein lay the problem with meat-eating: 'a piece of ground capable of supplying animal food sufficient for the subsistence of ten persons would sustain, at least, double that number with grain, roots, and milk.' On ten acres of land one could either grow crops to feed people directly, or one could raise animals, using some of the land for grazing and some for fodder crops. A certain proportion of any food given to animals was necessarily wasted (as faeces or heat, for example), thus leaving less nutrition in the end product. Furthermore, grasses grown for grazing were less productive plants than grain crops. Raising animals on land that could otherwise be used for arable agriculture was therefore a massive inefficiency.[4]

Adam Smith had made similar calculations in *The Wealth of Nations* (1776): 'A cornfield of moderate fertility produces a much greater quantity of food for man than the best pasture of equal extent.' Furthermore, a field of potatoes produced three times as much nourishment as a field of wheat. If the British were to change their staple from bread to potatoes, Smith ambitiously promised that the economy would expand: 'Population would increase, and rents would rise much beyond what they are at present.' He did not go as far as to suggest that people should relinquish eating meat in order to increase population;[5] but Paley transposed Smith's theory of economic expansion to the domain of Utilitarian morality, and thus revealed the ethical angle to society's choice of diet:

> In England, notwithstanding the produce of the soil has been of late considerably increased . . . yet we do not observe a corresponding addition to the number of inhabitants, the reason of which appears to me to be the more general consumption of animal food amongst us. Many ranks of people whose ordinary diet was, in the last century, prepared almost entirely from milk, roots, and vegetables, now require every day a considerable portion of the flesh of animals. Hence a great part of the richest lands of the country are converted to pasturage. Much also of the bread-corn, which went directly to the nourishment of human bodies, now only contributes to it by fattening the flesh of sheep and oxen. The mass and volume of provisions are hereby diminished, and what is gained in the amelioration of the soil is lost in the quality of the produce.
>
> This consideration teaches us that tillage, as an object of national care and encouragement, is universally preferable to pasturage, because the kind of provision which it yields goes much farther in the sustenation of human life.

By this argument, following the vegetable diet was patriotic – and it earned Paley a place in the vegetarian symposium satirically portrayed by Thomas Love Peacock in the *London Magazine*, where he appears seated alongside Shelley, Lambe, Ritson, Godwin, Thomas Taylor and Sir John Sinclair at a 'Dinner by the Amateurs of Vegetable Diet'.[6] Despite such contemporaneous mockery, however, Paley's agronomic principles are still broadly accepted today. The meat industry wasted resources and deprived untold numbers of people from existing.

In the context of this new Utilitarian emphasis on dietary ethics, the shining example of the Hindus was once again polished up with a new gloss. It was their strict vegetarianism, observed Paley, that allowed the Hindus to sustain populations that dwarfed those of Europe. If they were to develop a British taste for meat, they would have to 'introduce flocks and herds into grounds which are now covered with corn' and their population would necessarily decline.[7] (Indeed, it is precisely this shift towards Western levels of meat consumption in industrialising countries that is giving demographers today such anxiety about global food security.)

The comparative efficiency of different land uses had been apparent to agricultural peoples for millennia. Plato and St Jerome observed – and John Evelyn reiterated – that the demand for meat increased land hunger and thus led to disputes with neighbouring peoples. The most common argument against vegetarianism which had been used since Greek antiquity was the one about needing to kill animals to prevent them overpopulating. In the words of Porphyry's counter-vegetarian opponent, we had to eat animals, otherwise they would grow into such multitudes that they 'would damage our lives, both by standing and fighting us, as they are naturally well equipped to do, and simply by consuming what the earth produces for our food'. The seventeenth-century philosopher Samuel von Pufendorf saw this competition for resources as the basis of Hobbes' war in nature between man and the animals (another reason for Shelley to believe that the end of animal agriculture would bring an end to the war in nature). But this timeworn counter-vegetarian argument necessarily implied that breeding large numbers of farm-animals was a strain on resources, so it could just as easily be made into a case for vegetarianism. As Thomas Tryon observed in the seventeenth century, animals only existed in such great numbers because we bred them; the easiest way to curtail their population was therefore to stop bringing them into existence.[8] In the eighteenth century, following Tryon's lead, this classic *defence* of eating animals was transformed into an argument *against* eating so many of them. This itself reflects the fact that in the past meat was principally a by-product of agricultural systems in which animals were reared on otherwise unusable land and fed waste products. Traditionally, excess male calves of dairy herds and cows past milking age were killed as they would otherwise have continued to consume resources without returning anything to the system. But in the eighteenth century the meat industry was born: herds were bred for slaughter, and grain was grown exclusively to feed them.

In the fifteenth and sixteenth centuries vast swathes of the commoners' traditional arable land had been enclosed and converted into sheep-pastures by manorial lords keen to cash in on the booming wool industry. Works like Thomas More's *Utopia* complained that this greedy profit-chasing was depopulating the countryside. In the second half of the eighteenth century there was a new surge of enclosures conducted in the interests of agricultural improvement; and for the first time animals were raised on a large scale exclusively for the purpose of producing meat.[9] Arable land that had once provided food for people was being converted to grow pasture and fodder crops for animals. John Williamson of Moffat and John Oswald, who witnessed the effects of the infamous Highland Clearances, were among the first to build the critique of enclosures into a wholesale attack on meat production. By the 1780s it was common for established economists, agronomists and demographers to address the issue. The English enclosed their land much earlier than other European nations, where the practice only took hold in the nineteenth century. But even in France, Bernardin de Saint-Pierre pointed out that because grazing land was exempt from tithes, farmers had a counter-productive incentive to raise animals rather than growing food more efficiently with arable cultivation. The Chinese, he claimed, used their land much more sensibly by growing rice for human consumption and only feeding cattle with waste products like straw.[10]

In his *Zoonomia; or the Laws of Organic Life* (1794–6) and *Phytologia; or the Philosophy of Agriculture and Gardening* (1800), Erasmus Darwin demonstrated with dispassionate technical detail how these new objections to the meat industry had become compelling even for the most staunch admirer of British roast beef. Darwin stuck to his claim that humans were anatomically omnivorous; that vegetarianism made the Hindus 'feeble', and that vegetable diets did more harm than good to medical patients in Europe. But faced with the inefficiency of animal agriculture, he warned that Britons did need to curtail their meat consumption and revert to a more vegetable-oriented diet: 'perhaps tenfold the numbers of mankind can be supported by the corn produced on an hundred acres of land, than on the animal food which can be raised from it,' he claimed. 'This greater production of food by agriculture than by pasturage, shews that a nation nourished by animal food will be less numerous than if nourished by vegetable.'

Darwin explained that the rapid growth of the meat industry was fuelled by landowners' thirst for profit: pastoralism required less labour, and its products – meat, cheese and butter – being luxuries, fetched higher prices at market than arable produce. The increased profit margin provided a financial incentive to enclose arable land and revert it to animal pasturage. (This profit chasing is still seen by modern agronomists as the driving force behind the global rise in unsustainably high meat production.[11]) Since pasturage actually produced less food and employed fewer people, this quest for profit was responsible for emptying whole villages and starving the poor into slavery – scenes that Darwin vividly evoked by quoting Oliver Goldsmith's poem, *The Deserted Village*. Moderating Rousseau's critique, Darwin concluded that 'This inequality of mankind in the present state of the world is too great for the purposes of producing the greatest quantity of human nourishment, and the greatest sum of human happiness.'

The problem was exacerbated, said Darwin, by fermenting edible grain in the 'destructive manufactory' of liquor and strong beer, which basically meant 'converting the natural nutriment of mankind into a chemical poison'. He threatened a national catastrophe 'if the luxurious intemperance of consuming flesh-meat principally, and of drinking intoxicating liquors, should increase amongst us, so as to thin the inferior orders of society, by scarcity of food, and the higher ones by disease both of mind and body'. The only viable way of 'preventing a nation from becoming too carnivorous', he advised, was to ban the enclosure of arable land completely. Achieving this political imperative would ensure that Britain would progress to become 'more populous, robust, prosperous, and happy, than any other nation in the world'. In a vein of Godwin-like optimism, he looked forward to a time when things were reformed in such a way 'as may a hundred-fold increase the numbers of mankind, and a thousand-fold their happiness'.[12]

Although Darwin himself did not advocate giving up meat altogether, his authoritative statistics provided the basis for the new case for vegetarianism. George Nicholson quickly inserted quotes from Darwin into his vegetarian anthologies, and connected them with those of the popular physician William Buchan, who similarly thought that agronomic factors should be taken into consideration in medical discussions about diet. 'The excessive consumption of animal food,' said Buchan, inflamed thirst, disease and ferocity and 'is one great cause of the scarcity of grain. The food that a bullock affords, bears but a small proportion to the quantity of vegetable matter he consumes.'[13] Joseph Ritson also quoted Paley's arguments, so it is little surprise that Shelley underpinned his attack on political oppression with this new emphasis. Extending several lines of Darwin's logic into robust radicalism, Shelley realised that meat-eating was not just a sign of wealth, it was one of the tools with which the rich oppressed the poor. The carnivorous rich literally monopolised the land by taking over more of it than they needed. Pointing his accusatory finger at consumers (in contrast to Darwin's focus on agricultural producers), Shelley argued that the flesh gorged by the rich literally *was* the grain stolen from the mouths of the poor:

> The quantity of nutritious vegetable matter, consumed in fattening the carcase of an ox, would afford ten times the sustenance, undepraving indeed, and incapable of generating disease,

if gathered immediately from the bosom of the earth. The most fertile districts of the habitable globe are now actually cultivated by men for animals, at a delay and waste of aliment absolutely incapable of calculation.

Like Paley and Lambe, Shelley allowed that even the poor were to blame if they indulged a luxurious taste for meat: 'The peasant cannot gratify these fashionable cravings without leaving his family to starve.' Like Darwin – and Roger Crab and Thomas Tryon in the seventeenth century – Shelley pointed out that drinking alcohol carried the same implications, for it too was a superfluous luxury made from grain that could otherwise be eaten as food: 'the use of animal flesh and fermented liquors,' he wrote with characteristic bombast, 'directly militates with this equality of the rights of man.'[14]

William Lambe likewise saw arable agriculture as the key to social reform. 'By the exercise of this beneficial art,' he said, 'myriads of human beings are called into life, who could otherwise have never existed.' If people confined themselves to vegetables, he claimed, populations could be 'increased to an indefinite extent'. Echoing Darwin, he also suggested that arable agriculture encouraged the arts of peace: 'It seems no visionary or romantic speculation to conjecture, that if all mankind confined themselves for their support to the productions supplied by the culture of the earth, war, with its attendant misery and horrors, might cease to be one of the scourges of the human race.' Like Darwin (and in contrast to Paley's mixed-farming model), Lambe argued that the dairy industry was equally implicated in the culture of waste. Lambe was politically of a more moderate outlook than Shelley, but the agronomic arguments drew him into a radical position, for it was clear that meat and dairy were 'monopolised' by the rich. If everyone ate meat, a thriving population could not be sustained without resorting to the unstable and economically undesirable practice of importing food from abroad. Radicalism did not just lead to vegetarianism (as in Shelley's case); people could be led to radicalism by vegetarianism.[15]

Population studies had become one of the most important topics for Europeans from the late eighteenth century, and the formulations developed then remain the basic ingredients of the global agronomic debate even today. By far the most influential demographer of the period – and still regarded as the founder of the modern discipline – was the Reverend Thomas Robert Malthus (1766–1834). Malthus' father had been a friend of Rousseau, and brought his son up according to the principles of *Émile*. But by the age of thirty Malthus rejected his father's faith in the perfectibility of mankind, and he published one of the most shocking works of economic realism the world had seen. His seminal *Essay on the Principle Of Population* (1798) aimed to refute the utopianism of Shelley's father-in-law, William Godwin, and he specifically attacked the faith in the comparative efficiency of vegetarianism. In a game of political tit-for-tat, which stretched over three generations, Shelley and the Bracknell vegetarians took up the gauntlet and challenged the basis of Malthus' agronomic assumptions.

Malthus' most controversial observation was that populations had the potential to grow geometrically (at a rate of 1, 2, 4, 8, 16 and so on). Agricultural yields, meanwhile, were likely to decline as the soil became exhausted; even the greatest advocate of technological improvement, he suggested, could not expect yields to be increased at the same rate as populations. In the real world, populations were always limited by the means of subsistence: the poor stopped reproducing when they were so miserable they no longer had the capacity to sustain large families. If populations were encouraged to grow unchecked, he commented bleakly, a certain swathe of each population would occasionally have to die. If it wasn't plague that killed them, there would have to be a war, and if neither of those materialised then the population would simply outstrip the supply of food and there would be famine. If the poor had more children than they could support, they were destined to live in abject poverty; regardless of whether one successfully averted plague or war, the same number of deaths would necessarily occur. Even Britain's Poor Laws should be abolished or radically curtailed, he insisted. Institutionalised benevolence merely encouraged the poor to bring excess children into the world, which stretched food resources beyond their capacity, creating a dearth for everyone. It was better, he suggested, to leave people to the harsh laws of nature's 'order and harmony' until they learned to limit their procreation within their means.

A basic element of Malthus' population dynamics had in fact been propounded by the Comte de Buffon in his attack on Rousseau and the vegetarians decades earlier. If populations did not sustain regular deaths, said Buffon, they would multiply so that 'by their numbers, they would soon injure and destroy each other. For want of sufficient nourishment, their fecundity would diminish. Contagion and famine would produce the same effects.' Malthus' three instruments of population control are all there in Buffon – killing each other, disease and famine – with the only other alternative as decreased fecundity, which Malthus also allowed for. The disturbing difference is that Buffon wasn't talking about humans, but about fish, and the mass-deaths he was justifying were not accidental but deliberate massacres committed by humans and other predators.[16] Malthus' demographic model was like a sociological version of Buffon's ecological defence of predation, and both Buffon and Malthus were directing their arguments against vegetarians. Their *laissez-faire* attitude to natural checks and balances within ecological cycles – to which humans were subject as well as other animals – was in fundamental opposition to what they saw as the vegetarians' utopian attempt to circumvent nature's harsh laws. Some would say the analogy between Malthus and Buffon justified the accusation that Malthus complied with class-oppression by making famine and war look like natural phenomena rather than resulting from deliberate acts of political injustice. Indeed, Buffon's follower John Brückner (1726–1804) had explicitly declared that warfare, like natural predation, was a providential blessing which benefited the general good by controlling populations.[17] But in fact Malthus was more aware of the potential political abuse of population control than critics have allowed, and he warned that superficially philanthropic attempts to alleviate poverty would have the sinister effect of swelling armies and creating cheap labour from desperation.[18] Malthus insisted that the only safe way for populations to grow was to improve agricultural yields, so people would naturally have larger families as supplies became abundant.

William Godwin had imagined a society in which everyone shared in agricultural labour instead of slaving away in industrial cities. If everyone followed 'a frugal yet wholesome diet', Godwin argued, they would no longer have to labour to produce superfluous luxuries, and would thus only have to work for as little as half an hour a day. The result would be a happy populous society with no war, violence or crime.[19] For the sake of argument, Malthus allowed that Godwin's system of perfect equality would remove some of the ordinary checks to population growth, and that England's population could perhaps be doubled. However, he argued that as populations grew, everyone would have to become a vegetarian: 'The only chance of success would be the ploughing up all the grazing countries, and putting an end almost entirely to the use of animal food.' He readily acknowledged that 'It is well known that a country in pasture cannot support so many inhabitants as a country in tillage.' He also acknowledged Adam Smith's projection that 'if potatoes were to become the favourite vegetable food of the common people ... the country would be able to support a much greater population.' This was precisely what the vegetarians were arguing for, but Malthus thought that giving up meat was an undesirable eventuality. Apart from anything else, he objected that a purely arable system would not produce the manure required for improving soils in Britain. Animal agriculture, he implied, provided meat for the rich and shit for the poor.

But Malthus' principal objection was that once the object of doubling the population had been attained – in twenty-five years or so – the problem of the limitation of resources would present itself again. With the population doubled from seven million, 'the food, though almost entirely vegetable, would be sufficient to support in health the doubled population of fourteen millions.' But as people continued to multiply, they would eventually outstrip the capacity for food production and face the prospect of famine once again. Then Godwin's imagined reign of universal benevolence would give way to competition for resources: 'The mighty law of self-preservation expels all the softer, and more exalted emotions of the soul ... self-love resumes his wonted empire, and lords it triumphant over the world.'

To illustrate this, Malthus turned to the vegetarian Chinese and Indian masses championed by Paley and Adam Smith. These enormous populations, said Malthus, survived on the smallest possible quantity of resources produced in the most efficient way on the available land. While this might look like the kind of perfect situation Godwin and Paley imagined, Malthus argued that it was fatally precarious. Because the populations did not have any superfluous luxuries, he speculated that whenever they had a bad harvest, they must necessarily be hit with the most devastating famines: 'It is probable that the very frugal manner in which the Gentoos are in the habit of living contributes in some degree to the famines of Indostan.' Malthus regarded luxuries as a buffer against famine, and he imagined – with nearly as much idealism as the Godwinites – that wealthier classes would part with their luxuries in time of hardship and use their excess money to provide employment for the poor. Furthermore, Malthus did not agree with Paley and the others that large populations were in themselves desirable: bringing more people into a life of indigence merely multiplied the quantity of misery, not happiness.[20]

Godwin responded to this by pointing out that Malthus had refuted his utopian vision by arguing that once it had been achieved it would eventually be defeated by its own success. But this, said Godwin, ignored the value of achieving it in the first place, and it assumed that when a population reached its capacity for food production people would still be hell-bent on multiplying as fast as possible. On the contrary, Godwin insisted, at this point people would sensibly turn to family planning; men could be optionally sterilised or they would exercise moral restraint on their reproductive appetite. Thus, agricultural reform could achieve a doubling of the population without causing the famine Malthus predicted.[21] In later expanded editions of the *Essay*, Malthus did in fact put more emphasis on curbing populations through 'moral restraint', by which he meant late marriage and celibacy. As Southey and Coleridge pointed out in 1803 in their joint review of Malthus' *Principle of Population*, Malthus himself ended his essay with the paradoxical assertion that the Christian exercise of chastity could overcome the harsh laws of overpopulation. Nature itself, Malthus had said, encouraged the use of restraint. By conceding that nature would force people to control reproduction, said Southey, Malthus revealed himself to be no less of a utopian than Godwin, for he had the optimistic *laissez-faire* faith of Leibniz and Buffon that deregulated natural forces would establish their own harmony: 'Malthus also is an optimist, but of the Pangloss school,* holding that the present state of society is, with all its evils, the best of all possible states.' His inconsistent pessimistic attack on liberal reform, they argued, was really a sinister plan to reduce the poor to brutal slavery.[22]

Although Malthus was not in favour of being forced to give up meat to increase agricultural yields, he did seem to assent to the vegetarians' basic argument that populations could thereby be increased. Godwin pointed out that Malthus' statistics reaffirmed that 'much would be economised as to human subsistence, by the general substitution of the vegetable for the animal productions of the earth'.[23] Likewise, when Shelley came to refute Malthus, he did so by embracing the greater part of his arguments, but subtly manipulating the perspective: 'Without disease and war, those sweeping curtailers of popu-

---

* Dr Pangloss, the satirised teacher of Leibnizian optimism in Voltaire's *Candide* (1759).

lation,' he said, echoing the *Principle of Population*, 'pasturage would include a waste too great to be afforded.' If populations were not wiped out by war and disease, he implied, they would thrive so well that the meat industry would have to give way to the arable system to provide for all the people. The only reason why population growth had not forced a wholesale conversion to arable agriculture was because politicians allowed people to be oppressed by war, tyranny and disease. Shelley implicitly turned Malthus into a latent mass-murderer: he would prevent millions of people from coming into existence rather than make people give up flesh to increase food production.[24]

The vegetarian argument renegotiated Malthus' pessimism by denying his premise about the limited potential for increasing the carrying capacity of European agricultural land. Dismissing Malthus' warnings as hollow, the vegetarians remained convinced that if people gave up meat and turned to the more efficient produce of arable agriculture, there would immediately be an astronomic leap in available food, leaving ample room for populations to expand. John Frank Newton took on Malthus' anonymously published tract with exactly this argument:

> A writer on population of some celebrity has contended that the destructive operations of whatever sort by which men are killed off or got rid of, are so many blessings and benefits, and he has the triumph of seeing his doctrine pretty widely disseminated and embraced; although no point can be more clearly demonstrable than that the earth might contain and support at least ten times the number of inhabitants that are now upon it.[25]

Newton's sanguine projection that populations could be multiplied by ten went beyond even Godwin, Darwin and Shelley's estimation, and it dwarfed Paley's more sober calculation that they could be doubled. Although in his more visionary moments Darwin promised a hundredfold increase in populations, in his specific comments about agriculture he suggested that ten times the *food* could be produced on arable than on pasturage, and Shelley adopted this figure. But this did not imply, as Newton seems to have believed, that *populations* could be universally multiplied by ten, for that would assume that everyone currently ate meat exclusively. In 1811 Newton was still corresponding with Godwin about the exact statistics one could rely on.[26]

Intriguingly, the 'ten times' claim has remained pervasive right up to present – demonstrating just how directly this debate has been kept alive through the intervening two centuries. The problem faced by Malthus and the Bracknell vegetarians has not changed, perhaps it has only been postponed, partly by intensifying agriculture, but also by resorting to exactly the measure that seemed so undesirable in the early nineteenth century: importing food from abroad. In 2003 a Research Fellow of the London School of Economics, Colin Tudge, warned that the world would run out of agricultural space if growing levels of meat production are not curbed. Like Malthus and Saint-Pierre, Tudge pointed out that a small number of animals in a mixed farming system were in fact desirable because they harness otherwise unusable resources like chaff, straw and inedible cellulose-rich plants like grass; and they provide useful resources like manure. But the basic claim remains intact, that 'Vegetarians point out that a hectare of wheat or pulses, say, produces about ten times more protein or calories as would the same area dedicated to beef or sheep.'[27]

Shelley, Godwin and the Bracknell vegetarians imagined that Malthus' harsh law of population pressure could be overcome. Human societies could grow, competition could be eradicated, and humans could live in harmony with animals. The naturalists regarded the Romantics as absurdly ignorant of both ecology and agriculture, and Malthus, whose population dynamic was essentially an ecological model, agreed. Malthus' forebears were outspoken in their attack on the vegetarians' lack of realism. In the 1760s Buffon's follower John Brückner had pointed out the naïvety of the vegetarians' faith that arable agriculture could obviate the need to kill animals. Imagine asking the world's nomadic animal herders to convert to vegetarianism, he proclaimed: their land was not suitable for arable cultivation; the only way they could fit in with natural ecologies was as a sustaining carnivore. Both the animals and the humans depended on this relationship to survive. The naturalist-ecologists like Buffon, Brückner and, before them, the theodocists such as Archbishop William King, recognised that the relation between humans and their domestic animals was symbiotic. The vegetarians' desire to abolish these relationships was as absurd as it was unecological. 'Senseless and stupid mortal!' Brückner exclaimed, 'This perfect calm, this universal and uninterrupted felicity they wish to introduce into the world; this beautiful chimera, will always appear possible to those who judge of things according to their imagination only.' Brückner's own *laissez-faire* attitude was arguably far more ecological than the vegetarians' antipathy to predation. There was no sense in trying to separate humans from the rest of the ecological system. Humans had unique power, but it was both in their ecological interests and in their compassionate nature to use that power responsibly. Man, said Brückner, 'is the only creature on earth upon whose will the preservation, or total ruin, of a multitude of species finally depend.' Humans' natural compassion, as well as their self-interest, was what could mitigate their dominion over the rest of the world's species.[28]

William Smellie (1740–95) translated Buffon's work and in his *Philosophy of Natural History* (1790) he reiterated why Buffon's theory flawed the vegetarians' idea of harmonious nature. 'Nature, it must be confessed, seems almost indifferent to individuals, who perish every moment in millions, without any apparent compunction . . . But, by making animals feed upon each other, the system of animation and of happiness is extended to the greatest possible degree.' It was the destruction of *individuals*, observed Smellie, that facilitated the co-existence of so many *species*. Smellie's warning against trying to tamper with this law of nature was just like that of Buffon and later that of Malthus: 'If the general profusion of the animated productions of Nature had no other check . . . the whole would soon be annihilated by an universal famine'. Humans were inescapably part of this cycle. It may seem cruel that domestic animals were killed for food, but, Smellie insisted, 'This is not cruelty. He has a right to eat them: For, like Nature, though he occasionally destroys domestic animals, a timid and docile race of beings, by his culture and protections he gives life and happiness to millions, which, without his aid, could have no existence.'[29]

Buffon and his followers accepted the war in nature as a prerequisite for achieving the greatest number and greatest variety of species. This principle became their rallying cry. They can be charged with having fostered the 'Fascist' implications of ecological thought in their cool detachment from the plight of individuals in the struggle for survival.[30] But theirs was the system that valued biodiversity in ways that today would be regarded as 'ecological'. They valued biodiversity for its own sake, and their values were inherited from the ancient valorisation of 'plenitude' – the idea that God's greatness was manifested in His creation of an infinite variety and abundance of life. Carnivorism, parasitism and scavenging were all essential in the planet's ecological equilibrium. Predator and prey were intimately connected and dependent on each other: the one obtained food, the other had its populations helpfully controlled. Attempts to tamper with the intricate workings of natural ecologies invariably ended in disaster. If carnivores – humans among them – did not kill to survive, the carnivores would cease to exist and the prey species would suffer catastrophic overpopulation and subsequent annihilation.[31] The same was true of human populations. Just as the vegetarians wished to prevent mass deaths of animals by stopping human predation, so they ignored Malthus' stark observation that allowing human populations to grow unchecked would result in a devastating tragedy of mass death. This attitude, warned the counter-vegetarians, was a futile attempt to evade the human place in an ecological system of which death was an integral part.

In the 1800s, when Shelley revived the movement of Rousseauist vegetarianism, Buffon and Brückner's critique was once again reignited. This time by Shelley's acquaintance, Sir William Lawrence, the young radical materialist whose theories on spontaneous variation later assisted Charles Darwin's discoveries and earned him the undying respect of Darwin's 'bulldog', Thomas Huxley, for helping to 'break down the barrier between man and the rest of the animal world'.[32] In 1814 or thereabouts, Lawrence had participated in Shelley's vegetarian experiment and kept it up for about a year, and in 1815 William Lambe claimed that Lawrence acknowledged that it had improved his health. But when Shelley consulted Lawrence in 1815 with his chronic abdominal illness, Lawrence seems to have decided that vegetarianism was a dangerous fad and apparently instructed Shelley to eat some meat, which Shelley duly did for part of that year. Lawrence immediately went on to develop a thorough scientific attack on Shelley's vegetarian ideals in his notorious *Lectures on the Natural History of Man*, delivered to the Royal College of Surgeons in 1817 and published in a summarised form in the article on 'Man' in Abraham Rees' monumental thirty-nine-volume *Cyclopædia; or Universal Dictionary* (1819).[33]

Lawrence assented that human teeth and guts were similar to those of herbivores: 'In general, then, the human teeth and joint of the jaw resemble most those of herbivorous animals: and man approaches most nearly in these, as well as in other points, to the monkey race, which are, in their natural state, completely herbivorous.' (The Bracknell vegetarians seized on this concession and Lambe quoted it in his own vegetarian treatises.[34]) Lawrence also agreed that a serious scientific experiment needed to be conducted to test the effects of the vegetable diet, though on a broader spectrum than the domestic trial he had attempted with the Bracknell vegetarians; numerous people of different constitutions would have to be tested over three generations. But Lawrence went on to insist (and needless to say Lambe excised these points from his own discussion) that 'In stating these circumstances, we do not wish our readers to draw the inference, that man is designed by nature to feed on vegetables.' To make this deduction, he suggested, was to misunderstand the entire meaning of 'nature', for as the Bracknell crowd had always agreed, 'nature' and 'civilisation' were not distinct. It was perfectly natural for humans to use their hands and the art of cookery to procure animal food. Vegetarianism, he indicated, was inherently a primitivist attack on civilisation and society. Quoting Buffon, he ridiculed the vegetarians' beliefs 'that, in the golden age, man was as innocent as the dove . . . and always in peace both with himself and the other animals.' It was appalling, said Lawrence, that in the nineteenth century 'men are actually found, who would have us believe, on the faith of some insulated, exaggerated, and misrepresented facts, and still more miserable hypotheses, that the development, form, and powers of the body are impaired and lessened, and the intellectual moral faculties injured and perverted by animal diet.' Shelley thought his use of 'empirical' evidence defied the characterisation of him as a hyper-imaginative idealist – or 'Romantic' in the modern idiom; but Lawrence pointed out that people like Shelley and Lambe just manipulated facts to match their idealistic dream. Vegetarianism was not scientific and it was not ecological: it betrayed a total misunderstanding about how ecologies worked.[35]

It was from the counter-vegetarian naturalist tradition of Buffon, Brückner, Erasmus Darwin and Malthus that the modern understanding of the human place in nature eventually emerged. Their recognition that mass death was essential for sustaining the greatest possible biodiversity was an essential ingredient to Charles Darwin's discovery that it was mass death that created the variety of life in the first place. It was on reading Malthus' theory of mass death in 1838 that Charles Darwin had the epoch-making flash of realisation that natural selection was the driving force of evolution. This eureka moment is preserved in Darwin's notebooks, which reveal that it was the passage in which Malthus addressed the potential for population increase under the

Godwinite vegetarian utopia that triggered Darwin's discovery. In his *Autobiography*, Darwin explained that 'I happened to read for amusement Malthus' *Population*, and being well prepared to appreciate the struggle for existence . . . [it] at once struck me that under these circumstances favourable variations would tend to be preserved and unfavourable ones to be destroyed. The result would be a new species. Here then I had at last got hold of a theory by which to work.' When he finally published this theory in *The Origin of Species* (1859) and in *The Descent of Man* (1871), Darwin acknowledged that his theory of evolution rested on Malthus' observations on the 'struggle for existence'. The mass deaths that afflicted every generation, Darwin pointed out, were the pressures that drove natural selection and were thus responsible for creating biodiversity in the first place: 'It is the doctrine of Malthus applied with manifold force to the whole animal and vegetable kingdoms; for in this case there can be no artificial increase of food, and no prudential restraint from marriage.' The co-discoverer of natural selection Alfred Russel Wallace, also credited Malthus with having triggered his breakthrough.[36] Species evolved *because* great swathes of each generation died before maturity. The survival of the fittest depended on the death of the less fit. Attempting to cleanse ecologies of that dynamic would rupture the entire system of nature. The exoneration of mass deaths had always been a defence of predation against the ideals of the vegetarians. The theory of evolution sprang from the naturalist tradition which had traditionally been articulated against vegetarian idealism.

Modern preconceptions have led scholars to search among eighteenth- and nineteenth-century vegetarians and 'nature lovers' for the pioneers of ecological philosophy. If the anachronism of 'ecology' is to be used at all, it is vital to distinguish between the 'idealist' ecologies of the vegetarians and the 'realist' ecologies of the counter-vegetarians, as well as between the political implications of both. The confusion between these variant positions persists in modern thought, and underlies some of the paradoxes in the animal rights and environmental movements, as well as in the assumptions of those who oppose them. It is true that vegetarians helped to formulate the idea of valuing non-human creatures in their own right, and to drive home the realisation that humans were related to the apes. They were therefore crucial in the construction of modern sensibilities towards nature. The vegetarians nurtured the value of *life*, but this invariably led them to regard violent death as a destructive force. They focused on the value of individual animals. But this was broadly antithetical to the perspective of the ecological naturalists, who saw the death of individual animals as the prerequisite for the life of others. This was a fundamental axis of difference between the vegetarians and the counter-vegetarian ecologists.

These divergent traditions can be traced back to the seventeenth century. Hobbes used his theory of the 'war of all against all' to attack the idealist dream that nature was originally peaceful. Hobbes in turn was opposed by vegetarians like Thomas Tryon who idealised interspecific harmony. This was part of the ongoing dichotomy between an 'idealist' and 'realist' view of nature, and it was frequently deployed in the political debate between egalitarians and *laissez-faire* defenders of political hierarchies. This debate crystallised in the spat between Buffon and Rousseau, and it was carried forward into the Romantic era by Shelley and his friends on the one side and Lawrence, Smellie and Erasmus Darwin on the other. It subsists today in the ethical disputes between animal-lovers who attribute rights or value to individual animals, and ecologists who care more about the equilibrium within ecosystems. Idealist vegetarians, by and large, stood on the other side of the line from the ecologists. It was the counter-vegetarians who valued ecosystems in their own right, and who saw humans as an integral, dependent part of them – even while they participated in the brutal act of eating meat.

Vegetarianism and the Politics of Ecology: Thoreau, Gandhi and Hitler

In 1845 Henry David Thoreau (1817–62) renounced his comfortable metropolitan existence and moved into a log cabin at Walden Pond near his hometown in Concord, Massachusetts. Thoreau's solitary two-year experience in the wilderness, which he inscribed in his best-known work, *Walden*, went down in history as the archetypal realisation of the American dream. But although in modern America Thoreau is universally hailed as the quintessential man of nature, his idea of man's relationship with nature was chronically ambivalent and remains widely (sometimes wilfully) misunderstood.[1] Was he the peaceful, quasi-Hindu-Pythagorean protector of living things he is often made out to be? Or was he, rather, a savage wild man intent on retrieving from the depths of his psyche man's primeval hunting instincts?

Thoreau's friendship with Ralph Waldo Emerson, the revered leader of the 'New England Transcendentalists', brought him into contact with the foremost vegetarian reformers in America, Amos Bronson Alcott (1799–1888), his cousin William Alcott, and Sylvester Graham (mastermind of the modern breakfast cereal). Thoreau experimented with the 'raw grain' diet peddled by these men and their vision of humanity clearly rubbed off on him, for he claimed that before he arrived at Walden Pond, 'Like many of my contemporaries, I had rarely for many years used animal food, or tea, or coffee, &c.; not so much because of any ill effects which I had traced to them, as because they were not agreeable to my imagination.' The vegetarians in turn eulogised Thoreau's earthy knowledge of the outdoors; as Bronson Alcott put it: 'He knows more of Nature's secrets than any man I have known, and of Man as related to Nature.' As they observed Thoreau living in his wood cabin, the vegetarians no doubt hoped he would discover in nature what so many of them believed: that man was a gentle animal hard-wired for sympathy with all living beings.[2]

Thoreau did indeed experience that side of human nature, and Emerson, in his hagiographic obituary, described Thoreau as an Orphic figure who had such 'intimacy with animals' that 'Snakes coiled round his leg; the fishes swam into his hand, and he . . . took the foxes under his protection from the hunters.' But as Emerson pointed out, Thoreau was not partisan to one particular viewpoint, least of all that of the vegetarians. Thoreau was convinced that eating meat was nutritionally unnecessary, that vegetable food was cheaper, easier to acquire and, being a lighter diet, was well suited to the contemplative life, and he demonstrated this to the American nation by documenting his daily intake of rice and home-grown beans. But Thoreau distinguished his views from the cranky missionary zeal of the vegetarians. 'He liked and used the simplest food,' Emerson explained, 'yet, when some one urged a vegetable diet, Thoreau thought all diets a very small matter, saying that "the man who shoots the buffalo lives better than the man who boards at the Graham House."* . . . He confessed that he sometimes felt like a hound or a panther, and, if born among Indians,† would have been a fell hunter.'[3]

What Thoreau found by returning to nature was that both polar views of humanity's place in nature had some truth in them. On the one hand he experienced savage hunting instincts that apparently manifested man's rightful place at the top of the food chain. On the other, he recognised that civilisation cultivated the moral feelings that tied humans into societies, and bound them to the wider community of all living things.

These two poles relate directly back to the dual tradition represented by Thomas Hobbes' emphasis on man's brutal instinct of self-preservation in the war of all against all, and on the other side by Rousseau's contention that humans also had a fundamental instinct of sympathy from which all social virtues sprang. These two rival ecological traditions became philosophical foundations for the two great political movements of the nineteenth and twentieth centuries: the Left and the Right. The Right followed Malthus in viewing nature as a constant and pitiless struggle between individuals in which only

---

* Vegetarian boarding houses established by Sylvester Graham.
† North American Indians.

the most capable deserved to survive; in the wake of Charles Darwin's discoveries this became the dominant ideological view in the West. But the Left also used Darwin's arguments with less individualistic ramifications. Just as the Rousseauists fundamentally disagreed with the Hobbesians and the Malthusians, so in the post-Darwinian world some argued that cooperation and sympathy were also powerful forces in the ecological system.

Thoreau built these clashing ideas of man's place in nature into an evolutionary scheme in a chapter in *Walden* called 'Higher Laws' (it was originally entitled 'Animal Food'). He began the section with the provocative claim that on seeing a woodchuck he 'felt a strange thrill of savage delight, and was strongly tempted to seize and devour him raw'. 'I was never unusually squeamish;' he elaborated. 'I could some-times eat a fried rat with a good relish, if it were necessary.' In the modern urban world hunting has been portrayed as antithetical to ecological sensitivity, as it often has been, but like Rousseau, Thoreau saw that it at least brought people into unmediated contact with nature. Thoreau frequently supplemented his coarse diet at Walden with fish and other spoils of the hunt, and this satisfied what he saw as man's predatory niche in the ecological cycle: 'The perch swallows the grub-worm,' he explained, 'the pickerel swallows the perch, and the fisher-man swallows the pickerel; and so all the chinks in the scale of being are filled.'[4]

Despite occasionally dipping his tongue in gore, Thoreau did finally decide that the principle of living a peaceful bloodless existence was the 'Higher Law'. Human civilisation, he insisted, would inexorably progress from savagery into herbivorousness:

> Is it not a reproach that man is a carnivorous animal? . . . he will be regarded as a benefactor of his race who shall teach man to confine himself to a more innocent and wholesome diet. Whatever my own practice may be, I have no doubt that it is a part of the destiny of the human race, in its gradual improve-ment, to leave off eating animals, as surely as the savage tribes have left off eating each other when they came in contact with the more civilized.[5]

Although he recognised that hunting had its own bounded legitimacy, Thoreau exalted the transcendent life of the vegetarian. The meat-eater at the top of the food chain remains viscerally dependent on all the other animals, but the vegetarian attains a superior rank. Rather than being 'the fiercest and cruellest animal', Thoreau called on man to transcend the food chain: 'Does he perform his duty to the inferior races? Should he not be a god to them?'

Under the guidance of Emerson, who had inherited the Romantic spirit of Wordsworth and Shelley, Thoreau took a copy of the *Bhagavad-Gita* with him to the log cabin at Walden and enthused about the idea of transcending the material world. When in deep meditation he often imagined himself as an Indian ascetic, proclaiming that 'To some extent, and at rare intervals, even I am a yogi', while Robert Louis Stevenson compared him to a 'gymnosophist'. The food he ate was a special aspect of this persona; he wrote in *Walden* that 'It was fit that I should live on rice, mainly, who loves so well the philosophy of India.'[6]

Rather than presenting this ascent in traditional dualist terms of mind over body, Thoreau made it sound like the yearning for spiritual freedom was itself an innate force: 'The repugnance to animal food is not the effect of experience, but is an instinct,' he wrote. 'I believe that every man who has ever been earnest to preserve his higher or poetic faculties in the best condition has been particularly inclined to abstain from animal food, and from much food of any kind.' Both lobes of his imagination – the transcendent ascetic and the earthy hunter – were 'natural'; like Shelley, he thought that the height of civilisation could be as natural as the life of the primitive American Indian.

Thoreau's tussle between what he described as the opposing 'instinct toward a higher, or, as it is named, a spiritual life ... and another toward a primitive rank and savage one', is analogous to a similar struggle experienced by Thoreau's literary and political forebear in the great American tradition, Benjamin Franklin. Franklin too represented this struggle between meat-eating and vegetarianism as between two fundamentally opposed concepts of man's position in nature. As with Thoreau, it was during a reflection on the murderous food chain that Franklin decided to relinquish vegetarianism and eat some freshly caught cod.[7]

This tension between predatory instincts and 'altruistic' abstinence stands for a wider struggle of political affiliations. The presence of both tendencies in Thoreau's writing is what makes it possible for him to be claimed by the Left and the Right in modern America, and what arguably makes Thoreau, along with Franklin, the quintessential voice of the American tradition.

Thoreau repudiated the legitimacy of democracy because it stifled an individual's commitment to a 'Higher Law'. Instead, he wanted to see a reduction in the power of the State and an increase in individual liberty. But the higher law to which Thoreau himself was committed was far from individualistic: just as he believed that the progress of civilisation would fortify man's instinct of sympathy and respect for all living beings, so he also believed – like the anarchist William Godwin – that humans had a strong enough communitarian instinct to live harmoniously with one another without the interference of the State.

Thoreau focused on applying this higher law to the abolition of slavery, convinced that as an individual adhering to the clear law of conscience he could help to bring about the end of that crime against humanity. But he also accepted that one day there would be 'a benefactor of his race' (he was probably thinking of the Alcott cousins) who would lead humans away even from their crimes against animals. 'The faintest assured objection which one healthy man feels,' he promised, 'will at length prevail over the arguments and customs of mankind.' Thus, with his faith both in the integrity of the moral individual and in the ultimate possibility of awakening moral instincts in the whole of humanity, Thoreau marked out a path towards universal vegetarianism.[8]

In 1842 Emerson gave Thoreau's friend Bronson Alcott – the self-taught farmer's son who became an educational reformer and abolitionist – enough money to visit England. There Alcott stayed at a radical educational establishment led by the vegetarian James Pierrepont Greaves, whose inhabitants 'labor on the land, their drink is to be water, and their food chiefly uncooked by fire'. Such was the North American's effect on their community (or 'Concordium') that they named themselves Alcott House in his honour. It was also they who, in 1847, were among the key contributors to the formation of the Vegetarian Society.[9]

The other major group that helped to form the Vegetarian Society were the Bible Christians. This congregation had been established at the beginning of the nineteenth century when the Reverend William Cowherd started giving away hot vegetable soup in the industrial centre of Salford, near Manchester. Blending Emmanuel Swedenborg's mystical Christianity, Cheyne's medical arguments, Saint-Pierre's Rousseauist principles and Thomas Paine's radical politics, Cowherd encouraged his congregation to see God dwelling in all creatures:

Hold, daring man! thy hand restrain –
God is the life in all;
To smite at God, when flesh is slain –
Can crime like this be small?

After Cowherd's death his ministry was continued by the radical liberal mill-owner Joseph Brotherton (1783–1857), a founding patron of the *Manchester Guardian*, eventually MP for Salford and, in 1847, first chairman of the Vegetarian Society. Cowherd's other prominent follower, William Metcalfe (1788–1862), emigrated to the United States in 1817 where he allied himself to Bronson Alcott and Sylvester Graham, and eventually founded the American Vegetarian Society in 1850.

Forming a 'Society' was a characteristic of Victorian reform movements, but it could be said that cordoning themselves off into a distinct community was in fact counterproductive to the overall aim of reducing the number of meat-eaters and the amount of meat eaten. Precisely by making 'vegetarianism' a fixed identity – indelibly associated with crankiness as it was – the vegetarians must have put off many who might otherwise have seen the sense of arguments against meat-eating. It certainly opened them up to a new wave of mockery. The satirical periodical *Punch* guffawed after the Vegetarian Society's first annual meeting: 'We see by the papers that there is a Society in Manchester that devotes its entire energies to the eating of vegetables, and the members meet occasionally for the purpose of masticating mashed potatoes and munching cabbage leaves.'

In 1853 there were 889 members of the Vegetarian Society, half of whom were said to be labourers and tradesmen. These numbers were swelled in the 1880s when prominent members of the literary establishment lent their name to the cause. In 1881 the playwright George Bernard Shaw converted to vegetarianism after reading Percy Shelley's *The Revolt of Islam*. He thus consolidated the strong links between vegetarians and sandal-wearing socialists, and was quickly followed by Leo Tolstoy who wrote a resounding endorsement to a new edition of Howard Williams' large anthology of vegetarian writing.

By the late nineteenth century the teeming streets of Victorian London harboured several vegetarian restaurants. It was into this world that a young man from Gujarat arrived in 1888 to study law, and it was here that he would stumble across the Vegetarian Society, the ideology of which would become a linchpin in his transformation of global politics. If any man deserves Thoreau's title of 'benefactor of his race', then this was he: Mohandas K. Gandhi, later to be leader of the Indian independence movement. Western vegetarianism had been heavily influenced by Indian culture for more than 300 years; in Gandhi's hands it was re-exported to India as a core element in the great national freedom struggle.[10]

Gandhi had been brought up a strict vegetarian of the Bania caste in Gujarat, the heartland of *ahimsa*-endorsing Vaishnavite Hinduism. Ironically, however, in nineteenth-century India many modernising reformers had an anti-vegetarian agenda, and Gandhi was induced to eat meat secretly as a symbolic defiance of traditional Hindu conservatism and even British imperialism. Explaining that they had been inculcated with the old European dogma that vegetarianism made the Indians weak and feeble, Gandhi remembered many years later that 'It began to grow on me that meat-eating was good, that it would make me strong and daring, and that, if the whole country took to meat-eating, the English could be overcome.' However, struck with remorse about deceiving his parents and tormented by nightmares of animals bleating inside him, Gandhi soon abjured the experiment and decided to renounce meat-eating at least until his parents died.

Ambitious to get on in the world, Gandhi decided to finish his studies in London, despite the financial strain and the fact that his community leaders threatened him with loss of caste because 'We are positively informed that you will have to eat flesh and drink wine in England.' Having made a solemn vow to his mother not to succumb to such carnivorous British customs, Gandhi ignored the threats and embarked for London, resolutely clinging to his vegetarian vow despite his lasting conviction that meat-eating was the key to strengthening the Indian constitution 'so that we might defeat the English and make India free'.[11]

At first Gandhi found it extremely hard to accommodate himself to the insipid vegetables that he boiled up for himself – spice-free – in his lodgings. But he was saved when his landlady told him about the numerous vegetarian restaurants serving cheap dinners all over London. Gandhi chanced upon one of these on Farringdon Street and, filled with joy, sat down to his first hearty meal in months. As he satisfied his deprived stomach, his attention was drawn to the array of vegetarian books displayed in the window, among them Howard Williams' *The Ethics of Diet*, Dr Anna Kingsford's *The Perfect Way in Diet* and the works of Dr Allinson (whose name is still carried by a brand of wholemeal bread). By far the most important discovery for Gandhi was the recently published *Plea for Vegetarianism* by the socialist friend of John Ruskin and Edward Carpenter, Henry Salt. Salt wrote five books about Shelley and edited the *Vindication of Natural Diet*; his enthusiasm for Shelley's call for non-violent radical vegetarian protest (itself inspired by Hinduism) evidently rubbed off on Gandhi who mentioned both Salt and Shelley in his writings.[12]

Encountering these books in London was a turning point in Gandhi's life. He became a born-again vegetarian, abstaining from meat, as he explained, 'by choice' rather than under the constraint of his vow. Until this moment he had retained the desire to overthrow vegetarianism in India, but 'The choice was now made in favour of vegetarianism, the spread of which henceforward became my mission.'[13] Vegetarianism had been for Gandhi a badge of colonial humiliation; he now converted it into a symbol of resistance. Reviewing his attitude to the ancient Indian customs he had been taught to despise, Gandhi now clung to them as an antidote to the malaise of Western civilisation.[14]

Vegetarianism was Gandhi's first political cause; many of his earliest writings were articles in the journals of the Vegetarian Society and correspondence about his new vegetarian 'mission'. 'Full of the neophyte's zeal for vegetarianism' – as he put it – he quickly became an executive on the committee of the Vegetarian Society, and remained their agent long after leaving the UK, helping to establish centres of 'vegetarian propaganda' all over the world.[15] While in London he also started his own vegetarian club, of which Edwin Arnold was the vice-president. With these activities he cut his teeth in the organisation of political movements; they also drew him into the ideological environment of the vegetarians, who were often neo-Luddites, socialists and critics of imperialism, among them Shaw, Annie Besant and Henry Salt (who had resigned his post at Eton after deciding that his colleagues were 'cannibals, as devouring the flesh and blood of . . . animals . . . [and] living by the sweat and toil of the classes who do the hard work of the world').

Gandhi saw vegetarianism as a bridge that could unite the peoples of East and West. He advised Indians in London to treat the Vegetarian Society as a home from home, which would, he hoped, help to make India and Britain 'indissolubly united by the chain of love'. On moving to South Africa to work as a lawyer for his uncle, he tried to convert Boer children to vegetarianism in order to instil a reverence for life which would simultaneously break down racial barriers. Increasing arable agriculture in the region, he promised, would double the number of inhabitants the soil could support and thus dissolve the competitive strife between Europeans and Indians. Indeed, it was at dinner in a Johannesburg vegetarian restaurant that Gandhi first met his principal political associates, Albert West and Henry Polak, with whom he founded his rural vegetarian communes Phoenix (1904) and Tolstoy Farm (1910). Indeed, it was with these fellow vegetarians that Gandhi forged his movement of *satyagraha* (literally 'truth-firmness'), the struggle which started for the rights of Asians in South Africa and ended in Indian Independence.[16]

Although Gandhi was initially mainly interested in the health benefits and frugal economics of his diet, he eventually turned more to what he called the 'religious' and 'moral' reasons for vegetarianism.[17] *Ahimsa* (non-violence), an ethic that he identified at the core of both Hinduism and Christianity, became a central plank in his political philosophy, and vegetarianism was one of its most potent manifestations. Gandhi tried to shift the Western vegetarian tradition towards the core Indian doctrine of *ahimsa*.[18] But he also introduced Western arguments into the traditional debate about *ahimsa* in India. Once, after Gandhi put a calf out of its misery, an Indian critic complained that 'You should confess that your views about ahimsa are imported from the West.' Admitting that his mind was a fusion of Eastern and Western ideas, Gandhi defiantly replied: 'I have nothing to be ashamed of if my views on ahimsa are the result of my Western education.'[19] Indeed, it was in England, under the influence of the Theosophical Society, that Gandhi first took a serious interest in Hindu scriptures.[20]

Gandhi's adherence to *ahimsa* determined the non-violent basis of his protests against British colonial rule, from his championing of homespun cotton in place of imported British cloth through to the non-cooperation movement which brought India to an intermittent standstill from 1919 until his death in 1948. Gandhi simultaneously applied *ahimsa* to the minutiae of each individual's personal life. He hoped, like Thoreau, that by experimenting on his own body he could revolutionise the habits of his nation. Abstinence from meat, in this respect, was just the beginning; any food had a certain harmful impact – even eating vegetables and drinking water and milk killed microorganisms. This was to some extent unavoidable; but, he insisted, 'It is a sin if you eat two morsels when you can do with one.' Chewing thoroughly to make the most efficient use of food, he explained, could also 'automatically reduce the dietetic *himsa* [violence] that one commits to sustain life'.[21]

The ultimate *himsa*-reduced diet he advertised was the 'raw-food' of sprouted wheat, which he first experimented with in London in his twenties (following a tradition that can be traced back to Shelley's friends J. F. Newton and William Lambe, whose work Gandhi read about in Howard Williams' *Ethics of Diet*) and which he tried again (until it made him ill) in 1929. 'To be rid of disease it is necessary to do away with fire in the preparation of foods,' he declared. 'We must take everything in its vital state even as animals do.' By liberating people from the necessity of cooking, he promised that the raw food diet 'enables serious men and women to make revolutionary changes in their mode of living. It frees women from a drudgery which brings no happiness but which brings disease in its train.' The raw food diet, and other innovations such as abstinence from milk, were clearly fads which had roots in the Western vegetarian tradition, and numerous observers at the time pointed to Gandhi's debt to the West.[22] Throughout his life he acknowledged that 'The seed, however, for all of them [his various arguments for vegetarianism] was sown in England.'[23] What has not been recognised sufficiently (even perhaps by Gandhi) is that the vegetarian tradition he picked up in England was already infused with Indian philosophy.

Thoreau was one of Gandhi's most important inspirations in his political deployment of *ahimsa* and his entire strategy of civil resistance. Gandhi read Thoreau's seminal essay, 'Resistance to Civil Government' (1849) (later known as 'Civil Disobedience') when he was just beginning the *satyagraha* movement. Although Gandhi insisted that he had developed his method of civil resistance *before* reading Thoreau (despite some contemporaries' claims to the contrary), he readily acknowledged that Thoreau's 'ideas influenced me greatly'. In an appeal 'To American Friends', Gandhi reiterated that 'You have given me a teacher in Thoreau, who furnished me through his essay on the "Duty of Civil Disobedience" scientific confirmation of what I was doing in South Africa'; and to Franklin Delano Roosevelt in 1942 he wrote that 'I have profited greatly by the writings of Thoreau and Emerson.' Many regarded this as the prime example of Gandhi's re-export to India of

Eastern-influenced Western traditions. As one American journalist put it somewhat wilfully: 'It would seem that Gandhi received back from America what was fundamentally the philosophy of India after it had been distilled and crystallized in the mind of Thoreau.' Gandhi himself revealed something similar regarding his enthusiasm for Emerson's essays which, he said, 'contain the teaching of Indian wisdom in Western garb. It is refreshing to see our own sometimes thus differently fashioned.'[24]

Although Thoreau was interested in the principles of harmlessness and stoic forbearance, he was not actually as committed to non-violence as Gandhi's enthusiasm has led some to believe (he was, for example, the staunchest defender of John Brown's use of murder and violent insurrection against the slave trade).[25] But Gandhi was inspired by Thoreau's faith in the power and righteousness of individuals resisting unjust governments. Thoreau's personal adherence to a 'Higher Law' in the face of social injustice was a dogma with which Gandhi became familiar during his residence in London where it was commonly espoused by vegetarians and Suffragettes.[26] Indeed, Thoreau's prophecy that one solitary individual, like Shelley's Promethean hero, could lead mankind away from the barbaric practice of meat-eating appeared as the epigram with which Henry Salt opened his *Plea for Vegetarianism*, the work that inspired Gandhi with his new mission and committed him to a life of political protest.

Salt was Thoreau's greatest champion in England and clearly regarded Gandhi as Thoreau's representative on earth, for in 1929, having to his delight found that Gandhi in his *Autobiography* treated reading the *Plea for Vegetarianism* as a pivotal moment in his life, he wrote to him – by now a hero of political freedom movements across the world – humbly enquiring whether '*you* had been a reader of Thoreau, and had been at all influenced by him, as on many subjects your views and Thoreau's seem rather akin'. Gandhi replied by relating how he had translated parts of 'Civil Disobedience' into Gujarati for his journal *Indian Opinion* and that later he read *Walden* and Salt's biography of Thoreau 'with great pleasure and equal profit'. The following year Salt wrote a poem celebrating Gandhi, the 'one old, powerless, unresisting man' fighting Britain's 'alien law'; the year after that Gandhi reciprocated during his visit to London to discuss Indian independence with the British government, when he took the time to deliver an address to the London Vegetarian Society in which he honoured Salt

Henry Salt seated next to Mahatma Gandhi
at the Vegetarian Society, 1931

who sat proudly beside him.[27] This iconic moment – Gandhi journeying full circle back to the Vegetarian Society of which he was once an executive, and as a leader of a movement incomparably greater – encapsulates perfectly the centuries of cross-cultural fertilisation which made this moment possible.

Gandhi was interested by more than Thoreau's theory of protest, his chastity and his self-sufficient frugality.[28] He also stated that Thoreau's 'Civil Disobedience' 'contained the essence of his political philosophy, not only as India's struggle related to the British, but as to his own views of the relation of citizens to government'. Indeed, in his popular publications Gandhi quoted Thoreau's mandate 'That government is best which governs least.' The dissolution of State power, Gandhi claimed, would nurture 'a state of enlightened anarchy' in which 'everyone is his own ruler. He rules himself in such a manner that he is never a hindrance to his neighbour.'[29] Gandhi hoped to shift towards this situation in India by removing powers from the national government and replacing them with the sort of 'village republic' he modelled on his pacifist vegetarian self-sufficient ashrams. As with Thoreau, Gandhi's belief in the viability of an anarchistic state manifested his faith in the benevolence of human nature – and this provides a key to understanding where Gandhi's political theories belong in the historical heritage with respect to the nature of humans and their place in the ecological system.

Gandhi thought that history gave a distorted picture of human nature because it catalogued all the exceptional moments when people's normal placid existence had been interfered with and plunged into conflict and war; left to themselves, humans would live in a harmonious state of mutual love and respect. As Gandhi demonstrated with his animal-friendly ashrams, this mutual love and respect also applied to man's relationship with animals. One key passage in his autobiography is enough to reveal the source for Gandhi's new ideological way of framing this perennial question, and it points to an ecological theory developed as an antidote to the dominant right-wing manifestations of Social Darwinism. Explaining the humanitarian case for vegetarianism as it was presented in *fin de siècle* London – and as he later espoused it – Gandhi wrote that 'man's supremacy over the lower animals meant not that the former should prey upon the latter, but that the higher should protect the lower, *and that there should be mutual aid between the two as between man and man.*'[30] An explicit parallel is made between the relationship of 'man and man' and that of humans and animals; politics and ecology were one and the same.

Gandhi's phrase 'mutual aid' points to the philosophical origins of this line of thinking, and clearly sums up his political outlook. 'Mutual aid' was the catchphrase of a school of socio-ecological thought that emerged in London during Gandhi's residence there, according to which animal and human societies were founded on the instinct of cooperation. This movement was led by the Russian naturalist-anarchist Prince Petr Alekseevich Kropotkin (1842–1921) whose oft-reprinted *Mutual Aid: A Factor of Evolution* (published in 1902 but composed of essays published since 1890) provided the ecological foundation for socialist anarchy.[31] Kropotkin had escaped from a Russian jail and fled to England after being arrested for stirring up revolutionary socialism among Russian workers in 1872. In 1888 (the year Gandhi arrived in London) he co-founded the Sheffield Socialist Group along with H. M. Hyndman the Marxist, Annie Besant, the Theosophist, and Edward Carpenter, the critic of Western modernity who had a lasting influence on Gandhi's economic outlook. Carpenter – a vegetarian himself – was also responsible for translating the vegetarian essays of Prince Kropotkin's great collaborator and fellow anarchist-agitator Jean-Jacques Élisée Reclus (1830–1905), who expanded Kropotkin's communitarian ethics to encourage a co-operative relationship between humans and animals. Henry Salt befriended Kropotkin and absorbed his theories, so at the very least Gandhi will have received Kropotkin's ideas second hand.[32] Kropotkin was also friends with Gandhi's fellow vegetarian George Bernard Shaw, and Kropotkin's daughter ended up translating a number of Shaw's plays into Russian.[33] Furthermore, Kropotkin, like most of this medley of dissidents and socialists in London, was a great admirer of Leo Tolstoy and applauded him in his article in the 1911 *Encyclopædia Britannica* for his experimental anarchistic village-farm communities. Tolstoy's *The Kingdom of God is Within You* (1894), meanwhile, inspired Gandhi and led to a flourishing correspondence about vegetarianism and non-violence between the two.

Kropotkin's main complaint – shared by Tolstoy, Shaw and clearly by Gandhi – was that the theory of evolution had been misappropriated by Malthusian advocates of individualism and social competitiveness. Chief demon in this amoral tribe of Social Darwinists, according to Kropotkin, was Darwin's best-known disciple Thomas Huxley, who argued in his 1888 essay, 'The Struggle for Existence and its bearing on Man', that in the natural state 'the weakest went to the wall, while the toughest and shrewdest . . . but not the best in another way, survived. Life was a continuous free fight . . . the Hobbesian war of each against all was the normal state of existence.' In order to escape the ruthlessness of nature, Huxley claimed, humans had to overcome their natural bloody instincts. This scarcely concealed political commentary was repeated with alarming enthusiasm across the Western world, not least by leading ecologists such as Ernst Haeckel (1834–1919), the man who coined the word 'ecology', and declared that 'The raging war of interests in human society is only a feeble picture of an unceasing and terrible war of existence which reigns throughout the whole of the living world.'[34]

Kropotkin argued that Huxley's portrayal of human social instincts was an ideologically motivated distortion of ecological facts 'which has been too willingly repeated, without sufficient criticism, since the time of Hobbes'. Most organisms in the state of nature did not survive by fighting each other, Kropotkin insisted, but by clubbing together to overcome hardship and danger. Kropotkin did most of his zoological

fieldwork in the harsh climate of the Siberian tundra where competition within sparse populations was not very obvious, which helps to
explain the discrepancy between his viewpoint and that of Darwin,
who regarded the superabundant tropics as the archetype of his ecological model. In a hostile environment, Kropotkin explained, those
organisms that cooperated best were most likely to survive. Communitarian instincts brought important evolutionary benefits: 'sociability
is the greatest advantage in the struggle for life.' Humans were the
pre-eminent social species, always practising mutual aid, and that is
why the species had been so successful. Kropotkin urged (in line with
Rousseau, Thoreau and Gandhi) that this was the 'pre-human origin
of moral instincts' and the basis of altruism.[35] (Like Shelley, he did not
have a problem with calling an evolutionarily determined trait 'moral',
for, as his opponents abundantly demonstrated, it was still possible to
choose to ignore the principle of mutual aid, even though it was a law
of nature.) Kropotkin felt that his theory of mutual aid had obvious
implications for the effective organisation of society: '"Don't compete!
– competition is always injurious to the species, and you have plenty
of resources to avoid it! . . . Therefore combine – practise mutual aid!"
. . . That is what Nature teaches us,' he thundered. The death and
destruction resulting from Malthusian competitiveness – far from being
ruthlessly efficient – was in fact a waste of resources.

Most biologists today are still aligned in opposition to Kropotkin,
pointing out that for an instinct such as altruism to be selected by the
process of evolution it must increase the propagative success of the
individual carrier of the relevant gene, not just the species. However,
Kropotkin's attack on the ideological hi-jacking of evolutionary theory
was pertinent, and his zoological work has been continued by controversial naturalists such as Vero Wynne-Edwards.[36] In a chapter titled
'Kropotkin Was No Crackpot', Stephen Jay Gould admiringly concedes that 'Kropotkin therefore created a dichotomy within the general
notion of struggle – two forms with opposite import: (1) organism
against organism of the same species for limited resources leading
to competition; and (2) organism against environment, leading to
cooperation.'[37]

Kropotkin felt that Darwin and his followers had unduly under-
estimated the importance of sociability. They had instead focused
almost exclusively on the selfish struggle for survival which legitimised
ugly political attitudes. It was true that Darwin and Huxley endorsed

the view that inferior races would give way to European racial supremacy and that the evolutionary progress of the human species was being hindered, as Darwin put it, 'by the preservation of a considerable number of individuals, weak in mind and body, who would have been promptly eliminated in the savage state'.[38]

But Darwin had also drawn close attention to the principle of sociability in evolution, acknowledging that sympathy 'will have been increased through natural selection; for those communities, which included the greatest number of the most sympathetic members, would flourish best, and rear the greatest number of offspring.' Alfred Wallace, the co-discoverer of evolution, and Ernst Haeckel likewise believed that human sympathy and morality were the result of 'ethical instincts derived from our animal ancestors'. But like Adam Smith and indeed Hobbes before him, Darwin emphasised that the feeling of sympathy ultimately evolved from, or was at least strengthened by, the fundamental attribute of selfishness, for, as Smith had pointed out, we receive visceral pleasure from satisfying the sympathetic instinct, and Darwin elaborated that 'we are led by the hope of receiving good in return to perform acts of sympathetic kindness to others.' The instinct of sympathy and sociability in this case was not, as Rousseau proposed, the opposite of selfishness, but merely an adjunct to it.

Kropotkin distanced himself from the naïvety of what he called 'Rousseau's optimism', but his belief that humans could live harmoniously by the instinct of mutual aid without restraining laws or authoritative governments was in the tradition of Rousseauist-Godwinite idealism, and it was shared by the likes of Thoreau and Gandhi.[39] Kropotkin, like his ideological forebear William Godwin, saw the inefficient use of agricultural land as a misuse of society's shared resources. Grazing land, he said, was 'much inferior in productivity to a cornfield; and the fine breeds of cattle appear to be poor creatures as long as each ox requires three acres of land to be fed upon.' But Kropotkin did not call for the abolition of meat-eating for, he said, 'the dearest of all varieties of our staple food is meat; and those who are not vegetarians, either by persuasion or by necessity, consume on the average 225 lb. of meat'.[40] However, some of his followers found in Kropotkin's theories an ecological rationale for vegetarianism. If harmonious cooperation within a species was so beneficial, why should not the same apply between different species? Élisée Reclus, a veteran of the Paris Commune of 1871 who indulged in more flagrant Rousseauist utopian dreams than his friend Kropotkin, argued that there was indeed a strong survival benefit to inter-specific harmony. Humans, he claimed, had evolved to live in 'fraternal association' with animals, and this natural relationship – still evident in remote parts of the world and inscribed in ancient Indian scriptures – was of mutual benefit to all members of the ecosystem: 'The natural sympathy existing between all these creatures harmonised them in a broad atmosphere of peace and love,' he claimed. 'The bird would come and perch on the hand of man, as he does even today on the horns of the bull.' This harmonious relationship, he said, would be far more beneficial to humans than their current ecological niche as predators.[41]

Evolution had swiftly become the prism through which most social issues were discussed; accordingly, Kropotkin and Reclus' theories took on special importance for vegetarians. (Indeed, Alfred Russel Wallace himself, though he ate meat, thought that humans ought to turn to vegetarianism for moral, medical and agronomic reasons and he corresponded with Henry Salt about the virtues of Percy Shelley.[42]) In 1938 the London delegate to the International Vegetarian Union, Dugald Semple, remarked that 'We must not only study Darwin but also Kropotkin.' Sociability was an evolutionary advantage, said Kropotkin: therefore, Semple deduced, the herds of sociable herbivorous animals were taking over the world while carnivores were ever dwindling.[43] The prelapsarian dream of a bloodless ecology was still alive in the post-Darwinian era. Even Gandhi, who called lions 'ferocious and practically useless', seems to have been touched by its appeal.[44]

In Russia after 1917 the radical Left emerged supreme – and after the deposition of the Tsar, Kropotkin returned from exile to establish his biomoral theories in the new revolutionary State. Simultaneously in Europe the far Right was rising towards a fearsome prominence, and its proponents also used ecology to defend their political vision: that it was natural for certain groups to exert ruthless supremacy over others. The Nazis (Nationalsozialistische Deutsche Arbeiterpartei, or German National Socialist Workers' Party) believed that their quest to purify the human race from evolutionary 'runts' was justified by the ecological force that Hitler in *Mein Kampf* called 'the aristocratic principle, which is a fundamental law of nature'. Huxley and Haeckel can hardly be blamed for the Holocaust, but the Nazis' willingness to use eugenics to direct human evolution drew on a long tradition, not least from Malthus and William Lawrence who came to understand evolution by

studying farmers' selective breeding programmes, and who saw nothing wrong in applying the concept of 'selective breeding' to ensure the
'improvement' of the human species. Nazis took theories like these to
their apocalyptic extreme: arguing that Jews had to be extirpated from
society because they had taken up a parasitic niche in the social ecology
and were causing Germany's urban economic malaise.[45]

It may come as a surprise that vegetarianism was in fact as prominent in the Fascist Right as it was on the Left (especially since the
Malthusian view of ecology which they inherited had traditionally
been used to critique vegetarianism). But Fascists intent on cleansing
the human race were particularly attracted to the vegetarian rhetoric of
purification. The Nazis aspired to lead humanity back to 'nature', and
although their concept of 'nature' was abhorrent, it was one that was
chillingly compatible with the language of vegetarianism. Their keen-
ness for animal protection legislation also manifested their antipathy
to Judaeo-Christian anthropocentrism, which they used as another
front for persecuting the Jews. Their insistence that humans were just
another animal in the ecosystem, meanwhile, no doubt rationalised
their decision to treat some humans in ways which their own animal
protection laws would have proscribed.

To the great discomfort of many modern vegetarians, therefore –
and despite the understandable attempts to highlight real discrepancies
in the historical record – Adolf Hitler was a vegetarian. At the very least
he espoused a vegetarian philosophy and practised it much of the time.
Indeed, many Nazis were either vegetarian or interested in related
issues. SS supremo Heinrich Himmler believed that vegetarianism was
the key to health and long life. The deputy leader of the Nazi party
Rudolf Hess was such a strict vegetarian that he even refused to eat
meals specially prepared for him at the Chancellery by Hitler's qualified
diet-cook because he could only eat organically grown vegetables.
(One-upmanship on Hitler was not advisable, and in the words of one
onlooker Hitler 'bluntly informed him that in that case he should take
his meals at home'.) Hitler's powerful spin-doctor Martin Bormann ate
vegetarian food, if only to ingratiate himself while at table with the
Führer. Even Joseph Goebbels, in an entry in his diary, seems to have
agreed that on the issue of vegetarianism, Hitler's 'arguments cannot
be refuted on any serious basis. They are totally unanswerable.'[46]

The Nazi ideology is perhaps the most repellent product of European history, and it did not spring from nothing; it is sickening partly

because one can trace distinct historical continuities both forwards and backwards. Apparently innocuous cultural trends were easily mutated into Fascism in the crucible of a national crisis.

By the early twentieth century, the post-Rousseauist back-to-nature movement had sprouted into a thriving medley of naturopaths, nudists, mud-bathers, ecologists and vegetarians; this movement found its zenith in counter-culture nudist camps that promoted the idea that 'men could live a paradisal life in nature'. In nineteenth- and early twentieth-century Germany there was a focus on the reinvigoration of health and beauty in the face of the pathological effects of urbanisation; it drew inspiration from the Weimar period's *Lebensreform* (life reform) and the vibrant *Körperkultur* (body culture). People from wildly different positions on the political spectrum selected aspects of these practices: Zionists and Fascists, Social Democrats and proto-hippies, all experimented with them. Even the Jewish novelist Franz Kafka became a nudist vegetarian raw-food enthusiast.

In the 1860s Eduard Baltzer (1814–87) organised the vegetarian movement in Germany, using ideas from the earlier vegetarian tradition such as those of Goethe's friend Wilhelm Hufeland. The German nationalist Richard Ungewitter (1868–1958) carried this tradition into the twentieth century by coaxing his followers into severe vegetarianism and harsh regimes of communal naked callisthenics, promising that this was the way to resurrect the German *Volk* as a world military power – a quest that took on special urgency after Germany's humiliation in the First World War, which was believed to have reversed the process of natural selection by killing the nation's fittest men.[99] Ungewitter's dietary allies, Gustav Selss (president of the German Vegetarian Union) and the feminist Klara Ebert, also advocated vegetarianism as a means of cleansing corruption from German society. They all believed that those 'degenerates' who could not be purified should be banned from breeding or even exterminated to prevent their deformities passing to the next generation. Ungewitter, meanwhile, forged an alliance with a neo-pagan cult whose membership consisted solely of an 'Aryan aristocracy' of blond males. In parallel developments in the United States, John Harvey Kellogg, who promoted breakfast cereals as a vegetarian alternative to bacon and eggs, was also a leader of the eugenics movement which endorsed the involuntary sterilization of African-American male convicts and aimed to sterilize 15 million men over 20 years.

'Waldesfrieden' from Richard Ungewitter's
Nacktheit and Kultur (1913)

In early twentieth-century Germany the Fascists did not have to look far to find useful rhetoric among the vegetarians, and although the Nazis eventually suppressed nudist groups like Ungewitter's, they readily adopted their language.[47] Hitler himself believed that vegetarianism would help to purify his own 'bad blood' – an idea carrying implications for both physical health and breeding (he may have feared that he had a Jewish ancestor). He first gave up meat for a time in 1911 to treat a stomach complaint, and again to shed some weight in 1924, and, according to some unreliable reports, finally renounced meat in 1931 to purge himself of the psychological association that flesh had with the corpse of his niece Geli Raubal who shot herself with a gun Hitler had just given her.[48] Throughout his life Hitler continued to believe that abstaining from meat alleviated his chronic flatulence, constipation, sweating, nervous tension, trembling of muscles, and the stomach cramps that convinced him he was dying of cancer.[49] It was easy for such a man to insist that his personal experience must apply to the whole human race.

Hitler, echoing the vegetarian tradition going back through

'Heil Göring!' from *Kladderadatsch*, 3 September 1933

Rousseau, Gassendi and Plutarch, became convinced that it was not natural for humans to eat meat. According to transcripts of Hitler's conversations edited by Martin Bormann and published as *Hitler's Table Talk* (tr. 1953), Hitler frequently insisted to top Nazi officials that 'The monkeys, our ancestors of prehistoric times, are strictly vegetarian.' 'If I offer a child the choice between a pear and a piece of meat, he'll quickly choose the pear. That's his atavistic instinct speaking . . . Man, alone amongst the living creatures, tries to deny the laws of nature.' 'He believes more than ever that meat-eating is harmful to humanity,' wrote Goebbels in his diary in 1942, corroborating the reliability of Bormann's transcripts.[50]

As Robert Proctor showed in his ground-breaking book *The Nazi War on Cancer*, some medical professionals at the time claimed that eating meat, especially in excess, caused cancer, and that vegetable-eating peoples like the Indians were free from the disease. Accordingly, Nazis instructed Germans to adopt more natural diets based on whole-some roots, fruits and cereals, and legally obliged bakers to sell wholemeal bread – the patriotic food of the great German peasant. Failure to comply with the ordinances instructing the nation to clean up their diet and make themselves fit, slim and healthy resulted in persecution. Anyone who fattened themselves on excessive quantities of meat and fat, the Nazis insisted, 'robs other racial comrades of these foods; he is a debauchee and a traitor to his land and his country'. These policies attracted some improbable support from German The-osophists, George Bernard Shaw and from the Seventh Day Adventists, who rejoiced in 1933 that the nation was now being run by Hitler 'who has his office from the hand of God, and who knows himself to be responsible to Him. As an anti-alcoholic, non-smoker, and vege-tarian, he is closer to our own view of health reform than anybody else.'[51]

Hitler went still further and concluded (like Gandhi, Thoreau's friends, the Danish hygienist Jens Peter Müller,[112] and vegetarians since Wilhelm Hufeland and William Lambe) that cooking itself was an unnatural health risk. 'All sicknesses of civilisation are caused by man cooking food,' said Hitler, according to *Hitler's Table Talk*. 'Those who adopt a vegetable diet must remember that it is in their raw state that vegetables have their greatest nutritive value.'[52] Thus, while Gandhi and his followers experimented with sprouted wheat diets inspired by German naturopaths, the German army was prescribed sprouted wheat alongside their rations of flour made from soya beans (nicknamed 'Nazi Beans'). Ironically mirroring Gandhi's own aspirations for dietary reform, Hitler claimed that if life expectancy was on the rise, 'that's because people are again finding room for a naturistic diet. The raw-food movement is a revolution.'[53]

Within months of taking office as Chancellor, Hitler arranged a consultation with an eighty-year-old woman 'known up and down the Rhine as the Seniorin of vegetarianism, cold-water cures, and herbal healing'. Later on the same day, when his staff tried to draw him back to the political tasks in hand, he answered that there were 'far more important things than politics – reforming the human lifestyle, for example. What this old woman told me this morning is far more important than anything I can do in my life.' He frequently startled his colleagues in the party by diverting political meetings into disquisitions on the benefits of the vegetable diet. Even in the height of the war, in April 1942, Hitler took up valuable strategy-building time ranting about his pet topic. 'Of course he knows that during the war we cannot completely upset our food system,' wrote Goebbels in his diary. 'After the war, however, he intends to tackle this problem also.' 'Supposing the prohibition of meat had been an article of faith for National Socialism, it's certain our movement wouldn't have succeeded,' Hitler mused; and he reassured Admiral Fricke that he would not issue a decree forbidding the navy to eat meat.

Hitler wasn't willing to institute it during a war, but he did believe that vegetarianism could be a key to Germany's military success. Caesar's soldiers had lived exclusively on vegetables, he claimed, and 'The Vikings would not have undertaken their now legendary expeditions [if] they'd depended on a meat diet.'[54] Himmler concurred, and called for the Waffen-SS to convert to a non-smoking, teetotal vegetarian regime. Indian vegetarians, Himmler observed, had longer lives and better health than Europeans, and he fantasised that Aryan Germans could take over the world if only they returned to their original vegetarian diet.[55]

The old vegetarian argument against wastefully feeding grains to animals became increasingly important to the Nazis as they careered towards the food shortages of the Second World War. Hitler is said to have complained that thirty-seven per cent of German land was wastefully taken up by pasturage, 'So it's not man who eats grass, it's his cattle'; potatoes, on the other hand – the staple of the German diet – occupied only one per cent: 'If it was three per cent,' Hitler claimed, 'we'd have more to eat than is needed.' Göring accordingly published a vigorously blunt ordinance declaring that farmers who wasted their grain by feeding it to beef-cattle were 'traitors'. Franz Wirz, a member of the Nazi Committee on Public Health, similarly complained that it took about 90,000 calories of grain to produce just 9,300 calories of pork (thus wasting nearly nine-tenths of agricultural produce). Land currently used to grow grains for livestock, he insisted, should be converted to growing horticultural products for people.[56]

Vegetarianism once again rose to prominence in war time as it had in seventeenth-century England and in revolutionary France. In the face of food shortages, meat-eating was stigmatised as an unpatriotic indulgence and an inefficient use of resources. Malthus had predicted that populations would outstrip food supplies and that increasing agricultural output was the only way of feeding more people. Failing that, he warned, there would be famine or war until populations fell back to a sustainable level. To what extent were the Nazis – whose social theories were drenched in Malthusian rhetoric – fulfilling Malthus' theories? Gandhi, meanwhile, was developing the arguments of Malthus' vegetarian opponents who called for vegetarianism as a way of avoiding the grim prospect of war. But – as Malthus warned – were the Indians thereby nurturing a growing population unprotected by the buffer of the luxury of meat, and therefore vulnerable to famine? Both Malthus and his vegetarian opponents had always recognised that subsisting on arable produce could increase the carrying capacity of a nation's land. Gandhi and Hitler, it seems, had come to occupy this common ground.

If it seems relatively easy to accept that health promotion and urgent food production were part of the Nazis' Fascist regime, it may be harder to comprehend that Nazi Germany was the site of the strictest animal protection laws then in existence. The state that conducted unspeakable experiments on living humans before sending them in their millions to the gas chambers simultaneously protected animals from vivisection. The Nazis even promulgated instructions on the humane slaughter of fish and crustaceans which today are still unprotected by legislation. It was Hermann Göring (a keen but environmentally sensitive hunter) who ushered in the animal protection laws. But other Nazis were just as passionate about keeping animals from harm. Himmler allegedly detested the very idea of 'shooting from behind cover at poor creatures browsing on the edge of a wood, innocent, defenceless, and unsuspecting', and he called it 'pure murder'. Hitler himself renownedly loved animals; he was said to believe that they were intelligent, perhaps even capable of language, and he developed intense relationships with his dogs, notably Blondi. After he and Eva

Hitler as friend of animals: Nazi propaganda material

Braun ate their final vegetarian meal of spaghetti and tomato sauce in 1945 before killing themselves in their bunker, Hitler saved Blondi from living in a non-Nazi world by feeding it a trial dose of cyanide. (Ironically, the Russian forensics examining Hitler's charred remains claimed that it was his yellowed teeth, 'typical of a vegetarian', that gave them the clue that the body they were examining was his.)[57]

Hitler's concern for animal welfare has probably been exaggerated to emphasise the paradox of his appalling policies. Contemporaries were aware of the inconsistencies; one French vegetarian cookbook found in Hitler's library, for example, was ironically dedicated to 'Monsieur Hitler, the vegetarian, and thus the man of peace'.[58] But the disturbing fact remains that sentimental relations to animals are by no means incompatible with cruelty towards humans; indeed, they are frequently seen to coincide in misanthropic individuals who fail to incorporate satisfactorily into human society, and turn to animals for more compliant social interactions. Recent scholars have pointed out that the Nazis' animal protection laws reveal a distinctly xenophobic emphasis, for example in banning kosher and halal methods of slaughter. When writing about Hitler's vegetarianism, Goebbels noted that Hitler was 'anti-Christian as well as anti-Jewish' because 'Both have no point of contact to the animal element, and thus, in the end, they will be destroyed.' Nazi biology textbooks taught that 'there exist no physical or psychological characteristics which would justify a differentiation of mankind from the animal world.' The Reichsmarschall in 1933 threatened to commit to concentration camps 'those who still think they can treat animals as inanimate property'.[59]

Anthropocentrism had long been associated with the Judaeo-Christian tradition. The Nazis' animal protection legislation, their vegetarianism and the persecution of the Jews were all elements of one common Fascist front, centring on the purification of the human ecological system from what they perceived as 'unnatural' corruptions. In *Table Talk*, Hitler is alleged to have claimed – almost like Percy Shelley – that ugly organisms like toads were unnatural corruptions of nature (created when frogs ate unsuitable food). It was his planned global dietary revolution that would bring nature back to its pristine purity.[60] This aspect of Hitler's vegetarianism has often been traced (with limited evidence) to the influence of his ideological hero, the opera composer Richard Wagner (1813–83) who, like Shelley and Gandhi and even apparently Hitler, seemed to think that carnivores themselves were 'unnatural' or at least undesirable members of the ecosystem.[61] Wagner wrote in 1881 that returning to the natural vegetarian diet would help to purify humanity from the corruptions brought on by meat-eating and racial mixing and protect against Jewish aggression: 'true and hearty fellowship with the vegetarians, the protectors of animals, and the friends of temperance' was the only hope for humanity. 'I feel less fellow-suffering for people than for animals,' wrote Wagner, explaining that animals had no way of rising above their suffering as humans did. Hitler may have absorbed such views from Wagner; certainly the drive for Fascistic purification was a shared principle.[62]

The association of Judaism and anthropocentrism to bolster Fascist political fulminations has survived into the present day. There are still supporters of the Greek Fascist, Maximiani Portas alias Savitri-Devi (dubbed 'Hitler's Priestess' by the historian Nicholas Goodrick-Clarke). Savitri-Devi emigrated to India during the Second World War and tried to get Hitler to join forces with his 'Aryan' counterparts among high-caste Hindus. Her books – printed by a publisher involved in Holocaust denial and reissued as recently as 1991 – cobbled together an attack on Judaeo-Christian anthropocentrism with brutal Social Darwinism, based on the mandate that 'You cannot "de-nazify"

Nature.' Hindu scriptures, according to Savitri-Devi, reveal that humans have no special place in the natural world and thus there is no contradiction in eliminating non-Aryan humans while cherishing animals. She laments that ancient forests have been destroyed to build roads, cities and to grow food for 'more and more people who might as well never have been born'. She preferred the idea of wiping out humanity to seeing nature utterly destroyed.[63] It was precisely the idea that humans were part of the animal world, and thus inexorably caught up in the fight for ecological supremacy, that rationalised, within the Fascists' minds, some of their greatest atrocities.

Thus the Nazis – who occasionally cited the Indians to bolster their vegetarian arguments – fall in line with numerous other figures in the history of vegetarianism's assault on Judaeo-Christian anthropocentrism. They took previously constructive ideas to extremes that are hardly imaginable in their ferocity. Understandably, vegetarians have often found the association with Hitler uncomfortable. It has been argued that Hitler did sometimes eat meat and that the image of him as a celibate, ascetic leader was a cynical invention of his press officials.[64] (Ironically, this image of a leader whose austerities liberated his mind and body for the unbridled execution of patriotic duties, may have been inspired by Mahatma Gandhi, books on whom appear in Hitler's library.[65]) Of course, that Hitler was a vegetarian need be no more relevant to a vegetarian than the fact that other Nazis were meat-eaters is relevant to meat-eaters. Although vegetarianism was an integral part of Hitler's Fascist ideology, this does not imply that vegetarianism has anything intrinsically Fascist about it.

With such precedents in the history of both vegetarianism and ecology, the modern debate has become a minefield hemmed in by a Scylla on the Right and Charybdis on the Left. A thoroughly considered view, however, reveals that both vegetarianism and ecology had long histories before they were appropriated by either the Nazis or their ideological opponents. Disputing people's perceptions and treatment of the natural world has been one of the most pervasive lines of cultural production in human history. The idea of vegetarianism has played a significant role in this for centuries; it cannot be tied down to any one political viewpoint. European vegetarians challenged humanity's reckless exploitation of the animal kingdom. We owe to them – and especially the Indian philosophies that backed them up – some of the environmental sensibilities we enjoy today.

Arguments that rage now still follow many of the traditional lines. Among the prominent animal liberationists, Professor Peter Singer is a direct intellectual descendant of the Utilitarians, and like them objects to causing unnecessary suffering. He includes animal sensations in the sum of the greater common good, but in contrast to most of his Utilitarian forebears who justified meat-eating, he calculates that, at least for people living in developed countries, with a wide choice of alternative diets, the use of commercially raised and killed animals for food is unjustifiable.[66] Ecologists, whose views often clash with animal liberationists, are more difficult to define, partly because the term can be used to describe scientists who study ecosystems, political theorists who think human society should follow ecological laws, or people who simply attribute intrinsic value to ecologies. These last, often termed Deep Ecologists or biocentrists, have been perhaps most maligned, to the extent that it has become common to associate them with Fascism – an association no more necessary than vegetarianism and Nazism.

Ecologists – like myself – argue that Singer's election of sentience as the criterion for moral considerability is an extension (rather than obliteration) of the old anthropocentric speciesism which attributes moral worth to entities according to how similar they are to 'us'. Surely the only hope (and that a slim one) is to realise that all organisms are bound up in a web of mutual dependence; that regardless of the human attribution of 'rights' or 'moral worth', ecologies must be sustained if we – and any of the other elements of the biosphere – are to avoid severe hardship, or worse. This becomes an important issue when methods of acquiring food are at stake, and it is by no means clear that the prescriptions of animal liberationists of imposing universal vegetarianism would be either the most ecologically sensible or even the best way of reducing animal suffering. There are ecologically sustainable ways of procuring meat for human sustenance – not least the regulated culling of wild animals – which even from the animal welfare perspective causes less harm to animals than arable cultivation. Furthermore, there are vast tracts of the earth where properly managed grazing of domestic animals is the only way of symbiotically sustaining the lives of both the animals and the humans who depend upon them.

In any case, the principal argument against eating meat must surely be the one that unites both the animal welfare and ecological perspectives – as well as that of human self-interest. The world's remaining forests are currently being destroyed to make way for grazing and for the cultivation of soya beans. The bulk of these nutritious pulses are used to feed animals which end up on the dinner plates of the affluent West and, increasingly, China. This ecological devastation – coupled with the vast resource-use the meat industry engenders – threatens not just ecosystems and local people whose lives depend on the sustainable use of their land, but the whole of humankind. The equation is simple: if we ate less unsustainably produced meat we would destroy fewer forests, use less water, emit fewer greenhouse gases and conserve the world's resources for future generations.[67] Insofar as it is desirable to avoid serious problems for both the natural environment and our own food security, there are compelling reasons, at the very least, to reduce our consumption of meat.

ABBREVIATIONS

BIBLIOGRAPHY

NOTES

INDEX

ABBREVIATIONS

Reference Works

OED: *Oxford English Dictionary (Second Edition) on CD-ROM*, Version 2.0 (1999), Oxford University Press, Oxford

ODNB: Matthew, H.C.G. and Harrison, Brian, eds (2004), *Oxford Dictionary of National Biography*, 60 vols, Oxford University Press, Oxford

DNB: Stephen, Leslie and Lee, Sidney, eds (1885–1900), *Dictionary of National Biography*, Oxford University Press, Oxford

ESTC: *English Short Title Catalogue*, The British Library, London

Serials and Journals

CR = *The Critical Review or Annals of Literature*, A. Hamilton, London

GM = *The Gentleman's Magazine; or, Monthly Intelligencer* (1731–1914), London

EM = *The European Magazine and London Review* vols 11–9 (1787–1791), J. Sewell, London

PT = *Philosophical Transactions of the Royal Society*

PA = *A Perfect Account of The Daily Intelligence*, [London]

WIC = *The Weekly Intelligencer of the Common-Wealth*, [London]

MF = *Mercurius Fumigosus, or the Smoking Nocturnall,, Communicating Dark and Hidden Newes*, [London]

MPC = *Madras Public Consultations*

ANF = Roberts. A. and Donaldson, J., eds (1885–6), *Ante-Nicene Fathers*, American Edition, New York

NPNF1 = Schaff. P., ed. (1887–92), *Nicene and Post-Nicene Fathers, 1st Series*, 14 vols, American Edition, New York

NPNF2 = Schaff. P. and Wace, H., eds (1890–1900), *Nicene and Post-Nicene Fathers, 2nd Series*, 14 Vols, American Edition, New York

Newton Manuscripts and Library

Keynes = Newton Manuscripts in the Keynes collection, King's College Library, Cambridge, UK

Yahuda = Newton Manuscripts in the Yahuda Collection, Jewish National and University Library, Jerusalem, Israel

Tr/NQ = Books in Newton's personal library held in Trinity College, Cambridge, UK

(d) = the cited page is folded down, showing that Newton read and marked it

(d2) = the cited page is folded at the bottom

(ds) or (d2s) = a crease on the page suggesting the page was once folded over

Dating Systems

n.s. = the year according to the New (Gregorian) System of dating (Britain and British colonies changed to the Gregorian calendar in 1752, thus shifting the beginning of the 'legal' year from 25March to 1 January)

o.s. = Old System

The Letters Writ by a Turkish Spy

Spy, I-VIII = [Marana, Giovanni P. (et al.?)] (1691), *The First Volume of Letters Writ by a Turkish Spy*, 2nd edn, H. Rhodes, London

> Anon. (1692), *The Second Volume of Letters Writ by a Turkish Spy*, 3rd edn, H. Rhodes, London
>
> Anon. (1692), *The Third Volume of Letters Writ by a Turkish Spy*, 2nd edn, H. Rhodes, London
>
> Anon. (1692), *The Fourth Volume of Letters Writ by a Turkish Spy*, H. Rhodes, London
>
> Anon. (1692), *The Fifth Volume of Letters Writ by a Turkish Spy*, H. Rhodes, London
>
> Anon. (1694), *The Sixth Volume of Letters Writ by a Turkish Spy*, J. Hindmarsh, London
>
> Anon. (1694), *The Seventh Volume of Letters Writ by a Turkish Spy*, H. Rhodes, London
>
> Anon. (1694), *The Eighth and Last Volume of Letters Writ by a Turkish Spy*, J. Hindmarsh, London

Works by Percy Bysshe Shelley

Unless otherwise stated, Shelley's poems are quoted from Percy Bysshe Shelley, *Poetical Works*, ed. T. Hutchinson and G.M. Matthews (Oxford, 1971)

QM = 'Queen Mab'

PU = 'Prometheus Unbound'

Mg = 'Mazenghi' or 'Marenghi'

DW = 'The Daemon of the World'

Other works by Shelley quoted from Percy Bysshe Shelley (1926–30), *The Complete Works of Percy Bysshe Shelley*, eds. Roger Ingpen and Walter E. Peck, 10 vols (London and New York, 1926–30)

RI = 'The Revolt of Islam', later called 'Laon and Cythna'

V.Sys = 'Of the Vegetable System of Diet' (in vol. VI)

Vind = 'A Vindication of Natural Diet' (in vol. VI), originally published (1813) by J.Callow, et al., London

Libraries and Archives

BL = British Library, London

OIOC = Oriental and India Office Collections, in the British Library, London

NLS = National Library of Scotland, Edinburgh

CUL = Cambridge University Library

NRA = National Register of Archives

Transcription conventions

All quotations are in the spelling of the original work quoted, except that the use of i/j and u/v has been modernised; the old long s has been altered to 's'; contractions have been silently expanded where necessary; inserted emendations in manuscripts have been enclosed thus, > <; clarifications and authorial comments have been placed inside square brackets.

BIBLIOGRAPHY

Aaron, R.I. and Gibb, Jocelyn, eds (1936), *An Early Draft of Locke's Essay Together With Excerpts From His Journals*, Clarendon Press, Oxford
Aberdour, Alexander (1791), *Observations on the Small-pox*, Edinburgh
Abul Fazl (1783–6), *Ayeen Akbery*, tr. F. Gladwin, 3 vols, Calcutta
Abul Fazl (1993), *The Āīn-i Akbari*, tr. Blochmann, 2nd edn, 3 vols, Calcutta
Abul-Pharajio, Gregorio (1663), *Historia Compendiosa Dynastiarum*, tr. Edward Pococke, R. Davis, Oxford
Accoramboni, Girolamo (1726), *Tractatus de natura et usu lactis* in Sextus Placitus, *De Medicamentis ex Animalibus*, J. Petrium, Norimbergæ
Acheson, R.J. (1990), *Radical Puritans in England 1550–1660*, New York
Adair, James Makittrick (1772), *Principles and Practice of Physic*, London
Adair, James Makittrick (1786), *Medical Cautions*, Bath
Adair, James Makittrick (1787a), *Natural History of the Human Body*, R. Crutwell, Bath
Adair, James Makittrick (1787b), *Medical Cautions*, 2nd edn, Bath
Adair, James Makittrick (1799), *An Essay on Regimen*, Air
Adam, James (1789), *Practical Essays on Agriculture*, 2 vols, London
Adams, Carol (1990), *The Sexual Politics of Meat*, Polity Press, Cambridge
Adams, Stephen and Adams, Barbara (1990), 'Thoreau's Diet at Walden', *Studies in the American Renaissance*, 243–60
Addington, Anthony (1753), *An Essay on the Sea-scurvy*, Reading
Africanus (1788), *Remarks on the Slave Trade*, London
Agrippa, Heinrich Cornelius ([1630?]), *Opera*, 2 vols, Lugduni [Strasburg?]
Agrippa, Heinrich Cornelius (1651), *Three Books of Occult Philosophy*, tr. J[ohn] F[rench], R.W. for Gregory Moule, London
Agrippa, Heinrich Cornelius (1655), *Fourth Book of Occult Philosophy*, tr. R. Turner, J. Harrison, London
Agrippa, Heinrich Cornelius (1676), *The Vanity of Arts and Sciences*, S. Speed, London
Ahmed, Khaled Anis, ed. (1995), *Intercultural Encounter in Mughal Miniatures*, Lahore
Aikin, Arthur, ed. (1803), *The Annual Review . . . for 1802*, T.N. Longman, London
Aikin, John (1792), *John Howard*, London
Aitken, John (1779), *Systematic Elements*, Edinburgh
Aitken, John (1782), *Theory and Practice of Physic and Surgery*, London

Alam, Muzaffar and Alavi, Seema (2001), 'Introduction', in Antoine-Louis Henri Polier, *A European Experience of the Mughal Orient*, Oxford University Press, New Delhi, 1–73

Alberuni (1888), *Alberuni's India*, ed. E.C. Sachau, 2 vols, London

Alcott, Amos Bronson (1938), *Journals*, Little, Brown, Boston

Alexander, Meena (1996), 'Shelley's India: Territory and Text, Some Problems of Decolonization', in Bennet and Curran, eds, 169–77

Alger, John G. (1889), *Englishmen in the French Revolution*, London

Alger, John G. (1894), *Glimpses of the French Revolution*, London

Alger, John G. (1902), *Paris in 1789–94*, London

Ali, B. Sheik (1963), *British Relations with Haidar Ali (1760–1782)*, Raghavan, Mysore

Ali, Tariq (2003), *The Clash of Fundamentalisms*, London

Allen, David (2001), 'Greeks, Indians, and the Scottish Presbyterian: Dissident Arguments for Vegetarianism in Enlightenment Scotland', in Kevin L. Cope and Anna Battigelli, eds, *1650–1850: Ideas, Æsthetics, and Inquiries in the Early Modern Era*, New York, 265–98

Allen, John (1733), *The Whole Practice of Physick*, 2 vols, London

Allers, Rudolf (1944), 'Microcosmus from Anaximandros to Paracelsus', *Traditio: Studies in Ancient and Medieval History, Thought and Religion* 2, 319–407

Almond, Philip C. (1999), *Adam and Eve in Seventeenth-Century Thought*, Cambridge

Alter, Joseph S. (2000), *Gandhi's Body*, University of Pennsylvania Press, Philadelphia

Altherr, Thomas L. (1984), ' "Chaplain to the Hunters": Henry David Thoreau's Ambivalence Toward Hunting', *American Literature*, 56:3, 345–61

Altmann, Alexander (1987), 'Lurianic Kabbalah in a Platonic Key: Abraham Cohen Herrera's *Puerta del Cielo*', in Twersky and Septimus, eds, 1–38

Altmann, Alexander (1995), 'Eternality of Punishment', in Fine, ed., 270–87

Ammianus, Marcellinus (1609), *The Roman Historie*, tr. P. Holland, A. Islip, London

Ammianus, Marcellinus (1935), *Ammianus Marcellinus* tr. J.C. Rolfe, 3 vols, Cambridge, Mass.

Anastos, Milton V. (1948), 'Pletho's Calendar and Liturgy; Pletho and Islam', *Dunbarton Oaks Papers*, 4, 183–305

Anderson, Mark M. (1992), *Kafka's Clothes*, Clarendon Press, Oxford

Andhare, Shridhar (2004), 'Imperial Mughal tolerance of Jains and Jain painting in Gujarat', in Rosemary Crill, Susan Stronge, Andrew Topsfield, eds, *Arts of Mughal India, Studies in honour of Robert Skelton*, Ahmedabad, 223–33

Andree, John (1788), *Considerations on bilious diseases*, Hertford

Andry, Nicolas (1704), *Eclaircissement sur le livre De la generation*, Paris

Andry, Nicolas (1710), *Le Regime du Caresme*, J.B. Coignard, Paris

Andry, Nicolas (1737), *Traité des Aliments de Carême*, Paris, 1713

Anon. (1646a), *The Eating of Blood Vindicated*, W. Ley, London

Anon. (1646b), *A Bloudy Tenent Confuted*, H.S. and W.L., London

Anon. (1650a), *Declaration of the Ranters*, B.A. [London?]

Anon. (1650b), *The Ranters Declaration*, J.C., London

Anon. (1651a), *Proceedings at the Sessions Of the Peace 20. day of June, 1651*, London

Anon. (1651b), *The Ranters Creed*, J. Moxon, London

Anon. (1652a), *The Triall Of A Black-Pudding*, J. Hancock, London

Anon. (1652b), *The Ranters Monster*, G. Horton, London

Anon. (1654), *A List of Some of the Grand Blasphemers*, London

Anon. (1687), *A Seasonable Prospect for the View and Consideration of Christians*, L. Meredith, London

Anon. (1692), *The Visions of the Soul*, John Dunton, London

Anon. (1694a), 'Eyreneus Philoctetes', *Philadelphia, Or Brotherly Love*, T. Sowle, London

Anon. (1694b), *Seder Olam*, tr. J. Clark, T. Howkins, London

Anon. (1694c), *The Revolution Of Humane Souls*, Sarah Howkins, London

Anon. (1724), *Remarks on Dr Cheyne's Essay of Health and Long Life*

Anon. (1726), *It Cannot Rain But it Pours*, J. Roberts, London

Anon. (1730), *A Collection of Recipe's . . . for . . . Free-Masons*, T. Warner, London

Anon. (1773), *The Practice of the British and French hospitals*, London

Anon. (1786), *The Adventures of George Maitland*, 3 vols, J. Murray, London

Anon. (1790), *The Life of John Howard*, Newcastle

Anon. (1794), *The History of Robespierre*, 2nd edn, T. Boosey, London

Anon. (1796a), *Historical View of the French Revolution*, 2 vols, M. Angus, Newcastle

Anon. (1796b), *Abrégé chronologiques* (1796), Paris [i.e. London?], T. Boosey, London

Anon. (1797a), *Biographical Anecdotes of the Founders of the French Republic*, R. Phillips, London

Anon. ([1797b]), *Le Souvenir des Honnetes Gens*, 2 vols, Londres

Anon. (1799), *British and Irish Public Characters of 1798*, Dublin

Anon. (1800), *An Essay on the Nair System of Gallantry*, Ridgway & Symonds, London

Anon. (1898), *A Journal of the first Voyage of Vasco da Gama, 1497–1499*, ed. E.G. Ravenstein, Hakluyt Society, London

Apuleius, Lucius (1822), *Golden Ass*, tr. Thomas Taylor

Apuleius, Lucius (1853), *The Works of Apuleius*, H.H. Bohn, London

Aquinas, St Thomas (1975), *Providence* Part II, tr. V.J. Bourke in *Summa Contra Gentiles*, 5 vols, University of Notre Dame Press, London, vol. 4, book 3

[Aquinas, St Thomas, attrib.] (1966), *Aurora Consurgens*, tr. R.F.C. Hull, London

Arbuthnot, John (1731), *An Essay Concerning The Nature of Aliments*, Dublin

Arbuthnot, John (1732), *Practical Rules of Diet*, London

Arbuthnot, John (1733), *The Effects of Air on Human Bodies*, London

Archenholtz, J.W. von (1787–91), *The British Mercury*, 17 vols, Hamburg

Archer, Mildred and Falk, Toby (1989), *India Revealed*

Archer, W.G. (1973), *Indian Paintings from the Punjab Hills*, Delhi

Argens, Marquis D' (1739–40), *The Jewish Spy*, 5 vols, D. Browne, London

Armstrong, George (1783), *Diseases Most Incident to Children*, London

Armstrong, John (1737), *Cure of Venereal Diseases*, London

Armstrong, John (1992), 'The Art of Preserving Health', in *Miscellanies* [T. Cadell, London, 1770], Chadwyck-Healey, Cambridge

Arnobius (2005), *Against the Heathen* [*ANF*, vol. 6, 1886], http://www.newadvent.org/fathers/06317.htm

Arnold, Denis G. (1995), 'Hume on the Moral Difference Between Humans and Other Animals', *History of Philosophy Quarterly*, 12:3, 303–16

Aronson, Alex (1946), *Europe Looks at India*, Hind Kitabs, Bombay

Arrian (1933), *Anabasis Alexandri*, tr. E. Iliff Robson

Asiatic annual register, The (1800), J. Debrett, London

Astruc, Jean (1714), *Traité; de la cause de la digestion*, Toulouse

Athenian Society, A Member of The (1703), *The Athenian Oracle*, 4 vols, Andrew Bell, London

Atkins, John (1758), *The Navy Surgeon*, London

Atkyns, Arabella, ed. (1747), *The Family Magazine*, 3rd edn, J. Osborn, London

Aubrey, John ([1669–96]), *A Brief Life of Thomas Hobbes*, http://oregonstate.edu

Augustine of Hippo, St (2004a), *From Augustine to Januarius* [*NPNF 1*, vol. 1, 1887], http://www.newadvent.org/fathers

Augustine of Hippo, St (2004b), *On the Morals of the Manichaeans* [*NPNF 1*, vol. 4, 1887], http://www.newadvent.org/fathers

Augustine of Hippo, St (2004c), *Of the Morals of the Catholic Church* [*NPNF 1*, vol. 4, 1887], http://www.newadvent.org/fathers

Augustine of Hippo, St (2005), *Reply to Faustus the Manichaean* [*NPNF 1*, vol. 4, 1887], http://www.newadvent.org/fathers

Austen, Jane (1997a), *Sense and Sensibility*, 2nd edn, Oxford Text Archive

Austen, Jane (1997b), *Emma*, ed. R.W. Chapman, 2nd edn, Oxford Text Archive

Austen, Jane (1997c), *Letters to her sister Cassandra and others*, ed. R.W. Chapman, 2nd edn, Oxford Text Archive

Axon, William E.A. (1890), *Thomas Taylor, The Platonist*, London

Axon, William E.A. (1893), 'A Forerunner Of The Vegetarian Society',
   Vegetarian Messenger, 453–5

Bachmann, Peter R. (1972), *Roberto Nobili 1577–1656*, Rome
Bachstrom, J.F. (1734), *Observationes circa Scorbutum*, C. Wishof, Lugduni
Backscheider, P. (1976), 'Defoe's Women', *Studies in Eighteenth-Century
   Culture*, 5, 103–20
Bacon, Francis (1605), *The Twoo Bookes of Francis Bacon*, London
Bacon, Francis (1623), *Historia Vitæ & Mortis*, London
Bacon, Francis (1638), *The Historie of Life and Death*, Humphrey Mosely,
   London
Bacon, Francis (1640), *Of the Advancement and Proficience of Learning*,
   tr. G. Wats, Oxford
Bacon, Francis (1650), *The History Naturall and Experimentall, Of Life and
   Death*, William Lee and Humphrey Mosely, London
Bacon, Francis (1651), *Sylva Sylvarum*, ed. William Rawley, 6th edn,
   William Lee and Humphrey Mosely, London
Bacon, Francis (1854), *Novum Organum*, tr. Basil Montague in *The Works*,
   3 vols, Philadelphia
Bacon, Francis (1974), *The Advancement of Learning and New Atlantis*, ed.
   Arthur Johnston, Clarendon Press, Oxford
Bacon, Francis (1996), *The Works of Francis Bacon*, ed. James Spedding,
   Robert Ellis and Douglas Heath, 12 vols, London
Bailey, Margaret Lewis (1914), *Milton and Jakob Boehme*, Oxford University
   Press, New York
[Baillet, Adrien] (1691), *La Vie De Monsieur Des-Cartes*, 2 vols,
   D. Horthemels, Paris
Bailly, Jean Sylvain (1779), *Lettres sur l'Atlantide*, Londres
Baker, D.W. (1996), 'Topical utopias', *Studies in English Literature
   1500–1900*, 36
Ball, John (1762), *The Modern Practice of Physic*, 2 vols, London
Bancroft, Edward (1769), *An Essay on the Natural History of Guiana*, London
Bancroft, Edward (1770), *The History of Charles Wentworth*, 3 vols, London
Bardesanes (2004), *The Book Of The Laws Of Divers Countries* [*ANF*, vol. 8,
   1886], http://www.newadvent.org/fathers
Baricellus, Julius Caesar (1623), *De lactis, seri*, L. Scoriggium, Neapóli
Barilan, Y. Michael (2004), 'Medicine Through the Artist's Eyes',
   Perspectives in Biology and Medicine, 47:1, 110–34
Barkas, Janet (1975), *The Vegetable Passion*, Routledge & Kegan Paul,
   London
Barker, John (1747), *Ancient and Modern Physicians*, G. Hawkins, London
Barker, John ([1795?]), *Epidemicks*, Birmingham
Barker-Benfield, G.J. (1992), *The Culture of Sensibility*, Chicago
Barruel, A.A. (1798), *History of Jacobinism*, tr. R. Clifford, 2nd edn, 4 vols,
   London

Barry, Edward (1726), *Consumption of the Lungs*, Dublin

Barry, Edward (1759), *Three Different Digestions*, London

Barry, Jonathan (1985), 'Piety and the patient: Medicine and religion in eighteenth century Bristol', in Roy Porter ed., 145–75

Bate, Jonathan (1991), *Romantic Ecology: Wordsworth and the Environmental Tradition*, London

Bauthumley, Jacob (1650), *The Light and Dark sides of God*, London

Baxter, Richard (1696), *Reliquiæ Baxterianæ*, London

Bayle, François (1670), *Dissertationes . . . De usu lactis*, I. Pech, Tolosæ

[Bayle, Pierre] (1684), *La Republique Des Lettres*, H. Desbordes, Amsterdam

Bayle, Pierre (1710), *An Historical and Critical Dictionary*, C. Harper, London

Bayle, Pierre (1734–41), *A General Dictionary Historical and Critical*, ed. Lockman et al., G. Strahan, London

Bayly, C.A. (1990), *Indian Society and the Making of the British Empire*, Cambridge

Bayly, C.A. (1996), *Empire and Information*, Cambridge

Bayly, Susan (1992), *Saints, Goddesses and Kings*, Cambridge University Press

[Baynard, Edward] (1724), *Health, A Poem*, J. Roberts, London

Beach, Milo Cleveland (1974), *Rajput Painting at Bundt and Kota*, Ascona

Beavan, A.H. (1899), *James and Horace Smith*, Hurst and Blackett, London

Beer, I.A. (1735), *De usu lactis medico*, Praes. J.J. Geelhausen, J.J. Gerzabek, Pragae

[Behn, Aphra, ed.] (1685), *Miscellany*, J. Hindmarsh, London

Bellini, Lorenzo (1696), *Opuscula*, Cornelium Boutesteyn, Lugduni Batavorum

Bellini, Lorenzo (1720), *A Mechanical Account of Fevers*, London

Bellini, Lorenzo (1730), *De Urinis et Pulsibus*, Lugduni

Bellini, Lorenzo (1741), *Discorsi di Anatomia*, 3 vols, F. Moücke, Firenze

Belsham, William (1798), *History of Great Britain*, 4 vols, London

[Benedict, St], *The Rule of St. Benedict* (1998), tr. E.F. Henderson [*Historical Documents*, London, 1910], http://www.fordham.edu/halsall/sbook.html

Bennet, Betty T. and Curran, Stuart, eds (1996), *Shelley: Poet and Legislator of the World*, Baltimore and London

Bentham, Jeremy (1907), *Introduction to the Principle of Morals and Legislation* [Oxford], http://www.la.utexas.edu/labyrinth/ipml/index.html

Beranek, Andrea J. (2004), 'From Virtue to Sympathy', Ph.D. dissertation, McAnulty College and Graduate School of Liberal Arts, Duquesne University, http://etd1.library.duq.edu/theses/available/etd-03272004-095724/unrestricted/04Dissertation.pdf

Berckendal, Johann (1661), *Neue Schwarmgeister-Brut* [Hamburg?]

Berens, L.H. (1906), *The Digger Movement*, London
Bergerac, Cyrano de (1657), *Les Estats et Empires de la Lune*
Berkman, John (2004), 'The Consumption of Animals and the Catholic Tradition', *Logos*, 7:1, 174–90
Bernal, Martin (1987), *Black Athena, Volume 1*, Free Association Books, London
Bernier, François (1684), *Abrégé de la Philosophie de Gassendi*, 2nd edn, 7 vols, Anisson, Posuel & Rigaud, Lyon
Bernier, François (1694), *Three Discourses of Happiness, Virtue, and Liberty*, J. Churchill, London
Bernier, François (1890), *Lettres de François Bernier*, ed. H.C. des Fosses, Angers
Bernier, François (1992), *Abrégé de la Philosophie de Gassendi*, ed. S. Murr and G. Stefani, 2nd edn, 7 vols, Fayard
Bernier, François (1999), *Travels in the Mogul Empire AD 1656–1668*, ed. A. Constable and V.A. Smith, 2nd edn, Low Price Publications, New Delhi
Berrow, Capel (1762), *A Pre-existent Lapse Of Human Souls*, J. Whiston, London
Berrow, Capel (1772), *Theological Dissertations*, J. Dodsley, London
Berti, Silvia, ed. (1994), *Trattato Dei Tre Impostori*, Torino
Besant, Annie, ed. (2003), *Theosophist Magazine July 1933–September 1933*, Kessinger Publishing
Bethune, G.W. (1848), *The British Female Poets*, Philadelphia
Betts, C.J. (1984), *Early Deism in France From the so-called 'déistes' of Lyon (1564) to Voltaire's 'Lettres Philosophiques' (1734)*, The Hague
Bianchi, Giovanni (1752), *Se il vitto pitagorico di soli vegetabilis sia giovevole per conservare la sanita e per la cura d'alcune malatie*, Venice
Biggs, Penelope (1982), 'Hunt, Conquest, Trial', *Studies in Eighteenth-Century Culture*, 11, 51–64
Bigland, John (1816), *An Historical Display*, London
Billington, James (1980), *Fire in the Minds of Men*, Basic Books, New York
Biographical Dictionary (1767), *A Supplement to the New and General*, London
Biographical Dictionary (1795), *A New and General*, 8 vols, London
Birch, Thomas (1849), *James the First* [ed. R.F. Williams], London
Black, Joseph (1816), 'Case of Professor Ferguson', *Medico-Chirurgical Transactions*
Blackburne, Francis (1780), *Memoirs of Thomas Hollis*, 2 vols, London
Bloch, Chaim (1928), 'The Legends of the Ari', *The Menorah Journal*, 14:4, 371–84
Blount, Charles ([1680?]), *Great is Diana of the Ephesians*, Cosmopoli [London]
Blount, Charles (1680), *The Life of Apollonius Tyaneus*, London
Blount, Charles, Gildon, C. et al. (1693), *The Oracles of Reason*

Blundell, Thomas (1877), *A History of the Isle of Man (1648–56) Volume 1*, ed. William Harrison, Douglas, Isle of Man

Boas, George (1948), *Primitivism and Related Ideas in the Middle Ages*, Baltimore

Boas, George (1966), *The Happy Beast In French Thought of the Seventeenth Century*, New York

Boccage, M.A. du (1770), *Letters concerning England*, 2 vols, London

Boemus, Joannes Aubanus (1885–90), *The Fardle Of Facions* in Richard Hakluyt, ed., *The Principal Navigations*, 16 vols, Edinburgh

Boerhaave, Hermann (1719), *A Method of Studying Physick*, C. Rivington, London

Boerhaave, Hermann (1731), *Historia Plantarum*, London [i.e. Amsterdam]

Boerhaave, Hermann (1735), *Elements of Chemistry*, tr. T. Dallowe, 2 vols, London

Boerhaave, Hermann (1739), *Materia Medica*, W. Innys et al., London

Boerhaave, Hermann (1742–6a), *Praelectiones Academicae*, ed. A. Haller, 5 vols, Taurini

Boerhaave, Hermann (1742–6b), *Academical Lectures*, 6 vols, W. Innys, London

Boerhaave, Hermann (1751), *Methodus Studii Medici*, ed. A. Haller, 2 vols, Amsterdam

Boerhaave, Hermann (1962), *Correspondence*, ed. G.A. Lindeboom, 3 vols, Leiden

Böhme, Jacob (1640), *Mysterium Magnum* [Amsterdam]

Böhme, Jacob (1654), *Mysterium Magnum* [tr. J. Sparrow], H. Blunden, London

Böhme, Jacob (1894), *The Way to Christ* [Canterbury: G.T. Moreton], *www.ccel.org*

Böhme, Jacob (1909), *Threefold Life of Man*, ed. C.J. Barker, M. Watkins, London

Böhme, Jacob (1920), *Three Principles*, ed. Paul Deussen, London

Böhme, Jacob (1924), *Mysterium Magnum*, ed. C.J. Barker, London

Bondt, Jacob (1769), *Medicines of the East Indies*, T. Noteman, London

Bonnet, Jean Claude (1975), 'Le système de repas et de la cuisine chez Rousseau', *Poétique*, 6:22, 244–67

Bonno, Gabriel (1955), *Les Relations Intellectuelles de Locke avec la France*, Berkeley

Borello, Mark E. (2004), 'Mutual Aid and Animal Dispersion: An Historical Analysis of Alternatives to Darwin', *Perspectives in Biology and Medicine*, 47:1, 15–31

Borkfelt, Sune (2000), 'Cause and Effect: The Development of Ethical and Religious Arguments for Vegetarianism, in Great Britain before 1847', University of Aarhus, Denmark, http://home.worldonline.dk/borkfelt/vaerker/6.html

Boswell, James (1785), *The Journal of a Tour to the Hebrides*, 2nd edn, London

Boswell, James (1799), *The Life of Samuel Johnson*, 3rd edn, 4 vols, London

Boswell, James (1886), *Life of Johnson*, ed. G.B. Hill, 6 vols, London

Boswell, James (1970), *Journal of a Tour to the Hebrides*, ed. R.W. Chapman, Oxford

Bosworth, C.E., et al., eds (1993), *The Encyclopaedia of Islam*, New York

Bougainville, Louis-Antoine, Comte de (1772), *A Voyage round the world*, tr. J. Reinhold Forster, J. Nourse, London

Bougeant, G.H. (1740), *The Language of Beasts and Birds*, 2nd edn, T. Cooper, London

Bougerel, Joseph (1737), *Vie de Pierre Gassendi*, Jacques Vincent, Paris

Bourignon, Antoinette (1699), *An Apology*, H. Newman, London

Bourignon, Antoinette (1703), *The Light Risen in Darkness*, H. Newman, London

Bourignon, Antoinette (1707), *The Renovation* [tr. George Garden], J. Baker, London

Bouwsma, William J. (1957), *Concordia Mundi*, Cambridge, Mass.

Bowers, Rick (2003), 'Roger Crab: Opposition Hunger Artist in 1650s England', *Seventeenth Century* 18:1, 93–112

Bowler, Peter J. (1971), 'Preformation and Pre-existence in the Seventeenth Century', *Journal of the History of Biology*, 4:2, 221–44

Bowles, Geoffrey (1974), 'Physical, Human and Divine Attraction in the Life and Thought of George Cheyne', *Annals of Science*, 31:6, 473–88

Boyle, Robert (1744), *The Works of The Honourable Robert Boyle*, A. Millar, London

Boyse, Samuel (1747–8), *The Transactions of Europe*, 2 vols, Reading

Bradshaw, Penelope (1754), *The Family Jewel*, London

Bramwell, Anna (1985), *Blood and Soil: Richard Walther Darré & Hitler's 'Green Party'*, Bourne End

Brand, Michael and Lowry, Glenn D. (1986), *Akbar's India*, New York

[Brande, William T.?] (1822), *The Life . . . of the Celebrated Walking Stewart*, London

Brands, H.W. (2002), *The First American*, New York

Brandt, Carlos (*c*.1930), *The Frugivorous Nature Of Man*

Breck, Samuel (2002), *Recollections*, ed. H.E. Scudder, Washington DC

Brendel, J.G. (1751), 'De logarithmis parabolicis disputationem inauguralem *De victu salubri ex animalibus et vegetabilibus temperando*', in *Decanus Ordini Medici*, Gottingen

Brewster, David (1831), *The Life of Sir Isaac Newton*, John Murray, London

Brissot, Jacques-Pierre and Claviere, Etienne (1797) *The Commerce of America with Europe*, 2nd edn, J.S. Jordan, London

Brissot, Jacques-Pierre (1830–2), *Mémoires*, ed. M.F. De Montrol, 4 vols, Paris

Brissot, Jacques-Pierre (1912a), *Correspondance et Papiers*, ed. C. Perroud, Paris

Brissot, Jacques-Pierre ([1912b]), *Mémoires*, 2 + 1 vols, ed. C. Perroud, Paris

Brockliss, L.W.B. (1989), 'The medico-religious universe of an early eighteenth-century Parisian doctor: the case of Philippe Hecquet', in French and Wear, eds, 191–222

Bromfield, M. (1679), *A Brief Discovery Of . . . the Scurvy*, [London]

Bromley, Thomas (n.d.), *Catalogue of Mr. T. Bromley's Library*, (n.p.)

Bronson, Bertrand H. (1938), *Joseph Ritson: Scholar at Arms*, 2 vols, Berkeley

[Brothers, Richard] (1794), *A Revealed Knowledge of the Prophecies*, London

Brothers, Richard (1801), *A Description of Jerusalem*, G. Riebau, London

Brothers, Richard (1830), *The New Covenant*, Finleyson, London

Brougham, Henry (1803), Review of Ritson's *Essay, Edinburgh Review . . . for Oct. 1802 . . . July 1803*, 2 vols, A. Constable, Edinburgh, II.128–36

Brown, James W. (1978), 'The Ideological and Aesthetic Function of Food in *Paul et Virginie*', *Eighteenth-Century Life*, 4:3, 61–7

Brown, Judith M., Frykenberg, Robert Eric, Low, Alaine, eds (2002), *Christians, Cultural Interactions, and India's Religious Traditions*, Routledge

Brown, Stuart (1997), 'F.M. van Helmont: His Philosophical Connections and the Reception of his Later Cabbalistic Philosophy', in M.A. Stewart ed., *Studies in Seventeenth-Century European Philosophy*, Oxford, 97–116

Brown, Theodore M. (1981), *The Mechanical Philosophy and the 'Animal Economy'*, New York

Brown, Theodore M. (1987), 'Medicine in the shadow of the *Principia*', *Journal of the History of Ideas*, 48:4, 629–49

Browne, Sir Thomas (1672), *Pseudodoxia Epidemica* [1646], 6th edn, http://penelope.uchicago.edu/

Brückner, John (1768), *A Philosophical Survey of the Animal Creation*, tr. T. Cogan, J. Johnson, London

Buchan, William (1772), *Domestic Medicine*, 2nd edn, London

Buchan, William (1797), *Observations Concerning the Diet of the Common People*

Buchanan, Francis (1807), *A Journey from Madras*, 3 vols, London

Buehren, D.F. (1691), *Humani lactis, naturam & usum*, Praes. G. Eckardt, Groschianis, Erfordiæ

Buettner, J.G. (1727), *Dissertatio anatomico-pathologica de lactis*, Praes. C.G. Stentzel, Vitembergæ

Buffon, G.-L. Leclerc, Comte de (1753), *Histoire Naturelle*, Impr. Royale, Paris

Buffon, G.-L. Leclerc, Comte de (1780), *Natural History*, tr. W. Smellie, W. Creech, Edinburgh

Bugge, Henriette (1994), *Mission and Tamil Society*, Richmond

Buhr, Petrus H. (1780), *De Usu Opii Chirurgico*, J.H. Schulzii, Gottingen

Bulstrode, Whitelocke (1692), *An Essay of Transmigration*, T. Basset, London

Burde, Jyotsna (1963), 'Food and Food Habits in Vijayanagara Times', *The Journal of the Karnatak University*, 7

Burg, Hieronymus von der (1756), *De Acetariis*, Præs. C. Linnaeus, L.M. Höjer, Upsala

Burghardt, Walter J. (1944), 'Cyril of Alexandria on "Wool and Linen"', *Traditio: Studies in Ancient and Medieval History, Thought and Religion*, 2, 484–5

Burke, Edmund (1756), *A Vindication of Natural Society*, London

Burke, Edmund (1958–78), *The Correspondence*, ed. T.W. Copeland, J.A. Woods, P.J. Marshall et al., 10 vols, Cambridge

Burke, Edmund (1981), *The Writings and Speeches*, vol. V, ed. P.J. Marshall, Oxford

Burke, Peter (1999), 'The Philosopher as Traveller: Bernier's Orient', in Rubiés, Joan-Pau and Elsner, Jas, eds (1999), *Voyages and Visions: Towards a Cultural History of Travel*, London

Burke, S.M. (1989), *Akbar*, Manohar, New Delhi

Burkert, Walter (1972), *Lore and Science in Ancient Pythagoreanism*, tr. Edwin L. Minar Jr, Havard University Press, Cambridge, Mass.

Burkert, Walter (1983), *Homo Necans*, tr. Peter Bing, London [Berlin, 1972]

[Burnet, Thomas] (1691), *The Theory of the Earth*, 2nd edn, London

Burnet, Thomas (1729), *Archæologiæ Philosophicæ*, ed. Foxton, E. Curll, London

Burnet, Thomas (1736), *Doctrina Antiqua de Rerum Originibus*, tr. Mead and Foxton, E. Curll, London

Burthogge, Richard (1675), *Causa Dei*

Burtt, Ruth G. (1946), 'Quaker Books in the 18th Century From the point of view of a Country Quarterly Meeting', *The Journal of the Friends' Historical Society*, vol. 38, 7–18

Bushell, Thomas (1628), *The First Part of Youths Errors*, London

Bushell, Thomas (1659), *Abridgment Of . . . Mineral Prosecutions*, London

Bushell, Thomas (1660), *An Extract by . . . of his late Abridgement*, London

Busteed, H.E. (1908), *Echoes from Old Calcutta*, 4th edn, London

Butler, Alban (1774), *The Moveable Feasts, Fasts*, London

Butler, Marilyn (1996), 'Shelley and the Empire in the East', in Bennet and Curran, eds

Bynum, Caroline Walker (1988), *Holy Feast and Holy Fast*, University of California Press, Berkeley

Calendar of State Papers, Domestic Series 1651–2

Calvin, John (1999), *Commentaries on the first book of Moses called Genesis*, tr. John King, 2 vols [Calvin Translation Society: Edinburgh, 1847], http://www.ccel.org

Calvin, John (2002), *The Institutes of the Christian Religion*, tr. H. Beveridge, ed. R.J. Dunzweiler [Grand Rapids, Mich.], http://www.ccel.org

Cambridge University Library (2001–2), *Footprints of the Lion: Exhibition Catalogue*, Cambridge

Cameron, Kenneth Walter (1969), 'Thoreau's *Walden* and Alcott's Vegetarianism', *American Transcendental Quarterly*, 2, 27–8

Camões, Luis de (1776), *The Lusiad*, tr. William Julius Mickle, Jackson, Oxford

Campanella, Tommaso (1901), *The City of the Sun*, in *Ideal Commonwealths*, P.F. Collier, New York

Campbell, D. Grant (1990), 'Fashionable Suicide: Conspicuous Consumption and the Collapse of Credit in Frances Burney's *Cecilia*', *Studies in Eighteenth-Century Culture*, 20

Campbell, Donald (1797), *A Journey over India*, T. Dobson, Philadelphia

Cannon, Garland (1990), *The Life and Mind of Oriental Jones*, Cambridge

Carey, Dan (2004), 'Locke's Anthropology: Travel, Innateness, and the Exercise of Reason', *The Seventeenth Century*, 19:2, 260–85

Carlyle, Thomas (1998), *The French Revolution*, www.gutenberg.com

Carpenter, Edward (2003), *My Days & Dreams*, Kessinger Publishing

Carpenter, Kenneth J. (1986), *The History of Scurvy and Vitamin C*, Cambridge University Press, New York

Carpini, John de Plano and Rubruquis, William de (1903), *The Texts and Versions*, ed. C.R. Beazley, London

Carter, Francis (1788), *An Account of the Various Systems of Medicine*, 2 vols, London

Case, John (1682), *The Wards Of The Key to Helmont*, London

Case, John (1697), *The Angelical Guide*, London

Cassian, John (1491), *De Institutis Cenobiorum*, Venetas

Cassian, John (1894), *Institutes*, in *Nicene and Post-Nicene Fathers*, vol. XI, Oxford

Cassirer, E., Kristeller, P.O., Randall, J.H., eds (1948), *The Renaissance Philosophy of Man*, Chicago

Castro, Estevam Rodrigues De (1631), *Tractatus de sero lactis*, Florentiæ

Cattaneo, Arturo (1987), 'Dr Cheyne and Richardson: Epistolary Friendship and Scientific Advice', in Sergio Rossi, ed., *Science and Imagination in Eighteenth Century British Culture*, Milan, 113–32

Caulfield, James (1813), *Portraits, Memoirs, And Characters, of Remarkable Persons*, 3 vols, R.S. Kirby, London

Cavendish, Margaret (1653), *Poems and Fancies*, London

Cavendish, Margaret (2004), *Assaulted and pursued Chastity*, Kessinger Publishing

Celenza, Christopher S. (1999), 'Pythagoras in the Renaissance: The case of Marsilio Ficino', *Renaissance Quarterly* 52:3, 667–711

Celsus, Aulus Cornelius (1935–38), *De medicina*, tr. W.G. Spencer, 3 vols, London

Chabad.org (2001–6), 'The Chassidic Masters on Food and Eating', http://www.chabad.org/library/archive

Chakravarty, Gautam (2005), *The Indian Mutiny and the British Imagination*, Cambridge

Chamberlain, John (1939), *The Letters of John Chamberlain*, ed. N.E. McClure, 2 vols, Philadelphia

Chandra, Pramod (1960), 'Ustad Salivahana and the development of popular Mughal Art', *Lalit Kala*, 8, 25–46

Chanet, Pierre (1643), *Considérations sur la sagesse de Charon*, Paris

Charpentier, J. (1934) 'The Indian travels of Apollonius of Tyana', *Skrifter utgivna av K. Humanistiska Vetenskaps*, Uppsala

Charron, Pierre (1601), *De la Sagesse*

Chase, Alan (1980), *The Legacy of Malthus*, 2 vols, London

Cheselden, William (1723), *Operation of the Stone*, J. Osborn, London

Cheyne, George (1703), *Fluxionum methodus inversa*, J. Matthews, London

Cheyne, George (1705), *Philosophical Principles Of Natural Religion*, G. Strahan, London

Cheyne, George (1715 [1716]), *Philosophical Principles Of Religion: Natural and Reveal'd*, G. Strahan, London

Cheyne, George (1720), *Observations Concerning The Nature And Due Method Of Treating the Gout*, G. Strahan, London

Cheyne, George (1724), *An Essay of Health and Long Life*, G. Strahan, London

Cheyne, George (1733), *The English Malady*, G. Strahan, London

Cheyne, George (1738), *Treating the Gout . . . Also, Of the Nature and Cure of most Chronical Distempers*, 9th edn, G. Strahan, London

Cheyne, George (1740), *An Essay On Regimen*, C. Rivington, London; J. Leake, Bath

Cheyne, George (1742), *The Natural Method*, G. Strahan, London

Cheyne, George (1743), *Dr. Cheyne's own account of himself*, J. Wilford, London

Cheyne, George (1940), *The Letters of Dr. George Cheyne to the Countess of Huntingdon*, ed. Charles F. Mullett, San Marino, Calif.

Cheyne, George (1943), 'The letters of Doctor George Cheyne to Samuel Richardson (1733–1743)', ed. Charles F. Mullett, *The University of Missouri Studies*, 18

Cheyne, George (1990), *The English Malady*, ed. Roy Porter, Routledge

Child, Paul William (1992), 'Discourse and Practice in Eighteenth-Century Medical Literature', unpublished Ph.D. dissertation, University of Notre Dame, Ann Arbor

Choudhury, M.L.R. (1997), *Din-i-Ilahi*, New Delhi

Chrysostom, St John (2005a), *Homilies on Galatians*, etc. [*NPNF 1*, vol. 13, 1889], http://www.newadvent.org/fathers/

Chrysostom, St John (2005b), *Homilies on . . . Saint Matthew* [*NPNF 1*, vol. 10, 1888], http://www.newadvent.org/fathers

Churchill, Mary S. (1967), 'Seven Chapters, with explanatory notes', *Chymia*, 12, 29–57

Claeys, Gregory (2000), 'The "Survival of the Fittest" and the Origins of Social Darwinism', *Journal of the History of Ideas*, 61:2, 223–40

Clark, David L. (1939), 'The date and source of Shelley's "A Vindication of Natural Diet'", *Studies in Philology*, 36, 70–6

Clark, John (1773), *Diseases in Long Voyages to Hot Countries*, G. Nicol, London

Clarke, John (1720), *An Enquiry into the Cause and Origin of Evil*, London

[Clarkson, Lawrence] (1659), *Look about You*, W. Learner, London

Claudinus, J.C. (The Elder) (n.d.), *De natura et usu lactis*, n.p.

Clement of Alexandria, St (2004a), *The Stromata, or Miscellanies* [*ANF*, vol. 2 (1885)], http://www.newadvent.org/fathers http://www.angelfire.com/yt3/mxx/stromatabook3.htm

Clement of Alexandria, St (2004b), *The Instructor* [*ANF*, vol. 2 (1885)], http://www.newadvent.org/fathers

Cloyd, E.L. (1972), *James Burnett, Lord Monboddo*, Oxford

Cocchi, Antonio (1741), 'Preface', in Lorenzo Bellini, *Discorsi*, 3 vols, Florence

Cocchi, Antonio (1743), *Del Vitto Pitagorico*, Florence

Cocchi, Antonio (1745), *The Pythagorean Diet, of Vegetables Only, Conducive to the Preservation of Health, And the Cure of Diseases*, R. Dodsley, London,

Cocchi, Antonio (1750), *Du Regime de Vivre Pythagoricien* [with 'Preface' and notes(?) by Jean-Baptiste Sénac], C. Philbert, Geneva

Cocchi, Antonio (1762), *The Life of Asclepiades*, T. Davies, London

Cocchi, Antonio (1824), *Opere*, 3 vols, Milan

[Cocchi, Venceslao] (1871), *Biografia di Antonio Celestino Cocchi*, Roma

Cockburn, Henry (1856), *Memorials of his Time*, A. & C. Black, Edinburgh

C[ockburn], W[illiam] (1696), *Nature, Causes, Symptoms and Cure*, H. Newman, London

Cohen [Rosenfield], Leonora D. (1936), 'Descartes and Henry More on the Beast-Machine', *Annals of Science*, 1:1, 48–61

Cohn, Norman (1970), *The Pursuit of the Millennium*, 2nd edn, London

Coleridge, S.T. (1796), 'On The Slave Trade', in *The Watchman*

Coles, William (1657), *Adam in Eden*

[Collier, Ronald], Pauline Kohler ([1940]), *I Was Hitler's Maid*, London

Collingham, E.M. (2001), *Imperial Bodies: The Physical Experience of the Raj, c.1800–1947*, Polity Press, Cambridge

Combe, Andrew (1860), *The Physiology of Digestion*, ed. J. Coxe, 10th edn, Edinburgh

Compte, Louis Le (1697), *Memoirs and Observations*, B. Tooke, London

Conger, G.P. (1922), *Theories of Macrocsms and Microcosms*, New York

[Conway, Anne] (1692), *Ancient and Modern Philosophy*, tr. J. Clark, London

Conway, Moncure Daniel (1892), *The Life of Thomas Paine*, 2 vols, New York

Cooper, J.P., ed. (1971), *The New Cambridge Modern History, Volume IV*, Cambridge

Cope, Zachary (1953), *William Cheselden 1688–1752*, Edinburgh

Coppe, Abiezer (1651), *A Remonstrance of The sincere and zealous Protestation*, London

Coppin, Richard (1649), *Divine Teachings: In three Parts*, London

Costaeus, Joannes (1604), *De lactis*, Petrum Bartolum, Papiæ

Coudert, Allison (1975), 'A Cambridge Platonist's Kabbalist Nightmare', *Journal of the History of Ideas*, Temple University, Philadelphia, PA, 36:4, 633–52

Coudert, Allison (1976), 'A Quaker-Kabbalist Controversy: George Fox's Reaction to Francis Mercury van Helmont', *Journal of the Warburg and Courtauld Institutes*, 39, 171–89

Coudert, Allison (1997), 'Leibniz, Locke, Newton and the kabbalah', in Joseph Dan, ed., *Christian Kabbalah*, Cambridge, Mass., 149–81

Coudert, Allison (1999), *Impact of the Kabbalah in the Seventeenth Century*, Leiden

Coudert, Allison et al., eds (1998), *Leibniz, Mysticism, and Religion*, Kluwer, London

Couvray, Jean-Baptiste Louvet de ([1795]), *Quelques notices*, Paris [London]

Couvray, Jean-Baptiste Louvet de (1795), *An Account of the Dangers*, Perth

Coveney, John (2000), *Food, Morals and Meaning*, Routledge, London

C[oward?], W[illiam] (1705?), *The Just Scrutiny*, John Chantry, London

Cowley, Abraham (1777), *Poetical Works*, Edinburgh

Cowper, William (1785), *The Task, a Poem, in Six Books*, J. Johnson, London

Cowper, William (1812), *The Life and Letters*, 4 vols, J. Johnson, London

Cowper, William (1992), *The Works* [Baldwin & Craddock, London, 1835–7], Chadwyck-Healey, Cambridge

Cox, Edward G. (1952), 'The Compleat Angler of a Cromwellian Trooper', in Arnold Williams, ed., *A Tribute to George Coffin Taylor*, Chapel Hill

[Coxall, Samuel?] (1721), *The Secret History Of Pythagoras*, J. Brotherton et al., London

Crab, Roger (1655), *The English Hermite*, London

Crab, Roger (1657), *Dagons-Downfall* [London?]

Crab, Roger (1659a), *Gentle Correction For The High-flown Backslider*, London

Crab, Roger (1659b), *A Tender Salutation*, London

Crab, Roger (1745), 'The English Hermit, or Wonder of this Age', in *The Harleian Miscellany, Vol. IV*, T. Osborne, London

Crab, Roger (1990), *The English Hermite*, ed. Andrew Hopton, London

Craven, J.B. (1910), *Count Michael Maier*, Kirkwall

Crawford, Fred D., ed. (1995), *Shaw: The Annual of Bernard Shaw Studies*

Crawford, Fred D. (2000), 'Shaw in Translation Part I', *Shaw: The Annual of Bernard Shaw Studies*, 177–96

Creech, Thomas (1699), *Litus Lucretius Carus, His Six Books of Epicurean Philosophy*, 4th edn, T. Braddyll, London

[Créquinière, de La] (1705), *The Agreement of the Customs of the East-Indians with those of the Jews* [tr. John Toland], W. Davis, London

Croft, Herbert, Sir (1780), *Love and Madness*, new edn, London

Cronin, Vincent (1959), *A Pearl to India*, London

Cudworth, Ralph (1678), *The Intellectual System Of The Universe*, R. Royston, London

Cullen, William (1771), *Lectures on the Materia Medica*, London

Culpeper, Nicholas (1649), *A Physicall Directory*, London

Culpeper, Nicholas (1656), *Health for the Rich and Poor, By Dyet*, London

Culpeper, Nicholas ([1794?]), *Culpeper's English Physician*, ed. E. Sibly, London

Cunningham, Andrew (1981), 'Sydenham versus Newton: The Edinburgh Fever Dispute of the 1690s', *Medical History*, suppl. 1

Cuppage, Frances E., (1994), *James Cook and the Conquest of Scurvy*, London

Cureau de la Chambre, M. (1657), *The Knowledge of Beasts*, T. Newcomb, London

Cureau de la Chambre, M. (1658), *Les Characteres Des Passions, Vol. II*, Amsterdam

[D.F.] (1663), *Reason and Judgement*, J.W., Oxford

da Vinci, Leonardo (1956), *Selections from the Notebooks*, ed. I.A. Richter, Oxford

da Vinci, Leonardo (1970), *The Literary Works*, ed. J.P. Richter, 3rd edn, 2 vols, London

da Vinci, Leonardo (1987), *Leonardo's Kitchen Note Books*, tr. J. Routh, London

Daggett, Herman (1926), *The Rights of Animals* [1792], New York

Dahmen, Pierre (1924), *Un Jésuite Brahme: Robert de Nobili*, Paris

Dan, Joseph, ed. (2002), *The Heart and the Fountain*, Oxford

Daniell, Thomas (1797), *Oriental Scenery*, London

Darmon, Jean-Charles (1998), *Philosophie Épicurienne*, Paris

Darnton, Robert (1968), *Mesmerism and the End of the Enlightenment in France*, Harvard University Press, Cambridge, Mass.

Darnton, Robert (1984), *The Great Cat Massacre*, New York

Darwin, Charles (1882), *The Descent of Man*, 2nd edn, John Murray, London

Darwin, Charles (1885), *The Origin of Species*, 6th edn, John Murray, London

Darwin, Charles (1887), *The Life and Letters*, ed. F. Darwin, John Murray, London

Darwin, Erasmus (1794–6), *Zoonomia*, 2 vols, J. Johnson, London

Darwin, Erasmus (1797), *A Plan for the Conduct of Female Education*, Derby

Darwin, Erasmus (1800), *Phytologia*, London

Darwin, Erasmus (1803), *The Temple of Nature*, J. Johnson, London

Davis, Lockyer ([1783]), *A catalogue of several libraries* [London]

Dawson, P.M.S. (1996), '"The Empire of Man": Shelley and Ecology', in Bennet and Curran, eds, 232–9

Dawson, P.M.S. (1997), 'Review of *Shelley and the Revolution in Taste* by Timothy Morton', *Studies in Romanticism*, 36:3, 498–502

Debus, Allen G. (2001), *Chemistry and the Medical Debate*, Canton., Mass.

Debus, Allen G., ed. (1972), *Science Medicine and Society in the Renaissance*, 2 vols, London

Decker, Catherine H. (1995), 'Female Self-Treatment', at the Asesc Conference, Tuscon, http://locutus.ucr.edu/~cathy/sandtext.html

Decker, Herbert (1693), *De Motu cibi*, A. Elzevier, Lugduni Batavorum

Defoe, Daniel (1694), *The Englishman's Choice*, Salusbury, London

[Defoe, Daniel] (1718), *A Continuation of Letters Written by a Turkish Spy*, London

Degategno, Paul James (1975), '"The Letters Writ By a Turkish Spy" and the Motif of the Foreign Observer', Ph.D. dissertation, Pennsylvania State University

[Delany, Patrick] (1733), *Revelation Examined*, 2nd edn, 3 vols, C. Rivington, London

Delattre, Lucas (2005), *Spy at the Heart of the Third Reich*, New York

Della Valle, Pietro (1892), *The Travels . . . from the old English translation of 1664*, tr. G. Havers, ed. E. Grey, 2 vols, Hakluyt Society, London

Denison, Stephen (1627), *The White Wolf*, London

Deodatus, Claudius (1628), *Pantheum hygiasticum*, Bruntrati

Derham, William (1714), *Physico-Theology*, 2nd edn, London

Derrett, J. Duncan M. (1960), 'The History of "Palladius on the Races of India and the Brahmans"', *Classica et Mediaevalia: Revue Danoise de Philologie et D'Histoire*, 21, Copenhagen

Derrett, J. Duncan M. (2000), *The Bible and the Buddhists*, Sardini

Descartes, René (1897–1913), *Oeuvres*, ed. C. Adam and P. Tannery, Paris

Descartes, René (1952), *Rules for the Direction of the Mind, Discourse on the Method, Meditations on First Philosophy, Objections against Meditations and Replies, The Geometry*, tr. S. Haldane and G.R.T. Ross, Chicago

Descartes, René (1984–91), *Philosophical Writings*, tr. J. Cottingham et al., 3 vols, Cambridge

Deverell, Mary (1781), *Miscellanies in Prose and Verse*, 2 vols [London]

Dick, Steven J. (1980), 'The Origins of the Extraterrestrial Life Debate and its Relation to the Scientific Revolution', *Journal of the History of Ideas*, 41, 3–27

Dimock, Wai Chee (2003), 'Planetary Time and Global Transition', *Common Knowledge*, 9:3, 488–507

Diodorus Siculus (1559), Βιβλιοθηκης Ιστορικης Βιβλοι, ed. Henricus Stephanus [Geneva]

Diodorus Siculus (1604), *Bibliothecæ Historicæ*, ed. L. Rhodomanus, Hanoviæ

Diodorus Siculus (1700), *The Historical Library*, tr. G. Booth, A. & J. Churchill, London

Diodorus Siculus (1933), *Diodorus of Sicily*, tr. C.H. Oldfather, 10 vols, London

Diogenes Laertius (2000), *Lives of Eminent Philosophers*, tr. R.D. Hicks, 2 vols, Cambridge, Mass.

Disraeli, Isaac (1798), *Curiosities of Literature*, 4th edn, 2 vols, London

Dobbs, B.J. Teeter (1975), *The Foundations of Newton's Alchemy*, Cambridge

Dobbs, B.J. Teeter (1991), *The Janus Face of Genius*, Cambridge

[Docteurs de la Faculté] (1736), *Lettre . . . relative aux attestations abusives pour dispenses de carême*, Paris

Dodd, Martha (1939), *My Years in Germany*, London

Doddridge, Philip (1794), *Pneumatology, Ethics, and Divinity*, London

Doig, Andrew (1982), 'Dr Black', in A.D.C. Simpson, ed., *Joseph Black*, Edinburgh

Dole, George (1707), *De furia podagræ lacte victa*, Amsterdam

Dombrowski, Daniel A. (1984), *The Philosophy of Vegetarianism*, University of Massachusetts Press

Dombrowski, Daniel A. (1986), 'Thoreau, Sainthood and Vegetarianism', *American-Transcendental-Quarterly*, 60, 25–36

Doody, Margaret Anne (1974), *A Natural Passion*, Oxford

Doody, Margaret Anne (1990), 'Richardson's Politics', *Eighteenth-Century Fiction*, 2:2, 113–26

Doody, Margaret Anne (1999), 'Sensuousness in the Poetry of Eighteenth-Century Women Poets', in Isobel Armstrong and Virginia Blain, eds, *Women's Poetry in the Enlightenment*, London, 3–32

Doorschodt, Henricus (1737), *De lacte*, Praes. J.J. Vitriarius, J. Hasebroek, Lugduni

Dornavius, Caspar (1619), *Mathusala Vivax, hoc est, de causis longævitatis Patrum Primogenitorum dissertatio*, Hanoviæ

Douthwaite, Julia (1997), 'Homo ferus: Between Monster and Model', *Eighteenth-Century Life*, 21:2, 176–202

Dow, Alexander [or Firishtah] (1768–72), *The History of Hindostan*, 3 vols

Drayton, Richard (2000), *Nature's Government*

Drew, John (1998), *India and the Romantic Imagination*, Oxford University Press, Delhi

Drummond, J.C. and Wilbraham, Anne (1939), *The Englishman's Food*, London

Dryden, John (1700), *Fables Ancient and Modern*, Jacob Tonson, London

Dryden, John (1958), *The Poems*, ed. James Kinsley, 4 vols, Clarendon, Oxford

Dubois, Abbé J.A. (1999), *Hindu Manners, Customs and Ceremonies*, 3rd edn, Rupa, New Delhi

Duffy, Maureen (1989), *The Passionate Shepherdess: The Life of Aphra Behn 1640–1689*, Phoenix Press

Dufrenoy, Marie-Louise (1975), *L'Orient Romanesque*, Amsterdam
Dupleix, Scipion (1606), *Les Causes de la Veille et du Sommeil*, Paris
Dupleix, Scipion (1610), *L'Ethique Ou Philosophie Morale*, Paris
Dussinger, John A. (1974), *The Discourse of the Mind in Eighteenth-Century Fiction*, The Hague

Eaves, T.C. Duncan and Kimpel, Ben D. (1971), *Samuel Richardson*, London
Edelstein, Ludwig (1987), *Ancient Medicine*, tr. C.L. Temkin et al., Baltimore
Edwards, Bryan (1799), *The History . . . of the British colonies in the West Indies*, London
Edwards, John (1693), *The authority . . . of the Old and New-Testament*
Edwards, John (1699), *Dispensations and Methods of Religion*, 2 vols, D. Brown, London
Edwards, Thomas (1645–6), *Gangræna*, Ralph Smith, London
Edwards, Thomas (1646), *The Third Part of Gangræna*, London
Elias, Norbert (2000), *The Civilizing Process*, tr. E. Jephcott, ed. E. Dunning, Oxford
Elior, Rachel (1995), 'The Doctrine of Transmigration in *Galya Raza*', in Fine, ed., 243–69
Ellis, Markman (1996), *The Politics of Sensibility*, Cambridge
Ellis, William (1752), *The Country House-Wife's Family Companion*, London
Elmer, Peter (1989), 'Medicine, religion and the puritan revolution', in French and Wear, eds
Emerson, Ralph Waldo (1969), 'Thoreau', in *Selected Prose and Poetry*, ed. Reginald L. Cook, New York
Erasmus, Desiderius (1534), *The Forbedynge of Eatynge of Fleshe &c.*, n.p.
Erdman, David V. (1986), *Commerce des Lumières: John Oswald and the British in Paris, 1790–1793*, University of Missouri Press, Columbia
Etherington, John (1645), *The Blasphemous Doctrine of Familisme*, London
Eusebius Pamphili (1903), *Evangelicae Praeparationis*, ed. E.H. Gifford, Oxford
[Evelyn, John] (1659), *A Character of England*, 3rd edn, J. Crooke, London
Evelyn, John (1661), *Fumifugium*, W. Godbid, London
Evelyn, John (1669), *Kalendarium Hortense*, 3rd edn, J. Martin, London
Evelyn, John (1670), *Sylva, Or A Discourse of Forest Trees*, J. Martyn, London
Evelyn, John (1676), *A Philosophical Discourse of Earth*, J. Martyn, London
Evelyn, John (1699), *Acetaria. A Discourse of Sallets*, London
Evelyn, John (1850), *The History of Religion*, ed. R.M. Evanson, 2 vols, London
Evelyn, John (1995), *The Writings of John Evelyn*, ed. Guy de la Bédoyère, Woodbridge
Evelyn, John (1996), *Acetaria: A Discourse of Sallets*, ed. C. Driver and T. Jaine, Totnes

Evelyn, John (1997), *John Evelyn, Cook*, ed. C. Driver, Totnes

Evelyn, John (2000), *Elysium Britannicum, or The Royal Gardens*, ed. John E. Ingram, Philadelphia

Everard, Robert (1649), *The Creation and Fall of Adam reviewed*, London

Everett, Jennifer (2001), 'Environmental Ethics, Animal Welfarism, and the Problem of Predation', *Ethics & the Environment*, 6:1, 42–67

Eylon, Dina Ripsman (2003), *Reincarnation in Jewish Mysticism and Gnosticism*, Edwin Mellen Press, Lewiston

Ezra, Abraham ibn (1939), *The Beginning of Wisdom*, ed. Raphael Levy and Francisco Cantera, Baltimore, Maryland

Ezra, Abraham ibn (1988), *Ibn Ezra's Commentary on the Pentateuch: Genesis (Bereshit)*, tr. H.N. Strickman and A.M. Silver, New York

F., A. (1980), 'Il Primo Massone Italiano', *Hiram*, 2, 51; http://www.esoteria.org/ilprimomassoneitaliano.htm

Faber, George (1816), *The Origin of Pagan Idolatry*, 3 vols, F. & C. Rivington, London

Fabra, Aloysius a (n.d.), *De arthritide dissertatio, ac de saccari lactis usu observatio*, n.p.

Fairfax, Thomas (1647), *An Humble Remonstrance*, London

Falconer, William (1781), *Remarks on the Influence of Climate*, London

Falk, Toby and Archer, Mildred (1981), *Indian Miniatures in the India Office Library*, London

Farrukh, Omar A. (n.d.), 'Ikhwan al-Safa', www.muslimphilosophy.com/hmp/18.htm

Fasick, Laura (1993), 'The Edible Woman', *South Atlantic Review*, 58:1, 17–31

Ferguson, Adam and Playfair, John (1997), *James Hutton & Joseph Black*, ed. G.Y. Craig, Edinburgh

Ferguson, John (1975), *Utopias of the Classical World*

Festugière, A-J. (1936), 'Une source Hermétique de Porphyre', *Revue des Etudes Grecques*, 49, 586–95

Field, John (1685), *The Absurdity & Falsness Of Thomas Trion's Doctrine Manifested, In Forbidding to Eat Flesh*, Tho. Howkins, London

Field, John (1701), *Light and Truth discovering and detecting sophistry and deceit*, T. Sowle, London

Fielding, Henry (1973), *Shamela*, ed. A.R. Humphreys, London

Findly, Ellison B. (1934), 'Jahāngīr's Vow of Non-Violence', *Journal of the American Oriental Society*, 54:2, 243–60

Fine, Lawrence, ed. (1995), *Essential Papers on Kabbalah*, New York

Fine, Lawrence (2003), *Physician of the Soul, Healer of the Cosmos: Isaac Luria and His Kabbalistic Fellowship*, Stanford Studies in Jewish History and Culture

Fisch, Jörg (1985), 'A solitary vindicator of the Hindus: the life and writings of General Charles Stuart (1757/8–1828)', *Journal of the Asiatic Society*, 4:2–3, 35–7

Fischer, Daniel ([1745?]), *De remedio rusticano*, Erfordiæ

Floyer, John and Baynard, Edward (1715), *ΨΥΧΡΟΛΟΥΕΣΙΑ. Or, The History of Cold Bathing*, 4th edn, William Innys, London

Fontenelle, B. le Bovier de (1728), *The Life of Sir Isaac Newton*, J. Woodman, London

Forbes, James (1813), *Oriental Memoirs*, 4 vols, London

Force, James E. and Popkin, Richard H., eds (1990), *Essays on the Context, Nature, and Influence of Isaac Newton's Theology*, Dordrecht

Force, James E. and Popkin, Richard H., eds (1999), *Newton and Religion*, Dordrecht

Forster, Georg (1777), *A Voyage round the world . . . commanded by Capt. James Cook, during the years 1772, 3, 4, and 5*, B. White et al., London

Fosl, Peter S. (2000), 'Common Life and Animality in Hume', in Kevin L. Cope and Anna Battigelli, eds, *1650–1850: Ideas, Aesthetics, and Inquiries in the Early Modern Era 5*, New York

Foster, William, ed. (1999), *Early Travels in India 1583–1619*, LPP, Delhi

Fox, Adam (2000), *Oral and Literate Culture in England 1500–1700*, Oxford University Press, Oxford

Fox, Robin Lane (1997), *Alexander the Great*, The Folio Society, London

Franck, Richard (1687), *A Philosophical Treatise on the Original and Production of Things*, John Gain et al., London

Franck, Richard (1694), *Northern Memoirs*, Henry Mortclock

Franklin, Benjamin (1776–85), Letter to the Royal Academy of Brussels, in the Stevens Collection of the Franklin Mss at the State Department, Washington DC, http://www.pelagus.org/books/ PARIS_1776-1785,_by_Benjamin_Franklin_1.html

Franklin, Benjamin (1986), *Autobiography*, ed. K. Silverman, Harmondsworth

Franzero, Carlo Maria (1969), *Leonardo*, London

Frega, D.M. (1990), 'Pedagogy of the Perfect', Dissertation Abstract in *Dissertation Abstracts International*, 50:8, 2496A

Frega, D.M. (1998), *Speaking in Hunger*, South Carolina

French, Roger and Wear, Andrew, eds (1989), *The Medical Revolution of the Seventeenth Century*, Cambridge University Press, Cambridge

[Fréret, Nicolas] (1728), *Sir Isaac Newton's Chronology*, J. Peele, London

Fréret, Nicolas (1758), *Défense De La Chronologie*, Durand, Paris

Fryer, John (1909), *A New Account of East India and Persia . . . 1672–1681*, ed. William Crooke, 3 vols, Hakluyt Society, London

Fudge, Erica (2000), *Perceiving Animals: Humans and Beasts in Early Modern English Culture*, Illinois

Fuller, Francis (1711), *Medicina Gymnastica*, 4th edn, R. Knaplock, London

Gaitonde, P.D. (1983), *Portuguese Pioneers in India*, Popular Prakashan, Bombay

Gandhi, Mahatma (1944), *Ethics of Fasting*, ed. Chander, Indian Printing Works, Lahore

Gandhi, Mahatma (1999), *The Life and Works of Mahatma Gandhi*, 98 vols, CD-ROM, New Delhi

Garber, Daniel and Ayers, Michael, eds (1998), *The Cambridge History of Seventeenth-Century Philosophy*, 2 vols, Cambridge University Press, Cambridge

Garden, George (1699), *An Apology for M. Antonia Bourignon*, D. Brown et al., London

Garment, Joshuah (1651), *The Hebrews Deliverance at hand*, London

Garrett, Aaron V., ed. (2000), *Animal Rights and Souls in the Eighteenth Century*, 6 vols, Thoemmes Press

Garret, Aaron C. (forthcoming), 'Animals', in Goulder and Grayling, eds, *Encyclopedia of British Philosophy*, Thoemmes Continuum

Gassendi, Petri (1658), *Opera Omnia* [ed. H.L. Habert and F. Henri], 6 vols, Laurentii Anisson, Lugduni

Gatti, Hilary (1995), 'Giordano Bruno and the Stuart court masques', *Renaissance Quarterly*, 48:4

Gaudenzio, Paganino (1641), *De Pythagoraea Animarum Transmigratione*, Pisis

Geber [Jābir Ibn Haiyān] (1928), *The Works of Geber 1678*, tr. Richard Russel, ed. E.J. Holmyard, London

Geoffroy, Claude-Joseph (1732), 'Examen Chymique Des Viandes', *Histoire de L'Academie Royale Des Sciences. Année 1730*, L'Imprimerie Royale, Paris, 217–32

George, Mary D. and Stephens, Frederick G. (1978), *Catalogue of Political and Personal Satires . . . in the British Museum*, 7 vols, British Museum Publications, London

Gibbons, B.J. (1996), *Gender in Mystical and Occult Thought*, Cambridge

Gibbs, Robert (1888), *Worthies of Buckinghamshire*, Bucks Advertiser, Aylesbury

Giblin, James Cross (2002), *The Life and Death of Adolf Hitler*, Clarion Books

[Gildon, Charles] (1710), *The Golden Spy*, London

[Gildon, Charles] (1997), *The Post-boy rob'd of his Mail* [1692], Chadwyck-Healey, Cambridge

Giller, Pinchas (2001), *Reading the Zohar*, Oxford

Gillray, James ([1873]), *The Works of James Gillray*, ed. T. Wright, London

Gillray, James (1966), *Fashionable Contrasts*, ed. Draper Hill, Phaidon Press, London

Glacken, Clarence J. (1990), *Traces on the Rhodian Shore: Nature and Culture in Western Thought from Ancient Times to the End of the Eighteenth Century*, University of California Press, Berkeley

Glanius (1682), *A Relation of an Unfortunate Voyage in the Kingdom of Bengala*, Henry Bonwick, London

[Glanvill, Joseph] (1662), *Lux Orientalis*, London

Godwin, William (1793), *An Enquiry Concerning Political Justice*, J. Robinson, London

Godwin, William (1820), *Of Population*, London

Godwin, William (1831), *Thoughts On Man His Nature*, E. Wilson, London

Godwin, William (2005), *Imogen*, www.gutenberg.net

Goethe, J.W. von (1917), *The Sorrows of Werther*, www.bartleby.com

Goethe, J.W. von (1932), *Goethe's Autobiography*, tr. R.O. Moon, London

Goethe, J.W. von (1962), *Italian Journey*, London

Goldish, Matt (1998), *Judaism in the Theology of Isaac Newton*, Dordrecht

Goldsmith, Maurice (1986), 'Levelling by Sword, Spade and Word', in Colin Jones et al., eds, *Politics and People in Revolutionary England*, Oxford, 65–80

Goldsmith, Oliver (1774–[1785?]), *An History of the Earth*, 8 vols, J. Nourse, London

Goldsmith, Oliver (1996), *Collected Works*, ed. Arthur Friedman, Oxford

Goodrick-Clarke, Nicholas (1985), *The Occult Roots Of Nazism*, Aquarian Press, Wellingborough

Goodrick-Clarke, Nicholas (1998), *Hitler's Priestess*, New York University Press, New York

Goodspeed, Charles E. (1943), 'Richard Franck', in Deoch Fulton et al., *Notes and Studies Written and Gathered in Tribute to Harry Miller Lydenberg*, New York

Gordon, Alexander (1871), 'A Pythagorean of the Seventeenth Century', *Proceedings of the Literary and Philosophical Society of Liverpool*, 25

Gordon, Terri J. (2002), 'Fascism and the female form', *Journal of the History of Sexuality*, 11:1–2, 164–200

Gott, Samuel (1670), *The Divine History of the Genesis of the World*, A.C., London

Gough, J.W. (1932), *The Superlative Prodigall*, Bristol

Gould, Stephen J. (1991), *Bully for Brontosaurus*, London

Goulder, N. and Grayling, A., eds (forthcoming), *Encyclopedia of British Philosophy*, Thoemmes Continuum

Gourraigne, Hugues (1741), *Dissertatio de natura et causis fluiditatis sanguinis*

Goyal, S.R. (1985), *Kautilya and Megasthenes*, Kusumanjali Prakashan, Meerut

Goyal, S.R. (2000), *The Indica of Megasthenes*, Jodhpur

Graham, James (1775), *An Address to the Inhabitants of Great Britain*, G. Scott, London

Graham, James (1776), *The Christian's Universal Prayer*, 3rd edn, R. Cruttwell, Bath

Graham, James (1778), *Medical and Chirurgical Practice*, 6th edn, Bath

Graham, James (1783), *A Discourse Delivered*, Edinburgh

Graham, James ([1785?]), *The Guardian Goddess of Health*, London

Graham, James (1789), *The True Nature and Uses of the Bath Waters*, Bath

Graham, James (1790), *The Guardian of Health, Long-Life, and Happiness*, S. Hodgson, Newcastle

Graham, James (1793), *The Nature and Effects of Simple Earth*, Richardson, London

Graham, Maria (1813), *Journal of A Residence in India*, 2nd edn, Edinburgh

Graham, Maria (1814), *Letters on India*, Edinburgh

Grand, Antoine le (1672), *Institutio Philosophiae Secundum Principia Domini Renati Descartes*, J. Martyn, London

Grand, Antoine le (1694), *An Entire Body of Philosophy, According to the Principles of the Famous Renate des Cartes*, tr. R. Blome, S. Rycroft, London

Graves, Richard (1766), *The Festoon*

Graves, Richard (1996), *The Spiritual Quixote* [J. Dodsley, 1773], Chadwyck-Healey, Cambridge

Greaves, Richard L. and Zaller, Robert, eds. (1982–4), *Biographical Dictionary of British Radicals in the Seventeenth Century*, 3 vols, Harvester Press, Brighton

Green, Martin (1978), *The Challenge of the Mahatmas*, New York

Green, Martin (1983), *Tolstoy and Gandhi, Men of Peace*, New York

Green, Martin (1986), *The Origins of Nonviolence*, Pennsylvania

Greene, Edward L. (1909), 'Linnaeus as an Evolutionist', *Proceedings, Washington Academy of Sciences*, 11

Gregory, George (1788), *Essays Historical and Moral*, 2nd edn, London

Greisel, Johann Georg (1670), *De Cura lactis in Arthritide*, Vienna

Greisel, Johann Georg (1681), *Tractatus medicus de cura lactis in arthritide*, 2nd edn, Joh. Widischii, Andreae Richteri, Budissinae

Greville, Charles Francis (1793), *British India Analyzed*, 3 vols, London

Grieg, J.Y.T., ed. (1932), *The Correspondence of David Hume*, 2 vols, Oxford

Grose, John Henry (1766), *A Voyage to the East-Indies*, 2 vols, London

Gross, Gloria Sybil (1985), 'Dr. Johnson's Practice', *Studies in Eighteenth Century Culture*, 14, 275–88

Grotius, Hugo (1727), *Annotationes in vetus & novum Testamentum*, Jos. Smith et al., London

Grotius, Hugo (1901), *The Rights of War and Peace including the Law of Nature and of Nations* [1625], tr. A.C. Campbell, M. Walter Dunne, New York

Grove, Richard H. (1995), *Green Imperialism, Colonial Expansion, tropical island Edens and the origins of environmentalism 1600–1860*, Cambridge University Press

Gruman, Gerald J. (1966), *A History of Ideas about the Prolongation of Life, Transactions of the American Philosophical Society*, 56:9

Guerrini, Anita (1985), 'James Keill, George Cheyne, and Newtonian Physiology, 1690–1740', *Journal of the History of Biology*, 18:2, 247–66

Guerrini, Anita (1987), 'Archibald Pitcairne and Newtonian Medicine', *Medical History*, 31:1, 70–93

Guerrini, Anita (1989a), 'The Ethics of Animal Experimentation in Seventeenth-Century England', *Journal of the History of Ideas*, 50:3, 391–407

Guerrini, Anita (1989b), 'Isaac Newton, George Cheyne and the "*Principia Medicinae*"', in French and Wear, eds, 222–45

Guerrini, Anita (1993a), ' "A club of little villains": rhetoric, professional identity and medical pamphlet wars', in Roy Porter and M.M. Roberts, eds, *Literature and Medicine During the Eighteenth Century*, London, 226–44

Guerrini, Anita (1993b), 'Ether Madness: Newtonianism, Religion and Insanity in Eighteenth-Century England', in Theerman and Seeff, eds, 232–54

Guerrini, Anita (1995), 'Case History as Spiritual Autobiography', *Eighteenth Century Life*, 19:2

Guerrini, Anita (1999a), 'A Diet for a Sensitive Soul: Vegetarianism in Eighteenth-Century Britain', in *Eighteenth-Century Life: The Cultural Topography of Food*, ed. Beatrice Fink, 23:2, 34–42

Guerrini, Anita (1999b), 'The Hungry Soul: George Cheyne and the Construction of Femininity', *Eighteenth-Century Studies*, 32.3, 279–91

Guerrini, Anita (2000), *Obesity & Depression in the Enlightenment*, University of Oklahoma Press

Gueullette, Thomas Simon (1725), *Chinese Tales*, 2 vols, J. Brotherton and W. Meadows, London

Guglielmini, G.D. (1709), *Item L. Testi . . . De novo Sacchara*, Lugduni in Batavis

Guglielmini, G.D. (1719), *Opera Omnia mathematica*, 2 vols, Geneva

Guha, J., ed. (1976), *India in the Seventeenth Century*, Associated Publishing House, New Delhi

Guidi, Abbé (1782), *Ame des Bêtes*, Moutard, Paris

Gupta, Narayani (1998), *Delhi between Two Empires, 1803–1931*, Oxford University Press, Delhi

Guthrie, W.K.C. (1962), *A History of Greek Philosophy*, vol. 1 *The Earlier Presocratics and The Pythagoreans*, Cambridge University Press, Cambridge

Hacker, J., ed. (1976), *Studies in the Kabbala Literature*, Tel Aviv

Haeckel, Ernst (1876), *The History of Creation*, 2 vols, D. Appleton, New York

Haeckel, Ernst (1895), *Monism*, tr. J. Gilchrist, A. and C. Black, London

Haeckel, Ernst (1912), *The Evolution of Man*, tr. Joseph Mccabe, Watts, London

Haggerty, George E. (1990), 'Sir Charles Grandison and the "Language of Nature"', *Eighteenth-Century Fiction*, 2:2, 127–40

Hahn, Thomas, ed. (1981), *Upright Lives*, The Augustan Reprint Society Nos. 209–10, Los Angeles

Hakluyt, Richard, ed. (1885–90), *The Principal Navigations, Voyages, Traffiques and Discoveries*, ed. E. Goldsmid, 16 vols, Edinburgh

Haldane, Elizabeth S. (1905), *Descartes*, John Murray, London

[Halhed, Nathaniel Brassey] (1776), *A Code of Gentoo Laws*, London

Halhed, Nathaniel Brassey (1777), *A Code of Gentoo Laws*, London

Hall, A. Rupert (1980), *Philosophers at War*, Cambridge

H[all?]., G[eorge]. (1651), *The Declaration of John Robins*, London

H[all], J[ohn] (1694), *An Answer to some Queries propos'd by W.C.*, L. Lichfield, Oxford, Marlborough

Haller, Albrecht von (1751), *Primae Lineae Physiologiae*, A. Vandenhoeck, Gottingae

Haller, Albrecht von (1754), *Dr. Albert Haller's Physiology*, 2 vols, London

Haller, Albrecht von (1757), *On the Motion of the Blood*, London

Haller, Albrecht von (1772), *Usong. An Eastern Narrative*, 2 vols, J. Walter, London

Haller, Albrecht von (1773), *Usong. An Oriental History*, J. Wilkie, London

Haller, Albrecht von (1786), *First Lines of Physiology*, tr. W. Cullen, Edinburgh

Hamann, Brigitte (2000), *Hitler's Vienna*, Oxford University Press

Hamilton, Alastair (1981), *The Family of Love*, James Clarke & Co., Cambridge

Hamilton, Eliza (1796), *Translation of the Letters of a Hindoo Rajah*, London

Hamilton, W.D., ed. (1873), *Calendar of State Papers, Domestic Series, of the Reign of Charles I, 1639*, London

Harris, John, ed. (1705), *Voyages and Travels*, 2 vols, T. Bennet, London

Harrison, John (1978), *The Library of Isaac Newton*, Cambridge

Harrison, Mark (1994), *Public Health in British India*, Foundation Books, New Delhi

Harrison, Mark (1996), ' "The Tender Frame of Man": Disease, Climate, and Racial Difference in India and the West Indies, 1760–1860', *Bulletin of the History of Medicine*, 70:1, 68–93

Harrison, Mark (1999), *Climates and Constitutions: Health, Race, Environment and British Imperialism in India 1600–1850*, Oxford University Press, New Delhi

Harrison, Peter (1993), 'Animal Souls, Metempsychosis, and Theodicy in Seventeenth-Century English Thought', *Journal of the History of Philosophy*, 31:4, 519–44

Harrison, Peter (1999), 'Subduing the Earth: Genesis I, Early Modern Science, and the Exploitation of Nature', *The Journal of Religion*, 79:1, 86–109

Hartley, David (1749), *Observations on Man*, 2 vols, S. Richardson for J. Leake et al., London

Hartlib, Samuel (1652), *A Designe for Plentie, by an Universall Planting of Fruit Trees*

Harvey, Gideon (1672), *Morbus Anglicus*, London

Harvey, Gideon (1675), *The Disease Of London*, T. James, London

Harvey, William (1628), *De Motu Cordis*

Harvey, William (1847), *The Works of William Harvey*, tr. Robert Willis, London

Hasan, Abu Zaid and Sulaimān (1733), *Ancient Accounts of India and China*, tr. E. Renaudot, Sam. Harding, London

Haslewood, Joseph (1795), *The Secret History of the Green-Room*, 2 vols, London

Hastings, Hester (1936), *Man and Beast in French Thought of the Eighteenth Century*, Baltimore

Hastings, Hester (1946), 'Man and Beast: Lamartine's Contribution to French Animal Literature', *Publications of the Modern Language Association*, 1109–25

Hau, Michael (2003), *The Cult of Health and Beauty in Germany: A Social History, 1890–1930*, Chicago

Haussleiter, Johannes (1935), *Der Vegetarismus in der Antike*, Berlin

Hay, Stephen (1989), 'The Making of a Late-Victorian Hindu: M.K. Gandhi in London 1888–1891', *Victorian Studies*, 33:1, 75–98

Hayes, T. Wilson (1984), 'John Everard and the Familist Tradition', in Margaret Jacobs and James Jacob, eds, *Origins of Anglo-American Radicalism*

Haykel, Navina N. Haidar (2004), 'A Lacquer Pen-Box by Manohar: An Example of Late Safavid-Style Painting in India', in Rosemary Crill, Susan Stronge, Andrew Topsfield, eds, *Arts of Mughal India, Studies in honour of Robert Skelton Ahmedabad*, 177–86

Hazard, Paul (1953), *The European Mind (1680–1715)*, tr. J. Lewis May, London

Hearmon, Carolynne (1982), *Uxbridge*, Hillingdon Libraries, London

Hecquet, Philippe (1695), *An Chronicorum Morborum medicina, in Alimento?*

[Hecquet, Philippe] (1709), *Dispenses du Carême*, François Fournier, Paris

[Hecquet, Philippe] (1712), *De la Digestion*, Paris

Hecquet, Philippe (1724), *Hippocratis Aphorismi*

[Hecquet, Philippe] (1733), *La Medecine Théologique*, G. Cavalier, Paris

[Hecquet, Philippe] (1758), *La Medecine et Chirurgie des Pauvres* [Paris?]

Hecquet, Philippe (1990), *De l'Indécence aux hommes d'accoucher les femmes*, ed. Hélène Rouch, Paris

[Helmont, Franciscus Mercurius van] (1684), *Two Hundred Queries*, R. Kettlewell, London

Helmont, Franciscus Mercurius van [and J.B.] (1685), *The Paradoxal Discourses*, F. Collins, London

Helmont, Jan Baptista van (1664), *Van Helmont's Workes*, tr. J.C., L. Llyod, London

Hendrick, George (1956), 'The Influence of Thoreau's Civil Disobedience on Gandhi's *Satyagraha*', *New England Quarterly*, 29:4, 462–71

Hendrick, George (1977), *Henry Salt: Humanitarian Reformer and Man of Letters*, University of Illinois Press, Illinois

Heninger, S.K. (1974), *Touches of Sweet Harmony*, Huntington Library, San Marino

Heninger, S.K. (1977), *The Cosmographical Glass*, Huntington Library, San Marino

Herbert of Cherbury, Edward, Lord (1705), *The Ancient Religion of the Gentiles*, J. Nutt, London

Herbert, Sandra (1971), 'Darwin, Malthus, and Selection', *Journal of the History of Biology*, 4:1, 209–17

Herbert, Thomas (1634), *A Relation of Some Yeares Travaile*, J. Bloome, London

Herbert, Thomas (1638), *Some Yeares Travels into divers parts of Asia*, 2nd edn, London

Herodotus (1862), *The History of Herodotus*, tr. G. Rawlinson, Dutton & Co., New York, http://www.fordham.edu/halsall/ancient/herodotus-history.txt

Heyden, Hermannus van der (1653), *Synopsis discursuum . . . præcipue, seri-lactis in fluxu terminali*, Londini

Heydon, John (1662) *The Holy Guide*, T. Whittlesey, London

Heylyn, Peter (1625), *Mikrokosmos*, W. Turner, Oxford

Hierocles (1657), *The Golden Verses of Pythagoras*, tr. J. Hall, F. Eaglesfield, London

Hildrop, John (1742–3), *Free Thoughts upon the Brute-Creation*, 2 parts, R. Minors, London

Hildrop, John (1752), *The Husbandman's Spiritual Companion*, J. Rivington, London

Hill, Christopher (1980), *Some Intellectual Consequences of the English Revolution*, Weidenfeld and Nicolson, London

Hill, Christopher (1983), 'John Reeve and the Origins of Muggletonianism', in Christopher Hill, Barry Reay and William Lamont, *The World of the Muggletonians*, Temple Smith, London

Hill, Christopher (1986a), 'Till the conversion of the Jews', in *The Collected Essays of Christopher Hill. Volume Two*, Harvester Press, Brighton

Hill, Christopher (1986b), *Puritanism and Revolution*, Harmondsworth

Hill, Christopher (1990), *A Nation of Change and Novelty*, Routledge, London

Hill, Christopher (1991), *The World Turned Upside Down*, Harmondsworth

Hill, Christopher (1995), *Puritanism and Revolution*, Secker & Warburg

Hill, S.C., ed. (1905), *Bengal in 1756–1757*, 3 vols, London

Hilliard, Raymond F. (1990), 'Clarissa and Ritual Cannibalism', *Publications of the Modern Language Association of America*, 105:5, 1083–97

Himsel, Nicolaus (1751), *De victu salubri ex animalibus et vegetabilibus Temperando*, Praes. A. Haller, Gottingen

Hippocrates (1948), *Airs, Waters, Places*, tr. W.H.S. Jones, Cambridge, Mass.

Hippolytus, St (1921), *Philosophumena*, tr. F. Legge, 2 vols, London, New York

Hippolytus, St (2005), *The Refutation of All Heresies*, tr. J.H. Macmahon [*ANF*, vol. 5, 1886], http://www.newadvent.org/fathers

Hird, William (1751), *Disquisitio medica inauguralis de lactis natura et usu*, Edinburgi

Hirschhorn, Norbert et al. (2001), 'Abraham Lincoln's Blue Pills', *Perspectives in Biology and Medicine*, 44:3, 315–32

Hitler, Adolf, *Mein Kampf* (1943), Houghton Mifflin, Boston

Hitler, Adolf [and Picker, Henry, et al., eds] (1963), *Hitlers Tischespräche*, ed. P.E. Schramm, Stuttgart

Hitler, Adolf [and Picker, Henry, et al., eds] (2000), *Hitler's Table Talk 1941–1944*, tr. Cameron and Stevens, Phoenix Press, London

Hobbes, Thomas (1651), *Leviathan*, Andrew Crooke, London

Hobbes, Thomas (1676), *Leviathan, sive de materia, forma & Potestate civitatis ecclesiasticae et civilis*, Joannis Thomsonii, London

Hobbes, Thomas (1839–45), *The English Works*, ed. W. Molesworth, London

Hobbes, Thomas (1969), *The Elements of Law Natural and Politic*, ed. F. Tönnies, 2nd edn, London

Hobson, John M. (2004), *The Eastern Origins of Western Civilisation*, Cambridge

Hodder, Alan D. (2003), '"The Best of the Brahmans": India Reading Emerson Reading India', *Nineteenth-Century Prose*, 30:1, 337–68

Hogg, Thomas Jefferson (1858), *The Life of Percy Bysshe Shelley*, 4 vols, Edward Moxon, London

Holcroft, Thomas (1816), *Memoirs of Thomas Holcroft*, ed. Hazlitt

Holland, H[enry] (1596), *The Christian Exercise of Fasting*, W. Young, London

Holland, John (1650), *The Smoke of the Bottomless Pit*, London

Holmes, Richard (1974), *Shelley: the Pursuit*, Weidenfeld & Nicolson, London

Holwell, John Zephaniah (1766–7), *Interesting Historical Events*, 2nd edn, London

Holwell, John Zephaniah (1774), *India Tracts*, 3rd edn

[Holwell, John Zephaniah] (1776), *Primitive Religion Elucidated*, L. Bull,

Holwell, John Zephaniah (1779), *A Review of the Original Principles, Religious and Moral, of the Ancient Bramins . . . With A Dissertation on the Metempsychosis, commonly, though erroneously, called the Pythagorean Doctrine*, D. Steel, London

[Holwell, John Zephaniah] (1786), *On the Origin . . . of Intelligent Beings*, London

Holwell, John Zephaniah (1970), 'The religious Tenets of the Gentoos', in P.J. Marshall, ed., *The British Discovery of Hinduism*, Cambridge, 45–90

Holwell, John Zephaniah (1971), 'An Account of the Manner of Inoculating for the Small Pox in the East Indies' [1767], in Dharampal, ed., *Indian Science and Technology in the Eighteenth Century*, Impex India, Delhi

Hope, John (1780), *Thoughts, in Prose and Verse*, Stockton

Hopetoun House (1889), *Catalogue of the Library of the Right Honourable the Earl of Hopetoun*, n.p.

Hopetoun House (1962), *Hopetoun House Library*, ed. M.J. McKeeman, Edinburgh

Hopton, Andrew, ed. (1992), *The Declaration of John Robins*, Aporia Press, London

Hotham, Durand (1654), 'The Life of Jacob Behmen', in Jacob Böhme, *Mysterium Magnum* [tr. J. Ellistone and J. Sparrow], H. Blunden, London

Howells, Robin (1995), 'Voltaire, Rousseau and the Brahmin: a Small Correction on a Large Topic', *French Studies Bulletin*, 54, 6–8

Huddesford, George (1992), 'The Pythagorean', in *The Wiccamical Chaplet* [T. Burton, London, 1804], Chadwyck-Healey, Cambridge

Hudson, D. Dennis (2000), *Protestant Origins in India*, W.B. Eerdmans, Cambridge

Huet, Pierre-Daniel (1694), *Demonstratio Evangelica*

Hufeland, Christoph Wilhelm (1797), *Die Kunst Das Menschliche Leben zu Verlängern*, 2 vols, Franz Haas, Vienna

Hugot, Claudius ([1678]), *An inveteratæ et contumaci dysenteriæ lactis potio?*, Præs. F. Girard, Paris

Hume, David (1983) *An Enquiry Concerning the Principles of Morals*, ed. J.B. Schneewind, Indianapolis

Hume, David (1985), *A Treatise of Human Nature*, ed. E.C. Mossner, Harmondsworth

Hunt, John Dixon (1997), 'Evelyn's Idea of the Garden: A Theory for All Seasons', in O'Malley and Wolschke-Bulmahn eds

Hunt, Lynn (2004), *Politics, Culture, & Class in the French Revolution*, University of California Press

Husain, Mahdi (1987), *Bahadur Shah-II*, M.N. Publishers, New Delhi

Hutcheson, Francis (1755), *A System of Moral Philosophy*, 3 vols, Glasgow

Hutcheson, Francis (1764), *A Short Introduction to Moral Philosophy*, 3rd edn, 2 vols, A. Foulis, Glasgow

Hutchinson, Benjamin (1799), *Biographia medica*, London

Hutin, Serge (1960), *Les Disciples Anglais de Jacob Boehme aux XVIIe et XVIIIe Siècles*, Paris

Huxham, John (1759), *Observations on the Air and Epidemic Diseases*, London

Huxley, Thomas (1870), 'On Descartes' *Discourse*', *Macmillan's Magazine* 22, 69–80

Huxley, Thomas (1874), 'On the Hypothesis that Animals are Automata, and Its History', *Nature*, 10, 362–66, http://aleph0.clarku.edu/huxley/CE1/AnAuto.html

Huxley, Thomas (1888), 'The Struggle for Existence and its bearing on Man', in *The Nineteenth Century*

Huxley, Thomas (1968), *Collected Essays*, 9 vols, [Greenwood Press, New York] http://aleph0.clarku.edu/huxley/CE7/

Iamblichus (1818), *Life of Pythagoras or Pythagoric Life*, tr. Thomas Taylor, J. Valpy, London

Iamblichus (1989), *On the Pythagorean Life*, tr. Gillian Clark, Liverpool

Idel, Moshe (1987), 'Differing Conceptions of Kabbalah in the Early 17th Century', in Twersky and Septimus, eds, 137–200

Iliffe, Rob (1998), 'Isaac Newton: Lucatello Professor of Mathematics', in Christopher Lawrence and Steven Shapin, eds, *Science Incarnate*, Chicago

Ilive, Jacob (1736), *The Oration . . . Proving . . . That the Souls of Men are the Apostate Angels*, 2nd edn, J. Wilford, London

International Vegetarian Union (n.d.), 'Dr Gustav Selss', http://www.ivu.org/members/council/dr-selss.html

Irenaeus of Lyons, St (1868), *Adversus Heraeses*, in *The Writings of Irenæus*, tr. Rev. Alexander Roberts and Rev. W.H. Rambaut, Edinburgh

Irenaeus of Lyons, St (2004), *Adversus haereses* [*ANF*, vol. 1, 1885], http://www.newadvent.org/fathers

Isaacs, Ronald H. (2000), *Animals in Jewish Thought*, Northvale, New Jersey

Isez, Joannes Franciscus ([1741]), *An arthritide præcavendæ lactis diæta?*, Præs. H.F. Bourdelin, [Paris]

Israel, Jonathan (2001), *Radical Enlightenment*, Oxford University Press

Jacob, Margaret C. (1976a), 'Millenarianism and Science in the Seventeenth Century', *Journal of the History of Ideas*, 37:2, 335–41

Jacob, Margaret C. (1976b), *The Newtonians and the English Revolution 1689–1720*, Ithaca, New York

Jacob, Margaret C. (1981), *The Radical Enlightenment*, George Allen & Unwin, London

Jacob, Margaret C. and Lockwood, W.A. (1972), 'Political Millenarianism and Burnet's *Sacred Theory*', *Science Studies*, 2:3, 265–79

Jacobi, Ludovicus Conradus (1675), *Resp. Exercitatio de cura lactis, podagricorum solatio, et certo podagræ remedio*, Præs. J.J. Waldschmied, Marburgi Cattorum

Jaffer, Amin (2002), *Luxury Goods from India*, V&A Publications, London

Jaffer, Amin and Schwabe, Melanie Anne (1999), 'A group of sixteenth-century ivory caskets from Ceylon', *Apollo*, 149, 445

Jahangir (1968), *Tuzuk i Jahangiri*, tr. A. Rogers, ed. H. Beveridge, Delhi

James, Robert (1741), *The Modern Practice of Physic*, 2 vols, J. Hodges, London

James, Robert, ed. (1750), *Health Preserved*, 2nd edn, J. Woodyer, London

Jardine, Lisa and Stewart, Alan (1998), *Bacon, Hostage to Fortune*, London

Jefferson, Thomas (1958), *The Papers*, vol. 15, ed. J.P. Boyd, Princeton

Jenner, Mark (1998), 'Bathing and Baptism: Sir John Floyer and the Politics of Cold Bathing', in K. Sharpe and S. Zwicker, eds, *Refiguring Revolutions*, Berkeley, 197–216

Jenyns, Soame (1793), *The Works of Soame Jenyns*, 4 vols, T. Cadell, London

Jerome, St (2005a), *Against Jovinianus* [*NPNF 2*, vol. 6, 1893], http://www.newadvent.org/fathers

Jerome, St (2005b), *Letter 124: To Avitus* [*NPNF 2*, vol. 6, 1893], http://www.newadvent.org/fathers

Jha, D.N. (2002), *The Myth Of The Holy Cow*, Verso, London

Johnson, Daniel (1827), *Sketches of Indian Field Sports*, 2nd edn, Robert Jennings, London

Johnson, James (1813), *The Influence of Tropical Climates*, J.J. Stockdale, London

Johnson, James (1837), *The Economy of Health*, 2nd edn, London

Johnson, Samuel (1793), *Works*, Dublin

Johnson, Samuel (1952), *The Letters*, ed. R.W. Chapman, 3 vols, Oxford

Johnson, Samuel (1958), *Rasselas*, ed. Bertrand H. Bronson, New York

Johnson, Samuel (1970), *Journey to the Western Islands*, ed. R.W. Chapman, Oxford

Johnston, William M., ed. (2000), *Encyclopedia of Monasticism*, 2 vols, Chicago

Jones, Joseph (1957), 'Transcendental Grocery Bills: Thoreau's *Walden* and Some Aspects of American Vegetarianism', *Texas Studies in English*, 36, 141–54

Jones, Rufus M. (1909), *Studies in Mystical Religion*, London

Jones, Rufus M. (1914), *Spiritual Reformers in the 16th and 17th Centuries*, London

Jones, Stephen (1799), *A New Biographical Dictionary*, 3rd edn, London

Jones, Stephen E. (n.d.), 'Creation/Evolution Quotes: Social', http://members.iinet.net.au/sejones/social.html

Jones, William (1799), *The Works of Sir William Jones*, 6 vols, London

Jones, William (1807), *The Works*, ed. Teignmouth, 13 vols, London

Jones, William (1970), *The Letters of Sir William Jones*, ed. Garland Cannon, London

Jonson, Ben (1716–17), *The Works*, 6 vols, J. Walthoe et al., London

Jooma, Minaz (1996), 'The Alimentary Structures of Incest', Dissertation Abstract in *Dissertation Abstracts International* 57:2, 693A

Josephus, Flavius (1755), *The Works of Flavius Josephus*, tr. William Whiston, www.ccel.org

Jundt, Auguste (1875), *Histoire du Panthéisme Populaire au Moyen Age et au Seizieme Siècle*, Paris

Jung, C.G. (1974), *Psychology and Alchemy*, tr. R.F.C. Hull, 2nd edn, London

Kaempfer, Engelbert (1694), *Decadem Observationum Exoticarum*, A. Elzevier, Leiden

Kaempfer, Engelbert (1727), *The History of Japan*, tr. J.G. Scheuchzer, 2 vols, London

Kämper, Martin (1995), *Sir William Temples Essays* Upon Ancient and Modern Learning *und* Of Poetry, Peter Lang, Frankfurt

Katz, David S. (1982), *Philo-Semitism and the Readmission of the Jews to England 1603–1655*, Oxford

Kay, Donald (1973), 'Pamela and the Poultry', *Satire Newsletter*, 10:1, 25–7

Keay, John (1988), *India Discovered*, Collins

Keay, John (1993), *The Honourable Company*, London

Keith, George (1671), *The universall free grace of the Gospel asserted*, London

Keith, George (1678), *The way to the city of God described*, Netherlands and London [advertisement added later]

Kelly, Michael (1826), *Reminiscences*, Henry Colburn, London

Kemp, Martin (1981), *Leonardo da Vinci*, London

Kennedy, Gordon and Ryan, Kody (2003), 'Hippie Roots & The Perennial Subculture', http://www.hippy.com/php/article-243.html

Kenyon-Jones, Christine (2001), *Kindred Brutes: Animals in Romantic-period Writing*, Ashgate, Aldershot

Kershaw, Ian (1998), *Hitler 1889–1936: Hubris*, Allen Lane, Harmondsworth

Kershaw, Ian (2000), *Hitler: 1936–45: Nemesis*, Allen Lane, Harmondsworth

Kersten, Felix (1956), *The Kersten Memoirs: 1940–1945*, tr. C. Fitzgibbon and J. Oliver, Hutchinson, London

Keymer, T. (1995), 'Pamela's Fables', *Bulletin de la Société d'Études Anglo-Americaines des XVIIe et XVIIIe Siècles*, 41, 81–101

Kincaid, Dennis (1973), *British Social Life in India, 1608–1937*, ed. J. Lunt, London

Kindler, J.A. ([1742]), *Medica de lacte*, Præs. J.H. Schultze, J.C. Hilligeri, Halae Magdeburgicae

King, William (1731), *An Essay on the Origin of Evil*, London

Kircher, Athanasius (1987), *China Illustrata*, tr. Charles D. Van Tuyl, Oklahoma

Kirk, G.S. and Raven, J.E. (1960), *The Presocratic Philosophers*, Cambridge University Press, Cambridge

Kisbán, Eszter (1986), 'Food Habits in Change' in A. Fenton and E. Kisbán, eds, *Food in Change*, Glasgow, 2–10

Kish, John (1984), 'The Influence of Pierre Gassendi on John Locke's Theory of the Material World', Dissertation Abstract, Johns Hopkins University

Koch, Ebba (1988), *Shah Jahan and Orpheus*, Graz

Köhler, Joachim (2000), *Wagner's Hitler*, tr. R. Taylor, Polity, Cambridge

Kopf, David (1964), 'Orientalism and the Genesis of the Bengal Renaissance 1800–1830', Ph.D. thesis, University of Chicago, Illinois

Kristeller, Paul Oskar (1972), *Renaissance Concepts of Man and other Essays*, Harper Torchbook, New York

Kroll, Richard W.F. (1991), 'The Question of Locke's Relation to Gassendi', in Preston King, ed., *John Locke: Critical Assessments*, London, 397–418

Kroll, Richard W.F. (1984), 'The Question of Locke's relation to Gassendi', *Journal of the History of Ideas*, 43:3, 339–59

Kropotkin, Petr (1912), *Fields, Factories and Workshops*, London

Kropotkin, Petr (1914), *Mutual Aid: A Factor of Evolution*, W. Heinemann, London

Kuflik, Arthur (1998), 'Hume on Justice to Animals, Indians and Women', *Hume Studies*, 34:1, 53–70

Kuntz, Marion Leathers (1981), *Guillaume Postel*, The Hague

Kuntz, Marion Leathers (1999), *Venice, Myth and Utopian Thought*, Aldershot

Kurth-Voigt, Lieselotte E. (1999), *Continued Existence, Reincarnation, and the Power of Sympathy in Classical Weimar*, Camden House, Rochester

Lach, Donald F. (1971), *Asia in the Making of Europe, Volume I, Book One*, 2nd impression, Chicago and London

Lach, Donald F. and Kley, Edwin J. Van (1993), *Asia in the Making of Europe, Volume III: A Century of Advance; Book Two: South Asia*, Chicago

Lakowski, Romuald Ian (1999), 'Geography and the More Circle: John Rastell, Thomas More and the "New World"', *Renaissance Forum*, 4:1

Lamartine, Alphonse de (1832–3), *Souvenirs . . . pendant un voyage en Orient*, http://gallica.bnf.fr

Lamartine, Alphonse de (1849–51), *Confidences*, http://gallica.bnf.fr

Lambe, William (1805), *A Medical and Experimental Inquiry*, J. Mawman, London

Lambe, William (1809), *Reports on The Effects of a Peculiar Regimen*, J. Mawman, London

Lambe, William (1815), *Additional Reports on the Effects of a Peculiar Regimen*, J. Mawman, London

Lange, Carl Nicolaus ([1705]), *Idea historiæ naturalis lapidum figuratorum Helvetiæ, ejus viciniæ*, Lucernæ

Langer, Walter C. (1972), *The Mind of Adolf Hitler*, London

Laurentius, T.A. ([1749]), *Resp. Dissertatio inauguralis Medica de lactis discussione*, Præs. J.H. Kniphofio, Erfordiae

Lawrence, Bruce (1976), *Shahrastani on the Indian Religions*, Houton, The Hague

Lawrence, Christopher (1979), 'The Nervous System and Society in the

Scottish Enlightenment', in Shapin, Steven and Barnes, B., eds, *Natural Order: Historical Studies in Scientific Culture*, London

Lawrence, James Henry (1811), *Empire of the Nairs*, 4 vols, London

Lawrence, John ([1810]), *A Philosophical and Practical Treatise on Horses*, 2 vols, London

Lawrence, William (1819), *Lectures on Physiology*, J. Callow, London

Leach, Linda (1995), *Mughal and Other Indian Paintings from the Chester Beatty Library*, 2 vols, London

Lead, Jane (1695), *The Laws of Paradise*, London

Lead, Jane (1696), *A Message to the Philadelphian Society*, London

Leary, D.E. (1984), 'Nature, Art, and Imitation', *Studies in Eighteenth-Century Culture*, 13, 155–72

Leask, Nigel (1992), *British Romantic Writers and The East: Anxieties of Empire*, Oxford University Press

Leask, Nigel (2002), *Curiosity and the Aesthetics of Travel Writing, 1770–1840: 'From an Antique Land'*, Oxford University Press, New York

Ledel, Johann Samuel ([1713]), *Resp. Dissertatio . . . De arthritide, ejusque remedio saccharo lactis*, Præs. J.H. Slevogtio, Jenæ

Lee, Debbie (2002), *Slavery and the Romantic Imagination*, Philadelphia

Lee, Debbie (August 2002) 'Grave Dirt, Dried Toads, and the Blood of a Black Cat: How Aldridge Worked His Charms', in C. Rzepka, ed., *Obi: Romantic Circles Praxis Series*, http://www.rc.umd.edu/praxis/obi/lee/lee.html

Leeuwenhoek, A. van (1695), *Arcana Naturæ*, H. a Krooneveld, Delphis Batavorum

Leeuwenhoek, A. van (1722), *Opera Omnia*, J.A. Langerak, Lugduni Batavorum

Leeuwenhoek, A. van (1798), *The Select Works*, tr. Samuel Hoole, 2 vols, London

Leeuwenhoek, A. van (1962), *On the Circulation of the Blood*, Facsimile, Nieuwkoop

Leibniz, Gottfried Wilhelm (1686), *Discourse on Metaphysics*, tr. G.R. Montgomery, http://www.epistemelinks.com/Main/TextName.asp?PhilCode=Leib

Leibniz, Gottfried Wilhelm (1902), *Discourse on Metaphysics*, tr. G.R. Montgomery, Open Court Publishing, Chicago, www.class.uidaho.edu/mickelsen/texts/Leibniz%20-%20Discourse%20on%20Metaphysics.htm

Leibniz, Gottfried Wilhelm (1985), *The Monadology*, tr. Robert Latta [Garland, London], http://www.its.uidaho.edu/mickelsen/texts/Leibniz%20-%20Monadology.txt

Leibniz, Gottfried Wilhelm (2001), 'Reflections on the Souls of Beasts' [from *Epistolae ad diversos* (1734), ed. S. Kortholt, Lipsiae, p.189], tr. Donald Rutherford, http://philosophy2.ucsd.edu/~rutherford/Leibniz/beasts.htm

Lémery, Louis (1704), *A Treatise of Foods, in General*, London
Lempriere, J. (1808), *Universal Biography*, London
Lennon, Thomas M. (1993), *The Battle of the Gods and the Giants*, Princeton, New Jersey
León-Jones, Karen Silvia de (1997), *Giordano Bruno and the Kabbalah*, Yale University Press
Les Cases, Emmanuel de (1823), *Le Mémorial de Sainte-Hélène*, http://gallica.bnf.fr
Lesage, A.-R. (1977), *Histoire de Gil Blas de Santillane*, ed. R. Laufer, Paris
L'Espine, G.J. de (1723), *An Creatoris & Naturæ Legum imago, Carnisprivii Lex?* Praes. Philippe Hecquet
Lessius, Leonard, Cornaro, Luigi and Anon. (1634), *Hygiasticon . . . A Treatise of Temperance and Sobrietie . . . A Spare Diet*, Roger Daniel, Cambridge
Lessius, Leonardus (1742), *Hygiasticon*, London
Levine, Joseph M. (1997), 'John Evelyn: Between the Ancients and the Moderns', in O'Malley and Wolschke-Bulmahn, eds
Levy, Raphael (1927), *The Astrological Works of Abraham Ibn Ezra*, Baltimore, Maryland
Lilly, William ([1681]), *Doctor Lilly's last Legacy*, 3rd edn, J. Conyers, London
Linand, Barthelemy (1700), *L'Abstinence De La Viande Rendue Aisée*, P. Bienfait, Paris
Lind, James (1753), *A Treatise of the Scurvy*, Edinburgh
[Lind, James] Lindh, J. (1759), 'De Pingvedine Animali', Præs. C. Linnaeus, Upsala
Linnaeus, Carl (1781), *Select Dissertations from the Amœnitates Academicæ*, tr. F.J. Brand, 2 vols, G. Robinson, London
Linnaeus, Carl (1790), *Amoenitates Academicae*, 10 vols, J.J. Palm, Erlangae
Linschoten, John Huygen van (1988), *The Voyage . . . to the East Indies*, ed. A.C. Burnell, Asian Education Services, New Delhi
Litwack, David Michael (1977), 'Clarissa and La Nouvelle Héloïse', Dissertation Abstract, *Dissertation Abstracts International* 38
Lloyd, William (1699), *Account of the Life of Pythagoras*, H. Mortlock, London
Locke, John (1689), *A Letter Concerning Toleration*, A. Churchill, London
Locke, John (1690), *An Essay Concerning Human Understanding*
Locke, John (1692), *Some Thoughts Concerning Education*, http://www.fordham.edu/halsall/mod/1692locke-education.html
Locke, John (1858), *The Life and Letters of John Locke*, ed. Lord King, London
Locke, John (1994), *Second Treatise of Government* [1690], http://www.knuten.liu.se/bjoch509/works/locke.txt
Lockhart, J.G. ([1910]), *The Life of Sir Walter Scott*, 2 vols, London
Lockman, ed. (1743), *Travels of the Jesuits into Various Parts of the World*, London

Lonie, Iain M. (1981), 'Hippocrates the Iatromechanist', Medical History, 25:2, 113–50

Lonie, Iain M. (1985), 'The "Paris Hippocrates"', in Wear, French and Lonie, eds, 155–74

Lonsdale, Roger (1989), Eighteenth-Century Women Poets, Clarendon, Oxford

Lord, Henry (1630), A Display of two forraigne sects in the East Indies, F. Constable, London

Lorenzen, David N. (1996), 'Review of Vincent L. Wimbush and Richard Valantasis, eds, Asceticism (New York, OUP)', The Journal of Asian Studies, 55:4, 975–6

Lovejoy, A.O. (1933), 'Monboddo and Rousseau', Modern Philology, 30, 275–96

Lucian (1905), The Works of Lucian of Samosata, tr. H.W. Fowler and F.G. Fowler, 4 vols, Oxford

'Luria, Isaac' (1986), Gates of Reincarnation, Kabbalah Publishing

Lusane, Clarence (2003), Hitler's Black Victims, Routledge

Luxon, Thomas H. (1993), '"Not I, But Christ": Allegory and the Puritan Self', in ELH, 60:4, 899–937

Lynch, Jack (n.d.), 'Mary Shelley's Reading', http://www.english.upenn. edu/jlynch/FrankenDemo/MShelley/reading.html; accessed 2004

Lyne, Raphael (2001), Ovid's Changing Worlds: English Metamorphoses 1567–1632, Oxford University Press

Lysons, Daniel (1792–6), Environs of London

Macaulay, Catherine (1974), Letters on Education, ed. G. Luria, New York

Mack, Maynard (1985), Alexander Pope, A Life, New York

Maclaurin, Colin (1748), Isaac Newton's Philosophical Discoveries, ed. P. Murdoch, London

Maclean, Gerard, Landry, Donna and Ward, Joseph P., eds (1999), The Country and the City Revisited, Cambridge University Press, Cambridge

Maginus, Joannes Baptista (1670), De Podagra brevis disceptatio, in qua morbi idea, causa, et curatio ab usu lactis sine aliis cibariis proponuntur, Romæ

Maier, Michael (1617), Symbola Aureæ Mensæ Duodecim Nationum, Antonius Humius, Frankfurt

Maier, Michael (1619a), Tractatus de volucri arborea, Frankfurt

Maier, Michael (1619b), Verum inventum, Frankfurt

Maier, Michael (1656), Themis Aurea, N. Brooke, London

Maier, Michael (1687), Secreta naturae Chymica, Frankfurt

Maier, Michael (1717), Silentium post clamores, Frankfurt

Maimonides, Moses [Moses ben Maimūn] (1963), The Guide of the Perplexed, tr. Shlomo Pines, Chicago

Main, C.F. (1983), 'John Evelyn's Salads', Journal of the Rutgers University Libraries, 45:2, 82–93

Maistre de la Tour (1774 [i.e. 1784?]), *The History of Ayder Ali Khan*, 2 vols, W. Porter, Dublin

Majumdar, R.C., ed. (1960), *The Classical Accounts of India*, Calcutta

Makin, William Edward Anselm (1986), 'The Philosophy of Pierre Gassendi', Dissertation Abstract, Open University, UK

Malebranche, Nicolas (1694), *The Search after Truth*, tr. T. Taylor, London

Malebranche, Nicolas (1694[-5]), *Malebranch's Search after Truth*, tr. [R. Sault], 2 vols, S. Manship, London

Malebranche, Nicolas (1962), *Oeuvres Complètes*, ed. Geneviève Rodis-Lewis, Paris

Malebranche, Nicolas (1997), *The Search after Truth*, ed. T.M. Lennon and P.J. Olscamp, Cambridge

[Malthus, Thomas Robert] (1798), *Principle Of Population*, J. Johnson, London

Malthus, Thomas Robert (1826), *An Essay on the Principle of Population*, 2 vols, John Murray, London

[Mandeville, Bernard] (1714), *The Fable of the Bees*, J. Roberts, London

Mandeville, Bernard (1924), *Fable of the Bees*, ed. F.B. Kaye

Mandeville, Sir John (1900), *The Travels of Sir John Mandeville*, Macmillan

Manetho (1940) [*Works*], tr. W.G. Waddell, London; Cambridge, Mass.

Manners, V. and Williamson, G.C. (1920), *John Zoffany*, London

Manu (1794), *Institutes of Hindu law*, Calcutta

Manu (1971), *The Laws of Manu*, tr. G. Buhler, New York

Manucci, Niccolao (1965), *Storia Do Mogor*, tr. W. Irvine, 4 vols, Calcutta

Manuel, Frank E. (1963), *Isaac Newton, Historian*, Cambridge, Mass.

Manuel, Frank E. (1974), *The Religion of Isaac Newton*, Oxford

Marana, Giovanni P. [et al.?] (1970), [Selected] *Letters Writ by a Turkish Spy*, ed. A.J. Weitzman, London

– For the editions of *Turkish Spy* cited, see 'Abbreviations' page above.

Markley, Robert (1999), 'Newton, Corruption, and the Tradition of Universal History', in Force and Popkin, eds, 121–43

Marsay, C.H. Marquis St George de (1738), *Témoignage d'un Enfant . . . ou Explication des trois premiers chapitres de la Genese*, C.M. Regelein, Berlebourg

Marsay, C.H. Marquis St George de (1739) *Témoignage d'un Enfant . . . ou Explication mystique & literale De L'Acopalipse*, vol. I, C.M. Regelein, Berlebourg

Marsay, C.H. Marquis St George de (1749), *Spiritual Life*, T. & W. Ruddimans, Edinburgh

Marshal, John (1702), 'A letter from the East Indies', *Philosophical Transactions*, 22:268, S. Smith and Walford, London

Marshall, P.J., ed. (1970), *The British Discovery of Hinduism in the Eighteenth Century*, Cambridge

Marshall, P.J. (2000), 'The White Town of Calcutta Under the Rule of the East India Company', *Modern Asian Studies*, 34:2, 307–31

Martin, J.W. (1982), 'The Elizabethan Familists: A Separatist Group as Perceived by their Contemporaries', *Baptist Quarterly*, 29, 267–81

Masai, F. (1956), *Pléthon et le platonisme de Mistra*, Paris

Matton, Sylvian (1987), 'L'Egypte chez les "philosophes chymiques"', de Maier à Pernety', *Les Études Philosophiques*, 2–3, 207–26

Maty, M. (1755), *Life of Richard Mead*, J. Whiston, London

Mazza, M.F. and Tomasello, B. (1996), *Antonio Cocchi primo antiquario*, Modena

McCalman, Iain (1988), *Radical Underworld: Prophets, Revolutionaries and Pornographers in London, 1795–1840*, Cambridge University Press, Cambridge

McCalman, Iain (1995), 'New Jerusalems: Prophecy, Dissent and Radical Culture in England, 1786–1830', in Knud Haakonssen, ed., *Enlightenment and Religion: Rational Dissent in eighteenth-century Britain*, Cambridge University Press, Cambridge, 312–35

McCalman, Iain (1998), 'Newgate in Revolution: Radical Enthusiasm and Romantic Counterculture', *Eighteenth-Century Life*, 22:1, 95–110

McColley, Grant (1936), 'The Seventeenth-Century Doctrine of a Plurality of Worlds', *Annals of Science*, 1:4, 385–430

McCrindle, J.W. (1960), *Ancient India*, Calcutta

McDowell, Paula (1996), 'Tace Sowle (London: 1691–1749) Andrew Sowle (London: circa 1660–circa 1690)', in J. Bracken and J. Silver, eds, *The British Literary Book 1475–1700*, Gale, Detroit, 249–57

McDowell, Paula (2002), 'Enlightenment Enthusiasms and the Spectacular Failure of the Philadelphian Society', *Eighteenth-Century Studies*, 35:4, 515–33

McGuire, J.E. and Rattansi, P.M. (1966), 'Newton and the "Pipes of Pan"', *Notes and Records of the Royal Society of London*, 21:2, 108–43

McKee, David Rice (1941), *Simon Tyssot de Patot*, Baltimore

McLane, Maureen N. (1996), 'Literate Species: Populations, "Humanities," and Frankenstein', *ELH*, 63:4, 959–88

Mead, G.R.S. (1931), *Fragments of a Faith Forgotten*, 3rd edn, London

Mead, Richard (1751), *Medical Precepts and Cautions*, tr. T. Stack, W. Smith, Dublin

Mead, Richard (1755), *Medica Sacra*, tr. T. Stack, J. Brindley, London

Mead, Richard (1762), *The Medical Works*, 2 vols, C. Hitch, London

Medwin, Thomas (1913), *The Life of Percy Bysshe Shelley*, ed. H. Buxton Forman, Oxford University Press

Mellor, Anne K. (1993), *Romanticism & Gender*, London

Mercerus, Joannes (1598), *In Genesin . . . Commentarius*, ed. Theodorus Beza [Geneva]

Mercier, Louis Sébastien (1800), *New Picture of Paris*, 2 vols, H.D. Symonds, London

Merrett, Robert James (1991), 'Natural History and the Eighteenth-Century Novel', *Eighteenth-Century Studies*, 25:2, 145–70

Mertans, C. de (1809), 'Scurvy', *Philosophical Transactions . . . Abridged*, C. & R. Baldwin, London

Midelfort, H.C.E. (1994), *Mad Princes of Renaissance Germany*, Charlottesville

[Mickle, W.J.] (1787), 'Review of Holwell's *Intelligent Beings*', *The European Magazine*, vol. 11, March, London

Mill, John Stuart (1848), *Principles of Political Economy*, Boston

Mill, John Stuart (1969), *Essays on Ethics, Religion and Society*, ed. J.M. Robson, Routledge & Kegan Paul, London

Miller, Philip (1731), *The Gardeners Dictionary*, London

Miller, Webb (1938), *I Found No Peace*, New York

Milner, John (1700), *An account of Mr. Locke's religion*

Milton, Giles (2002), *Samurai William*, London

Milton, J.R. (2000), 'Locke and Gassendi: A reappraisal', in M.A. Stewart, ed., *English Philosophy in the Age of Locke*, Oxford, 87–111

Milton, John (1667), *Paradise Lost*, Peter Parker et al., London

Mirandola, Giovanni Pico della (1496), *Oratio de hominis dignitate*, Bologna, http://www.brown.edu/Departments/Italian_Studies/pico/oratio.html

Mirandola, Giovanni Pico della (n.d.), *Oration on the Dignity of Man*, http://cscs.umich.edu/crshalizi/Mirandola/

Miskolczy, Ambrus (2003), *Hitler's Library*, Budapest

Mitter, Partha (1977), *Much Maligned Monsters*, Oxford

Moffet, Thomas (1746), *Health's Improvement*, ed. C. Bennet, T. Osborne, London

Mohammed, Ovey N. (1984), *Averroes' Doctrine of Immortality*, Ontario

Molyneux, William (1709), *Dioptrica Nova*, 2nd edn, London

Monboddo, James Burnet, Lord (1773–92), *Of the Origin and Progress of Language*, 6 vols, A. Kincaid et al., Edinburgh

[Monboddo, James Burnet, Lord] (1795), *Antient Metaphysics*, IV, Bell, Edinburgh

[Monboddo, James Burnet, Lord] (1797), *Antient Metaphysics*, V, Bell, Edinburgh

Monro [I], Alexander (1744), *Comparative Anatomy*, John Nourse, London

Monro [I], Alexander (1783), *Comparative Anatomy*, ed. Alexander Monro [II], G. Robinson, Edinburgh

Montaigne, Michel de (1991), *The Complete Essays*, tr. M.A. Screech, Harmondsworth

Montaigne, Michel de (1999), *Montaigne's Essays*, tr. John Florio, Renascence Editions

Montenegro, F., and Jerónimo, B. (1780), *Essays*, tr. J. Brett, 4 vols, London

Montesquieu, Charles de (1914), *The Spirit of the Laws*, tr. Thomas Nugent [1752], revd J.V. Prichard, http://www.constitution.org/cm/sol.txt

Montluzin, Emily Lorraine de (n.d.), 'Attributions of Authorship in the

European Magazine, 1782–1826', http://etext.lib.virginia.edu/bsuva/euromag/

Moon, Elaine (1985), ' "Sacrific'd to my sex" – The Marriages of Samuel Richardson's Pamela and Mr B., and Mr and Mrs Harlowe', *Journal of the Australasian Universities Language and Literature Association*, 63, 19–32

Moor, Edward (1810), *The Hindu Pantheon*, J. Johnson, London

Moore, Charles (1790), *A Full Inquiry into the Subject of Suicide*, 2 vols, London

Moore, John (1669), *Moses Revived*, Gyles Meddowes, London

More, Henry (1662), *Philosophical Writings*, 2nd edn, J. Flesher, London

More, Henry (1682), *Annotations upon . . . Lux orientalis*, London

More, Henry (1712), *Philosophical Writings*, 4th edition, London

More, Louis Trenchard (1934), *Isaac Newton*, New York

More, Lucy (2000), *Amphibious Thing*, Auckland

Morgan, J. (1732), *Phœnix Britannicus*, 6 vols, London

Morgan, Thomas (1725), *Philosophical Principles of Medicine*, J. Darby, London

Morgan, Thomas (1735), *The Mechanical Practice of Physick*, T. Woodward, London

Mortimer, Russell S. (1948), 'The First Century of Quaker Printers, Part I', *The Journal of the Friends' Historical Society*, 40, 37–49

Morton, A.L. (1970), *The World of the Ranters*, London

Morton, Timothy (1994), *Shelley and The Revolution in Taste: The Body and The Natural World*, Cambridge University Press, Cambridge

Morton, Timothy (1998a), 'Blood Sugar', in Peter J. Kitson and Timothy Fulford, eds, *Romanticism and Colonialism: Writing and Empire, 1780–1830*, Cambridge, 87–106

Morton, Timothy (1998b), 'The Pulses of the Body: Romantic Vegetarian Rhetoric and its Cultural Contexts', in Kevin Cope, ed., *1650–1850: Ideas, Aesthetics, and Inquiries in the Early Modern Era*, 4, New York, 53–88

Morton, Timothy (2000), *The Poetics of Spice*, Cambridge

Morton, Timothy (2002), 'The Plantation of Wrath', in Timothy Morton and Nigel Smith, eds, 64–85

Morton, Timothy and Smith, Nigel, eds (2002), *Radicalism in British Literary Culture, 1650–1830: From Revolution to Revolution*, Cambridge University Press, Cambridge

Moseley, Benjamin (1800), *A Treatise on Sugar*, 2nd edn, London

Moss, Jean Dietz (1975), 'The Family of Love and English Critics', *The Sixteenth Century Journal*, 6:1, 35–52

Moss, Jean Dietz (1981), ' "Godded with God": Hendrik Niclaes and His Family of Love', *Transactions of the American Philosophical Society*, 71:8

Muddford, Peter G. (1968), 'William Lawrence and *The Natural History of Man* (1819)', *Journal of the History of Ideas*, 430–6

Muggleton, Lodowick (1699), *The Acts of the Witnesses of the Spirit*, London

Mullan, John (1988), *Sentiment and Sociability*, Clarendon, Oxford

Mullan, John (2001), 'The lonely goatherd', *Times Literary Supplement*, no. 5135, 31 August, p.22

Mullett, Charles (1937), 'A letter by Joseph Glanvill on the Future State', *Huntington Library Quarterly*, 1:4, 447–56

Murr, Sylvia (1987), *L'Inde Philosophique entre Bossuet et Voltaire*, 2 vols, Paris

Murr, Sylvia (1992), 'Bernier et le gassendisme', in *Bernier et les Gassendistes: Corpus: revue de philosophie*, 20–1, ed. Sylvia Murr, 115–35.

Murr, Sylvia (1993), 'Gassendi's scepticism as a religious attitude', in Richard H. Popkin and Arjo Vanderjagt, eds, *Scepticism and Irreligion in the seventeenth and eighteenth centuries*, Leiden, 12–31

Murray, Alexander, ed. (1998), *Sir William Jones 1746–1794*, Oxford University Press, New York

Murray, John J. (1957), 'The Cultural Impact of the Flemish Low Countries on Sixteenth and Seventeenth-Century England', *The American Historical Review*, 62:4, 837–54

Murti, Vasu (n.d.), *They Shall Not Hurt or Destroy*, Oakland, Calif.

Nashe, Thomas (1592), *Pierce Penilesse*, Abell Jesses, London

Nashe, Thomas (1599), *Lenten Stuffe*, N.L. and C.B., London

Nauert, Charles G. (1965), *Agrippa and the Crisis of Renaissance Thought*, University of Illinois Press, Urbana

Nehora.com (n.d.), 'Rabbi Yitzchak Luria Ashkenazi – The Ari', www.judaicaplus.com

Neill, Stephen (2002), *A History of Christianity in India 1707–1858*, Cambridge University Press

Nelson, Robert (1739), *A Companion For The Festivals and Fasts*, 17th edn, London

Newton, Isaac (1713), *Principia Mathematica*, 2nd edn, Cambridge

Newton, Isaac (1728), *The Chronology of Ancient Kingdoms Amended*, T. Longman, London

[Newton, Isaac] (n.d.), *Reponse aux Observations sur la Chronologie de M. Newton*, n.p.

Newton, Isaac (1950), *Theological Manuscripts*, ed. H. McLaclan, Liverpool

Newton, Isaac (1959), *The Correspondence*, ed. H.W. Turnbull, Cambridge

Newton, John Frank (1821), *Three Enigmas*, Thomas Hookham, London

Newton, John Frank (1897), *The Return to Nature* [1811], ed. C.W. Forward, London

Nicholl, Charles (2004), *Leonardo da Vinci*, Harmondsworth

Nichols, Ashton (1991), 'The Loves of Plants and Animals: Romantic Science and the Pleasures of Nature', *Romantic Circles Praxis Series*:

Romanticism and Ecology, http://www.rc.umd.edu/praxis/ecology/
nichols/nichols.html

Nicholson, E.B. (1879), *The Rights of an Animal: A New Essay in Ethics*,
London

[Nicholson, George, ed.?] (1796), *Preceptive, moral, & sentimental pieces*,
G. Nicholson, [Manchester]; Whitrow, London

Nicholson, George (1797), *On The Conduct of Man to Inferior Animals*,
G. Nicholson, Manchester; Whitrow, London

[Nicholson, George, ed.?] (1798), *Moral philosophy*, G. Nicholson,
Manchester

Nicholson, George, ed. (1803), *On Food*, George Nicholson, Pougnill; H.D.
Symonds, London

Nicholson, George (1999), *George Nicholson's On the Primeval Diet of Man
(1801)*, ed. Rod Preece, New York

[Niclaes, Hendrik] (1574), *Peace upon Earth*, [Amsterdam?]

Niclaes, Hendrik ([1575a?]), *Terra Pacis*, [Amsterdam?]

Niclaes, Hendrik ([1575b?]), *The Proverbes of HN*, [tr. C.Vitell],
[Amsterdam?]

Niclaes, Hendrik (1649), *An Introduction To The Holy Understanding*,
London

Nizami, Khaliq Ahmad (1991), *Shaikh Nizam-u'd-din Auliya*, Idarah-i
Adabyat-i Delli, Delhi

Nobili, Roberto de (1971), *Adaptation*, ed. S. Rajamanickam,
Palayamkottai

Norwood, Captain Robert (1651[-2]), *Proposals for the propagation of the
Gospel, Offered to the Parliament*, London

Nuttall, Geoffrey F. (1954), *James Nayler*, Friends' Historical Society,
London

O'Flaherty, Wendy Doniger (1976), *The Origins of Evil in Hindu Mythology*,
Berkeley

O'Flaherty, Wendy Doniger, ed. (1980), *Karma and Rebirth in Classical
Indian Traditions*, Berkeley

O'Malley, Therese and Wolschke-Bulmahn, Joachim, eds (1997), *John
Evelyn's 'Elysium Britannicum' and European Gardening*, Washington

Obeyesekere, Gananath (1980), 'The Rebirth of Eschatology and its
Transformations', in Wendy Doniger O'Flaherty, ed., 137–64

Odes, by George Dyer . . . &c. ([c.1802]), G. Nicholson, Ludlow; H.D.
Symonds, London

Oerlemans, Onno (1994), ' "The meanest thing that feels":
Anthropomorphizing animals in Romanticism', *Mosaic*, 27:1

Oerlemans, Onno (2002), *Romanticism and the Materiality of Nature*,
Toronto

Offer, Avner (1991), *Agrarian History of the First World War*, Oxford

Olearius, Adam (1669), *Voyages and Travels*, 2nd edn, J. Starkey, London

Oliphant, Charles (1702), *A Short Answer To Two Lybels*, [Edinburgh?]

Origen (2005), *Against Celsus* [*ANF*, vol. 4, 1885], http://www.newadvent. org/fathers

Oswald, John, ed. (1788), *The British Mercury*, new edn, J. Ridgway, London

[Oswald, John] Silvester Otway (1789), *Poems . . . The Humours of John Bull*, J. Murray, London

Oswald, John (1791), *The Cry of Nature; Or, an Appeal to Mercy and to Justice, on Behalf of the Persecuted Animals*, J. Johnson, London

Oswald, John ([1792]), *Review of the Constitution of Great-Britain*, 3rd edn [Paris]

Oswald, John (1793), *Le Gouvernement du Peuple*, L'Imprimerie des Révolutions, Paris

O[verton], R[ichard] (1643), *Mans Morallitie*, J. Canne, Amsterdam [i.e. London]

Ovid (1567), *The. xv. Bookes of P. Ovidus Naso, entytuled Metamorphosis*, tr. Arthur Golding, ed. B.F., London, www.elizabethanauthors.com

Ovid (1632), *Ovid's Metamorphosis*, tr. George Sandys, http:// etext.virginia.edu/

Ovid (1717), *Ovid's Metamorphoses*, ed. Samuel Garth, J. Tonson, London

Ovington, John (1929), *A Voyage to Surat in the Year 1689*, ed. H.G. Rawlinson, Oxford

Owenson, Sydney, Lady Morgan (1811), *The Missionary*, 2nd edn, 3 vols, London

Oxford Dictionary of National Biography (2004), ed. H.C.G. Matthew and Brian Harrison, Oxford University Press, Oxford [*ODNB*]

Pagel, Walter (1982), *Joan Baptista Van Helmont*, Cambridge

Pagès, F.X. (1797), *Secret history of the French Revolution*, 2 vols, London

Pagès, P.M.F. de (1791–2), *Travels round the world*, 3 vols, J. Murray, London

Pailin, David A. (1984), *Comparative religion in seventeenth- and eighteenth-century Britain*, Manchester

Pal, Pratapaditya (1994), *The Peaceful Liberators*, New York and Los Angeles

Paley, William (1785), *Elements of Moral and Political Philosophy*, London

Palladius et al. (1665), *De Gentibus Indiæ et Bragmanibus*, ed. Edward Bysshe, T. Roycroft, London

Pallierius, Paulus Franciscus (1663), *De vera lactis genesi et usu*, Genuæ

Paracelsus (1656), *Dispensatory And Chirugery*, tr. W.D., T.M., London

Paracelsus (1979), *Selected Writings*, tr. N. Guterman, ed. J. Jacobi, Princeton University Press, New York

Parker, Thomas (1782), *Evidence of our transactions in the East Indies*, London

Parry, Graham (1992), 'John Evelyn as Hortulan Saint', in M. Leslie and

T. Raylor, eds, *Culture and Cultivation in Modern England – Writing the Land*, Leicester

Passmore, John (1974), *Man's Responsibility for Nature*, New York

Passmore, John (1975), 'The Treatment of Animals', *Journal of the History of Ideas*, 36:2, 195–218

Pasta, Giuseppe (1795), *La Tolleranza . . . Lettere Inedite del . . . Antonio Cocchi*, 3rd edn, Venezia

Patris, B. Combes De (1930), *Des Gardes Françaises a la Convention: Valady (1766–1793)*, E. Boccard, Paris

Patrizi, Francisco (1593), *Pampsychia, in Nova de universis philosophia*, Venice

Payne, Robert (1973), *The Life and Death of Adolph Hitler*, London

Peacock, Thomas Love (1909), *Memoirs of Shelley*, ed. H.F. Brett-Smith, London

Peacock, Thomas Love (2001), *Letters*, ed. Nicholas A. Joukovsky, 2 vols, Oxford University Press

[Pemberton, Henry] (1728), *Sir Isaac Newton's Philosophy*, S. Palmer, London

Penny, A.J. (1912), *Studies in Jacob Böhme*, John M. Watkins, London

Perkins, David (2003), *Romanticism and Animal Rights*, Cambridge University Press, Cambridge

Perry, Ruth (1999), 'Colonizing the Breast: Sexuality and Maternity in Eighteenth-Century England', in R. DeMaria, ed., *British Literature 1640–1789*, Blackwell, Oxford, 302–32

Pettus, Sir John (1674), *Volatiles from the History of Adam and Eve*

Philanthropos, N.N. [pseud.] (1690), *A Letter To a Gentleman*, A. Churchill, London

Phillips, Richard (1826), *Golden Rules of Social Philosophy*, London

Philosophical Transactions (1700 [o.s.]), *For the Month of January 1700*

Philosophical Transactions (1702), *For the Years 1700 and 1701*, vol. XXII, S. Smith and Walford, London

Philosophical Transactions (1716), *and Collections To the end of the Year 1700*, Abridg'd, ed. John Lowthorp, 2nd edn, R. Knaplock et al., London

Philosophical Transactions (1721) *(From the Year 1700 to the Year 1720)*. Abridg'd, vol. V, Part i, ed. Henry Jones, G. Strahan, London,

Philosophical Transactions (1734), *(From the Year 1719, to the Year 1733)* Abridged, vols VI–VII, ed. J. Eames and J. Martyn, J. Brotherton et al., London

Philostratus, Flavius (1709), *Vita Apollonii*, ed. G. Olearius, Lipsiae

Philostratus, Flavius (1912), *The Life of Apollonius of Tyana*, tr. F.C. Conybeare, 2 vols, London

Picart, Bernard (1733–7), *Ceremonies and Religious Customs*, 6 vols, C. du Bosc, London

Pigott, Charles (1795), *A Political Dictionary*, D.I. Eaton, London

Pigott, Robert ([1792]), *Discours . . . contre le grand usage du pain*, [Paris?]

Pillai, Ananda Ranga (1907–28), *The Private Diary*, tr. J.F. Price, 12 vols, Madras

Pillei, A. Muttusamu (1840), 'A Brief Sketch of the Life and Writing of Father C.J. Beschi', *Madras Journal of Literature and Science*, 250–300

Pinson, DovBer (1999), *Reincarnation and Judaism*, J. Aronson, Northvale

Piolet, J.-B. (1901), *Les Missions Catholiques Françaises au XIXe Siècle*, Paris

Pitcairne, Archibald (1701), *Dissertationes Medicæ*, Regneri Leers, Rotterdam

Pitcairne, Archibald (1713), *Dissertationes Medicæ*, R. Freebairn, Edinburgh

Pitcairne, Archibald (1715), *The Works* [tr. G. Sewell], E.Curll, London

Pitcairne, Archibald (1718a), *The Philosophical and Mathematical Elements Of Physick*, J. Osborn, London

Pitcairne, Archibald (1718b), *Elementa Medicinæ Physico-mathematica*, H. Scheurleer, Hague

Pitcairne, Archibald (1722), *Opera Omnia*, new edn, 2 vols, H. Scheurleer, Hagae

Pitcairne, Archibald (1727), *The Whole Works*, 2nd edn, J. Innys, London

Plard, Henri (1970), 'La Médiatrice Cosmique: La Vierge Sophie de Jacob Böhme', in *L'Univers à la Renaissance*, Bruxelles

Plat, Sir Hugh (1608), *Floraes Paradise*, William Leake, London

Plato (1956), *The Republic*, tr. P. Shorey, 2 vols, London; Cambridge, Mass.

Pletho [George Gemistos] (1689), 'Oracula magica Zoroastris', in *Sibyllina Oracula*, ed. J. Opsopoeus, Paris

Pletho [George Gemistos] (1754), *Zoroastreorum et Platonicorum dogmatum compendium*, in J.A. Fabricius, *Bibliotheca Graeca*, vol. 14, Hamburg

Pletho [George Gemistos] (1858), *Traité des Lois*, tr. A. Pellissier, Paris

Plomer, Henry R. (1968a), *Dictionary of the Booksellers and Printers . . . From 1641 to 1667*, Oxford

Plomer, Henry R. (1968b), *Dictionary of the Printers and Booksellers . . . 1668 to 1725*, ed. A. Esdaile, Oxford

Plotinus (1952), *Enneads*, tr. Stephen MacKenna and B.S. Page, Chicago

Plutarch (1928), *The Lives of the Noble Grecians and Romanes*, tr. J. Amyot and T. North, 8 vols, Houghton Miflin, New York

Plutarch (1995), *Moralia*, vol. XII, tr. H. Cherniss and W.C. Hembold, Loeb, Cambridge, Mass.; London

Pococke, Edward (1650), *Specimen Historiae*, H. Hall, H. Robinson, Oxford

[Pococke, Edward] (1674), *Oriental Philosophy*, (n.p.)

Polak, Henry S.L. (1953), 'Gandhi and Thoreau', *Thoreau Society Bulletin*, 45, 3–4

Polak, Millie, (2005), 'Interview', BBC Radio 4 Broadcast

Poliakov, Léon (1974), *The Aryan Myth*, tr. E. Howard, London

Pollock, Sheldon (1993) 'Rāmāyana and Political Imagination in India', *The Journal of Asian Studies*, 52:2, 261–97

Polo, Marco (1972), *The Travels*, tr. R.E. Latham, Harmondsworth

Ponsonby, D.A. (1949), *Call a Dog Hervey*, London

Poole, Kristen (2000), *Radical Religion from Shakespeare to Milton*, Cambridge

Poole, William (2004), 'Seventeenth-Century Preadamism', *The Seventeenth Century*, 19:1, 1–35

[Pope, Alexander] (1729), in *The Guardian*, 2 vols, J. Tonson, London, no. 61, 21 May 1713, I, 259–64

Pope, Alexander (1993), *Alexander Pope*, ed. Pat Rogers, Oxford

Popkin, Richard H. (1979), *The History of Scepticism from Erasmus to Spinoza*, Berkeley

Popkin, Richard H. (1987a), *Isaac La Peyrère (1596–1676)*, New York

Popkin, Richard H. (1987b), 'A late seventeenth-century attempt to convert the Jews to Reformed Judaism', in Shmuel Almog et al., eds, *Israel and the Nations*, Jerusalem, xxv–xlv

Popkin, Richard H. (1990a), 'Polytheism, Deism, and Newton', in Force and Popkin, eds, 27–42

Popkin, Richard H. (1990b), 'The Crisis of Polytheism and the answers of Vossius, Cudworth, and Newton', in Force and Popkin, eds

Popkin, Richard H. (1992), *The Third Force in Seventeenth-Century Thought*, Leiden

Popkin, Richard H. (1998), 'The religious background of seventeenth-century philosophy', in D. Garber and M. Ayers, eds, *The Cambridge History of Seventeenth-Century Philosophy*, 2 vols, Cambridge, I.393–422

Porphyry (1823), *Select Works of Porphyry*, tr. Thomas Taylor, T. Rodd, London

Porphyry (2000), *On Abstinence from Killing Animals*, tr. Gillian Clark, Duckworth, London

Porritt, Jonathon (2006), 'Hard to Swallow', *Guardian: Society Guardian*, 4 January

Porter, Roy (1982), 'The Sexual Politics of James Graham', *British Journal for Eighteenth-Century Studies*, 5, 199–206

Porter, Roy (1984), 'Sex and the Singular Man: The Seminal Ideas of James Graham', *Studies on Voltaire and the Eighteenth Century*, 228, 3–22

Porter, Roy, ed. (1985), *Patients and Practitioners*, Cambridge University Press, Cambridge

Porter, Roy and Roberts, Mary Mulvey, eds (1993), *Literature and Medicine During the Eighteenth Century*, London

Postel, Guillaume (1553?a), *De originibus, seu, de varia et potissimum orbi Latino ad hanc diem incognita*, Basel

Postel, Guillaume (1553?b), *Des merveilles du monde, et principalement des admirables choses des Indes et du nouveau monde*, [Paris?]

Postel, Guillaume (1969), *Le Thresor des Prophéties De l'Univers*, ed. François Secret, The Hague

Postel, Guillaume (1981), *Postelliana*, ed. François Secret, Nieuwkoop

Postel, Guillaume (1986), *De Etruriae Regionis Originibus Institutis Religione et Moribus*, ed. Giovanni Cipriani, Rome

Pottle, Frederick A. (1966), *James Boswell. The Earlier Years 1740–1769*, London

Powicke, Frederick A., ed. (1926), 'The Reverend Richard Baxter's Last Treatise', *Bulletin of the John Rylands Library*, 10

Prasad, R.C. (1968), *Early English Travellers in India*, London

Pratt, Samuel Jackson (1779), *Shenstone-Green*, 3 vols, R. Baldwin, London

Pratt, Samuel Jackson (1781), *Sympathy*, 2nd edn, London

Pratt, Samuel Jackson (1786), *The Triumph of Benevolence*, J. Nichols, London

Pratt, Samuel Jackson (1788), *Humanity, or The Rights of Nature*, T. Cadell, London

Preece, Rod (2003), 'Darwinism, Christianity, and the Great Vivisection Debate', *Journal of the History of Ideas*, 64:3, 399–419

Pressick, George (n.d.), *A briefe Relation of some of the most Remarkable Passages of the Anabaptists*, n.p.

Prest, John (1981), *The Garden of Eden*

Price, Richard (1787), *Sermons on the Christian Doctrine*, London

Priestley, Joseph (1782), *Disquisitions Relating to Matter and Spirit*, 2nd edn, 2 vols, Birmingham

Priestley, Joseph (1799), *A Comparison of the Institutions of Moses with those of the Hindoos*, Northumberland

Primatt, Humphrey (1776), *A Dissertation on the Duty of Mercy and Sin of Cruelty to Brute Animals*, J. Dodsley, London

Primaudaye, Pierre de la (1618), *The French Academie*, London

Proctor, Robert N. (1999), *The Nazi War on Cancer*, Princeton University Press, Princeton

Pryme, Abraham de la (1880), 'Memoirs of Thomas Bushell "The Recluse of the Calf"', in *Manx Miscellanies Vol. II*, ed. W. Harrison, *The Manx Society*, 30, Douglas, Isle of Man

Pseudo-Clement (2005a), *Recognitions of Clement* [*ANF*, vol. 8, 1886], http://www.newadvent.org/fathers

Pseudo-Clement (2005b), *The Clementine Homilies* [*ANF*, vol. 8, 1886], http://www.newadvent.org/fathers/

Pufendorf, Samuel Freiherr von (1749), *The Law of Nature and Nations*, 5th edn, London

Purchas, Samuel, ed. (1625), *Purchas his Pilgrimes*, W. Stansby, London

Purchas, Samuel (1626), *Purchas his Pilgrimage*, 4th edn, H. Fetherstone, London

Purchas, Samuel, ed. (1905–7), *Hakluytus Posthumus*, 20 vols, Glasgow

Purchase, Graham (2003), 'Peter Kropotkin: Ecologist, Philosopher and Revolutionary', Ph.D. dissertation, University of New South Wales, Sydney, Australia, http://www.library.unsw.edu.au/~thesis/adt-NUN/uploads/approved/adt-NUN20041011.094306/public/02whole.pdf

Quasten, J. (1942), 'A Pythagorean Idea in Jerome', *American Journal of Philology*, 63, 207–15

Quincey, Thomas De (1890), *The Collected Writings*, ed. D. Masson, 14 vols

Quintilius, J.P. (n.d.), *Responsio medica philosophica*, n.p.

Raben, Joseph (1963), 'Shelley's *Prometheus Unbound*: Why the Indian Caucasus?', *Keats-Shelley Journal*, 12, 95–106

Radcliffe, Ann (1980), *The Mysteries of Udolpho*, ed. B. Dobree, Oxford

Radcliffe, Ann (1993), *A Sicilian Romance*, ed. Alison Milbank, Oxford

Radcliffe, A. and Thornton, P. (1978), 'John Evelyn's Cabinet', *Connoisseur*, 197, 254–62

[Radicati, Alberto] (1730), *Christianity Set in a True Light*, J. Peele, London

Radicati, Alberto (1734), *Twelve Discourses Concerning Religion and Government*, 2nd edn, London

Radicati, Alberto (1737), *A Succinct History of Priesthood*, H. Gorham, London

Rajamanickam, S. (1967), *Roberto de Nobili and Adaptation*

Ramsay, Chevalier Andrew Michael (1727), *The Travels of Cyrus*, 2 vols, J. Peele, London

Ramsay, Chevalier Andrew Michael (1730), *The Travels of Cyrus*, 4th edn, London

Ramsay, Chevalier Andrew Michael (1748), *Natural and Revealed Religion*, 2 vols, R. Foulis, Glasgow

Ramsay, John (1888), *Scotland and Scotsmen*, ed. A. Allardyce, 2 vols, Edinburgh

Ramsay, John (1966), *Letters*, ed. B.L.H. Horn, Edinburgh

Ramsay, John (1996), *Scotland and Scotsmen*, Bristol

Rattansi, Piyo (1972), 'Newton's Alchemical Studies' in Debus, ed., II.183–98

Rauschning, Hermann (1939), *Hitler Speaks*, London

Rauschning, Hermann (2004), *Voice of Destruction*, Kessinger Publishing

Ravenstein, E.G., ed. (1898), *The First Voyage of Vasco da Gama*, London

Rawlinson, John (1612), *Mercy to a Beast*, Oxford

Ray, John (1717), *The Wisdom of God Manifested in the Works of the Creation*, 7th edn [W. Inys, London], www.jri.org.uk/ray

Raynal, Abbé W.T. (1783), *A Philosophical and Political History . . . of the Europeans in the East and West Indies*, rev. edn, tr. J.O. Justamond, 8 vols, W. Strahan, London

Reclus, Élisée (1901), 'On Vegetarianism', *Humane Review*, www.veginfo.dk/eng/texts/reclus.html

Reclus, Élisée (1927), 'The Great Kinship', tr. Edward Carpenter in J. Ishill, ed., *Élisée and Élie Reclus*, New Jersey, 51–4

Redlich, Fritz (1998), *Hitler: Diagnosis of a Destructive Prophet*, Oxford University Press, Oxford

Rees, Abraham et al., eds (1819), *The Cyclopædia; or Universal Dictionary*, 39 vols, Longman et al., London

Reeve, John [and Lodowicke Muggleton?] (1711), *Transcendent Spiritual Treatise*, [London?]

Regan, Marie Marguerite (2001), 'The Roasting of John Bull: Vegetarian Protest in Eighteenth Century English Literature', unpublished Ph.D. dissertation, University of Arkansas

Reid, Thomas (1795), *Directions for Warm and Cold Sea-bathing*, Dublin

Reid, Thomas (1798), *Phthisis Pulmonalis*, 3rd edn, London

Reinders, Eric Robert (2004), 'Blessed Are the Meat Eaters: Christian Antivegetarianism and the Missionary Encounter with Chinese Buddhism', *Positions: East Asia Cultures Critique*, 12:2, 509-37

Renbourn, E.T. (1960), 'The Natural History of Insensible Perspiration', *Medical History*, 4:2, 135-52

Reuchlin, Johann (1983), *De Arte Cabalistica*, tr. Sarah Goodman, New York

Reynolds, John (1725), *Three Letters to the Deist. I. Demanding his Warrant for Eating of Flesh*, London

[Rheims, The English College of] (1582), *The New Testament of Jesus Christ*, John Fogny, Rhemes

Rhodiginus, L.C. [Richerius] (1542), *Lectionum Antiquarum* [ed. C. Richier], Basil

Richards, John F. (2000), *The New Cambridge History of India*, I.5: *The Mughal Empire*, Cambridge

Richardson, Samuel (1742), *Pamela: Or, Virtue Rewarded* [Parts 3 and 4], 3rd edn, J. Rivington, London

Richardson, Samuel (1749), *Meditations Collected from the Sacred Books*, printed privately

Richardson, Samuel (1754), *Sir Charles Grandison*, Chadwyck-Healey, Cambridge

Richardson, Samuel (1985a), *Pamela* [Parts 1 and 2], ed. Peter Sabon, Harmondsworth

Richardson, Samuel (1985b), *Clarissa*, ed. Angus Ross, Harmondsworth

Richardson, Samuel (1996a), *Familiar Letters* [J. Rivington, London, 1750], Chadwyck-Healey, Cambridge

Richardson, Samuel (1996b), *Sir Charles Grandison* [J. & J. Rivington, London, 1754], Chadwyck-Healey, Cambridge

Ridderus, Franciscus (1669), *De Beschaemde Christen door Het Geloof en Leven van Heydenen en anderer natuerlijcke Menschen*, Joannes Bortius, Rotterdam

Rifkin, Jeremy (1992), *Beyond Beef*, New York

Ritson, Joseph (1802), *An Essay on Abstinence from Animal Food as a Moral Duty*, Richard Phillips, London

Ritson, Joseph (1833), *The Letters of Joseph Ritson* [ed. Joseph Frank], London

Robertson, Alexander ([1752?]), *Poems, on Various Subjects and Occasions*, C. Alexander, Edinburgh

Robertson, William (1802), *An Historical Disquisition concerning The Knowledge which the Ancients had of India*, 4th edn, T. Cadell, London

Robinson, Catherine (2000), 'Druids and Brahmins: A Case of Mistaken Identity?', *Diskus*, 6, http://www.uni-marburg.de/religionswissenschaft/journal/diskus

Rocher, Rosane (1983), *Orientalism, Poetry and the Millennium: The Checkered Life of Nathaniel Brassey Halhed, 1751–1830*, Motilal Banarsidass, Delhi

Rocher, Rosane (1993), 'British Orientalism in the Eighteenth Century', in C.A. Breckenridge and P. van der Veer, eds, *Orientalism and the Postcolonial Predicament*, Philadelphia

Rodger, N.A.M. (2004), *The Command of the Ocean*

Rodgers, J. (1986), 'Sensibility, Sympathy and Benevolence', in L.J. Jordanova, ed., *Languages of Nature*, London

Rodis-Lewis, Geneviève (1998), *Descartes*, tr. J.M. Todd, Ithaca

Roe, Thomas (1990), *The Embassy of Sir Thomas Roe to India 1615–19*, ed. William Foster, New Delhi

Roe, William? (1662), *Christian Liberty*, W[illiam].H[all]., Oxford

Roerer, J.G.J. (1739), *Circa noxium et salutarem usum lactis*, Præs. A.E. Büchner, Heringii, Erfordiæ

Roger, Jules (1889), *Hecquet*, Retaux-Bray, Paris

Rogerius, Abraham (1651), *De Open-Deure*, F. Hackes, Leyden

Rogerius, Abraham (1663), *Offne Thür*, Johann Andreas Endters, Nürnberg

Rogerius, Abraham (1670), *La Porte Ouverte*, tr. T. la Grue, J. Schipper, Amsterdam

Rogers, Frederick (1903) 'One of Cromwell's Soldiers', *The Treasury*, I, 1082–6

[Rogers, John] (1579), *The Displaying of an horrible Secte*, London

Roland, Manon Philipon (1835), *Lettres Autographes*, E. Renduel, Paris

Roland, Manon Philipon (1902), *Lettres, 1788–1793*, ed. C. Perroud, Paris

Ronconius, Joannes (1631), *De seri lactis natura*, F. Honofrij, Florentiæ

Rosenfield, Leonora (née Cohen) (1968), *From Beast-Machine To Man-Machine*, New York

Rosenroth, Knorr von, et al., eds (1677), *Kabbala Denudata*, A. Lichtenhaleri, Sulzbaci

Rosenroth, Knorr von, et al., eds (1684), *Kabbalæ Denudatæ*, [II], J.D. Zunneri, Frankfurt

Rosenroth, Knorr von (1991), *The Kabbalah Unveiled*, tr. S.L.M. Mathers, Harmondsworth

Rossi, Sergio, ed. (1987), *Science and Imagination in Eighteenth Century British Culture*, Milan

Rostvig, Maren-Sofie (1954), *The Happy Man*, Oxford

Rousseau, G.S. (1976), 'Nerves, Spirits, Fibres: Towards Defining the Origins of Sensibility', in R. Brissenden and J.C. Eade, eds, *Studies in the Eighteenth Century III*, Canberra, 137–57

Rousseau, G.S. (1988), 'Mysticism and Millenarianism: "Immortal Dr. Cheyne"', in Richard H. Popkin, ed., *Millenarianism and Messianism*, New York, 81–126

Rousseau, Jean-Jacques (1754), *The Origin Of Inequality*, tr. G.D.H. Cole, http://www.constitution.org/jjr/ineq05.htm

Rousseau, Jean-Jacques (1755), *L'Origine et les Fondements de l'Inegalite*, M.M. Rey, Amsterdam, http://un2sg4.unige.ch/athena/rousseau/jjr_ineg.html

Rousseau, Jean-Jacques (1953), *The Confessions*, tr. J.M. Cohen, Harmondsworth

Rousseau, Jean-Jacques (1973), *Les Confessions*, ed. B. Gagnebin et al., Gallimard, Paris

Rousseau, Jean-Jacques (1979), *Emile or On Education*, tr. Alan Bloom, Harmondsworth

Rousseau, Jean-Jacques (1997a), *Julie, Or The New Heloise*, tr. P. Stewart and J. Vaché, London

Rousseau, Jean-Jacques (1997b), *The Discourses*, tr. Victor Gourevitch, Cambridge

Rousseau, Jean-Jacques (1998), *The Social Contract*, tr. H.J. Tozer, Hertfordshire

Roy, Parama (2002), 'Meat-eating, Masculinity, and Renunciation in India: A Gandhian Grammar of Diet', *Gender & History*, 14:1, 62–91

Roy, Rammohun (1997), *The Correspondence*, ed. D.K. Biswas, Saraswat Library, Calcutta

Rubiés, Joan-Pau (2000), *Travel and Ethnology in the Renaissance*, Cambridge

Rubiés, Joan-Pau and Elsner, Jas, eds (1999), *Voyages and Visions: Towards a Cultural History of Travel*, London

Rudrum, Alan (1989), 'Henry Vaughan, the Liberation of the Creatures, and Seventeenth-Century English Calvinism', *The Seventeenth Century*, 4:1, 33–54

Rudrum, Alan (2003), 'Ethical Vegetarianism in Seventeenth-Century Britain', *The Seventeenth-Century*, 18:1, 76–92

Runt, Roseann (1978), 'Nurture and Culture', *Eighteenth-Century Life*, 4:3

[Rust, George?] (1661), *A Letter Of Resolution Concerning Origen*, London

[Rust, George?] (1721), 'A Letter of Resolution', in *A Collection of Choice, Scarce, and Valuable Tracts*, G. Strahan, London

Ryan, Cornelius (1999), *The Longest Day*, Ware

Ryland, John (1776), *The Preceptor, or Counsellor of Human Life*, London

Sabinus, George (1584), *Fabularum Ovidii Interpretatio*, Cambridge

Sade, Marquis de (2003), *Incest*, tr. Andrew Brown, Hesperus Press, London

Said, Edward (1978), *Orientalism*, Harmondsworth

Saint Étienne, J.-P.R. and Cretelle, J.C.D. de la (1795), *An Impartial History of the French Revolution*, new edn, 2 vols, R. Morison, Perth

Saint-Pierre, J.-H. Bernardin de ([n.d.]), *Paul and Virginia* and *The Indian Cottage*, Joseph Smith, London

Saint-Pierre, J.-H. Bernardin de (1791a), *La Chaumière Indienne*, Paris

Saint-Pierre, J.-H. Bernardin de (1791b), *The Indian Cottage*, John Bew, London

Saint-Pierre, J.-H. Bernardin de (1798), *Studies of Nature*, tr. H. Hunter, 2 vols, Dublin

Saint-Pierre, J.-H. Bernardin de (1818), *Œuvres Complètes*, Paris

Saint-Pierre, J.-H. Bernardin de (1826), *Correspondance*, 3 vols, Paris

Saint-Pierre, J.-H. Bernardin de (1836), *Oeuvres*, ed. L. Aimé Martin, A. Desrez, Paris

Saint-Pierre, J.-H. Bernardin de ([1879]), *The Indian Cottage*, Routledge, London

Saint-Pierre, J.-H. Bernardin de (1997a), *Etudes de la nature* [Deterville, Paris, 1804], http://gallica.bnf.fr

Saint-Pierre, J.-H. Bernardin de (1997b), *Harmonies de la nature* [*Oeuvres Posthumes*, Ledentu, Paris, 1840, vol. 2], http://gallica.bnf.fr

Salmon, Joseph (1651), *Heights in Depths, and Depths in Heights*, London

Salt, Henry (1930), *Company I have Kept*, London

Salt, Henry (2000), *Life of Henry David Thoreau*, Illinois

Salter, George (1659), *An Answer to Roger Crabs Printed paper*, London

Sarasohn, Lisa T. (1996), *Gassendi's Ethics*, Ithaca and London

Sax, Boria (1997), 'Are there Predators in Paradise', *Terra Nova*, 2:1, 59–68

Sax, Boria (2000), *Animals in the Third Reich*, New York

Scaliger, Julius Caesar (1592), *Exotericarum Exercitionum*, Frankfurt

Schaffer, Simon (1993), 'Comets & Idols: Newton's Cosmology and Political Theology', in Theerman and Seef, eds, 206–31

Schama, Simon (1989), *Citizens: A Chronicle of the French Revolution*, London

Schama, Simon (1995), *Landscape and Memory*, London

Schechner, Sara (1999), *Comets, Popular Culture, and the Birth of Modern Cosmology*, Princeton University Press, New Jersey

Schenck, Ernst-Günther (1989), *Patient Hitler: Eine medizinische Biographie*, Dusseldorf

Schenck, Ernst-Günther (1970), *Ich sah Berlin Sterben*, N. Verlagsbuchhandlung, Herford

Scher, Amy (1993), 'Praying for the prey: perceptions and treatment of animals in the *Gentleman's magazine*, 1731–40', Dissertation Abstract, Indiana

Scheuer, J.L and Bowman, J.E. (1994), 'The health of the novelist and printer Samuel Richardson (1689–1761)', *Journal of the Royal Society of Medicine*, 87:6, 352–5

Schiebinger, Londa (2004), *Nature's Body*, Beacon Press, New Jersey

Schimmel, Anne Marie (2003), *Mystical Dimensions of Islam*, Lahore

Schnorrenberg, B.B. (1984), 'Medical Men of Bath', *Studies in Eighteenth Century Culture*, 13, 189–205

Schofield, Roger (1985), 'The Impact of Scarcity and Plenty on Population Change in England, 1541–1871', in R.I. Rotberg and T.K. Rabb, eds, *Hunger and History*, Cambridge, 67–93

Scholem, Gershom (1941), *Major Trends in Jewish Mysticism*, New York

Scholem, Gershom (1987), *Origins of the Kabbala*, tr. A. Arkush, ed. R.J. Zwi Werblowsky, Princeton University Press

Scholem, Gershom (1991), *On The Mystical Shape of the Godhead*, New York

Schreiber, Roy (n.d.), 'Samuel Pepys and His Cookbooks', http://flan.utsa.edu/conviviumartium/SamuelPepys.htm

Schuler, Robert M. (1980), 'Some spiritual alchemies of seventeenth-century England', *Journal of the History of Ideas*, 41, 293–318

Schwab, Raymond (1934), *Vie D'Anquetil-Duperron*, Paris

Schwab, Raymond (1984), *The Oriental Renaissance: Europe's Rediscovery of India and the East, 1680–1880*, tr. G. Patterson and V. Reinking, New York

Schwartz, Stephan A. (2001), 'Dr. Franklin's Plan', *Smithsonian Magazine*, http://www.stephanaschwartz.com/HTML/dr_franklins_plan.htm

Scobell, Henry (1657–8), *Acts and Ordinances*, London

[Scott, Sarah] (1986), *Millenium Hall*, ed. Jane Spencer, Harmondsworth

Scott, Walter (1932–7), *Letters*, ed. H. Grierson [Constable, London], http://www.walterscott.lib.ed.ac.uk/etexts/etexts/letters1.PDF

Scott, Walter (1999a), *Guy Mannering* [Edinburgh, 1830], Chadwyck-Healey, Cambridge

Scott, Walter (1999b), *Kenilworth* [Edinburgh, 1831], Chadwyck-Healey, Cambridge

Scott, Walter (1999c), *St. Ronan's Well* [Edinburgh, 1832], Chadwyck-Healey, Cambridge

Scott, Walter (1999d), *The Antiquary* [Edinburgh, 1830], Chadwyck-Healey, Cambridge

Scott, Walter (1999e), *Waverley* [Edinburgh, 1830], Chadwyck-Healey, Cambridge

Scull, Andrew (2000), 'The Madhouse of Dr Monro', *Times Literary Supplement*, 27 October

Sedlar, Jean W. (1982), *India in the Mind of Germany*, Washington DC

Selden, John (1640), *De Iure Naturali & Gentium*, R. Bishop, London

Selden, John (1725), *Jurisconsulti Opera Omnia*, ed. D. Wilkins, 3 vols, London

Seneca (1917–25), *Moral Epistles*, tr. Richard M. Gummere, 3 vols, Loeb, Cambridge, Mass.

Serjeantson, R.W. (2001), 'The Passions and Animal Language, 1540–1700', *Journal of the History of Ideas*, 62:3, 425–44

Seward (1795), *Anecdotes Of Some Distinguished Persons*, 2nd edn, 4 vols, T. Cadell, London

Shahrastânî (1951–5), *Kitâb al-milal wa al-nihal*, ed. M. b. Fatah Allah Badrân, 2 vols, http://www.religiousstudies.uncc.edu/jcreeves/shahra_on_manichaeans.htm

Shakespeare, William (1990), *The Complete Works*, ed. Wells and Taylor, Oxford

Shapin, Steven (1998), 'The Philosopher And The Chicken: On the Dietetics of Disembodied Knowledge', in Christopher Lawrence and Steven Shapin, eds, *Science Incarnate*, Chicago

Shapin, Steven (2000), 'Descartes the doctor: rationalism and its therapies', *British Journal for the History of Science*, 33, 131–54

Shapin, Steven (2003), 'Trusting George Cheyne', *Bulletin of the History of Medicine*, 77:2, 263–97

Sheffey, Ruthe T. (1962), 'Some Evidence for a New Source of Aphra Behn's *Oroonoko*', *Studies in Philology*, 59:1, 52–63

Shelley, Harriet (1889), *Letters from Harriet Shelley to Catherine Nugent*, London

Shelley, Percy Bysshe (1926–30), *The Complete Works of Percy Bysshe Shelley*, ed. Roger Ingpen and Walter E. Peck, 10 vols, London

Shelley, Percy Bysshe (1964), *The Letters of Percy Bysshe Shelley*, ed. F.L. Jones, 2 vols, Oxford

Shelley, Percy Bysshe (1971), *Poetical Works*, ed. T. Hutchinson and G.M. Matthews, Oxford

Sherman, Sandra (2002), 'An Eden on a Plate', *Petits Propos Culinaires*, 69

Sherwood, Joan (1993), 'The Milk Factor', *CBMH/BCHM*, 10, 25–47

Scheuer, J.L. and Bowman, J.E. (1994), 'The health of the novelist and printer Samuel Richardson (1689–1761): a correlation of documentary and skeletal evidence', *Journal of the Royal Society of Medicine*, 87:6, 352–5

Shimi, Safa Fadel (1973), 'Portrait of a Seventeenth-Century Spy, Giovanni P. Marana: "Letters Written by a Turkish Spy"', Unpublished Ph.D. dissertation, Florida State University

Shoulson, Jeffrey S. (2000), 'The Embrace of the Fig Tree: Sexuality and Creativity in Midrash and in Milton', *ELH*, 67:4, 873–903

Shugg, Wallace (1968a), 'Humanitarian Attitudes in the Early Animal Experiments of the Royal Society', *Annals of Science*, 24, 227–38

Shugg, Wallace (1968b), 'The Cartesian Beast-Machine in English Literature (1663–1750)', *Journal of the History of Ideas*, 29:2, 279–92

Shuttleton, David E. (1992), '"My Own Crazy Carcase": The Life and Works of Dr George Cheyne (1672–1743)', Unpublished Ph.D. Dissertation, University of Edinburgh

Shuttleton, David E. (1995), 'Methodism and Dr George Cheyne "More Enlightening Principles"', in Roy Porter, ed., *Medicine and Enlightenment*, Amsterdam, 316–35

Shuttleton, David E. (1996), 'Jacobitism and Millennial Enlightenment', *Enlightenment and Dissent*, 15

Shuttleton, David E. (1999a), '"Pamela's Library": Samuel Richardson and Dr. Cheyne's "Universal Cure"', *Eighteenth-Century Life*, 23:1, 59–79

Shuttleton, David E. (1999b), '"All Passion Extinguish'd": The Case of Mary Chandler, 1687–1745', in I. Armstrong and V. Blain, eds, *Women's Poetry in the Enlightenment*, London, 33–49

Sieveking, Paul (1988), 'Saint Roger or, The Song of the Hermit Crab', *Fortean Times*, 50, London

Sinclair, John (1802), *An Essay on Longevity*, A. Strahan, London

Sinclair, John (1807), *Code of Health and Longevity*, 4 vols, A. Constable, Edinburgh

Singer, Peter (1975), *Animal Liberation*, New York

Singer, Peter (1980), 'Utilitarianism and Vegetarianism', *Philosophy and Public Affairs*, 9, 325–37

Sinha, H.N., ed. (1957), *Fort William–India House Correspondence (Public Series) Volume II 1757–1759*, Delhi

Sinha, N.K. (1959), *Haidar Ali*, 3rd edn, A. Mukherjee & Co., Calcutta

Sinha, Samita (1993), *Pandits in a Changing Environment*, Calcutta

Sinner, Johann Rudolph (1771), *Essai sur les Dogmes de la Métempsychose*, Berne

Skinner, Quentin and Kessler, Eckhard, eds (1988), *The Cambridge History of Renaissance Philosophy*, Cambridge University Press, Cambridge

Smellie, William (1790–9), *The Philosophy of Natural History*, Edinburgh

Smith, Adam (1759), *The Theory of Moral Sentiments*, J. Bell, Edinburgh

Smith, Adam (1776), *The Wealth of Nations*, 2 vols, London

Smith, Charles (1774), *The County and City of Waterford*, 2nd edn, Dublin

Smith, Eliza (1753), *The Compleat Housewife*, 15th edn, London

Smith, Nigel (1989), *Perfection Proclaimed*, Clarendon Press, Oxford

Smith, Nigel (1990), Review of Jonquil Bevan, *Izaak Walton's The Compleat Angler*, *The Review of English Studies*, 562–3

Smith, Nigel (1993), 'Oliver Cromwell's Angler', *The Seventeenth Century*, 8:1, 51–65

Smith, Nigel (1994), *Literature & Revolution in England, 1640–1660*, London

Smith, Nigel (1999), 'Enthusiasm and Enlightenment: Of Food, Filth and Slavery', in G. Maclean, D. Landry and J.P. Ward, eds, *The Country and the City Revisited*, Cambridge, 106–18

Smith, Virginia (1983), 'Thomas Tryon's regimen for women; sectarian health in the seventeenth century', in London Feminist History Group, ed., *The Sexual Dynamics of History*, London, 47–65

Smith, Virginia (1985), 'Prescribing the rules of health: Self-help and advice in the late eighteenth century', in Roy Porter, ed., *Patients and Practitioners*, Cambridge University Press, Cambridge, 249–82

Smollett, Tobias (1961), *Roderick Random*, Folio Society, Chatham

Smollett, Tobias (1978), *Ferdinand Count Fathom*, ed. D. Grant, Oxford

Smollett, Tobias (1996a), *Peregrine Pickle* [London, 1751], Chadwyck-Healey, Cambridge

Smollett, Tobias (1996b), *Adventures of an Atom* [1769], Chadwyck-Healey, Cambridge

Smuts, Malcolm, ed. (1996), *The Stuart Court and Europe*, Cambridge

[Southey, Robert] M.A. Espriella (1807), *Letters from England*, London

Snobelen, Stephen D. (1999), 'Isaac Newton, heretic: the strategies of a Nicodemite', *BJHS*, 32, 381–419

Snyder, Louis L. (1998), *Encyclopedia of the Third Reich*, Wordsworth Editions

Society in Edinburgh, A (1787), *Medical Commentaries, for the years 1781–2*, 2nd edn, 8 vols, London

Society of Jesus (1707–76), *Lettres édifiantes*, 34 vols, Paris

Spang, Rebecca L. (2000), *The Invention of the Restaurant: Paris and Modern Gastronomic Culture*, Cambridge, Mass.

Speed, John (1646), *The Most Famous Parts of the World*, J. Legatt, London

Speer, Albert (1970), *Inside the Third Reich*, tr. R. & C. Winston, London

Spencer, Colin (1993), *The Heretic's Feast*, London

Spencer, Colin (2000), *Vegetarianism: A History* [repr. of above], London

Spencer, Jane (2000b), *Aphra Behn's Afterlife*, Oxford University Press, New York

Spencer, John (1685), *De Legibus Hebræorum*, R. Chiswell, Cambridge

Spengler, Joseph J. (1942), *French Predecessors of Malthus*, Durham, N. Carolina

Spink, J.S. (1960), *French Free-Thought from Gassendi to Voltaire*, London

Spinoza, Benedict de (2000), *Ethics*, tr. G.H.R. Parkinson, Oxford University Press, New York

Spitzer, L. (1943), 'Additional note on "Wool and Linen" in Jerome', *American Journal of Philology*, 64, 98–9

Spurr, David (1996), 'Writing in the Wake of Empire', *MLN*, 111:5, 872–88

Srivastava, Sanjeev P. (2001), *Jahangir: A Connoisseur of Mughal Art*, New Delhi

St Clair, William (1989), *The Godwins and the Shelleys*, London

Stanley, Thomas (1655–60), *The History of Philosophy*, 3 vols, H. Moseley, London

Stansky, Peter (1999), *From William Morris to Sergeant Pepper: Studies in the Radical Domestic*, Palo Alto, Calif.

Stark, William (1788), *The Works*, ed. J.C. Smyth, London

Staudenmaier, Peter (n.d.), 'Ambiguities of Animal Rights', http://www.social-ecology.org/article

Stavorinus, Johan Splinter (1798), *Voyages to the East-Indies*, 3 vols, London

Stevenson, Robert Louis (1880), 'Henry David Thoreau: His Character and Opinions', *Cornhill Magazine*, 41, 665–82; http://eserver.org/thoreau/stevens2.html

S[teuar]t, James (1757), *Apologie du Sentiment de . . . Newton*, J.B. Eichenberg, Francfort

Stewart, John (1794), *Good Sense*, J. Owen & Baldwin, London

[Stewart, John] ([1795] or 1813?), *The Revelation of Nature*, New York

[Stewart, John] (1808), *Apocalypse of Human Perfectuability*, S. Gosnell, London

Stewart, John ([1818?]), *The Book of Nature*, London

Stillingfleet, Benjamin, ed. (1759), *Miscellaneous Tracts relating to Natural History*, R. and J. Dodsley et al., London

Stone, Lawrence (1977), *The Family, Sex And Marriage In England 1500–1800*, Harper & Row, New York

Stoneman, R., ed. (1991), *The Greek Alexander Romance*, London

Stoneman, R (1994), 'Who are the Brahmans? Indian lore and Cynic doctrine in Palladius' *De Bragmanibus* and its models', *Classical Quarterly*, 44:2, 500–10

Stoneman, R. (1995), 'Naked Philosophers: the Brahmans in the Alexander Historians and in the Alexander Romance', *Journal of Hellenic Studies*, 115, 99–114

Stott, Rosalie (1987), 'Health and Virtue: Or, How to Keep out of Harm's Way. Lectures on Pathology and Therapeutics by William Cullen c.1770', *Medical History*, 31:2, 123–42

Strabo (1707), *Rerum geographicorum*, ed. Casaubon, 2 vols, Amstelædami

Strasser, Otto (2005), 'Hitler as I knew Him: Some Introductory Revelations', in Kurt Krueger, *I was Hitler's Doctor: His Intimate Life*, Kessinger Publishing

Strother, Edward (1725), *An Essay on Sickness and Health*, London

Stroumsa, Sarah (1999), *Freethinkers of Medieval Islam*, Leiden

Strype, John (1720), *A Survey Of the Cities of London and Westminster*, 2 vols, London

Strype, John, ed. (1824), *Annals of the Reformation*, II, i, Clarendon Press, Oxford

Stuart, Tristram (2002), '"This proud and troublesome Thing, called *Man*": India and Concepts of Nature in Seventeenth-century England', Conference on the Environmental History of Asia, 4–7 December, Jawarharlal Nehru University, New Delhi

Stuart, Tristram (2003), 'Body of Evidence', *Biblio: A Review of Books*, New Delhi, 8:3–4, 5–6

Stukeley, William (1936), *Memoirs of Sir Isaac Newton's Life*, ed. A. Hastings, London

Subrahmanyam, Sanjay (2000), 'The Career of Colonel Polier and late eighteenth-century orientalism', *Journal of the Royal Asiatic Society of Great Britain and Ireland*, Third Series, 10:1, 43–60

Sutton, Samuel (1749), *An Historical Account of A New Method For extracting the foul Air out of Ships*, 2nd edn, J. Brindley, London

Svensson, Isacus (1757), 'Dissertatio Academica, De Pane Diætetico', Præs. Carl Linnaeus, L.M. Höjer, Upsala

Sweeting, C.G. (2002), *Hitler's Personal Pilot*, Brassey's

Sweetman, Will (2001), 'Unity and Plurality: Hinduism and the Religions of India in Early European Scholarship', *Religion*, 31, 209–24, www.ncl.ac.uk/rs/Hinduism.pdf

Swieten, G. (1744–73), *Aphorisms of Dr. Herman Boerhaave*, 18 vols, London

Swift, Jonathan (1726), *Gulliver's Travels*, London

Sydenham, Thomas (1722), *The Whole Works*, tr. John Pechey, 8th edn, J. Darby, London

Taine, Hippolyte A. (2001), *The French Revolution*, www.gutenberg.com

[Tany, Thomas] (1651), *Theauraujohn His Theousori Apokolipikal*, London

Tany, Thomas (1988), *The Nations Right*, ed. Andrew Hopton, Aporia Press, London

Targhi, M.T. (1996), 'Orientalism's Genesis Amnesia', *Comparative Studies of South Asia, Africa and the Middle East*, 16:1, 1–14

Tavernier, Jean-Baptiste (1995), *Travels in India*, tr. V. Ball, 2nd edn, 2 vols, New Delhi

Taylor, John (1651), *Ranters of both Sexes, Male and Female*, J. Hammon, London

Taylor, John (1825), *The Old, Old, Very Old Man*, H. Gosson, London

Taylor, John (1832), *Records of my Life*, 2 vols, E. Bull, London

Taylor, Rachel A. (1927), *Leonardo the Florentine*, London

Taylor, Thomas (1788–9) [tr.], *Commentaries of Proclus*, 2 vols, T. Payne et al., London

[Taylor, Thomas] (1792), *A Vindication of the Rights of Brutes*, E.J. Miller, London

[Taylor, Thomas] (1799), 'Thomas Taylor', in *British and Irish public Characters of 1798*, Dublin

[Taylor, Thomas] (1966), *A Vindication of the Rights of Brutes*, ed. L.S. Boas, Gainesville

Taylor, Thomas (1969), *Selected Writings*, ed. K. Raine and G.M. Harper, London

Teltscher, Kate (1995), *India Inscribed*, Oxford University Press, Delhi

Teltscher, Kate (1996), '"The Fearful Name of the Black Hole": the Fashioning of an Imperial Myth', in Bart Moore-Gilbert, ed., *Writing India, 1757–1990*, Manchester

Teltscher, Kate (2000), '"Maidenly and Well nigh effeminate": constructions of Hindu masculinity and religion in seventeenth-century English texts', *Postcolonial Studies*, 3:2, 159–70

Temple, Sir William (1680), *Miscellanea*, E. Gellibrand, London

Temple, Sir William (1690), 'An Essay upon the Ancient and Modern Learning', in *Miscellanea, The Second Part*, R. & R. Simpson, London

Temple, Sir William (1701), *Miscellanea. The Third Part*, Benjamin Tooke, London

Terasaki, Hiroaki (1995), 'The Educational Thought of Thomas Tryon –

Embryo Education in Seventeenth Century England', *Bulletin of the Faculty of Education, the University of Tokyo*, 34

Terry, Edward (1655), *A Voyage to East-India*, J. Martin, London

Tertullian (2004a), *Apology* [*ANF*, vol. 3, 1885], http://www.newadvent.org/fathers

Tertullian (2004b), *On fasting* [*ANF*, vol. 4, 1885], http://www.newadvent.org/fathers

Testi, Luigi (n.d), *De novo saccharo lactis*, n.p.

Testi, Luigi (n.d), *De saccharo lactis relatio*, n.p.

Theerman, Paul and Seeff, Adele F. (1993), *Action and Reaction*, London

Theophrastus (1644), *De Historia Plantarum*, ed. J.C. Scaliger, revd J.B. a Stapel, H. Laurentius, Amsterdam

Theophrastus (1916), *Enquiry into Plants*, tr. A. Hort, 2 vols, Loeb, New York

Thomas, Apperley (1731), *Observations in Physick*, London

Thomas, Keith (1971), *Religion and the Decline of Magic*, Weidenfeld & Nicolson, London

Thomas, Keith (1983), *Man and The Natural World: Changing Attitudes in England 1500–1800*, Harmondsworth

Thomson, James (1736), *The Works of Mr. Thomson*, 2 vols, [H. Woodfall], London

Thomson, James (1746), *The Seasons*, [H. Woodfall], London

Thoreau, Henry David (1973), *Reform Papers*, ed. Glick, Princeton

Thoreau, Henry David (1989), *Walden*, ed. J. Lyndon Shanley, Princeton

Thune, Nils (1948), *The Behmenists and the Philadelphians*, Uppsala

Tissot, S.A.D. (1774), *Advice to People*, 6th edn, 2 vols, J. Potts, Dublin

Titley, Norah M. (1983), *Persian Painting*, London

Todd, Janet (1996), *The Secret Life of Aphra Behn*, André Deutsch, London

Todes, Daniel P. (1989), *Darwin without Malthus: The Struggle for Existence in Russian Evolutionary Thought*, Oxford University Press, Oxford

Toepfer, Karl (2003), 'One Hundred Years of Nakedness in German Performance', *The Drama Review*, 47:4, 144–88

Toland, John (1704), *Letters to Serena*, Bernard Lintot, London

Toland, John (1976), *Adolf Hitler*, New York

Toomer, G.J. (1996), *Eastern Wisedom and Learning: The Study of Arabic in Seventeenth-Century England*, Oxford

Topsfield, Andrew, ed. (2000), *Court Painting in Rajasthan*, Mumbai

Towers, Joseph (1766–72), *British Biography*, 10 vols, [Sherborne]

Townsend, Joseph (1781), *Free Thoughts*, London

Trautmann, Thomas (1997), *Aryans and British India*, Berkeley

Trevus, Persius (1634), *Exercitationes*, 2nd edn, Romæ

Tryon, Thomas (1682a), *A Treatise Of Cleanness*, L. Curtis, London

Tryon, Thomas (1682b), *Healths Grand Preservative*, L. Curtis, London

[Tryon, Thomas] Philotheos Physiologus (1683), 'A Dialogue Between An East-Indian Brackmanny or Heathen-Philosopher, and a French

Gentleman', in *The Way to Health, Long Life and happiness*, Andrew Sowle, London

[Tryon, Thomas] Philotheos Physiologus (1684a), *Friendly Advice To The Gentlemen-Planters*, Andrew Sowle, [London]

[Tryon, Thomas] Philotheos Physiologus ([1684b]), *The Good Houswife Made A Doctor*, Andrew Sowle, London

[Tryon, Thomas] Philotheos Physiologus, ([1684c]), *The Country-Man's Companion*, Andrew Sowle, London

T[ryon], T[homas] (1684d), *Modest Observations*, G. Larkin, London

[Tryon, Thomas] (1685), *The Way to make all People Rich*, Andrew Sowle, London

Tryon, Thomas (1688), *Monthly Observations*, Andrew Sowle, London

[Tryon, Thomas] Philotheos Physiologus ([1688?]), *The Country-Man's Companion* [repr.], Andrew Sowle, London

Tryon, Thomas (1690), *A New Art Of Brewing Beer*, T. Salusbury, London

Tryon, Thomas (1691a), *The Way To Health, Long Life and Happiness*, 2nd edn, D. Newman, London

Tryon, Thomas (1691b), *Wisdom's Dictates*, Thomas Salusbury, London

Tryon, Thomas (1691c), *Pythagoras His Mystick Philosophy Reviv'd* [Reissue of *A Treatise of Dreams & Visions*], Tho. Salusbury, London

[Tryon, Thomas] (1695a), *Averroeana: Being A Transcript Of Several Letters From Averroes . . . Also Several Letters from Pythagoras to the King of India*, T. Sowle, London

Tryon, Thomas (1695b), *A New Method Of Educating Children*, J. Salusbury and J. Harris, London

[Tryon, Thomas et al.?] ([1695?]), *The Way to Save Wealth*, G. Conyers, London

Tryon, Thomas (1696), *Miscellania*, T. Sowle, London

Tryon, Thomas (1697), *The Way To Health*, 3rd edn, H. Newman, London

Tryon, Thomas [?] (1699), *England's Grandeur, And Way to get Wealth* [a reissue of *Some General Considerations* (London, 1698)], J.Harris and G.Conyers, London

Tryon, Thomas (1700), *Tryon's Letters, Upon Several Occasions*, Geo. Conyers and Eliz. Harris, London

[Tryon, Thomas] (1702), *A Brief History of Trade in England*, E. Baldwin, London

Tryon, Thomas (1703), *The Knowledge Of A Man's Self . . . Or, The second part of the Way to Long Life*, T. Bennet, London

Tryon, Thomas (1704), *The Knowledge of a Man's Self . . . Or, The third part*, etc., T. Bennet, London

Tryon, Thomas (1705a), *Some Memoirs*, T. Sowle London [British Library Shelfmark, VII.32.70]

Tryon, Thomas (1705b), *Some Memoirs*, T. Sowle, London [ESTC: N23690], [18 new pages inserted between pp.34 and 35, and 'Epitaph' after p.128]

[Tryon, Thomas and Palladius et al.] (1707), *Letters from an Arabian philosopher . . . To which are added, the entertainments of an Indian King with Pythagoras* [reprint of Tryon (1695a)]: *and Alexander's conference with Dindimus the Brachman* [reprint of *Upright Lives* [1683]], 2nd edn, J. Sowle, [London?]

[Tryon, Thomas, Cheyne, George et al.] (1726), *The Way to Health and Long life*, G. Conyers, London

Tryon, Thomas (1761), *Some Memoirs of . . . Tho. Tryon*, [ed. John Lovell], London [Philadelphia]

Tudge, Colin (2003), *So Shall We Reap*, London

Tull, H.W. (1989), *The Vedic Origins of Karma*, SUNY Press

Tull, H.W. (1996), 'The killing that is not killing', *Indo-Iranian Journal*, 39:3, 223–44

Tulpius, Nicolaus (1672), *Observationes Medicae*, D. Elzevirius, Amsterdam

Turner, James (1980), *Reckoning with the Beast: Animals, Pain, and Humanity in the Victorian Mind*, Johns Hopkins University Press, Baltimore and London

Twersky, Isadore and Septimus, Bernard, eds (1987), *Jewish Thought in the Seventeenth Century*, Cambridge

Tyson, Edward (1699), *Orang-Outang, sive Homo Sylvestris*, Thomas Bennet et al., London

Tyson, Edward and Wallis, John (1702), 'On Man's feeding on Flesh, and of Carnivorous Animals'; first published in *Philosophical Transactions For the Month of February 1700*, no. 269; thence repr. in *Philosophical Transactions . . . For the Years 1700 and 1701*, vol. 22, S. Smith, London, 769–85

Tyson, Edward, and Wallis, John (1721) [abridgement of the above] *Philosophical Transactions (From the Year 1700 to the Year 1720.) Abridg'd*, vol. V, Part i, ed. Henry Jones, G. Strahan et al., London, 1–9

[Tyssot de Patot, Simon] 'Pierre Bayle' (1743), *James Massey*, 2nd edn, J. Watts, London

Tyssot de Patot, Simon (1997), *Voyages et avantures de J. Massé* [Jaques l'aveugle, Bourdeaux (La Haye), 1760], http://gallica.bnf.fr/

U.S. Army Infantry School (1941), 'The Modern Ration of the German Armed Forces', *Infantry School Mailing List*, vol. 21, ch. 11 (Item No.10184), http://www.military-info.com/Aphoto/Subjectlist/A030c.htm

Ulmer, Gregory L. (1972), 'Clarissa and La Nouvelle Héloïse', *Comparative Literature*, 24, 289–308

Ungewitter, Richard (1979a), *Die Nacktheit* [1907], Stuttgart

Ungewitter, Richard (1979b), *Nacktheit und Kultur* [1913], Arzte-Verlag, Köln

Upright Lives of the Heathen Briefly Noted, The ([1683]), Andrew Sowle, London

Upright Lives of the Heathen Briefly Noted, The ([1740]), ed. C. Woolverton,
  A. & W. Bradford, Philadelphia
Upright Lives of the Heathens briefly noted, The (1786), T. Lord, Clonmel

Valady, [Christian d'Yzarn de Freissinet, Marquis de] (1935), *La Maison
  d'Yzarn-Freissinet-Valady*, Rodez
[Vaughan, Thomas] Eugenius Philalethes (1650), *Magia Adamica*,
  London
Vaughan, Thomas (1984), *The Works*, ed. A. Rudrum and J. Drake-
  Brockman, Oxford
Vaughan, William (1600), *Directions for Health*, R. Bradocke, London
Vaughan, William (1630), *The Newlanders Cure*, F. Constable, London
[Vaughan, William] (1633), *Directions for Health*, 7th edn, J. Harison,
  London
Veer, Peter van der, ed. (1995), *Nation and Migration*, Pennsylvania
Venner, Tobias (1660), *Via Recta Ad Vitam Longam*, 4th edn, London
Vickers, Brian, ed. (1984), *Occult and Scientific Mentalities in the Renaissance*,
  Cambridge University Press, Cambridge
Victoria and Albert Museum (1982), *The Indian Heritage*, London
Viereck, Pieter (1961), *Metapolitics: The Roots of the Nazi Mind*, 1961;
  Capricorn, New York
Vital, Chaim (n.d.), 'Introduction of *Shaar HaHakdamot*', tr. M. Miller,
  www.ascent.org.il
Vital, Chayyim (1999), *The Tree of Life*, tr. D.W. Menzi et al., Northvale,
  New Jersey
Volckerstorff, Engelbertus von (1721), 'Liber de causis longævitatis
  hominum ante Diluvium', in B. Pez, *Thesaurus Anecdotorum novissimus*
Voltaire (1756), *Essay sur l'histoire générale et sur les moeurs et l'esprit des
  nations*, Cramer, Genève
Voltaire (1764), *Dictionnaire Philosophique Portatif*, Londres
Voltaire (1765a), *Dictionnaire Philosophique*, 5th edn, www.voltaire-
  integral.com
Voltaire (1765b), *La Philosophie de l'Histoire* [London?]
Voltaire (1768), *The Princess of Babylon*, London
Voltaire (1769), *Lettre Anonyme Écrite A M. De Voltaire Et La Réponse*,
  www.voltaire-integral.com
[Voltaire] (1770), *Les Lettres d'Amabed*, tr. Tamponet, Geneve
[Voltaire] (1775), *Lettre Philosophique*, London
Voltaire (1777), *La Bible Enfin Expliqée*, www.voltaire-integral.com
Voltaire (1779–80), *The Works of M. de Voltaire*, tr. W. Kenrick et al.,
  5 vols, London
Voltaire (1779–81), *The Age of Louis XIV*, ed. R. Griffith, 3 vols, Walker,
  London
Voltaire (1937), *Fragments on India*, tr. F. Bedi, Lion Press, Lahore
Voltaire (1980–), *The Complete Works of Voltaire*, Oxford

Voltaire (1998), *Letters on the English*, http://www.fordham.edu/halsall/mod/1778voltaire-lettres.html

Vosgien (1799–1801), *An Historical and Biographical Dictionary*, 4 vols, Cambridge

Vossius, Gerard Johann (1641), *De Theologia Gentili*, C. Blaev, Amsterdam

Wagar, W. Warren, ed. (1982), *The Secular Mind*, London

[Wagener, Otto] (1978), *Hitler – Memoirs of a Confidant*, tr. R. Hein, ed. H.A. Turner Jr, Yale University Press, New Haven

Waite, R.G.L. (1971), 'Adolf Hitler's Guilt Feelings', *Journal of Interdisciplinary History*, 1:2, 229–49

Waite, R.G.L. (1977), *The Psychopathic God: Adolf Hitler*, New York

Walbridge, John (2001), *The Wisdom of the Mystic East*, SUNY Press, Albany

Walker, D.P. (1954), 'The Prisca Theologia in France', *Journal of the Warburg and Courtauld Institutes*, 17, 204–59

Walker, D.P. (1964), *The Decline of Hell*, London

Walker, D.P. (1972), *The Ancient Theology*, London

Wallace, Alfred Russel (1916), *Letters and Reminiscences*, ed. J. Marchant, London

Wallace, Alfred Russel (2004), *My Life*, Kessinger Publishing

Walli, Koshelya (1974), *The Conception of Ahimsā*, Bharata Manisha, Varanasi

Walters, Kerry S. and Portmess, Lisa, eds (1999), *Ethical Vegetarianism from Pythagoras to Peter Singer*, State University of New York Press, Albany

Warren, George ([1667?]), *A Full and Impartial Description of Surinam*, (n.p.) [BL 1061.g.82]

Wear, A., French, R.K. and Lonie, I.M., eds (1985), *The Medical Renaissance of the Sixteenth Century*, Cambridge

Webb, John (1669), *A Probability That the Language of the Empire of China is the Primitive Language*, N. Brook, London

Webster, Charles (1975), *The Great Instauration*, London

Webster, Charles (1982), *From Paracelsus to Newton*, Cambridge

Wellesz, Emmy (1952), *Akbar's Religious Thought*, London

Wells, K.D. (1971), 'Sir William Lawrence (1783–1867); A Study of Pre-Darwinian Ideas on Heredity and Variation', *Journal of the History of Biology*, 4:2, 319–61

W[elsh], J.J. (1831), *A Brief Notice of Mr. Thomas Taylor*, G. Balne, London

Weltzien, J.C. (1789), 'De Affectuum Animi usu Medico', J.C. Dietrich, Gottingae

Wesley, John (1776), *Explanatory Notes on the Whole Bible*, http://www.studylight.org/com/

Wesley, John (1872), *Works*, London

Wesley, John (1931), *The Letters of the Rev. John Wesley*

Westfall, Richard S. (1958), *Science and Religion in Seventeenth-Century England*, New Haven

Westfall, Richard S. (1980), *Never at Rest: A Biography of Isaac Newton*, Cambridge University Press, Cambridge

Westfall, Richard S. (1984), 'Newton and Alchemy', in Vickers, ed., 315–35

Wexelman, David M. (1999), *The Jewish Concept of Reincarnation and Creation*, Jason Aronson, Northvale, New Jersey

Wheaton, Barbara Ketcham (1983), *Savouring the Past*, Chatto and Windus, London

White, Benjamin ([1770]), *A new catalogue of books* [London]

White, Gilbert (1789), *The Natural History and Antiquities of Selborne*, T. Bensley, London

White, Michael (1997), *Isaac Newton*, Fourth Estate, London

Whiting, C.E. (1968), *Studies of English Puritanism*, London

Whytt, Robert (1755), *Physiological Essays*, Edinburgh

Whytt, Robert (1765), *Disorders which have been commonly called Nervous, Hypochondriac, or Hysteric*, 2nd edn, Edinburgh

Wild, Wayne (2001), 'Medicine-by-post in eighteenth-century Britain', unpublished Ph.D. dissertation, Brandeis University

[Wilkins, Charles, tr.] (1787), *Le Bhaguat-geeta*, tr. J.P. Parraud, Londres [i.e. Paris]

Willett, C. and Cunnington, P. (1957), *Handbook of English Costume*, London

Williams, David (1789a), *Lectures on Education*, 3 vols, John Bell, London

Williams, David (1789b), *Lectures on the Universal Principles and Duties of Religion and Morality*, 2 vols, J. Dodsley et al., London

Williams, E.F. (1976), 'The Development of the Meat Industry', in D. Oddy and D. Miller, eds, *The Making of the Modern British Diet*, London, 44–57

Williams, Helena Maria (1795), *The Politics of France*, J. Chambers, Dublin

Williams, Howard (1883), *The Ethics of Diet*, J. Heywood, London

Williamson, George (1961), 'The Context of Marvell's "Hortus" and "Garden"', *Modern Language Notes*, 76:7, 590–8

Willich, A.F.M. (1799), *Lectures on Diet*, London

Willis, Thomas (1681), *The Remaining Works*, tr. S[amuel]. P[ordage]., T. Dring et al., London

Willis, Thomas (1683), *Two Discourses concerning The Soul of Brutes*, London

Wilmot, John, Earl of Rochester (1964), *Poems*, ed. V. de Sola Pinto, 2nd edn, London

Wilson, Daniel (2005), 'Imperfect Necessity. Aspects of Violence: The Unabomber, Thoreau and John Brown', unpublished M.Phil. dissertation, Birkbeck College, University of London (publication forthcoming)

Wilson, G.H. (1813), *The Eccentric Mirror*, London

Wilson, Thomas (1745), *The Lord's Supper*, 9th edn, M. Pilkington, Corke

Winge, Johannis Olai (1696), *Positiones medicae de lacte*, Praes. Lucas van de Poll, F. Halma, Rhenum

Winstanley, Gerrard (1649), *Truth Lifting up its head above Scandals*, London

Winstanley, Gerrard (1941), *Works*, ed. G. Sabine

Winstanley, Gerrard (1973), *The Law of Freedom and other Writings*, ed. Christopher Hill, Cambridge University Press, Cambridge

Wollstonecraft, Mary (1792), *A Vindication of the Rights of Woman*, J. Johnson, London

Woodhouse, C.M. (1986), *George Gemistos Plethon*, Oxford

Woolman, John (1922), *Journal and Essays*, ed. A.M. Gunmere, Philadelphia

Wordsworth, William (1981), *The Poems*, ed. John O. Hayden, 2 vols, New Haven

Worster, Donald (1985), *Natures's Economy: A History of Ecological Ideas*, Cambridge

Wotton, William (1697), *Reflections upon the Ancient and Modern Learning*, 2nd edn, J. Leake, London

Wright, John P. (1991), 'Locke, Willis, and the seventeenth-century Epicurean soul', in Margaret J. Osler, ed., *Atoms, Pneuma, and Tranquility: Epicurean and Stoic Themes in European Thought*, Cambridge, 239–58

Wynne-Edwards, V.C. (1983), 'Self-regulation in Populations of Red Grouse', in J. Dupâquier and A. Fauve-Chamoux, eds, *Malthus Past and Present*, London, 379–91

Wynter, John (1725), *Cyclus Metasyncriticus*, J. Leake, Bath

Yates, Frances (1964), *Giordano Bruno and the Hermetic Tradition*, London

Young, Art (1975), *Shelley and Nonviolence*, The Hague

Young, J.T. (1998), *Faith, Medical Alchemy and Natural Philosophy*, Aldershot

Yule, Henry, ed. (1915), *Cathay and The Way Thither*, 2nd edn, Hakluyt Society, London

Ziegler, Joseph (1998), *Medicine and Religion c. 1300*, New York

Zimmerman, Francis (1987), *The Jungle and the Aroma of Meats: An Ecological Theme in Hindu Medicine*, University of California Press

Zohar, The (1931–4), tr. Harry Sperling and Maurice Simon, London

Županov, Ines G. (1999), *Disputed Mission*, Oxford University Press, New Delhi

NOTES

INTRODUCTION

1 Mandeville (1924), I.173–81
  (Remark P); ([Mandeville] (1714),
  Remark O, pp.146–57).
2 Passmore (1974), pp.13–14;
  Harrison, P. (1999); Schama
  (1995), pp.14, 18–19; Burkert
  (1983), pp.7–11, 17–22, 38;
  Burkert (1972), pp.180–1.
3 See especially the overviews in
  Mercerus (1598), pp.34–5, 195–7;
  Evelyn (1996), pp.80–1; Edwards
  (1699), I.91–9, 113–18; Almond
  (1999), pp.23–6, 118–22, 199;
  Prest (1981), pp.71–4 (the
  'Vertumnus' poem Prest repeatedly
  quotes is by Abel Evans); Milton,
  J. (1667), X.185–9.

CHAPTER 1

1 This is John Aubrey's version
  which he claims to have received
  from Thomas Hobbes. Jardine and
  Stewart (Jardine & Stewart (1998),
  pp.502–5) say that Bacon's
  reference to his experiment on the
  'conservation and induration of
  bodies' refers to living bodies
  which they take to be Bacon's own
  body; however it could apply to
  dead bodies (such as the chicken)
  and would therefore corroborate
  Aubrey's version rather than
  contradicting it. Jardine and
  Stewart suggest, rather, that the
  experiment in question was Bacon
  inhaling nitre (salt-petre) or
  opium to preserve his own life.
  They do not explain why Bacon
  would go to Highgate to inhale
  opium or nitre, whereas Highate
  Hill is where one would go to

fetch snow in March. If Aubrey's
version is a fabrication, it is an
odd coincidence that it
corroborates a legitimate reading
of Bacon's private comments. It
would also be odd if Bacon said
that his attempt to preserve his life
went 'excellently well' when it was
followed by a coughing fit so
fierce that he was forced to take
refuge in Arundel's house.
2 Bacon (1996), I.i.58; IV.247–8;
  Webster (1982), pp.48–9, 65–9;
  Webster (1975), pp.1, 4–5, 12,
  15–16, 21–7 and *passim*; Almond
  (1999), p.23; Popkin (1998),
  p.395; Markku Peltonen, 'Bacon,
  Francis, Viscount St Alban
  (1561–1626)', *ODNB*.
3 Gruman (1966), pp.80–2.
4 Celsus (1935–8), I.43 (I.i.2);
  Venner (1660), p.230; Boerhaave
  (1742–6b), I.98–101n.6, VI.241;
  Boerhaave (1742–6a), I.65–7;
  Mead (1751), pp.207–8; Sinclair
  (1807), III.483; cp. Cheyne (1733),
  pp.152–3, 159–60. Aubrey
  (1669–96); Nicholson (1999),
  p.87. cf. Webster (1975),
  pp.246–323; Shapin (2000),
  p.134; Shapin (1998), pp.35–6,
  which treats Bacon's comments as a
  novel 'twist'; Bacon was siding with
  Celsus as he often did; cf. Bacon
  (1854), III.343–71 (Aphorism
  73); Celsus (1935–8), 'Proem'.
5 See n.8 below.
6 Jardine and Stewart (1998),
  pp.464–5.
7 Bushell (1628), 'Epistle
  Dedicatory', pp.58–61
  [mispaginated 54–5], and *passim*;
  cf. Bacon (1650), p.18ff.;
  [Vaughan, W.] (1633), p.62.

8 Bacon (1650), pp.7, 13–26, 32, 35–6, 40–3, 46, 51. Compare, for example, Bacon (1623), pp.103–4, 146 (where *'solum'* is not translated). cf. Bacon (1651), p.156; Bacon (1638), p.209; Lessius, Cornaro and Anon. (1634), sig.5v; and ms. marginalia in Bacon (1638) [British Library: 535.a.6], pp.214–5.

9 Bushell (1659), 'Letter to. . .Fairfax', p.3; 'Minerall Overtures', pp.3–4; 'Condemned men', pp.2–3; 'Fellow-Prisoners', p.7; '[Bacon's] New Atlantis', pp.5, 29, 31–2; 'Post-Script', pp.4–21, espec. pp.6–8 for Bushell's continued vegetarianism in Oxford; Bushell (1660), pp.14–18, 34–7; Bushell (1628), 'Epistle Dedicatory', pp.13, 20, 30, 58, 70, 74, 84, 99, 109, 111, 138; Blundell (1877), pp.34–5; Pryme (1880), vol.30, pp.8, 11–17+n.; Gough (1932), pp.4–18, 27–30, 34; Thomas, K. (1983), pp.289–90; George C. Boon, 'Bushell, Thomas (b. before 1600, d. 1674)', *ODNB*; Rostvig (1954).

10 Jerome (2005a), Bk II, ch.15, Bk I, ch.18; cf. Pseudo-Clement (2005b), Hom. viii, ch. 15–17; Boas (1948), pp.25–6, 32, 84, 114–6; Bynum (1988), pp.35, 44, 109, 320n.5.

11 Pettus (1674), pp.146–7; *cit.* Sherman (2002), pp.88–9.

12 John Calvin (1999), vol.I, Genesis I.xxix and 9.iii; cf. Evelyn (1996), pp.80–1; Almond (1999), pp.118, 199; Browne (1672), Bk III, ch.xxv, pp.189–94; Edwards (1699), I.91–9, 113–8.

13 Bushell (1660), 'Post Script', pp.20–1, 34–7; cf. Bushell (1659), '[Bacon's] New Atlantis', p.29.

14 Ovid (1632), Bk I. cp. the 'lothsome bramble berries' of Golding's translation, Ovid (1567), Bk I, ll.115–21. Dryden's later translation is still more enthusiastic than Sandys' (Ovid (1717), p.5). However, even Golding's translation expanded Ovid's list of five fruits to twelve, Lyne (2001), pp.75–7. For the variant traditions of idealised and despised primitivism, cf. Boas (1948), pp.140n., 150.

15 Ovid (1632), Sandys' commentary, Bk I and Bk XV.

16 Bushell (1659), 'To the reader', sig.A3r.

17 Bushell (1659), 'Post-Script', pp.4–8; cf. Hill (1991), p.27. For Rosicrucian vegetarianism, cf. e.g. Heydon (1662), Bk I.14, Bk III.1, 26–32, 106.

18 cf. e.g. Dornavius (1619); Volckerstorff (1721), I.i.

19 Bacon does not explicitly state this view, but see Bacon (1650), pp.15ff, 21.

20 Culpeper (1656), p.21; cf. Parkinson (1629) and especially Tryon (1691a), p.217.

21 Coudert (1999), p.74.

22 Passmore (1974), pp.18–20; Webster (1975), pp.25–7; Garber and Ayers eds (1998), p.395.

23 Bacon (1640), p.382; Turner (1980), p.3n; Proverbs 12:10; Almond (1999), pp.124–5; Ray (1717), pp.55–6. Bacon's subsequent comments on the kindness of Turks to animals could have come from George Sandys (1610–11) repr. in Purchas ed., (1905–7), VIII.135–6. For Bacon's other comments on Pythagoras and the Brahmins, cf. e.g. Bacon (1996), II.640–1; V.422 and especially IV.377.

24 Powicke ed., (1926), p.197; *cit.* Almond (1999), p.119.

CHAPTER 2

1 Garment (1651), p.4; Anon. (1651a), pp.3, 7–9, 12–13; H[all?], G. (1651), pp.2–3; *PA* (1651) no. 21, p.166; Taylor (1651), p.2; Reeve [and Muggleton?] (1711), pp.6, 9–13; Muggleton (1699), pp.20–2, 45–6; Hill (1983), p.67; Ariel

Hessayon, 'John Robins', *ODNB*; Greaves and Zaller eds, (1982–4), III.100–1; Hopton, ed. (1992). Jacob Böhme and George Fox similarly tried to speak the Adamic language; cf. Thune (1948), pp.63–4, 159–60.

2 Katz (1982), p.120.

3 Hill, Reay and Lamont (1983), pp.18–19, 68–70; Hill (1990), pp.160–73; H[all?]., G. (1651); Berckendal (1661); Muggleton (1699), p.47.

4 Reeve [and Muggleton?] (1711), p.12; H[all?]., G. (1651), p.2; cf. Muggleton (1699), p.22.

5 Reeve [and Muggleton?] (1711), p.11; cf. Muggleton (1699), p.45.

6 Muggleton (1699), pp.46–7; H[all?]., G. (1651), p.4; Katz (1982), pp.114–5; Thomas Tany was also accused of witchcraft, (Hill, Reay and Lamont (1983), p.69), as was Roger Crab.

7 Reeve [and Muggleton?] (1711), p.13.

8 Hopton, ed. (1992), p.12; *PA* (1651) no.21, p.166; Reeve [and Muggleton?] (1711), p.12.

9 Hill, Reay and Lamont (1983), pp.18–19; cf. Thune (1948), p.146. The Robins sect were compared to the Adamites and Familists in Taylor (1651), pp.2–4. For the Adamites and other radical nudists, see Cohn (1970), pp.180–1, 210, 218–21. The frontispiece woodcut in H[all?]., G. (1651) showing naked dancing was used before in Anon. (1650b), which reveals that one of the figures represented was Dr Pordage, the associate of John Robins' collaborator Thomas Tany, cf. p.3 and Anon. (1650a), p.6.

10 Muggleton (1699), pp.22–3; Hill (1983), p.68; cf. Hill (1986b), p.63; Katz (1982), p.109.

11 Garment (1651), p.6.

12 Muggleton (1699), pp.20–1; Revelation 7:4.

13 Garment (1651), pp.3–4; Katz (1982), pp.107–26.

14 Hill, Reay and Lamont (1983), p.69; Hill (1995), p.128. Pythagoras was also said to have circumcised himself, cf. e.g. Ovid (1632), Bk XV, Sandys' commentary.

15 Muggleton (1699), pp.20–1, 43–4; *PA* (1655 [n.s.]), no.210, p.1680; *WIC* (1655 [n.s.]) 9–17 Jan., pp.154–5; *WIC* (1655 [n.s.]) 2–9 Jan, pp.151–2, 158; *MF* (1655 [n.s.]) no.32, 3–10 Jan, front page, p.252 and espec. p.256; *PA* (1654) no.209; Katz (1982), pp.107–26; Hill, Reay and Lamont (1983), p.69; Hill (1995), pp.128+n, 284; Hill (1990), p.160; Hill (1986a), p.281 and *passim*; Popkin (1998), p.395; Smith (1989), p.233+n.; Luxon (1993), p.900; Tany (1988), pp.4–8+n.; Hopton, ed. (1992).

16 Norwood (1651[–2]), p.17; Hill (1995), p.128; Cooper, ed. (1971), p.571; cf. Katz (1982), pp.107–26 espec. p.110.

17 It has been argued that Blake was a member of, or was influenced by, the Muggletonians, a sect that grew out of, or in opposition to, the Robins sect (cf. Hill (1990), p.323).

18 H[all?]., G. (1651), p.5.

19 *PA* (1651) no.21, p.166.

20 H[all?]., G. (1651), pp.2–3; cf. Garment (1651), p.4; Muggleton (1699), pp.20–1.

21 Katz (1982), pp.109–10; Hill (1995), pp.128, 282; Morton (1970), p.92; Almond (1999), p.121; Thomas, K. (1983), pp.289–90; Spencer (1993), pp.204–5; Hopton, ed. (1992); Luxon (1993), p.900; Prest (1981), p.74.

22 Nigel Smith, 'Foster, George (*fl.* 1650)', *ODNB*.

23 H[all?]., G. (1651), p.5.

24 H[all?]., G. (1651), p.5.

25 Muggleton (1699), pp.46–7.

26 Reeve [and Muggleton?] (1711), p.13; cf. Muggleton (1699), pp.46–7.

27 Field (1685), p.8; [Vaughan, W.] (1633), p.62.
28 Reeve [and Muggleton?] (1711), p.13; cf. Muggleton (1699), pp.46–7; cf. Field (1685), p.8; cf. pp.A2r, 15, 17; 1 Timothy 4:1–5; cf. St Hippolytus (2005), Bk. vii, ch.12 and Bk. viii, ch.13 (pp.326–7); Jerome (2005a), Bk II, ch.16.
29 Garment (1651), pp.4–7; H[all?], G. (1651), pp.2–3; Muggleton (1699), pp.20–1; Hill, Reay and Lamont (1983), p.69; Genesis 14:18; Hebrews 6:20; cf. Böhme (1924), pp.398–9; Whiting (1968), pp.255, 316.
30 Garment (1651), pp.3, 6; cf. Niclaes (1649), pp.143–4 (ch. 11. vs 51–2); Coppe (1651), p.3.
31 Isaiah 65:25; cf. Isaiah 11:6–9.
32 Anon. (1650a), pp.4–5; Katz (1982), pp.18–30; Chamberlain (1939), II.140n.; Birch (1849), II.65; Hamilton, W.D., ed. (1873), pp.466–7. Mrs Traske may or may not have been in prison since the time of her husband's first conviction. cf. Vaughan, W. (1630), p.56.
33 Scobell (1657–8), pp.124–5, 149–50; Hill (1990), p.157ff.; Hill (1991), p.208; Jones (1909), p.478.
34 H[all?]. (1651), pp.2–3; Anon. (1651a); Taylor (1651); *PA* (1651), no.21, p.166; Anon. (1651b), pp.1–5; Katz (1982), pp.111–12; Hopton, ed. (1992); Tany (1988).
35 Scobell (1657–8), pp.124–5, 149–50; Hill (1990), p.157; Hill (1991), p.208; Jones (1909), p.478.
36 Hopton, ed. (1992), p.12.
37 Records based on official interrogation reports (which Christopher Hill considered often biased) state that he and his followers believed he was God. The two pamphlets not relying on government sources report that he and some of his followers explicitly denied he was God

(Garment (1651) and H[all?]. (1651)). However, these statements were made after his arrest and could have been tailored to avoid conviction for blasphemy. Garment also denied that they were pantheists, another doctrine outlawed by the Blasphemy Act. Garment (1651); H[all?]., G. (1651), p.6; Anon. (1651a), pp.1–14; Anon. (1651b) Anon. (1654); Hopton, ed. (1992), pp.10–12; Luxon (1993), p.900; cf. Webster (1975), p.13.
38 Katz (1982), pp.113–14; H[all?]., G. (1651), pp.2–3; Anon. (1651a).
39 *Calendar of State Papers, Domestic Series 1651–2*, p.114, which may be referring to John Robins; Reeve [and Muggleton?] (1711), pp.6–14; Muggleton (1699), pp.38–9, 45–7; Katz (1982), p.115.
40 Scobell (1657–8), pp.124–5; cf. e.g. Anon. (1650b), p.2; [Clarkson] (1659), p.98ff.; Baxter (1696), p.76.
41 Bauthumley (1650), pp.3–9; Holland (1650), p.5. cf. O[verton] (1643), pp.17–19; Ecclesiastes 3:19; Böhme (1654), ch. 22, § 4, pp.97–8; Salmon (1651), pp.37–8; Coppin (1649), title page. Hill (1991), pp.204–27; Morton (1970), p.73; Acheson (1990), p.66; Whiting (1968), p.272.
42 Winstanley (1973), pp.84, 90, 94; Smith (1994), p.334.
43 Winstanley (1941), pp.82, 157; Hill (1991), pp.139–40, 206; Winstanley (1649), pp.2–4; cf. Mss Rawlinson (Bodleian) D 833, fol.105r–v; Harrison, P. (1993), p.530; cp. Smith (1989), p.258; cf. Winstanley (1973), pp.19, 219; Coppin (1649), Part I, pp.9–10; Bauthumley (1650), pp.4–6; Morton (1970), pp.70–1; Jacob (1981), p.224; Lennon (1993), pp.323–6n.
44 Winstanley (1649), pp.4, 9–10; *cit.* Harrison, P. (1993), pp.538–9;

cf. Winstanley (1973), pp.219–20, 250; Winstanley (1941), p.156. Hill (1986b), p.90; Böhme (1920), p.426; see 'Golden Rule' under 'Animals' in index. On Winstanley's ideas of the Fall, see Winstanley (1973), p.99; cf. Böhme (1894), ch. 4, § 109–10; and compare Winstanley (1942), pp.156–7 with Böhme (1920), p.426.

45 Winstanley (1973), p.224; cp. Smith (1994), p.334; Smith (1989), pp.258, 266. It may have been as a result of the conflation of pantheism and vegetarianism that Nigel Smith says that Thomas Tany was vegetarian without providing any evidence (Smith (1999), p.110). There is a danger of reading back into Winstanley views held by others with similar beliefs, like Thomas Tryon; cf. e.g. Tryon (1700), p.86, 127 and pp.63–5 (which Smith cites (Smith (1999), pp.108–9); cf. [Tryon] (1684b), pp.91–4; cf. e.g. Spencer (1993), pp.204–5.

46 Bauthumley (1650), pp.3–9.

47 Smith (1994), p.334.

48 Niclaes (1649), pp.1, 23, 57, 143–4; [Niclaes] (1574), sig.A2v–A5r; Romans 12:18–19; Hebrews 12:14; Exodus 20; Matthew 5; [Niclaes] (1575a?), sig.52v–53r; [Rogers] (1579), sig.Hv.v; Thomas More, *Utopia, cit.* Williams, Howard (1883), p.93; Hamilton (1981), p.133; Moss (1975); Jundt (1875), p.201. Niclaes did not say that God was limited to the universe, making him a panentheist rather than pantheist.

49 [Niclaes] (1575a?), sig.55r; cf. sigs.7r, 9v; Niclaes (1575b?), sig.17r, 45r; Isaiah 11:6–9, 65:25; Hosea 2:18.

50 Edwards (1645–6), Bk I, p.80; *cit.* Thomas, K. (1983), pp.290–1. cf. [Niclaes] (1649), p.1. Marshall also preached universal salvation, like John Robins.

51 Edwards (1645–6), Bk I, pp.21,

35, 80; cf. Edwards (1646), pp.25, 35–6. Edwards echoes Etherington (1645), p.1; cf. Thomas, K. (1983), p.139. For links between Winstanley and the Family of Love, see e.g. Hill (1991), pp.27, 110–87; Berens (1906), *cit.* Bailey (1914), p.113.

CHAPTER 3

1 For Crab's practices and beliefs which indicate that he was a Baptist, see Edwards (1646), p.110; Crab (1655), pp.8–9; Crab (1657), pp.5–6, 15.

2 Edwards (1646), p.110; Edwards is often regarded as unreliable (Woolrych (1986), p.97), but in this case the evidence is corroborated by a Parliamentary report.

3 Fairfax (1647), p.5. This document helps to confirm Crab's affiliation with the Levellers which Christopher Hill suspected (Hill (1995), p.283). Andrew Hopton and Rick Bowers, who also did not know about these sources, take at face value the claim of Crab's publisher that Crab was 'neither for the Levelers, nor Quakers, nor Shakers, nor Ranters'. But the publisher had an interest in making his client as acceptable to the public as possible and by 1655 affiliation with these groups would have been unpopular and dangerous. Bowers (2003), p.93.

4 PA (1655), no.210, p.1680.

5 Hessayon, 'Roger Crab', *ODNB*.

6 Crab (1655), pp.1, 15; Crab (1657), p.17; cf. Winstanley (1973), pp.12, 127; Winstanley (1942), p.188; cf. Crab (1990), p.6.

7 Hessayon, 'Roger Crab', *ODNB*.

8 Crab (1655), p.1. For Ranters in Uxbridge cf. Whiting (1968), p.273.

9 Crab (1655), p.12; cf. Purchas, ed. (1905–7), VIII.211. Crab's allusion to John the Baptist as a Leveller recalls Winstanley saying

in 1650 that 'Jesus Christ . . . is the head Leveller', Hill (1995), p.287.

10 cf. Goldsmith (1986), pp.70–1.

11 Crab (1655), pp.7–8; Hill (1995), pp.286–7; Tryon (1700), p.236. Crab even pointed out that shirt-starching was a waste of flour (Crab (1657), p.19).

12 Crab (1990), pp.4–5.

13 William Lilly, Bodleian Library, Oxford, Ashm. 427, f.51v; cf. Ashm. 210, f.107v; *cit.* Thomas, K. (1971), p.373.

14 Crab (1655), 'To the Reader', p.[i].

15 Crab (1990), p.4.

16 O[verton] (1643), pp.17–19, 38, 49–51; Harrison, P. (1993), pp.538–9n.; cf. Hildrop (1742–3), p.42; Ecclesiastes 3:19; Thomas, K. (1983), p.139; Harrison, P. (2001), p.210; Bauthumley (1650), pp.3–9; Hill (1991), p.207; Coppin (1649), Part III, p.8; Cudworth (1678), pp.44–5; [Vaughan, T.] (1650), pp.12–13, 15–16; Rudrum (1989).

17 Crab (1990), pp.4–5.

18 Crab (1655), p.[ii]; Hill (1995), pp.128, 282–4; Rogers (1903), p.1084; cp. Bowers (2003), p.96; Ariel Hessayon, 'Robert Norwood', *ODNB*.

19 James Caulfield (1813), II.155–6.

20 Winstanley (1973), p.18.

21 Crab (1990), p.6.

22 Crab (1655), p.15; Winstanley (1973), pp.289–90; *cit.* Goldsmith (1986), pp.75, 77. This idea of personal agrarian reform was revived by radicals at the end of the eighteenth century; cf. Shelley, *Vind.*15.

23 cf. e.g. Crab (1657), title page; Hill (1995), pp.286–7.

24 Strype (1720), II, Appendix 1, p.99; Winstanley (1942), p.111; *cit.* Harrison, P. (1993), pp.539; Crab (1657), pp.6–7; Goldsmith (1986), pp.67, 70–1.

25 Woolman (1922), p.306; Turner (1980), pp.6–7, 9.

26 Christopher Hill says many ex-Leveller Quakers did the same (Hill (1995), p.286).

27 Crab (1655), p.3.

28 Crab (1655), pp.3–4; cf. Aquinas (1975), ch.112, § 12–13, pp.118–19. Crab developed this idea further in his description of butchers as bloodthirsty. The reviling of butchers, as a scapegoat for human cruelty to animals, was common; Thomas More's Utopians gave the job of butchering only to their criminalised bondsmen; cf. also ch. 16 below; Mercerus (1598), 'Genesis 9:4', p.197; Hartley (1749), II.222; Blount ([1680?]), pp.58–9; Edwards (1699), I.117–19: 'Butchers, who kill Beasts, are generally cruel and bloody to Men; and for that reason the Law suffers them not to be on the Jury of Life and Death'; Bernard Mandeville parallels Crab's reasoning closely in his argument that the consumer is guilty as well as the butcher Mandeville (1924), Remark P, I.173–81; Rousseau was building on Mandeville and probably inherited this idea from him (Rousseau, J.-J. (1979), pp.153–4); Jeremy Bentham in turn repeated Rousseau's maxim (see ch. 24 below). Keith Thomas says that this common notion that butchers were not allowed to be jurymen has no basis in fact (Thomas, K. (1983), p.295; cf. Fudge (2000), p.132).

29 Crab (1655), p.4.

30 Crab (1655), p.3; cf. e.g. 1 Peter 2:11.

31 Crab (1655), pp.[ii], 1, 3.

32 Ironically, later in the century, John Edwards, the son of Crab's anti-vegetarian foe, Thomas Edwards, would come to the same conclusion, Edwards (1699), I.113, 117; cf. e.g. Dupleix (1606), p.189; Browne (1672), Bk III, ch.xxv, pp.189–94; cp. [Hecquet] (1733), I.xiii–xix, 7–8, 16–18, 21, 42–4, 104–10; Reynolds (1725), pp.92–3.

33 Crab (1657), p.20; Crab (1655),

p.3; cf. Rostvig (1954); Smith (1994), p.335; Morton (2002), p.64.

34 Exodus 16:2–3; Numbers 11:33; cf. Jerome (2005a), Bk I, ch.18, Bk II, chs.15, 17; [Hecquet] (1709), pp.29–30; [Hecquet] (1733), I.27–9.

35 Crab (1655), pp.[i], 11; also the Rechabites; Ezekiel 4:9; Isaiah 20; Jeremiah 35:6.

36 Jerome (2005a), Bk II, ch.15.

37 Crab (1655), pp.12–13.

38 Isaiah 7:15; Crab (1655), 'To the impartial Reader', p.9.

39 Crab (1655), p.9. The distinction is reminiscent of Catholic fast laws which forbade land, but not aquatic, animals.

40 Matthew 15:11; Mark 16:18; I Corinthians 10:25; I Timothy 4:1–4; Crab (1655), pp.4–5; Aquinas (1975), ch.127, p.158.

41 Crab (1657), p.17; cf. Crab (1655), title page; Romans 14:21; 1 Corinthians 8:13.

42 1 Timothy 4:5.

43 Crab (1655), p.10. Crab's reliance on voluntary levelling action in the department of diet was like the Levellers' insistence that landowners should not be commanded to give up their property but should do so voluntarily (Goldsmith (1986), p.74). He also echoes Philostratus (1912), II.305–7.

44 Romans 14:2–3; Crab (1657), p.16.

45 Crab (1655), p.[iv]; Crab (1657), p.3; Bowers (2003), p.97, n.14; Hearmon (1982), p.28.

46 Crab (1655), p.7; Crab (1657), pp.3–4, 17, 19, 24–8.

47 PA (1655 [n.s.]), no.210, p.1680; cit. Crab (1990), p.5.

48 Crab (1655), p.1.

49 Roger Crab's contemporaries and later generations emasculated his 'radicalism' by constructing it as 'eccentricity'; so effective was this that it is claimed that Lewis Carroll's 'Mad Hatter' in *Alice's Adventures in Wonderland* was based on Roger Crab, and Christopher Hill even going as far as to claim that the phrase 'Mad as a Hatter' was invented as a title for Crab. Others have speculated that Crab's head-wound could explain his unorthodox opinions. Morgan, J. (1732), I; Crab (1745); Lysons (1792–6), III.438, 454–6; Lempriere (1808); Caulfield (1813), II.154–6; Wilson (1813), I.46–8; Gibbs (1888), pp.116–17; Rogers (1903); Hill (1995), pp.282–9; Sieveking (1988); cf. Bowers (2003).

50 Crab (1659a), p.4; cf. Smith (1994), p.335.

51 Crab (1659a), pp.3–4; Crab (1659b); Hessayon, 'Roger Crab', *ODNB*; Salter (1659), p.5.

52 Strype (1720), II, Appendix 1, p.99; Gibbons (1996), pp.114–5; Walker (1964), p.218; Revelation 1:11, 3:7.

53 Hill (1995), p.284; Elmer (1989), p.23; Rogers (1903), p.1085; Ariel Hessayon, 'John Pordage', *ODNB*.

54 Baxter (1696), pp.76–8 ; Moss (1981), pp.58, 60, 63; Etherington (1645), p.10; Nuttall (1954), pp.3–9; Hamilton (1981), pp.136–9; Hill (1995), p.284; Hill (1991), pp.224, 284, 289; Thune (1948), pp.36–43, and *passim*; Jones (1914), pp.227–34; Whiting (1968), p.299; Mss Rawlinson (Bodleian) D 833, fol.63r; Anon. (1650b), p.3; Anon. (1650a), p.6 (Pordich and Buckeridge = Pordage).

55 Mss Rawlinson (Bodleian) D 833, fols.12v, 86v.

56 Thune (1948), pp.79, 92, 94; Lead (1695), p.4; Almond (1999), p.118.

57 Mss Rawlinson (Bodleian) D 833, fols.105r–v, 227r; Crab (1655), p.13.

58 Timothy Morton told me of a Philadelphian vegetarian by the name of 'Bathsheba Bowers' (sp?), but I have found no references to such a person.

59 Thune (1948), pp.48, 156; cf.

p.150; Mss Rawlinson (Bodleian) D 833, fols.1v, 6v–7r, 14r, 69, 85r, 190r; Nuttal (1954), pp.7–16; Whiting (1968), p.301; Hill, Reay and Lamont (1983), p.69; Rousseau, G.S. (1998), p.101; McDowell (2002), p.515; Crab (1655), p.3.

60 Mss Rawlinson (Bodleian) D 833, fol.63r.

61 Mss Rawlinson (Bodleian) D 833, fols.48r, 77, 165v–r, 185r, 223v.

62 Thune (1948), pp.36–7, 42–3, 48, 63–4, 72–4, 80–1, 117, 141, 150 and *passim*; Walker (1964), pp.218–30; Whiting (1931). pp.321–2; Lead (1695), pp.4, 64; Lead (1696), pp.54–5; Whiting (1968), p.299, 309–10 ; Bromley (n.d.), pp.4–5 (Pythagoras' *Golden Verses*), p.10 (History of the Waldenses, probably by Perrin); Jones (1914), pp.208, 219–11, 223, 227–34; Plard (1970), p.145.

63 Boehme (1909), p.225.

64 Böhme (1924), pp.150–1; Böhme (1640), p.107, (21.16–17); cf. Tryon (1691b), p.130. Cf. Spencer (1993), pp.237–8, 253.

65 Crab (1657), pp.20–2; Böhme (1654, 1924), pp.31–3; Gibbons (1996), pp.114–15; cf. e.g. Tryon (1705a) [128, [2]pp.; 12°; CUL VIII.32.70], pp.23–4; Thune (1948), p.119. Compare also Crab (1657), pp.14, 18 with Böhme (1654, 1924), ch.27, v.46, pp.231–2.

66 Strype (1720), II, Appendix 1, p.99.

67 Hessayon, 'Roger Crab', *ODNB*.

CHAPTER 4

1 Della Valle (1892), p.99; Gaudenzio (1641), p.41; Mitter (1977), pp.28–31, 49ff.; Tavernier (1995), II.142; Fryer (1909), II.100; Blount (1680?), pp.14–15; Temple (1690), pp.17–18.

2 cf. e.g. Terry (1655), p.A7v; Locke (1858), pp.251–3.

3 The debate about Orientalist constructions of the Indian 'Other'

has deepened the understanding of how the European acquisition of knowledge about India was motivated by a desire to acquire, and was in itself an expression of exerting, power over India (Said (1978), pp.21, 37 and *passim* and e.g. Teltscher (1995)). But we have lost sight of the genuine influence which Indian culture had on Europe. Recent academic work has returned to the question of 'genuine influence' and has begun to erode the megalithic assumption that travellers only projected onto the Orient those prejudices they carried with them, e.g. Rubiés (2000), pp.x–xiv+n., 367n., and *passim*; Mitter (1977), p.51; Popkin (1990a), pp.33–5; cf. Hazard (1953), pp.8–12; Sarasohn (1996), p.178; Reinders (2004). Drew (1998) tackles this issue from a different angle.

Europeans encountered Jains and Buddhists, but there was little understanding about their status, and so the different traditions were often conflated under the umbrella terms 'Gentoo', 'Hindoo', 'Banian'. 'Hinduism' itself can be argued to be a category of Western invention, misleadingly projecting onto the heterogeneous Indian religious traditions a homogeneity equivalent to that of Christianity. However, since the development of European thought is the object of examination, it is pertinent to refer to categories which they conceptualised. Thus they were interested in 'Hinduism' even if Hinduism can be said not to exist. Although suggestions can be made about exactly which groups were encountered by particular individuals, the conclusions are often doubtful since the travelogues were partly (and sometimes entirely) composed of invention, exaggeration, misapprehension, projection and plagiarism. Recent scholars have pointed out that Vaishnavism and Jainism are intermixed in western India, that many Banians in western India are Jain, and that most Jain merchants still call themselves Hindus. However, such comments have often relied upon the speculative work of nineteenth-century scholars who sometimes assumed that Indian culture had remained static for two millennia and that nineteenth-century practices provided a perfect picture of conditions in previous centuries. cf. Lach and Kley (1993), p.645n. who cite Yule and Burnell, *Hobson Jobson* (n.18), pp.63–4; Prasad (1968), pp.324–25, n.7 who in turn repeats the comments of Monier Williams, *Modern India*, 2nd edn, p.74. See also Linschoten (1988), I.252–5n.; Goyal (2000), pp.117–18, 122, 131. Stoneman (1994), p.507; Stoneman (1995), p.108. On this confusion, see e.g. Rubiés (2000), p.29.

4 Pyrrho appears to have absorbed Indian thought on a visit there, and even Socrates was said to have met Indian philosophers sojourning in Athens. Democritus and Lycurgus were said to have derived part of their philosophy from India. Herodotus (484–c.435 BC) had written of Indians who 'refuse to put any live animal to death . . . Vegetables are their only food.' Ctesias the Cnidian (b. c.416 BC), the Greek physician, picked up enough while staying in Persia to write a book about India full of stories of the justice-loving Indians living disease-free lives of up to 200 years, feeding exclusively on sweet roots and milk (Herodotus (1862), III.100; Kämper (1995), pp.159–60; Stoneman (1995), pp.99–100, 103–4; Stoneman (1994), p.507; Ferguson (1975), pp.47, 64; cp. Sedlar (1980)).

5 Majumdar, ed. (1960), p.278. This and other such observations show

that Europeans were aware of the problems of interpreting alien cultures; see e.g. Della Valle (1892), pp.76–7.

6 cf. Palladius et al. (1665), sig.c2r.

7 On karmic rebirth in Hinduism, and its similarity to Pythagorean 'ethicized' metempsychosis, see e.g. O'Flaherty, ed. (1980), pp.14, 21; Obeyesekere (1980), pp.137–8, 151; Spencer (1993), p.77. On those doctrines in Indian and Greek religion respectively, see Tull (1989), p.31ff. Kirk and Raven (1960), pp.222–3; Guthrie (1962), pp.194–5; Heninger (1974), pp.267+n.; Kämper (1995), p.160; Ovid, *Metamorphoses*, XV.

8 Kämper (1995), pp.159–85; Ammianus (1935), II.366–9 (xxiii. 6, 32–33). Most previous commentators have focused on the claim that Pythagoras took his philosophy from Egypt, though Egypt was often seen only as an intermediary between Pythagoras and India, cf. Kirk and Raven (1960), p.224; Guthrie (1962), p.160; Heninger (1974), pp.268–9.

9 Apuleius (1853), pp.377–8, 388–9; cf. pp.272, 278–9; Walbridge (2001), pp.5–8; Stoneman (1994), p.507.

10 Guthrie (1962), pp.186–195; Celenza (1999); Burkert (1972), pp.180–1; Mitter (1977), p.49ff.

11 On the Egyptian origin of Greek Philosophy, see Bernal (1987), pp.70–2, 105–6, 110, 117–20, 135–6, 230 and *passim*. On Indian primacy see the excellent collection of ancient and early modern references in Kämper (1995), pp.146 (Egyptian origin of Greek culture); 148, 159 (Pythagoras' travels); 149–50 (Brahmins); 151 (Pythagoras learning from the Brahmins); 152 (Egypt was a colony that came from India, citing Homer, Strabo, Pliny, Ptolemaios, Herodotus (an erroneous citation, cf. VII.70),

Arrian, Eusebius of Cæsarea, Philostratus, and from the seventeenth century P.D. Huet, C. Helvicus, J. Ludolph; see also Manetho (1940), Appendix IV, 159–61, 171–2; Lucian (1905), IV.97–8; Creech (1699), sig.Ar; Lloyd (1699), p.vi. cp. Diodorus Siculus (1604), Bk III, p.144.

12 Anti-sacrifice was a Pythagorean position; there are conflicting stories, however, that Pythagoras offered a sacrifice of oxen when he worked out his famous theorem about the hypotenuse of a right-angled triangle. Diogenes Laertius (2000), II.331–2; Burkert (1972), pp.180–1; cf. Athenaeus of Naucratis, *Deipnosophistae*, Bk. 1; Reuchlin (1983), pp.173–9; Lord (1630), pp.47–9; Guthrie (1962), pp.188–91. For a review of the parallels between Buddhist and Christian sacrifice-reforms, see Derrett (2000).

13 Philostratus (1912), I.3, 5, 257–69, 291, 307; II.39–51, 303–7, 315, 339, 537–41; Drew (1998), pp.85–90; Stoneman (1994), p.504; Stoneman (1995), p.108–9; Mitter (1977), p.49ff.

14 Sedlar (1980), pp.199–207; Stoneman (1994), pp.503–4; Schwab (1984), p.3.

15 St Irenaeus (1868), Bk I, ch.25, sect.4, pp.95–6; Mead (1931), pp.23, 26, 77, 274, 7, 37, 205, 231–2, 339; Spencer (1993), pp.55, 113, 117, 130–42.

16 cf. Manu (1971), v.56; Porphyry (2000), pp.113–15+nn. Clark notes the accuracy of Porphyry's description of the Brahmins, but not his description of the 'renouncers', which does not come from Strabo and therefore attests the verity of Bardesanes' claims of a real encounter. Rajumdar (1960), pp.425–31; Stoneman (1995), p.109; Drew (1998), pp.80–1.

17 Rajumdar (1960), pp.439–40; McCrindle (1960), pp.103–4; Clement of Alexandria (2004a),

Bk I, ch.15; cf. Bk II, ch.18; Bk III, ch.7; Bk VII, ch.1; Clement of Alexandria (2004b), Bk 2, ch.1 'On eating'.

18 Hippolytus (2005), Bk I, ch.21, pp.59–60; Bk VII, ch.16; Bk VIII, ch.13, pp.326–7; Rajumdar (1960), p.443; Stoneman (1994), pp.503–4; Genesis 3:19.

19 Rajumdar (1960), pp.431–4; cf. Herodotus (1862), III.106.

20 cf. Drew (1998), pp.164–6; Prest (1981), pp.27–37; Grove (1995), pp.96–100, 153; Rubiés (2000), pp.36, 147–9.

21 Rajumdar (1960), p.446; cf. Boas (1948), pp.140n., 150; cf. Voltaire (1779–80), I.43–4.

22 Bardesanes (2004), p.730; Eusebius (1903), Bk VI, Ch. 10, Vol.III, pp.295–300 (col.273a–278a); p.442 (col.410d); pp.502–3 (col.471a); (cf. Porphyry (2000), p.113n.). Exactly the same passage from Bardesanes was used by the influential text which Eusebius had also read: Pseudo-Clement (2005a), Bk IX, ch.20; cf. chs. 25, 27; and used again in Pseudo-Origen, repr. in Rajumdar (1960), p.443.

23 Jerome (2005a), Bk II, chs.13–15; Rajumdar (1960), p.440; Derrett (1960), p.67; Origen (2005), p.36.

24 Stoneman (1994), p.503; cf. Hahn, ed. (1981), f.97r; Tryon (1696), p.125.

25 Stoneman (1991), pp.131–3, 178–9; Stoneman (1995), pp.99, 113–4; Stoneman (1994). For discussions on the history of 'the virtuous Brahmin', see Boas (1948), pp.137–51 and Mitter (1977), p.49ff.

26 Rubiés (2000), p.82.

27 Polo (1972), pp.261, 267, 271, 277–80; cf. pp.255–6, 265; Polo recognised that India was not entirely vegetarian, p.272; Rubiés (2000), pp.54–72.

28 Polo (1972), p.281ff; cf. Linschoten (1988), I.78–9; Lockman, ed. (1743), I.383n.

29 Drew (1998), pp.164–6; Grove (1995), pp.96–100, 153; Rubiés (2000), pp.36, 147–9.

30 Yule, ed. (1915), III.220, 226–60; cf. II.171; cf. Rubiés (2000), pp.65, 74n.

31 On Bacchus in India, see Rajumdar (1960), pp.195, 273–82; Goyal (2000), pp.117–32; McCrindle (1960), pp.68, 227; Goyal (1985), p.105; Stoneman (1995), pp.103–9; cf. Rubiés (2000), pp.83–4, 98; Lach and Kley (1993), p.648.

32 Rubiés (2000), pp.83–4, 106–21.

33 Boemus (1885–90), Vol.VI, Bk. ii, ch.8; Rubiés (2000), pp.126+n.; Mitter (1977), p.48. Compare Boemus with Boas (1948), pp.148–9.

34 Mandeville (1900), ch. 32.

35 Rubiés (2000), p.146; Lakowski (1999), pp.13–14, 17, 19; Yates (1961), p.233; Derrett (1960), p.67.

36 Spink (1960), p.50; McGuire and Rattansi (1966), p.129.

37 Campanella (1901); cf. Polo (1972), pp.279–80.

38 Swift (1726), Pt. IV, Ch.2.

39 Mitter (1977), pp.27–8; Drew (1998), p.47; Rubiés (2000), pp.7–9, 83–4, 155–62; Županov (1999), pp.35–7.

40 Mitter (1977); da Vinci (1970), II.103–4n.; da Vinci (1956), p.382; Nicholl (2004), p.43; Annand (1927), p.414.

41 da Vinci (1956), p.246; da Vinci (1970), II.103–6+n., 179, 216, 298–9, 315, 341–2+n., 369; cf. II.94, 221, 242+n., 245, 258, 289, 292–308; Kemp (1981), pp.44, 52, 159, 177, 343–4; Franzero (1969), pp.107–8 (treat with caution); da Vinci (1987), pp.20–3, 26 (extremely dubious authenticity); Spencer (1993), pp.190–2, who is incorrect to suggest that the issue was only mentioned by one of sixty biographies in the London Library. Blount (1680), pp.2–3. Cf. Ovid (1632), Bk XV and Sandys'

commentary; Gaitonde (1983), pp.36–7.

42 Anon. (1898), pp.45, 58, 132; cf. 49–59, 57, 138–9; Purchas, ed. (1905–7), II.71; Rubiés (2000), pp.161, 165–70, 267+n.; Burde (1963). cf. Lord (1630), p.41.

43 For a polemic discussion of non-vegetarian traditions in ancient Indian texts, see e.g. Jha (2002) (published and pulped in New Delhi as *Holy Cow: Beef-eating in Indian Dietary Traditions*, 2001).

44 Findly (1934).

45 Zimmerman (1987), pp.182–92.

46 Manu (1971), v.29.

47 Manu (1971), v.46.

48 Linschoten (1988), I.297–9; Roe (1990), pp.274–5; Tavernier (1995), p.158; Foster (1999), p.14.

49 Mitter (1977), pp.1–55. Though cf. the humanist interpretations of Della Valle (1892), pp.73–4. Della Valle echoes Plutarch's *Isis and Osiris* and Porphyry, cf. Bernal (1987), pp.117–19; Rubiés (2000), pp.357–8; Ovington (1929), pp.168–70; Manuel (1963), pp.107–8.

50 Lach (1971), I.i.439–40; Foster (1999), pp.14, 22–3; Roe (1990), p.275; Bernier (1988), pp.326–7; Fryer (1909), I.138; Picart (1733–7), VI.ii.162–3; Lockman, ed. (1743), I.361n.; Mitter (1977), pp.22, 50, 62; Radicati (1737), pp.41; Herbert (1634), p.39; Anon. (1898), pp.45, 132; Rubiés (2000), p.167; [Créquinière] (1705), p.55; Terry (1655), pp.327, 352.

51 Glanius (1682), pp.168–70; cf. Rubiés (2000), p.371+n.; Kircher (1987), p.137; Yates (1961), p.68; Diodorus Siculus (1700), p.43; Picart (1733–7), VI.ii.162–3.

52 Yule, ed. (1915), II.137–8; Rubiés (2000), pp.75–6; Mitter (1977), p.50; Polo (1972), pp.279–80.

53 Lach (1971), I.i.439–40; Foster (1999), p.14; Linschoten (1988), I.257–8; Lord (1630), pp.60–1; Tavernier (1995), pp.164, 169,

199; Manucci (1965), I.151–3;
Ovington (1929), p.186; Picart
(1733–7), IV.ii.15; Manucci
(1965), I.151–3, III.39–42.
54 Polo (1972), pp.265, 276, 279;
Rubiés (2000), p.60; Mitter
(1977), p.50; cf. Linschoten
(1988), I.257–8, 300–1; Della
Valle (1892), pp.68–71, 86–7+n.;
Ovington (1929), pp.168–70; cf.
pp.138, 177+n., 219.
55 Bernier (1988), pp.326–7; Fryer
(1909), I.94.
56 Aquinas (1975), pp.157–8; cf.
Diodorus Siculus (1700),
pp.44–5; Maimonides (1963),
p.581 (III.xlvi); Browne (1672), Bk
III, ch.xxv, pp.189–94.
57 See ch. 19 below; cf. Jerome
(2005a), Bk II. ch.7; Browne
(1672), Bk III, ch.xxv,
pp.189–194+nn.; Maimonides
(1963), p.581 (Pt III, ch.46).
58 Mitter (1977), p.49; Gaitonde
(1983), pp.31–3; Linschoten
(1988), I.253–4; Ovington
(1929), p.176; Kincaid (1973),
p.13; Terry (1655), pp.326–7.
59 Gaitonde (1983), pp.31–3, 36–7;
Lach (1971), pp.360, 399–401; cf.
Polo (1972), pp.277, 280;
Linschoten (1988), I.253–4; Roe
(1990), pp.92, 270–1; Mitter
(1977), p.49ff; Manucci (1965),
I.151–3, 379+n.; Fryer (1909),
I.231, 211–12+n.; Ovington
(1929), p.175; Picart (1733–7),
IV.ii.15; Teltscher (2000), p.161;
Purchas (1905–7), IV.443, IX.46;
Herbert (1634), p.38. On
apparently Jain concern for
microscopic organisms, cf.
Ovington (1929), pp.195–6; the
preposition in Ovington's
statement seems to have been
misunderstood in [Créquinière]
(1705), p.55; cf. Lach (1971),
I.459–60; Lord (1630), pp.74–6;
Lach and Kley (1993), p.649; Fryer
(1909), II.107–8+n. Missionaries
debunked vegetarianism by using
microscopes to show Indians that
they 'committed many murders'
every time they drank water:

Teltscher (1995), p.95 (see ch. 20
and 25 below); O'Flaherty, ed.
(1980), pp.223–5; Walli (1974),
pp.56–7.
60 Linschoten (1988), I.251–6+n.; cf.
I.205–7, 246, 248; Gaudenzio
(1641), pp.39–42; Della Valle
(1892), pp.68–71.
61 Ovington (1929), pp.177–8; Roe
(1990), p.105; Manucci (1965),
I.151–3; Fryer (1909), I.138, 257,
350, II.25; cf. I.196, II.73.
62 Anon. (1687), pp.55, 63.
63 cf. e.g. Lord (1630), pp.74–6;
Della Valle (1892), pp.68–71;
Manucci (1965), I.151–3; Kircher
(1987), p.143; [Créquinière]
(1705), p.55; Hasan (1733),
Notes, Part 2, p.35.
64 Foster (1999), p.25; cf. pp.14–19,
28; cf. Linschoten (1988),
I.253–4+n..
65 Ovid (1632), Bk XV; Ovington
(1929), pp.177–8; cf. *Spy*,
V.87–90; Tryon (1691a),
pp.371–2.
66 Tertullian (2004a), ch.48; Lord
(1630), p.52; Linschoten (1999),
p.212; Teltscher (2000),
pp.161–5. Mughals had noticed
the similarity too: Alberuni
(1888), I.68–88; Abul Fazl
(1783–86), III.96; Drew (1998),
pp.53–4.
67 Tyson & Wallis (1721), p.4.
68 Fryer (1909), I.94, 108, II.79,
100–2, 167; cf. I.118.
69 Purchas, ed. (1905–7), I.205,
217–43, III.69; V.200; IX.45ff, 89;
Roe (1990), pp.270–1, 105; cf.
Gaitonde (1983), p.39; Linschoten
(1988), I.251–2+n.; Bondt
(1769), pp.156–7.
70 These claims may have arisen due
to the traditional medieval Islamic
claim that Hinduism had been
established in India by Pythagoras,
a story that would have been well
known in Mughal India. The sixth/
twelfth-century theologian
Shahrastānī – exceptional in his
openness to Hinduism – claimed
that a student of Pythagoras called
Calanus (*Qalānus*) travelled to

India and divulged
Pythagoreanism to 'Barākhmīn'
who then became 'the leader of all
the Indians and urged men to
purify their bodies and rectify their
souls'. The historical Calanus,
whose legend was recorded in
numerous ancient and early
modern texts, was in fact an
Indian 'gymnosophist' who
returned from India with
Alexander as far as Persia before
burning himself on a funeral pyre;
cf. Walbridge (2001), pp.70–2;
Lawrence (1976).

71 Della Valle (1892), pp.75–7; cf.
Bayle, P. (1734–41), VIII.618;
Mitter (1977), pp.28–31, 49;
Rubiés (2000), pp. 354–8, 363,
370–2+n., 382. Della Valle stated
that Philostratus claimed that
Pythagoras taught metempsychosis
to the Indians, whereas the Greek
text of Philostratus says the
opposite (as far as can be
ascertained): that the Indians
taught it to Pythagoras. This
crucial priority reversal is repeated
by Athanasius Kircher and Father
Bouchet. I am extremely grateful
to Joan-Pau Rubiés for pointing
out to me what he does not
explain in Rubiés (2000), that the
origin of this 'error' lies in the
standard Latin translation of the
problematic Greek manuscript of
Philostratus edited at the turn of
the sixteenth century, and two
separate Italian translations of
1549, all of which declared that
Pythagoras taught the doctrine to
us (the Indians), rather than to
you (the Greeks). Whether these
editors mistranslated that one
Greek word wholly inadvertently,
or whether they did so wilfully
because *they* did not think it
possible or desirable that the
Indians taught Pythagoras, their
decision epitomised a priority
dispute with far-reaching
significance which raged for
centuries, and in a different
framework is still openly debated

today. In 1532 a humanist critic
noted the manuscript variant in a
footnote, but without corrrecting
the translation. Rubiés' statement
that Philostratus had 'completely
reversed' the usual derivation 'by
giving primacy to India', however,
does not seem to take account of
the Neoplatonic tradition
represented by Apuleius (see
above). Philostratus (1912), I.269,
II.303–5, 339; Kircher (1987),
p.138; Picart (1733–7),
IV.ii.159–67. cp. e.g. Gueullette
(1725), pp.xv–xvi; Lloyd (1699),
p.vi.

72 Lord (1630), Title Page,
Dedication, Introduction, pp.4,
31–5, 43–53, 59, 71, 76ff, 83–94;
Rubiés (2000), p.7; Tertullian
(2004a), ch. 48; Teltscher (2000),
p.161; Teltscher (1995), pp.23–4,
92, 98; Polo (1972), pp. 277, 280;
Rhodiginus (1542), pp.496–9,
715–16; cf. [Créquinière] (1705),
p.55. cf. also Mitter (1977), pp.50,
53n., 243; Lach (1971),
pp. 439–40; Lach and Kley
(1993), pp.644–9; Schwab
(1984), pp.135–8; Anon. (1687),
pp.11–12.

73 Mitter (1977), pp.51–4; Rubiés
(2000), pp.309, 312; Rogerius
(1651); Rogerius (1670); another
French edition, 2 vols (J. Schipper,
Amsterdam, 1761); Rogerius
(1663); another German edition
(1683); Sweetman (2001), p.209;
Picart (1733–7), III; Schwab
(1984), pp.138–41, 145, 151–2;
Rubiés (2000), pp.345–6.

74 Kircher (1987), pp.141–5; Rubiés
(2000), pp.345–7. cf. Hasan
(1733), Notes, Part 2, pp.31–2;
[Créquinière] (1705), p.56;
Compte (1697), pp.323–32;
Gueullette (1725), pp.vi–xxiii.
Walker (1972), p.194 and *passim*.

75 [Palladius et al.] (1665); Mitter
(1977), p.191; Derrett (1960),
p.67; Fox (1997), pp.344–5; John
Keay, *India: A History*, p.77;
Rajumdar (1960), p.277; cf.
Boemus (1885–90), Part II, ch.8.

76 Walli (1974), pp.15, 39, 53–4, 56–7; Terry (1655), pp.326–30, 336–7, 341–2, 348–52; cf. sigs. A2r–A4r, A6r–v, A8r, A8v, [*]r; Terry substantially expanded his account in 1655 to recreate it as a sermon against schism and excess. cf. Lord (1630), p.41; Anon. (1687), pp.10–11.

77 Burke (1999); Rubiés and Elsner (1999), p.50; Murr (1993).

78 Bernier (1988), pp.326–7; cf. Tavernier (1995), II.30; cp. e.g. Rubiés (2000), pp.377–8+n.; Fryer (1909), I.177–80+n., I.209–10, II.83–4, 114–15, 120; cf. I.94, II.79–80, 100; cf. [Tryon] (1684a), pp.54–5.

79 Diogenes Laertius (2000), II.331–2; cf. Celenza (1999); Reuchlin (1983), pp.173–9; Sabinus (1584), pp.604–6; Ovid (1632), Sandys' commentary, Bk XV; [Rust?] (1661), pp.53–4; Cudworth (1678), pp.38–9; Blount (1680), pp.2–3; Bulstrode (1692), pp.115–16, who cites Iamblichus, *Life of Pythagoras* as his authority; Tryon (1691a), pp.28–9; Athenian Society (1703), I.19; Toland (1704), p.57; [Créquinière] (1705), p.57; Cocchi (1745), pp.29–33; Ritson (1802), p.170; Harrison, M. (1999), pp.85–6. See below ch. 17 note 7 and ch. 5 notes 97 and 107.

80 Aquinas (1975), pp.118–19, 157–8; Picart (1733–7), IV.ii.15.

81 Bernier (1988), pp.381–2; cf. pp.334–5; McCrindle (1960), p.68 (Strabo, XV i.53–6); Boemus (1885–90), Vol.VI, Bk.ii, ch.8; Linschoten (1988), I.200+n.; *Spy*, VI.5–7; Rubiés (2000), p.198; Tavernier (1995), I.311; cf. I.225, II.137, 143.

82 Ovington (1929), pp.163–4; Manucci (1965), I.151–3; cf. Jerome (2005a), Bk II, ch.11.

83 Regan (2001); Teltscher (2000), pp.162–3; Glacken (1967), p.86; Tryon (1705a), pp.37–8; Lambe (1815), pp.18–20; Falconer (1781), pp.236–9.

84 E.g. Terry (1655), pp.248–59.

85 cf. e.g. Purchas, ed. (1905–7), XVI.56; Lockman, ed. (1743), I.111, 190, 234, 402–3; Prest (1981), p.74; Anon. (1687), pp.56–7; Adair (1787b), pp.268–9; Africanus (1788), pp.46–7; cf. Boas (1948), *passim*.

86 Purchas, ed. (1905–7), V.384, 389, 443–4, 519; VII.14–15, 26–9; VIII.135–6; XII.381, 461; XV.158 (cf. Warren (1667?), pp.19–20, 23, 26–7); Fryer (1909), II.282–3, III.146–9.

87 Manucci (1965), I.151–3, III.39–42, 232; cf. Fryer (1909), I.59, 120–1, II.107–8+n; Teltscher (2000), p.165.

88 Tavernier (1995), I.57–8, 93–4, 140, 193; II.50, 59, 144, 146, 154, 156, 162–3 192–7; cf. Ovington (1929), p.202; Lach (1971), pp.439–40.

89 Ovington (1929), pp.163–4, 168–70, 175–9, 184, 186–7, 202; Harrison, M. (1999), pp.51–2; Lach (1971), pp.441–2. cf. Teltscher (2000), p.160. cf. Bernier (1988), pp.253–4. On the ancient history of Indian religion, cf. Ovington (1929), pp.139, 168–72; Temple (1690), pp.10–13; Drew (1998), pp.50–1; Robinson (2000), who does not mention Ovington. In his explanation of metempsychosis, Ovington translated sections straight out of Porphyry (2000), p.112. Compare the parallel passages in *Spy*, III.88, IV.18–20 (see ch. 9 below).

CHAPTER 5

1 Tryon (1700), pp.189–90; Tryon (1699), pp.11–12; Tryon (1691a), p.361; [Tryon] ([1688?]), pp.76–7, 133–4; [Tryon] (1684a), p.96. Tryon used slave dialect words such as 'bukra' (white man), 'okra' and 'gumbo' (okra stew) up to 120 years before their first recorded use in the *Oxford English Dictionary*: [Tryon] (1684c),

pp.43–4; [Tryon] (1684a),
pp.150–1; cf. Warren (1667?),
pp.6–7, 15; cf. also pp.19–20,
26–7.

2 [Tryon] (1684c), pp.100–6,
115–22, 128; [Tryon] (1685),
pp.39–40; [Tryon] (1684a), pp.1,
3, 194, 198–9; cf. Penn (1683); cf.
Hahn, ed. (1981), p.iv.

3 Tryon (1705a), pp.7–8, 12–25;
Gordon trusted Tryon and
therefore did not find the entry for
his birth in the Bibury Parish
Register for 6 September 1635
(Gordon ([1871]), pp.280–1+n.;
http://www.theleefamily.org/
Ancestry/wc12/wc12370.htm;
Terasaki (1995); Fox (2000)).

4 cf. Pressick (n.d.), pp.2, 20; Smith
(1983), p.53.

5 Tryon (1705a), pp.26–9.

6 Both were 'vegan': Tryon (1705a),
pp.41–2; both their bodies
'rebelled' but resuscitated: Tryon
(1691a), p.46; Tryon (1705a),
p.26 with Crab (1655), title page,
pp.1–2. See also the possible
connection between [Tryon]
(1684a), p.72 and Crab (1655),
pp.1–2; cf. 'Insurrections' in Tryon
(1696), p.125; cf. the same
passage in Tryon (1691a), p.41.
Both said alcohol was a waste of
grain: Tryon (1700), pp.229–33,
236; and e.g. [Tryon] ([1684c]),
pp.115–16; [Tryon] (1684b),
p.185; Crab (1655), p.7. Both said
vegetarianism enhanced psychic
acuity: Crab (1655), p.3; Tryon
(1705a), p.26. Compare also
Böhme (1894), 'Of Regeneration',
§ 107; Hotham (1654) in Böhme
(1654).

7 For Crab and Tryon's similarities
with Böhme and the (not
exclusively Behmenist) 'Seven
Grand Properties': Tryon (1691a),
sig.A4r, pp.13, 82, 321–2; Tryon
(1705a), pp.23–4; Crab (1657),
pp.20–2; Crab (1655), p.3; cp.
Hutin (1960), p.72n. cf. Agrippa
(1651), III.459; Tryon (1691a),
p.252; Böhme (1924), pp.5–33,
344–5 (Ch.35.30–34); cf. e.g.

Case (1682), p.16; Case (1697),
pp.31, 34–6, 39–42 (This book
was dedicated to Tryon:
sig.a2r–a3v; cit. Thomas, K.
(1971), pp.376–7). Both Crab and
Tryon thought eating flesh
attracted flesh-destroying spirits:
Crab (1655), pp.[iv], 4; Tryon
(1691a), pp.314–17, cf. p.46;
Tryon (1691b), p.38; Baxter
(1696), pp.76–8. Tryon started
writing in 1682, immediately after
the death of Crab (1680) and
John Pordage (1680–1). See also
Rudrum (2003). Crab had given
up his hat-trade by this time, but
as a Baptist he was aligned with
the Anabaptists; it is possible that
Crab and Tryon crossed paths.
G.S. Rousseau says Tryon joined a
splinter group of the
Philadelphian Society (Rousseau,
G.S. (1998), p.101; I have found
no mention of the Philadelphians
in the copies I have seen. He may
be referring to Tryon (1705b),
pp.10–11 (in the 18 pages
inserted between pp.34 and 35).

For Crab and Tryon's similar
flesh-proscribing astro-medicine,
see Crab (1655), p.4; Tryon
(1688), pp.8–9 and *passim*; Tryon
(1691a), pp.53, 58, 71, 103,
267–8; Jerome (2005a), Bk II,
ch.11; [Tryon] (1684b), pp.1–8,
44, 218–19; cf. e.g. Paracelsus
(1979), pp.19–20; Culpeper
(1656), sig.A2r, pp.5–6, 20, 21,
38–9; Case (1682), pp.10–11;
Harvey (1672), pp.236–7; Willis
(1683), pp.115, 224; Smith
(1983); Smith (1985), pp.259–61
(Smith argues that Tryon is
indebted to Hippocratic medicine,
which is true, but so were
innumerable contemporaneous
mainstream physicians, so it is not
his most distinguishing feature).
Tryon may have been encouraged
in using meatless medicine by the
example of the Indian physicians
who renownedly specialised in
dietary remedies; like Tryon they
were also said to specialise in

ointments and herbal plasters (cf.
e.g. Rajumdar (1960), p.276, and
see ch. 11 below. For other
similarities between Tryon and
Crab, compare Strype (1720), II,
Appendix 1, p.99, line 5 with
Tryon (1691a), pp.59–60; [Tryon]
(1685), p.11 with Crab (1655),
[pp.ii–iii]; Tryon (1691a), pp.27,
254 with Crab (1655), pp.3–4;
[Tryon] (1685), p.74 and [Tryon]
(1684a), pp.152–8 with Crab
(1655), pp.12–13; Tryon (1691c),
p. 50 with Crab (1655), p.12;
[Tryon] (1685), p.81 and [Tryon]
(1684c), p.138 with Crab (1657),
p.20; Tryon (1705a) [128, [2]pp.;
12°; CUL VIII.32.70], pp.23–4
with Crab (1655), p.4.

8 Tryon (1691b), p.82; Tryon
(1691a), pp.42, 126–7, 264,
283–90, 359–60, 458–9; [Tryon]
(1684c), pp.90, 97; [Tryon]
(1685), pp.31, 86; Tryon (1691b),
pp.35–6; cf. Winstanley (1973),
p.99. On Tryon's utopian
community, see Tryon (1691a),
pp.337–62; cf. Hotham (1654);
cp. Tryon (1691a), p.331;
Diogenes Laertius (2000), II.323.

9 On Moses: Tryon (1682b), pp.14,
19; Tryon (1691a), pp.28–32, 60,
72, 73, 75, 101–2, 188, 194, 251,
257–8, 322–5, 353, 370–1;
Numbers 11:4, 18, 22. Compare
Tryon (1691a), pp.154–5 with
Evelyn (1699), pp.74–5, 128; *Spy,*
IV.109–10; Lémery (1704), p.6;
[Hecquet] (1733), I.33–6, 63–4,
68; Cheyne (1740), pp.72–5;
Wesley (1776), 'Numbers 11:4';
St Jerome (2005a), Bk II, ch.15.
Compare Böhme (1909), p.225
with Tryon (1691a), p.73; cf.
pp.39–40; Clement of Alexandria
(2004b), Bk 2, ch.1 'On eating'.
On the prohibition of blood:
[Tryon] ([1684c]), p.168; [Tryon]
(1685), p.57; [Tryon] (1684a),
pp.165–75. On Jesus: [Tryon]
(1685), p.66. Others: Tryon
(1691a), pp.38–9; compare
Tryon's rhetoric about Daniel to
Crab on John the Baptist (Crab

(1655), p.12); cf. also Tryon
(1691c), pp.104–5; Eusebius
(1903), II.2–3; St Augustine
(2005), Bk 22, ch. 3; *cit.* Williams,
Howard (1883); *Spy,* VI.278–9;
Smith (1774), pp.373–4. On the
Wrath: Tryon (1691a), pp.309–10;
cf. p.217; [Tryon] ([1684c]),
p.120; Tryon (1700), pp.69–72.

10 [Tryon] ([1684b]), pp.94–5[b],
119, 185; [Tryon] ([1684c]),
pp.115–6; Tryon (1700), pp.63,
70–1, 86; Tryon (1691a), pp.46,
249–51, 280–3, 320–1, 346;
Tryon (1691b), pp.38, 134–6;
[Tryon] (1685), pp.45, 60; Tryon
(1703), pp.72–3; Tryon (1682b),
p.13; [Tryon] (1695a), pp.68–9;
Almond (1999), pp.121–2; cf.
Crab (1655), p.[iv]. Böhme
lamented that since the Fall 'man
is become a wolf to them [in
devouring the beasts]' (Böhme
(1920), p.426; cf. also e.g. Böhme
(1924), pp.150–1); Winstanley
(1941), pp.156–7; [Hecquet]
(1733), I.4–6.

11 Tryon (1691a), pp.496–7; Tryon
(1691c), pp.38–9, 42; Tryon
(1705b), pp.10–11 (in the 18
pages inserted between pp.34 and
35). On the extension of 'do as
you would be done by' to animals,
cf. e.g. Tryon (1691a), pp.251;
Tryon (1705a), p.79; and see ch.
3, 4, 6, 8, 9 above and below.

12 Tryon (1705a), pp.41–4.

13 Tryon (1705a), pp.54–6; cf. Jacob
Böhme: 'When I consider and
think why I write thus . . . I find
that my spirit is kindled in this
matter . . . and it is laid on me as a
work which I must exercise.' *cit.*
Penny (1912), p.75.

14 Defoe (1694); Plomer (1968b),
pp.30, 146, 217; for Tryon's other
publishers cf. pp.15–16, 30–1, 80,
96, 146–7, 183–4, 253, 260, 284.

15 Tryon against revolution: [Tryon]
(1685), pp.78–80; cf. pp.21–2,
36–7, 75; Tryon (1703), p.54;
Tryon (1691b), pp.125, 134;
[Tryon] (1684a), pp.140–1, 202;
[Tryon] (1702), pp.210–11.

16 Tryon (1691b), pp.141–53;
[Tryon] ([1684b]), p.49; Tryon
(1700), p.233; Tryon (1691a),
pp.153–6, 160, 165; [Tryon]
([1695?]), pp.3–19; cf. Evelyn
(1699), p.128; Evelyn (1996),
pp.74–5; Lémery (1704), p.6.

17 Tryon (1691a), pp.35, 50, 62,
105–6, 147–8, 154, 221, 248;
Tryon (1700), pp.24, 98; Tryon
(1691b), pp.103, 108–9; Tryon
(1690), pp.67–9, 70–1; [Tryon]
([1684c]), pp.86, 96; [Tryon]
([1684b]), pp.29–32, 50, 79, 81,
86, 97, 117; Tryon (1696), p.144;
Tryon (1688); cf. Lessius, Cornaro
and Anon. (1634), p.59; Evelyn
(1699), p.126.

18 Tryon (1691a), pp.59–60, 78–89;
Tryon (1682a); cf. Clement of
Alexandria (2004b), Bk 2, ch.1
'On eating'.

19 Todd (1996), p.49; Spencer
(2000b), p.225. Behn and Tryon
published works simultaneously
with the same bookseller, e.g.
Thomas Benskin published Behn's
The City-heiress (1682), *The
Roundheads* (1682), *Romulus and
Hersilia* (1683) and *The young king*
(1683) at the same time as Tryon's
Healths Grand Preservative (1682)
(cf. Plomer (1968b), pp.30–1);
Duffy (1989), p.241; [Behn ed.]
(1685). The collection, devised
and signed by 'A.Behn', includes
this poem with the same signature
'Mrs A.B.' as several other poems
in the collection. The appearance
of the name 'Mrs. Ann Behn' in
one of Tryon's versions must be an
error (Tryon (1697), sig.A4r–v); a
variant version of the poem in
[Tryon] (1685), pp.[i–iii]; cf. also
Smith, 'Tryon', *ODNB*. It is
difficult to follow Sheffey's
suggestion that Tryon's epitaph,
printed in one of the editions of
Tryon's *Memoirs*, was written by
Behn who died 14 years before
Tryon (Tryon (1705b), p.[129];
Sheffey (1962), p.54). Behn's
verses to Creech and Lestrange are
similarly hyperbolic. (cf. also the

descriptipn of George Cheyne as
'Man's Saver': Cheyne (1943),
p.128, 137).

20 Tryon (1697), sig.A4r–v; cf. Ovid's
Metamorphoses, I and XV; Field
(1685), sig.A2r, pp.19–20.

21 Tryon (1705a), pp.40–2, 86; Field
(1685), pp.14, 20, 24; Tryon
(1691b), pp.83–4.

22 Tryon (1705a), pp.40–2, 86;
Tryon (1691b), pp.83–4; Tryon
(1691a), pp.68–9, 83; Field
(1685), sig.A2r, A3r, pp.14, 20,
24, 27.

23 On Tryon's construction of natural
religion, see [Tryon] ([1684c]),
pp.68–70; [Tryon] (1684a),
pp.116–22, 151–2, 188–9, [192];
[Tryon] (1695a), pp.11, 66–7,
101–2, 105–6; Tryon (1691a),
pp.34, 253, 258–9; Tryon
(1695b), pp.1–2; Tryon (1682a),
pp.19–20; [Tryon] (1685),
pp.9–10; Tryon (1703),
pp.59–60; Tryon (1700), p.147.
The name of Tryon's Ethiopian
'Sophy' implies that he has
inherited knowledge from the
'gymnosophists'. cf. Hahn, ed.
(1981), pp.iii–v; Young (1998),
p.110; Dobbs (1975), p.60; Drew
(1998), p.90; Philostratus (1912),
II.39, 303–5; Dryden (1958),
'Religio Laici', ll.178–211; Warren
(1667?), pp.19–20, 23, 26–7;
Fryer (1909), II.24+n.

24 Agrippa (1651), III.342, 347–8,
477, 524–5; Agrippa (1655),
Preface; Agrippa ([1630]),
II.ii.994; Agrippa (1676), p.110;
compare e.g. Agrippa (1651),
III.347–8 with Tryon (1691c),
pp.191–3; cf. e.g. Lucian (1905),
IV.97–8; Fryer (1909), II.101. On
the *prisca sapientia* or *theologia*, see
e.g. Mirandola [1496], § 212, 220,
283; Agrippa (1655), pp.[i–iv];
Yates (1961), pp.5, 14–15, 78, 80,
84–90; Heninger (1977), p.90;
Walker (1954); and Walker
(1972). There was even a
traditional claim, made by
Clearchus of Soli, that the Jews
were descendants of the Indian

philosophers, the *Kalanoi*, who
were themselves descendants of
the Persian Magi (cf. Walbridge
(2001), pp.70–2).

25 [Tryon] (1683), pp.18–19; cf.
Edwards (1699), pp.91–9,
113–18; Browne (1672), Bk III,
ch.xxv, pp.189–94; Selden (1640),
p.19. For the contemporaries,
Nebuchadnezzar and Pythagoras,
and the relevance this had for
theories of transmigration, cf.
Ovington (1929), pp.171–2.

26 [Tryon] (1695a), pp.87–8, 107,
128–9; Tryon (1691a), pp.28–9,
75. For his blanket term 'Wise
Ancients' cf. Tryon (1691c),
pp.151–2, 232; [Tryon] (1684a),
pp.66–7; Tryon (1691a), pp.180,
338, 365; [Tryon] ([1684c]),
pp.67, 94.

27 'Brackmanny' is from Βραχμάνε.

28 [Tryon] (1683), p.2. On the
Francophobia in this piece, cf.
Hahn, ed. (1981), pp.vi–viii;
Tryon (1691a), p.138. cf. also
[Tryon] ([1684c]), pp.151–2.

29 [Tryon] (1683), p.19.

30 The Brahmin voices Tryon's
(probably Behmenist) creation
story according to which a
dialectic of powers caused the
'strife' between the Forms,
Qualities and Properties of the
hidden Nature (e.g. [Tryon]
(1683), p.13).

31 Field (1685), p.12; [Tryon]
(1683), p.20; Tryon (1703), p.49.

32 Tryon (1691a), pp.258–9.

33 Walli (1974), pp.53–4.

34 Ovid (1632), Bk XV, Sandys'
commentary; [Tryon] (1683),
pp.2, 9–10, 16–17, 21–2; Tryon
(1691a), p.280; cp. *Spy*, III.300;
Ovington (1929), pp.175, 178–9.

35 [Tryon] (1683), pp.16–17.

36 [Tryon] (1683), pp.9–10; [Tryon]
(1685), pp.83–4; Tryon (1691a),
pp.258–9. cf. Bernier (1988),
pp.253–4. On the savageness of
the non-vegetarian Indians,
compare *Upright Lives* [1683],
pp.9–10; Pseudo-Clement
(2005a), Bk 9, ch.20; Tryon

probably read about them in
Eusebius (1903), III.297
(col.275a–b).

37 On Tryon's prelapsarian vegetarian
vision cf. also Tryon (1691a),
pp.217, 251, 266, 336, 341–63,
499; Tryon (1700), p.47; [Tryon]
([1684c]), p.170; Tryon (1703),
pp.59–60; Tryon (1691b), pp.28,
41–2, 68–9, 105. On Adamic
pansophia: Tryon (1691a),
pp.337–62; cf [Tryon] (1683),
pp.9–10.

38 For the Sowle family publishers
see McDowell (1996); Plomer
(1968a), pp.168–9; Plomer
(1968b), pp.277–8; Burtt (1946),
pp.16–17; Mortimer (1948),
pp.37–9, 47; www.mith.umd.
edu/fellows/king/change.htm; cf.
e.g. Thune (1948), pp.60–1,
87.

39 [Tryon] (1683), pp.9–10; [Tryon]
(1684a), pp.176–7; [Tryon]
(1685), pp.72–5; [Tryon]
([1684c]), pp.100–2; Roe (1990),
pp.270–1; Foster (1999), p.320ff;
Fryer (1909), I.274–5, II.276, 293;
cf. I.93, 177; Manucci (1965),
II.219; Thune (1948), pp.60–1,
87; Hahn, ed. (1981), p.viii.
Compare [Tryon] (1684a),
pp.179–80 with [Tryon] (1683),
p.12. On Marco Polo's
approbation of Kublai Khan's
toleration policies, see Rubiés
(2000), p.72. Locke (1689); cp.
Locke (1858), p.73.

40 [Tryon] (1685), pp.74–84; cf.
Plutarch (1995), pp.557–9
(995F–996A); Lord (1630),
p.83.

41 On reincarnation, cf. Thomas, K.
(1983), pp.138–9; Purchas, ed.
(1905–7), XII.127–8. On
communism see ch. 2. The
Pythagoreans, Essenes and Indian
monks were *loci classici* of
communist vegetarian sects, cf. e.g.
Diogenes Laertius (2000), II.329;
Iamblichus (1989), p.11+n.; Baker
(1996), n.53; Bayle, P. (1734–41),
VIII.612; Stanley (1655–60),
III.46; Josephus (1755),

'Antiquities of the Jews', Bk II, ch.8; Lord (1630), pp.74–6; Boemus (1885–90), vol.VI, Bk. ii, ch.8; Drew (1998), p.166; and see ch. 2 above. On pacifism: Tomé Pires, *Suma Oriental* (1512–15) in Gaitonde (1983), pp.31–7; cf. e.g. Lord (1630), p.83.

42 Gaudenzio (1641), pp.70–1.

43 Majumdar (1960), pp.273–5, 278; cf. Plutarch, 'Life of Alexander' in *ibid.*, p.195; Goyal (2000), pp.120, 122, 126–7; [Palladius et al.] (1665), sig.c2r; Stoneman (1991), pp.131–3, 178–9; Stoneman (1994), p.508; Rhodiginus (1542), p.716; Manucci (1965), III.27–8. On Pythagoras' analogous pantheism see e.g. Philostratus (1912), I.307; Blount (1680), pp.2–3; Bacon (1996), vol.II, Part 2, pp.640–1; Heninger (1974), pp.202–4; Ovid (1632), Bk I and XV, Sandys' Commentary.

44 Tryon (1691a), pp.139, 225; Rousseau, J.-J. (1979), p.127.

45 [Créquinière] (1705), pp.87–8; cf. Bayle, P. (1734–41), I.238–40; Picart (1733–7), VI.i.185–7. Picart was a member of a Masonic group associated with John Toland who published similar comments in 1705 (cf. Jacob (1976b), pp.224–6).

46 Purchas (1626), pp.547–9; cf. Majumdar (1960), pp.278, 443; McCrindle (1960), pp.69, 71, 121; Della Valle (1892), p.105; Tavernier (1995), II.150ff; Hudson (2000), pp.8–9; Teltscher (1995), pp.44, 51; Teltscher (2000), pp.165–8; Rubiés (2000), pp.219, 299–300n., 363; Gaitonde (1983), p.39; Acheson (1990), p.66. For an analysis of the Puritan self-representation of austerity being undermined by criticism of sensual hypocrisy, cf. Poole (2000).

47 Boemus (1885–90), VI, Bk ii, ch.8.

48 Keith (1671), pp.126–9. Keith was also published by the Sowle family, and Tryon's books were advertised in Keith's books (George Keith, *The way to the city of God described* (Netherlands, and London, 1678 [advertisement added later]); cf. Field (1701). On Keith and the kabbalist reincarnation see ch. 7 below.

49 cf. e.g. *Upright Lives* [1683], p.7.

50 cf. e.g. Ridderus (1669), pp.590, 610–12, 635, 644, 655, 660, 675, 694–7, 700, 706, 713, 717; Terry (1655), pp.A6r–v.

51 *Upright Lives* [1683]; [Tryon and Palladius et al.] (1707); *Upright Lives* (1740); Hahn ed. (1981), pp.iii–xiii: Hahn discusses the textual relation between the *Upright Lives* [1683] and Tryon's *Brackmanny* (1683), but did not know Tryon was the author of the latter.

52 Anon. (1687), p.55; cf. pp.10–12, 30–1, 37–8, 43–4, 50, 55–7; Proverbs 12:10; and e.g. Lord (1630), p.41. The author of this interesting treatise ignored Terry and Lord's more derogatory statements.

53 [Tryon] (1695a), [sig.A6r]. Virginia Smith lists this among the three of Tryon's works 'not yet found', all of which I have identified (Virginia Smith, 'Tryon, Thomas (1634–1703)', *ODNB*). (Tryon's *magnum opus, The Way to Health* (1683) is not, as Smith says, a reprint of the short pamphlet, *Health's Grand Preservative* (1682).) Tryon refers to the *Letters From Averroes* in his other writings, maintaining the myth of their authenticity (Tryon (1696), p.11). In the last year of his life, Tryon published a list of his writings in which the work is alluded to obscurely as 'Averroes Letter to Pythagoras' (Tryon (1703), [sig.A5v]). As was his habit, Tryon recycled numerous passages from his previous works (e.g. [Tryon] (1695a), pp.74–5 = [Tryon] (1683), p.8; [Tryon] (1695a), pp.25–6 = [Tryon] (1690), pp.115–6). He re-used further

passages in his later works ([Tryon] (1695a), pp.66–7 = Tryon (1695b), pp.1–2). The only correct bibliographical identification I have come across is in Sinclair (1807), II.298. [Tryon and Palladius et al.] (1707); the catalogue of Duke University, North Carolina, which holds the only known copy of this edition, notes that the letters of Averroes 'are of questionable authenticity'!

54 [Tryon] (1695a), pp.80–4, 140–1; cf. Philostratus (1912), II.303–5 (Bk VIII, ch.7).

55 [Tryon] (1695a), pp.149–50. Compare [Tryon] (1695a), p.84 with [Tryon] (1683), p.19.

56 [Tryon] (1695a), p.116; cf. e.g. Linschoten (1988), I.252–5; Ovington (1929), pp.177–9.

57 [Tryon] (1695a), pp.116–17.

58 [Tryon] (1695a), p.117; cf. Tryon (1700), p.84 (cp. p.86); Tryon (1691a), pp.60–1, 209, 370–80; cf. e.g. Ovington (1929), pp.168–70, 202; Numbers 22:28–30; cf. Hildrop (1752), pp.28–9.

59 [Tryon] (1695a), p.118.

60 [Tryon] (1695a), p.123; cf. [Tryon] (1683), p.20; Tryon (1700), p.184; cf. e.g. Lord (1630), pp.65, 70; Tavernier (1995), II.49, 144–5; Ovington (1929), pp.165, 168–70; Boemus (1885–90), Vol. VI, Bk ii, ch.8; Rubiés (2000), pp.101–2; Foster (1999), p.322; *Spy*, III.332–5; Herbert (1634), p.38.

61 [Tryon] (1695a), p.122; cf. also p.120 and Porphyry (2000), p.113.

62 Tryon (1705a), pp.82–6, 126–8. On the questionable existence of Tryon's followers cf. Field (1685), sig.A2r. 8, 12–13, 15, 17, 25; Gordon (1871), pp.277–9. Tryon also gathered whatever he could from other sources on Pythagoreanism: for example, eating local food; not laughing; silence and solitude (Agrippa (1651), III.459, 524–5; Lord

(1630), pp.73–4); a special taboo against wool (sheep excrement), preferring linen (Agrippa (1651), III.520; Tryon (1691a), pp.39–40; Tryon (1691c), pp.198–200; Philostratus (1912), I.3, 261, II.39, 41, 303–7; Kirk and Raven (1960), p.220; Guthrie (1962), p.160; Burghardt (1944), pp.484–5; Quasten (1942); Spitzer (1943); Eusebius (1903), IV.471a and note; Lord (1630), 'Introduction'; Della Valle (1892), p.74; Yahuda, 16.1; Tryon (1691a), p.359); a belief in the symbolic powers of numbers and music ([Tryon] ([1684c]), p.81; Agrippa (1651), III.522–3 with e.g. Tryon (1691a), pp.23–4, 36–7; [Tryon] (1684b), p.8; Tryon (1691c), p.103).

63 Smith (1774), pp.371–4; Julian C. Walton, 'Robert Cook', *ODNB*; cf. Tryon (1691b), pp.139–40.

64 [Tryon] (1695a), pp.149–50.

65 Hobbes (1893–45), V.185–8; Hobbes (1651), Part I, ch.xiv, pp.64–9.

66 [Tryon] (1695a), p.156.

67 Hobbes (1839–45), II.113–4; V.166, 185–8; Hobbes (1969), pp.130–1; cf. Tryon (1691b), pp.131–3.

68 Tryon (1703), p.36; [Tryon] ([1684c]), pp.8, 101–4, 128; [Tryon] (1685), p.44.

69 Tryon (1691a), p.280.

70 [Tryon] ([1684c]), p.118; Tryon (1705a), pp.82–4.

71 Tryon (1703), p.61.

72 [Tryon] (1684a), pp.107–8, 151–2.

73 [Tryon] ([1684c]), pp.59–61; Tryon (1691a), pp.365–6; compare the similar views expressed in Patrizi (1593), fols. 57v–58r (to which compare especially Tryon (1691a), pp.373–4); cf. Serjeantson (2001), p.435; cf. also Almond (1999).

74 Tryon (1691a), pp.367–81; cf. Numbers 22:28–30.

75 [Tryon] ([1684c]), p.146.
76 Tryon (1691a), pp.258–9; cit. Spencer (1993), p.206.
77 Tryon (1700), p.146.
78 [Tryon] ([1684c]), pp.11, 167; Tryon (1700), p.280; Tryon (1691a), pp.279–82.
79 Tryon (1691a), pp.52–3, 124–31, 184–5; cf. Tryon (1682b), pp.16–17; Harvey (1675), pp.103–4; Evelyn (1699), p.132.
80 Tryon (1691a), p.168.
81 Tryon (1684c), p.155.
82 Tryon (1700), p.280.
83 Tryon (1691a), pp.331–3; cf. pp.49, 267, 336; [Tryon] (1685), pp.52–3.
84 [Tryon] (1684b), p.213.
85 Tryon (1700), p.119; [Tryon] (1685), pp.4–5; [Tryon] ([1684b]), pp.84–9, 119, 175–7, 181, 183, 213; Tryon (1696), p.125; Tryon (1682b), p.13; Tryon (1691a), pp.52–3, 124–131, 126–7, 163–4; [Tryon] (1702), pp.236–7; cf. Harvey (1672?), pp.133–4. On the topos of ransacking the world cf. Diogenes Laertius (2000), II.331–2; Ovid, Metamorphoses, Bk.1; Seneca (1917–25), III.66–71, Epistle 95; Lessius, Cornaro and Anon. (1634), pp.61–2; Blount (1680), pp.2–3; Evelyn (1996), pp.88–9; Cheyne (1733), pp.49–51; Rousseau, J.-J. (1979), p.59; Williams, Howard (1883), p.166.
86 Cf. [Tryon] (1684a), pp.48–52, 60–1; Palladius et al. (1668); Rajumdar (1960), pp.431–4, 443–4; Upright Lives [1683], p.3; Hippolytus (2005), pp.59–60; Tryon (1696), p.125; Tryon (1682b), p.13.
87 Cf. Tryon (1703), pp.72–3; Tryon (1700), p.139; cf. e.g. Lord (1630), p.41.
88 Hitherto scholars have labelled Tryon a disciple of Böhme. Some of Tryon's ideas which scholars have assumed came from Böhme, like the Seven Grand Properties, are more similar to popular astrology: Hutin (1960), pp.71–3; Thomas, K. (1971), p.376; Spencer (1993), p.206; Guerrini (1999a), p.35ff; Smith (1999), pp.107–8; Morton (2002). The argument has been more sophisticatedly developed by Gibbons (1996), pp.114–5.
89 Agrippa (1651), II.263; Agrippa (1630?), I.190; Tryon (1682b), p.6. Even Tryon's division of the universe and God into a light and dark side, the former characterised by love, the latter by wrath – a hallmark of Böhme – might have been partly influenced by Agrippa: compare e.g. Agrippa (1651), III.473–4 with [Tryon] (1695a), pp.71–9.
90 Agrippa (1651), Bk III, Ch.55, pp.522–3; Agrippa (1630?), I.378–9; cf. Philostratus (1912), II.41–3.
91 Tryon (1691c), pp.232–3; cf. Tryon (1691a), p.41; Tryon (1691b), pp.74, 78. Tryon (1696), p.125; compare Stoneman (1994), p.503; Hahn, ed. (1981), f.97r.
92 Agrippa (1655), pp.[i–iv]; Hill (1991), p.179.
93 Hotham (1654), sig.C2r–v.
94 On the ancient magicians, especially the Indian wise men, see Agrippa (1676), ch.42, p.110; Agrippa (1651), Bk III, Chs.55, 58; Agrippa (1676), 'The Censure: Of Magick'; Madaurensis (1853), pp.272, 278–9; Pseudo-Clement (2005a), Bk IV, ch.27; Porphyry (2000), p.112; Kämper (1995), pp.149, 166, 184–5; Origen (2005), Bk I, ch.25; Polo (1972), p.261; Vaughan, T. (1984), pp.482–6; Della Valle (1892), pp.106–7; Tavernier (1995), I.55, II.142; Fryer (1909), III.86–7; Boemus (1885–90), II.vii; Linschoten (1999), p.212; Rubiés (2000), pp.106, 110–11; Arnobius (2005), Bk IV.13; Arrian (1633), VIII.xi; Spy, IV.336–7; Blount (1680), pp.2–3; Postel (1553?b),

pp.18v–19r; *The Zohar* (1931–4), II.33–34; Temple (1690), pp.19, 44–5; Ammianus (1935), II.366–9 (xxiii.6.32–3), III.96–9 (xxviii.1.13).

95 [Créquinière] (1705), p.102; Locke (1858), p.252.

96 Vaughan, T. (1984), p.484; Nauert (1965), pp.326–7, 330–1.

97 Plato, *Timaeus*, 30a; Skinner and Kessler, eds. (1988), pp.312–15; Allers (1944); Conger (1922); Heninger (1977), pp.144–9; Kemp (1981), p.114. On Moses see note 9 above. On Pythagoras: Tryon (1691b), pp.130–1; Tryon quotes from Hierocles (1657), p.12. Mirandola [1496], espec. § 28–30, 35, 37, 44; Tryon (1691a), pp.28–9 (compare Bernier's comments in ch. 4 pp.56–7 and note 79 above); Tryon (1695b), p.101; Tryon (1688). For other echoes of Pico cf. Tryon (1700), p.84 and Tryon's perennial emphasis on *sympatheia*, 'Nothing in excess', 'Know thyself' (e.g. Tryon (1691a), p.1). cf. Heninger (1974), p.268+n.; Kristeller (1972), pp.10–16; Cassirer, Kristeller, Randall, eds (1948), p.389; Celenza (1999); Agrippa (1651), III.459; Reuchlin (1983), pp.173–9; Primaudaye (1618), p.584; [Rust?] (1661), pp.53–4; Cudworth (1678), pp.38–9; Toland (1704), p.57; [Créquinière] (1705), p.57; Hasan (1733), Notes, Part 2, pp.31–2; Teltscher (2000), pp.162–5. Interpreting metempsychosis as Pico did was related to the tradition of denying that Pythagoras was vegetarian at all, which Aristotle had maintained according to Plutarch (Guthrie (1962), pp. 188–91); see ch. 17 note 7 below.

98 Tryon (1700), pp.23, 82, 87, 126; [Tryon] (1685), pp.66–7; Tryon (1691c), pp.27, 66–7;

99 Tryon (1691a), pp.14, 70, 186; [Tryon] ([1684c]), p.170; [Tryon] (1695a), pp.12–13; Tryon (1695b), pp.1–3; cf. Agrippa (1651), III.458.

99 Tryon (1682b), p.6; Tryon (1682b), p.14; Tryon (1691a), pp.27, 189, 192. Compare Agrippa (1651), III.459–60 with [Tryon] (1683), p.8; Tryon (1691a), pp.186, 268, 353. For Ficino, Pico and Agrippa's use of the *sympatia* cf. Yates (1961), pp.68–9, 88–90, 109–17, 131–41.

100 Tryon (1696), pp.35–40; cf. Gassendi (1658), VI.21; Tryon (1700), p.151; Tryon (1703), p.37; Guerrini (1999a), p.35; Böhme (1920), p.347; Lémery (1704), pp.146–7; Helmont, J.B. (1664), pp.797–8.

101 Tryon (1691a), p.293; cf. [Tryon] (1685), pp.55–6; Tryon (1696), pp.150–1. [Tryon] (1684b), pp.198–9; cf. Aristotle, *On the Soul*, II.iv.

102 Tryon (1691a), p.268; cf. Tryon (1700), p.87; Festugière (1936), pp.586, 593–4; Pseudo-Clement (2005b), Homily VIII, chs 15–17.

103 Tryon (1691a), p.261; cf. pp.189, 197–8.

104 [Tryon] (1685), p.58.

105 Tryon (1691a), p.99; cf. Agrippa (1651), III.520; Tryon (1696), pp.ii–iv.

106 [Tryon] (1683), pp.16–17; Tryon (1688); Tryon (1682b), pp.13–17; Tryon (1691a), pp.60–1, 64–5, 209; Tryon (1700), p.86; Tryon (1695b), p.101; Clement of Alexandria (2004b), Bk 2, ch.1 'On eating'; Clement of Alexandria (2004a), Bk I, ch.15; Bk II, ch.18; Bk VII, ch.1; Manu (1971), v.49.

107 [Tryon] (1695a), pp.71–9, 93–4, 115; Tryon (1700), p.139; Agrippa (1651), III.473–4, 480, cp. p.481; Agrippa (1630?), Vol.1, Bk iii, ch. 41. For some of Tryon's other numerous

quotations from Agrippa on this system, compare Agrippa (1651), III.479 with Tryon (1691c), pp.194–5; and Agrippa (1651), III.478–9 with Tryon (1691c), p.71. Note the difference between Agrippa (1651), III.480 and Tryon (1691c), p.198; cf. also pp.65–6. Johann Reuchlin also tried to reconcile Pythagoras' teaching with Christianity by saying that the bodies a soul takes on after death 'were imaginary and figurative, but nevertheless real' (Reuchlin (1983), p.173). Plato, *Phaedo*, 81E–82A; cf. Plato, *Timaeus*, 91D–92C; *cit.* Porphyry (2000), p.125 n.29; Plotinus (1952), III.iv.2, IV.iii.12; Harrison, P. (1993), pp.535–6n.; see also ch. 7 below. In 1656 Margaret Cavendish, Duchess of Newcastle, warned of a very similar afterlife in which 'the bodily part' of those who displease the gods 'may be tormented out of one shape into another, and be perpetually dying or killing with all manner of torments, and yet never dye; as . . . in the shape of a Bull, knocks on his head, or the like; in the shape of a Hart, Arrows in the haunch, or the like; in the shape of a Fish, Hooks tearing the jaws', Cavendish (2004), p.23 (thanks to Zoe Hawkins). As a friend of Gassendi, and interested in Lucretian-Epicurean atomism, Cavendish's system is corporal in contrast to Tryon's mental-spiritual 'Other World'. Though Cavendish does not say that these punishments are for the sin of meat-eating (as Tryon does), there is an implied sense of retribution for the suffering mankind inflicts upon animals. Tryon's system of natural justice works without God's active intervention; cf. Smith (2004); More, H. (1682), pp.16, 126; Harrison, P. (2001), p.206nn. See

the relation to deist thought in ch. 9 below.

108 O'Flaherty, ed. (1980), pp.4, 14, and *passim*; Terry (1655), pp.351–2; Fryer (1909), I.94, 108; Manucci (1965), III.232; Kircher (1987), p.142; Compte (1697), p.330; Stanley (1655–60), III.105; Ovington (1929), pp.171–2; Blount (1680), pp.2–3, n.1; Blount (1678?), pp.59–60; Anon. (1692), p.86; Toland (1704), pp.57–8. [Tryon] (1695a), p.86. Tryon did not claim (as others did) that the Hindus' value of animal life derived from the belief that they contained human souls.

109 Tryon (1691c), pp.198–9; cf. Mohammed, O. (1984), pp.35, 111, 128–9, 136.

110 Revelation 22:15; Tryon (1700), pp.135–6, 146; Tryon (1691a), pp.328–9; Tertullian (2004a), Ch.48.

111 Field (1685), p.13.

CHAPTER 6

1 Franck (1694), p.207; cf. Smith (1994), pp.335–6; Smith (1990); Smith (1993); Cox (1952); Goodspeed (1943). Franck prepared *Northern Memoirs* in 1685, the same year that Tryon published his 'Dialogue Between Sophronio and Guloso', [Tryon] (1685).

2 Franck (1687), pp.142, 151–60; Terry (1655), pp.205–6, 326–30; Culpeper (1656), sig.A2r.

3 Levine (1997), p.62n.; [Evelyn] (1659), pp.38, 57–8.

4 Evelyn (1997), pp.10–11.

5 Main (1983); Murray (1957), pp.851–2. cf. Bacon (1650), p.41.

6 Evelyn (1699), sig.[A8v].

7 Evelyn (1699), pp.146–7, 149, 157–9; Evelyn (1850), II.16.

8 Evelyn (1699), pp.190–1.

9 Prest (1981); Drayton (2000); O'Malley and Wolschke-Bulmann, eds (1997); Parry (1992).

10 Coles (1657), 'Epistle to the Reader'; *cit.* Almond (1999), pp.23–4.

11 Evelyn (2000), pp.30–1.

12 Evelyn (1669), p.5; Evelyn (2000), p.421; cf. Hunt, J. (1997), p.272+n.; Sherman (2002), pp.72–5.

13 Evelyn (1699), pp.4–5.

14 Evelyn (1699), pp.119–20.

15 Thomas, K. (1983), p.159.

16 Prest (1981), p.52; Schama (1995), pp.537–8; cf. Manucci (1965), I.151–3.

17 Koch (1988), p.40nn.32, 33, 36, pl.27; Radcliffe and Thornton (1978), pp.254–62.

18 *PT* (1668), III, no.40, p.799; Sherman (2002), p.70.

19 Almond (1999), pp.91–4; Rostvig (1954), p.179.

20 Williamson (1961), p.592.

21 Boyle (1744), V.398.

22 Browne (1672), Bk III, ch.xxv, pp.189–94; Grotius (1727), Genesis 1:29–30 and 9:3; cf. Grotius (1901), Bk II, ch. 2, § 2.

23 Levine (1997), p.57.

24 [Tryon et al.] (1695?), p.19. Morton assumes a connection between Evelyn and Tryon, stating that Evelyn's use of the phrase '*Health* and *Long Life*' was derived from Tryon (whose *magnum opus* was called *The Way to Health, Long Life and happiness*, which Morton calls *The Way to Health and Long Life*) (Morton (2002), p.79). But Evelyn would have frequently used Ralph Austen's *A Treatise of Fruit–Trees . . . most conducing to Health and Long–Life* (Oxford, 1657) and the phrase was a generic label for works on health, appearing in the title of at least ten works of the period and in the text of innumerable others. The phrase derived from the Latin key phrase '*sanitate et longævitate*' and was widespread since Galen's seminal treatise, *De sanitate tuenda*.

25 Schreiber (n.d.).

26 Evelyn (1699), pp.153, 190–1, O2r–v.

27 Evelyn (1699), pp.164–5; Almond (1999), p.120; Morton (2002), p.80.

28 Evelyn (1997), pp.13–20 and *passim* (in which Evelyn described 207 flesh-free dishes and 118 dishes including animal products).

29 Webster (1975), *passim*; Webster (1982), pp.48–9, 65–8.

30 Jacob (1976a), pp.338–40; cf. Jacob and Lockwood (1972).

31 Evelyn (1699), pp.179, 190.

32 Evelyn (1670), pp.226, 233; Evelyn (2000), pp.150–2; Evelyn (1850), II.17–20; Gaudenzio (1641), p.31ff.

33 Evelyn (1699), pp.137–8, 150–1.

34 Webster (1982), pp.65–8; Levine (1997), p.68; cf. Hippolytus (2005), pp.59–60; Burthogge (1675), pp.374–5, 378–81; Postel (1986), pp.39–40, 91–2; Hartlib (1652). Others tried to trace pantheism to the Bible: e.g. Salmon (1651), pp.37–8; Coppin (1649), Part III, title page and p.8. cf. Vaughan, T. (1984), p.491; [Vaughan, T.] (1650), pp.12–13, 15–16.

35 *PT* (1702), pp.729–38 (Evelyn's copy in the British Library, Eve.a.149).

36 Evelyn (1699), pp.79–81; Evelyn (2000), pp.343–4; pp.417–18; Evelyn (1670), pp.231–2.

37 Evelyn (1699), pp.153–4, 163–4.

38 Evelyn (1699), pp.124, 150.

39 Evelyn (2000), pp.54, 343–4; see ch. 4 above.

40 Evelyn (2000), pp.150–7, 418–19; Evelyn (1670), pp.225–33; cf. Lord (1630), pp.58–9; Yule, ed. (1915), III.242–3; Fryer (1909), I.59, 110.

41 Evelyn (1670), pp.228, 246–7 and 'Pomona', p.3; Evelyn (1995), p.223n.; Schama (1995), pp.158–9; Tryon (1691a), p.361; [Tryon] ([1688?]), pp.76–7, 133–4.

42 Evelyn (1661); Evelyn (1699), pp.131–2; cf. Tryon (1691a), pp.184–5.

43 Evelyn (1699), pp.151, 153.

44 Ovid (1632), Sandys'
commentary, Bk XV.
45 [Burnet] (1691), p.190; cf. Evelyn
(1699), pp.150, 163–4; Almond
(1999), pp.25–6; Pseudo-Clement
(2005b), Homily VIII, chs 15–17;
Bacon (1650) [Eve.b.30], p.13;
Lambe (1815), pp.102–7.
46 cf. Levine (1997), p.74.
47 Temple (1690), pp.13–23; Temple
(1680), p.189ff.; Temple (1701),
pp.112–15; cf. Mitter (1977)
p.191; Drew (1998), p.47.
48 Wotton (1697), pp.94–7, 148–65.

CHAPTER 7

1 For Helmont, Locke and the
Kabbala, see Coudert (1997),
pp.153, 157; Coudert (1999),
pp.272–302; Brown, S. (1997),
pp.109–10; 'F.M. van Helmont',
ODNB
2 More, H. (1662), 'Immortality',
pp.110–11, 121; More, H. (1712),
'Atheism', pp.207, 231n. cp.
Cudworth (1678), pp.43–6; cf.
312–14 on the relation between
Egyptian, Pythagorean and Indian
'Brachman' systems of
metempsychosis. See also
Cudworth (1678), pp.38–9, which
echoes [Rust?] (1661), p.54.
3 More, H. (1662), 'Immortality',
pp.113–14.
4 This is necessarily a hugely
simplified scheme of a complex
and varied set of beliefs. For
Jewish kabbalists on *gilgul* in
humans and its origin, see e.g.
Scholem (1987), pp.90, 113, 123,
154, 176, 188–98, 456–60, 467;
Scholem (1941), pp.280–4;
Scholem (1991), pp.197–9,
205–15 (Scholem thought the
most likely source was medieval
Gnostic Jewish sects in the Middle
East, where Gnostic Christian,
Jewish and Islamic groups did –
and in Iraq still do – believe in
reincarnation, though cf. Eylon
(2003), pp.26–7, 30–1+n.,
36n.70, 67–9+nn., on a passage
which could be interpreted as an

allusion to ethicised (i.e. 'karmic')
reincarnation in midrashic and
talmudic literature, though her
argument is less than convincing);
Giller (2001), pp.35–69; Elior
(1995), pp.243, 262+n.82; Dan,
ed. (2002), pp.204–5; Rosenroth
et al., eds (1684), this is vol. 2;
section three in the second
pagination sequence pp.243–478
contains the 'De Revolutionibus
Animarum', attributed here to
Luria, whose doctrines it explains;
cf. Rosenroth et al., eds (1677),
I.236; Part II, e.g. pp.256, 268;
Vital (1999), pp.243–4;
Wexelman (1999), pp.71–2,
109–12; Fine (2003) (not seen).
5 On the original Adam out of
whom the whole creation 'fell', see
e.g. Scholem (1991), pp.220–1,
229–33; Scholem (1941),
pp.278–82; Coudert (1975),
p.638 (Coudert says it is Adam
Kadmon, whereas I think this
story usually refers to Adam Ha-
Rishon, the Adam of the Bible);
Anon. (1694c), pp.17, 20, 31–3,
39 (all souls contained in Adam
and their hereditary transfer).
6 Rosenroth et al. (1677), I.ii.294;
cf. Scholem (1991), pp.227–8+nn.
Coudert (1975), p.642; Scholem
(1991), pp.237–8.
7 The claim that God regulated the
killing of beasts to ensure the
passage of the soul into a human
was formulated in the *Temunah* (AD
c.1300). *Gilgul* for animals and the
corollary of compassion to
animals seems to have come to
the sixteenth-century kabbalists via
Rabbi Joseph of Shushan's Sefer
Ta'amei ha-Mitsvot (c.1300),
circulated in Salonica c.1520 by
Rabbi Isaac ibn-Fahri. On the role
of slaughter and consumption in
tikkun, and compassion for
animals, see Elior (1995),
pp.253+n.51, 257, 259+n.79;
Scholem (1987), pp.188–98,
468–9; Scholem (1991), pp.218,
225–6 (Scholem rightly
distinguished reincarnation

systems which enjoin vegetarianism and care to animals from those, such as kabbalist *gilgul*, which encourage slaughter of animals. But in fact the Kabbala – like the Vedic system where ritual slaughter was believed not to cause death or suffering – encourages both); Harrison, P. (1993), p.540n; Altmann (1987), pp.29–30; Giller (2001), pp.41–2+nn.; Isaacs (2000), pp.84–5. Compare e.g. Manu (1971), v.40.

8 Nehora.com (n.d.); Vital (n.d.); Bloch (1928), p.384; Murti (n.d.).

9 See also Helmont, F.M. (1685), pp.105–9, 145; cf. Blount (1678?), pp.59–60.

10 Helmont, Anne Conway and the anonymous 'Helmontians' did not deny damnation, they just reserved it for sinners who refused to repent over several incarnations. For the role of transmigration in the Christian eternal damnation debate, see Walker (1964), pp.134–41 and Coudert *opera cit.*

11 [Helmont, F.M.] (1684), preface.

12 Scholem (1991), pp.237–8; cf. Scholem (1987), pp.176, 189–90; Altmann (1995), pp.280–3.

13 Helmont, F.M. (1685), pp.129–30; cf. Coudert (1999), p.268. On Christians and the salvation of animals and all creation by *gilgul*, see Coudert (1976), p.178n. Peter Harrison is incorrect to suggest that Helmont did not believe that animal souls worked their way up into humans. Harrison says instead that Lady Anne Conway was alone in adopting fully blown animal-to-human metempsychosis, whereas it is likely that Conway received the doctrine from Helmont. Walker and Kurth-Voigt also omit Helmont's belief that animal spirits could work their way up to human existence and thence to heaven (Walker (1964), pp.141–2; Kurth-Voigt (1999), pp.36–8; Harrison, P. (1993), pp.533–8,

541). Harrison says that Origen believed that human souls could degenerate into animals, but that seventeenth-century thinkers would not go that far, whereas the reverse is true. Origen, and his seventeenth-century redactor, expressly denied that Origen believed in metempsychosis between humans and animals (see above). On the other hand, a number of seventeenth-century Christians went beyond Origen and did believe that human souls could enter animal bodies, including Franciscus Mercurius van Helmont, Lady Anne Conway, Joseph Glanvill (who considered it at any rate) and, in an altered fashion, Thomas Tryon.

14 [Helmont, F.M.] (1684), p.165.

15 Coudert (1976), pp.185–6; Coudert (1999), pp.254–8, 276–7); H[all] (1694), pp.15–16, 35.

16 Woodhouse (1986), pp.54–6, 63, 75, 257, 326–7, 334–5, 355, 357–9; Pletho (1858), pp.30–3, 78–9, 251–9; Anastos (1948), pp.281–9; Masai (1956), pp.136–8. For Pletho's comments on animals and food, see Woodhouse (1986), p.343; Pletho (1858), pp.13, 81–3.

17 e.g. Pletho (1689) and Pletho (1754).

18 For the counterpart to this debate among Jewish kabbalists, see Idel (1987), pp.155–62; Altmann (1987), pp.29–30. Some, like Rabbi Joseph Solomon of Kandia, denied that Pythagorean metempsychosis and kabbalist *gilgul* were similar.

19 [Helmont, F.M.] (1684), pp.153–8, 163–4. The authorship of this pamphlet should perhaps be reconsidered in the light of Anon. (1694c), pp.31–3; Tertullian (2004a), ch.48. Coudert (1975), pp.634–5; Coudert (1999), p.73; cf. [Philanthropos] (1690), p.52.

20 H[all] (1694), pp.15–16, 35–6; cf.

Anon. (1692), p.86; Gueullette (1725), p.xxi.

21 Coudert (1976), pp.180–1.

22 Coudert (1999), pp.244–9.

23 [Rust?] (1661), pp.14, 22–3, 37–9, 47–9, 51–3, 68–70, 75, 100–1, 105; Walker (1964), pp.134–5. cf. ch. 5, n.107 above.

24 [Rust?] (1661), pp.4, 53–4, 84–7; Origen (2005), Bk V, chs. 39, 41, 49; Bk VII, ch.7; Bk VIII, chs. 28–30; cf. Bk I, ch.20; Bk III, ch.75; Bk V, ch.29; Jerome (2005b), § 4, 7, 15.

25 Huet (1678); Edwards (1693), p.250; Bayle, P. (1734–41), VIII.614 'Pythagoras', Note H; Hazard (1953), pp.45–6; Walker (1972), pp.214–20; cf. Ramsay (1748), pp.[463–4].

26 Picart (1733–7), IV.ii.159–67; Lockman ed. (1743), II.266, 277.

27 [Glanvill] (1662), sig.Bv–[B5v], C4v, pp.1–3, 33–4, 48–9, 52–4.

28 Allison Coudert suggested that *Lux Orientalis* discussed pre-existence in a non-Kabbalist way (Coudert (1975), p.639); but cf. especially [Glanvill] (1662), p.9.

29 [Glanvill] (1662), sigs[A8r–v], [B8v]–Cr; pp.4, 5–6, 9, 33–5, 44, 47, 52–6, 59–61, 68–9, 84.

30 Mullett (1937); *cit.* Harrison, P. (1993), pp.535–8; cf.also Walker (1964), pp.134–5; [Glanvill] (1662), p.68 may suggest that when writing *Lux Orientalis*, Glanvill did not think human souls could reincarnate into animals (bodies 'more *squallid* and *ugly*').

31 Coudert (1976), p.179n.; Coudert (1975), pp.639, 645.

32 [Conway] (1692), pp.48–9, 65–6, 69–70, 153; Daniel 4:31–3. cf. Coudert (1999), p.268. Rabbi Israel Baal Shem Tov (1700–60), leader of Hasidism in eastern Europe, said that when an animal or plant was eaten in accordance with the rules of the Torah the spark trapped within it was released to its spiritual origins (Scholem (1991), pp.241–7).

Rabbi Schneur Zalman of Liadi (1745–1812), founder of Chabad Hasidism, explained that unclean foods were forbidden (literally, 'bound') by the Torah precisely because their shell of matter was impenetrable and the spark could not be released (Chabad.org (2001–6), chs 7 and 8). On medicinal punishment, cf. Brown, S. (1997), p.101.

33 [Conway] (1692), pp.48–76; cf. Walker (1964), pp.138–42; Harrison, P. (2001), pp.212–13; Harrison, P. (1993), pp.538–9. Compare [Conway] (1692), pp.69–70 with [Tryon] (1695a), p.72. This force of sympathetic attraction is related to More, H. (1662), 'Immortality', pp.118–24, 156; More, H. (1682), pp.16, 123–6, where More says that a soul's 'Natural Congruity' could operate simultaneously with 'the Spirit of Nature attracting such a soul as is most congruous to the predelineated Matter which it has prepared for her' (Harrison, P. (2001), p.206+n.; Cohen (1936), p.54). The idea is implicit in Greek myth (Tantalus is an example), and was built into a theodicy by Plato and then Plotinus. It was thence developed by Bruno, Agrippa, Conway and Tryon; Agrippa (1651), III.480. Helmont conceived of a magnetic force which drew particles to the soul in the womb, ensuring that the same material was used for each of a soul's incarnations (H[all] (1694), pp.26–7). A similar idea occurs in Giordano Bruno (León-Jones (1997), pp.85, 123–4, 155–6). The *Turkish Spy* and other deist texts developed their own form of the same idea. A similar force was later described by the mystic Charles Hector Marquis St George de Marsay and adapted by George Cheyne to the Newtonian concept of 'electricity' (see ch. 9 and 13 below); Berrow (1762), p.38. This carefully

directed retribution seemed preferable to the blunter punitive instrument of eternal damnation. John Hall pointed out that such pedantic retaliation would result in infinite repetition of sins and ridiculed the claim that the verse 'he that killeth with the sword must be killed with the sword' (Revelation 13:10) meant that murderers would be born again to suffer the crimes they committed (H[all] (1694), pp.1–4, 20). cf. Agrippa (1651), III.473–4, where Agrippa collates Origen's gloss of the same verse with 'the Ethnick Philosophers'' concept of 'retaliation' whereby 'he which hath polluted his hands with blood, should be compelled to undergo retaliation; he that lived a brutish life, should be precipitated and revolved into a brutish body' and Plotinus' belief that 'those who use sense especially together with wrath, do arise wild beasts'; Field (1685), p.23, satirising Tryon's application of Revelation 13:10 to bird-murderers; [Tryon] ([1684c]), pp.130–1, 160; [Tryon] (1695a), pp.70–8. Thomas Tryon was harsher than these Helmontians: the retributive suffering and the animal form taken on in the next life was a punishment without end, whereas with the Helmontians it was a purgative step towards salvation (cf. e.g. Tryon (1691c), pp.198–9); and ch. 5 n.107 above. cf. also [Tryon] (1695a), pp.112–13; Lockman, ed. (1743), I.463; Manu (1971), v.33; cf. e.g. Isaacs (2000), pp.84–5. It is interesting that two of the most prominent women philosophers of the seventeenth century – Anne Conway and Margaret Cavendish – both proposed deeply unorthodox and very similar systems of reincarnation (see ch. 5 above). For other similarities between Tryon and the Christian kabbalists, cf. [Conway] (1692),

pp.137, 140–2, 142–3; Brown, S. (1997), pp.105–6; cf. also Ramsay (1727), II.ii.135–6. Tryon might have been connected to Conway and the Helmontians through the Quaker George Keith (see pp.68–9). Thomas and Sarah Howkins, who published John Field's attack on Tryon, also produced the books of Helmont and the anonymous 'Helmontians'. Tryon shared Helmont's prelapsarianism and passion for reclaiming the Adamic language and his interest in Jacob Böhme (Coudert (1999), pp.74, 146–7; Coudert (1976), pp.171–2) and Tryon's use of revelation for medical guidance is also similar to Helmont's techniques (cf. Coudert (1999), pp.157–8).

34 Conway considered all creatures to be connected as parts of one body 'united with one another, by means of Subtiler Parts, interceding or coming in between, which are the Emanations of one Creature into another, by which also they act one upon another at the greatest distance; and this is the Foundation of all Sympathy and Antipathy' ([Conway] (1692), pp.29, 55–6). For a similar notion in Hinduism of a universal force like electrical energy or fluid connecting all living things through which karma is transferred, see O'Flaherty, ed. (1980), p.58. Conway's requirement for the care of domestic animals may have derived directly from one of Luria's own edicts; cf. Nehora.com (n.d.); Bloch (1928), p.384.

35 [Conway] (1692), pp.30ff., 55–6, 68.

36 Anon. (1694b), pp.12–13; cf. Walker (1964), p.141n. (Walker attributes the work to Conway or Rosenroth edited by Helmont); Harrison, P. (2001), pp.210–11.

CHAPTER 8

1 McGuire and Rattansi (1966), pp.112, 119–21; [Pemberton] (1728), sig.[a1]r–v.
2 Stukeley (1936), pp.60–1; Keynes 136, p.7 [Typescript, pp.16–17]; cf. Keynes 136, Mead to Conduitt (7 July 1727); Keynes 135, 14 Feb 1727/8, side 1; More, L.T. (1934), p.206.
3 Keynes 130.5, sheet 1r [Transcript p.1]; Keynes 130.6, Notebook 4 [f.4v–5r]; *cit.* Westfall (1980), pp.103–4; Keynes 135, Second Letter (14 Feb 1727/8), side 2–3 [Typescript pp.2–3]. For the reference to Robert Sanderson, Bishop of Lincoln, cf. [D.F.] (1663), p.16.
4 Stukeley (1936), pp.66–7; cf. Keynes 130.7 [Transcript pp.15–16].
5 Keynes 135, 14 Feb 1727/8, side 2–3 [Typescript, p.3].
6 Newton (1959), II.
7 Keynes 129A, [pp.23–5]; Westfall (1980), pp.580–1; Brewster (1831), p.320; White (1997), p.132; Fontenelle (1728), pp.22–3, 26; Manuel (1968), pp.382–3. Mead was very cautious in administering vegetable diets (Mead ([1751]), pp.134, 157–9), but cf. Cheyne (1720), pp.13–15; Cheyne (1733), 'Preface', pp.vi–vii. On Newton's bladder surgeon, William Cheselden, cf. Keynes 130.6 Notebook 2, [f.15v]; Cheselden (1723); Cope (1953), p.36; Cheselden (1723), p.109.
8 Harrison (1978), pp.117–18, 125; cf. Iliffe (1998); cp. Keynes 129A, [p.23]; CUL Add. Ms. 3996, f.43.
9 See 'Abbreviations' for notes on Newton's Library; Maier (1687) [Tr/NQ 16.88], p.27 (d2s); cf. pp.5–6 (ds); cf. Maier (1617), p.144; Jung (1974), p.273.
10 Cheyne (1943), p.69; Cheyne (1742), p.81; Westfall (1980), pp.103–4; Shapin (1998), pp.40–1.
11 Haller, *Elementa Physiologiae*

Corporis Humani, VI.198, *cit.* Williams, Howard (1883) and Newton, J.F. (1897), p.33n.; Nicholson (1999), p.40; Falconer (1781), p.240ff; Adair (1787b), pp.268ᵗ–9.
12 Combe (1860), p.149.
13 Keynes 129A, p.18; Westfall (1980), pp.580–1; Shapin (1998), pp.21, 44.
14 Keynes 129A, p.[23].
15 Keynes 130.6, Notebook 2, f.15v; cf. Keynes 130.7, f.[3r] [Transcript p.6]; Keynes 130.6, Notebook 1; [Pope] (1729), I.263.
16 Voltaire (1980–), XV.222–3.
17 Westfall (1982), p.16; Manuel (1968), pp.349, 377; Manuel (1974), p.49; McGuire and Rattansi (1966), p.108; Force and Popkin, eds (1999), pp.xvi–xvii; cp. Newton (1728), 'Dedication', p.vi; Fontenelle (1728), p.22.
18 Harrison (1978), p.59 (Newton owned at least 46 travelogues).
19 Locke (1690), Bk I, ch. 3; Carey (2004); cp. Voltaire (1980–), XV.218–23. Yahuda 17.3, f.10–12; cf. Westfall (1958), p.207; Westfall (1982), pp.24–30; Popkin (1998), p.413; Webster (1982), pp.2, 10. Westfall emphasised Newton's deistic intimations (Yahuda 41, f.7; cf. Bacon (1974), p.201). Newton repeatedly stresses that the original divine knowledge was 'instituted by God in yᵉ beginning', though his frequent allusions to the 'God of Nature' could suggest a deist subtext (Yahuda 41, f.4r, 8).
20 Newton (1728), p.187; Yahuda 17.3, f.7–9.
21 Yahuda 41, f.4r; Newton (1728), p.187. Newton traced the establishment of the *holocaust*, or burnt sacrifice back to Cain and Abel, but other records of antediluvian religious practice were scanty (Keynes 7, side 1).
22 Westfall (1982), p.29; Manuel (1963), pp.61–2; Snobelen (1999); Yahuda 1.1, f.1–10; 10.3, f.27v.

23 Westfall (1982), pp.24–7; Bernal (1987), p.167; Newton (1728), pp.40–1, 174–9, 328; Yahuda 41, f.1r, 6–7; Yahuda 16.1; Yahuda 17.3, f.10–11; Vossius (1641), pp.648–52; Carpini and Rubruquis (1903), pp.109–10; Purchas (1625), III.4.

24 Yahuda 41, f.3–4, 8; cf. Yahuda 17.3, f.10. Thomas Burnet said of the Brahmins that 'Tis really a most wonderful thing that a Nation half barbarous should have retained these Opinions from the very times of *Noah*: for they could not have arrived to a Knowledge of these things any other way, than by Tradition; nor could this Tradition flow from any other Spring, than *Noah*, and the Antediluvian Sages' (Blount, Gildon et al. (1693), p.82).

25 Yahuda 41, f.4r.

26 cf. Leviticus 3:17, 17:12.

27 Manuel (1963), p.112+n.; cf. also McGuire and Rattansi (1966), pp.122–3+n.

28 Kenyon-Jones (2001), p.85; cf. e.g. Mandeville (1924), Remark P, I.180–1; *Spy*, III.110–11.

29 Yahuda 15.5, f.79v; cf. Keynes 3, p.30. cf. [Anon] (1646), p.5; [Delany] (1733), I.14, 132, II.5.

30 Selden (1725), 'Gentium', Bk I, ch.10, col.158, 163–4; Bk VII, ch.12, I.755; cp. Goldish (1998), pp.42, 49–50.

31 Newton (1728), pp.189–90; Yahuda 26.2, f.37–38. So unusual is Newton's emphasis that when R.S. Westfall quoted from a scrap of paper, which he did not realise was a draft of this passage, he thought that Newton was discussing the laws of loving God and one's neighbour, rather than the law of mercy to animals; Westfall (1982), p.28.

32 Keynes 3 'Irenicum, or Ecclesiastical Polyty tending to Peace' (post-1710), p.5; see ch. 2, 3, 5, 6 and 9 above; Tryon (1703), p.61; and cf. Terry (1655), pp.348–9.

33 Newton's desire to identify this pattern might explain his decision to maintain the pre-Copernican number of seven planets, and his readiness to categorise the spectrum into the seven 'primary' colours even though he could see each merged seamlessly into the other. There may also have been a chemical dimension, cf. Churchill (1967).

34 Keynes 3, p.35; cf. ch. 13 below.

35 Newton (1728), 'Dedication', p.vii; cf. Maclaurin (1748), pp.13–16.

36 Clarke (1720), pp.273–6. Clarke used this interpretation of the blood prohibition as part of a counter-vegetarian argument (see ch. 16 below), but it does not seem to have served this purpose for Newton.

37 Maimonides (1963), pp.585–6 (III.xlvi), 598–600 (III.xlviii); cf. Edwards (1699), I.117–19 (who misrepresents Maimonides). Sune Borkfelt writes (without providing evidence) that Maimonides was a vegetarian (Borkfelt (2000)). Ezra (1988), pp.121–3; cf. p.47 for ibn Ezra on antedeluvian vegetarianism; cf. Keynes 49; Keynes 25, f.1r. Compare Spinoza's eirenic seven laws, e.g. Betts (1984), p.76.

38 Bacon (1640), p.382; cp. Bacon (1974), p.104 (Bk 2, IX.1).

39 Keynes 130.7, f.[3r] [Transcript, p.6]; cf. Keynes 130.6, Notebooks 1; [Pope] (1729), I.263.

40 Clement of Alexandria (2004a), Bk II, ch. 17; cf. Aquinas (1975), pp.118–19; see ch. 5 above.

41 Calvin (1999), I, 'Genesis 9:3'; Mercerus (1598), 'Genesis 9:4', p.197; cf. e.g. Anon. (1652a), pp.4–5.

42 Edwards (1699), I.117–19. On the nutritional motive cf. Moore (1669), pp.35–6; Evelyn (1996), pp.78–80; Maimonides (1963), p.598 (III.xlviii); Mead (1755), p.26.

43 Patrick Delany later came to the

44 cf. e.g. Roe (1662), pp.125–6; Anon. (1646a), p.6; Calvin (1999), I, 'Genesis 9:3'; Edwards (1699), Vol. II, ch.18.
45 Yahuda 15.5, f.79v; cf. Keynes 3, p.30.
46 Holland (1596), pp.105–6.
47 Anon. (1646b), p.5.
48 Anon. (1646b), p.6.
49 Anon. (1652a), p.4.
50 Roe (1662), p.5.
51 Moore (1669), p.25. cf. Thomas, K. (1983), pp.289–90+n.
52 Evelyn (1996), pp.78–80; Evelyn (1850), II.17–18, 23.
53 [Tryon] ([1684c]), p.168; [Tryon] (1685), p.57; [Tryon] (1684a), pp.165–75; cf. Williamson, 'Just Complaint', f.7v.
54 Keynes 130.7, f.[7v] or 'Sheet 4' [Transcript, pp.13–14]; cf. Maclaurin (1748), pp.13–16; Westfall (1980), p.850.
55 On the Judaists, see ch. 2 above; Spy, III.110–11, 245–7; IV.21–3, 110; V.305; VI.28–30; VII.301–2.
56 Almond (1999), pp.25–7.
57 cf. e.g. Romans 14:20.
58 Rodis-Lewis (1998), p.182.
59 On the Golden age, see Yahuda 41, f.12; cf. Newton (1728), pp.163–5, 182; cf. e.g. Browne (1672), Bk III, ch.xxv, pp.189–94. Sacrifices were used from the beginning, but they were holocausts: Yahuda 26.2, f.33; Yahuda 41, f.4r; cp. the Jewish sacrifice (Newton, I. (1728), p.337, and Keynes 3, p.5); cf. Edwards (1699), p.115; Evelyn (1996), pp.75–6; Evelyn (1850), II.16; [Delany] (1733), I.124–5. cf. [Hecquet] (1709), pp.32–3.
60 Newton (1728), pp.241–2; Yahuda 25.1 a), f.'38'; cf. Yahuda 25.1 f), f.1r; Diodorus Siculus (1700) [Harrison, J. (1978), item 518], pp.2–3, 22–3, 37–45; Diodorus Siculus (1604) [Harrison, J. (1978), item 517], Bk 1, pp.42–3; Diodorus Siculus

(1559), p.29; cf. Diodorus Siculus (1933), I.29–31 (Bk I.viii).
61 Newton (1728), pp.241–2; cf. pp.161–2, 182, 197–8; Yahuda 25.1 a), f.'38'; cf. also Yahuda 25.1 f), f.1r. For other sources on Egyptian vegetarianism, cf. e.g. Edwards (1699), I.96–7.
62 Fréret (1758), pp.246, 285–7; Fréret (1728), pp.10–11, 89–91; Newton (1728), pp.201–4; Yahuda 25.1 e), f.10–12; S[teuar]t (1757), p.160; [Newton, I.] (n.d.), p.8; PT (1734), VII.ii, pp.4–6; Manuel (1968), p.353. See the contradictions in Yahuda 25.1 e), f.11r; Yahuda 25.1 f), f.31v.
63 He (inconsistently) argued that the 'Shepherds' referred to in various ancient sources were not the Israelites but the 'ignoble' human-sacrificing Canaanites. Yahuda 25.1 e), f.10r–11r, 12r; Yahuda 25.2 c), f.1, 3–4; Yahuda 25.2 a), f.25; Yahuda 25.2 b), f.4–5, 31 (cp. f.13); Newton (1728), pp. 11, 20, 191, 198, 201–2, 205–6, 215–16; Porphyry (2000), II.lv (not, as Newton writes, I.lv), p.77; Manetho (1940), fragment 85, pp.198–201; Diodorus Siculus (1700), pp.27–8; Philostratus (1707) [Tr/NQ 11.2–3], II.720–2 (d). Newton was less consistent in his identification of Ammon with Ham than Westfall implies; cf. e.g. Newton (1728), pp.205–6, 241–2.
64 Yahuda 41, f.5r; Yahuda 25.2 b), f.10.
65 John Spencer had brought upon himself furious and widespread accusations of atheism merely for suggesting that God had designed Moses' religion with some features deliberately like those of the Egyptians in order to hijack those rites from the Egyptian devil-worshippers and convert them to the use of the true God instead: Yahuda 41, f.5r; Spencer (1685), Bk 3; Edwards (1699), I.245–51; cf. DNB, 'John Spencer'; Maimonides (1963), p.581 (III.xlvi).

66 Harrison (1978), pp.117, 186, 223, 228, 248; Rogerius (1670), pp.42, 59, 61, 95. Newton's *Jan[ua]. reserat[a]* ('The unlocked door') is a Latin shorthand reference to Rogerius' work. There appears to have been a Latin version of this, circulating under the title *Gentilismus Reseratus* (Leiden, 1651?) which I have not traced; cf. Schwab (1984), p.138 and www.missionstudies.org/asia/india.htm. The title of Jan Amos Comenius' *Janua linguarum reserata* may have influenced Newton's shorthand.

67 Vossius (1641), pp.648–52; Yahuda 41, f.3–4, 8. See ch. 4 above.

68 Strabo (1707) [Tr/NQ 11.2–3], II.1007 (d2s), 1027 (d2s), 1031, 1035 (d2s), 1043 (d2s); Philostratus (1709) [Tr/NQ.18.13], pp.105–6 (d2s).

69 Genesis 25:6; Newton (1728), pp.347–50; cf. Yahuda 41, f.25; see also ch. 9 below. Bouwsma does not note the biblical source, and without referring to Abraham ibn Ezra, suggests that the source of this theory was probably the Zohar which speaks of the 'other sons' of Abraham who 'inhabit the mountains of the East, where they instruct the sons of men in the arts of magic and divination' (*Zohar* (1931–4), II.33–4). On the Abrahaman genealogy, see Hakluyt, ed. (1885–90), Vol.VI, Bk.ii, ch.8; Hudson (2000), pp.8–9; [Créquinière] (1705), p.100. Pailin (1984), p.57; Manuel (1963), p.111; Pseudo-Clement (2005a), Bk I, ch. 33. It was refuted by others: Lord (1630), p.71; cf. Schwab (1984), pp.138, 152; Županov (1999), p.70; Camões (1776), pp.291–3n.; Voltaire gave credence to it in one place, and in another lambasted Bouchet for positing it (Schwab (1984), p.152).

70 Maier (1617), p.7, slightly misremembering Agrippa (1630?),

II.ii.1077–8; cf. 1 Chronicles 1:32–3, Genesis 25:1–6 (in King James (1611), the name is rendered Hanoch and Henoch; Enoch in the *Biblia Sacra Vulgata*); Levy (1927), p.16; Ezra (1988), p.245; Ezra (1939), pp. 57, 155–7, 160, 183; Ezra (1947), pp.48, 75+n., 101. For Newton on Hermes, cf. Yahuda 25.2 a), f.26; Yahuda 25.2 b), f.9v–10.

71 Newton (1728), pp.40–1, 347–50; Yahuda 25.2 b), f.10; Yahuda 41, f.3–4; Ammianus (1935), II.366–9 (xxiii.6.32–33) (Newton, and the seventeenth–century translator, took Ammianus' *'qui'* to refer back to Hystaspes rather than (as modern translators) to Zoroaster); Ammianus (1609), p.231; cf. pp.235–6; cf. Maier (1617), p.8.

72 Newton (1728), pp.24, 252–3, 327; Yahuda 25.2 a), f.21; Yahuda 25.1 a), random page order, facing a page marked 20 [i.e. f.19v]; cf. Diodorus Siculus (1700), pp.13, 42; Manuel (1974), pp.43–4.

73 Newton (1728), pp.347–50; Madaurensis (1853), pp.388–9; Philostratus (1709) [Tr/NQ.18.13], pp.3+n., 247 (d2s), 347; Maier (1717) [Tr/NQ 10.148(2)], p.48; Maier (1617), pp.8, 113–14.

74 Keynes 3, pp.5–6; reproduced in Goldish (1998), Appendix A, p.167; cf. pp.42, 49–50. The version at Keynes 3, p.27 also includes 'the flesh' of living animals, apparently meaning 'of animals still alive' (as in the Mosaic law against cutting off limbs while the animal is still alive); other versions only mention 'the blood', e.g. Newton (1950), p.29. cf. Maier (1717) [Tr/NQ 10.148(2)], p.53; Philostratus (1709) [Tr/NQ.18.13], pp.3+n.; Strabo (1707) [Tr/NQ 11.2–3], II.1043 (d2s).

75 Metempsychosis arose from the corrupt belief that the seven planets and then that animals

could be animated by souls:
Yahuda 17.3, f.8r–9r, 11, 15;
Yahuda 25.2 a), f.25; Yahuda 25.2
b), f.31; Westfall (1982), p.16;
Newton (1950), p.50.
76 Yahuda 17.3, f.11; Manuel (1963),
p.112+n., Plate 10; McGuire and
Rattansi (1966), pp.109,
122–3+n. and *passim*; Westfall
(1982), p.15; Schaffer (1993),
p.220; Maclaurin (1748),
pp.31–3.
77 For Newton's interest in
Pythagorean works, cf. e.g.
Harrison (1978), pp.159, 166,
207, 217, 219; Philostratus (1709)
[Tr/NQ.18.13], p.120.
78 Huet (1694); Edwards (1693),
p.250; cf. Lockman, ed. (1743),
II.266, 277; Bayle, P. (1734–41),
VIII.614; Hazard (1953), pp.45–6;
Vossius (1641); Popkin (1990a),
pp.28–31; Markley (1999),
pp.126–7. For the claim that
Pythagoras learned from the Jews,
cf. Clement of Alexandria (2004a),
Bk I, ch.15; Josephus (1755),
'Against Apion', Bk I, section 22;
Blount (1678?), pp.13–15;
Dupleix (1610), p.8; Burthogge
(1675), pp.374–5, 378–81;
[Créquinière] (1705), p.100;
McGuire and Rattansi (1966),
pp.129–34; Heninger (1974),
pp.201–2+n.
79 Clement of Alexandria (2004a),
Bk II, ch.18; Exodus 22:30;
Manuel (1963), pp.93–4;
Mercerus (1598), 'Genesis 9:4',
p.197; Selden (1640), pp.14–22,
43–5, 82–3; Selden (1725),
I.193–4, II.333, 880–91, III.1735;
Selden (1665), pp.117, 313,
830–1.
80 Roe (1990), pp.274–5; Gaitonde
(1983), pp.31–3; Linschoten
(1988), I.253+n.; Purchas, ed.
(1905–7), X.218–318; Ovington
(1929), pp.178–9; Lockman, ed.
(1743), II.240, 266, 277; Herbert
(1634), p.38; cf. ch. 19 below.
81 Schaffer (1993), pp.222–5.
82 Westfall (1980), pp.530–1;
Westfall (1982), p.18; Westfall

(1984); Vickers, ed. (1984),
pp.8–9, 15, 20–2.
83 McGuire and Rattansi (1966);
Dobbs (1975), pp.15, 20, 90,
105–6, 108–10, 180–1; Dobbs
(1991), p.150; Manuel (1963) (3,
n.72), pp.112–16; Craven (1910),
pp.65–6, 71–5; Agrippa (1676),
p.110; Anon. (1694a), sig.[a4r];
Churchill (1967), pp.38–9;
Rattansi (1972); Matton (1987);
[Glanvill] (1662), pp.1–3, 33–4;
Harrison (1978), pp.184, 188–9;
Keynes 32, p.3; Cambridge
University Library (2001–2).
84 Maier (1617), pp.7, 38–44,
113–14, 120; Maier (1717) [Tr/
NQ 10.148(2)], pp.38, 47 (ds),
48–55; cf. Maier (1656),
pp.10–11, 96–7; Maier (1687)
[Tr/NQ 16.88], p.57 (ds); Maier
(1619a) [Tr/NQ 10.148(1)],
pp.109 (ds), 136 (d); Maier
(1619b) [Tr/NQ 10.148(3)], p.214
(ds); Maier (1618)[Tr/NQ
10.148], pp.177 (ds), 178, 179
(d2s), (the pages on the *prisca
sapientia* are among the only
marked pages in this book).
85 Isaac Newton (1728), pp.305,
347–50; cf. Porphyry (2000),
p.112 (4.16.2); Philostratus
(1709) [Tr/NQ.18.13], pp.3+n.,
85–8 (d2s); Harrison (1978),
p.84, 217; Keynes 67, f.7r–10r;
White (1997), pp.119–20.
86 Ben Jonson, *The Alchemist*,
II.ii.96ff. *cit.* Coudert (2000),
pp.84, 86; Anon. (1694a), pp.3–4,
31, 56–7; Geber (1928), p.30;
[Aquinas attrib.] (1966),
pp.107–8+n., 115–16, 336; Jung
(1974), pp.270–1; Schuler (1980);
Holland (1596), sig.A1v, A2r,
pp.101–2. Holland's information
on the Persian Magi's diet of
'farina and olus' was probably
derived from Jerome (2005a), Bk
II, ch.14, cf. Porphyry (2000),
p.112n.
87 Josephus (1755), 'Antiquities of
the Jews', Bk X, Ch.10.2; Daniel 1.
88 Keynes 130.6, Notebook 2,
f.[9r–v]; Manuel (1968), p.173;

cp. Dobbs (1975), p.15; cf. Iliffe (1998), p.148.

89 cf. Keynes 135, First Letter (17 Jan. 1727/8), side 3.

90 cf. Harrison (1978), pp.215, 232; Westfall (1980), p.531n. cites Newton's note in *Sanguis naturae* (1696) about Tace/Tacy Sowle as one of the three pieces of evidence that Newton continued an interest in alchemy after 1693 (though Westfall misnames her 'Stacy Sowles' and exaggerates her role in alchemical publishing). Tacy inherited her business from her father Andrew Sowle who died in 1695. Furthermore, if Newton, who referred to her as 'a Quaker Widow in White Hart Court', is right that she was a widow at the time he wrote the note, he must have written the note in or after 1723 which seems very surprising. It seems more likely that Newton was mistaken; Tacy was a spinster until 1706 and it was probably before then that Newton wrote his note; or Newton was talking about Jane Sowle, Andrew's widow, under whose name Tacy continued to publish after her marriage.

CHAPTER 9

1 Spinoza (2000), Part 1, Prop. 14, p.85, cf. pp.22, 55–7. Israel downplays the influence of the mid-century English republican 'pantheists' by contrasting Spinozism with Winstanley's 'poetic' pantheism (Israel (2001), pp.162, 177, 187, 601–3, 610); but Winstanley was not a pantheist. More relevant predecessors were the true pantheists like Bauthumley and those borderline atheists – familiarly alluded to in short-hand by horrified contemporaries and outlawed by the Blasphemy Act (1650) – who held that 'there is no God, but Nature only' (cf. e.g. Muggleton (1699), pp.18–20; Collins (1651), p.6; Anon.

(1650a), pp.1–4, 6; Anon. (1650b), pp.2–3; Anon. (1652b), pp.4–5. The Family of Love were accused of this (Hayes (1884), pp.58–67; [Rogers] (1579), sig. H.v.v.; Strype, ed. (1824), p.563; Hill, Reay and Lamont (1983), pp.18–19; Hill (1990), pp.155, 165; Hill (1991), pp.204–5, 209; Whiting (1968), p.273).

2 On the question of authorship, cf. Popkin (1987b), p.xxix; Popkin (1998), p.396; Marana (1970), pp.ix–xi, 'Bibliography'; Disraeli (1798), II.121–5 (Disraeli presents evidence that the whole work was written by Marana); Boswell (1799), pp.207–8+n.; cf. Boswell (1785), p.427. C.J.Betts shares the view of Almansi and Warren that all eight volumes were authored by Marana: Betts (1984), p.97+n. (citing Guido Almansi, '"L'Esploratore turco" e la genesi del romanzo epistolare pseudo-orientale', *Studi secenteschi* 7 (1966), 35–65 and G. Almansi and D.A. Warren, 'Roman épistolaire et analyse historique: l'"Espion turc" de G.P. Marana', *XVIIe Siècle* 110 (1976), 57–73; Shimi (1973), pp.2–5 [only first 20 open-access pages seen]); cf. note 20 on parallels in Ovington below.

3 Marana (1970), p.vii; Drew (1998), p.205; Disraeli (1798), II.121–5.

4 All these authors used the perspective of Indian vegetarianism to critique Western mores; as did Oliver Goldsmith's similar *Citizen of the World* (see ch. 16 below); cf. Hamilton (1796), espec. I.xv, xvii–xviii, II.222–6. For literature on the *Spy*'s impact on this literary genre, cf. Disraeli (1798), II.121–5; Shimi (1973), pp.11–12; Douthwaite (1997); Degategno (1975) (not seen); Dufrenoy (1975), III.18ff.

5 Marana (1970), pp.xiii–xiv; Disraeli (1798), II.121–5; cp. Popkin (1987a), p.120. Part of the

threat of deism in the *Turkish Spy* was defused by Mahmut's non-republican and even royalist sympathies, cf. *Spy*, II.84–5, 318–24; III.231–3, 290, 347, 357; Marana (1970), p.ix. Even this royalism, however, may have been sardonic, since he comments that the greatness of kings like Louis of France consisted in oppression, fleecing the rich and keeping the poor powerless (II.176, 275–7).

6 *Spy*, V.A5v, 319; VII.17; VIII.83–9, 254–6.

7 *Spy*, II.325–31, where he both repudiates but also defends this theory; V.165–6, where he is acutely equivocal; VI.253–5, where he equivocally defends it; and VIII.88 and 188, where he asserts it; cf. VII.242; VIII.A3v–A4v, where the editors deny he is atheist but sound sardonic; cf. III.A4r–v. Compare *Spy*, VIII.83–9 with Thomas Burnet, 'An Appendix Concerning the Modern Brachmins in the Indies, Together with their generally received Opinions', in Blount, Gildon et al. (1693), p.82. On the virtue of atheists, cf. *Spy*, II.325–33; IV.90–2; cf. also I.49; II.19; IV.207; Marana (1970), p.104n. For the radical sceptics' use of Epicurus' quasi-vegetarian frugality, cf. e.g. Berti (1994), ch. 9, p.138+n.; cf. ch. 11 below.

8 *Spy*, V.169–71; cf.II.114–18, 174–5; III.255–61; IV.354–9; V.303–4; VI.32–8; Marana (1970), pp.122–6n.; cf. [Defoe] (1718), pp.199ff., 218ff.; cp. IV.201 and cp. Betts (1984), p.114. The authors of the *Turkish Spy* may have derived information from the works of Edward Pococke, see Toomer (1996), pp.123, 220. Some views in the *Turkish Spy* are similar to the vegetarian sceptical Muslim poet-scholar Abū al-ʿAlāʾ al-Maʿarrī (AD 973–1058), and his predecessor Ibn Al-Rāwandī who described the freethinking philosophy of the

Barāhima (almost certainly the Indian Brahmins) apparently as a cover for his own heretical views. (Stroumsa (1999), pp.145–7, 162–3, 240–1; *Encyclopædia Britannica*, 'Islamic art: the new style', 'Abu al-Ala al-Ma'ari'; Ali (2003), pp.55–6). The *Turkish Spy*'s interest in India is also reminiscent of the sixth/twelfth-century Baghdad-based Islamic theologian, Shahrastānī, who shared many views with the Ikhwan al-Safa. The Ikhwan al-Safa also gave voice to the complaints of animals against the abuses of mankind; cf. Titley (1983), p.148.

9 *Spy*, V.A4r; Marana (1970), p.ix; cf. [Defoe] (1718), p.v; Popkin (1987b), p.xliii. For a catalogue of persecution meted out against the protagonists of the Radical Enlightenment, though omitting the *Turkish Spy*, see Israel (2001).

10 *Spy*, III.116–19, 185–6; VII.203, 262–4; V.258. C.J. Betts dismisses this recurrent, powerful and cogent critique of the Bible as 'little more than local colour, a necessity of the *genre*', 'not intended to do more than give verisimilitude to the fiction that a Muslim is the author'; Betts (1984), pp.100–3, 114.

11 *Spy*, VIII.119–24.

12 *Spy*, VI.254. On the claim that the law of nature, regardless of religion, will lead to virtue and salvation, cf. I.31; II.332–5; III.14, 179, 292; IV.262–4, 320; V.302–3, 341–3; VII.14–15, 188–9. On Mahmut's desire to reconcile all religions, cf. I.129, 226; II.109–10, 114–18; III.87; IV.101–9, 295–301; V.102, 186; VI.32–8, 274–6, 278–9, 282; VI.114; VII.162–6. Popkin (1987b), pp.xlii–xliii. This was also consistent with the aims of the Ikhwan al-Safa (cf. Farrukh (n.d.)).

13 On the Brahmins, cf. *Spy*, I.32; II. 21ff., 77–8, 325–31; III.A4r, 14,

116–19, 286, 291–4, 297, 299; IV.203, 205, 260, 354–9; V.303–5; VI.32–8; VIII.119–24; Marana (1970), p.vii; [Defoe] (1718), p.152ff. cf. e.g. Blount (1680), pp.19–20; cf. Betts (1984), pp.76, 101. On the vacillations between Mahmut's eirenic and partisan statements on the Sunni–Shia conflict, see *Spy*, II.114–8; IV.101–9; VI.32–4; cp. V.43–4; cf. Marana (1970), p.8n.

14 *Spy*, I.[A5r]; III.A4r–v; VI.274–6; cf. the mirror image in Mahmut's defence of Christians against the bigotry of his Turkish friends: *Spy*, II.55, 109–10; III.179, 255–61; VIII.197–201. In another vein, however, Mahmut's deist and Islamic voices combine to attack Christianity vigorously (cf. III.51).

15 *Spy*, I.26, 27–9, 196, 285, 355, 368; II.48–51, 129, 132–5, 224, 226–9, 273; III.124, 207–17, 260–1, 279–80, 295, 321–2, 332–5; IV.309–10, 342–3; V.128–130, 247, 289–91; VI.18ff., 77–80, 181–5; VII.17, 286–91; VIII.138, and further notes below. See also related fascination with China whose culture the *Turkish Spy* regards as largely contiguous with that of India, IV.87–98; V.31. Marana's first volume exhibits interest in travel literature, especially from India but nothing like the enthusiastic Indophilia and vegetarianism which commences in the second volume (*Spy*, I.26, 27–9, 62, 78, 99, 133, 175, 196, 199, 203, 206, 219, 230, 253, 258, 261, 285, 322–3, 355, 368).

16 *Spy*, I.196; II.48–51, 133–5, 226–9; III.207–17; IV.86–7, 164–5; VI.191–6; VIII.25–8.

17 On Mahmut's fascination for Eastern chronology, cf. *Spy*, IV.354–9; cf. IV.166–7, 193–4; V.216; VI.144–8, 246–9; VII.96, 104–7, 190–7, 249ff.; VIII.248, and especially 313–29. The *Turkish Spy's* use of foreign cultures, especially the antiquity of

China, to undermine the claims of Christian orthodoxy relate to similar techniques employed by La Peyrère and Guillaume Postel. On the Eastern testimony to the eternity of the earth, cf. *Spy*, VI.246–9; VII.104–7, 190–7; VIII.325–9. On the eternity of the earth in general, cf. III.216–17, 318; VI.191–6, 246–9; VIII.83–9. On Pre-Adamism, cf. III.315–22, 360; VI.191–6; VIII.336–9. cf. Patot (1760), II.146–7; D'Argens (1739–40), I.281–4. Newton did the opposite by trying to prove that such claims of antiquity were exaggerated (Newton (1728), *passim*; Manuel (1968), pp.351–2). On Sanskrit as the first language, cf. *Spy*, III.216–17, 321–2; VI.191–6; cf. Webb (1669). Guillaume Postel appears to have thought the ancient Brahmins had retained antediluvian books (Postel (1553?a), pp.72–3). For the *Spy's* cultural relativism, cf e.g. *Spy*, I.258; III.150; VI.77–80, 135–40; VII.188–9, 219; VIII.108–15; Marana (1970), pp.xiii–xiv. For the interest in travel in general, cf. *Spy*, II.35–7, 229–35; IV.253, 303–5; V.44, 186, 338; VI.135–40, 177–9; VII.143, 188–9, 226. Popkin (1979), pp.215–19, 224, 228; Popkin (1987a), pp.127–31; Popkin (1987b), pp.xxxix–xl; Popkin (1990a); Rubiés (2000), p.347; Drew (1998), p.47; Popkin (1998), p.414; Popkin (1990b), pp.20–1; Hazard (1953), pp.8–12; Rubiés (2000), pp.220n., 309, 312, 343, 347–8, 354–7+n., 378–85; Walker (1972), pp.194–230, espec. 214–15; Shimi (1973), p.10. In contrast to the active role that Popkin, Rubiés and Hazard and I attribute to the impact of travel literature, C.J. Betts takes the view that 'Knowledge of foreign societies seems to have determined the forms and setting of deistic literature rather than its content' (Betts (1984), p.75).

18 Even though C.J. Betts acknowledges that Mahmut 'returns to the question in other letters, as if he took it seriously,' he dismisses this central concern as the 'anti-climax when Mahmut asks whether to abstain from meat' (Betts (1984), pp.100–1). Richard H. Popkin's discussion of Mahmut's vegetarian mission is much more sensitive, Popkin (1987b).

19 *Spy*, IV.218; cf. IV.78, 109–10; V.16–17; VI.15.

20 *Spy*, V.87–90; cf. IV.18–21, 193–4; V.303–4; VI.191–6; VII.17; Ovington (1929), pp.168–70, 175, 177–9; Porphyry (2000), p.112; Evelyn (2000), p.154. Whether the several curious parallel passages in Ovington and the *Turkish Spy* are the result of either of them directly borrowing from the other, or both of them borrowing from a prior common source, the linguistic similarities could well be strong evidence that the anonymous volumes of the *Turkish Spy* were originally written in English. cf. also *Spy*, IV.305–10, 348–50; V.168; VII.145–54.

21 *Spy*, III.118; IV.16–22; VI.347–51; VII.17, 76; cf. Ovington (1929), pp.175, 178–9. Like Spinoza, Winstanley and other radicals, Mahmut emphasised that there was no landed property in the state of nature; cf. Israel (2001), p.271; and Ovid, *Metamporphoses*, Bk XV. On primitivism, cf. *Spy*, II.114–18, 168; IV.109–10; V.309, VI.347–51.

22 *Spy*, I.175, III.150–2; IV.306–8, 321–2; V.210; VIII.84, 97, 101; cf. Crab (1655), pp.12–13.

23 *Spy*, IV.109–10. The *Turkish Spy*'s portrayal of Muhammad is reminiscent of the medieval Islamic romantic figure of Majnun in the desert.

24 Purchas (1905–7), VIII.135–6; cf. Bacon (1640), p.382; Marana

(1970), p.45n.; [Pope] (1729), I.262.

25 *Spy*, IV.14–15.

26 *Spy*, IV.16–17, 62–7; V.87–90; an echo of La Peyrère (cf. Popkin (1979), p.217). On Bible textual criticism in this period cf. e.g. Popkin (1998), p.413.

27 *Spy*, VI.284–93; cf. Williamson, 'Just Complaint', f.7v. On the lost tribes, cf. VI.317; VII.96; VIII.116ff. and the letters, apparently a (mock?) emulation of La Peyrère's Postellian Messianism, at VII.307–14; VIII.18, 83–9 and cp. II.229–35; cf. Popkin (1979), pp.216–28; Popkin (1990a), pp.33–4; Popkin (1987b), pp.xxxviii–xlii. cf. also Montenegro and Jerónimo (1780), III.351–6; Patot (1760), I.17–21.

28 *Spy*, VII.145–54; cf. V.199; Matthew 3:4; Mark 1:6.

29 *Spy*, VI.278–9; VI.28–30.

30 *Spy*, IV.300–1; cf. Israel (2001), p.651. On the vegetarian Essenes, cf. Josephus (1755), 'Antiquities of the Jews', Bk XV, ch.10.4; Josephus (1755), 'The Wars Of The Jews', Bk II, ch. 8; Lord (1630), pp.74–6; Evelyn (1850), II.48–9; Grotius (1901), Bk II, ch. 2, § 2.

31 *Spy*, VI.246–9. For Mahmut's Neoplatonism, see *Spy*, I.39; II.332–5; III.80–1; V.23–5, 169–71, 359; VII.76, 121–6; VIII.253; Marana (1970), pp.122–6; contrast I.39 with VI.36–8. On his favourite philosopher, Porphyry, *Spy*, IV.196–7; V.319; cf. II.93–6; III.14–23; V.303–4; VII.236–41; VIII.253; and cf. Lloyd (1699), p.v. For Mahmut's reverence of Egypt: *Spy*, V.53, 64, 103, 128–9, 212–13, 216; VI.34–8; cf. Marana (1970), p.109n. For Mahmut's reverence for ancient religions other than his favourites, Egypt and India, see *Spy*, II.189–90, 323; III.158–60, 173, 255–61, 278; IV.297–8, 336–7; V.117; VII.286–91. Daniel Defoe completely reneges on the agenda

of the *Turkish Spy* by subsuming ancient paganism into Hebraic myth ([Defoe] (1718), pp.81ff., 152ff.).

32 Spy, VII.145–54; cf. e.g. I.32, 120; VII.16, VIII.222–3; Radicati (1734), p.44; Popkin (1987b), p.xliv; cf. Shahrastânî (1951–5), I.619–30.

33 *Spy*, IV.354–9; cf. IV.21–3, 303–5, 310; V.272; VI.144–8.

34 *Spy*, VIII.18–23; 170–6; cf. V.17–19.

35 *Spy*, IV.217–22; cf. IV.21–3; V.16–17, 250; VI.5–7, 28–30; VII.145–54; compare V.87–8 with Ovington (1920), pp.178–9.

36 *Spy*, V.16–17; cf. Tryon (1696), p.125.

37 *Spy*, III.66–70, 93–4; cf. II.142; IV.15–16, 78, 109–10; V.196; VIII.181–5.

38 *Spy*, VI.86–9.

39 *Spy*, VII.208; cf. V.69 and Drew (1998), p.205. For other vegetarians see *Spy*, I.261; II.312–13; III.260–1; and cf. I.38, 39, 213–14, 261, 322–3, 343–4; II.21ff., 197–9, 241–2; III.93–4. See also Mahmut's other comments on abstinence: II.4, 33–4, 72–3, 172, 226; III.192–3; IV.109–10; Marana's first volume shares this theme (*Spy*, I.38, 39, 213–14, 261, 322–3, 343–4) but exhibits contempt for Pythagorean vegetarianism (I.62, 230). cf. [Defoe] (1718), p.54. Mahmut seems to allude to the anchoritic community of Munastir in Tunisia (IV.109–10; cf. Bosworth et al., eds (1993), VII.227–9).

40 *Spy*, VII.145–54; cf. III.66–70; IV.16–17, 23, 109–10, 218, 331–2; V.15; VI.30, 347–51; VII.121–8, 145–54; Weitzman was simplifying the fraught issue when he said that Mahmut *was* a vegetarian (Marana (1970), p.xi–xii).

41 *Spy*, VII.126–7.

42 *Spy*, IV.109–10; cf. Ovington (1929), p.178; and *Spy*, III.110–11, 120, 181, 278.

Mahmut eats flesh even though it is polluted with blood: *Spy*, III.245–7: VI.28–30; cf. V.3–5. Mahmut initially abstained from wine, but eventually becomes an alcoholic: *Spy*, II.48–9, 354, 357–9; IV.348–9; V.53–5; VI.49–51; VIII.181–5; cf. [Defoe] (1718), p.74ff.

43 *Spy*, VII.145–54; cf. VI.191–6; VII.276–7; VIII.7–12.

44 *Spy*, VII.127–8, 208, 145–54; cf. III.260–1, VII.201–4; for anti-monasticism cf. VII.162–4; VIII.25–8; Bernier (1988), p.320. The *Turkish Spy* may have been influenced by Bernier's two-pronged technique of snidely ridiculing Christian practices under the guise of criticising similar Indian superstitions.

45 *Spy*, VIII.7–12.

46 *Spy*, IV.331–2; cf. VII.145–54.

47 *Spy*, IV.109–10.

48 Calvin (1999), I, Genesis 1:29 and 9:3.

49 Reynolds (1725), p.95, and pp.1–96.

50 Betts (1984), pp.11–12nn.

51 Popkin (1979), pp.215–19, 224, 228; Popkin (1990a), pp.33–4; Popkin (1987a), pp.78, 115–20, 128–32; Rubiés (2000), p.347. cf. Patot (1760), II.146–7; Hasan (1733), Notes, ii.254–5; Poole (2004), p.3 and *passim*.

52 Postel (1553?a), pp.68–70, 72; Postel (1986), pp.39–40, 91–92, 140; Postel (1981), pp.100, 102, 240–73; Postel (1969), pp.188–90+n., 206, 229+n.; Postel (1553?b), pp.4v–5r, 11r–12r, 16v–20r, 29v, 32v, 45v–60r, 65r, 66r–67v, 86v–87r (my translations from a facsimile of the edition in the Bibliothèque Nationale de France with Postel's ms emendations); Bouwsma (1957), pp.58, 61–2, 206–12, 252, 298; cf. pp.43, 51, 275–7; Lach (1977), pp.41, 266–70; Kuntz (1981), pp.6, 27, 34, 50–2, 83–4, 96–7, 104–5, 172; Kuntz (1999), II.278, 280–1, IV.34, XIII.171, XIV.445;

Scholem (1991), p.199; Popkin (1992), p.287; cf. Herbert of Cherbury (1705), pp.358–9; cp. Bayle, P. (1734–41), III.560.

53 *Spy*, VI.A5v; VII.A3r–v.

54 Blount, Gildon et al. (1693), p.82 and *passim*; Blount (1680), sig.[A3r].

55 Bayle, P. (1734–41), II.101–2; cf. Lloyd (1699), I.xii, xvii–xxvi, xxxvi–xlv.

56 Blount (1680), pp.1–4; Blount ([1680?]), pp.19–20, 40–1, 51, 58–9; cf. Ovid, *Metamorphoses*, Bk XV; Clement of Alexandria (2004a), Bk VII, ch.1; cp. [Delany] (1733), pp.124–5; [Coxall?] (1721), pp.21–2; cf. pp.16–18, 26–7.

57 Blount (1680), pp.3–4, 110; Blount ([1680?]), pp.49–50; cf. [Créquinière] (1705), p.30; Blount, Gildon et al. (1693); cf. Burnet (1729), IV, 'Modern Brachmans'; Burnet (1736), p.16ff.; Edwards (1699), I.95–6.

58 Blount (1680), pp.2–3, 69, 88–90; cf. p.152; Diogenes Laertius (2000), II.331–2; Blount ([1680?]), p.22. Compare Blount (1680), p.17 with Philostratus (1912), II.303–5 (Bk VIII, ch.vii).

59 Blount ([1680?]), p.22.

60 Blount (1680), pp.23–4.

61 Toland (1704), pp.21–2, 31–3, 38–9, 53, 57–8, 191; Ovington (1929), pp.195–6; *Spy*, IV.176; VI.253–4; VII.45; Reuchlin (1983), pp.169, 179; cf. Ovid (1632), Bk XV, and cf. Sandys' commentary; Cudworth (1678), pp.40–2; Kurth-Voigt (1999), pp.38–40; cf. [Créquinière] (1705), pp.30, 54–7, 99–100, 102–3; Kircher (1987), pp.141–5; Hasan (1733), Notes, Part 2, pp.31–2; cf. Betts (1984), pp.235–7; Jacob (1981), pp.215–21.

62 Jacob (1976b), pp.233–4 (cf. pp.212–13, 227, 231; Creech (1699), sigs.Ar–v, p.90; León-Jones (1997), pp.33, 83–91, 123–4, 149–53. León-Jones does

not solve the question to what extent Bruno understood metempsychosis as individual souls reincarnating in different bodies, rather than as the eternal cycling of matter and spirit. Stanley (1655–60), III.105; Porphyry (2000), Bk I.6, p.33n.29. cf. Blount (1678?), pp.8–9, 59–66, 92; Blount (1680), pp.2–3, Note 1; Blount (1680?), pp.25–6; cf. Anon. (1692), p.86; Helmont, F.M. (1685), p.145; [Glanvill] (1662), e.g. pp.52–3.

63 *Spy*, V.105–7; VI.250–2, 341–6; VII.242 and IV.218; V.23–5; VIII.250; and Mahmut's other discussions of metempsychosis: I.39; II.335–6; IV.16–17, 110, 202, 348–9; V.247, 295; VII.96, 145–54; Disraeli (1798), II.493–4. C.J. Betts denies that Mahmut gives metempsychosis such high priority, Betts (1984), p.109; Kurth-Voigt (1999), pp.38–40. Mahmut also tried to show that metempsychosis was compatible with Islam; *Spy*, V.105–8; Pococke (1650), pp.134–5; cf. Hasan (1733), Notes, Part 2, pp.31–2; Abul-Pharajio (1663), pp.33, 50; cf. Blount (1678?), p.66; Ovington (1929), pp.171–2; Scholem (1987), pp.191–4. See also the Spinozists' interest in Pococke's Latin translation of the Arabic pantheistic novel, the *Life of Hai Ebn Yokhdan*, which presented the origin of flesh-eating as an accident ([Pococke] (2001), p.198). Compare other attempts to reconcile reincarnation and resurrection in ch.5 and ch.6, and Gott (1670), p.477.

64 Yates (1961), p.249; Gatti (1995); Temple (1690), pp.22–3; Locke (1858), pp.128–30; Israel (2001), p.136.

65 Lloyd (1699), I.v; Fréret (1758), p.379. On Buddhism as atheism, see e.g. Locke (1690), Bk.I, Ch.iii; Radicati (1737), pp.36–7; Israel (2001), pp.647, 654, 660, 675.

66 [Gildon] (1710); Marana (1970),
   pp.xvi–xvii.
67 Blount, Gildon et al. (1693),
   p.182; cf. *Spy*, IV.193–4; cf. e.g.
   Heylyn (1625), p.692; Speed
   (1646), p.38; Olearius (1669),
   p.188. John Locke drew from the
   same source as Gildon when he
   commented in his notebook that
   'The Brahmins estimate that in the
   year 1639 of the Christian era the
   world had existed for 3,892,739
   years' (Bonno (1955), p.55; Locke
   (1858), pp.70, 73, 251–3).
   Suprisingly John Marshall's
   apparently independent report
   chronologically tallies with Locke's
   source, in saying that a 1670
   Sanskrit almanac reckoned the
   world was 3,892,771 years old (a
   point Evelyn marked in his own
   copy) (Marshall (1702), p.733; cf.
   Temple (1690), pp.19–20).
68 Gordon (1871), pp.277–8.
69 *Spy*, III.245, 272; V.251, 323;
   VI.250–2, 347–51; VII.2–5;
   VIII.18–23; cf. e.g. Tryon (1691a),
   pp.99, 186. For other Tryonist
   echoes in *Turkish Spy* see e.g.
   Tryon's pantheism (Tryon
   (1691a), pp.29–30; [Tryon]
   (1685), pp.66–7; Tryon (1703),
   pp.40, 62); the echo of Tryon's
   title in Mahmut's phrase, 'Health,
   long Life, and Happiness' (*Spy*,
   II.122, 217); and microcosm and
   pansophia (*Spy*, II.197–9).
70 This (and Tryon's Quaker
   precedents) revises the view of
   Drew and Popkin that the *Turkish
   Spy* is 'the first work in which the
   Orient serves as the basis for a
   satire on European manners and
   morals' (John Drew (1998),
   pp.79–80, 90; Popkin (1987a),
   p.115). For deist-like views, cf.
   [Tryon] (1695a), pp.5, 11, 90–5;
   Tryon (1691a), p.261; Tryon
   (1691b), pp.130–1; Agrippa
   (1651), III.473–5; *Spy*, III.300.
   Mahmut also goes through a
   phase of mystical Quietism which
   he compares to the spirituality of
   the Brahmins, a comparison that

had already been made by
François Bernier, John Locke and
Pierre Bayle: *Spy*, VII.236–41,
VIII.92–6; cf. [Defoe] (1718),
p.270ff.; Bernier (1890),
pp.19–20; Bernier (1988),
pp.316–19; Betts (1984),
pp.107–8; Aaron and Gibb, eds
(1936), p.119; Bayle, P.
(1734–41), III.563–4. McDowell
(2002), pp.524, 527; cf. e.g. *Spy*,
II.139–42.

CHAPTER 10

1 Cohen (1936), p.53; Malebranche
   (1694[–5]), I.ii.77; II.798–9;
   Passmore (1974), pp.204–5.
2 Malebranche (1694[–5]),
   II.249–51, 776–7.
3 When Thomas Huxley came to
   defend Charles Darwin's
   revolutionary theories, it was to
   Descartes he turned as the founder
   of their line of thought: Huxley
   (1874); Huxley (1870).
4 Shugg (1968b); Rosenfield (1968);
   Malebranche (1997), Bk V, ch.III,
   pp.352–3; *Spy*, VII.220–5; Ray
   (1717), I.54–7.
5 Thomas Hobbes, 'Objections', in
   Descartes (1952), p.136.
6 Hobbes (1839–45), II.113–14;
   V.166, 185–8; Hobbes (1969),
   pp.130–1; *cit.* Thomas, K. (1983),
   p.171; Hobbes (1651), Part I,
   ch.xiv, pp.64–9.
7 'The Hunting of the Hare', in
   Cavendish (1653), pp.112–13; see
   also Cavendish's anti-meat poem,
   'Nature's Cook' and Cavendish
   (2004), pp.18, 64, for a world in
   which meat-eating equals
   cannibalism and where she
   castigates Aristotle because 'his
   Knowledge was got by untimely
   Deaths, and cruel Dissections'. cf.
   Sarasohn (1996), pp.170–1;
   Thomas, K. (1983), p.170; Smuts
   ed. (1996), p.191; Spencer (1993),
   pp.211–12; Regan (2001), p.100.
8 Tryon once indirectly addressed
   the Cartesian debate in his attack
   on the Earl of Rochester, Tryon

(1691b), pp.131–3; Wilmot (1964), 'Satyr against Mankind' [1680], pp.118–24.

9 Tyssot de Patot fused sections from both Hobbes' and Gassendi's 'Objections' to Descartes *Meditations*: Tyssot de Patot (1997), I.43, 207; [Tyssot de Patot] (1743), pp.28–9; cf. Betts (1984), p.187; [Gildon] (1997), Letter 54, pp.[181–3], 170–2; McKee (1941), pp.80–4.

10 *Spy*, IV.310.

11 Ovington (1929), pp.168–70; cf. La Mettrie, *L'Homme–Machine* (1748).

12 *Spy*, IV.310; Israel (2001), pp.270–1; cf. Bergerac (1657).

13 Pufendorf (1749), pp.361–2.

14 Cohen (1936); Rosenfield (1968), pp.16–17, 52, 54; Passmore (1975), pp.204–5; Thomas, K. (1983), p.34+n. Henry More's Platonist colleague, Ralph Cudworth, agreed that even Pythagoreanism was 'more Reasonable and Tolerable', though he assuaged the anxiety of 'those, who are so much burthened with this difficulty', by explaining that animal souls did not reincarnate, but were reabsorbed into the world soul: Cudworth (1678), pp.38–46.

15 Williams, Howard (1883), p.102.

16 [Baillet] (1691), II.447–9 and p.xxvi; cf. Descartes (1897–1913), V.184, 199–201; Haldane (1905), p.360; Rodis-Lewis (1998), pp.xiii, 182; Gruman (1966), pp.77–9; Descartes (1984–91), III.75, 131, 136, 237, 275, 353; and the invaluable article Shapin (2000), which says that Descartes was not actually vegetarian; this may be the case, but it leaves unanswered, for example, why his diet was spoken of in terms of the fleshless Lenten fast.

17 Montaigne (1991), pp.505–9; Descartes (1897–1913), X.219; Descartes (1952), 'Discourse On The Method', § v; cf. Cureau de la Chambre (1658), p.587;

Serjeantson (2001), p.437+n.74; Boas (1964), pp.56–61; cp. Rosenfield (1968), pp.3, 19; Charron (1601); Rodis-Lewis (1998), pp.44–7.

18 Malebranche (1694[-5]), Bk II (part 3), Vol.I.i.253–63 (ch. 5); Malebranche (1962), I.368–9n.295.

19 This mechanical theory was a radical alternative to the belief, espoused by Francis Bacon, that sympathy was an ethical principle imprinted by God on every human soul (see ch. 1).

20 This idea that women were susceptible to intense sympathy and even vegetarianism was excoriated and idolised in turns throughout the eighteenth century.

21 Malebranche (1694), pp.56–8; Malebranche (1997), Bk 5, ch.3, pp.352–3; cf. Malebranche (1962), XVII.i.513–18.

22 Seward (1795), II.171–2; Ritson (1802), pp.180–1.

23 Even Malebranche acknowledged that somatic sympathy 'gives check to our Malice and Cruelty'; in this he anticipated the moral-sense school's refutation of Hobbes (see ch.15 below).

24 Mandeville (1924), I.173–81.

CHAPTER 11

1 Tyson (1699) [Eve.b.17], sig.A1r, pp.1, 5, 22–3, 28, 30, 42 (ms marginalia), 51–2, 55; Thomas, K. (1983), pp.129–30, 132; *PT* (1700 [o.s.]), no. 268 [Eve.a.149, vol. 1699–1701], pp.338–41; Serjeantson (2001), p.441; cf. Descartes (1952), 'Discourse On The Method', § v; Cureau de la Chambre, (1657), pp.262–3; Schiebinger (2004), pp.44, 78–88.

2 Wallis & Tyson (1702), pp.769–85; Wallis & Tyson (1721), pp.1–9.

3 Sarasohn (1996), p.178; Rosenfield (1968), pp.114–18; Darmon (1998).

4 Bougerel (1737), pp.413, 425,
  455; Makin (1986).
5 Bernier (1964), VII.453–69;
  Garber and Ayers, eds (1998),
  I.569–71, 585–8; Lennon (1993),
  pp.3–7.
6 Bernier (1694), pp.162–3; cf.
  Stanley (1655–60), III.ii.244–6.
  On Epicurus' frugality, cf. e.g.
  Jerome (2005a), Bk II, ch.11;
  Reynolds (1725), pp.55–6.
7 Bernier (1992), pp.303–11;
  Descartes (1952), 'Discourse On
  The Method', § v, Hobbes,
  'Objection 4', p.136 (cp. Objection
  6, p.138); Pierre Gassendi, 'Fifth
  Objections', pp.171–209, espec.
  p.176; Rosenfield (1968), p.9;
  Serjeantson (2001), pp.437–8;
  Bernier (1964), VI.312–28 (which
  retreats somewhat from Gassendi's
  earlier position). cf. [Tyssot de
  Patot] (1743), pp.28–9; McKee
  (1941), pp.80–4; Voltaire
  (1980–), XXXV.411–15; Darmon
  (1998), pp.109–18.
8 Plutarch (1995), pp.551–3
  (994F–995B), 571–3 (998B).
9 Compare the discussion in
  Doddridge (1794), I.208. Thomas
  Moffet countered Plutarch's point,
  insisting that it was not 'nature'
  that made us shrink from killing,
  but unnaturally over-cultivated
  'Niceness and Conceit', Moffet
  (1746), pp.132–5; cf. Montaigne
  (1991), p.509.
10 Gassendi (1658), III.76; Celsus
   (1935–8), I.51 (I.iii); Plutarch, *De
   Sanitate Tuenda* (132A); *cit.*
   Plutarch (1995), p.537; Williams,
   Howard (1883), p.104.
11 Gassendi (1658), II.301–2,
   VI.19–23; cf. III.75–6; Bougerel
   (1737), pp.45–57; Bernier (1684),
   V.581–6; VII.466–7; Williams,
   Howard (1883), pp.101–4;
   Newton, J.F. (1897), pp.32, 61,
   63; Pufendorf (1749),
   pp.359–60+n.
12 Grand (1694), pp.274–5; cf.
   shorter version in Grand (1672),
   p.293; cf. Pufendorf (1749),
   pp.359–60+n.
13 Murr (1992).
14 Bernier (1684), V.585.
15 Bernier (1694), pp.147–72; cf.
   pp.280–3; Sarasohn (1996),
   p.178.
16 Bernier (1999), p.338. For related
   comments on Indian medical
   practice, cf. Majumdar (1960),
   p.276; Polo (1972), pp.278–9;
   Boemus (1885–90), Vol.VI, Bk ii,
   ch.8; Linschoten (1988), I.248;
   Foster (1999), p.310; Lord (1630),
   p.50; Tavernier (1995), I.198–9;
   Gaitonde (1983), p.44. cf.
   Harrison, M. (1996), p.78ff.;
   Harrison, M. (1994), pp.40–2. In
   fact, ancient Sanskrit medical
   texts do prescribe rich meat broths as
   the most strengthening diet for the
   sick, but this practice was later
   frowned upon by supporters of
   vegetarianism (Zimmerman
   (1987), pp.182–92).
17 Bernier (1684), V.585–6 [my
   translation]; corresponding to
   Gassendi (1658), II.302 (where
   this passage is, of course, absent).
18 Bernier (1694), p.165.
19 Bernier (1988), pp.253–4; Bonno
   (1955), pp.39–41, 55, 67, 80, 82,
   215–16; Milner (1700), pp.6–7.
20 Locke (1997), I.133–40 (II.x.10,
   II.xi.5, 7, 9–11); cf. IV.239–40,
   IX.283; Cureau de la Chambre
   (1658), pp.561, 597–8, cf.
   pp.571, 591; Cureau de la
   Chambre (1657), sig.A3r, p.7, cf.
   sig.A4r, pp.3, 9, 13–14, 18, 21–2,
   29–31, 34, 85–6, 256, 262–5,
   278–9; Locke (1858), pp.70, 73,
   128–30, 251–3. cf. Rosenfield
   (1968), pp. 18–19, 44; Lennon
   (1993), p.92–6, 158–9, 314–26
   (where Lennon says that Chambre
   uses the chain of being to argue
   that since 'there is a rational soul,
   there must also be a (merely)
   sensitive soul', whereas it seems to
   me that Chambre is arguing that
   there must be a degree of *reason*);
   [Bayle, P.] (1684), pp.19–20;
   Chanet (1643), espec. Part II,
   Ch.2; Charron (1601), espec. Bk
   II, Ch.8; Sarasohn (1996),

pp.170–3, 177; Spink (1960),
p.107; Kish (1984) (Abstract only
seen); Kroll (1984).
21 Locke (1692), Part I, § 13–14;
Part II, § 29; cf. V.583.
22 For a summary of, and hostile
response to, this 'standard view',
see Milton (2000); cf. Kroll
(1984); Wright (1991), pp.242–3;
and see note 20 above.
23 Tyson (1699), pp.31–2; Plate 6.
24 Tyson & Wallis (1702), p.783.
25 Tyson & Wallis (1702),
pp.769–85; Tyson & Wallis
(1721), pp.1–9; cf. Clarke (1720),
p.271.
26 *PT February 1700* [i.e. 1701], no.
269 [Eve.a.149 (vol. 1699–1701)],
pp.777, 784; cf. Porphyry (2000),
Bk I.13.5, p.36.
27 Boerhaave (1742–6a), I.63–4; cf.
Falconer (1781), pp.231–2.
28 Arbuthnot (1731), pp.100–2.
29 Cocchi (1745), p.47; cf. also *The
Universal Spectator*, (20 Feb. 1731),
no.124, p.1 and Moffet (1746),
pp.62–6. cf. Reynolds (1725),
p.76.
30 See e.g. Wilmot (1964),
pp.118–24 'Satyr against
Mankind' [1680]; Cheyne (1724),
p.91; Hastings (1936), pp.254–7,
263; Williams, Howard (1883),
p.166; Oswald (1791), p.33;
Haller (1754), pp.122–3;
Brückner (1768), pp.26–7,
60–4+n.; Holwell (1970),
pp.85–6; Nicholson (1999),
pp.95–7; Ritson (1802), pp.41–2;
Shelley, *Vind.*, pp.7–8, *V.Sys*,
p.340; Sinclair (1807), I.428–9.
31 *Cit.* Williams, Howard (1883),
p.106; Spencer (1993),
pp.211–12; Almond (1999),
pp.23–4. cf. Ray (1717), p.20ff.
(pp.53–7); *Catholic Encyclopedia*
(2003, www.newadvent.org),
'Physical Effects of Abstinence'.
32 Schiebinger (2004), pp.40–74.
33 Linnaeus to Johann Gmelin,
February 1747; *cit.* Greene (1909),
pp.25–6.
34 Linnaeus (1790), X.8–9; *cit.*
Lambe (1815), p.176.

35 Svensson (1757), p.5; cf. Lind
(1759); Burg (1756), pp.2–3;
Linnaeus (1781), I.115, 118–9.
36 cf. e.g. Kaempfer (1694), p.36;
Aberdour (1791), pp.80–1;
Goldsmith (1774 –[1785?]),
VIII.428; Willich (1799),
pp.308–10; Adair (1787b),
pp.268–9.
37 Haeckel (1912), ch.1.5.
38 Lémery (1704), pp.5–6, 136,
144–9; Lémery (1702), pp.8–10.
39 Lémery (1704), p.147.

CHAPTER 12

1 Clement of Alexandria (2004b),
Bk II, ch.1 'On eating'; Pseudo-
Clement (2005b), Homily VIII, ch.
15–17; Tertullian (2004b), ch.1;
Cassian (1491), Bk V, ch.21;
Cassian (1894), Bk IV, ch.22;
Bk. V, ch.5; Bynum (1988),
pp.35–9, 45, 82.
2 St John Chrysostom (2005b),
Homily 49, § 3; St John
Chrysostom (2005a), Homily 13
on 1 Timothy 5.
3 St John Augustine (2005), Bk
XVI.6, XXII.3; cf. e.g. Pseudo-
Clement (2005b), Homily XII, ch.
6; Pseudo-Clement (2005a), Bk
VII. ch.6; Eusebius (1903), II.2–3;
Berkman (2004).
4 Clement of Alexandria (2004b),
Bk II, ch.1 'On eating'; St John
Chrysostom (2005b), Homily 25,
§ 2, p.1098. cf. Manu (1971),
v.56.
5 Pseudo-Clement (2005b), Homily
III, ch. 36; Homily VII, ch. 4 and
Homily VIII, ch. 19. For gluttony
cf. Pseudo-Clement (2005a), Bk
IV, ch. 17.
6 cf. St Irenaeus (2004), Bk I, ch.24,
§ 2; Bk I, ch.28, § 1. St Augustine
(2004a), XX.36; St Augustine
(2004b), ch.15; St Augustine
(2005), Bk VI.6–8; Bk XIII.18; Bk
XVI.6.
7 Origen (2005), Bk V, ch.49; cf. Bk
V, ch.39 and 41, Bk VIII, ch.30;
Augustine (2004c), ch.31,
§ 65–67.

8 Passmore (1975), p.197.
9 Kisbán (1986), pp.3–4; Bynum (1988), pp.35–45, 61; Thomas, K. (1983), p.289; for an interesting vegetarian discussion of eating fish, see Pufendorf (1749), pp.360–1.
10 Calvin (2002), 'Prefatory Address' § 4; Bk 4, ch.12, § 21.
11 Erasmus (1534), pp.45–6; cf. Agrippa (1676), p.311.
12 Holland (1596), sigs.A1v–[A4r], pp.1, 35, 95–104, 108–9; cf. Thomas, K. (1971), pp.229, 271, 479, 485–7, 593.
13 Nashe (1599), p.31; cf. Nashe (1592), 'The complaint of Gluttonie'; Vaughan, W. (1630), pp.9, 14–15, 56–8.
14 John Donne, 'The Liar', *cit.* Main (1983), pp.84–6; cf. Browne (1672), Bk III, ch.xxv, pp.189–94; Fryer (1909), II.282–3; Poole (2000), pp.7–8, 45–69.
15 Holland (1596), sig.A2v–A3r, pp.105–6; cf. [Vaughan, W.] (1633), p.62; [Hecquet] (1710), pp.524–5; [Rheims, The English College of] (1582), p.142 ('Luke 2', n.37 (not n.17 as noted by Henry Holland)); cf. p.330 ('Acts 13', n.3).
16 Vaughan, W. (1630), pp. 4–5, 9–10, 15–18, 38–45, 49, 53, 55; [Vaughan, W.] (1633), pp.1–2, 50–4, 61–2, 121–2; cp. Vaughan, W. (1600), p.45; [Hecquet] (1710), p.518. cf. e.g. Edwards (1699), I.131–2.
17 Benedict (1998), ch. 39.
18 Johnston ed. (2000), pp.483–4, 1056, 1298–1300.
19 When Rousseau and Voltaire came to advocate the vegetarian diet, one of the most radical aspects of their arguments was that they encouraged it *without* appealing to the Catholic Church for support. Voltaire's complaint that the Trappists were the only people in France to abide by Porphyry's vegetarian teaching was a deliberately provocative irony. cf. also Diderot (1966), pp.34, 70.
20 Linand (1700), sigs.a.iiir–v, e.iir–v, e[iv]r–v, pp.1–14; Boerhaave (1751), p.701.
21 [Hecquet] (1709), sig.a.iiiv.
22 Cf. e.g. [Hecquet] (1741), I.[a.xi v]; [Hecquet] (1758); Roger (1889), pp.67–8.
23 Roger (1889), p.21; [Hecquet] (1733), I.160–1; Brockliss (1989), p.193.
24 Roger (1889), pp.21–3, 25–8. Condé's father, Louis Bourbon, spent several years on a milk diet trying to cure his gout: [Coste] (1693), II.194, *cit.* Cheyne (1720), pp.13–15.
25 [Hecquet] (1710), pp.479–512, 513–25; [Hecquet] (1709), sig.a.ivr, pp.2, 11–14; Roger (1889), pp.46–8, 57–8; cf. L'Espine (1723).
26 Harvey (1628); Descartes (1952) 'Discourse On The Method', § v.
27 cf. e.g Bellini (1696), pp.68–9; Guerrini (1985), p.249. Guerrini cites Cunningham (1981), p.89, who says that Pitcairne replaced Cartesian physiology with what he believed to be Newtonian principles. But Pitcairne was regarded as a follower of Bellini the Cartesian and they remained close friends, cf. Pitcairne (1715), p.x; Pitcairne (1701), sig.*2r; Cocchi (1741), I.xiii–xiv.
28 cf. e.g. Pitcairne (1715), pp.111–12; Cheyne (1733), pp.4–5; Cheyne (1705), II.229–30.
29 Pitcairne (1722), sig.***3v, Definition 2.
30 Theodore M. Brown says that the excessive or diminished circulation, according to Pitcairne, were the sole causes of disease, while those other interruptions – blockages and so forth – were Cheyne's later additions; Brown (1987), p.634. But cf. e.g. Pitcairne (1718a), pp.101–2 (NB in the obvious place, *'quantity'* is an error for 'quality' cf. Pitcairne (1718b), p.68: *'qualitata'*; Pitcairne (1722), sig.[***4r], Definition 30).

31 [Mead] (n.d.), pp.74, 79.
32 Leeuwenhoek (1962), pp.17–20; Leeuwenhoek (1695), I.165ff., 189ff; cf. e.g. [Cheyne] (1701), p.108.
33 [Hecquet] (1733), I.65, 68–72, 76–7, 146; cf. Cheyne (1740), pp.72–3; Haller (1757), p.17; cf. Reynolds (1725), pp.50–1.
34 [Hecquet] (1733), I.124, 132–7, 147–9, 156–8, 197–9; Bellini (1696), p.235, cf. 207–8, 210, 229–31, 235–6, 251; Bellini (1730), pp.369–70, 503–4; Bellini (1741), I.xxiii–xxiv, 93.
35 Decker (1693); Pitcairne (1715), sig.A2v–[A3v], pp.130–4; [Hecquet] (1733), Vol.II, Appendix 'An Funtiones'; [Hecquet] (1709), pp.15–18, 22; [Hecquet] (1712); [Hecquet] (1733), I.75; Cheyne (1943), p.49. Hecquet was opposed by the defenders of the fermentation system: Andry (1710), pp.12–13, Astruc (1714); Pitcairne (1713), espec. 'Lector' and p.257. Boerhaave tried to reconcile the chemists and mechanists: Boerhaave (1742–6b), I.184–6. On Pitcairne and Hecquet's friendship, cf. [Hecquet] (1733), II.13, 188; Pitcairne (1727), p.iv; Pitcairne (1718b), p.283. cf. Debus (2001), pp.154–6.
36 The United States National Library of Medicine, 'Philippe Hecquet correspondence and medical notes', Ms C 168 (not seen).
37 [Hecquet] (1709), pp.15–27; [Hecquet] (1733), I.98–101, 143, 145.
38 [Hecquet] (1733), I.78, 94–5; [Hecquet] (1709), pp.26–9.
39 [Hecquet] (1733), I.68–9, 81–3, 102–4, 134–5; cf. Reynolds (1725), p.47.
40 [Hecquet] (1733), I.81–3; Geoffroy (1732), p.217, cit. Cheyne (1740), pp.56–60; [Hecquet] (1709), 'Approbation'.
41 Hecquet (1695); Roger (1889), pp.43–6, 71; Hecquet (1724); Brockliss (1989), p.201n.; cf. also

[Hecquet] (1733), I.2–3; Lonie (1981); St Jerome (2005a), Bk II, ch.11; Reynolds (1725), pp.52–3; Edelstein (1987), p.303; Barker (1747), pp.87–9, 94–5, 158; Bacon (1650), p.7; Vaughan, W. (1630), pp.15–16; Powicke, ed. (1926), p.198; Deodatus (1628) (it was disingenuous of Baxter to cite Venner, who was an enemy of dieting for ordinary people, Venner (1660), p.230). For the emergence of the neo-Galenic vegetarian diet in sixteenth-century Germany, see the case of Philip of Mecklenburg (1514–57), in Midelfort (1994). For the rise of Hippocratic medicine in sixteenth-century Paris, see Lonie (1985). For the impact of sixteenth- and seventeenth-century translations of Galen on diet, see Boerhaave (1807), II.i.175–6. (Arnau de Vilanova credited the longevity of Carthusian monks to their vegetarian diet, Ziegler (1998).)
42 [Hecquet] (1733), I.2–3; I cannot explain how L.W.B. Brockliss came to the conclusion that 'Hecquet, even in his later works, showed no awareness of the vegetarian prophylaxis of the English early eighteenth-century doctor, George Cheyne (1671–1743)' (Brockliss (1989), p.202n.). Hecquet's later works are full of adulatory remarks about Cheyne; e.g. [Hecquet] (1733), I.81–3, 102–3, 120–3, II.200. On the neurological impact of meat-induced 'plethora', for example, which Hecquet took from Cheyne, cf. [Hecquet] (1733), I.xxiv–xxvii, 79–81, 299, 314, II.13; cf. Pitcairne (1718a), pp.142–4, 173–9.
43 [Hecquet] (1733), I.76–7, 95–7, 119; cf. Cheyne (1724), pp.30–3; PT (1716), III.306–11 (the man of 169 was Henry Jenkins). Harvey (1847), pp.587–92; Gruman (1966), pp.68–73. Parr was incorporated into the canon of vegetarian apologia, cf. Taylor, J.

(1825), pp.16–18; Tryon [1684], pp.19–20; Temple (1701), p.124; Floyer & Baynard (1715), p.407; Adair (1787a), p.220; Oswald (1791), p.18; Hufeland (1797); Ritson (1802), pp.156–7; Shelley, *Vind.*19–20; Newton, J.F. (1897), pp.56–7; Caulfield (1813), II.135.

44 [Hecquet] (1709), pp.31–3; cf. [Hecquet] (1733), I.52.

45 [Hecquet] (1709), pp.2, 24–5, 30–3; [Hecquet] (1733), I.xiii–xix, 40–1. cf. *Biblia Sacra Vulgata, Liber Iesu filii Sirachi [Ecclesiasticus]* c.39.v.31; *The Holy Bible, King James version* (http://etext.lib. virginia.edu/relig.browse.html), The Apocrypha, *Prologue to Sirach* 40:26: 'The principal things for the whole use of man's life are water, fire, iron, and salt, flour of wheat, honey, milk, and the blood of the grape, and oil, and clothing.' cf. [Tryon] (1685), p.107.

46 [Hecquet] (1733), I.159–60.

47 [Hecquet] (1733), I.xiii–xix, 4–7, 13–15, 22–5, 54, 70–2, 151, 562–3; [Hecquet] (1709), pp.29–30; St Jerome (2005a), Bk II, ch.15; cf. Bk I, ch.18; Cheyne (1724), pp.91–4; cf. chs 3 and 5 above.

48 [Hecquet] (1741), 'Approbation', 'Avis', sig.[a.xᵛ]–b.iᵛ.

49 Hecquet knew Lémery personally: he joined the Paris medical Faculty four years before Lémery, he had been taught chemistry by Louis' father, and got Louis to write an approbation of his mechanical work, *De la Digestion* (1712); cf. Brockliss (1989), p.221.

50 Andry (1710), pp.1–3, 12–19, 27–8, 32–45; Andry (1704); Andry (1705); Andry (1737); [Docteurs de la Faculté] (1736); cf. Aristotle, *On the Parts of Animals*, IV.x. Hecquet was unrepentant: cf. [Hecquet] (1710), I.48–50; [Hecquet] (1733), I.38–9. Hecquet and Andry seem to have been reconciled later: Andry approved of [Hecquet] (1733),

(end of vol.I); cf. Brockliss (1989), p.220n.

51 Lesage (1977), Bk II, chs 2–5.

52 *Nouvelle Biographie Générale* (Paris, 1858), Vol.23; Roger (1889), pp.34–6, 40–1.

CHAPTER 13

1 Mack (1985), p.371.

2 An ell was 45 inches.

3 Cheyne (1943), p.7; Shuttleton (1992), pp.26, 154–5; Ponsonby (1949), p.158.

4 Cheyne (1733), pp.325–6.

5 Oliphant (1702), pp.4–5; cf. Guerrini (1993a).

6 Cheyne (1943), pp.76–8; cp. Cheyne (1733), p.342; Child (1992), pp.192–99; Guerrini (1995).

7 Keynes Ms 130.7, [f.2r] [Transcript pp.3–4]; Keynes Ms 130.6, Notebook 2, f.6v–7r; Cheyne (1703).

8 Cheyne (1733), pp.325–7.

9 Cheyne (1733), pp.6–9, 192–203, 245–54; Guerrini (2000), pp.5–7.

10 Cheyne (1733), pp.331–2; Shuttleton (1992), pp.50–100, espec. pp.54, 75–6; Shuttleton (1996); Mss Rawlinson (Bodleian) D 833, f.26r [illeg. 'Cheny'?]. There are similarities between Cheyne's and Tryon's beliefs, but Nigel Smith's statement that Tryon's books introduced Cheyne to Jacob Böhme is rash: there is no firm evidence that Cheyne read any of Tryon's books and Tryon never mentions Böhme in any case. Even Timothy Morton's view seems to be contradicted by Shuttleton (Smith (1999), pp.107–8; Morton (2002), p.81; Shuttleton (1992), p.112; Gibbons (1996), p.186); cf. Rousseau, G.S. (1998), p.101.

11 The mystical authors he read also recommended abstinence: Bourignon (1737), pp.49, 57, 60; Bourignon (1707), p.11; *cit.* Guerrini (2000), pp.15–19; Shuttleton (1992), pp.57–8;

Shuttleton (1999a), p.70;
Bourignon (1699), pp.326–7; cf.
Garden (1699), p.43; Bourignon
(1703), II.74–7, III.65–70; Marsay
(1749), pp.13, 22.

12 Cheyne (1733), pp.335–7; cf.
pp.253–4; Cheyne (1738),
pp.102–4; Cheyne (1724), p.32;
Cheyne (1940), pp.52–3, 88;
Cheyne (1943), pp.31–2, 76–8,
81, 102–4. There is no reason to
believe Shuttleton's suggestion
that Dr Taylor was 'was probably
an adherent of the Pythagorean
doctrines flourishing amongst
dissenters'. Cheyne says Taylor got
the diet from Dr Thomas
Sydenham (see below) (Shuttleton
(1992), pp.54–5+n.)

13 Cheyne (1733), pp.335–8;
Cheyne (1943), pp.82–5, 105.
Contrary to Cheyne's claims,
Pitcairne did not say the milk diet
was an 'infallible Cure', nor the
only one, and the three disorders
Cheyne says Pitcairne used it for
were all in fact the same thing
according to Pitcairne. Despite
Pitcairne's new medical theories,
most of the remedies he
prescribed were inherited from the
old pharmacopia: Pitcairne
(1718a), pp.77, 101–2, 181–2,
304–6. In a later publication
Pitcairne recommends water
drinking for the scurvy but does
not mention the milk diet:
Pitcairne (1715), p.259.

14 Playing with the common pun on
vegetable (which the gardener
Philip Miller said was 'deriv'd
from the Latin, *vegeto* to *quicken*,
to *refresh*, to *make lively and
strong*'), Cheyne announced that
since taking up vegetables 'I am
more alive than I ever was'.
(Indeed, as a believer in the
Adamic language, Cheyne may
have thought the etymology of
vegetables revealed their true
nature.) Cheyne (1733), pp.88–9,
361–2; Miller (1731), p.vi;
Boerhaave (1742–6a), I.54; cf.
Lémery (1704), pp.20, 47, 67, 84,

87, 134; Evelyn (1996), p.92;
Evelyn (1676), p.9; Tryon
(1691a), pp.39, 99.

15 Cheyne (1733), pp.330–1, 337–8.
He suffered another crash into
suicidal depression in the early
1720s – no doubt exacerbated by
the bursting of the South Sea
Bubble, the mother of all boom-
and-bust insider-dealing scandals,
on which Cheyne lost his
investments – but his recovery
became just another opportunity
to confirm the therapeutic powers
of the vegetable diet. Cheyne to
Lord Harley 1720 (copy) BL
Add.4291 f.237; cf. Shuttleton
(1992), pp.25–6, 134, 155, 216;
Guerrini (2000), p.106.

16 Towers (1766–72), VII.182;
Biographical Dictionary (1767),
p.95; Hutchinson (1799),
pp.197–8; Jones, Stephen (1799),
'Cheyne' [n.p.]; *Biographical
Dictionary* (1795), III.249; Vosgien
(1799–1801), 'Cheyne' (contains
gross errors); *GM* (March 1735),
Vol.V. p.123; *GM* (April 1743)
Vol.XIII, p.218.

17 Cheyne (1943), p.127.

18 Cheyne (1733), pp.364, 370. The
phrase '*casual Hints*' – God's
means of directing Cheyne's path
– refers to the clergyman's '*Hint*
accidentally dropt' which led him
to Dr Taylor and the milk diet.

19 Cheyne (1733), p.370; cf. Cheyne
(1943), pp.76–8; Cheyne (1715
[1716]), II.112. Compare also
Tryon's reverence for the colour
white in milk among other things
e.g. Tryon (1700), p.18. Another
layer of meaning to the 'light diet':
Cheyne explained that God was
the '*Sole Object*' of a soul's desire,
punning on 'soul', 'sole' and 'Sol',
the Latin for 'Sun' which, as the
centre of gravity, was analogous to
God attracting souls to Him, a
process Cheyne believed was
facilitated by the 'light diet' (see
below).

20 Cheyne (1990), p.xxxi; Guerrini
(2000), 'Bibliography'.

21 Wild (2001); Shuttleton (1992), pp.125–9; Guerrini (2000), pp.80, 89, 95; Wood (1769), pp.286–7; Rousseau, G.S. (1988); Shuttleton (1999a), p.59; Coveney (2000), pp.16, 62, 66–7, 89.
22 Shuttleton (1992), p.152.
23 Shuttleton (1995); Cattaneo (1987), p.131n.; Barry (1985), pp.166–7+n.
24 Cheyne (1943), p.116.
25 Robertson (1752?), pp.271–4, 241–7; cf. p.63; *Bath Miscellany for the Year 1740* (London, 1741), p.67; *Poetical Epitome* (London, 1792), p.355; *Compleat Family-piece*, 3rd edn (London, 1741), p.7; Bradshaw (1754), pp.92–3; Smith (1753), pp.354–5; *Family Guide to Health* (London, 1767), p.218; Ryland (1776), p.349; Atkyns, ed. (1747), p.xiii, II.15, 57, 91, 109; Reid (1798), pp.273–5.
26 Anon. (1724); *cit.* Guerrini (2000), p.129.
27 *Grub Street Journal* 86 (26 August 1731); *cit.* Shuttleton (1992), p.184+n.
28 Goldsmith (1996), III.364.
29 Armstrong, J. (1992); Strother (1925); Shapin (2003), p.273.
30 Shuttleton (1992), pp.151–2, 194, 217–18.
31 Arbuthnot (1731), 'Preface' and pp.100–2; Cheyne (1733), pp.149–50. Arbuthnot thought that the alkaline qualities of meat and the acid of vegetables could be used to keep each person's different constitutions in balance.
32 Morgan (1725), p.432; Morgan (1735), pp.73–4, 90–2, 101–4, 116; Maty (1755), pp.47–8; Mead (1751), pp.157–9, 170, 178; Richard Mead, 'On the Scurvy', in Sutton (1749), pp.112–13, 116; Mead (1762), II.476; Cheyne (1990), pp.ix–x; Wynter (1725), pp.xv–xvi, 4–5, 30, 42, 47–58, 86, 99; *London Magazine* 26 (1757), p.510; Graves (1766); Graves (1996), II.19, 77; Falconer (1781), pp.231–2; Apperley

(1731), pp.142, 192; Arbuthnot (1733), p.211; Arbuthnot (1732), p.429; Barry (1759), p.92.
33 Cheyne (1733), pp.34, 49–50; Cheyne (1724), p.28; Cheyne (1943), p.58; Guerrini (2000), pp.107–14.
34 Cheyne (1943), pp.78–81, 86–8; cf. [Hecquet] (1733), I.29–33; Tryon (1691a), p.314; [Tryon] (1685), pp.39–40; [Tryon] (1684c), pp.121–2. For other provocatively radical comments cf. e.g. Cheyne (1724), pp.30–1, 39, 192, 222; Cheyne (1740), pp.65–7; Cheyne (1943), pp.74–5, 76–8; cp. Cheyne (1990), p.xxxi.
35 Cheyne (1733), p.368. Cheyne largely avoided the Brahmin connotations of the vegetable diet, though he often spoke of the frugality of the Southerns and Easterns and once called the vegetable diet 'Eastern' (Cheyne (1943), p.121).
36 [Tryon, Cheyne et al.], *The Way to Health and Long life* (London: G. Conyers, 1726), p.53. George Conyers had published a number of Tryon's works, and it was Conyers, probably, who masterminded this popular health manual which cromprises an amalgamation of extracts from Cheyne and Tryon (including the spoof *Averroeana*). The extracts from Tryon are not attributed, but they illustrate the extent to which the mystical Indian and medical vegetarian discourses had merged. Tryon's books are, however, advertised in the text, revealing that his works were still readily available in the 1720s. Compare e.g. p.5 with Tryon (1688), pp.64–5; pp.9–10 and 24ff. with Tryon (1691a), chs 3 and 4, especially pp.59–60; p.24 with Cheyne (1724), pp.91–5; pp.53–6, 65 with Tryon (1695a), pp.6–22, 39–40, 57–8.
37 cf. e.g. Atkyns (1747), p.109; Oswald (1791), pp.17–18+n.

(pp.95–6); Nicholson (1999), pp.44–5; Ritson (1802), pp.49–50.

38 Anon. (1726); *cit.* Shuttleton (1992), pp.169–70.

39 Cheyne (1733), p.iii; cf. Cheyne (1740), p.xiii.

40 Willis (1683), pp.2–4, 23; Rousseau, G.S. (1976). Whytt (1755), p.168n.; Locke (1690), II.i.1–4, I.i.15; cf. Lawrence (1979), p.24; Wright (1991), pp.243–57.

41 [Cheyne] (1701), pp.9, 11, 12–14, 16, 35, 80–1; Cheyne (1705), II.212–13; Cheyne (1715 [1716]), I.303–6, 316–17; Bellini (1696); Bellini (1720); Shuttleton (1992), pp.139, 141.

42 Cheyne (1738), pp.91–5; Cheyne (1724), p.78; Cheyne (1733), pp.77–89; cf. Bellini (1696), pp.229, 236; Newton (1713), p.484; Guerrini (1993b), pp.244, 248; Guerrini (1985), pp.260, 265; Guerrini (2000), pp.124, 133–4, 146–7, 170–1; Dussinger (1974), p.28; cp. Boerhaave (1742–6b), III.310–11ff.

43 Cheyne (1720), pp.78–80; Cheyne (1724), pp.27, 98, 177; cf. Spang (2000), p.35+n.

44 Cheyne (1733), p.325; Cheyne (1943), p.94; cf. pp.86–8; cf. Whytt (1755), p.190.

45 Goldsmith (1966), IV.29; *cit.* Rousseau, G.S. (1976), pp.156; cf. e.g. Radcliffe (1980), p.79–80.

46 Austen (1997a); cf. Radcliffe (1993), p.4+n.

47 Cheyne (1724), p.163. On Cheyne's reading of, and perhaps contribution to, Newton's *De Natura Acidorum* and additions to *Opticks*, cf. e.g. Shuttleton (1992), pp.32–3; Guerrini (2000), pp.38–9, 120, 133–4; Guerrini (1993b), p.236; Guerrini (1987), p.74; Guerrini (1989b), p.240.

48 Cheyne (1740), pp.56–60; Geoffroy (1732), p.217; Cheyne (1742), p.54; cf. Ritson (1802), pp.62–3; Cheyne (1724), pp.20–1, 184; Cheyne (1705),

ii.163–4; Cheyne (1715 [1716]), p.255; Michele Pinelli, 'Concerning the Causes of the Gout', tr. Joh. James Scheutzer, *PT*, no.403, Vol.XXXV, pp.490–4; *cit.* Cheyne (1733), pp.39–42 (incorrectly writing no.433 instead of no.403).

49 Cheyne (1724), p.21; cf. Morgan (1725), pp.411–12; Gu[g]lielmini (1719), I.67–104, II.73–200, espec. I.77–9, 93, 99; II.39, 87, 91, 166, 173, 174, 179; *cit.* Cheyne (1733), pp.38–42; cf. also Cheyne (1705), ii.145–7; Cheyne (1715 [1716]), p.255; cf. Webster (1982), p.6.

50 Cheyne (1733), pp.118–23.

51 Cheyne (1733), pp.118–23; cf. Guerrini (2000), p.67; cp. Willis (1683), p.108.

52 Cheyne (1733), pp.6–9, 15–17; cf. Cheyne (1724), pp.19–20, 25, 177–85; Cheyne (1943), pp.75–6. Elsewhere Cheyne had stated that flesh particles were larger. cf. [Hecquet] (1709), p.25.

53 Cheyne (1724), pp.177–85; Cheyne (1943), pp.90–1.

54 Rifkin (1992), p.54; *cit.* Regan (2001), pp.8–10; Drummond and Wilbraham (1939), pp.245–61.

55 The medical dietary tracts of previous generations had actually warned that drinking water (rather than ale) was dangerous: Venner (1660), pp.31–2.

56 Cheyne (1733), p.170; Cheyne (1724), p.180; Cheyne (1740), pp.56–60.

57 [Cheyne] (1701), pp.106–7; Cheyne (1733), pp.128–37.

58 Cheyne (1740), p.78.

59 Harvey (1672?), pp.132–8, 210; Cheyne (1990), p.xxxvi; cf. Reynolds (1725), pp.52–3.

60 Willis (1683), pp.107–8, 115, 135, 144, 160, 174, 189, 204, 207, 224, 233; Willis (1681), III.6; cf. Tryon (1700), p.34.

61 Floyer & Baynard (1715), pp.74–5, 418; cf. [Baynard] (1724), pp.11, 19–20, 35; Cheyne (1733), pp.340–1; cf. pp.307–11;

PT (1716), pp.306–9. For
Baynard's reading on
vegetarianism, cf. *A catalogue of the
Libraries of Edward Baynard*
([London], 1721), pp.2, 10, 13,
18, 19, 33, 35. For
recommendations Cheyne shared
with Fuller: Fuller (1711),
sig.[A4v–A7r], [B7v–B8r],
pp.243–55 (compare Cheyne
(1733), pp.325–7). cf. Temple
(1701), p.189.

62 Boyse (1747–8), I.413; cf. e.g.
Wynter (1725), pp.50–3; Sinclair
(1807), II.i.169–70; Barker
(1747), pp.87–9, 94–5, 158, 171,
193, 236–9; Cocchi (1745), p.27;
Cheyne (1943), p.136; Shuttleton
(1992), pp.134–5.

63 Cheyne blamed the decline of
ancient dietary medicine on the
followers of Paracelsus
(1493–1541) and Jan Baptista van
Helmont who vaunted
(al)chemical panaceas and elixirs
in preference to, as one chemist
put it, 'submitting to Dr.
Boerhaave's milk-diet' (Ellis, W.
(1752), 'Diseases and Medicines').
Cheyne's conspiratorial allegations
were, however, somewhat unjust
since Paracelsus *had* recommended
dietary moderation, and Helmont
agreed with Hippocrates that the
sick should abstain from flesh, fish
and eggs. Cheyne (1733), p.154;
Cheyne (1740), pp.x–xi; cf.
Cheyne (1943), pp.47, 96–8;
[Hecquet] (1733), I.470;
[Hecquet] (1733), 'Barfeknecht,
An quos morbos'; Vaughan, W.
(1630), pp.2, 9, 44–5, 53;
Boerhaave (1742–6b), VI.271–5,
297–9; Tryon (1691a), p.71;
Paracelsus (1656), 'A Treatise
concerning long Life', pp.371, 393,
397, 406; Pagel (1982),
pp.115–16; Helmont, J.B. (1664),
ch. 58, pp.450–4; ch. 99, p.702;
index 'Flesh to be shun'd'; Barker
(1747), p.171; cf. Buhr (1780),
Thesis no.9; Lilly (1681), p.2;
Culpeper (1649), p.71; Culpeper
(1656), sig.A2r, p.20.

64 Cheyne (1740), pp.xiii–xvi;
Cheyne (1724), p.36; Cheyne
(1733), p.iii; Shapin (2003),
pp.273, 283–5; cf. Pitcairne
(1715), p.106; cp. Shuttleton
(1992), pp.166–7.

65 Silvanus Bevan to Cheyne 3 July
1733, with notes by Bevan;
Cheyne to Bevan 1736
(Colchester, Essex Record Office:
D/DU 161/369–370). The
notebook catalogued as 'Medical
Notes on Fevers *c.*1725, by
Cheyne or one of his followers' is
almost certainly not Cheyne's (D/
DU 161/371, 2 vols.). This
Silvanus Bevan (b.1698/9) should
not be confused with the Quaker
apothecary Silvanus Bevan FRS
(1691–1765).

66 Wesley (1931), II.285–6; *cit.*
Shuttleton (1995), n.11.

67 Galen, *De Methodus Medendi*, Bk V,
ch. 12; James (1741), pp.6–7.

68 [Vaughan, W.] (1633), p.41; cp.
Wynter (1725), pp.58–61; cf.
p.114 ff. Harvey (1672?),
pp.232–7; Harvey (1675),
pp.257–8; Boerhaave (1739), p.1;
Royal College of Physicians of
Edinburgh, Cullen Mss, #30 'Dr
William Cullen's Consultation
Letters', 21 vols; vol.2 (1764–70),
letter 30, ff.32r–v. cf. e.g. Hecquet
(1990); Weltzien (1789), Thesis
no.8 (p.43). See also Maginus
(1670); Jacobi (1675); Isez
(1741); cf. also Accoramboni
(1726); Costaeus (1604);
Baricellus (1623); Ronconius
(1631); Castro (1631); Trevus
(1634); Heyden (1653); Pallierius
(1663); Bayle, F. (1670); Hugot
(1678); Greisel (1681); Buehren
(1691); Winge (1696); Lange
(1705); Francis Slare in Dole
(1707); Guglielmini (1709); Ledel
(1713); Buettner (1727); Beer
(1735); Doorschodt (1737);
Roerer (1739); Gourraigne (1741);
Kindler (1742); Fischer (1745?);
Laurentius (1749); Hird (1751);
Claudinius (n.d.); Fabra (n.d.);
Testi (n.d.a); Testi (n.d.b);

Quintilius (n.d.). Kleinian psychoanalysts would no doubt be interested in Cheyne's claim that milk returned people to childlike innocence, Cheyne (1943), p.101.

69 Sydenham (1722), pp.324, 365–6; cf. Boerhaave (1742–6b), VI.241. Willis, Harvey, Wynter, Mead, Arbuthnot and even Pitcairne agreed with Sydenham (and Celsus before him) that pure 'milk and seed' diets should be used with extreme caution; they allowed their patients at least a small portion of flesh: Willis (1683), pp.115, 135, 144, 160, 189, 197, 207, 224, 233; Wynter (1725), pp.54–8, 99; Mead (1751), pp.157–9; Mead (1762), II.476; Harvey (1672?), pp.236–7; Sydenham (1722), pp.364, 374–5; [Hecquet] (1733), II.197. Others, such as the Indophile Sir William Temple, retorted that such trepidation was totally unnecessary: [Temple] (1680), pp.221, 229–30, 232–3; Temple (1701), pp.112–15; Temple (1690), pp.15–16, 18–23; Cheyne (1724), p.47; cf. Shuttleton (1992), pp.134–5, 166–7; Boerhaave (1742–6b), VI.241. When Cheyne promoted his own milk and vegetable diet, he repeated Sydenham's warnings verbatim: Cheyne (1720), pp.13–15; Cheyne (1733), pp.234–6. Elsewhere, Cheyne exaggerated Sydenham's enthusiasm for the milk diet (Cheyne (1733), pp.335–7).

70 Cheyne (1733), pp.164–5; Cheyne (1943), pp.74–5, 78–9, 82–4, 86–8. Old Parr was the prime illustration of this warning: he was said to have been a Pythagorean vegetarian until brought to court where his diet changed and he quickly died (Newton, J.F. (1897), pp.56–7); cf. Floyer & Baynard (1715), pp.408–9; Cheyne (1733), p.136; cf. [Hecquet] (1733), I.119–20; Jenner (1998).

71 Cheyne (1940), pp.52–3; Shapin (2003), pp.285–6; Shuttleton (1995), pp.323–4; cf. Shuttleton (1992), pp.217–18. Cheyne (1733), pp.253–4; cp. Cheyne (1738), pp.102–4.

72 cf. Ponsonby (1949), pp.158, 162–3.

73 More, Lucy (2000), pp.10, 20, 36, 42, 195.

74 Ponsonby (1949), p.48; Cheyne (1990), pp.x–xi.

75 More, Lucy (2000), p.10n.; cf. p.21.

76 Cheyne (1740), pp. 18–19, 61, 64–5.

77 Cheyne (1943), p.94; Thomas, K. (1983), p.175ff.; Turner (1980), pp.6–7; cf. Whytt (1765), pp.219–20; Whytt (1775), p.163; (compare e.g. Radcliffe (1980), p.109); Richardson (1754), III.374.

78 Willis (1681), II.61, 183, 186–7 and plates; Willis (1683), pp.13–14, 17, 20–3, 44. On the vivisection issue, cf. e.g. Whytt (1755), pp.108–9; Thomas, K. (1983), p.174, 178; Shugg (1968a); Guerrini (1989a).

79 Mandeville (1924), I.173–81.

80 Malebranche (1694), Bk II, ch.vii, pp.56–8.

81 Cheyne (1724), pp.91–4; Cheyne (1740), p.xvi. cf. Lawrence (1979), pp.24–5; Rodgers (1986); Shuttleton (1996), pp.51–2; Smith, A. (1759), Part III, ch.iii. Rousseau, G.S. (1988), p.83. Some have argued that it was Arbnuthnot that Hume consulted.

82 Cheyne (1740), pp.70–1; cf. pp.64–5, 70–1, 85. 'Custom' and 'habit' – seen as the unreflective aspects of human culture – were regularly blamed for making men go against their 'nature' (in this case, their herbivorous nature); cf. Ovid, *Metamorphoses*, Bk XV; Mandeville (1924), I.173; Cheyne (1733), pp.39–42; Cheyne (1943), pp.57, 71; [Hecquet] (1709), pp.6–7; Tryon also repeatedly blamed custom and habit.

83 Cheyne (1736), sig.[Aa5r]; Cheyne (1715 [1716]), II.45–6, 74, 78, 85–93, 98, 113–15; Cheyne (1724), pp.149–50; Cheyne (1733), pp.291–3, 325–7.

84 Cheyne (1724), pp.92–3; cf. [Tryon] ([1684c]), p.120; [Tryon, Cheyne, et al.] (1726), p.24; *The Family Magazine: in two parts* (London, 1747), p.109; Oswald (1791), pp.95–6.

85 Cheyne (1740), p.xvi; cf. pp.6–10, 23–6, 54–5, 61; Cheyne (1733), p.364; cf. Tertullian (2004b), ch.4: 'the primordial sin might be the more expiated by the operation of a greater abstinence in the (midst of the) opportunity of a greater licence.' Cheyne conceded that human bodies had been altered to deal with meat (Cheyne, *ER* (1740), p.53). cf. Almond (1999), p.23.

86 Cheyne (1740), pp.xiii–xv; Cheyne (1943), pp.102–4.

87 Shuttleton (1992), pp.151–2; cf. Cheyne (1943), pp.99–100.

88 Cheyne (1733), pp.366–7; cf. Shuttleton (1992), p.179; Cheyne (1943), pp.84–5, 110–11, 117, 94, 86–8.

89 Cheyne (1733), p.298. Cheyne later softened this a little: Cheyne (1740), p.76.

90 cf. e.g. Cheyne (1740), pp.88–9; Cheyne (1724), pp.159–60; Cheyne (1733), pp.20–1, 368; cf. e.g. Tryon (1691a), p.314.

91 Cheyne (1733), pp.325–7. On the unconscious convulsions of natural conscience cf. e.g. Tryon (1700), pp.22–4, 82.

92 Cheyne (1740), pp.18–19, 26, 31; cf. Cheyne (1705), II.229–30; Kurth-Voigt (1999), p.28.

93 Cheyne (1740), pp.2, 31; Cheyne (1705), II.232–3; Leeuwenhoek (1695), I.42; Leeuwenhoek (1722), II.168; cf. Leeuwenhoek (1798), I.118–19, Plate V, fig.3, II.181.

94 For a related idea of comets, see *Spy*, IV.251–2; cf. Schechner (1999), pp.183–4, 193–4.

95 Cheyne (1740), pp.32–4; cf. pp.41–9; Cheyne (1943), p.101; Shuttleton (1992), pp.120–3, 234.

96 Cheyne (1740), pp.26, 83–4; Cheyne (1943), p.101; cf. pp.40–1; Cheyne (1715 [1716]), II.74–5, 209–10; Dussinger (1974), p.116.

97 Cheyne (1740), pp.26, 69, 86–7; cf. Romans 8:4–22. Compare Joseph Glanvill's position in ch. 6 above.

98 Cheyne (1740), pp.64–5, 69–70; St Augustine (2005), Bk VI.6; Ramsay (1727), II.ii.2–5; cf. Blount (1680?), pp.24–5; Manu (1971), v.40; Tull (1996). For Cheyne's possible exposure to the ideas of F.M. van Helmont, cf. e.g. Shuttleton (1992), p.289.

99 Cheyne (1705), II.150–1; cf. II.26–9, 46, 108–10, 120–2, 199, 208–9; Cheyne (1715), I.290–1, II.89–90; cf. e.g. Cheyne (1740), pp.105–7; Cheyne (1715 [1716]), pp.244–6 and pp.209–10 where Cheyne again applies the multiple world theory to the system of rewards and punishments; cf. Cheyne (1736), sig.[Aa5v], pp.209–10.

100 Cheyne (1740), pp.6–10; Cheyne (1705), II.229–32; Cheyne (1715 [1716]), I.321–3, II.130; Cheyne (1733), pp.86–7; Leibniz (1985), § 72–4, 82; Leibniz (2001), § 11 [p.189]; Leibniz (1686), ch. 34. For Leibniz, Helmont and the Kabbalah, see Coudert (1995); Coudert (1999), pp.320–1, 328–9; Coudert et al., eds (1998); Coudert (1997); Brown, S. (1997), pp.97–9, 113–14.

101 Extra-terrestrial life: Cheyne (1705), II.110; McColley (1936), pp.386–8, 406–9, 416, 422–4, 428–9, see espec. Molyneux (1709), pp.278–9; Dick (1980), p.22; Cheyne had read most of the authors cited by Steven J. Dick, cf. e.g. Cheyne (1705), II.115–16, 177, 196; Cheyne (1715 [1716]), p.221. cf. also More, H. (1662), 'Immortality', p.123ff.; Kämper

(1995), pp.127–8. Animal Souls: Ray (1717), pp.20ff., 53–7; Cheyne (1740), pp.6–10; cf. Marsay (1749), pp.27–8. Animal Heaven: Thomas, K. (1983), p.140; Shugg (1968b), pp.289–90; Wesley (1872), VI.241–52; Garrett, ed. (2000); Hildrop (1742–3), II.9–15, 42, 47, 77; Shuttleton (1992), pp.121–3, 208–9; Turner (1980), p.8; Almond (1999), pp.112–13.

102 Reynolds (1725), pp.60–5; Thomas, K. (1983), pp.139–40.

103 Marsay (1938), pp.105, 223–5ff., 245–8; Marsay (1739), pp.86–9; Marsay (1749), pp.23–4, 28–32; Cheyne (1740), p.50; Cheyne (1943), pp.123–4. Cheyne considered his theory of universal salvation similar to Marsay's, but Marsay can hardly have been a source for Cheyne because, according to Marsay, God only revealed this system to Marsay in 1735, whereas Cheyne had come up with his ideas by 1705 when Marsay was only seventeen; cp. Guerrini (2000), p.172; Shuttleton (1996), p.39 and *passim*; Shuttleton (1992), p.96n.; Ramsay (1730), subscription list; Ramsay (1727), II.ii.98–127; cf. e.g. the Cheynian passage at I.90. Cheyne's publisher, George Strahan, printed the Origenist tract [Rust?] (1721).

CHAPTER 14

1 Cheyne (1943), pp.62, 72; cf. pp.50, 58, 60–1, 71, 72, 78–9, 88, 94, 116.

2 Cheyne (1943), pp.32–3 (9 Aug 1735). It seems that the issue of mercury poisoning may not have been raised previously partly because of Mullet's oversight in translating Cheyne's Latin prescription of Aethiop mineral as 'black mineral powder' without noting that this was one of Cheyne's favourite mercurial compositions.

3 Hirschorn et al. (2001).

4 [Cheyne] (1701), pp.106–7; cf. Shapin (2003), p.277; Guerrini (2000), p.132.

5 Cheyne (1733), pp.125–34; Huxham (1759), p.25.

6 Cheyne (1943), pp.42, 49, 54, 58, 62, 66, 108, 115. On Richardson's withdrawing from social contact, see e.g. Eaves and Kimpel (1971), p.157. This could provide an interesting perspective to the antisocial tendencies of 'sensibility' documented in Mullan (1988).

7 Cheyne (1943): further mercurial prescriptions made in June 1738 (p.38) (Mercury Alcalisatus, three pills morning and evening); again in September (p.42); and the same again in May 1739 to be continued morning and night until midsummer (p.49); Cinnabar of Antimony and Antimony Diaphoretic in February 1741 (5 pills morning and night) (p.66).

8 Scheuer and Bowman (1994); cf. Eaves and Kimpel (1971), p.84.

9 Cheyne (1733), pp.238–9.

10 Cheyne (1943), 16 July 1739, p.54; cf. p.59.

11 Cheyne (1943), pp.78–9, 104–5; cf. 59, 61, 88–9, 90–1, 92.

12 Cheyne (1943), 20 April 1740, pp.75–6.

13 Cheyne (1943), 1735–41, pp.32–3, 38, 42, 47, 48, 49, 50, 52, 54, 57, 58, 59–60, 64.

14 Cheyne (1943), p.66.

15 Cheyne (1943), Letter 62, n.d., pp.96–8. In Mullett's edition this letter has been printed as 'Letter 62' which would mean it was written between 2 and 17 May 1742; but in fact it was obviously written immediately after Letter 47 (dated 15 November 1741) and immediately before Letter 48 (2 December 1741) (p.73). In Letters 48 and 49 Cheyne refers to a recent letter in which he has suggested that Richardson take up the vegetable diet; it has hitherto been assumed that this letter was

missing, but it is really referring to the mis-positioned 'Letter 62' in which Cheyne does first suggest the vegetable diet (which would make no sense if it had been written in May 1742, four months after Richardson adopted the diet). Letter 48 refers to 'my last letter' with details about book deals which actually appear in the misplaced 'Letter 62' (£125+£80 for his books). Also in 'Letter 62' Cheyne asks for a copy of *Pamela* which he thanks Richardson for in Letters 48 and 49. cf. also p.109.

16 Eaves and Kimpel (1971), pp.154, 157.

17 Cheyne (1733), pp.286–90.

18 Cheyne (1733), pp.238–9, 343; cf. Fuller (1711), pp.243–6: Fuller says his own giddiness and convulsions were caused by poisoning from the mercury he applied to a skin condition; Cheyne (who seems to have used Fuller as a guide) used the same application for his leg ulcers and experienced giddiness and convulsions (see Fuller, ch.13, p.175+n.61 above). [Cheyne] (1701), pp.90–127.

19 Cheyne (1943), 22 June 1738, p.37.

20 Hirschorn et al. (2001).

21 Coudert (1999), pp.156–7.

22 Cheyne (1943), pp.76–8, 81.

23 Cheyne (1943), 7 December 1741, pp.74–5; cf. Shapin (2003), pp.282–8.

24 Cheyne (1943), pp.74–8, 94.

25 Cheyne (1943), pp.74–5, 76–8, 78–9, 80, 90, 120.

26 Cheyne (1943), p.100.

27 Cheyne (1943), pp.58, 74–5, 76–8, 78–9, 80, 84–5, 93, 94, 97, 101 ('our' food), 110–11, 112, 114, 116, 117.

28 Cheyne (1943), pp.74–5, 82–4, 105, 121; cf. Shapin (2003), pp.286–7.

29 Cheyne (1943), pp.74–9, 82–4, 86–8, 95, 120.

30 Cheyne (1943), pp.78–9.

31 Cheyne (1943), p.101; cf.

pp.78–89, 96, 107; Matthew 18:3; Böhme (1924), p.158.

32 Cheyne (1943), pp.99–100, 113, 123.

33 Eaves and Kimpel (1971), pp.154–6.

34 Richardson (1749) [my emphasis], quoted in Shuttleton (1992), p.278; cf. Lockyer (1783), p.147; White (1770), p.122.

35 Cheyne (1943), pp.32–5, 42.

36 Richardson (1985b), pp.738, 799, 895, 1054, 1058, 1059; Richardson (1985a), pp.133, 136, 165, 299, 373, 392, 436, 495; cf. Fielding (1973), pp.1, 22, 29; cf. Rousseau, J.-J. (1997a), p.136+n.

37 Richardson (1985a), pp.49, 57, 65, 69, 165, 206, 223, 282, 308, 311, 316, 323, 331, 340, 355, 363, 364, 378, 380, 397+n., 399–400, 408, 425, 428, 436, 443, 446–8, 491; Richardson (1985b), pp.263–4, 525, 532–3, 573, 581, 639–41, 799; Eaves and Kimpel (1971), p.123.

38 Richardson (1985a), p.230+n.; Richardson (1985b), p.108+n. (cf. e.g. p.429); Plutarch (1928), III.162; cf. pp.210–11. Eaves and Kimpel (1971), pp.121, 94. On the fraught issue of Richardson's politics, see Keymer (1995), pp.94–96+n.; cp. Doody (1990).

39 Richardson (1985a), pp.47, 73, 112–13, 230; cf. pp.45, 58, 66, 68, 70, 95, 102, 108, 228, 268–9, 294.

40 Cheyne (1943), p.76; Richardson (1985b), pp.263–4.

41 Richardson (1985b), pp.1117–18, 1129; Cheyne (1943), pp.76, 81, 86, 100; cf. Fasick (1993), p.25; Dussinger (1974), pp.116–21; Shuttleton (1992), p.278.

42 Richardson (1985b), p.1129.

43 cf. e.g. Cheyne (1724), p.36; Cheyne (1733), pp.166–7; Cheyne (1740), p.xxix; Cheyne (1943), p.77. Richardson (1985b), pp.746, 932, 979, 980, 1012, 1081, 1158, 1127, 1167, 1198, 1380, 1470–1; Richardson (1754), III.373–4; Haggerty (1990), p.133;

Willis (1683), p.194ff.; Harvey
(1672?), p.55; Gross (1985),
pp.284–5; Frega (1998),
p.119+n.13
44 Cheyne (1943), pp.99–100; cp.
p.95.
45 Cheyne (1943), p.87. Cheyne's
defence ironically fulfils J.B. van
Helmont's warning that diet-
doctors 'do oftentimes hope to get
occasion of excusing death, by the
disobedience of the sick, about the
rules of diet not being strictly
observed' (Helmont, J.B. (1664),
p.451).
46 Cheyne (1943), pp.74–5.
47 Shuttleton (1992), pp.269–70;
Shuttleton (1999b); cf. Fasick
(1993), p.25.
48 Cheyne (1733), pp.viii, 20;
Cheyne (1724), p.91.
49 Pamela as animal: Richardson
(1985a), pp.96, 97, 169, 176, 224;
cf. pp.56, 57, 202, 204, 456. Rakes
as carnivorous beasts: Richardson
(1985a), pp. 71, 169, 207, 216,
233–4, 472; Richardson (1742),
IV.33; Richardson (1985b),
pp.165, 823, 891, 1089, 1437;
predation: pp.196, 267, 418–19,
574, 887, 891, 1089; hunting:
pp.165, 181, 209, 323, 557, 706,
792, 795, 803, 814; sacrifice:
pp.67, 70, 85, 133, 162, 674;
trapping: pp.119, 133, 144, 145,
199, 517, 557, 710; fishing: p.85.
cf. Hume (1985), II.xi;
Backscheider (1976); Eaves and
Kimpel (1971), pp.84, 90; Hilliard
(1990); Haggerty (1990), p.137;
Keymer (1995); Biggs (1982).
Clarissa consoled herself on her
sacrificial status by reflecting on
Christ's sacrifice; she could have
received succour from Wilson's
Lord's Supper, one of the books
that she is 'not a little pleased
with' when she discovers it in her
closet at Sinclair's, which says that
sinners were reformed 'when they
saw, that their Sins could not be
forgiven, *but by the Death of an
innocent Creature*, bleeding and
dying before their Eyes, to make

Atonement for their Sin'
(Richardson (1985b), p.525;
Wilson (1745), pp.8, 21; cf.
Nelson (1979), p.5, 433, 439.
Shuttleton (1995), p.325; [Delany]
(1733), pp.144–6; Cheyne
(1740), pp.70–1).
50 Richardson (1985a), pp.136,
221–2, 249–50, 290, 332, 410,
447–9; cf. pp.61, 65, 112–13,
423; Richardson (1985b), pp.66,
77, 294, 591, 911; cf. Fasick
(1993), pp.19–20, 30n.8; Jooma
(1996); Moon (1985), p.32; Frega
(1990); Eaves and Kimpel (1971),
p.104; cf. Doody (1974), p.51; cp.
Robert James Merrett, 'Natural
History and the Eighteenth-
Century Novel', *Eighteenth-Century
Studies*, 145–70, pp.161–3; Kay
(1973).
51 Richardson (1985b), p.1202; cf.
pp.857, 1363; Harvey (1672?),
pp.236–7.
52 Richardson (1985a), pp.159, 168;
cf. Fielding (1973), pp.31–2:
Shamela identifies with the hares
being hunted by the country
gentlemen, and tries to protect
them.
53 Richardson (1985b), p.557; cf.
p.610. Richardson (1985a), pp.97,
114, 149, 218.
54 Richardson (1985b), p.1125–6.
55 Montaigne (1991), pp.502, 539.
56 cf. e.g. Cheyne (1943), p.76;
Richardson (1985b), pp.263–4;
and Ellis (1966), pp.65–6.
57 'Nervous distempers' and their
influence on literature have
received much attention from G.S.
Rousseau, Roy Porter, John Mullan
and Barker-Benfield. Barker-
Benfield (1992), p.7; Eaves and
Kimpel (1971), p.156. But the
dietary cures have been
insufficiently discussed, which
deprives Cheyne's construction of
nervous disorders of its means for
the reformation of moral action,
which Richardson in turn adapted
for his novels. The fact that many
nervous sufferers – both real and
fictional – were given dietary

restrictions, effectively cutting them off from conviviality with mainstream society, but binding them together in smaller intimate circles, should also be seen alongside the anti-sociability of sensibility discussed by Mullan (1988) and Spang (2000), p.59.

58 Gross (1985), p.285; Eaves and Kimpel (1971), p.84.

59 Eaves and Kimpel (1971), p.142.

60 Richardson (1985b), pp.931, 957, 973, 1023, 672–3, 1201, 1431–3, 612–16, 1225–6, 55, 1157, 828, 1476, 1378, 1434, 659, 1476, 1217, 1491, 560, 543, 606, 888; Richardson (1996a), pp.105–6; Richardson (1985a), pp.290–2, 295; Mrs Jewkes escapes this fate and Pamela remarks how lucky she is to have repented before reaching the inevitable sick-bed.

61 Richardson (1985b), pp.539, 543, 934, 1088–9, 1123, 1227, 1431; cf. Pope (1993), 'Essay on Man', III.165–6; Campbell, D.G. (1990), p.137; Keymer (1995).

62 Richardson (1985b), p.1426.

63 Richardson (1985b), p.1429; cf. also Richardson (1985a), pp.99, 212, 231, 251.

64 Richardson (1985b), p.838.

65 Richardson (1985b), p.659.

66 Mandeville (1924), Remark P, I.173–81. cf. Coleridge (1796); George and Stephens (1978), VI. § 8081; Radcliffe (1980), pp.79–81.

67 Richardson (1985b), p.609; cf. pp.559, 605, 833, 838; cf. Hilliard (1990).

68 Richardson (1985b), pp.543, 614, 1226.

69 Smollett (1978), pp.235–6. For more similarities with Clarissa cf. pp.237–41. cf. the regulated lifestyle of love-sick, melancholy, isolated and suicidal Nekayah in *Rasselas* (1759), Johnson (1958), pp.578, 580; Gross (1985), pp.284–5.

70 Smollett (1978), pp.237, 330, 334, 354, 361; cp. p.351.

71 Smollett (1978), p.149; cf. Smollett (1996b), I.17–23.

72 Barker-Benfield (1992); Smollett (1996a), Vol.II, ch.75, p.295; cf. ch.98.

73 Smollett (1961), pp.170–3; cf. Ovingdon (1696), p.310.

74 Schnorrenberg (1984), pp.191–5; cf. Shuttleton (1992), pp.127–9; cf. Smollett (1996a), Vol.II, ch.75, pp.291–5.

75 Austen, J. (1997c), pp.20–2, 39, 45, 70–1.

76 Austen, J. (1997b), p.19.

77 Austen, J. (1997b), pp.24–5; cf. pp.213, 391; cf. Austen, J. (1997a), p.185.

78 Austen, J. (1997c), p.466, cf. pp.71–2. On her mock-macabre sympathy for animals, cf. pp.3, 6, 10, 12, 15, 35–6, 57–8, 68, 72, 280, 336, 344.

CHAPTER 15

1 cf. Willett and Cunnington (1957), pp.119–32, 268–75; *cit.* Sherwood (1993), p.27.

2 Schama (1989), pp.217–20; Spang (2000), pp.27+n.67, 63.

3 Rousseau, J.-J.(1997b), pp.134–5, 140–2 (I follow this edition, though I have changed some words and phrases, in consultation with Rousseau's original (Rousseau, J.-J. (1755)) and the translation of G.D.H. Cole. In this case I have given *'également'* a literal translation to restore the resonance with the essay's title). Centuries earlier, Pico della Mirandola had seen the absence of a fixed nature as man's God-given free-will; Montaigne had seen it as his pathetic deficiency; Rousseau, on the other hand, presented it as an *adaptation* which liberated humans from slavish adherence to either herbivorous or carnivorous instincts. Like Tyson, Wallis and Jan Baptista van Helmont, Rousseau considered omnivorousness a manifestation of man's special – even

microcosmic – status: Mirandola [1496], ch.4–5, § 10–23; Montaigne (1991), p.502; Gassendi (1658), VI.21; cf. Aquinas (1975), pp.116–17; Skinner and Kessler, eds. (1988), pp.313–15; Leary (1984), p.167; cf. ch. 11, pp.145, and n.9; ch.14, p.192–3 (Belford's comment) above. cf. Monboddo (1773–92), I.204; [Monboddo] (1797), p.135. On omnivorousness as a special human characteristic, cf. ch.18, p.257–8 below; Lawrence (1819), pp.210–11.

4 Rousseau, J.-J. (1997b), pp.141–2, and Note X, pp.205–6; cf. Jerome (2005a), Bk II, ch.13; Rousseau, J.-J. (1979), p.151.

5 Rousseau, J.-J. (1997b), p.134 and Note V, pp.193–4; Cocchi (1745), p.47; cit. Rousseau, J.-J. (1979), p.58n.; Ritson (1802), pp.41–2; cf. Kenyon-Jones (2001), p.126.

6 Bonnet (1975), pp.265–6.

7 Schiebinger (2004), pp.40–74.

8 Rousseau, J.-J. (1997b), Note V, pp.193–4; Lovejoy (1933), pp.285–6; cf. ch.18 below; cp. Jenyns (1793), III.186–93; Ritson (1802), p.233+n.

9 Rousseau, J.-J. (1997b), Note VIII, p.196 and Note XII, pp.213–14; cf. Note X, pp.205–6.

10 Schama (1989), pp.148, 769–75; Schiebinger (2004), pp.40–74; Hunt (2004), pp.93–4.

11 Rousseau, J.-J. (1997b), pp.152–3; Hobbes (1651), Part I, ch.xiv, pp.64–9.

12 See discussion of Mandeville above and Hume below, pp.179, 225+n.26.

13 Grotius (1901), Bk I, ch.1, § 11.

14 Rousseau, J.-J. (1997b), Preface, pp.127–8; Rousseau, J.-J. (1754); cf. Morton (1994), p.30; Bentham pp.362–2.

15 Ovid (1717), Bk XV, p.514.

16 Hobbes (1676), p.66 (Pt. I, ch. xiv).

17 Rousseau, J.-J. (1997b), p.134; Rousseau, J.-J. (1979), pp.56–8; Bonnet (1975), p.265.

18 Schiebinger (2004), pp.40–74.

19 cf. Pufendorf (1749), p.361; Hastings (1994), ch.3, § 32.

20 Buffon (1780), III.423–6; Buffon (1753), IV.437–42, 'Le Boeuf'; Oswald (1791), pp.113–15; Rees et al. (1819), 'Man', sig.Ss4r; Williams, Howard (1883), p.166; Hastings (1936), pp.254–61.

21 Rousseau, J.-J. (1997b), pp.229–30; cf. Stillingfleet, ed. (1759), p.98.

22 Rousseau, J.-J. (1997b), pp.230–1; cf. Richardson (1742), IV.17–18; Monboddo (1773–92), I.215.

23 Buffon (1780), IV.164–94; Buffon (1758), VII.3–38, 'Les Animaux Carnassiers'; cit. Hastings (1936), pp.254–61; cf. King (1731), pp.118–19.

24 Hastings (1936), pp.254–61.

25 Williams, Howard (1883), p.177n.

26 Ulmer (1972); Litwack (1977). Compare for example Rousseau, J.-J. (1997a), pp.599–600, 604+n.134; Richardson (1985b), pp.1360–3; Clarissa's post-mortem letters (pp.1367, 1371–7, 1425–7) and Julie's (p.608 ff.).

27 Rousseau, J.-J. (1997a), p.599.

28 Rousseau, J.-J. (1997a), IV.x.373; cf. pp.444, 470, 496.

29 Rousseau, J.-J. (1979), p.395; cf. Rousseau's description of himself and Mme Warens, Rousseau, J.-J. (1953), pp.21, 105–6. Richard Graves' Charlotte Woodville, with her 'artless freedom' and 'native simplicity', resembles Rousseau's Sophie (Graves (1996), II.13).

30 Rousseau, J.-J. (1997a), p.372; cf. [Hecquet] (1733), I.124–8; Rousseau, J.-J. (1979), pp.56–8+n., 151; Richardson (1985b), pp.41ff., 532; Spang (2000), p.54. This is not necessarily Rousseau's own opinion. Saint–Preux may, as usual, be misinterpreting the extent of Julie's naturalness. Sugar was an exotic, colonial product, at odds with Julie's self-sufficiency; and most of her foods – even her milk-based sweets – do not

include it. In *Émile*, Sophie's affection for sugar is a (minor) flaw in her character; one that Rousseau as a child shared (Rousseau, J.-J. (1953), p.21). cp. Spang (2000), pp.44–5. On the masculinisation of meat, cf. Adams (1990).

31 Rousseau, J.-J. (1997a), pp.306–7, 363, 444, 450.

32 Rousseau, J.-J. (1997a), pp.390–3; cf. Godwin (2005), Bk vi.

33 Evelyn (2000), p.154; *Spy*, V.II.iii.88–90.

34 Rousseau, J.-J. (1997a), IV.xvii.422; cf. pp.495–6.

35 Linnaeus also encouraged mothers to nurse their own infants; Schiebinger (2004), pp.40–74; Sherwood (1993), p.27; Mellor (1993), p.81ff.; Perry (1999); Stone (1977), pp.257–70.

36 Schiebinger (2004), pp.40–74.

37 Rousseau, J.-J. (1979), pp.56–8; Locke (1692), Pt I, § 13; cf. Rousseau, J.-J. (1979), p.55 and Locke (1692), Pt II, § 29; Richardson (1742), IV.10–29, 139, 256, 331–2; Vaughan, W. (1630), p.90; [Hecquet] (1733), I.124–8, 522–3; Hecquet (1990), pp.21–5 *et passim*; Morgan (1735), p.305.

38 Bernier (1964), V.583–4 (Gassendi (1658), II.301–2); cf. Evelyn (1996), pp.74–5. Rousseau may have read these arguments in Pufendorf (1749), pp.359–60.

39 Rousseau, J.-J. (1979), pp.153+n.; cf. Rousseau, J.-J. (1998), pp.81–2; Smellie (1790–9), I.60–1; *cit.* Thomas, K. (1983), p.292; Bonnet (1975), p.250.

40 Rousseau, J.-J. (1979), pp.222–5; cf. p.320.

41 Rousseau, J.-J. (1979), pp.153–5; cf. Plutarch (1995), pp.551–3 (994F–995B)ff.; cf. Rousseau, J.-J. (1997b), pp.274–5.

42 Rousseau, J.-J. (1979), pp.320, 351.

43 Rousseau, J.-J. (1979), pp.59, 190–1, 345; Spang (2000), pp.51–2. Rousseau and Plutarch

regard the repulsion to the act of slaughter and butchery as 'natural'. 'Civilisation' creates the distance and disguise which allows those acts to occur out of sight. (In Rousseau's case the development of sensibility to animals was natural *and* ought to be cultivated (Rousseau, J.-J. (1979), pp.222–3).) George Cheyne made an analogous attempt to 'disgust the stoutest stomach' by highlighting the process of producing animal food in cramped and noxious agricultural practices (Cheyne (1733), pp.49–50 and Cheyne (1724), p.28). Norbert Elias identifies the putting 'out of sight' as the tool of the progress of civilisation; however, he does not regard disgust as 'natural' but as the product of civilisation, linking it to the human suppression of everything in them 'of an "animalic character"' (Elias (2000), pp.102–3).

44 Bonnet (1975), pp.249–50; Barkas (1975), pp.75–8; Wheaton (1983), pp.224–6. Morton (1994), pp.42–3, 97; Thomas, K. (1983), p.176. In her otherwise illuminating discussion, Rebecca L. Spang misrepresents Rousseau's dietary ethic and aesthetic by aligning him with the promoters of the *nouvelle cuisine* in not celebrating 'the dark bread of peasant fare' but instead '(comparatively expensive) fruits and dairy products' (Spang (2000), p.42). Rousseau did celebrate peasant fare and brown bread (*pain bis*) (see note 45 below; and Rousseau, J.-J. (1979), pp.190–1). Julie's dairy foods and fruits which Rousseau celebrated were home-grown as part of a self-sufficient domestic economy and therefore, while privileged (although shared among the servants), they cost nothing ('Our own commodities alone grace our table', Rousseau, J.-J. (1997a),

pp. 372–3, 450). The restaurants did seize on Rousseauist appeals to natural food by serving fruits and dairy-foods, alongside their refined meat soups. But Spang puts her own comments right by observing how at odds Rousseau really was with the restaurant's sophisticated, urban food and their rhetoric of 'simplicity' (Spang (2000), pp.57, 59–61). On her death-bed Julie does not take the restorative *consommé* of the type served in restaurants, and instead opts for locally caught fish (Rousseau, J.-J. (1997a), pp.496, 599).

45 Rousseau, J.-J. (1973), p.111.

46 Rousseau, J.-J. (1953), Bk iv; cf. Runt (1978), p.68ff.; Saint-Pierre (1997a), II.19.

47 Spang (2000), pp.21–8, 34–65.

48 On Rousseauist education, see Darnton (1984), pp.215–56; Kenyon-Jones (2001), pp.59–65; Spang (2000), pp.58–9.

49 Sade (2003), pp.10–11; Bonnet (1975), p.250n.

50 Saint-Pierre (1826), I.212–13; Saint-Pierre (1836), pp.755, 765.

51 Saint-Pierre (n.d.), p.103.

52 Saint-Pierre (n.d.), pp.46, 50, 111; Brown (1978).

53 Saint-Pierre (1791a), pp.48–58; cf. pp.ix–x, xii–xv, xxi, xxiv–xxviii, 25; Saint-Pierre (1791b), pp.26–8, 46–8, 69, 79–81, 100, 105, 117.

54 cf. Rousseau, J.-J. (1997b), pp.192–3, Note 4; Monboddo (1773–92), I.254; Voltaire (1779–80), I.37.

55 Saint-Pierre (1836), p.178; Grove (1995), pp.9, 248, 252–3; Schwab (1984), p.102.

56 Saint-Pierre (1997b), I.51–2, 98–100; Kaempfer (1727), I.103, 113, 120, 124–5, 128, 132–41, 218, 297; cf. Cocchi (1745), p.87. On soil fertility cf. Rousseau, J.-J. (1997b), pp.192–3, n.4; cf. Evelyn (1670); Kenyon-Jones (2001), pp.132–3; cf. Saint-Pierre (1798), II.398; Pigott, R. (1792); Ritson (1802), pp.64–5; Lambe (1815),

pp.230–1. For Byron's bread-fruit eating utopia in *The Island* see Kenyon-Jones (2001), pp.132–3. Lambe could have been a source for Byron. On the related ideas of Linguet see e.g. Schama (1989), p.197.

57 Williams, Howard (1883), pp.175–6; Bigland (1816), pp.66–7; cf. Saint-Pierre (n.d.), p.99; Saint-Pierre (1997a), I.168, II.145–6, 441–4, III.70; Saint-Pierre (1826), III.316.

58 Saint-Pierre (1826), II.180–1; cf. III.10.

59 Saint-Pierre (1826), III.169; cf. III.109–10, 172–3; Haller (1754), I.xxvi, xxxiv, xxxviii, II.340, 346, 360–1, 369, 423–4.

60 Goethe (1932), p.286; cf. pp.303, 534.

61 Goethe (1962), p.358; Nichols (1991), § 9; Nicholson (1999), p.xviii; Teltscher (1995), pp.5, 213; Schwab (1984), pp.60, 141.

62 Goethe (1917), Bk 1, § 64, 21 June; § 68, 1 July.

63 See ch. 18 below.

64 Williams, Howard (1883), p.184.

65 Lamartine (1849–51), pp.73–5; cf. Lamartine (1832–3), p.229; Williams, Howard (1883), p.245; Hastings (1946), p.111n.

CHAPTER 16

1 Mack (1985), pp.590, 800; cf. 73, 621, 757.

2 Borkfelt (2000); Williams, Howard (1883), pp.129–32; Spencer (1993), pp.216–19; Allen, D. (2001), p.290+n.

3 The quote comes from the otherwise very sensitive article, Oerlemans (1994). The attitude is pervasive.

4 Dryden (1700), p.529; Thomas, K. (1983), p.292; Dryden (1958), IV.1736, 2080 (ll.705–6); Terry (1655), p.327. Dryden's Pythagorean section of Book XV was incorporated into the oft-reprinted full translation of Ovid (1717).

5 Thomson (1746), 'Spring', ll.236–41; Ovid (1717), pp.512–17; Williams, Howard (1883), pp.116–19.

6 Thomson (1746), 'Spring', ll.340–68; cf. l.789; Alexander Pope (1993), 'Essay on Man', III.152; Evelyn (1669), p.[3].

7 Oswald (1791), pp.18–19.

8 Thomson (1746), 'Spring', ll.370–78; cf. l.785 ff.; Morton (1994), p.92.

9 Thomson (1736), 'Liberty', iii.60–70.

10 [Pope] (1729), I.259–64; for the authorship see sig.A4v; Plutarch (1928), III.168; Seneca (1917–25), Epistle 95, III.66–71; Pope (1993), 'Essay on Man', I.111–12, III.21–4.

11 Plutarch (1995), p.565 (996F–997A); cf. Cheyne (1733), pp.49–50. cf. also Browne (1672), Bk III, ch.xxv, pp.189–94 and Pliny, XI.210–11.

12 *The Guardian* (J. Tonson, London 1729), no.6, I.30–4; *The Tatler* (14–16 Feb. 1709 [1710]), no.134; Scher (1993).

13 *The Universal Spectator*, (20 Feb. 1731), no.124; cf. (10 July 1731), no 144; *GM* (Feb. 1731), Vol. 1.ii, p.62.

14 Pope (1993), 'Essay on Man', III.151–4. The Indian in Pope's 'Essay on Man' I.111–12 resembles the opening scene in the Hindu epic, the *Ramayana*; but it seems unlikely that Pope would know of this.

15 Pope (1993), 'Essay on Man', III.159–68; cf. Seneca (1917–25), Epistle 95, III.66–71; [Tryon] ([1684b]), pp.217–18.

16 Pope (1993), 'Essay on Man', III.49–70; cf. I.81–6, III.195–6, 264–6. cp. Borkfelt (2000), Williams, Howard (1883), pp.131–2; Spencer (1993), pp.216–19. Morton observes that the passages in Pope he calls 'vegetarian' are balanced by a resignation to fate; I think the counter-vegetarian thrust is more

forceful than 'resignation', cf. Morton (1994), pp.91–2.

17 Pope (1993), 'Essay on Man', I.81–4; Ovid (1717), Bk XV [ll. 686–7], pp.530–1. cf. Rousseau, J.-J. (1979), pp.153–4, 225; cf. Beranek (2004), pp.68–71.

18 Graves (1996), I.245, 260; II.10, 15, 19; Shuttleton (1999a), p.61; Shuttleton (1995), pp.319–20. Graves may also have modelled his 'Graham' character on James Graham the vegetarian doctor.

19 Graves (1996), I.235–40; *Measure for Measure* in Shakespeare (1990), III.i.76–9.

20 Brückner (1768), pp.134–5, 141–6; see *CR*, Vol.26 (August 1768), p.50.

21 Oswald (1791), pp.41–3; Erdman (1986), pp.52–5; see ch. 26 below.

22 Clarke (1720), p.271 (my emphasis).

23 I quote from the punchier translation in Pufendorf (1749), p.361n.; cf. King (1731), pp.118–20+n.; Clarke (1720), pp.273–85; Doddridge (1794), I.207–9; cf. Thomas, K. (1983), pp.20–1.

24 Cheyne would be one such 'great name', though the assertion that natural reason can establish the right to eat meat without Scripture goes back to Thomas Hobbes' dispute with Bishop Bramhall (see ch.10 above); Hutcheson (1764), I.156–9; Hutcheson (1755), I.309–17+n. Hutcheson and Rousseau are clear precedents to the later animal rights theories of Humphrey Primatt and Thomas Young, for which see Garrett (2000), I.v–xxiv; Garrett (forthcoming); cf. Regan (2001), p.121; Thomas, K. (1983), p.179; Passmore (1975), p.209; Turner (1980), pp.6–7.

25 Hume (1985), II.I.xii, p.375; II.II.xii, pp.444–5; cf. II.II.v, pp.411–12.

26 Thomas, K. (1983), pp.175–6; Hume (1983), III.i. pp.25–6; cf.

Montaigne (1999), Bk II, ch. xi 'Of Crueltie': 'Unto men we owe Justice, and to all other creatures that are capable of it, grace and benignity'; Plutarch (1928), III.168: 'nature teacheth us to use justice onely unto menne, but gentlenesse sometimes is shewed unto brute beastes'. Hume (1985), II.I.xii, p.375; II.II.xii, pp.444–5; cf. II.II.v, pp.411–12; cf. 'An Apology for Raymond Sebond' in Montaigne (1991), pp.525–6; Passmore (1975), p.209; Fosl (2000); Arnold (1995); Kuflik (1998).

27 Hartley (1749), II.222–4 (II.ii.2.§.52); cf. I.404, II.140; Cheyne (1724), p.91; King (1731), pp.118–20; Doddridge (1794), I.208; Thomas, K. (1983), pp.140, 155, 295, 298; Perkins (2003), p.118. Hartley's statements were mutilated by Williams and thus misrepresented by all the 'vegetarian' historians who have relied on him: Williams, Howard (1883), pp.138–9; Spencer (1993), pp.217–19; Borkfelt (2000); http://www.vegdot.org/ quotes. For Cheyne and Hartley, cf. Shuttleton (1992), pp.96, 213, 220, 234–5; Shuttleton (1999a), p.69.

28 The World, 19 Aug. 1756, 190; cit. Ritson (1802), pp.225–6, Williams, Howard (1883), pp.125, 139–41; Thomas, K. (1983), p.295.

29 Jenyns (1793), III.186–93 (my emphasis); Turner (1980), p.8; Ritson (1802), pp.228–36; Nicholson (1999), pp.103–4; cf. Nicholson (1797), pp.37–9.

30 Ritson (1802), pp.90–1; Williams, Howard (1883), pp.110–11, 178; Mullan (2001), p.22; Morton (1994), p.89; Morton refers to 'the vegetarian Task VI (759–817)'; cf. Morton (2002), p.82.

31 Cowper (1785), pp.259–60; cf. pp.249–55.

32 Cowper (1812), I.206, 213–14, 221, 273–4, 293; II.44–50, 73,

98; III.70, 114, 149, 150, 160–2, 164, 360–2.

33 Cowper (1812), I.213; II.165; IV.157, 314–20.

34 Cowper (1992), Vol.X, 'Elegy VI. To Charles Deodati'; Williams, Howard (1883), pp.110–11, 178; Morton (1994), p.107+n.

35 Cowper (1785), pp.251, 254, 260–1.

36 Pratt (1788), pp.38–41; Pratt (1786), pp.7–8, 11; Plutarch (1995), p.565 (996F–997A); cf. Pratt (1779), III.119–20; Pratt (1781), p.[v]; cp. Morton (1994), pp.94–6. On Howard's vegetarianism, see Anon. (1790), p.18; Aikin (1792), p.40; EM (March 1790), XVII.163–4.

37 Doody (1999); [Nicholson, ed.?] (1798), pp.27–8. In Richardson's novels, women team up with animals in defiance of their male aggressors; this is not easily distinguishable from the objections to male cruelty to women and animals made by contemporaneous women writers.

38 [Scott, S.] (1986), pp.4–5, 17–19, 21, 59, 63, 67, 155–6. Isaiah 11:6–9; Thomson (1746), 'Spring', l.786; cf. Pope (1993), 'Essay on Man', III.151–4; Morton (1994), p.75; Cowley (1777), p.34, 'The Wish', I.20; Bancroft (1770), III.70–6; Bancroft (1769), pp.260–2; Burke (1756), p.99.

39 Deverell (1781), I.240–51.

40 Darwin, E. (1797), pp.46–8.

41 Darwin, E. (1794–6), II.384–5.

42 Thomas, K. (1983), p.301; Goldsmith may have been thinking of his acquaintance, the 'doctor' George Cheyne, or more probably he is lampooning the theodicy of the Jesuit Father Guillaume Hyacinthe Bougeant who thought devils were imprisoned in animals before being sent to hell (see ch. 20 below). cf. Goldsmith's 'The Hermit'.

43 cf. Thomas, K. (1983), pp.185–6; Kenyon-Jones (2001), p.92;

Schama (1989), p.186; Mandeville (1924), I.173–81; Evelyn (1699), pp.119–20.

CHAPTER 17

1 Mazza & Tomasello (1996); [Cocchi, V.] (1871); Aikin (1799–1815), III.45.
2 Rousseau, J.-J. (1979), pp.56–8+n.; Bianchi (1752).
3 Pasta (1795), pp.173–5; cf. pp.40–1, 134–6, 146; Cocchi (1745), pp.66–7.
4 Cocchi (1824), III.2–3; cf. Morgan (1735), pp.90–1.
5 Cocchi (1741), I.xiii–xiv.
6 Cocchi (1745), pp.47–51; cf. pp.53, 58–9, 61, 68; Lind (1753), pp.302–5+n.
7 Cocchi (1745), pp.29–33 (Cocchi (1743), p.32; Cocchi (1824), I.211). cf. Diogenes Laertius (2000), II.331–2: 'The Sameness of the Nature of the Soul was indeed a Pretence for the forbidding the eating of Animals: But the Truth was, that he intended by such a Prohibition to accustom Men to content themselves with such a Diet as was every where to be Found with Ease, (which they might eat without dressing) and with drinking only pure Water; all which is highly conducive both to the Health of the Body, and the Alacrity of the Mind'; Cocchi also cites Plutarch's defence of vegetarianism without recourse to Pythagorean metempsychosis and Plato's *Timaeus*: 'We restrain Mankind by false Reasons . . . if they will not let us guide them by the true. Whence arises the Necessity of talking of those strange Punishments of Souls, as if they passed out of one Body into another.' cf. Blount (1680), pp.2–3 'Thus *Ovid* in the 15ᵗʰ. Book of his *Metamorphosis*, gives us a full and admirable Character of all *Pythagoras's Tenents*, whereof the abstaining from Flesh-meats

was one: however not out of Superstition, as some would have it, but rather (as *Laertius* observes) for conveniency and healths-sake, as thinking all those sanguinary Meats too gross and stupifying for the Brain; and therefore most disagreeable with the study of Philosophy'. cf. also Bulstrode (1692), pp.115–16: 'But did not *Pythagoras* abstain from Flesh-Meat, for fear of eating his Parents, according to the gross Notion of Transmigration? Most certainly not; for *Jamblicus* in the Life of *Pythagoras*, tells us That he being the Disciple of *Thales*, one of the chief Things *Thales* advised him, was, to husband his Time well; upon which account, he abstained from Wine and Flesh, only eating such things as were light of Digestion'; Ritson (1802), p.170. On the Epicurean-influenced tradition of denying Pythagoras and/or the Hindus believed in reincarnation, and the related claim that they abstained from meat with more 'rational' motives, such as the preservation of health, see ch. 4 note 79; ch. 5 notes 97 and 107; and ch. 19 note 25.
8 Cocchi (1745), p.78; Butler (1774), pp.234–6n.
9 Cocchi (1745), p.87; Kaempfer (1727), I.103, 124–5, 128, 211–12; cp. pp.133ff., 141.
10 Jean-Baptiste Sénac, 'Preface' in Cocchi (1750).
11 Cocchi (1745), p.39.
12 Cocchi (1745), pp.79–80.
13 A.F. (1980), p.51; Cocchi (1745), pp.30, 35, 63; Anon. (1730), p.4ff.
14 Gibbon (1796), II.350–9; Johnson, S. (1793), I.283; Boccage (1770), p.170; Blackburne (1780), I.222.
15 Cocchi (1824), I, e.g. p.309; Cocchi (1762).
16 Cocchi (1745), p.27.
17 Cocchi (1745), pp.66–7; Dole (1707); Greisel (1670), p.179; Greisel (1681). Hecquet regarded the sixteenth-century Parisian

physicians, such as Guillaume Baillou (1538–1616), as the modern progenitors of Hippocratic medicine (Lonie (1985)). Cheyne focused on the late seventeenth-century debate as articulated by Sydenham. Opinions varied on the origins of the revival of dietary medicine, but all the vegetarian doctors considered themselves part of this renaissance.

18 Cocchi (1745), p.88.
19 Cocchi (1750), pp.105–11; Carpenter, K. (1986), pp.46–51.
20 cf. e.g. Harvey (1675); Cheyne (1990), pp.xxxvi–xl.
21 cf. e.g. [Hecquet] (1733), II.385–8.
22 Thomas, K. (1971), pp.6–7; incidents of scurvy dropped between 1720 and 1760, but rose again after the Enclosure Acts according to Drummond and Wilbraham (1939).
23 Carpenter, K. (1986), pp.45–6; Rodger (2004), p.308; Cuppage (1994), p.11.
24 Vaughan, W. (1630), pp.51, 53, 63–4; [Vaughan, W.] (1633), p.53; cf. Carpenter, K. (1986), p.45.
25 Ravenstein, ed. (1898), pp.20–1, 35, 39, 89, 93, 124; Carpenter, K. (1986), pp.1–2; Cuppage (1994), pp.9, 12.
26 Bushell (1659) '[Bacon's] New Atlantis', p.5.
27 Bromfield (1679), pp.2–3; Carpenter (1986), pp.11–12, 17–18, 20–3, 32–3.
28 Harvey (1672), p.19; Harvey (1675), pp.10–11, 89, 103–4, 107–8, 112, 222, 257–8.
29 Pitcairne (1715), pp.252–9; Pitcairne (1718a), pp.300–6; Willis (1681), 'Pathology of the Brain', III.6; cf. Cheyne (1733), pp.183–90.
30 C[ockburn] (1696); Wynter (1725), pp.4, 39–42; Floyer & Baynard (1715), Part I, pp.10, 74–5; [Temple] (1680), p.200; Temple (1701), pp.163–4, 182, 185; Morgan (1735), pp.117–18,

119–20, 274–6, 350–62; cf. Morgan (1725), pp.411–15, 434–5; Ray (1717), I.114; cf. Carpenter, K. (1986), pp.14, 46.
31 Carpenter, K. (1986), p.46.
32 Evelyn (2000), p.105 ('Endemical' replaces Evelyn's 'Endemial'); Evelyn (1699), pp.14, 19, 23, 46, 63, 89–90; cf. [Tryon] ([1684b]), p.191. cf. also [Hecquet] (1733), I.109–10; Ritson (1802), p.151.
33 [Tryon] ([1684b]), pp.191, 216–19; cp. pp.45, 74, 88, 216, 217–21; Tryon (1691a), pp.51, 122, 143, 184; cf. Tryon (1682a), pp.2–3; Tryon (1691a), pp.143–4.
34 Carpenter, K. (1986), p.17.
35 Bachstrom (1734), p.39.
36 Cocchi (1745), p.71; cf. Cocchi (1824), III.73, 82, 97ff.
37 Swieten (1744–73), XI.323–4+n.
38 cf. Jerome (2005a), Bk II.11.
39 Cocchi (1750), pp.105–11.
40 Article 'Scurvy'. The mention under 'Medicine' is more nuanced.
41 Carpenter, K. (1986), pp.52–63, 69–71, 96; cf. Addington (1753), pp.15–16.
42 Lind (1753), pp.303–4+n.
43 Clark (1773), pp.281, 335–6; cf. p.332; Richard Mead, 'On the Scurvy' in Sutton (1749), pp.112–13, 116, 173–8; Buchan (1772), pp.80, 171, 501–4; Ritson (1802), p.147; Jefferson (1958), p.482; Newton, J.F. (1897), p.73; Lambe (1815), pp.177–9; [Stewart] (1795], pp.22–4; Mertans (1809), XIV.401; Carpenter, K. (1986), pp.59–60, 68, 75–98.

CHAPTER 18

1 Guerrini (1999a), p.34.
2 For a selection of over one thousand texts that address the use of the vegetable diet, cf. Aberdour (1791), pp.54, 80–1; Buchan (1772), pp.56, 80, 87, 171, 218, 226–7, 245, 309, 380, 391, 398, 420, 424, 426, 433, 446, 473, 495–6, 501–4, 541, 545, 624, 659; Culpeper ([1794?]), II.125–6,

150, 152, 163, 168, 179, 183–4, 208; Atkins (1758), pp.23–9, 46, 170, 319; James, ed. (1750), p.7; Tissot (1774), I.69, 86, 119, 135, 151; Willich (1799), pp.43, 227, 300–1, 308–10, 358, 364, 603–4; Carter (1788), I.9–10, 30, 102, II.22–4, 45–8; Adair (1799), pp.18–19–23, 123; Adair (1786), p.88; Adair (1787b), pp.194–5, 209, 248, 257, 268–9, 368–70, 374–5; Adair (1772), pp.89, 90; Addington (1753), pp.16, 31; Anon. (1786), I.30–4; Aitken (1782), p.365; Aitken (1779), p.126; Allen (1733), pp.37–8; Adam (1789), II.523; Reid (1798), p.275; Reid (1795), pp.15–16; *The Aberdeen Magazine*, 3 vols (Aberdeen, 1788–90), I.548, 648; Armstrong (1783), pp.113–14, 194–5; Armstrong (1737), pp.317, 321; Anon. (1773), p.91; Ball (1762), I.310; Barker ([1795?]), pp.131–2; Barry (1726), p.154.

3 Boerhaave (1742–6b), I.96–104. For the original Latin, which includes the interesting bibliographic references, see Boerhaave (1742–6a), I.54ff.

4 Boerhaave (1742–6b), I.96–7.

5 Boerhaave (1742–6b), I.101–2, 104, 224–5, 309; cp. I.257; Boerhaave (1735), II.205–9.

6 Boerhaave (1742–6b), I.96–101, 257, VI.246–7; Boerhaave (1742–6a), I.65–7; Boerhaave (1735), II.205; Boerhaave (1731), p.422.

7 Theophrastus (1916), I.312–15; Theophrastus (1644), pp.347–53. I have not deciphered Boerhaave's reference 'histor stirp.' ('the history of stems'?); his reference to p.337 may be intended to be Theophrastus (1644), p.347 (p.337 is mispaginated as p.343). Porphyry claimed that Theophrastus himself was a vegetarian (cf. Haussleiter (1935), pp.237–45). On the paradisiacal *Ficus Indicus* and its alternate identification with the Banian Tree and the banana, see Tavernier

(1995), p.197+n.; Saint-Pierre (1997b), p.52; Lord (1630), p.58; Purchas (1626), p.17; Prest (1981), pp.78–81; Evelyn (2000), pp.418–19; Shoulson (2000), p.892.

8 Boerhaave was drawing on Tulpius (1672), pp.296–7.

9 cp. Boerhaave (1742–6b), VI.241. Boerhaave collected innumerable vegetarian sources; cf. Boerhaave (1742–6a), I.54, 63–9; Boerhaave (1719), pp.279–81; Sinclair (1807), II.i.168–9.

10 Boerhaave (1742–6b), I.101–2; Boerhaave (1962), II.352–7, III.37–9, 247, 251.

11 Haller (1754), I.iv–v.

12 Haller (1754), II.123; Drummond and Wilbraham (1939), pp.276–7.

13 Haller (1754), I.xxvi, xxxiv, xxxviii, II.340, 346, 360–1, 369, 423–4; Sinclair (1807), II.i.169–70; Newton, J.F. (1897), p.33.

14 Haller (1772), I.29, 34; Haller (1773), p.iii; Haller (1786), I.85–9, and see ch.18, pp.274–5 below.

15 Haller (1754), II.119–23; cf. Himsel (1751); Haller (1751), ch.22, p.373; cf. Brendel (1751); Haller (1786), I.v–vi, 85–9+n.

16 Haller (1751), pp.688–707.

17 Shuttleton (1992), p.47.

18 [Monro] (1744), pp.14–18; cf. Brückner pp.82–5; (1768), pp.61–2+n.

19 Monro (1783), pp.20–3; cf. Scull (2000), pp.14–15.

20 Brandt (c.1930); I have not been able to trace the source of Darwin's comment.

21 Royal College of Physicians of Edinburgh, Cullen Mss, #18 'Lectures on physiology', 5 vols (c.1770), V.77–81; cf. V.73–5.

22 Royal College of Physicians of Edinburgh, Cullen Mss, #30 'Dr William Cullen's Consultation Letters', 21 vols, vol.2 ([1764]–1770), second pagination sequence, pp.2–6; cf. first pagination sequence: ff.1r, 2v, 18r–19r, 25r–26r, 32r–v.

23 Cullen Mss, #30.

24 Cullen used abbreviations heavily, and I have expanded these to modern usage. Cullen Mss, #18, V.77–81; cf. V.73–5. Rosalie Stott says that Cullen thought meat was less easily digested. But Cullen says that meat's putrescency aids its digestion ('it is this putrescency yt converts it in to a State fit to be thrown out of ye Body' (V.77–8)). Indeed, he thought that a little bit of meat could help the digestion of less putrescent vegetable food: 'I suspect there is a peculiar fluid or menstruum [in the stomach] beginning putrefaction, & that power is freq[uent]ly too weak, so not able to Digest vegetable food, & therefore it requires ye Assistance of Animal food' (V.81).

25 Cullen Mss, #18, I.78, 127; IV.55–7, 63, 135; V.9–10, 37, 45, 47, 74, 80–2; Cullen (1771), p.20; William Cullen, 'The art of health', unpublished Mss, Glasgow University, Cullen/Thomson Mss; William Cullen, 'An essay on the hypochondriac disease', unpublished Mss, Glasgow University, Cullen/Thomson Mss, e.g. pp.54, 74; quoted in Stott (1987).

26 Stott (1987).

27 Smith, A. (1776), I.200–2, 235, II.492; cf. I.122–3, Bigland (1816), pp.66–7. cf. also Tryon (1695b), p.63; Ritson (1802), pp.81, 192–5; Lambe (1805), p.36; Lambe (1815), p.220.

28 Fania Oz-Salzberger, 'Ferguson, Adam (1723–1816)', ODNB; 'Joseph Black', DNB; Allen, D. (2001), p.276n.; Doig (1982), pp.39–41; Cockburn (1856), pp.48–51; Ferguson & Playfair (1997), pp.85, 87, 93, 95, 103, 113–17; Black (1816), VII.230–5.

29 Sinclair (1807), I.430.

30 Stark (1788), pp.ix–xi, 92–3.

31 Franklin (1986), pp.17, 39–40, 52, 93, 244, 252, 259; Schwartz (2001); Morton (2002), pp.82–4; Barkas (1975), p.135; Brands (2002), pp.33, 40–1, 57, 76, 100, 624; Combe (1860), p.148; Franklin did occasionally return to the vegetable diet after the cod episode (Spencer (1993), p.232). In Philadelphia Franklin apparently knew the printer William Bradford (the son-in-law of Tryon's publisher Andrew Sowle) and published works by Charles Woolverton who also produced for Bradford Sowle's Upright Lives of the Heathen (Upright Lives [1740]).

32 Ramsay (1966), p.xx.

33 Ramsay (1966), p.xxi; cf. Fuller (1711), sig.[A6v–A7r].

34 Ramsay (1966), pp.204–5, 237; cf. pp.163, 194, 212, 216–17, 274–5.

35 Ramsay (1966), pp.204–5, 207; Sinclair (1802), p.4; Sinclair (1807), I.377–8, 396, 400–1, 422–30.

36 Ramsay (1966), p.147.

37 Ramsay (1966), p.261; cf. pp.137, 237, 274–5.

38 Ramsay (1966), p.213.

39 Ramsay (1966), p.261; for Keir's health cf. pp.xxii, 85, 87, 89, 292. Sinclair (1802), p.4; though Sinclair had also written that the diet of the studious 'ought to consist chiefly of vegetables' (Sinclair (1807), I.427–8).

40 Ramsay (1966), p.261; cf. p.23.

41 Ramsay (1966), p.184.

42 For Gregory in Ramsay's letters, see Ramsay (1966), pp.49, 97–8.

43 Ramsay (1966), pp.204–5; cf. p.xxvi.

44 Ramsay (1966), pp.204, 287–8, 292; cf. Leask (2002), pp.205–18.

45 Graham (1813), p.63; cf. pp.24–5, 27; Graham (1814), p.276.

46 Graham (1813), p.15+n.; cf. p.viii; cit. Leask (2002), p.216; cf. Graham (1814), pp.282n., 371.

47 Hope (1780), pp.46–8, 180–3, 200, 339.

48 Ramsay (1888), II.327–35; cf. Ramsay (1996), I.v–viii.

49 Ramsay (1888), II.327–35; Allen, D. (2001), p.271.

50 Allen, D. (2001); [John

Williamson], 'A Just Complaint', National Library of Scotland: Adv. Ms 23.6.3. The manuscript is entered in the printed copy of *Catalogue of the Library of the Faculty of Advocates*, 3 vols (Edinburgh, 1742–1807), III.459, which can be viewed online at ECCO.

51 Williamson, 'Just Complaint', f.7v.

52 Williamson, 'Just Complaint', f.1v, 6v; Allen, D. (2001), pp.286–7.

53 Williamson, 'Just Complaint', f.9r–v.

54 Allen, D. (2001), pp.278–9+n.; see ch. 16 above; [Tryon] ([1684b]), pp.217–18.

55 Williamson, 'Just Complaint', f.2r–v, 4r; Allen, D. (2001), pp.286–7; cf. ch.5 p.76–7 above. Allen's article (Allen, D. (2001)) interprets Williamson's providentialism as a manifestion of Scottish Calvinist evangelical Presbyterianism. A Calvinist background might have made Williamson more open to Tryon's puritanical austerity, but Williamson's Providence acts principally through the laws of nature; it is unmistakably Tryonist and is nearer to deism than Calvinism. Allen appears to believe John Ramsay's testimony that Williamson believed in metempsychosis, even though Williamson says nothing about metempsychosis (he speaks of souls as rays of divinity (f.5r–v, 8r)). Allen cites Tryon's *Way to Health* in a discussion of metempsychosis, though that work says nothing about metempsychosis either. Allen does not mention the fact that Williamson names Tryon (perhaps because Williamson, or the transcriber of his manuscript, mis-spelled him 'Tyron'). Allen does not mention George Cheyne either, perhaps again because Williamson used the variant spelling 'Chein'. Cheyne and Tryon provide the principal context for Williamson's vegetarian providentialism. Allen also says that Williamson 'reaches out unexpectedly to Stoicism' by citing Arrian and Strabo; Williamson cites them because they were the principal authorities on the ancient Brahmins. Allen also says that Pope was vegetarian and Arbuthnot espoused vegetarianism, neither of which are true: the latter vigorously opposed Cheyne's vegetarianism (see chs 13 and 16 above). Allen's discussion is also hampered by regular misreading of the manuscript, especially his confusion of the letters 'r', 'n', and 'm'; for example, reading Banians as 'Barians', Arianus as 'Ariarrus', Porphirius as 'Porphinus', Josephus as 'Josephius' etc. Allen says that Williamson's nickname 'Brachman' was the term used to refer to all eighteenth-century vegetarians, whereas it was in fact rare; the label suited Williamson in particular because he openly revered the Brahmins. cf. also Ramsay (1727), II.i.6–7, II.ii.2–5, 42, 123–6, 127–31; Ramsay (1748), II.311–12, 323–5, [463–4].

56 Williamson, 'Just Complaint', f.6v. Allen, D. (2001), p.293.

57 Tryon (1697) [NLS, RB.s.381]; Allen mentioned the Tryon work with the Hopetoun bookplate, but did not reveal its location. Thanks to Graham Hogg at the NLS for help in identifying the contents of the Hopetoun Library. For Williamson's method of acquiring vegetarian books, cf. Ramsay (1888), II.327–8. In addition to Tryon's, Williamson could have found many works relating to vegetarianism in the Hopetoun House Library, notably those of Pythagoras, Plutarch, Ovid, Lessius, Floyer, Josephus and many ancient and modern accounts of India including A. and J. Churchill's collection which he

mentions; see for example Hopetoun House (1962), [Press No: Shelf No.] A:4, A:5, B:4, C:6, D:1, D:2, D:3, T:8; Hopetoun House (1889), p.32 (Item 510), p.74.

58 Williamson, 'Just Complaint', f.8v–10v; *The Royal Magazine* (J. Coote, London, August 1759), I.61–3; Crab, R. (1745). On Robert Cook see ch. 5 above.

59 Williamson, 'Just Complaint', f.7v–9r.

60 Harris (1705).

61 Williamson, 'Just Complaint', f.7r.

62 Williamson, 'Just Complaint', f.3v.

63 Williamson, 'Just Complaint', f.3v–4v; Allen, D. (2001), pp.276–7.

64 Williamson, 'Just Complaint', f.5v–6r; Stoneman (1991), pp.132–3; Tryon (1691a), p.369.

65 Williamson, 'Just Complaint', f.10r; Allen, D. (2001), p.286.

66 Tudge (2003), pp.145–6.

67 *GM* (August 1787).

68 Ramsay (1966), pp.25, 75, 147, 260–1; Ritson (1802), pp.195–8; Ritson correctly argued that Williamson did not believe in reincarnation.

69 Lovejoy (1933), p.275+n.

70 Pottle (1966), p.4; cf. pp.20, 33–5; Thomas, K. (1983), p.295.

71 Pottle (1966), p.26.

72 Thomas, K. (1983), pp.159–60.

73 Pottle (1966), p.133; Stone (1977), p.356.

74 Johnson, S. (1952), II.350, 375; cf. I.329, II.282, 306, 328, 338, 349, 344; cf. Johnson (1970), p.76; Ritson (1802), p.154.

75 Thomas, K. (1983), p.178.

76 Buffon (1753), IV.437–42; William King, Frances Hutcheson, Pufendorf, John Clarke all concurred with Buffon and Jenyns (see ch. 16 above).

77 Thomas, K. (1983), p.298.

78 Monboddo (1773–92), I.204–15, 223–4+n., 227–9, 251–60; Lovejoy (1933).

79 [Monboddo] (1797), pp.1–29, 34, 41; [Monboddo] (1795),

pp.288–94. Oglethorpe actually only lived to 88 (1696–1785). Cloyd (1972), pp.60, 126–8, 169–70; Douthwaite (1997).

80 Cloyd (1972), pp.58–9.

81 Boswell (1799), ch.31, 1777.

82 Boswell (1786), pp.205–11, cf. pp.187–8, 230, 311, 326, 427; Johnson, S. (1952), I.344.

83 Boswell (1886), V.122.

CHAPTER 19

1 Lach (1971), I.439–40.

2 That Hindu asceticism exceeded Western asceticism was proverbial; see e.g. Yule, ed. (1915), III.260; cf. Teltscher (1995), pp.86–7; Lorenzen (1996).

3 Rubiés (2000), pp.5–10; Lach (1971), I.245, 250, 258–61, 278, 280, 292–9, 679–80; Milton (2002), pp.94–8.

4 Nobili (1971), pp.12–13 and *passim*; Rajamanickam (1967), pp.2–5; Cronin (1959), frontispiece drawing, pp.51, 56–7, 69–71+n., 73–5, 79–80, 127, 133, 147, 153, 224, 230, 251; Županov (1999), pp.3–5, 22–9, 34, 47–71 and *passim*; Lach (1971), I.280, 328–9; Rubiés (2000), p.317; Teltscher (1995), pp.74–6; Bayly, S. (1992), pp.390, 393–4; Hudson (1994), pp.23–4+n., 44; Schwab (1984), pp.28–9, 147, 155; Neill (1985), pp.75–9, 90; Piolet (1901), II.187–8; Bachmann (1972), pp.45–9+nn., 53; Dahmen (1924), frontispiece portrait showing Nobili wearing a sacred thread, pp.22–30, 43–53.

5 Pillei (1840), based on the 1798 mss by the poet Saminda Pillei; *cit.* Hudson (2000), p.23; Neill (1985), p.87.

6 Manucci (1965), III.303–5, 341, IV.69–70; cf. Bachmann (1972), pp.47–8+n.

7 Hudson (2000), pp.8–9.

8 Forbes (1813), I.406; Buchanan (1807), II.391; Bayly, S. (1992), pp.284–5; cf. p.348. Susan Bayly

suggests that this was a recent move by the Syrian Christians to distance themselves from Kshatriyas and strengthen their relations with Brahmans, for example by claiming that they were descended from Brahmans converted by St Thomas. This may be so, but Hindu infiltrations into the community, such as belief in transmigration, had been criticised for centuries (Lach (1971), I.268–9). cf. Fryer (1909), II.14, 282–3.

9 Lord (1630), II.40; Fryer (1909), I.293+n.

10 Collingham (2001), pp.26–8; Bayly, C. (1990), pp.157–8; Hudson (2000), p.23; Bugge (1994), p.65; Bayly, S. (1992), pp.284–5; Dubois (1999), pp.213–14.

11 Pollock (1993), pp.276–7.

12 Conversation with Dr Yunus Jaffery, December 2002; Tavernier (1995), I.218. The continuities between the European and Mughal responses to India are yet to receive full treatment; see Rubiés (2000), e.g. pp.38–9, 70–1, 286; Alam and Alavi (2001), e.g. pp.34–5; Targhi (1996).

13 Abul Fazl (1783–6), I.371; Findly (1934), pp.252–3.

14 This passage is based on the 1780s translation, but I have added one clause from the complete modern translation which emphasises Akbar's objections to cruelty: Abul Fazl (1783–6), I.84; Abul Fazl (1993), I.61, 64–5; cf. Richards (2000), p.47; Husain (1987), pp.36–7; Nizami (1991). For Sufic fasting practices generally, see e.g. Schimmel (2003), pp.114–17.

15 Burke (1989), p.123 (cf. ch. 8 above); Andhare (2004), pp.224–6; Choudhury (1997), pp.19, 123, 144; Wellesz (1952), pp.15–16; V&A (1982), pp.12–13.

16 Jahangir (1968), I.45, 240; Burke (1989), p.126; Koch (1988), p.33; Findly (1934); Chandra (1960); Andhare (2004).

17 Srivastava (2001), Plate 25, pp.25, 33–5, 39–40, 98; cf. Chandra (1976), p.87, Plate 27; Brand and Lowry (1986), pp.63, 67, 104, 153; Koch (1988), pp.8, 31 and *passim*; Ahmed, ed. (1995), pp.14–25, 33, 39, 44–6; V&A (1982), p.14; Srivastava (2001), Plate 57. Thanks to the late Nausheen Jaffery. Jesuit missionaries presented Akbar with a copy of the multi-lingual Bible that had been produced by Christopher Plantyn, the printer who collaborated with Guillaume Postel and the Family of Love in an attempt to unite disparate religions (see chs 2 and 8 above). The frontispiece bore the Isaiahan image of the wolf and lion in peaceful company with the lamb and the ox, a symbol of millenarian peace. Akbar and Jahangir adapted this into one of their favourite imperial icons, and Aurungzeb even had a live lion and goat paraded in public, suggesting that his reign had pacified even the animals. For Indian painting representing animals approaching musicians and ascetics see e.g. Topsfield, ed. (2000), pp.4, 66; Archer (1973), pp.24, 28, 72, 302; Beach (1974), VIII. Fig.4; Falk and Archer (1981), pp.376–7, 492.

18 Haykel (2004); Leach (1995), II.949–52, col. pl.137.

19 Tavernier (1995), I.296+n., 309–10; cf. Manucci (1965), II.309–10; Ritson (1802), p.156.

20 Husain (1987), pp.36–40; cf. 43, 44, 56, 284.

21 Marshall, ed. (1970), pp.107–27.

22 Harrison, M. (1999), pp.82–3; Collingham (2001), pp.27–8.

23 Chakravarty (2005); Husain (1987), pp.162, 166–7. My thanks also to John Lennard; Bayly, C. (1996); Dubois (1999), p.214ff+n.; Gupta (1998); Brown, Frykenberg and Low, eds (2002), p.205; Neill (2002), pp.360–1;

Collingham (2001), pp.55–6, 188; Bayly, C. (1990), pp.165–7.

24 cf. Goldsmith (1774 –[1785?]), II.179–80.

25 Dubois (1999), pp.xvi–xvii, xxvii–xxviii; 210–19, 631–6; Montesquieu (1914), Bk XIV, ch.15; Bk XXIV, chs 21, 24; cf. Bk XIV, chs 2, 10; Bk XXV, ch.4. Montesquieu was following Bernier (1999), pp.326–7, see ch. 4 note 79 above. The vegetarian friend of Percy Bysshe Shelley, Dr William Lambe, later observed that Montesquieu's comments about the relation between Asian despotism and vegetarianism were indebted to Hippocrates who had written that their vegetable diet made Asians effeminate and unwarlike, and thus easy to oppress; Lambe (1815), pp.18–20; Hippocrates, *Liber de Aere, Aquis et Locis*, xxxi, xxxii, xxxix, liii–liv. cf. Pseudo-Clement (2005a), Bk IX, ch.27 which argued that the doctrine of climatic determination was untenable because, for example, 'in the one country of India there are both persons who feed on human flesh, and persons who abstain even from the flesh of sheep, and birds, and all living creatures'. cf. Aronson (1946), p.30ff; Neill (1985), p.277; Rubiés (2000), p.202+n.; Murr (1987), vol.II, ch.1.

26 Teltscher (2000), pp.160–4; Harrison, M. (1999), p.168.

27 Fryer (1909), I.177–80+nn., cf. I.209–10. Fryer, however, thought it a more important factor that Europeans had a fixed natural constitution which was unsuited to the climate; cp. Harrison, M. (1999), p.51. In his *De medecina indorum* (Leiden, 1642), Jacob Bondt, a physician in the Dutch settlement of Batavia, allowed tropical travellers to eat all sorts of flesh, though he reckoned that the Indians were, of all people, 'the most careful of preserving their health, and observe a regular and temperate course of diet', living 'almost entirely upon vegetables, after the manner of Pythagoras' (Bondt (1769), pp.129, 133–4, 156–7).

28 Tryon (1691a), pp.94–5; cf. pp.143–4; [Tryon] (1684a), pp.48–61, 68; Tryon (1682b), p.8; [Tryon] (1702), pp.183–4, 199–200, 206–7, 215–16, 234–7.

29 Harrison, M. (1999), pp.51–2; Polo (1972), pp.278–9; Bernier (1999), pp.253–4, 327; Ovington (1929), pp.186–7.

30 Clark (1773), p.332; Bondt (1769), pp.133–4; Fryer (1909), III.146–9; Edwards (1799), pp.127–8; Moffet (1746), p.34; Andree (1788), p.12; Falconer (1781), pp.iv–v, 231–2; Gregory (1788), p.54.

31 Harrison, M. (1996), pp.73–8; Harrison, M. (1999), Preface, pp.11, 47–9, 81–2, 86 and *passim*; Harrison, M. (1994), pp.36–40 and *passim*; Collingham (2001), pp.25–8; Glacken (1990), pp.565–610.

32 Armstrong (1992), pp.32–3; Juvenal, Satire 14, ll.98–9; Darwin, E. (1803), IV.419–28.

33 Johnson (1813), pp.433–7; cf. pp.444–5; Johnson (1837), pp.10–11; Harrison, M. (1999), pp.81–2, 85; Collingham (2001), pp.26–8; Stuart, T. (2003), pp.5–6; Cullen Mss, #18, V.77–81. Cullen also acknowledged that a sparse diet could make people more susceptible to contagions (V.81–2). The idea relates to the standard notion of the vegetable being insufficient to maintain strength, which Sydenham and others grappled with a hundred years earlier (see ch.13 above). cf. also Adair (1787b), pp.268–9; Johnson (1827), pp.136, 138–9.

34 Teltscher (1995), p.96; Lach (1971), I.439–40; Tavernier (1995), I.195–6+n., 203; Linschoten (1988), I.252–5; Sinha (1993), pp.28–9.

35 Pillai (1907–28), XI.79.

36 Pillai (1907–28), IV.52, 144–152+n.; cp. V.334–5, 416.

37 Pillai (1907–28), IX.93, 325, XI.20–3, 90, 250, 255.

38 Pillai (1907–28), VI.179; IX.252–3, 258–9; X.166, 340; XI.311–12, 334.

39 Pillai (1907–28), VIII.401, IX.xii–xiii, xxii.

40 Not unusually, Ananda Ranga endorsed animal sacrifice, Pillai (1907–28), X.285.

41 Pillai (1907–28), III.388, X.56; cf. XII.16.

42 Pillai (1907–28), III.325–6, 388; IV.100, 164, 290, 373–5; V.412, 440, 449; VII.286; VIII.238, 332, 340, 344, 369; IX.286; XII.84, 127.

43 Pillai (1907–28), XI.372–4.

44 Pillai (1907–28), VI.267, IX.150–1, XI.162–3.

45 Pillai (1907–28), VI.264–5; cf. IX.189, 399–400. This practice continued into the twentieth century, see Collingham (2001), pp.55–6, 188.

46 Pillai (1907–28), VIII.296–7; I have changed the translations 'animal food' to 'animal fodder' to avoid the misleading sense of 'animal food' as 'meat'.

47 Pillai (1907–28),VII.354, he comments about Frenchmen getting drunk; and X.374 criticises Europe bringing their own fierce warfare to India.

48 Pillai (1907–28), II.70–2; cp. Pillai (1907–28), V.346, VII.267, XII.163.

49 Pillai (1907–28), V.300–10, IX.6–12; cf. III.247–9, V.334–5.

50 Burke (1958–78), IV.344, 356–7, 361–2, 367–8, 371–2 + nn. cf. IV.411–12, V.200; Burke (1981), pp.13–14, 392–400.

51 Burke (1958–78), I.45–7.

CHAPTER 20

1 For Records of Holwell's private trading, cf. Sinha (1957), e.g. pp.193–5, 303.

2 For a sample of Holwell's heroic reputation, cf. Croft (1780), p.30;

Greville (1793), II.436–7; Townsend (1781), p.47; Parker (1782), ch.7; Grose (1766), II.452–61; Belsham (1798), I.455.

3 Marshall (2000), pp.319–20.

4 Holwell (1766–7), Pt I.

5 Sinha (1957), pp.xliv, 20–1, 33–4. For Holwell's rhetorical use of Mughal tyranny, see e.g. Holwell (1779), I.21, II.13.

6 Holwell's monument was moved to an inconspicuous site in the grounds of St John's Church. On Holwell, the sack of Calcutta, the incident of the Black Hole, and subsequent controversies see e.g. *CR* (1767), vol.23, pp.155–7; Hill, ed. (1905), e.g. I.xxiii, xliv, 50–1, III.413–14; Sinha (1957), pp.38–9, 82, 83, 193–5, 203; Busteed (1908), pp.47–52; *GM* (February 1767), Vol.XXXVII, pp.79, 84; and the following manuscripts in OIOC: Mss Eur/Orme IV.17, pp.1003–26; IV.18, pp.1027–33; Mss Eur/Orme XII.1 (7), e.g. p.3077; Mss Eur/Orme J.6, p.67; Mss Eur/Orme J.14, pp.97–102; Mss Eur/Orme OV 19.16, pp.167–8; Mss Eur/Orme OV 21.2–5 (espec. 21.2 (1), pp.5–8; 21.2 (2), pp.9–12; 21.2 (4), p.17; 21.2 (5), pp.21–37; 21.3, pp.41–56; 21.4, pp.57–9); Mss Eur/Orme OV 28.1 (3), pp.45–56; Mss Eur/Orme OV 222.12, p.11; Mss Eur/Orme OV 222.13, p.12; Mss Eur/Orme OV 222. 93, p.68; Mss Eur/Orme OV 293.22, pp.87–90; Mss Eur/Orme OV 293.26, pp.101–5; Sutton Court Collection, Mss Eur F 128, p.135; Clive collection, Mss Eur G 37; Mss Eur B165; Mss Minutes of House of Commons 27 Mar–13 Apr 1766–7; Mss Eur D804; Mss Eur D 1018; Keay (1993), pp.299–313; Spurr (1996); Teltscher (1995), p.120; Teltscher (1996). For the British use of 'Mughal despotism' to justify their own colonial conquest, see e.g. Mss Eur/Orme VI.11, p.1493, where it is anticipated that 'the

whole Gentoo race . . . would
rejoice to submit to any other
masters, & especially to the
English'; Mss Eur/Orme IV.19,
pp.1034–50, p.1034; Camões
(1776), p.ix; Teltscher (1995),
pp.229–59.

7 Priestley (1799), pp.2, 10, 30,
34–5, 56–7, 121, 150, 174,
187–8, 192, 211, 279; cf. Priestley
(1782), I.304–7; cf. e.g. [Halhed]
(1776), pp.15–17; [Wilkins,
Charles, tr.] (1787), pp.lxiii–xci;
Moore (1790), I.11–12.

8 On karmic rebirth in Hinduism,
and its similarity to Pythagorean
'ethicized' metempsychosis, see ch.
4, note 7 above.

9 Holwell (1779), I.131, 143–4.

10 Holwell (1779), I.4–5; for Holwell
on the four ages, see also II.158,
169, 173–5, 179–80. The
universality of the story of the
golden age also inspired John
Oswald (1791), pp.65–8+nn.; cf.
Ramsay (1727), II.i.6–9, 136–7;
II.ii.127–31; Ramsay (1748),
II.283. On the possible exchange
between Iran, India and Greece
between the eighth and third
centuries BC of the myth of the
four ages which decline in virtue,
see O'Flaherty (1976), p.18.

11 Holwell (1779), II.109; cp.
Holwell's later criticism of nations'
vying for greater antiquity in
Holwell (1786), p.62.

12 In the equation of Birmah and
Christ, Holwell was
simultaneously adapting and
contesting Baldaeus' suggestion
that the Hindu belief that 'Brama'
was the son of God in human
form had derived 'from what they
have heard (tho' perhaps
confusedly) of Jesus Christ'.
Holwell simply pointed out that
the Hindu myth was antecedent to
Christianity and therefore the debt
was likely to be the other way
round (Mss Eur/Orme VI.11,
pp.1424–99, Holwell, '[Account
the Shastah] Druga, or the
religious principles of the

Gentoos' (1750), p.1431). Also
revising Baldaeus, Holwell
disaggregated the Hindu God
Bramah into three entities – Brum
the divine spirit, Birmah the
personal god figurative of creation,
and Bramah the prophet (which
he sometimes considered an
incarnation or avatar of Birmah)
(Holwell (1970), p.90; Holwell
(1779), I.5, 12; II.71–2, 76, 90,
110; cf. [Mickle] (1787), p.166).

13 Holwell (1970), pp.72–4. John
Marshall referred to demons and
gods as the good and evil 'dewta'
in Marshall, J. (1702), (no. 268),
pp.731, 733; cf. Manucci (1965),
III.28.

14 Holwell's source may have been
Ramsay (1727), II.ii.2–5; cf. ch. 7,
13 and 16 above.

15 Holwell (1970), pp.85–6.

16 Holwell (1779), II.160–2. For
Holwell's eschatology and place in
the history of Orientalism, see
Holwell (1970), pp.46, 62–3,
72–90; Holwell (1779), 'Preface',
I.5, 12–15, 22, 151–2; II.1–227;
Marshall (1970), pp.5–6, 26–7;
Murray, ed. (1998), p.98–9;
Trautmann (1997); Schwab
(1984), pp.7, 29–30, 33, 77,
149–53.

17 Asiatic Annual Register (1800),
pp.25–31; Holwell (1971); cf.
Aitken (1782), p.365; Tissot
(1774), I.135; Aberdour (1791),
pp.54, 80–1; Saint-Pierre (1826),
III.169; Society in Edinburgh
(1787), VIII.231–2.

18 Holwell (1779), II.97–8, 119–20;
see ch. 17 note 7 above.

19 Edward Said, 'Foreword' in
Schwab (1984), pp.xi–xii.

20 Holwell (1779), II.97–9, 104,
143; [Mickle] (1787), p.165.

21 Holwell cites Ilive in Holwell
(1779), II.39, 99, 143; Colin
Haydon, 'Sherlock, Thomas
(1677–1761)', ODNB; Ilive
(1736), pp.1, 7–8, 15–32, 60–2;
Revelation 12:4–9; 2 Peter 2:4
(not 2:14 as Ilive says). Holwell,
giving a harsher sentence, said

that those who had not repented before the end of the world would be plunged into the fiery *Onderah* forever (Holwell (1779), II.200–1).

22 Berrow (1772), § i and iii; Berrow (1762), p.75n.; cf. Cheyne (1740), pp.26, 31, 86–7. For St Augustine's analogous doctrine that animal suffering could have no purpose, see Passmore (1975), p.205; James A. Herrick, 'Ilive, Jacob (bap. 1705, d. 1763)', *ODNB*; A.B. Grosart, 'Berrow, Capel (1715–1782)', rev. S.J. Skedd, *ODNB*. Berrow believed that all souls would be saved after passing through a purgatorial fire: Berrow (1772), II.11, 15, 19–20. Holwell cites and quotes from Berrow (1779), II.37–8, 124–5, 131, 133–5.

23 Ramsay (1727), II.ii.98–127. On Ramsay's blend of deism and mysticism, especially his association with Cheyne's Quietist guru, Mme Guyon, and even the similarity of his hybrid theology to the *Turkish Spy*, cf. Betts (1984), pp.107–8, 235–7.

24 Ramsay (1727), I.71, 85, 89–90; II.ii.2–5, 10–12, 42, 98–102, 110, 121–42. Ramsay repeated this work and elaborated on his own beliefs in a later work which Holwell may also have seen: Ramsay (1748), II.217–19, 225, 234–7, 242, 244–7, 252–3, 274–83, 304, 311–14, 323–7, 354–6, [463–4].

25 Ramsay (1727), II.ii.125–6.

26 Bougeant (1740), title page, pp.1–26 and *passim*; cf. Rosenfield (1968), pp.22, 136–41; Serjeantson (2001), pp.439–42; Voltaire (1765a), 'Brachmanes'; Passmore (1975), pp.204–5; Hildrop (1742–3), I.14–15, 52; II.7–15, 38, 40, 42–3, 47–9, 72–3, 77. cf. O[verton] (1643), pp.49–51; [Hildrop] (1722), pp.28, 30–1, 41–2, 44, 70; Hildrop (1752), pp.5–6, 26–33. Hildrop

studiously avoids the thorny issue that the end of husbandry is the abattoir. When he lists the uses of domestic animals, he mentions labour, woollen clothes, and milk; he does not mention the use of their flesh. cf. Guidi (1782), pp.7, 106; Thomas, K. (1983), p.140; Turner (1980), p.8.

27 Holwell (1971), pp.155–6; O'Flaherty, ed. (1980), pp.29, 223–5. O'Flaherty (1976), pp.57, 65–70, 78, 230, 258; Festugière (1936), pp.593–4; Walli (1974), p.75.

28 Marshall, ed. (1970), pp.6–7, 26–7.

29 *GM* (September 1765), vol.XXXV, pp.413–17, *GM* (November–December & Supplement 1766), Vol.XXXVI, pp.542–3, 566–9, 608–10.

30 Raynal (1783), I.52, 83, 86–90; Teltscher (1995), p.162.

31 Sinner (1771); Kurth-Voigt (1999), pp.53–6; Schwab (1984), pp.149–52.

32 Camões (1776), pp.291–300n.; [Mickle] (1787), p.169; Mss Eur/ Orme OV 8.14, pp.67–103, *Mémoires de l'origine et etablissement de Siks* (before 1772), p.83.n.9; cf. ch. 4 note 59 above and ch. 25 below; Cheyne (1724), p.91.

33 *CR* Vol.20 (1765), pp.145–8; *CR* Vol.22 (1766), pp.340–2; *CR* Vol.23 (1767), pp.155–7; *CR* Vol.26 (1768), pp.81–90, 182ff., 241ff.; cf. Holwell (1779), II.75; Schwab (1984), p.149.

34 *GM* (1798), vol.LXVIII, pt.ii, pp.998–9; cf. *Asiatic Annual Register* (1800), pp.25–31.

35 H.G.K., 'J.Z. Holwell', *DNB* (1891); D.L. Prior, 'J.Z. Holwell', *ODNB*.

36 *Monthly Review* (Dec 1771), XLV.428; *cit.* John Drew (1998), p.80n.

37 [Holwell] (1786), pp.20–3, 34, 49–51 and *passim*; see the similar forces described by Plotinus,

Agrippa, Henry More, Glanvill, Tryon, Conway, Cheyne and Marsay *et al.* chs 5, 7, 13 above; [Holwell] (1776), *passim*; Marshall (1970), p.6; Holwell (1779), II.16, 72–4.

38 [Holwell] (1776), pp.32–3.
39 Mickle (1787), pp.165–9; Montluzin (n.d.); Camões (1776), p.295n.
40 Marshall, ed. (1970), pp.7, 23; Alexander Dow, 'A Dissertation concerning the Customs, Manners, Language, Religion and Philosophy of the Hindoos', in Marshall, ed. (1970), pp.107–27; Dow (1768–72); Sinner (1771); Kurth-Voigt (1999), pp.53–6; Schwab (1984), p.149.
41 Schwab (1984), pp.29–30, 156–7; Subrahmanyam (2000).
42 Schwab (1984), pp.xxiii, 4, 7, 24, 136–45, 158–61; Mitter (1977), pp.106–7; Schwab (1934), e.g. p.51; Williams, Howard (1883), pp.208–10; Targhi (1996).
43 Collingham (2001), pp.26–8, 32–41; Fisch (1985), pp.35–7; Liz Woods, 'Stuart, Charles (1757/8–1828)', *ODNB*; Archer and Falk (1989), p.46.
44 Voltaire (1937), p.24; Montesquieu (1914), Bk XXIV, ch.21; Bernier (1988), p.310; cp. Voltaire (1756), I.38–42; Voltaire (1765b), pp.101–2; Holwell (1779), II.84; Voltaire (1779–81), III.190–3; Williams, Howard (1883), pp.149–50.
45 Voltaire (1980–), XXXV.411–15; Voltaire (1775), pp.10–13; Voltaire (1768), p.38; cf. [Tyssot de Patot] (1743), pp.28–9; Tyssot de Patot (1997), ch. 2, I.43; McKee (1941), pp.80–4.
46 Voltaire (1937), pp.43–4; Voltaire (1779–81), III.190–3; Voltaire (1779–80), I.35, 42; Voltaire (1988), Letters 1–4, 17; Voltaire (1769); Voltaire (1777), n.26.
47 Voltaire (1765a), 'Brachmanes, Brames' cf. 'Ézourveidam', 'Métamorphose, Métempsycose';

Voltaire (1937), pp.2–3, 19–20, 24, 43–4+n.; Williams, Howard (1883), pp.149–54; cf. Aronson (1946), pp.16–28; Kopf (1964), p.46; Schwab (1984), pp.149–53; Poliakov (1974), ch. 9; Murray, ed. (1998), p.99.
48 Voltaire (1768), pp.38–42 (I have inserted the word 'acrid' as a correction from the French).
49 [Voltaire] (1770), p.84; cf. pp.12–13; Ecclesiastes 3:18–19.
50 Jones, W. (1970), I.251–2, II.430–1.
51 Jones, W. (1970), II.742, 756–8; cf. II.780; Jones, W. (1807), III.37; Teltscher (1995), pp.195–227; Schwab (1984), pp.158–61.
52 Manu (1794), pp.xviii, 129; Teltscher (1995), p.198.
53 Jones, W. (1970), II.764–6; Cannon (1990), pp.99, 281; cf. Price (1787), p.217; cf. pp.12, 22–3, 77.
54 Jones, W. (1970), II.750–3; Jones, W. (1799), I.153–4; Williams, Howard (1883), p.240; Keay (1988), p.34.
55 Jones, W. (1970), II.783; cf. II.743, 756, 793, 812–13.
56 Manu (1794), p.129.
57 Jones, W. (1970), Letter 147, to Viscount Althorp, Temple, 30 Nov [1777]; I.251–2, II.632–3, 637, 657, 687, 719, 772, 783. Jones' wife Anna also suffered ill health and followed a temperate diet which included fish and chicken broth (II.710, 726, 730).
58 Leask (1992); Kate Teltscher argued that William Jones, despite his dabbling in native customs and religion, never lost his original cultural identity. He did not lose his identity, but Indian customs did alter that identity: Teltscher (1995), p.201.

CHAPTER 21

1 Oswald, ed. (1788), No.1, 12 May 1787, p.31.
2 Erdman (1986), pp.13–20, 50,

119; for a discussion of the uncertain role of the British massacres in Oswald's resignation, cf. pp.24–31. Oswald ([1792]), p.46; Oswald, ed. (1788), No.2, May 1787, p.52. For later developments along these lines in India, cf. Roy (1997), II.1110; Kopf (1964), pp.10–16; Leask (1992), p.119.

3 Erdman (1986), p.7.

4 Haslewood (1795), II.222–5n.; cit. Ritson (1802), pp.198–200; Erdman (1986), pp.90–1.

5 Doddridge (1794), I.208n.

6 EM, XVII.198–9, cf. p.172, XI.169; Erdman (1986), pp.12, 36; Archenholtz (1787–91), VII.303ff.

7 Erdman (1986), p.7.

8 EM, XV.18–19; EM, XVII.116, 118, 162–5; EM, XIX.9–13, 169ff., 249–52, 329–33.

9 Erdman (1986), pp.118–19.

10 Haslewood (1795), II.222–5n.

11 Erdman (1986), pp.3, 8–9.

12 Wordsworth (1986), pp.3, 7, 21, 33, 100, 288–9; Oerlemans (1994).

13 Oswald (1791), pp.4–5+n., (pp.83–90); 52–8+nn.; Oswald ([1792]), pp.39–40; Erdman (1986), p.100.

14 Oswald (1791), Advertisement, p.ii; cf. Bentham (1789); ch. 24, p.360 below.

15 Oswald (1791), pp.1–10+n., (pp.90–2), 61–3+n., (pp.124–5) cf. pp.78–81. Oswald spent years writing his own 'Account of the Manners, Customs, History, Religion, Philosophy, &c. of Hindostan', which never reached the press and is now lost (Erdman (1986), pp.22–3, 32, 34). He had read and quoted from Alexander Dow, William Jones, the Abbé Raynal's adaptation of Holwell's Hinduism and various travel narratives; Raynal (1783), I.52, 83, 86–90.

16 Oswald (1791), p.28; cf. pp.3–10+nn., 66–73+nn.; Oswald ([1792]), p.8; Erdman (1986), pp.22–3; Passmore (1975).

17 Oswald, ed. (1788), No.1, 12 May 1787, p.6; No.2, May 1787, pp.37, 42. Compare his use of the common idea that hunting makes men ferocious, and agriculture makes them peaceful (Oswald (1791), pp.16–17).

18 Oswald (1791), pp.12–38+nn. (pp.92–113); Cheyne (1724), p.91.

19 Oswald (1791), pp.10–12, 18–19, 26, 41–3, 48–52; cf. Andrew Marvell, 'Nymph Complaining for the Death of her Faun'; Plutarch (1995), pp.551–3 (994F–995B).

20 Oswald ([1792]), pp.7, 11–12, 15, 16, 26, 31, 33, 41–2 (quote from p.49); Oswald (1791), pp.15–16, 33; cf. Schama (1989), p.27; cf. Darwin, E. (1794–6), II.669–71.

21 Schama (1989), pp.77, 82, 197, 260, 558.

22 Schama (1989), pp.43–4, 171, 258, 339; Erdman (1986), p.77; Ritson (1802), pp.70–7.

23 Franklin (1776–85), pp.6–7.

24 Spang (2000), pp.113, 133, 143; Erdman (1986), pp.77, 90–1; Schama (1989), pp.14, 339.

25 George and Stephens (1978), IV, § 4476, 4516, 4527, 4541, 4477, 4527, 4619, 4531; V, § 5028, 5611–12, 5081; VI, § 6508.

26 Smollett (1978), pp.130–1; George and Stephens (1978), VI, § 8145; cf. VII, § 8284, 8288–90, 8293, 8609; Morton (2000), p.113ff.

27 Oswald ([1792]), pp.41–2; Oswald (1791), pp.70–3+nn. (pp.132, 145–7); Porphyry (2000), Bk. II. paras 29–30; pp.66–7; cf. Spy, IV.16–17; Oswald, ed. (1788), No.2, May 1787, p.49.

28 [Oswald] (1789), pp.84, 92–3, 97ff., 101–3.

29 [Oswald] (1789), p.86.

30 cp. Erdman (1986), pp.56–60, 98–9; Morton (1994), pp.25–6.

31 Erdman (1986), pp.1–4, 9–10, 34–55, 73, 83, 88, 96–7, 118–19, 151.

32 Erdman (1986), pp.7, 91–4, 98, 113; Oswald ([1792]); Oswald (1793).

33 Erdman (1986), pp.73–6, 116–17, 124; Billington (1980), p.50.

34 Erdman (1986), pp.204–9.

35 Erdman (1986), pp.3–4, 120, 161, 187–265.

36 Erdman (1986), pp.90–1, 246.

37 Erdman (1986), pp.8–9.

38 Brougham (1803), II.134.

39 Erdman (1986), pp.8–11, 90–1, 171–80, 267–89; Conway (1892), II.97.

40 Erdman (1986), Preface, p.vii; Billington (1980).

CHAPTER 22

1 Patris (1930), p.145; Breck (2002), pp.61–2, 82–4, 220–2; Anon. (1797a), pp.150–4.

2 Breck (2002), p.220.

3 Anon. (1794), pp.84–5; Brissot (1830–2), I.234–5; cf. Breck (2002), pp.82–4. Valady had published an anti-war poem in 1783 in Chansons choisies, 4 vols (Londres [i.e. Paris], 1783), IV.98–9.

4 Patris (1930), pp.25–7, 132–3; Breck (2002), p.226.

5 Breck (2002), p.223; Anon. (1797a), pp.150–4; Anon. (1794), p.84; Patris (1930), p.148. In 1788 Valady subscribed to Bell's edition of Shakespeare, 20 vols (John Bell, London, 1785–80).

6 Patris (1930), pp.27–30; Breck (2002), pp.221–2.

7 Breck (2002), pp.225–7. The only source for this journey is the memoirs of Samuel Breck and it is therefore not found in Patris. Its authenticity is supported by Breck's claim that he has a letter from Valady dated from London 1787. On the French assistance to the Dutch Patriots, see Schama (1989), pp.251–3.

8 Patris (1930), pp.30–4; Breck (2002), pp.225–7.

9 Patris (1930), pp.138–40. All translations from Valady's letters are my own.

10 Anon. (1797a), pp.154–7. On Phillips' vegetarianism, see Medical Journal, 27 July 1811 and Phillips (1826).

11 Ritson (1802), p.81; Thomas Seccombe, rev. M. Clare Loughlin-Chow, 'Richard Phillips', ODNB.

12 Pigott, R. (1792).

13 Robert Pigott, 'Liberté de la Presse', Le Patriote François, 10 février 1790 et Supplement, pp.4–6, and another separate print at the end of the volume in the edition at the British Library. I have not seen the vegetarian appendix mentioned by J.G. Alger: J.G. Alger, rev. Stephen M. Lee, 'Robert Pigott', ODNB; Alger (1894), pp.103–6; Alger (1899), pp.39–45, 76–7; Alger (1902), pp.58–9, 79; Morton (2002), p.65; cf. Erdman (1986), pp.159, 174, who I think mistakenly mentions an 'Arthur Piggot' at a meeting of the Society of the Friends of the People.

14 Brissot ([1912?]), I.350.

15 Brissot (1912a), pp.249+n., 252–4; Roland (1835), pp.94, 100, 105–6, 112, 116, 119; Roland (1902), II.58+n., 77–8, 97, 102, 150, 156, 161–2, 177, 179, 182–3, 185, 188, 191, 193, 679–80, 695, 698–700, 732+n., 733, 743, 746.

16 [Southey] (1807), III.193–4; Anon. (1797a), pp.154–7.

17 Saint-Pierre to Brissot [probably in reply to a letter from Brissot dated 23 April 1788], Brissot (1830–2), III.72–3.

18 Patris (1930), pp.37–8.

19 Williams, Howard (1883), pp.175–6; cf. Ritson (1802), pp.83–4.

20 Saint-Pierre (1826), I.212–13.

21 They were in the Society of the Blacks together (Brissot (1830–2), III.88+n.; Brissot ([1912b]), II.86–7n.) and Valady entrusted his library and belongings to him

when he sent them over to America in advance of his planned journey in October 1788: Patris (1930), pp.137, 147–8; Valady to Thomas Jefferson, Paris 26 September 1789, Jefferson (1958), p.483, in which Valady asks Jefferson to forward a letter to Crèvecœur ensuring the safety of his 'Trunks filled with Books and things' which 'I have been at great trouble and expence to collect' and which he hopes Jefferson's 'love of learning and Philosophy will bring you to sympathize with the Sollicitude of a Young man, and to excuse the irregularity of his address'; cf. Roland (1902), II.34+n. Crèvecœur introduced Breck to Brissot (Breck (2002), pp.82–4), and since Valady had known Breck before coming to Paris, it was perhaps through these two that Valady first caught the revolutionary fire.

22 Patris (1930), pp.138–40.
23 Patris (1930), p.146; Anon. (1797a), pp.154–7.
24 Patris (1930), pp.138–40.
25 Anon. (1794), pp.84–5. Phillips based his account on the same material as *The History of Robespierre*, but he claimed that Pigott, rather than Oswald, was Valady's vegetarian guru because Valady thanked his conversion to Pigott in a letter to Thomas Taylor (see below).
26 For the multiple connections between Pigott, Oswald and Lanthenas, cf. Alger (1899), pp.76–7; Alger (1902), p.326; Brissot (1830–2), III.88+n.; Brissot ([1912b]), II.86–7n.; Roland (1902), II.34+n., 695, 698–700, 744; Darnton (1968), p.134; Erdman (1986), pp.1, 73–6, 124, 132.
27 Alger (1894), pp.71–3.
28 Breck (2002), pp.225–7.
29 Brissot ([1912b]), II.86–7n.; Patris (1930), pp.34–5. Volney argued that Christianity was a third hand derivative of more ancient

Egyptian and Hindu religions claiming, for example, that Christ was etymologically connected to 'Christna' and Abraham and Sarah were derived from 'Brahma' and 'Saraswadi'. This was an attitude recycled by Shelley in *Queen Mab* (1813) and in *Revolt of Islam* (Schwab (1984), p.172; Leask (1992), pp.104–6, 114–15). Volney was a significant part of the education of Frankenstein's 'monster', who was vegetarian (McLane (1996)).

30 Brissot ([1912b]), II.83–7n.; Brissot (1912a), pp.xlv–xlvi, 172–5; Brissot (1830–2), III.54–5+n., 88+n.; Mercier (1800), p.197; Roland (1902), II.695; Barruel (1798), II.449.
31 Brissot (1830–2), III.72–4; Brissot ([1912b]), II.83–4; Brissot (1912a), p.249.
32 Brissot (1912a), pp.xlv–xlvi, 174–5; Patris (1930), pp.51–2, 148; St Clair (1989), pp.262–3; Morton (1994), pp.65–6.
33 Brissot (1912a), pp.195, 244–5. Perroud thinks that the first letter does not refer to Valady, though in the light of the second letter it obviously does. Furthermore, Valady was indeed planning to travel for a short time to London in July 1788 and thence to travel to America, as the letter indicates. cf. Brissot (1912a), pp.172–3, cf. pp.426–8.
34 Patris (1930), p.137.
35 Anon. (1797a), pp.154–7. On this visit he stayed with Brissot's friend, Sir Garlek, later Lord Auckland, Governor General of British India: Brissot (1912a), pp.140–1.
36 Patris (1930), pp.34–41.
37 Taylor, T. (1788–9), pp.213–320, cf. e.g. p.217; cf. Porphyry (1823), pp.vi–viii.
38 [Southey] (1807), III.193–4; [Taylor, T.] (1966), pp.viii, xii–xiii; Axon (1890), pp.1, 9. The stories of animal sacrifices have been dismissed, but from the

internal evidence of Taylor's writing it does not seem implausible. Taylor conditionally advocated much of the content of the texts he translated. When he did not agree, he often made an editorial note. For example, in the *Abstinence from Animal Food* when Porphyry condemns animal sacrifice, Taylor butts in with a counter-quote from Iamblichus who argues that while sacrifices are not appropriate for immaterial gods, they are appropriate for those gods that infuse matter (Porphyry (1823), pp.72–4n.; cf. p.156n).

39 [Taylor, T.] (1799), pp.72–4; [Southey] (1807), III.193–4; W[elsh] (1831), p.4.

40 Valady to Taylor, 12 December 1788; this letter was published in a biographical article on Valady in *Biographical Anecdotes of the Founders of the French Republic* (R. Phillips, London, 1797) (henceforth Anon., (1797a)), pp.150–60. Boas' claim that Taylor authored this article (cf. Taylor, T. (1969), p.127n.) is unlikely since the report was written by a radical republican sympathiser, which Taylor was not. The supposition that the article was an original account by an acquaintance is doubtful since most of the material is a verbatim reproduction of the account of Valady (written by an author hostile to republicanism) in *The History of Robespierre*, 2nd edn (T. Boosey, London, 1794) (henceforth Anon. (1794)). It may have been authored by the publisher of the *Biographical Anecdotes*, Richard Phillips, the radical republican vegetarian who was friends with Taylor from whom he may have obtained Valady's letter to Taylor (supposing that letter is authentic).

41 Anon. (1797a), pp.157–60.

42 [Southey] (1807), III.193–7;

[Taylor, T.] (1966), pp.viii, xii–xiii; Axon (1890), pp.7–9; *Fraser's Magazine*, New Series, 12:71 (Nov. 1875), pp.647, 649; Iamblichus (1818), p.xi; Porphyry (1823) (some of which was originally translated in [Taylor, T.] (1792), along with passages from Plutarch's 'Whether Land or Sea Animals are Cleverer'); Porphyry (1823), pp.100n., 122n. Taylor's other translations relating to Pythagoreanism and animals include Apuleius (1822) (see e.g. I. 322), the *Political fragments of Archytas . . . and other Ancient Pythagoreans* (1822), Aristotle's *History of Animals* (1809), Iamblichus, *On the mysteries of the Egyptians* (1821), Julian, *Two orations*, the *Hymns of Orpheus* (1792), Plato's writings on metempsychosis in the *Timaeus* and *Phaedrus*, Plotinus, *On the Beautiful*, and a summary of Porphyry's *Life of Plotinus*. Raine and Boas both refer to Taylor as a vegetarian: Taylor, T. (1969), pp.40, 127n.

43 Taylor, T. (1969), pp.8, 49–102; Axon (1890), p.2.

44 Porphyry (1823), pp.ix–xi.

45 [Taylor, T.] (1792), pp.iii–iv, 18–20. For Taylor on the Brahmins see [Taylor, T.] (1792), pp.59–67; Porphyry (1823), p.158n.; Taylor, T. (1788–9), p.213.

46 cf. ch. 23, note 15 below. Turner (1980), pp.9, 13.

47 [Taylor, T.] (1792), p.103; Taylor, T. (1969), p.127; [Taylor, T.] (1799), pp.81, 88; Morton (1994), p.30.

48 [Taylor, T.] (1792), p.20; cf. Oswald (1791), pp.52–8+nn., 83–90.

49 [Taylor, T.] (1792), pp.vi–vii; [Taylor, T.] (1966), pp.xiii–xiv; Taylor, T. (1969), p.47.

50 [Taylor, T.] (1799), p.85.

51 Anon. (1797a), pp.157–60; [Southey] (1807), III.193–4.

52 Anon. (1794), p.86; Pagès (1797),

I.96; Carlyle (1998), 1.5.III. Carlyle also mentions Valady at 1.4.IV, 1.5.VI. Brissot was in D'Orleans' pay, cf. Brissot (1912a), pp.xl–xli.

53 Patris (1930), pp.41–56; Anon. (1797a), pp.157–60; Anon. (1796a), I.143–5; Saint Étienne and Cretelle (1795), I.76; Pagès (1797), I.96; Les Cases (1823), I.v..625, II.iii.285–368; Anon. ([1797b]), I.42 (which reports that Brissot voted in favour of regicide).

54 Breck (2002), pp.228–9; Brissot and Claviere (1797), p.xlvi; Anon. (1794), p.87.

55 Quoted in Schama (1989), p.723.

56 Breck (2002), pp.228–31; Schama (1989), pp.722–6; Taine (2001), p.103.

57 Brissot ([1912b]), II.74–5.

58 Anon. (1797a), opp. title page; Anon. (1796a), II.259–60; Anon. (1794), p.74; Williams (1795), p.41; Schama (1989), pp.803–5.

59 Couvray (1795), pp.139–51; Breck (2002), pp.232–45.

60 Anon. (1797a), pp.157–60; Anon. (1796a), II.272; Anon. (1796b), p.87; Breck (2002), p.246; *Bulletin de la Société Historique et Archéologique Du Périgord*, 20 (1893), p.356; 21 (1894), p.34.

61 Valady (1935), p.311.

62 Patris (1930), pp.153–9; Breck (2002), p.223.

CHAPTER 23

1 Erdman (1986), pp.73–6, 160–1; Roland (1902), II.204+n., 299, 699, 744; *Fraser's Magazine*, New Series, 12:71 (Nov. 1875), pp.649–50; Schama (1989), p.474; [Southey] (1807), III.189.

2 Brissot ([1912?]), I.350–1.

3 See ch.16 above.

4 Williams (1789b), pp.48–61; Williams (1789a), I.84–8, 104; III.201.

5 Brissot ([1912?]), I.350–1.

6 Graham (1789), pp.29–30; Porter (1984); Graham (1793), pp.3–4.

7 Graham (1778), p.27; Graham (1776), p.9.

8 Graham (1790), p.1; cf. Graham (1776), Title Page, p.11.

9 Graham (1790), p.4; cf. p.20 'Wisdom's Dictates'.

10 Graham (1790), p.5. For more details on his dietary advice, in which he often permitted certain sorts of meat, cf. Graham (1790), p.2; Graham (1793), pp.3–4, 20–1; Graham ([1785?]), pp.2–6, 30; Graham (1778), pp.12, 18–19, 22–3, 29. Porter (1984) and Porter (1982), esp. pp.201–3, simplify Graham's varied dietary advice by saying that he recommended vegetarianism, as does McCalman (1998) and, by implication, Decker (1995).

11 Graham (1775), p.3; Graham (1778), pp.27–8. See ch. 18 above.

12 Graham (1793), p.25ff.; cf. Schnorrenberg (1984), pp.191–5; Graham (1778), pp.30–1.

13 For a letter from Graham to Macaulay, see Graham (1778); cf. Decker (1995); McCalman (1998).

14 Regan (2001), pp.129–34; Kenyon-Jones (2001), pp.59–65. It seems disingenuous of Regan to suggest that Macaulay did not advocate vegetarianism because she was 'writing at a time when the discourse of vegetarianism was only moving towards its formulation'. There were plenty of fully formulated vegetarian arguments available which Macaulay could have adopted had she wished – not least those made by her acquaintances James Graham and Benjamin Franklin. Surely the same applies to Regan's claim that '[Mary] Hays never reaches the point of explicit recommendations for a vegetarian diet largely because there was no precedent for this. But, as we have seen, writers like Macaulay did makes moves in this direction.' As I have argued in chapter 16, many authors who have been assumed

to be 'moving in the direction of vegetarianism', should really be considered 'counter-vegetarian': they show how sympathy for animals could be adopted *without* going to the extreme of vegetarianism.

15 Wollstonecraft (1792), ch.1 + note; ch.12; cf. Nicholson (1797), pp.39–40; Turner (1980), p.12; Oerlemans (1994); cp. Regan (2001), pp.127–9, 138. Surely Regan misrepresents Wollstonecraft by claiming that she provided a 'theoretically justifiable indifference toward animals'. Regan is bemused about, and even implicitly condemnatory of, Wollstonecraft: 'How, then, could she turn a deaf ear to the growing regard for the suffering of animals?' Although Wollstonecraft's perspective can be called anthropocentric, I think it ahistorical for Regan to suggest that Wollstonecraft's denial of 'reason' or 'equality' to animals – in line with the vast majority of her contemporaries – was an 'oversight' or a failure to espouse the 'obvious' alliance between feminism and animal-rights advocacy. Wollstonecraft did in any case articulate the familiar parallel between patriarchal cruelty to women and animals ('This habitual cruelty is first caught at school, where it is one of the rare sports of the boys to torment the miserable brutes that fall in their way. The transition, as they grow up, from barbarity to brutes to domestic tyranny over wives, children, and servants, is very easy'). What Wollstonecraft objected to – perfectly legitimately – was the system of sentimental education which encouraged women to exhibit a 'parade of sensibility' (what Coleridge called 'a false and bastard sensibility') by fawning over their pets, while ignoring the acute suffering of humans *and other animals* (in her illustrative example she mentions the neglected horses as well as the coachman).

16 Brissot ([1912b]), I.350–3.
17 [Southey] (1807), II.348–9.
18 Kenyon–Jones (2001), pp.42–3; [Southey] (1807), III.185–94; I.164–70, cf. I.3, II.300ff.
19 McCalman (1995), p.322; McCalman (1998); McCalman (1988); Morton (2002), pp.68–70.
20 Brothers (1830), pp.22–3; [Brothers] (1794), I.13; Brothers (1801), p.64.
21 Brothers (1801), pp.43, 48, 86–7.
22 Brothers (1801), p.63; Morton (2002), pp.68–70.
23 Rocher (1983), pp.39–40, 215, 242, 305; Rocher (1993), pp.226–7; Morton (2002), pp.68–70; Halhed (1777), pp.ix, xxxvii–xxxviii, lxiv.
24 Brothers (1801), pp.82–3; [Southey] (1807), III.254–65.
25 [Brothers] (1794), II.45.
26 Pigott, C. (1795), pp.7–8; cf. pp.1, 10, 28–9. Archenholtz (1787–91), IV.2.
27 Billington (1980), p.50; Darnton (1968), chs 3–4; Erdman (1986), pp.73–6, 118+n.; Bronson (1938), pp.30–3; Nicholas Roe, 'John Tweddell', *ODNB*.
28 Morton (1994), pp.15–16; Lawrence ([1810]); McCalman (1998); Sebastian Mitchell, 'John Lawrence', *DNB*; Turner (1980), p.13+n.
29 Nicholson, ed. (1803); cf. *Odes, by George Dyer . . . &c.*[c.1802]); Nicholson, ed.? (1796) (Franklin's *Way to wealth* probably owed its name to Tryon's work with a similar title (Tryon [?] (1699))).
30 Lambe (1815), pp.128–9; cp. Newton, J.F. (1897), pp.14–15n.; Thomas, K. (1983), p.296. See 'Epilogue' below.
31 Moseley (1800), pp.159–68; Lee (2002), pp.178–9; Lee (August 2002); Morton (2000), p.190; Morton (1998a), pp.96. 87–106, p.96.

32 Bruce E. Graver, 'Wakefield, Gilbert (1756–1801)', *ODNB*.
33 Kenyon-Jones (1983), pp.83, 87.
34 Kenyon-Jones (1983), pp.79–108; Sheridan proposed a similar conspiracy to Charles Blount (see ch.9, p.126 above); Thomas, K. (1983), pp.184–5; Mitchell, 'John Lawrence', *ODNB*.
35 Cheyne (1742); cf. Ritson (1802), p.159. Gillray ([1873]), pp.148–50; Gillray (1966), pp.63–4; Morton (1998b); cf. George and Stephens (1978), VI, § 6967.
36 Oswald ([1792]), p.35; Erdman (1986), p.97; cf. pp.43, 69–71.

CHAPTER 24

1 Erdman(1986), pp.118–19.
2 Quincey (1890), III.105–6.
3 OIOC P/240/25 *MPC, Jan–June 1767*, p.377, 488 (missing?).
4 W.P.C., 'John Stewart', *DNB* (1897). His letter of resignation should be in the second half of the *Madras Public Proceedings* 1769; OIOC's copy is missing; I have not looked for this document in Madras. The letter is mentioned in the index in P/240/28 *MPC, Jan–July 1769*, pp.906, 907, 911.
5 Quincey (1890), III.94; Taylor, J. (1832), pp.285–6.
6 John Stewart, 'Mr. Stuart's account of the battle between Hydra Ally and the Morattoes', OIOC Mss Eur/Orme OV 8.10, pp.51–4 (Stewart's holograph original); and a copy, John Stewart, 'Battle Between Hyder and the Morrattoes, written by Mr.Stuart, who was in it', at Mss Eur/Orme XIII.64, pp.3771–3. In the original, one can see Stewart's fib-weaving in action where the claim that 'I walkd over the Field' is crossed out as being incompatible with the claim that he was taken prisoner. Sinha, N.K. (1959), pp.102–8 corroborates Stewart's account with Indian sources.
7 [Brande?] (1822), p.13.

8 John Stewart, 'Mr John Stuart's Travels', OIOC Mss Eur Orme XVII.42, pp.4932–7. The letter in Mss Eur Orme.71.2, pp.41–9 appears to be Stewart's own holograph draft. This report does not differ hugely from the account in his letter of apology in P/240/32 *MPC*, 22 Oct. 1771; P/240/31 *MPC*, Jan–Aug 1771, pp.702–9 (not p.609 as listed in the index); receipt entered on p.699. cf. Ali (1963), pp.155–61. The story does not agree with the that of Colonel Wilks (*cit.* W.P.C., 'John Stewart', *DNB*) and may have been partly inspired by Maistre de la Tour (1774 [i.e. 1784?]); cf. *GM*, Vol.68.ii.998–9 and Vol.54.ii.519–21, 531.
9 From John Stewart to Warren Hastings (24 December 1784), BL Add.Mss. 29167 f.259. This could have been on the separate journey mentioned in Kelly (1826), I.247–9; *EM* (March 1790), XVII.198–9.
10 Taylor, J. (1832), p.287; Quincey (1890), III.108; Barry Symonds, 'Stewart, John (1747–1822)', *ODNB*.
11 Quincey (1890), III.99.
12 Stewart, J. (1794), pp.9–10; cf. Stewart, J. ([1818?]), pp.43–4, 51–3; Stewart, J. ([1795] or 1813?), pp.xii–xiv, xxix–xxx, 101; Stewart, J. (1808), p.15; [Brande?] (1822), pp.7–9.
13 Quincey (1890), III.107–8; Taylor, J. (1832), p.288.
14 Morton (1994), p.68; Stewart, J. ([1795] or 1813?), p.101. The British Library catalogue calculates the publication date as 1813, apparently taking it as five years from the publication of *The Apocalypse of Nature* (1808). But *The Apocalypse of Nature* was first published in 1789–90, making the date of this *Revelation of Nature* more like 1795. This dating is supported by a ms. notation on the British Library copy of this edition which reads 'Charles

Goberl, . . . No.154. Broad-way, New York. to M.Callanano Philadelphia 1796'.

15 Stewart, J. ([1818?]), pp.xxiv, 54, 95–8, 211; Stewart, J. ([1795] or 1813?), pp.32–5, 82, 87; Quincey (1890), III.109, 116; Stewart, J. (1808), pp.11–12; Nigel Leask refers to him as a Scots Jacobin; Morton says he was not a reactionary monarchist; Leask (1992), p.178; Morton (1994), p.68.

16 Stewart, J. ([1795] or 1813?), pp.60, 82. Stewart's ideas relate to those of Paley, Malthus and Godwin; see ch.27.

17 [Brande?] (1822), p.14; Taylor, J. (1832), p.294; Quincey (1890), III.109.

18 Stewart, J. (1794), p.63; cf. Oswald (1791), pp.6–7; Taylor, J. (1832), p.289.

19 Quincey (1890), III.109.

20 *The Annual Biography and Obituary for the Year 1823* (1823), pp.101–2; Taylor, J. (1832), I.284–5; Kelly (1826), I.247–9; Jane Girdham, 'Michael Kelly (1762–1826)', *ODNB*.

21 Quincey (1890), III.113–20; Leask (1992), p.178.

22 Stewart, J. ([1818?]), pp.8–10; Stewart, J. (1808), pp.11–12.

23 Stewart, J. ([1818?]), pp.153, 258–9; Stewart, J. ([1795] or 1813?), pp.xii–xiv; Stewart, J. (1794), p.63; Quincey (1890), III.98–9, 109; Stewart, J. (1808), p.13; cf. Reuchlin (1983), p.179. Stewart was thus not strictly a pantheist or animist as he has been referred to hitherto (Leask (1992), p.178; Morton (1994), p.68). In an otherwise edifying article, Ian McCalman says that Oswald and Stewart 'depicted an animistic universe in which all parts interpenetrated and corresponded through vitalist energies, sympathies, and antipathies' (McCalman (1998), p.102). Stewart's material universe had sense, not soul and therefore cannot be called animist. He was contemptuous of all metaphysics and 'the ridiculous doctrine of spiritualism' (i.e. all systems containing souls, spirits or gods). Neither Oswald nor Stewart believed in vitalist corresponding sympathies and antipathies. The 'sympathy' that bound their universe together was based on somatic emotion.

24 Stewart, J. ([1818?]), Title Page; Stewart, J. ([1795] or 1813?), pp.19, 39.

25 Stewart, J. (1808), pp.18–19; Stewart, J. ([1818?]), pp.36–7; cf. Pal (1994), p.59.

26 Stewart, J. ([1818?]), p.2.

27 Stewart, J. ([1818?]), p.84; cf. pp.1, 145–6, 149–50; Stewart, J. ([1795] or 1813?), Title Page, pp.xii–xiv; Alexander Pope, *Essay on Man*, III.vi; III.i, cf. I.ix, IV.i; cf. Pratt (1788), pp.38–41.

28 cf. Stewart, J. ([1795] or 1813?), pp.xii–xiv, 41; cf. p.27; Taylor, J. (1832), pp.284–5.

29 Stewart, J. ([1795] or 1813?), pp.iv, 21–5, 63; Armstrong (1992), Vol.1; e.g. Bk II, ll.345–6; cf. Oswald, (1791), pp.17–18.

30 Stewart, J. ([1795] or 1813?), pp.iv, 25, 58. He may have been adapting Thomas Morgan who said that in the countryside where people have open air, exercise and live plainly, women do not suffer so much sickness in breeding. Morgan (1735), p.219.

31 Stewart, J. ([1818?]), pp.1, 8–10; cf. Stewart, J. (1794), p.6.

32 Bentham (1907), ch.17, no.IV.+n. In another text (*Traités de Legislation Civile et Pénale* (1802)) Bentham seems to have slipped into the much more conventional idea that cruelty to animals was undesirable only insofar as it encouraged cruelty to humans. And in yet another text (*Constitutional Code*) he switched the emphasis from their sentience to their intelligence. cf. Passmore (1975), pp.211, 217; Thomas, K.

(1983), pp.175–6. I think I am justified in rejecting Passmore's suggestion that Bentham's differing statements on the moral status of animals was a *progression* rather than inconsistency. Although the works Passmore cites are in chronological order, the 'earliest' statement is not revised even in the final edition in Bentham's lifetime (1823).

33 Thomas, K. (1983), p.176; Turner (1980), p.13; Singer (1975); Singer (1980).

34 Dombrowski (1986), p.29; Regan (2001), p.123. Regan misleadingly implies that 'Blake, Bentham, Barbauld and numerous others' 'were setting the stage for the acceptance of a vegetarian platform predicated on animal rights.'

35 Thomas, K. (1983), pp.175–6; Turner (1980), p.13; Doddridge (1794), I.207–9; Sedlar (1982), p.176.

36 Thomas, K. (1983), pp.178–9.

37 See ch.27 below.

38 Nichols (1991); Darwin, E. (1803), IV.189–96nn., 419–28.

39 Buffon (1780), III.423–5, IV.165, 191–2; Kenyon-Jones (2001), pp.61–2.

40 Quincey (1890), III.103.

CHAPTER 25

1 Ritson (1833), II.22–4.

2 Ritson (1833), II.7; Bronson (1938), I.150–1.

3 For Ritson's republican activities and friendship with Godwin, see Bronson (1938), pp.144–71; St Clair (1989), pp.130, 165, 189, 217, 260–1; McCalman (1998), p.99; Hogg (1858), II.444–7; Morton (1994), p.63. cf. e.g. Lambe (1809), pp.21–2, which copies Ritson (1802), pp.150–4. For Shelley's borrowings from Ritson, see Clark (1939). Newton shows little direct influence from Ritson; for a few echoes (which could equally come from elsewhere), see Newton, J.F. (1897), p.14 and Ritson (1802), reverse side of title page and p.235n.; pp.24–5+n; p.27; 120n. Godwin and Newton were acquainted well before Morton's dating of 1809 (Morton (1994), p.65); cf. St. Clair (1989), pp.262–3+n. Godwin (2005), Bk VI; Godwin (1831), xxi.3; vi; John Milton, *Paradise Lost*, XI.483–8; cf. Ritson (1802), p.39; *Vind*.5; Medwin (1913), p.136; Morton (1994), p.58.

4 Ritson (1833), II.12, 22–4, II.194.

5 Ritson (1812), p.131; Ritson (1833), I.40–1; cf. Cheyne (1733), pp.39–42.

6 Ritson (1802), pp.1–32, 187–9, 226n.; Ritson (1833), I.32–3; cf. *QM*. VII.25–30.

7 Ritson (1802), p.233n.; cf. pp.41–2, 44, 47–50, 231–2n.; cp. e.g. Brückner (1768), pp.60–4. cp. Morton (1994), pp. 152–8. Timothy Morton, in agreement with *The Edinburgh Review* ((1803–4), II.129), says that Ritson's first chapter 'attempts to show how unnatural (in the sense of refined, civilized) vegetarianism is, and that the second chapter is concerned to show how unnatural (in the sense of unrefined, savage), meat–eating is.' According to my reading, the first chapter is devoted to arguing that there is no benevolence or 'God' in nature, and argues that man should be 'just, mild, mercyful, benevolent, humane, or, at least, innocent or harmless, whether such qualitys be natural or not' (p.40). In the second chapter, I understand Ritson (who does not agree on every point with Monboddo) to argue that vegetarianism is natural (in the sense of unrefined, harmless), and that meat-eating is a vicious and unnatural product of civilisation (i.e. in the sense of civilised, savage). Man was naturally vegetarian not in the sense that God had made him to

be gentle and benevolent, but because he was not naturally formed for the killing and eating of animals.

8 Ritson was following Porphyry in blaming priests for introducing sacrifice, and may also have had Oswald's use of Porphyry in mind. Ritson knew about Oswald (Ritson (1802), pp.198–200) but Erdman says he did not know Oswald's *Cry of Nature* (Erdman (1986), p.90). It seems odd that Ritson – capable of turning up the most obscure references to vegetarians hundreds of years before – would have been unaware of the vegetarian work of a fellow Jacobin-sympathiser contemporaneously residing in London with several mutual acquaintances, including John Stewart. Since Ritson deliberately ignored Stewart's 'absurd' vegetarian arguments in his anthology, it seems plausible that he also had reasons for remaining judiciously silent about Oswald's. Ritson also makes no mention of the third major vegetarian anthologist, George Nicholson, whom he may well have derived some information from; so perhaps Ritson – a notoriously jealous scholar – was disguising his debt to these antiquarian predecessors. For parallels that may (inconclusively) suggest that Ritson had read Oswald's *Cry of Nature*, see e.g. Ritson (1802), pp.41–2=Oswald (1791), p.33+n. (pp.113–14), pp.44–5+n. (pp.114–15); Ritson (1802), pp.60–2+n., 87+n.=Oswald (1791), pp.103–9 (they quote some of the same passages from Arbuthnot, but use different editions); Ritson (1802), pp.103ff=Oswald (1791), pp.68–71+nn. (pp.132ff.); Ritson (1802), pp.105–7=Oswald (1791), pp.145–7.

9 Ritson (1802), pp.30–2.

10 Ritson (1802), pp.40, 51.

11 Ritson (1802), pp.206–8; cf.

pp.77, 86, 181–3, 208–16, 236. Like Volney and Rousseau, Ritson derided the Brahmin priesthood and their religion, but nevertheless admired their principles (Rousseau, J.-J. (1979), pp.153+n.); cf. Rousseau, J.-J. (1998), pp.81–2; cf. Volney in ch.22 above. He contortedly argued that vegetarianism made people 'gentle' but did not diminish their 'valour' in battle.

12 Ritson (1802), pp.72–8, 183–9, 192–5.

13 Ritson (1833), I.46–7ff.; cf. I.32–3, 38–9, 66.

14 Ritson (1833), I.39–41.

15 Ritson (1802), pp.201–2; cf. Shelley (1858), II.414.

16 Ritson (1802), p.35n.

17 For Ritson and his nephew's vegetarian antics, see Ritson (1833), I.30–1, 39–41, 62, 86, 95, 97, 101, 104, 105; Bronson (1938), pp.93–100, 297.

18 Everett (2001).

19 [Southey] (1807), III.191–2.

20 Bronson (1938), pp.295–9.

21 S.L., 'Joseph Ritson', *DNB* (1896); Stephanie L. Barczewski, 'Joseph Ritson', *ODNB*.

22 Brougham (1803), II.128–36.

23 Teltscher (1995), p.95; cf. ch. 4 note 59 above. Indian scriptures do in fact deal with the problem of unavoidable violence, and speak of limiting *himsa* (violence) as far as possible; cf. Gandhi (1999), XXIV.27–8.

24 Cheyne (1724), pp.91–5.

25 Bronson (1938), pp.295–9.

26 Ritson (1833), p.lxxvii; cf. Huddesford (1992), ll.31–6, p.207.

27 Bronson (1938), pp.134–7+nn.

28 Ritson (1833), p.lxxviii; Scott (1999e), pp.iv–v; S.L., 'Ritson', *DNB*; Lockhart (1910), I.87–92 [Ch.3, 1801]; Scott (1932–7), I.199, 205, 262, 298, 355–6.

29 Scott (1999d), II.184–5; cf. II.293; Scott (1999c), I.116–17+n., 296; Scott (1999a), II.127; cf. Scott (1999b), I.343. See ch. 18 above.

CHAPTER 26

1 Shelley (1926–30), VI.17n., 348;
Hogg (1858), II.287–8; Newton,
J.F. (1897), pp.46–7; cf. Rousseau,
J.-J. (1997a), p.167; cf. Newton,
J.F. (1897), pp.83–4; Shelley
(1971), p.828.
2 Lambe (1809), p.18.
3 *Vind*.17n.
4 Shelley (1964), II.92. For most of
the information on Godwin I have
relied on St Clair (1989),
pp.259–64, 337–8, 343, 356–7;
cf. also Morton (1994), pp.59,
65–9, 76, 133; Drew (1998),
pp.274–6+nn.; *Vind*.17n.;
McCalman (1998), p.103+n.;
Medwin (1913), pp.94–9+n.
5 Shelley (1964), II.187–8.
6 Morton (1994), p.65.
7 BL Add Ms.37232.(F), Hogg to
Newton, London, 11 Feb. 1832,
f.44.
8 Hogg (1858), II.412–35, 448,
469–70, 485–7; Morton (1994),
pp.67–9; Shelley (1971), p.830;
Vind.11.
9 Morton (1994), pp.65, 69; Clark,
D.L. (1939), p.71.
10 Lawrence (1811); Medwin (1913),
p.94–9+nn.; Morton (1994),
pp.65–6, 133; St Clair (1989),
pp.262–3; Drew (1998),
pp.274–6+nn.; cf. Anon. (1800);
McCalman (1998), p.103+n.
11 St Clair (1989), pp.356–7.
12 Peacock (2001), II.380, 475;
Forster's testimony on Lawrence is
corroborated by Lambe (1815),
pp.128–9 (see below).
13 Morton (1994), p.47; McLane
(1996), pp.979–80. Morton finds
vegetarianism in Mary Shelley's
The Last Man (Morton (1994),
pp.51–6).
14 Byron, *Don Juan*, II.529–34;
Kenyon-Jones (2001), pp.123–5;
cf. Lambe (1809), p.12. For a
context to Byron's *Cain*, cf.
Darwin, E. (1800), p.468.
15 Peacock (2001), II.475.
16 Lambe (1809), pp.v, 4–12, 18,
21–2; Lambe (1815), pp.117–18,

280–1; Newton, J.F. (1897),
pp.vii, ix, xi, 84–5; *Vind*.12–13; cp.
Lambe (1805), pp.36, 53, 138–9,
167. cf. Tryon (1691a), pp.267–8;
Jerome (2005a), Bk II, ch.11.
17 Lambe (1809), p.8; Lambe
(1815), p.119.
18 Lambe (1809), pp.21–2, which
copies Ritson (1802), pp.22–31,
150–4. Lambe (1815), p.96,
which could have come from
Ritson (1802), pp.150–3; Lambe
(1815), pp.98, 101–2, 128–9,
148, 161ff., 519–22. Lambe may
have been alerted to Cocchi's
existence by Sir John Sinclair's
Code of Health; cf. Newton, J.F.
(1897), pp.xii, 23–5+n., 60–3, 82;
Newton, J.F. (1821), pp.137–8;
Vind.8, 15–16; *V.Sys*.340; Rees et
al., eds (1819), f.Ss3v–Ss4v.
19 Lambe (1815), pp.105–8.
20 Lambe (1815), pp.18–21, 91–3,
99–108, 139, 192–4, 203–20,
244; Lambe (1809), pp.6–8;
Lambe (1805), p.36. cf. Newton,
J.F. (1897), pp.45–6, 50, 73–7;
Morton (1994), p.168; cf. also
Ritson (1802), pp.192–5.
21 Newton, J.F. (1897), *passim*; cf.
Nicholson (1999), p.96; Cheyne
(1724), pp.91–4; *Vind*.5–7; Raben
(1963), pp.104–5+n.; Porphyry
(2000), Bk I.13, p.36; Morton
(1994), pp.65–7; Hogg (1858),
II.421–2. Newton, J.F. (1897),
p.73 and Lambe (1815),
pp.177–9, citing authorities on
the nutritional value of raw
potatoes.
22 Newton, J.F. (1897), pp.21–3+n.,
33, 82–3; cf. pp.60–1, 189;
Temple (1690), pp.14–16;
Newton, J.F. (1821), p.112,
117–20+n, 127–8, 138–9; see chs
8 and 20 above.
23 Newton, J.F. (1821), pp.v–vi,
127–8; Faber (1816), pp.vii–ix.
24 Newton, J.F. (1821), *passim*.
25 Newton, J.F. (1897), pp.21–3;
QM, VI.45–6+n.; *Vind*.5; Drew
(1998), pp.259–60+n. Though he
finds no direct link, Drew suggests
a possible debt to Holwell. The

similarities are probably explained by their shared set of cultural assumptions and intermediary sources such as Monboddo.

26 Newton, J.F. (1897), pp.87–9, 42–3. D.L. Clark was taking his argument that Shelley was influenced by Ritson rather than Newton too far when he claimed that 'Both Ritson and Shelley considered that man's physical and moral depravity was due to an unnatural diet, while Newton emphasized only the physical' (Clark, D.L. (1939), pp.72–3).

27 Lambe (1809), p.10; Lambe (1805), pp.230–2.

28 *Vind.*11–14; Shelley (1971), p.830.

29 *Vind.*19–20; Ritson (1802), pp.72–7, 156–7. Despite innumerable borrowings, Shelley only ever cites Ritson in an unpublished draft manuscript (*V.Sys.*341 and 342 where his note 'See Essay' refers to Ritson (1802), pp.72–7, 156–7). Ritson was kept out of any published work.

30 Shelley, H. (1889), p.4; Lambe (1815), pp.41–6, 109–10, 222–7, 232–3, 245–6; Lambe (1809), pp.26–7; Newton, J.F. (1897), pp.91–2+n.; Morton (1994), pp.67–9; Hogg (1858), II.412–35, 448, 469–70, 485–7; Shelley (1971), p.830; *V.Sys.*341–3; *Vind.*11.

31 Hogg (1858), I.120–3 (cf. ch. 16 above), II.446–7; Morton (1994), pp.73–5, 104–5; Shelley (1964), I.368; Drew (1998), p.260n.; *Vind.*17; Shelley (1971), p.359+n.; William Wordsworth, *The Excursion*, VIII.568–71; William Wordsworth, 'Hart-Leap Well', ll.178–80; Oerlemans (1994).

32 Lambe (1815), pp.237–8; *Vind.*7–8; *V.Sys.*341–3; Ritson (1802), pp.33–4; Clark, D.L. (1939), p.74; Tryon (1691a), pp.371–2.

33 *V.Sys.*343–4. This makes sense of Harriet Shelley's comments (Shelley (1964), I.368) and Hogg's

(Hogg (1858), II.469–70), and Shelley's (*QM*, VI.198n.), and even shows that Shelley's eventual abandonment of the vegetable diet on the firm recommendation of his doctors need not necessarily be seen as contrary to his original *moral* argument.

34 cf. Adams, C. (1990); Morton (1994), pp.78–9; cf. Voltaire ch. 20, p.292 above.

35 Morton (1994), pp.65, 73, 75, 79; cf. Nicholson (1797), pp.41–2, 44; Shelley (1964), I.337.

36 Oerlemans (2002), p.117.

37 *QM*, VII.43–8, VIII.191–3.

38 *QM*, VIII.211–27; cf. *The Daemon of the World*, ll.443–60; *Vind.*12; Newton, J.F. (1821), pp.136–7. For Shelley's depiction of harmony with the cosmos, cf. e.g. *QM*, VI.42–3, VIII.15–18, 64–9; *Alastor*, ll.651–3; *Mg*, ll.133–5; Morton (1994), pp.84–7, 106.

39 *Vind.*12–13. He was more hesitant in the text of the footnote to *QM* than in the *Vindication*; cf. Newton, J.F. (1897), pp.40–3.

40 Shelley (1964), I.347, 368; *Vind.*9–13, 16; Lambe (1809), pp.6–8, 12–16; Lambe (1815), pp.101–12, 121–9, 140; Newton, J.F. (1897), pp.xiii, 14–15n., 38–43, 51–3, 88; Medwin (1913), pp.190–1. In Hogg (1858), II.429, was Hogg thinking of the 'Epicurean materialist', John 'Walking' Stewart? [Southey] (1807), III.193; Evelyn (1699), p.123.

41 Pindar's use of 'dome' resembles Shelley's frequent use of the word to express both 'home' and the wider 'dome' of the world; the 'radical domestic' employed by Pindar and Shelley shows how the power of an individual could map out onto the anthropocentric macrocosmic universe; cf. e.g. Shelley, *Alastor*, l.435; 'Mont Blanc', ll.104, 140.

42 Morton (1994), pp.62–3.

43 *QM*, VIII.124–8; cf. VIII.77–87; and Shelley (1926–30), V.254;

Morton (1994), pp.89–90, 212, 227.

44 Oerlemans (2002), pp.143–7.

45 *QM*, IV.89–99, 104, 111–12, 117–18; Shelley (1971), pp.271–4.

46 Oerlemans (2002), pp.104–7; Sax (1997), pp.62–3 (Sax makes very misleading quotations from Smellie and Buffon); Godwin (1831), ch. 21, 'Of Astronomy', § iii; Ritson (1802), pp.37–40.

47 On Shelley's later mystical pantheism, cf. Leask (1992), pp.120–1.

48 cf. Dawson (1997).

49 Bougainville (1772), pp.39–40; Monboddo (1773–92), I.205–7; Morton (1994), p.154; Darwin, E. (1794–6), I.158–61; White (1789), pp.214–16; Moseley (1800), pp.167–8. For a contemporary example, see *Deep Trouble* (BBC/WW, 2003) where Joanna Sarsby writes of fish in a marine reserve that, 'once scared of man, the fish are now perhaps a little over-friendly' (a fish nibbles a scientist's pen). For the alternative fantasy that humans were carnivorous by bestial agreement, Ben Jonson, 'The Forest: To Penshurst', ll.19–39 'The painted Partridge lies in ev'ry Field,/ And for thy Mess is willing to be kill'd' (Jonson (1716–17), III.178); Juvenal, 4th Satire.

50 Primatt (1776), p.295, quoted in Garrett ed. (2000), I.v–xxiv.

51 Forster (1777), I.127–8; Nicholson (1797), pp.8–12, 23–5.

52 Bougainville (1772), pp.39–40; *cit.* Nicholson (1797), p.10.

53 *V.Sys.*340; cf. *Vind.*7–8; Morton (1994), p.65; Shelley (1964), I.337. See ch. 11 above.

54 Forster (1777), I.127–8.

55 Lambe (1815), pp.232–3.

56 Pagès (1791–2), II.22–3; cf. II.27; Ritson (1802), pp.208–16; cf. Stavorinius (1798), II.488–91.

57 Medwin (1913), pp.152–3.

58 *QM*, VII.25–30, 35–9; *RI*, X.xxxi; Leask (1992), pp.114–15; cf. Drew (1998), p.272+n.; Clark (1939). If Shelley read Bailly (1779), he would have found there Voltaire's eulogy of, and borrowing from, Holwell (pp.2–6).

59 Robertson (1802), pp.233, 239–40, 247, 252–3; cf. pp.342–3.

60 Janet Browne, 'Forster, Thomas Ignatius Maria (1789–1860)', *ODNB*.

61 Drew (1998), p.235+n.; Shelley (1964), II.361+n.5; Shelley (1971), 'Letter to Maria Gisborne', ll.236–7, p.368; Young (1975), pp.20–2.

62 Drew (1998), pp.235–60, 267n., 282; Raben (1963), p.99; Jones, ed. (1807), IX, *Sacontala*, Acts I, III, IV, e.g. pp.454, 473–4; Owenson (1811), I.87, II.114–15.

63 Morton (1994), pp.70–1; Drew (1998), p.282; Shelley (1964), I.380; Hogg (1858), II.480–2. Newton, J.F. (1897), pp.58–9; cp. Morton (1994), p.107+n. Morton says that Shelley would have known Cowper's translation of Milton's *Elegia Sexta* from Ritson (1802), pp.90–2. Ritson quotes from Cowper's *The Task*, but I find no mention of *Elegia Sexta* in Ritson. Newton's translation is different from Cowper's. cf. Crab (1990), pp.4–5.

64 Shelley (1971), pp.271–4; cf. *QM*, VI.33.

65 *Vind.*10–11.

66 *Alastor*, ll.100–2; Morton (1994), pp.104–5; Drew (1998), pp.256–7n.; cf. *RI*, X.ii.

67 *Mg*, ll.133–41; cf. ll.73–4.

68 Morton (1994), pp.116–18; *Mg*, ll.106–11.

69 Nicholson (1797), pp.23–5.

70 *Vind.*12–13 [my emphasis].

71 *QM*, III.192–6, 226–37; 'Ode to the West Wind', ll.53–4, 63–7; Oerlemans (2002), pp.117–21.

72 *RI*, V.xv, xxvi, xxxiv, xxxvii, xl–xli,

xlv, xlviii, li, VI.vi, X.xxiii; cp. *RI,* VIII.xviii; Morton (1994), pp.103, 215. cf. *PU,* I.49–54; 'Mont Blanc', l.104; and another work which Shelley, as well as J.F. Newton, had read on related topics: Moor (1810), pp.xi, 28, 64, 175, 259–60, 269, 388–9; Leask (1992), pp.72–9, 116–18, 133–4; Butler (1996); Drew (1998), pp.231–5+nn., 257, 271n.

73 *RI,* V.li, verse 5, pp.323–5; cf. *RI,* V.lv–lvi; Morton (1994), pp.110, 113–16.

74 *QM,* III.44–9; *RI,* V.xxxii, ll.284–5, V.lv; *PU,* I.i.618ff., III.iii.84–7, III.iv.180–9; Morton (1994), p.123. On the origins of fear and vanquishing it, cf. Shelley, *The Daemon of the World,* l.450; *PU,* I.6–9, 55, III.iii.84–107, III.iv.180–9; *RI,* I.20–2, IV.xxvi, X.xl, X.xlii; Oswald (1791), pp.70–1; Wordsworth, 'The Prelude', passages on stealing ravens' eggs and the 'elfin pinnace'; Tryon (1700), pp.134–6; Cheyne (1715 [1716]), II.88; Kenyon-Jones (2001), p.114; Drew (1998), pp.271–2.

75 *RI,* X.xlii, XII.xiii, xvii; Owenson (1811), III.164–90; cf. Drew (1998), pp.260n., 263n. For related issues in *PU,* see Raben (1963); Drew (1998), pp.231–2, 238; Faber (1816), I.314–56; Owenson (1811), I.130–42, II.252, III.17, 22–3; Drew (1998), pp.242, 250, and see the related themes in Shelley's *Alastor* and 'The Sensitive Plant'; Leask (1992), p.122+n.; Drew (1998), pp.201–6, 234–5+nn., 254–5, 257; Morton (1994), p.109; Raben (1963), p.97.

76 Morton (1994), pp.62, 71–9; cf. Lambe (1815), pp.109–10.

77 Drew (1998), pp.231–2+n.; *PU,* I.450, IV.400–5, 573–4; Morton (1994), pp.122–5; Oerlemans (2002), p.122; Owenson (1811), II.114–15.

78 *PU,* III.iii.90–107; III.ii.19; III.iv.180–9; II.iv.55–8; cf. Drew (1998), p.279; *RI,* V.l, p.322; *QM,* VIII.77–87; Morton (1994), p.112.

79 *PU,* III.iv.36–85; cf. *QM,* VIII.129–30; Dawson (1997).

80 Shelley (1971), pp.272–3; cf. Morton (1994), p.119.

81 *RI,* V.li, verse 5, pp.323–5; *QM.* VIII.221; Kenyon-Jones (2001), pp.111–12; Buffon (1780), III.183–5.

82 cf. Morton (1994), pp.226–7; Bate (1991), pp.36–7.

83 Shelley (1971), pp.207, 274; Morton (2002), pp.69–70, 85; Stansky (1999), pp.vii–viii; Morton and Smith, eds (2002), p.13.

CHAPTER 27

1 Lambe (1815), pp.241–3; cp. Morton (1994), pp.162, 221.

2 Schofield (1985); Morton (1994), p.222.

3 [Southey] (1807), III.193 (my emphasis); Lambe echoes Southey in Lambe (1815), pp.171–2.

4 Paley (1785); Williams, Howard (1883), pp.169–72; Pufendorf (1749), pp.360–1; *Encyclopædia Britannica,* 'William Paley'; cp. Hutcheson, ch. 16 p.225 above.

5 Smith (1776), I.184, 200–2.

6 Morton (1994), pp.18–19; *London Magazine* (1821), repr. in *The Medical Adviser* (1824). I think Morton is wrong to identify 'Sir J.S.' as John 'Walking' Stewart, who was not a Sir. I take it to refer to the eccentric Sir John Sinclair, who – as president of the Board of Agriculture – advocated the conversion of 'grass-lands into tillage' and whose *Code of Health and Longevity* (1807) included an anthology and bibliography of dietetic writing including the vegetarians Tryon, Oswald, Cheyne and Cocchi. Lambe frequently cited Sinclair's work to support vegetarianism. Sinclair

(1807), II.vi+n., 205, 298–9;
Lambe (1815), pp.166, 186–7,
522–3; cf. pp.200–1; Aikin
(1803), p.755.

7 Paley (1785), pp.xii, 11; Williams,
Howard (1883), p.169.

8 Plato (1956), I.76–7; Jerome
(2005a), Bk II, ch.11; Evelyn
(1996), pp.88–9; Pufendorf
(1749), p.361; Porphyry (2000),
pp.35, 52, 111; Tryon (1691a),
pp.49, 267, 331–3, 336; [Tryon]
(1685), pp.52–3; Tryon (1696),
p.125; cf. Ritson (1802),
pp.81–5+nn.; Doddridge (1794),
I.207; Morton (2000), pp.96–9;
Morton (1994), p.162+n.

9 Williams, E.F. (1976), pp.47, 49.

10 Saint-Pierre (1798), II.398; cf.
Rousseau, J.-J. (1755), Note 4; and
see ch.15, 18 and 21 above;
Spengler (1942), pp.257–8.

11 Tudge (2003), p.77.

12 Darwin, E. (1794–6), II.292, 660,
669–71; Darwin, E. (1800),
pp.466–9; Thomas, K. (1983),
p.295n.; Lambe (1815),
pp.278–9, 518–19.

13 Nicholson (1999), pp.xviii–xix,
28–9, 48–50; Oswald (1791),
p.16; Thomas, K. (1983), p.295n.;
Buchan (1797), pp.7, 11–12. On
the sparse population of the
Amerindians, see Oswald (1791),
pp.15–16; Darwin, E. (1794–6),
II.669–71; [Malthus] (1798), ch.
3.

14 *Vind.*13–14+n.; Hogg (1858),
II.412; Ritson (1802), pp.84–5;
Thomas, K. (1983), p.295+n.;
Crab (1655), p.7; Tryon (1700),
p.236.

15 Lambe (1815), pp.171–2, 220,
238–43, 518–19; Morton (1994),
p.162+n. For Lambe's other
negative comments on milk, see
Lambe (1809), pp.21–2, 34–6;
Lambe (1815), p.160; cp. p.167;
cf. also Newton, J.F. (1897),
pp.31, 64–5.

16 Buffon (1780), IV.166–8. John
Brückner extended Buffon's
argument to humans (Brückner
(1768), pp.85–122). The idea was

a demographic slant on the
common remark that if people did
not eat the animals they would
overrun the land. Even Thomas
Tryon had retorted to this counter-
vegetarian argument by asking
whether, if war were eradicated,
there would be too many people
([Tryon] (1685), pp.52–3).

17 Brückner (1768), pp.85–122; *CR*
Vol.26 (August 1768), pp.49–50.

18 [Malthus] (1798), ch.7.

19 Godwin (1793), II.806; Morton
(2000), p.110.

20 [Malthus] (1798), chs 3, 7, 10,
p.187; Malthus (1826), II.25–7;
Morton (1994), pp.208–12; Green
(1978), p.20; Paley (1785),
pp.587–8.

21 Godwin (1820), pp.453–4.

22 Aikin, ed. (1804), pp.292–301; cf.
J.M. Pullen, 'Malthus, (Thomas)
Robert (1766–1834)', *ODNB*
(2004).

23 Godwin (1820), p.497.

24 *Vind.*13–14+n.

25 Newton, J.F. (1897), p.38; cf. e.g.
Lambe (1815), p.518; Shelley
(1926–30), I.242.

26 BL Add Ms. 37232.(F), William
Godwin to J.F. Newton 1811,
ff.38–42.

27 Tudge (2003), pp.77, 333–5.

28 Brückner (1768), pp.54–60,
134–5, 148–9; *CR* Vol.26 (August
1768), p.46; Aikin ed. (1804),
p.295.

29 Smellie (1790), pp.389–98; cf.
Stillingfleet (1759), pp.95–105;
Derham (1714), pp.169–74.

30 cf. e.g. Smellie (1790), p.398.

31 Brückner (1768), pp.xvii, 40–1,
46–54, 64–84, 131–3, 136ff.; cf.
CR Vol.26 (August 1768),
pp.46–9; cf. Oerlemans (2002),
pp.104–7; da Vinci (1970),
II.258; Kropotkin (1914), pp.1–2.

32 Wells (1971); Huxley (1968), VII
'Preface'; Muddford (1968),
pp.432–3; cf. Malthus (1826),
II.12.

33 Peacock (2001), II.475; Lawrence
(1819), pp.208–22; Lambe
(1815), pp.128–9, 519–22;

Holmes (1974), pp.286–7, 290, 294; Morton (1994), p.72; Morton writes that Lawrence 'translated' the article on 'Man'; he later indicates that Lawrence authored it, Morton (1994), pp.65–6, 133–4.

34 Lambe (1815), pp.519–22; cf. pp.148, 512; Lambe (1809), pp.22–31; Newton, J.F. (1897), pp.xii, 23–4+n., 137–8; Vind.8; V.Sys.340.

35 Rees et al. (1819), sig.Rr1v–Tt3v–Tt4r.

36 Herbert (1971). Darwin seems to attribute to Malthus a recognition that the survival of the fittest was the power driving a species' adaptation to its competitive environment. This seems to respond to Malthus (1798), ch. 3: 'Want pinched the less fortunate members of the society . . . Young scions were then pushed out from the parent-stock . . . The peaceful inhabitants of the countries on which they rushed could not long withstand the energy of men acting under such powerful motives of exertion. And when they fell in with any tribes like their own, the contest was a struggle for existence . . . Till at length the whole territory . . . was peopled by a various race of Barbarians, brave, robust, and enterprising, inured to hardship, and delighting in war.' Darwin regarded Malthus' theory as analogous to his theory of intraspecific adaptation by natural selection; he wrote that 'The final cause of all this wedging, must be to sort out proper structure, and adapt it to changes. – to do that for form, which Malthus shows is the final effect (by means however of volition) of this populousness on the energy of man.' Darwin, C. (1887), I.83; Darwin, C. (1885), pp.50–1; Darwin, C. (1882), pp.44–8 (Part I, ch.2, 'Rate of Increase', 'Natural

Selection'); Claeys (2000), pp.223–4.

EPILOGUE

1 Dombrowski (1986).

2 Thoreau (1989), pp.214–15; Alcott (1938) p.318.

3 Emerson (1969), p.256ff.; Adams (1990), pp.243–4.

4 Thoreau (1989), pp.210, 217, 283–4; Dombrowski (1986), p.32+nn.16, 18, 19 (a misleading article).

5 Thoreau (1989), pp.215–16; cf. pp.210, 212–14; Altherr (1984).

6 Thoreau (1973), p.22; Worster (1985), pp.104–5; Hodder (2003); Stevenson (1880); Adams (1990), pp.243–4.

7 Thoreau (1989), pp.210, 214–15; see ch. 18, p.248 above.

8 Thoreau (1989), p.216. On Thoreau, Alcott and vegetarianism, cf. Altherr (1984); Adams (1990), pp.245–6; Jones, J. (1957); Cameron (1969).

9 Emerson (1842), III.227–47; Axon (1893).

10 Spencer, C. (2000), pp.238–70; Alexander Gordon, 'Cowherd, William (1763–1816)', rev. Ian Sellers, ODNB; Peter Shapely, 'Brotherton, Joseph (1783–1857)', ODNB; Julia Twigg, 'Prospectus of Concordium. The Vegetarian Movement in England 1847–1981', Unpublished Ph.D Dissertation, London School of Economics (not seen); Gandhi (1999), XLIV.92, 105–10, 125–8, 133–43; Roy (2002), p.82.

11 Gandhi (1999), I.45–7, XLIV.92, 105–8. Subversive reformers such as the atheist Eurasian professor in Calcutta, Derozio, encouraged caste Hindus to eat beef as a sign of their rejection of caste laws and pagan superstition.

12 Salt (2000), pp.xiv–xvi. Salt wrote five books and four articles on Shelley and edited the 'Vindication of Natural Diet' and other prose; for a bibliography see

http://www.henrysalt.co.uk/
indexold.html. Gandhi (1999),
I.21–2, 39, 91, 310; XLIV.127–8;
Alexander (1996); Oerlemans
(2002), p.113; Young (1975),
pp.19–33; Spencer (2000), p.273.
13 Gandhi (1999), XLIV.125–8;
I.47–9; XLVII.243.
14 Roy (2002), pp.70, 82.
15 Gandhi (1999), I.18–28, 34–52,
64–5, 80, 90–100, 126, 136–42,
176–7, 184, 206–7, 239–40,
307–11; XLIV.136–8; Salt
(2000), p.xvi; Hay (1989),
pp.87–94; Green (1986),
pp.65–72.
16 Gandhi (1999), I.40, 80–1,
239–40 (cf. Kropotkin (1912),
ch.5), 307–9; IV.151–2+n.; cf.
V.149, 476, 493; Alter (2000),
pp.9–10; Millie Polak, 'Interview'
(2005), BBC Radio 4 Broadcast;
Alter (2000), pp.7–8; Roy
(2002), pp.74–5.
17 Gandhi (1999), I.307–9;
XLIV.127–8, 136; cp. I.48–9;
Alter (2000), pp.3, 161 n.14 and
passim.
18 Walters and Portmess, eds
(1999), p.143; cf. Alter (2000),
pp.161–2n.18. Compare the
ambivalence to health motives
for vegetarianism in Élisée
Reclus' 'search for truth': Reclus
(1901).
19 Gandhi (1999), XLIII.84. On the
diasporic provenance of some of
Gandhi's ideas, cf. Roy (2002);
Veer, ed. (1995), pp.1–16.
20 Gandhi (1999), XLIV.142–3; Hay
(1989), pp.83–7.
21 Gandhi (1999), I.100;
XXIV.27–8; XLI.39, XLIII.225,
and the partly contradictory,
L.446; Alter (2000), pp.34–5; cf.
Roy (2002), pp.74–5.
22 Williams, Howard (1883),
pp.198–206; Gandhi (1944),
pp.41–53; Gandhi (1999), I.19,
34, 64–5, 136; Roy (2002),
p.75n.
23 Gandhi (1999), XLIV.136.
24 Gandhi (1999), XLVII.243;
LXVII.400; XCIV.125; Dimock

(2003); Miller (1938), pp.238–9;
Hendrick (1956); Hodder (2003),
p.357.
25 Wilson (2005).
26 Gandhi (1999), VII.181–2;
XII.23–4; XXI.14–15; cf. Polak
(1953); Hay (1989), pp.91–2;
Young (1975), pp.32–3.
27 Gandhi (1999), XLVII.243;
Hendrick (1977), pp.109–13,
160; Walters and Portmess, eds
(1999), pp.141–4.
28 cf. e.g. Gandhi (1999), I.25–7,
100; Thoreau (1989), pp.219–20;
Alter (2000), p.4.
29 Hendrick (1956), p.462; Thoreau,
'On the Duty of Civil
Disobedience'; Gandhi (1999),
LIII.4–5.
30 Gandhi (1999), XLIV.133 (my
emphasis).
31 Kropotkin (1914), pp.xv–xvi.
32 Green (1930); Carpenter (2003),
pp.100, 264.
33 Crawford (2000).
34 Huxley (1888), p.165; cf.
Kropotkin (1914), pp.77–8;
Kropotkin (1912), ch. 4; Claeys
(2000), pp.226–8; Borello
(2004), p.19; Haeckel (1895),
pp.73–4; Gandhi (1999),
LXXIX.87–8; LXX.260.
35 Kropotkin (1914), pp.ix–xii, xv,
57, 74–5; Preece (2003), p.403;
Todes (1989), pp.123–42.
36 Borello (2004); Wynne-Edwards
(1983).
37 Gould (1991), p.335.
38 Darwin, C. (1874), ch.2, 'Natural
Selection'; cf. Jones, S.E. (n.d.).
39 Purchase (2003), p.76; Darwin,
C. (1874), ch.4, 'Sociability';
Kropotkin (1914), pp.5, 77–8.
40 Kropotkin (1912), ch. 3; cf. ch.5.
41 Purchase (2003), pp.20–1, 68;
Reclus (1927), p.52; cf. Reclus
(1901). Kropotkin did, in
passing, mention inter–specific
mutual aid: Kropotkin (1914),
p.xi.
42 Wallace (2004), p.309; Wallace
(1916), p.158; Wallace to Salt
(26 Sept. 1897 and 11 Jan.
1898), Alfred Russel Wallace

Collection, American Philosophical Society B W15a (www.amphilsoc.org/library/mole/w/wallacear.htm)

43 *Vegetarian Messenger*, August 1938 (www.ivu.org/history); Kropotkin (1914), pp.77–8; Todes (1989), pp. 130–1.

44 Gandhi (1999), I.309–11.

45 Hitler (1943), chs 3, 4, 13; Haeckel (1876), I.170; Claeys (2000); Bramwell (1985), pp.171–9; Köhler (2000), pp.199–201; Wells (1971), pp.326–7, 339, 353–6; [Wagener] (1978), pp.40–1, 68–9, 145.

46 Speer (1970), pp.119–20; Sweeting (2002), p.86; Proctor (1999), p.136.

47 Gordon (2002), pp.185–7+n.; Anderson (1992), pp.25, 51–2, 74–85; Ungewitter (1979b), pp.25, 69; Ungewitter (1979a), pp.11, 69; Chase (1980), I.85–138; II.18–19; Lusane (2003), pp.130–3 (Kellogg thus provided inspiration for both Hitler and Gandhi: Gandhi (1999), LXVII.284); Hau (2003), pp.120–3; cf. pp.1, 4, 23, 27, 110; Hamann (1999), pp.367–8; International Vegetarian Union (n.d.); Toepfer (2003), pp.144–8, 180; Kennedy and Ryan (2003); [Wagener] (1978), pp.40–1, 145; Proctor (1999), p.127.

48 [Wagener] (1978), pp.222, 226; Kershaw (1998), pp.261–2, 345+n.; Toland (1976), p.256; Waite (1971), pp.232–6.

49 Schenck (1998), pp.261–2, 345; Hitler (2000), pp.230–1 (22/1/1942); Waite (1977), pp.25–6.

50 Hitler (2000), pp.152, 230–1, 442–3 (cf. chs 11 and 15, pp.145, 209 above); Kershaw (2000), p.509. Although the authenticity of some aspects of the *Table Talk* transcripts is doubtful, the views attributed to Hitler on vegetarianism which I quote are either corroborated by separate sources, or at the very least, in the case of land-use efficiency measures for example, they accord with policies implemented by Hitler's administration. The disquisition he gave on vegetarianism in April 1942, for example, is corroboratively recorded in *Table Talk* and in Goebbels (1993–8), IV.175–7; Hitler (1963), pp.294–5.

51 Proctor (1999), pp.26–7, 130–3+n.; Hamann (1999), pp.367–8; Redlich (1998), p.128; Crawford (1995), p.217; Besant (2003), pp.616–17.

52 Anderson (1992), pp.77–84; Proctor (1999), pp.26–7+n.; Redlich (1998), pp.77–8; Hitler (2000), pp.114–15, 230–1, 442–3 (I have adjusted the translation 'vegetarian' to 'vegetable' to avoid the implication that Hitler actually used the jargon of the 'vegetarian' movement). cf. Alter (2000), p.98; Gandhi (1999), I. 206–7; Gandhi (1944), p.44.

53 U.S. Army Infantry School (1941); Hitler (2000), pp.114–15, 442–3; Proctor (1999), pp.26–7, 135.

54 Hitler (2000), pp.114–15, 230–1, 442–3; Kershaw (2000), p.509; Proctor (1999), pp.134–5.

55 Proctor (1999), pp.137–8; Schenck (1970), p.18; Kersten (1956), pp.41–3. Compare the surprisingly similar ideas prevalent in post-Holocaust Germany: Barilan (2004), pp.124–5; cf. Goodrick-Clarke (1985), pp.198–9, 218–20.

56 Proctor (1999), pp.120–1, 131–2; Offer (1991); Hitler (2000), pp.230–1.

57 Sax (2000), p.121; Hitler (2000), pp.164–5, 232, 247–8; Köhler (2000), p.265; Kershaw (1998), pp.92–3; Redlich (1998), pp.216–17; Proctor (1999), p.134.

58 Miskolczy (2003), p.64.

59 Sax (2000), pp.110–13;

Staudenmaier (n.d.); Proctor (1999), pp.129, 136.

60 Hitler (2000), pp.114–15.

61 Hitler (2000), pp.230–1; cf. p.391 above; Walters and Portmess, eds (1999), p.91; Gandhi (1999), I.309–11.

62 Rauschning (2004), p.229; Viereck (1961), pp.107–8, 119; Walters and Portmess, eds (1999), pp.89–95. See Köhler (2000), p.265. In support of his overwrought thesis, Köhler claims that 'it was chiefly due to Wagner that Hitler became a vegetarian'; to back up this claim he merely cites Waite (1977), p.26, who in turn quotes from Rauschning's exaggerated and fabricated memoirs. Even Robert Proctor's otherwise illuminating discussion of Nazi vegetarianism has been contaminated by drawing on Rauschning (Proctor (1999), p.136).

63 Goodricke-Clarke (1998), pp.1–4, 8, 92, 106–7, 230–1.

64 Much has been made of various records suggesting that Hitler either ate roast pigeon, liver dumplings and/or ham; but while some of these stories may be true, they mostly refer either to the period before Hitler renounced meat, or were quoted by unreliable sources. In any case, if reported lapses disqualify individuals from consideration, then along with Hitler must go other vegetarian 'heroes' such as Percy Shelley, Thomas Tryon, Joseph Ritson, Pythagoras, and the Buddha. (Nevertheless, there is an entire book dedicated to denying Hitler's vegetarianism and an ongoing furious debate on the Internet.) Evidence for Hitler's vegetarianism is abundant; in addition to sources cited above, cf. e.g. Kershaw (1998), pp.47, 343; Redlich (1998), pp.77–8, 81, 128, 216–17, 249, 283, 285; Speer (1970), p.119; Hitler (2000), pp.219, 230–1; Proctor (1999), pp.26–7, 134–6; Payne (1973), p.346; Langer (1972), pp.49, 51, 93; Dodd (1939), pp.182–3, 193; Strasser (2005), p.xv; Ryan, (1999), p.82n.; Delattre (2005), p.55; Giblin (2002), p.175; Snyder (1998), p.105; Sweeting (2002), pp.86, 162; [Collier] ([1940]), pp.47–9 (a spurious memoir); Rauschning (1939), pp.66–7 (a spurious memoir).

65 Miskolczy (2003), pp.63–4; Hamann (1999), pp.367–8; Roy (2002), pp.75–6. The interest was mutual: Gandhi (1999), LXVII.444.

66 See chs 23 and 24 above.

67 Porritt (2006), p.9.

INDEX

Page numbers in *italics* refer to in-text illustrations.

Further praise for *The Bloodless Revolution*

"The book is a magnificently detailed and wide-ranging collection of scholarship on what has been said to justify either refraining from meat or consuming it. . . . The history of vegetarian (and anti-vegetarian) thought neither adds up nor goes anywhere, except in the sense that it goes everywhere that people disposed to reflection have explored when asking what it means to be human and to be good. It's a history of human morality, but it's no less a history of human ingenuity in moral argumentation." —Steven Shapin, *The New Yorker*

"Tristram Stuart's thought-provoking book is not a global history of this taboo. Instead, it revolves around the vegetarian movement that began in 17th-century England—the name first came into use in the 1840s—and that remains strong today. But there is nothing narrow about the author's focus. Both scholarly and entertaining, *The Bloodless Revolution* is a huge feast of ideas." —Mark Kurlansky, *Washington Post Book World*

"An astonishing examination of mankind's changing perception of its place in the natural world and of what it means to be human." —*Boston Globe*

"As Stuart points out in his marvelously researched, deeply revealing, minutely considered history of vegetarianism, it was not till the nineteenth century and the founding of Britain's Vegetarian Society that Western Society seriously confronted its conflicted attitudes toward the eating of meat. . . . Students of this phenomenon will be forever grateful for Stuart's immense bibliography." —Mark Knoblauch, *Booklist*

"Voraciously researched, densely detailed, beautifully written." —Laura Shapiro, *Slate*

"The word 'vegetarian' wasn't coined until the 1840s, but Stuart's magisterial social history demonstrates how deeply seated the vegetarian impulse has been in Western culture since the 17th century. . . . Stuart offers a masterful social and cultural history of a movement that changed the ways people think about the food they eat."

—*Publishers Weekly*

"A fascinating, ambitious work of intellectual history."

—Barbara Davenport, *San Diego Union Tribune*

"Stuart demonstrates not only the extraordinary length and depth of the vegetarian tradition, but also the fascinating fact of its connection with radical politics and the most refined spiritual philosophy. . . . Stuart writes with flair and intelligence, and this debut shows that he is destined to be a luminous presence in his literary generation."

—A. C. Grayling, *The Independent on Sunday*

"Far from being merely a lengthy panegyric to vegetarianism—as I with carnivorous prejudice thought it must be on first sight—the book is a rich and complex history of a movement whose influence has been felt far beyond the table."   —Katherine A. Powers, *Boston Sunday Globe*

"An epic of non-carnivorous restraint. Stuart, a young British scholar, offers portraits of often little-known figures who would not eat anything with a mother or a face, and he blends these character studies with smart analysis of historical trends and transmission of ideas. . . . Culinary and cultural history intertwined: readable, and endlessly interesting."   —*Kirkus Reviews*

"[A]n accomplished exposition of the way in which vegetarianism has been used as a way of writing about society's ills . . . well-crafted and amusing. . . . Surprising and delightful . . . this well-written book is essential reading for anyone who wishes to get to grips with the philosophical history of the vegetarian debate."

—Lizzie Collingham, author of *Curry: A Tale of Cooks and Conquerors*

"[A] very fine achievement, covering an enormous amount of ground and written with verve and enthusiasm. [*The Bloodless Revolution*]

draw[s] the different strands of the subject together in a way that has never been done before."
—Keith Thomas, author of *Man and the Natural World*

"*The Bloodless Revolution* is a wonderful book, crammed with original research and written with verve, wit and passion. The most enthralling work of cultural history I have read in years, it brings out the political, ethical and environmental implications of our dietary choices without any preachiness."
—Chandak Sengoopta, *The Independent* (London), author of *Imprint of the Raj: How Fingerprinting Was Born in Colonial India*

"Brilliant: juicy, full-blooded, witty and acute prose; fast-paced without losing weight; and rich in surprising and compelling ideas."
—Dr. Hannah Dawson, Edinburgh University

"Despite his serious approach, Mr. Stuart has a relaxed, semi-anecdotal style which repays both careful engagement and lighter dipping."
—*The Economist*

"The brilliance of Stuart's book is to demonstrate that the study of attitudes towards food is the gateway to appreciating how people understood their place in society, their relationship to their environment and the significance of being human. . . . Stuart navigates many fascinating bywaters and eddies in the history of ideas and provides so many acute analyses that it's impossible to do complete justice to the breadth and depth of his study in a single review. This is intellectual history at its most scintillating, as passionate and vibrant as any swashbuckling romp or perilous adventure."
—Jonathan Beckman, *The Observer*

"[*The Bloodless Revolution*] is a beautifully written work of impressive scholarship, perhaps the most erudite yet to appear on the subject of vegetarian history."
—Michael O'Donnell, *San Francisco Chronicle*